HUMAN RESOURCE MANAGEMENT

We work with leading authors to develop the strongest educational materials in business, bringing cutting-edge thinking and best learning practice to a global market.

Under a range of well-known imprints, including Financial Times Prentice Hall, we craft high quality print and electronic publications which help readers to understand and apply their content, whether studying or at work.

To find out more about the complete range of our publishing please visit us on the World Wide Web at: www.pearsoneduc.com

Fifth Edition

HUMAN RESOURCE MANAGEMENT

Derek Torrington

Laura Hall

Stephen Taylor

FINANCIAL TIMES

An imprint of **Pearson Education**

Harlow, England • London • New York • Boston • San Francisco • Toronto • Sydney • Singapore • Hong Kong
Tokyo • Seoul • Taipei • New Delhi • Cape Town • Madrid • Mexico City • Amsterdam • Munich • Paris • Milan

Pearson Education Limited
Edinburgh Gate
Harlow
Essex CM20 2JE
England

and Associated Companies throughout the world

Visit us on the World Wide Web at:
www.pearsoneduc.com

First published in Great Britain under the Prentice Hall Europe imprint in 1987
Second edition published 1991
Third edition published 1995
Fourth edition published 1998
Fifth edition published 2002

© Prentice Hall Europe 1987, 1991, 1995, 1998
© Pearson Education Limited 2002

The rights of Derek Torrington, Laura Hall and Stephen Taylor to be
identified as authors of this work have been asserted by them
in accordance with the Copyright, Designs, and Patents Act 1988.

ISBN 0 273 64639 7

British Library Cataloguing-in-Publication Data
A catalogue record for this book can be obtained from the British Library.

Library of Congress Cataloging-in-Publication Data
Torrington, Derek, 1931–
   Human resource management / Derek Torrington, Laura Hall, Stephen Taylor.-- 5th ed.
     p. cm.
   Includes bibliographical references and index.
   ISBN 0–273–64639–7 (alk. paper)
    1. Personnel management. I. Hall, Laura, 1952-II. Taylor, Stephen. III. Title.

HFF5549.T675 2001
658.3--dc21   2001040542

10 9 8 7 6 5 4 3
06 05 04 03 02

Typeset by 3 in 9.5/12pt Stone Serif.
Printed and bound by Scotprint, East Lothian, Scotland.

In memory of Stewart Seddon, Laura's father,
who has been a constant source of support and
encouragement and who died on 6 April 2001.

Brief contents

Contents

Part II ORGANISATION

Part IV PERFORMANCE

Part VII PAY

Preface

The objective of this text is to provide a comprehensive and practical introduction to the human resource function and the human resource processes in and around a business, supporting this through extensive illustrative material and evidence from company practices.

In response to market research and in order to assist continuity and familiarity with the organisation of the text for those recommending it for courses, we have maintained the overall structure of the book with its logical flow in a seven-part structure, with the core of the text covered in the 35 chapters which comprise Parts II–VII. Each of these parts begins with an opening chapter reviewing the strategic aspects of the human resource function that is the subject of that part, thereby reflecting the current interest in strategy and making the necessary link to the concept of HRM, but without becoming involved in its sometimes incoherent lack of agenda. This is followed by several chapters each describing and discussing the core operational aspects. The final chapter in each part addresses the practical interactive skills required by HR people in relation to the heart of the function.

Our publisher had the text of the 1998 fourth edition extensively reviewed and a synthesis of the reviewers' suggestions has led to the following changes:

- Part I (Introduction) reverts to three chapters by the inclusion of a new chapter on contemporary issues in HRM.
- Part II (Organisation) has communication and information condensed from two chapters to one and the chairing of meetings has been introduced as the interactive skill feature. The material on presentation has been shortened and moved to Part V.
- Part III (Resourcing) has a new chapter on retention.
- Part IV (Performance) has a new chapter on leadership and motivation and the management of diversity is expanded to two chapters.
- Part VIII (Ethics) in the fourth edition has been dropped.

Parts II to VII maintain the now well-established pattern of:

- **STRATEGY**   - **OPERATION**   - **INTERACTION**

We have comprehensively updated and revised the material to encompass legislative changes, emerging issues of professional and academic debate, findings and commentary from our own recent research into contemporary business practices, and other recent data and survey findings.

There is a range of assessment material and new illustrations, as well as several design features to assist further both full-time and part-time students in using and learning from the text; these include:

- **Integrated Window on Practice boxes** provide a range of illustrative material throughout the text, including examples of real company practice, survey results, anecdotes and quotes, and court cases.

- **Integrated Activity boxes** encourage students to review and critically apply their understanding at regular intervals throughout the text, either by responding to a question or by undertaking a small practical assignment, individually or as part of a group. In recognition that this text is used on both professional and academic courses, many of the exercises reflect the fact that many undergraduate students will have little or no business experience. Others may appear to exclude students who are not in employment by asking readers to consider an aspect in their own organisation; however, the organisation could be a college or university, the students' union, a political body or sports team.
- **Discussion topics**: at the end of each chapter there are two or three short questions intended for general discussion in a tutorial or study group.
- **Case study problems**: at the end of each part we have included one short case study and several questions to enable students to review, link and apply their understanding of the previous chapters to a business scenario.
- **Examination questions**: at the end of each part of the text we have included eight sample questions from past examinations, each of which has been graded to indicate its level: introductory undergraduate, intermediate/advanced undergraduate, masters and professional.
- **Website**: The most obvious change from the fourth edition is an enhanced and enlarged website *http://www.booksites.net/torrington*, with much more material, including a case study or exercise for each chapter and more support for both tutor and student. The HRP exercise is directly referred to in Chapter 5, as this is an integral part of the chapter. This exercise is a case study giving worked examples of how the techniques have been used.

Each part of the text includes a brief introduction to its scope and purpose. The extensive end-of-chapter references and bullet-point summary propositions from previous editions have been retained and updated. In previous editions at the end of each of the interaction chapters, there were two or three role-play style exercises intended for students to practise the skills which have been covered. These have now been moved to the much enlarged website.

A major change from previous editions is that this is now a three-author text. Stephen Taylor prepared the website material for the fourth edition and helped considerably with the main text. This time he has played a much larger part in the design and writing of the text and now lies in bronze medal position.

Lecturer support material

This edition has an improved content and range of supplementary materials to assist lecturers in the preparation and delivery of courses using the text. All of the following items are available on application to the publisher:

- **Resource Manual** – includes comprehensive lecture and seminar outlines for both one- and two-semester courses; and indicative answers and debriefs for all the text exercises and case study problems.
- **OHP Masters pack** – includes over 100 black/white A4 sheets containing a variety of specially prepared bullet-point material, and selected enlarged illustrations, figures and tables from the text.
- **PowerPoint slides** – includes the above material on CD-ROM in full-colour presentation format.
- **Website address**: http://www.booksites.net/torrington

Acknowledgements

We should like to thank the reviewers who helped in the development of this new edition: Patricia Chase, Alf Crossman, Alastair Evans, Roger Fagg, Andrew LeLeux, Ed Snape and Lynn Thurloway.

We are grateful to the following for permission to reproduce copyright material, fully credited in the text: David Guest for Figures 3.2 and 16.1; Table 3.1 from *Academy of Management Executive;* The Free Press, a Division of Simon and Schuster, for Figure 3.3; Figure 3.4 and Figure 3.5 from *Strategic Human Resource Management* copyright © 1984 John Wiley & Sons Inc. (Fombrun *et al.* 1984); Taylor and Francis for Figure 3.6; Figure 9.2 from 'Strategic determinants of managerial labour markets' in *Human Resource Management*, Vol. 27, copyright © 1992 John Wiley & Sons Inc. (Sonnenfield *et al.* 1992), Figure 22.1 from 'Baxter Healthcare Corporation' in *Human Resource Management* Vol. 31 copyright © 1992 John Wiley & Sons Inc. (Jackson, B.W. *et al.* 1992), Table 25.2 and Table 25.3 from *The Competent Manager*, copyright © 1982 John Wiley & Sons Inc (Boyatzis, R. 1982). This material is used by permission of John Wiley & Sons Inc; Figure 9.1 from 'Manpower strategies for flexible organisations' in *Personal Management*, Personnel Publications Ltd (Atkinson, J. 1984); The Random House Group Ltd for *The Preying Mantis* on p. 164; Manchester University Press for Table 13.1; the Chartered Institute of Personnel and Development for Figures 13.1 and 25.1; McGraw-Hill Europe for Figures 17.1 and 17.3; Addison-Wesley Longman for Figure 17.2; Idea Group Publishing for Figure 19.2; Gulf Publishing for Table 20.1; Prentice-Hall for Table 20.2 and Paul Miller for Table 24.1; Figure 19.2 from *Partners not Competitors* copyright © 1992 Idea Group Publishing, reprinted with permission (Oliva, L.M. 1992); Table 20.2 adapted from *Managerial Organizational Behavior* © copyrighted material, adapted/reprinted with permission of Center for Leadership Studies, Escondido, CA 92025, all rights reserved (Hersey, P. and Blanchard, K. 1988); Table 20.3 adapted from 'Leadership that gets results' in *Harvard Business Review* copyright © 2000 by the Harvard Business School of Publishing Corporation, all rights reserved (Goleman, D. 2000); Figure 22.2 adapted from *Equal Opportunities Review* Butterworths Division of Reed Elsevier (UK) Ltd (EOR, 1999); Table 24.1 from 'A strategic look at management development' in *Personnel Management* © the author (Managing Director of Trends Business Research) reprinted with permission from Personnel Publications Ltd (Miller, P. 1991); Table 26.1 adapted from 'Planned and emergent learning: a framework and a method' in *Executive Development*, MCB University Press Ltd (Megginson, D. 1994).

Whilst every effort has been made to trace the owners of copyright material, in a few cases this has proved impossible and we take this opportunity to offer our apologies to any copyright holders whose rights we may have unwittingly infringed.

Derek Torrington, Laura Hall and Stephen Taylor
Manchester, February 2001

A Companion Website accompanies
HUMAN RESOURCE MANAGEMENT

Visit the *Human Resource Management* Companion Website at www.booksites.net/torrington to find valuable teaching and learning material including:

For Students:
■ Study material designed to help you improve your results
■ Multiple choice questions to test your learning
■ Extra case studies and exercises
■ Search for specific information on the site

For Lecturers:
■ A secure, password-protected site with teaching and assessment material
■ A downloadable version of the full *Lecturer's Manual*
■ Debriefs of case studies in the book
■ Answers to exercises and debriefs to extra case studies found on the Student site
■ A syllabus manager that will build and host a course web page
■ A brief overview of each chapter in the book

Guided tour

Chapter openings
Each chapter is categorised in one of three ways – strategy, operation or interaction, to help students understand the approach of the material contained within the chapter.

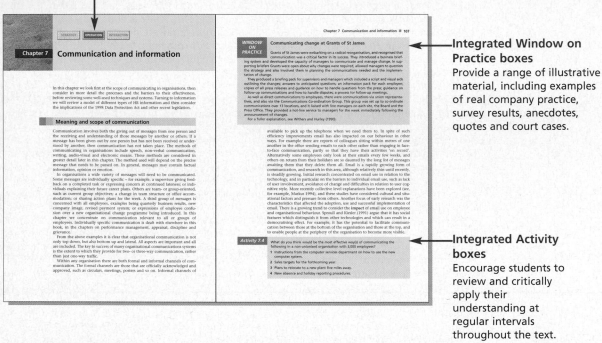

Integrated Window on Practice boxes
Provide a range of illustrative material, including examples of real company practice, survey results, anecdotes, quotes and court cases.

Integrated Activity boxes
Encourage students to review and critically apply their understanding at regular intervals throughout the text.

Summary propositions
Each chapter ends with summary propositions to consolidate students' learning.

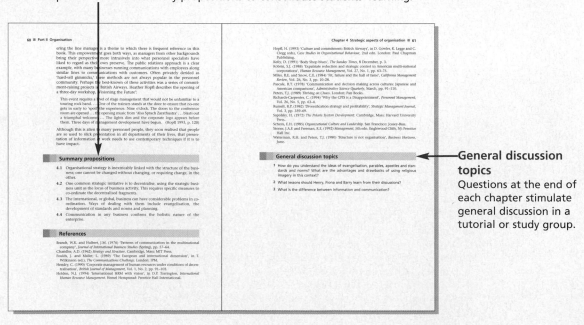

General discussion topics
Questions at the end of each chapter stimulate general discussion in a tutorial or study group.

Case study problem

At the end of each Part, a short case study helps students to review, link and apply their understanding of the previous chapters to a business scenario

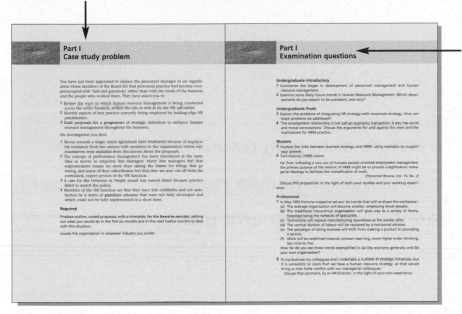

Part I
Case study problem

Examination questions

Each Part ends with 8 sample questions from past examinations – undergreduate, masters and professional.

Website

A companion website, available at **http://www.booksites.net/torrington** contains much more material for both lecturers and students, including an extra case study or exercise for each chapter.

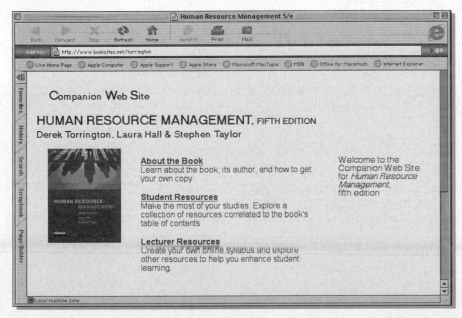

Screen shot reprinted by permission from Microsoft Corporation.

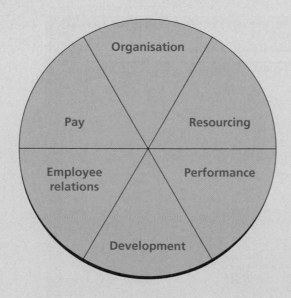

PART I

INTRODUCTION

The first part of the book has only three chapters and forms the basis for all that is to follow. Chapter 1 sets the scene by describing the way in which human resource management works today and then explains how it has evolved to its present form over the hundred years of its existence as a separate function of management. It shows that present-day practice is not only a response to contemporary business demands and social expectations, but also an amalgam of different features which built up throughout the twentieth century. At the close of the chapter there is a model of the remainder and a philosophy for human resource management.

Chapter 2 takes a range of issues in contemporary human resource management, analysing the arguments that relate to them.

Chapter 3 concentrates on strategy in personnel and human resource management. We see the way in which personnel specialists make their strategic contribution, drawing a distinction between a human resource strategy and strategic human resource initiatives.

Chapter 1

The nature of human resource management

The years since the first edition of this book was published in 1987 have witnessed profound developments in jobs, careers and the whole experience of employment. The fundamental change is the steady and clearly perceptible reversal of a trend that has lasted more than 200 years. During that time the organisation has been not only the central feature of economic activity, but also the boundary within which most people work, in which they find their personal security, their career prospects and the means to meet their work related needs. While this remains the case for many, there is no longer the same certainty. What we now witness is a far greater diversity in the size and shape of organisations, and the growth of newer, 'non-standard' approaches to the employment relationship.

Organisations are getting smaller and less reliable. Entrepreneurs are less likely to found a dynasty for their children to inherit, and more likely to launch a project to be developed, exploited and then closed down or sold on within two or three years. The movement and availability of investment capital is less at the disposal of the tycoon following a dream with remorseless determination and more disposed of by 9–5 manipulators of yield ratios yawning in front of computer terminals. Organisations are becoming leaner and smaller. We have delayering and downsizing, rightsizing and outplacement, core/periphery workforces, subcontracting and temporary contracts, a growth in self-employment and part-time working. The organisation as a readily defined entity to which employees 'belong' is becoming less common. In its place the above terms have arrived in the management vocabulary to describe a process whereby businesses compete by being as small and flexible as possible. For those whose job is the effective and efficient management of people at work this gives rise to significant challenges.

New forms of working

Consider the following imaginary scenario. There are six people to watch among the crowds thronging the railway station. First is Charles, Personnel Director, who is on his way to London for yet another strategy meeting. There is the possible closure of the plant in South Korea in order to take advantage of the lower labour costs in Sri Lanka. Then there is the meeting with the executive search consultants to review the candidates for the Chief Executive post in the new subsidiary at Luton before flying out to Los Angeles to propose that the design function should be relocated to Rome – they won't like that!

Also walking briskly along the first-class section of the London train is Sam, a freelance consultant specialising in management development, setting off to run a three-day event for a large company that is rapidly developing its overseas activities and needs her expertise to bring some of the senior executives up to date on European issues. During the journey Sam hopes to do some more work on the web-based distance learning package that the business school has requested.

On a different platform Sharon has got off her commuter train and is hurrying towards the office, hoping that the computer system is working properly, so that she can pull off those reports that are needed for the management meeting later in the day. She is Personnel Administration Manager for her company and is regularly required to produce personnel projections and analyses for meetings. She has just spotted Adrian and has decided to dodge round the other side of the platform to avoid him. Adrian has been hired on a temporary six-month contract to develop the new IT system applications, but he seems more interested in developing his own career and making sure that his work cannot possibly be finished in the time allotted.

John and Mary are some way ahead and exchanging views on what its like to be a line manager. There used to be quite a lot of expertise in the personnel department to help with things like absence, discipline, performance management and all the range of matters relating to people at work, but now everything seems to be left to 'the line'. The Chief Executive called it 'empowerment'. John and Mary feel that it is having responsibility dumped on you without really knowing what you are doing, and without much reward either.

Charles, Sam, Sharon, Adrian, John and Mary could well be going to work that day for the same company, but it is not an organisation by which they are all employed on anything like the same terms. Their contractual relationships are highly diverse both in legal and in psychological terms. The organisation itself operates globally, expanding and contracting in different ways and at different rates in different locations. It is a small fish in a large global pool, unable to exercise any real control over its business environment, competing fiercely on a number of fronts and continually having to improve its performance in order to survive. Once it may have been able to employ all its people on a full-time, long-term basis, and this had great advantages in many ways. Staff returned the favour by showing considerable loyalty to the company. Careers were developed internally, while people in search of secure, pensionable employment actively sought to become long-serving employees. They performed the same basic job tasks in the same way for years on end. But that was when the firm was the dominant player in a predominantly national product market. Now it has to compete with many other lean players operating globally. It has merged with one competitor, formed a strategic alliance with another and has been through successive waves of reorganisation as new technologies have permitted the achievement of ever-greater efficiency. Flexibility and responsiveness to change are the keys to its present and future prosperity.

The experiences of this company and of the people it employs illustrate many of the changes that have taken place in the field of employment in recent years. As has been demonstrated in successive versions of the British Workplace Employment Relations Surveys (see Cully *et al.* 1999 and Milward *et al.* 2000) there has been a solid growth in non-standard forms of employment in the UK over the best part of two decades. While a majority are still employed in full-time jobs and on open-ended contracts, over a quarter are now working on a part-time basis. The number of organisations reporting increased use of staff on temporary or fixed-term contracts, subcontractors and freelancers to carry out tasks that once would have been the preserve of permanent full-timers grew significantly during the 1990s. A clear trend is thus discernible, and it is one that has led many to look forward with a mixture of apprehension and excitement to a twenty-first century in which the world of work differs very considerably to that we have been used to:

> The employee society is on the wane. New models are needed, new role players who will make the new ways less frightening. Political society will also have to make changes: resolving once and for all that children grow up with something to sell the world . . . and that the helpless and the failures of this new order do not suffer too much, or bring too much suffering. (Handy 1995, p. 31)

Handy's reference to 'the employee society' reminds us of the irony that we now regret the passing of a form of life which our early nineteenth century predecessors resisted: the factory system. Regular employment was virtually unknown and the idea of spending all one's working life in a specific place outside the home was unpalatable to most people, even though the alternative of a very hard, indigent life in agriculture was so gruelling. The early factory owners resorted to harsh discipline and long hours as a crude method of converting men, women and children to this radically new way of working:

> The new virtues that the workers were persuaded to adopt were those requisite for a material civilisation: regularity, punctuality, obedience, thrift, providence, sobriety and industry. (Chapman and Chambers 1970)

The practice of personnel management has followed changing patterns of employment and, as the new millennium dawns, contemporary HR specialists – perhaps – stand ready to be Handy's 'new role players to make the new ways less frightening'.

New directions for organisations

Many commentators believed that the arrival in the 1980s of a new approach they labelled 'human resource management' was to be the great change in emphasis, but that was no more than rethinking the processes inside the organisation; we now have to think beyond the organisation as a clearly defined, stable entity. Personnel management has grown and developed with the increasing size and variety of organisations. It is in the throes of fundamental change because the established process has gone into reverse and organisation *as entity* is in decline. We are rediscovering organisation *as a process*.

Activity 1.1	We use the word 'organisation' to describe an entity when we are describing the place where we work ('my organisation'), a particular business enterprise ('Shell is an international organisation') or as a general term to describe undertakings ('over 200 organisations were represented at the conference'. Organisation as a process describes how something is done ('the organisation of the conference was very efficient'; 'the project failed due to poor organisation'). Think of examples of personnel work which are organisation as a process.

The result is a major shift in emphasis for human resource managers. Less and less do they administer the contract of **employment**: more and more they administer the contract for **performance**, and the performance may come from employees, but is just as likely to come from non-employees. A business which seeks to be as lean and flexible as it can needs to reduce long-term cost commitments and focus its efforts on the activities which are the basis of its competitive advantage. Over the long term it is often both a cheaper and more flexible option to buy in standard business services, as well as expertise, from specialist providers. Performance standards can be unambiguously agreed and monitored, while the contract can be ended a great deal more easily than is the case with a department full of employees. In moving towards such models personnel specialists often lead the way from within their own ranks with the contracting out of much of their traditional work. Training functions have been dismantled and the specialist work of developing skills, competences and capacities has been contracted out to consultants and specialist suppliers. The administration of payment arrangements is now frequently carried out by an external subcontractor, as are aspects of recruitment and selection. Activities such as outplacement are typically handed to consultants, while the newer concept of employee assistance programmes is usually regarded as needing to be contracted out if it is to be credible.

WINDOW ON PRACTICE

Macclesfield, in the north of England was the centre of silk manufacture from the beginning of the eighteenth century through to the middle of the twentieth. The town's heritage museum portrays vividly how people were engaged in making silk buttons, working individually or as small family units in garrets producing buttons to the order of merchandisers and being paid by the piece, as and when there was an order. They were all home workers.

Ten miles away the village of Styal developed around a mill which represented a different mode of working. Instead of work being put out to people, people were brought in to the work. There is an apprentice house, where foundlings were housed and both cared for and exploited during their teen years. Begun in 1783, the firm employed 2000 people by 1834 (Rose 1986, p. 13). This was the beginning of a trend that was to continue uninterrupted until very recently. The entity of the organisation was the focus for economic activity and it was also the vehicle for our working lives. We became employees, the organisation took over responsibility for our jobs and our livelihood, our training and our security in old age. Welfare officers were invented and later turned into personnel officers. Trade unions developed. We acquired elaborate structures of authority and lines of responsibility.

Today Styal Mill is a textile museum still surrounded by the village of houses built by the mill owner for his employees. It is owned by the National Trust and visited by thousands of people every year. It is a flourishing, successful business, but it employs only a handful of people on a full-time, permanent basis. Many more are temporary, part-time employees or volunteers.

Defining human resource management

The term 'human resource management' is not easy to define. This is because it is commonly used in two different ways. On the one hand it is used generically to describe the body of management activities covered in books such as this. Used in this way HRM is really no more than a more modern and supposedly imposing name for what has long been labelled 'personnel management'. On the other hand, the term is equally widely used to denote a particular approach to the management of people which is clearly distinct from 'personnel management'. Used in this way 'HRM' signifies more than an updating of the label; it also suggests a distinctive philosophy towards carrying out people-oriented organisational activities: one which is held to serve the modern organisation more effectively than 'traditional' personnel management. We explore the substance of these two meanings of human resource management in the following paragraphs, referring to the first as 'HRM mark 1' and the second as 'HRM mark 2'.

HRM mark 1: the generic term

The role played by human resource functions is best explained by identifying the key objectives that they seek to achieve on behalf of organisations either singly or with the help of other departments. Four objectives form the foundation of all HR activity. We describe each in turn before looking at how the HR function can be organised so as to best ensure that they are met.

Staffing objectives

Human resource managers are first concerned with ensuring, as far as is possible, that the organisation is appropriately staffed and is thus able to draw on the human resources it needs. This involves designing organisation structures, identifying under what type of contract different groups of employees (or subcontractors) will work, before recruiting, selecting and developing the people required to fill the roles: the right people, with the right skills to provide their services when such services are needed. There is a need to compete effectively in the employment market by recruiting and retaining the best, affordable workforce that is available. This involves developing employment packages that are sufficiently attractive to maintain the required employee skills levels and, where necessary, disposing of those judged no longer to have a role to play in the organisation.

Performance objectives

Once the required workforce is in place, human resource managers seek to ensure that individuals are as well motivated and committed as possible so as to maximise their performance in their different roles. Training and development has a role to play here, as do reward systems which maximise effort and focus attention on performance targets. In many organisations, particularly where trade unions play a significant role, human resource managers negotiate improved performance with the workforce. The achievement of performance objectives also requires HR specialists to assist in disciplining employees effectively and equitably where individual conduct and/or performance standards are unsatisfactory. Welfare functions can also assist in achieving and maintaining high performance standards by providing constructive assistance to people whose performance has fallen short of their potential because of illness or difficult personal circumstances. Last but not least, there is the range of employee involvement initiatives which are sponsored by human resource functions as a means of raising levels of commitment and engaging employees in the development of new ideas.

Change-management objectives

A third set of core objectives in nearly every organisation relates to the role played by the human resource function in the effective management of change.

For a good proportion of organisations change no longer comes along in readily defined episodes precipitated by some external factor. Instead it is endemic and well-nigh continuous, generated by a continual need to innovate as much as from definable environmental pressures. Change comes in different forms. Sometimes it is merely structural, requiring reorganisation of activities or the introduction of new people into particular roles. At other times cultural change is sought; a more general objective being the need to alter attitudes, philosophies or long-present organisational norms. In any of these scenarios the HR function can play a central role. Key activities include the recruitment and/or development of people with the necessary leadership skills to drive the change process, the employment of change agents to encourage acceptance of change and the construction of reward systems which underpin the change process. Timely and effective employee involvement is crucial here too because 'people support what they help to create'.

Administration objectives

The fourth type of objective is less directly related to achieving competitive advantage, but is no less necessary in the contemporary business environment. It is essentially administrative in nature and is focused on underpinning the achievement of the other forms of objective. In part it is simply carried out in order to facilitate an organisation's smooth running. Hence there is a need to maintain accurate and comprehensive data on individual employees, a record of their achievement in terms of performance, their attendance and training records, their terms and conditions of employment and their personal details. However there is also a legal aspect to much administrative activity, meaning that it is done because the business is required by law to comply. Of particular significance is the requirement that payment is administered professionally and lawfully, with itemised monthly pay statements being provided for all employees. There is also the need to make arrangements for the deduction of taxation and national insurance, for the payment of pension fund contributions and to be on top of the complexities associated with Statutory Sick Pay and Statutory Maternity Pay. Additional legal requirements relate to the monitoring of health and safety systems and the issuing of contracts to new employees. Accurate record keeping is central to ensuring compliance with a variety of new legal obligations such as the National Minimum Wage and the Working Time Regulations.

Activity 1.2

Each of the four types of HR objective is important and necessary for organisations in different ways. However, at certain times one or more can assume greater importance than the others. Can you identify types of situation in which each could become the most significant or urgent?

Delivering human resource management objectives

The larger the organisation, in theory, the more scope there is for the employment of people who specialise in particular areas of HRM. Some organisations, for example, employ employee relations specialists to look after the collective relationship between management and employees. Where there is a strong tradition of collective bargaining, the role is focused on the achievement of satisfactory outcomes from ongoing negotiations. Increasingly, however, employee relations specialists are required to provide advice about legal developments, to manage consultation arrangements and to preside over employee involvement initiatives.

Another area where some degree of specialisation is the norm is in the field of training and development. Much of this kind of work is now undertaken by external providers, but there is still a role for in-house trainers and particularly for specialists in management development. Increasingly the term 'consultant' is being used instead of 'officer' or 'manager' to describe the training specialist's role, indicating a shift towards a situation in which line managers determine the training *they* want rather than one in which the training section organises a standardised portfolio of courses. The other major specialist roles are in the fields of recruitment and selection, health, safety and welfare, compensation and benefits and human resource planning.

In addition to the specialist roles many people are employed as human resources or personnel generalists. In the less extensive organisations, working alone or in small teams, they carry out the range of HR activities and seek to achieve all the objectives outlined above. In larger organisations generalists either look after all personnel matters in a particular division or else are employed at a senior level to develop policy and take responsibility for HR issues across the organisation. In more junior roles, organisations continue to employ human resource administrators and assistants to undertake many of the administrative tasks we identified as necessary above.

Figure 1.1 HRM roles and objectives

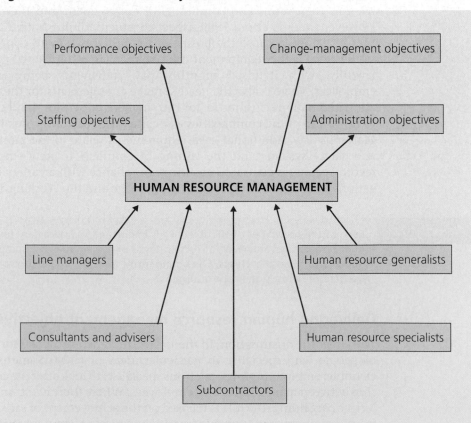

Most HR practitioners working at a senior level in UK organisations are now professionally qualified, having secured membership of the Chartered Institute of Personnel and Development (CIPD). The wide range of elective subjects which can now be chosen by those seeking qualification through the Institute's examinations has made it as relevant to those seeking a specialist career as to those who prefer to remain in generalist roles. However, many smaller organisations do not need, or cannot afford HR managers at all. They may use consultants, they may use the advisory services of university departments, they may use their bank's computer to process the payroll, but there is still a human resource dimension to their managers' activities.

Activity 1.3

Which of the various HR roles described above would you be most interested in undertaking? The generalist role, a specialist role or perhaps that of a consultant or subcontractor?

What are the main reasons for your choice?

WINDOW ON PRACTICE

The rock-hard, steely-eyed film star Clint Eastwood has appeared in several films as tough cop Harry Callaghan, whose approach to law and order is to shoot first and not bother asking too many questions afterwards. On one occasion he had killed rather a lot of people even by his own standards, so that he was becoming politically embarrassing to the authorities. Something had to be done. The Chief of Police nerved himself and called Harry into his office, taking care that there was a large table between them, and gave him the news that he was being transferred to personnel. There was a moment of electric silence. A nervous tic flickered briefly on Harry Callaghan's right cheek. His jaw locked and those famous cold-blue eyes gave the Chief a look that could have penetrated armourplate as he hissed his reply through clenched teeth: 'Personnel is for assholes'. Whereupon he left the room, slamming the door with sufficient vigour to splinter the woodwork in several places.

Being a man of few words, Harry Callaghan did not explain further, but we can interpret his view as being the common one that personnel work is typically undertaken by deviant innovators who have their own 'soft' agenda of being nice to people and who shirk the hard, competitive world of marketing, the precision of finance, or the long hours and hard knocks of manufacturing. It is soft, ineffectual and unimportant.

HRM mark 2: a distinctive approach to the management of people

The second meaning commonly accorded to the term 'human resource management' denotes a particular way of carrying out the range of activities discussed above. Under this definition, a 'human resource management approach' is something qualitatively different from a 'personnel management approach'. Commentators disagree, however, about how fundamental a shift is signified by a movement from personnel management to human resource management. For some, particularly those whose focus of interest is on the management of collective relationships at work, the rise of HRM in the last two decades of the twentieth century represents something new and very different from the dominant approach in earlier years. A particular theme in their work is the contention that personnel management is essentially *workforce centred*, while HRM is *resource centred.* Personnel specialists direct their efforts mainly at the organisation's employees; finding and training them, arranging for them to be paid, explaining management's expectations, justifying management's actions, satisfying employees' work-related needs, dealing with their problems and seeking to modify management action that could produce an unwelcome employee response. The people who work in the organisation are the starting point, and they are a resource that is relatively inflexible in comparison with other resources, like cash and materials.

Although indisputably a management function, personnel management is not totally identified with management interests. Just as sales representatives have to understand and articulate the aspirations of the customers, personnel managers seek to understand and articulate the aspirations and views of the workforce. There is always some degree of being in between management and the employees, mediating the needs of each to the other.

HRM, by contrast, is directed mainly at management needs for human resources (not necessarily employees) to be provided and deployed. Demand rather than supply is the focus of the activity. There is greater emphasis on planning, monitoring and control, rather than mediation. Problem solving is undertaken with other members of management on human resource issues rather than directly with employees or their representatives. It is totally identified with management interests, being a general management activity, and is relatively distant from the workforce as a whole. David Guest (1987) emphasises the differences between the two approaches in his model illustrating 'stereotypes of personnel management and human resource management' (see Figure 1.2).

An alternative point of view, while recognising the differences, downplays the significance of a break between personnel and human resources management. Such a conclusion is readily reached when the focus of analysis is on what HR/personnel managers actually do, rather than on the more profound developments in the specific field of collective employee relations. Legge (1989 and

Figure 1.2 Personnel versus HRM

	Personnel management	*Human resource management*
Time and planning perspective	Short term, reactive, ad hoc, marginal	Long term, proactive, strategic, integrated
Psychological contract	Compliance	Commitment
Control systems	External controls	Self-control
Employee relations perspective	Pluralist, collective, low trust	Unitarist, individual, high trust
Preferred structures/systems	Bureaucratic/mechanistic, centralised, formal defined roles	Organic, devolved, flexible roles
Roles	Specialist/professional	Largely integrated into line management
Evaluation criteria	Cost minimisation	Maximum utilisation (human asset accounting)

1995), concludes that there is very little difference in fact between the two, but that there are some differences that are important; first, that human resource management concentrates more on what is done to managers rather than on what is done by managers to other employees; second that there is a more proactive role for line managers; and third, that there is a top management responsibility for managing culture – all factors to which we return later in the book. From this perspective, human resource management can simply be seen as the most recent mutation in a long line of developments that have characterised personnel management practice as it evolved during the last century. HRM is therefore the latest new dimension to be added to a role which has developed in different directions at different stages in its history. Below we identify six distinct stages in the historical development of the personnel management function. HRM, as described above, is a seventh.

Activity 1.4	While the use of the term 'personnel management' is still widespread in organisations, people working in the field increasingly prefer to use the term 'HRM' and to label themselves as 'Human Resource Managers'. This has occurred even where the role itself has not changed to any great degree. Why do you think this trend has occurred? What consequences, if any, does it have for the way the management specialism is perceived?

The evolution of personnel/HRM

Stage 1: the social reformer

The origins of personnel management lie in the nineteenth century, deriving from the work of social reformers such as Lord Shaftesbury and Robert Owen. Their criticisms of the free enterprise system and the hardship created by the exploitation of workers by factory owners enabled the first personnel managers to be appointed and provided the first frame of reference in which they worked. Such concerns are not obsolete. There are still regular reports of employees being exploited by employers flouting the law, and the problem of organisational distance between decision makers and those putting decisions into practice remains a source of alienation from work.

Stage 2: the acolyte of benevolence

In the late nineteenth and early twentieth centuries some of the larger employers with a paternalistic outlook began to appoint welfare officers to manage a series of new initiatives designed to make life less harsh for their employees. Prominent examples were the progressive schemes of unemployment benefit, sick pay and subsidised housing provided by the Quaker family firms of Cadbury and Rowntree, and the Lever Brothers' soap business. While the motives were ostensibly charitable, there was and remains a business as well as an ethical case for paying serious attention to the welfare of employees. This is based on the contention that it improves commitment on the part of staff and leads potential employees to compare the organisation favourably *vis-à-vis* competitors. The result is higher productivity, a longer-serving workforce and a bigger pool of applicants for each job. It has also been argued that a commitment to welfare reduces the scope for the development of adversarial industrial relations. The more conspicuous welfare initiatives promoted by employers today include pension schemes, childcare facilities and health-screening programmes.

Stage 3: the humane bureaucrat

The third phase marked the beginnings of a move away from a sole focus on welfare issues towards the meeting of various other organisational objectives. Personnel managers began to gain responsibilities in the areas of staffing, training and organisation design. Influenced by social scientists such as F.W. Taylor (1856–1915) and Henri Fayol (1841–1925) personnel specialists started to look at management and administrative processes analytically, working out how organisational structures could be designed and labour deployed so as to maximise efficiency. The humane bureaucracy stage in the development of personnel thinking was also influenced by the Human Relations School, which sought to ameliorate the potential for industrial conflict and dehumanisation present in too rigid an application of these scientific management approaches. Following the ideas of thinkers like Elton Mayo (1880–1949), the fostering of social relationships in the workplace and employee morale thus became equally important objectives for personnel professionals seeking to raise productivity levels.

Stage 4: the consensus negotiator

Personnel managers next added expertise in bargaining to their repertoire of skills. In the period of full employment that followed the Second World War labour became a scarce resource. This led to a growth in trade union membership and to what Allan Flanders, the leading industrial relations analyst of the 1960s, called 'the challenge from below'. Personnel specialists managed the new collective institutions such as joint consultation committees, joint production committees and suggestion schemes set up in order accommodate the new realities. In the industries that were nationalised in the 1940s, employers were placed under a statutory duty to negotiate with unions representing employees. In order that this could be achieved, the government encouraged the appointment of personnel officers and set up the first specialist courses for them in the universities. A personnel management advisory service was also set up at the Ministry of Labour, which still survives as the first A in ACAS (the Advisory, Conciliation and Arbitration Service).

Stage 5: organisation man

The late 1960s saw a switch in focus among personnel specialists, away from dealing principally with the rank-and-file employee on behalf of management, towards dealing with management itself and the integration of managerial activity. This phase was characterised by the development of career paths and of opportunities within organisations for personal growth. This too remains a concern of personnel specialists today, with a significant portion of time and resources in many organisations being devoted to the recruitment, development and retention of an elite core of people with specialist expertise on whom the business depends for its future.

Stage 6: the manpower analyst

The final stage prior to the advent of human resource management in the 1980s involved personnel specialists developing the capacity to undertake the techniques of manpower or workforce planning. This is basically a quantitative activity, boosted by the advent of information technology, which involves forecasting the likely need for employees with different skills in the future. According to Message (1974) it comprises three main processes:

1 Assessing what manpower of what different grades, categories and skills will be needed in the short and long term (i.e. manpower demand).
2 Deciding what manpower an organisation is likely to have in the future, based on current trends and anticipated external circumstances (i.e. manpower supply).
3 Taking action to ensure that supply meets demand.

Manpower planning (now commonly referred to as human resource planning) remains a task undertaken by some HR specialists. Increasingly however, the unpredictability of some business environments has made accurate forecasting difficult, leading to its abandonment as a formal management activity in a number of organisations.

Activity 1.5   Think of an HR management role with which you are familiar. To what extent can you identify in it the presence of activities inherited from each of the six stages in the development of modern HRM?

A philosophy of human resource management

The philosophy of human resource management that is the basis of this book has been only slightly modified since it was first put forward in 1979 (Torrington and Chapman 1979, p. 4). Despite all the changes in the labour market and in the government approach to the economy, this seems to be the most realistic and constructive approach, based on the earlier ideas of Enid Mumford (1972) and McCarthy and Ellis (1973). The original was:

> **Personnel management is most realistically seen as a series of activities enabling working man and his employing organisation to reach agreement about the nature and objectives of the employment relationship between them, and then to fulfil those agreements.** (Torrington and Chapman 1979, p. 4)

Our definition for 1995 was as follows:

> **Personnel management is a series of activities which: first enables working people and the organisation which uses their skills to agree about the objectives and nature of their working relationship and, secondly, ensures that the agreement is fulfilled.** (Torrington and Hall 1995, p. 21)

With the exception of a shift in title from 'personnel management' to 'human resource management' this remains our philosophy. Only by satisfying the needs of the individual contributor will the business obtain the commitment to organisational objectives that is needed for organisational success, and only by contributing to organisational success will individuals be able to satisfy their personal employment needs. It is when employer and employee – or business and supplier of skills – accept that mutuality and reciprocal dependence that human resource management is exciting, centre stage and productive of business success. Where the employer is concerned with employees only as factors of production, personnel management is boring and a cost that will always be trimmed. Where employees have no trust in their employer and adopt an entirely instrumental orientation to their work, they will be fed up and will make ineffectual the work of any HR function.

Human resource managers are great grumblers, and some will react to the last paragraph by saying that they do not get the support they deserve. HR decisions are always taken last, never get proper resources and so forth. Sometimes this is correct, but all too often it is a self-fulfilling prophecy, because the human resources people are pursuing the wrong objectives, or carefully keeping out of the way when things get really tough; which was exactly Harry Callaghan's point.

Figure 1.3 represents the contents of this book in the six main parts. After the three-chapter introduction in Part I come the six parts, which each have the same format: strategic aspects, operational features and a keynote chapter on an interaction that is central to that set of operations. This is the HRM process, a strategic core with operational specialist expertise and a strong focus on dealing with people face to face.

Human resource managers are like managers in every other part of the organisation. They have to make things happen rather than wait for things to happen, and to make things happen they not only need to have the right approach; they also have to know their stuff. Read on!

Figure 1.3 The personnel/HR process

Summary propositions

1.1 Human resource management is undergoing its biggest ever change *as organisation as entity* declines and we rediscover *organisation as process*.

1.2 It is possible to identify two distinct definitions of the term 'human resource management'. The first describes a body of management activities, while the second signifies a particular approach to carrying out those activities.

1.3 Human resource managers are concerned with meeting four distinct sets of organisational objectives. These relate respectively to staffing, performance, change management and administration.

1.4 Organisations carry out HRM activities in a variety of different ways through various forms of organisational structure. In some larger organisations HR generalists work alongside specialists in particular HR disciplines.

1.5 Human resource management can be characterised as the latest in a series of incarnations that personnel practitioners have developed since the origins of the profession over 100 years ago.

1.6 The philosophy of human resource management in this book is that it is a series of activities which: first enables working people and the business which uses their skills to agree about the nature and objectives of their working relationship; and, second, ensures that the agreement is fulfilled.

References

Chapman, S.D. and Chambers, J.D. (1970) *The Beginnings of Industrial Britain*, quoted in Quarry Bank Mill Trust (1986) *Mill Life at Styal*. Willow Publishing: Altrincham, Cheshire.

Cully, M., Woodland, S., O'Reilly, A. and Dix, G. (1999) *Britain at Work as depicted by the 1998 Workplace Employee Relations Survey*. London: Routledge.

Guest, D.E. (1987) 'Human resource management and industrial relations', *Journal of Management Studies*, Vol. 24, No. 5.

Handy, C.B. (1995) *Beyond Certainty*. London: Random House.

Lawler, E.E. (1971) *Pay and Organizational Effectiveness: A Psychological View*. New York: McGraw-Hill.

Legge, K. (1989) 'Human resource management: a critical analysis', in J. Storey (ed.), *New Perspectives on Human Resource Management*. London: Routledge.

Legge, K. (1995) *Human Resource Management: Rhetorics and Realities*. London: MacMillan.

McCarthy, W.E.J. and Ellis, N.D. (1973) *Management by Agreement*. London: Hutchinson.

Message, M.C. (1974) 'Manpower Planning', in D.P. Torrington (ed.), *Encyclopedia of Personnel Management*. Aldershot: Gower.

Milward, N., Bryson, A. and Forth, J. (2000) *All Change at Work? British employment relations 1980–1998, as portrayed by the Workplace Industrial Relations Survey series*. London: Routledge.

Mumford, E. (1972) 'Job satisfaction: a method of analysis', *Personnel Review*, Vol. 1, No. 3.

Rose, M.B. (1986) *The Gregs of Quarry Bank Mill*. Cambridge: Cambridge University Press.

Torrington, D.P. and Chapman, J.B. (1979) *Personnel Management*. Hemel Hempstead: Prentice Hall.

Torrington, D.P and Hall, L. (1995) *Personnel Management: A New Approach*. Hemel Hempstead: Prentice Hall.

General discussion topics

1 In what ways does the decline of the 'organisation as an entity' make working more attractive, and in what ways does it become less attractive?

2 How do you understand the suggestion that the contract of employment is gradually changing to a contract for performance?

3 The philosophy of HRM set out at the end of this chapter makes no reference to the customer. David Ulrich, a professor at Michigan Business School, believes that it is important to refocus HR activities away from the firm towards the customer so that suppliers, employees and customers are woven together into a value-chain team. What difference do you think that would make?

Chapter 2 | Current issues in human resource management

The world in which human resource managers exist and with which they inter-act is continually changing, generating new issues and conundrums to consider. While in most cases managers have a fair degree of choice about how to deal with new ideas and new sets of circumstances, the choices themselves are often diffi-cult. Our aim in this chapter is to introduce readers to a number of these issues in general terms. All raise themes to which we will return at various stages later in the book.

Responding to intensified competition

The most significant general issue facing HR managers in the current environ-ment concerns the appropriate response to intensified competition in product markets. For many, the gut reaction is to react by simply maintaining a contin-ual downward pressure on costs. This may mean fewer people, in which case the HR function is faced with the need to cut jobs and develop new means of inten-sifying work. It may also mean keeping pay levels down at or below market rates. Where this second line is taken, it becomes harder to recruit and retain staff, and a good deal more difficult to maintain motivation and commitment. In the long run, however, depending on the nature of the competition faced, it may be the best way of ensuring the security of the jobs that are left. Provided the process of cutting out 'fat' does not go too far, so that the organisation becomes overly lean (i.e. weak and anorexic) for its own good, such an approach is feasible.

Cost cutting is not, however, the only approach available. The alternative involves seeking to compete on grounds other than cost, accepting that prices charged to customers will be higher than those of some competitors, but provid-ing greater overall value. The result is the production of 'high value-added' goods and services, which appeal because of their high quality or because they are inno-vative in some shape or form. In such situations there remains a need to operate efficiently, but there is less continual downward pressure on staffing costs. Instead there is a need to find and subsequently motivate high-quality per-formers. A more sophisticated set of HR practices is thus needed. Recruitment happens less often than it does in an organisation competing primarily on cost, but it matters more when it does because of the need to secure the services of highly capable people. A sophisticated approach to employee development is also necessary, as is a commitment to employee involvement.

Whatever approach is taken, there is a clear need to develop a greater capacity for flexibility and agility than has previously been the case. Whether the 'low-cost' or 'high value-added' strategy is adopted there has to be a fundamental change in the expectations of employees about the role they play and what the organisation is able to give to them in return. A widespread development has thus been a change in what is known as 'the psychological contract' between employers and the people they employ. Whereas a legal contract of employment sets out terms and conditions of employment, remuneration arrangements and the basic rules that are to govern the employment relationship, the psychological contract concerns broad expectations about what each side will gain from the other. Unquestionably shifts in this area have been some of the most important in employment in recent years as organisations have had to face increased competitive pressure. Central to the shift is the ending of any expectation of long-term or life-time employment. The old psychological contracts can be summed up as follows from the employee perspective:

> I will work hard for and act with loyalty towards my employer. In return I expect to be retained as an employee provided I do not act against the interests of the organisation. I also expect to be given opportunities for promotion should the circumstances make this possible.

By contrast, the new psychological contract takes the following form:

> I will bring to my work effort and creativity. In return I expect a salary that is appropriate to my contribution and market worth. While our relationship may be short term, I will remain for as long as I receive the developmental opportunities I need to build my career.

Another significant effect of increased competition on the operation of the HR function has been greater pressure for it to justify its own existence. The presence of an HR department or HR managers in an organisation can no longer be accepted as a given necessity. They survive and gain influence only where they can show that they add value by making a real contribution to the achievement of business objectives. There has thus been an upsurge in interest recently in ways of measuring the HR contribution, or where this is not possible, in finding other means of carrying out effective evaluation. A range of alternative approaches is used, including benchmarking outcomes such as absence rates, employee turnover rates and productivity per head against those of other organisations. Attitude surveys among staff and line managers are also more frequently carried out to establish what their perception of the function is and how it can be improved, while HR managers are considerably more inclined to set targets for themselves against which their performance can subsequently be evaluated.

Managing international operations

As was stated above, one of the chief causes of intensified competition in recent decades has been the growth of the global economy. Most organisations now have to compete, at least to some extent, with rivals based in other countries. If a firm itself is not a large exporter, it is usually faced with competition from overseas organisations importing products or services into the home market. Particular challenges are posed for organisations based in the older industrialised countries by competitors with far lower cost bases in newly industrialising areas of the world. An important consequence of globalisation is the growth in the number and size of multinational organisations. As a result, a growing proportion of HR specialists work in organisations which are owned and controlled from overseas or are home based with substantial international operations.

The key decision to take here is how far it is necessary or desirable to have in place HR practices which are cross-national and which operate in the same way in all divisions across the world. In principle it is often considered desirable to standardise policy, practices and philosophy in all countries so as to develop a clear, single international identity and corporate culture. Global standardisation also facilitates the movement of individuals from one country to another, as well as permitting the sharing of 'best practice' on an international basis. However, a number of problems arise when such a path is taken. First, it is not always possible to operate in the same way across the world because of important institutional variations between countries. Tax regimes are different, as are training and qualification systems. Above all there are diverse systems of employment law in place, requiring organisations to operate differently in different locations. In some countries, for example, collective agreements are legally binding, while in others (including the UK) they are 'binding in honour only'. There are also major differences in the areas of dismissal and discrimination law. In the USA the doctrine of 'employment at will' means that there is little by way of statutory protection for people who consider themselves to have been unfairly dismissed. In the UK there is a measure of protection for some but not for all, while in Holland employers can only dismiss lawfully once they have gained the permission of a state official so to do (Hepple 1998, p. 291).

In addition to institutional restrictions there is a need to take account of cultural differences. As has been shown by Hofstede (1980 and 1991) and others, the way that different peoples approach work and workplace relations can vary substantially from country to country. Approaches which seem entirely natural in one place thus often travel badly when they are transplanted abroad. A good example is the standard Anglo-Saxon approach to performance appraisal, with annual reviews at which managers and subordinates talk frankly about what individuals have achieved and ways in which performance can be improved. As a method of managing individual performance, appraisal works well in most UK-based organisations – but this is not always the case elsewhere. Across much of the world it simply does not fit with prevailing cultural norms, managers and staff being reluctant to speak frankly and directly to one another about such matters (see Ling Sing Chee 1994, p. 154; Sparrow and Hiltrop 1994, pp. 558–60; Fletcher 1997, p. 97). A balance therefore has to be struck between global and local HR practices. It is usually possible to put in place an international HR strategy and, with certain limitations, to develop a global HR philosophy. By contrast, their application at the local level has to vary considerably depending on what is appropriate in the country concerned.

Activity 2.1

In the literature on international HRM there is a divide between those who see institutional differences as being the most significant determinants of varying HR practices across the globe, and those who stress the importance of cultural differences. The former believe that working cultures can be altered by making institutional changes, while the latter argue that culture is deeply entrenched and that it is responsible for the shape that institutions take. What is your view on this debate?

Riding waves of technological innovation

Developments in the fields of information technology, telecommunications, biotechnology and laser-based applications, often used in collaboration, continue to provide opportunities for organisations as well as posing problems. From an HR perspective it is possible to identify three distinct types of challenge that arise from these developments. First there are direct effects in the way in which the HR function goes about its business:

■ the use of email and intranet as tools of information provision and communication;
■ the rise of the internet as a major new method for recruitment;
■ the development of web-based approaches to training and learning;
■ the use of computer databases to hold staff information and to generate reports;
■ the application of computer technologies to established tasks such as human resource planning and pay-roll administration.

Second, technology brings change more generally to an organisation in terms of its structure, job duties, work allocation and even its culture. Technological change thus drives organisation change, requiring action of different kinds from the HR function. Recruitment and selection processes have to reflect the need to bring in people with different skills and attributes, the purpose and type of training activities will often have to evolve in new directions, while it may also be necessary to make redundancies. In some situations technology can drive radical change in a short space of time, changing forever long-established ways of carrying out an organisation's core functions. A good example is the revolution that took place in newspaper and magazine publishing during the mid-1980s. Whatever the pace of technological development, there is a role for HR professionals to play in planning it and subsequently in its implementation.

The third way in which technological developments affect HRM activity relates to the need to find new ways of managing staff who are employed in research and development (R&D) functions, and whose job is to drive technological development to the advantage of the organisation. It has been convincingly argued that the nature of this work is fundamentally different in key respects from that performed by others in an organisation, and that established management practices are often inappropriate. The following quotation illustrates this point:

> The principles of high task specialization, unity of command and direction, high division of labour, and equality of responsibility and authority all address the problems of structuring work systems and information flows in clear, repetitive ways. They are geared toward the resolution of familiar problems and the facilitation of productivity and control through formal lines of positional and hierarchical authority or through job standardisation. And organizations that are designed and managed for doing the same things well repetitively, as in manufacturing, are not particularly appropriate for doing something well once, as in R&D.
>
> (Katz 1998, p. viii)

A theme of research carried out into the management of staff in research and development environments is the need to move away from approaches which serve to enhance management control and which tend to work against the development of teams. In their place there is a need for structures which promote collaboration between individuals, exchange of ideas and sharing of knowledge.

Activity 2.2

What are the main ways in which technological developments are currently affecting the management of human resources in your organisation or one with which you are familiar? What do you think will be the most significant new developments over the next ten years?

Meeting the expectations of the law

Another major trend with which the HR profession has had to contend in recent years is the growth in the amount of legislation covering employment matters. Prior to 1970, with one or two exceptions, there was no statutory regulation of the employment relationship in the UK. An individual's terms and conditions of employment were those that were stated in the contract of employment and in any collective agreements. The law did not intervene beyond providing some basic health and safety protection, the right to modest redundancy payments and a general requirement on employers and employees to honour the contractual terms agreed when the employment began. Since 1970 this situation has wholly changed. The individual contract of employment remains significant and can be enforced in court if necessary, but there has been added to this a whole range of statutory rights which employers are obliged to honour. The most significant are in the fields of health and safety, equal pay, sex and race discrimination and unfair dismissal. The following have recently been added to these longer-established rights:

- disability discrimination law (in operation since 1997);
- working time regulations (since 1998);
- the national minimum wage (since 1999);
- new maternity regulations (since 1999);
- parental leave and the right to time off for family emergencies (since 1999);
- the right to trade union representation at serious disciplinary and grievance hearings (since 2000);
- new trade union recognition procedures (since 2000).

Unfair dismissal law itself has also been strengthened with the reduction in the qualifying period to one year's service and in the raising of the maximum compensation level to £50,000 from 1999. Further new law on discrimination and consultation is due to be placed on the statute books before 2003.

The extent to which HR practitioners, and managers generally, should welcome the growth in regulation remains a matter of debate. One view, expressed most frequently by those working in smaller firms, deplores much of the legislation. While accepting the laudable motives behind it, they see the long-term effect as being to increase the costs associated with employing people, while decreasing the flexibility managers enjoy in the running of their businesses. This results in a reluctance to create jobs in the first place and a tendency for international organisations to site operations in other, less highly regulated countries. According to proponents of this school of thought, regulation provides more social justice, but does so at a price – namely higher unemployment than would otherwise be the case.

An alternative view starts with the proposition that the burden of regulation in the UK remains a good deal less onerous on employers than is common in many industrialised countries, and that it is not extensive enough to have a detrimental effect. Indeed it can be persuasively argued that UK employment legislation does no more than require employers to treat their employees equitably and reasonably, and that good employers thus have no reason to complain. A third point of view is that UK labour law does not in fact go far enough and that further, rather tougher legislation would be beneficial. The argument here rests on the belief that the UK can no longer compete globally by producing 'low cost – low value-added' products and services because of competition from the newly industrialising countries and the former eastern bloc. Instead there is a need to develop a more highly skilled labour force and to focus activity on producing quality goods and services, on new technologies and on the development of a knowledge economy. Legislation, in requiring employers to pay relatively high wages and in making it difficult to dismiss without good reason, helps force them down such a path. The result, so it is argued, is a situation in which a high level of statutory employment protection is entirely compatible with the operation of a successful economy.

Activity 2.3	What is your position in the debate about employment protection legislation? Would you like to see more or less regulation in this field? What additional measures would you welcome? Which would you like to see removed from the statute book?

Managing with or without trade unions

The Employment Relations Act 1999 requires employers to recognise trade unions and to bargain with them in good faith where a majority of the workforce in an identifiable bargaining group indicate that this is what they want. To an extent the law thus now restricts how far managements can choose whether or not they deal with a trade union. However, for many there remains a choice because of the reluctance of employees in many sectors of the economy to become trade union members in sufficient numbers to force recognition. According to the most recent UK Workplace Employee Relations Survey (Cully *et al.* 1999, p. 87) as many as 47 per cent of workplaces employ no one at all who is a union member, while membership covers fewer than half the workforce in the case of a further 25 per cent of organisations. There is also scope within the legislation for employers to resist recognition, even where there are plenty of union members, by seeking to persuade them that a system of collective bargaining is not in the organisation's interests.

For many organisations a good management case can be made against the recognition of trade unions. For smaller firms particularly there is often a well-founded desire to manage employee relations informally and on an individual rather than a collective basis. In other situations the case is based on fears that unions will restrict the freedom of action enjoyed by managers, that they will resist necessary change, preventing it from occurring, or that a damaging adversarial relationship between employees and management will become established. There are also, however, good reasons for managers to welcome or even to encourage a trade union presence:

> Trade unions also fulfil a number of important managerial functions which help explain why a number of foreign-owned companies coming into the UK have been willing to recognise them. One is the agency function which is especially important where there are large numbers of employees engaged in relatively homogeneous activities: management escapes the time-consuming and costly process of dealing with employees individually and also avoids inconsistencies which can be a major problem. A second is that trade unions voice the grievances and complaints of employees (Freeman and Medoff, 1984). In the words of Henry Mond, who had a significant influence on ICI's early policy towards trade unions, 'the trade unions are extremely useful to us in bringing to our notice matters that we would not otherwise be aware of' (quoted in Reader, 1973: 66). A third, and in many respects the most important, function that trade unions perform is in helping to manage discontent by legitimating procedures and management prerogative. (Sisson and Storey 2000, p. 193)

What is important from a management point of view is that a healthy and productive relationship should be established with one or more unions which enhances rather than detracts from the long-term success of the organisation. Such thinking underpins the growth in interest over recent years in forms of **partnership** arrangement – an approach favoured and encouraged by government. The key factor which distinguishes partnership from more traditional types of union relationship is an acceptance that both sides are working towards the same ultimate goals. The role of the union is not one of perpetual opposition but is instead supportive and constructive of legitimate management initiatives. In return for such support, managers treat union representatives as partners in decision-making processes and employees as key stakeholders in the organisation's future. Consultation occurs before new programmes are announced, while in other areas there will be an element of joint decision making. Partnership agreements do not restrict a union's freedom to criticise management

WINDOW ON PRACTICE

An interesting effect of the recent legislation on union recognition has been the way it has encouraged employers to review their employee relations practices ahead of time in order to avoid being forced to make changes by the regulators. Much activity in this area occurred between February 1999 (when the government issued its White Paper entitled 'Fairness at Work') and July 2000 (when the new legislation became active). Two rather different examples were reported in *People Management* in June 2000. The first concerned Eurotunnel, which tried to pre-empt a claim for compulsory recognition by signing a single-union agreement of the 'partnership' kind with the Transport and General Workers Union. The aim was to avoid a situation in which the company dealt with several different unions representing different groups of staff. The other example concerned Richard Branson's empire, in which unions were recognised in the Virgin Trains company but not in the Virgin Atlantic Airline. Here, before possibly being forced to do so under the terms of the Employment Relations Act, Virgin themselves organised a ballot of staff in order to establish whether or not there is any great desire for union recognition among employees of the airline. The article reported that were the staff survey to indicate support for recognition, some form of single-union deal would be sought and signed.

or to seek better terms and conditions for employees, but they do imply the fostering of an understanding mindset on the part of representatives which respects management's right to manage and accepts that the ultimate goal of an enterprise is commercial success.

Ethical questions

Personnel/human resource management has always had an ethical dimension. The odd thing is that practitioners have for so long been trying to bury this aspect, while academic commentators have grumbled that HR practitioners fail to deliver on it. Thirty years ago it was possible to write a chapter in a book on personnel management with the title 'The Social Role of Personnel' (Torrington 1968, pp. 147–60) and generate a series of reviews that all vehemently disagreed with the implicit proposition that there actually *was* a social role for the personnel manager in the business. Since then there has been a resurgence of interest in ethics, but now it is not a vain attempt of the 'nice' personnel people to act as the conscience of the company. Instead it is a much more general management interest.

On a practical day-to-day basis, as well as when determining issues of policy and strategy, human resource managers are faced with ethical dilemmas. Situations often arise in which there is a conflict of some kind between what is strictly in the interests of the organisation and what individuals consider to be 'right' according to their own consciences or ethical principles. Interestingly the lack of ethicality arises as often from a failure to act as from a positive decision to take a particular course of action. Some examples are as follows:

- dismissing someone for a reason other than gross misconduct, such as ill health;
- failing to dismiss a senior manager or a particularly able employee who has committed an act of gross misconduct (such as sexual harassment);
- maintaining payment arrangements in which groups which are predominantly female are less well remunerated than those dominated by men;
- offering training opportunities to some while denying them to others;
- putting pressure on someone to change working hours or to move location when this will be disruptive for them or their families;
- failing to compensate disabled workers or those from ethnic minorities for possible disadvantages suffered in appraisal or recruitment processes;
- discriminating on grounds of age;
- minimising pay awards despite the organisation having the ability to pay more;
- failing to tell the 'whole truth' when giving evidence at an Employment Tribunal;
- failing to give wholly honest answers about a workplace or job to potential recruits in order to secure their services;
- turning a blind eye to the need to make costly alterations for health and safety reasons.

More generally, an organisation's overall stance on HR issues can often be criticised on ethical grounds. Some of the recent developments outlined earlier in the chapter can be seen as being responsible for a reduced interest on the part of employers in managing ethically. Significant examples include the pressure placed on people to work longer hours than is good for them, the decline in job security resulting from increased competitive pressures, and investment in new technologies which directly result in job losses. Some forms of cultural change may also be considered unethical, an example being a shift away from a culture based on excellence in customer service to one which is oriented towards hard-selling.

How far then should HR practitioners allow ethical questions to colour their judgement when making decisions? For some commentators the answer is 'not at all', since they believe that the long-term interests of society in terms of wealth creation are best served by unfettered competition between firms. Milton Friedman went as far as to contend that managers who devoted corporate resources to pursue personal interpretations of social need might be misguided in their selection and would unfairly 'tax' their shareholders, employees and customers in the process:

> There is one and only one social responsibility of business: to use its resources and energy in activities designed to increase its profits as long as it stays within the rules of the game, engaging in open and free competition, without deception and fraud.
>
> (Friedman 1963, p. 163)

The problem with such a position is that it pushes to one side consequences, such as inequity, inequality, insecurity and abuse of power, that arise in organisations when the pursuit of profit is placed ahead of all other considerations. Whatever its merits in purely economic terms, in putting expediency before ethicality, Friedman's position ignores altogether the role employers can play in promoting social justice. It is also a position with which many managers are understandably uncomfortable.

Such is reflected in the stance of the influential Chartered Institute of Personnel and Development (CIPD). One of its key objectives is the establishment, monitoring and promotion of standards and ethics for HR practitioners in the UK. In pursuing this objective it is seeking to prescribe standards of professional conduct such as those that exist in the medical, legal and accountancy professions. The problem is that HR people do not have a separate professional existence from the management of which they are a part. Human resource management must be a management activity or it is nothing. Doctors, lawyers and accountants, even when employed by a large organisation, can maintain a non-managerial professional detachment, giving advice that is highly regarded, even when it is unpopular. Furthermore they advise; they do not decide. HR specialists are employed in no other capacity than to participate closely in the management process of a business. They can not, therefore, be expected to take up a full-fledged, independent, professional stance. Were they to retreat to an ivory tower and maintain a purist position on ethical matters theirs would be a voice in the management wilderness that no one wanted to hear, let alone provide a salary or provide a company car in order to hear.

The need therefore is for HR people to argue vigorously in favour of a combination of efficiency and justice, remembering that they can only argue vigorously if they are present when decisions are made. They must ensure that they are valued by their managerial colleagues for the wholeness of their contribution and be prepared to accept the fact that they will often lose the argument. They cannot do it by masquerading as an unrepresentative shop steward. In practice what has to be done is to make a strong business case for taking an ethical line wherever it is credible to do so. Invariably this will be based on the long-established ideas of the Human Relations School outlined above; namely the belief that a business can only maintain its competitive edge if the people who work there are committed to its success and that commitment is volitional. In order to maintain the good will and enthusiastic co-operation of employees while also attracting good quality applicants from outside the organisation, there is a need for fair dealing, openness and consistency in the way people are treated.

Activity 2.4	What ethical dilemmas have you faced in the workplace? How far were you able to influence the direction that events took? To what extent can you justify to yourself the course of action that you took?

Best practice v. best fit

The final general issue of significance we discuss at this stage is another that has consequences across the field of human resource management. As well as being a managerial issue it concerns one of the most significant academic debates in the HR field at the present time. At root it is about whether or not there is an identifiable 'best way' of carrying out HR activities which is universally applicable. It is best understood as a debate between two schools of thought, although in practice it is quite possible to take a central position which sees validity in both the basic positions.

Adherents of a best practice perspective argue that there are certain HR practices and approaches to their operation which will invariably help an organisation in achieving competitive advantage. There is therefore a clear link between HR activity and business performance, but the effect will only be maximised if the 'right' HR policies are pursued. A great deal of evidence has been published in recent years, using various methodologies, which appears to back up the best practice case (e.g. Pfeffer 1994; Huselid 1995; Wood and Albanese 1995; Delery and Doty 1996; Fernie and Metcalf 1996; Patterson *et al*. 1998; Guest *et al*. 2000). While there are differences of opinion on questions of detail, all strongly suggest that the same basic bundle of human resource practices or general human resource management orientation tends to enhance business performance in all organisations irrespective of the particular product market strategy being pursued. According to David Guest this occurs through a variety of mechanisms:

> human resource practices exercise their positive impact by (i) ensuring and enhancing the competence of employees, (ii) by tapping their motivation and commitment, and (iii) by designing work to encourage the fullest contribution from employees. Borrowing from elements of expectancy theory (Vroom 1964, Lawler 1971), the model implies that all three elements should be present to ensure the best outcome. Positive employee behaviour should in turn impact upon establishment level outcomes such as low absence, quit rates and wastage, as well as high quality and productivity.
> (Guest 2000, p. 2)

The main elements of the 'best practice bundle' that these and other writers identify are those which have long been considered as examples of good practice in the HRM field. They include the use of the more advanced selection methods, a serious commitment to employee involvement, substantial investment in training and development, the use of individualised reward systems and harmonised terms and conditions of employment as between different groups of employees.

The alternative 'best fit' school also identifies a link between human resource management practice and the achievement of competitive advantage. Here, however, there is no belief in the existence of universal solutions. Instead all is contingent on the particular circumstances of each organisation. What is needed is HR policies and practices which 'fit' and are thus appropriate to the situation of individual employers. What is appropriate (or 'best') for one will not necessarily be right for another. Key variables include the size of the establishment, the dominant product market strategy being pursued and the nature of the labour markets in which the organisation competes. It is thus argued that a small organisation which principally achieves competitive advantage through innovation and which competes in very tight labour markets should have in place rather different HR policies than a large firm which produces low-cost goods and faces no difficulty in attracting staff. In order to maximise competitive advantage, the first requires informality combined with sophisticated human resource practices, while the latter needs more bureaucratic systems combined with a 'low cost – no frills' set of HR practices.

The best fit or contingency perspective originated in the work of Joan Woodward and her colleagues at Imperial College in the 1950s. In recent years it has been developed and applied to contemporary conditions by academics such as Randall Schuler and Susan Jackson, John Purcell and Ed Lawler. In addition, a number of influential models have been produced which seek to categorise organisational contingencies and suggest what mix of HR practices are appropriate in each case. Examples are those of Miles and Snow (1978), Fombrun *et al.* (1984) and Sisson and Storey (2000) – a number of which we look at in more detail in Chapter 3.

To a great extent the jury is still out on these questions. Proponents of both the 'best practice' and 'best fit' perspectives can draw on bodies of empirical evidence to back up their respective positions and so the debate continues.

Summary propositions

2.1 Organisations respond in different ways to intensified competitive pressures. Whatever the response there is a need to become more flexible and to place the employment relationship on a different psychological footing.

2.2 In international organisations it is necessary to strike a balance between human resource strategies which operate globally and human resource policies which vary from country to country to reflect local institutional and cultural expectations.

2.3 New technologies give HR specialists opportunities to develop fresh approaches to their work. They also require new thinking about change processes and the management of people in technologically specialised roles.

2.4 Developments in employment law over recent years have substantially restricted the freedom of employers to manage their workplaces. While the law does little more than require compliance with basic good practice, there are also administrative and procedural requirements which reduce flexibility and increase costs.

2.5 While trade union recognition remains much less common than was the case in the 1980s, there remains a good business case for working with trade unions in certain circumstances. This is particularly true of relationships based on the principles of partnership.

2.6 Human resource managers are regularly faced with ethical dilemmas. HR professionals must argue for justice and equity, but will not be listened to unless they put forward a convincing business case.

2.7 Opinion is divided about whether or not it is possible to identify 'best practice' in the various activities that make up HRM. Adherents of the 'best fit' perspective argue that what is 'best' for some organisations is often inappropriate elsewhere.

References

Cully, M., Woodland, S., O'Reilly, A. and Dix, G. (1999) *Britain at Work as depicted by the 1998 Workplace Employee Relations Survey*. London: Routledge.

Delery, J. and Doty, D.H. (1996) 'Modes of Theorising in Strategic Human Resource Management: Tests of Universalistic, Contingency and Configurational Performance Predictions', *Academy of Management Journal*, Vol. 39, No. 4.

Fernie, S. and Metcalf, D. (1996) 'Participation, Contingent Pay, Representation and Workplace Performance: Evidence from Great Britain', *Discussion Paper 232*, Centre for Economic Performance, London School of Economics.

Fletcher, C. (1997) *Appraisal: routes to improved performance*, 2nd edn. London: IPD.

Fombrun, C., Tichy, N.M. and Devanna, M.A. (1984) *Strategic Human Resource Management*. New York: Wiley.

Freeman, R.B. and Medoff, J.L. (1984) *What do Unions Do?* New York: Basic Books.

Friedman, M. (1963) *Capitalism and Freedom*. Chicago: University of Chicago Press.

Guest, D.E. (2000) 'Human resource management, employee well-being and organisational performance', Paper given at the CIPD Professional Standards Conference, University of Warwick.

Guest, D.E., Michie J., Sheehan, M. and Conway, N. (2000) *Employment Relations, HRM and Business Performance: An analysis of the 1998 Workplace Employee Relations Survey*. London: CIPD.

Hepple, B. (1998) 'Flexibility and Security of Employment', in R. Blanpain and C. Engels (eds), *Comparative Labour Law and Industrial Relations in Industrialized Market Economies*, 2nd edn. The Hague, Netherlands: Kluwer.

Hofstede, G. (1980) *Culture's Consequences: International differences in work-related values*. Beverly Hills: Sage.

Hofstede, G. (1991) *Cultures and Organizations: Software of the mind*. London: McGraw Hill.

Huselid, M. (1995) 'The impact of Human Resource Management practices on Turnover, Productivity and Corporate Financial Performance', *Academy of Management Journal*, Vol. 38, No. 3.

Katz, R. (ed.) (1998) *The Human side of managing technological innovation: A collection of readings*. Oxford: Oxford University Press.

Lawler, E.E. (1971) *Pay and Organizational Effectiveness. A Psychological View*. New York: McGraw-Hill.

Ling Sing Chee (1994) 'Singapore Airlines: strategic human resource initiatives', in D.P. Torrington (ed.), *International Human Resource Management: Think Globally, Act Locally*. London: Prentice Hall.

Miles, R.E. and Snow, C.C. (1978): *Organizational Strategy, Strategy and Process*. New York: McGraw Hill.

Patterson, M.G., West, M.A., Lawthom, R. and Nickell, S. (1998) *Impact of People Management Practices on Business Performance*. Issues in People Management No 22. London: IPD.

Pfeffer, J. (1994) *Competitive Advantage Through People*. Boston: Harvard Business School Press.

Reader, W.J. (1973) *The First Quarter Century 1926-1952. Imperial Chemical Industries: A History. Vol. 2*. Oxford: Oxford University Press.

Sisson, K. and Storey, J. (2000) *The Realities of Human Resource Management: Managing the Employment Relationship*. Buckingham: Open University Press.

Sparrow, P. and Hiltrop, J.M. (1994) *European Human Resource Management in Transition*. London: Prentice Hall.

Torrington, D.P. (1968) *Successful Personnel Management*. London: Staples.

Vroom, V.H. (1964) *Work and Motivation*. New York: Wiley.

Wood, S. and Albanese, M. (1995) 'Can We Speak of High Commitment Management on the Shop Floor?', *Journal of Management Studies*, Vol. 32, No. 2.

General discussion topics

1 What other issues, aside from those discussed in this chapter, do you think are significant for human resource managers? Which do you consider will become more important in years to come?

2 How far do you think it is possible to agree with *both* the 'best fit' and 'best practice' perspectives on HRM? In what ways are they compatible with each other?

3 It could be argued that the most effective means of forcing employers to treat their employees ethically is to pass more restrictive employment law and to police it more rigorously. How far do you agree with this point of view?

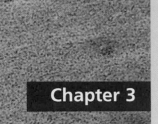
Chapter 3 Strategic human resource management

There is a strong lobby propounding the view that human resources are *the* source of competitive advantage for the business, rather than, say, access to capital or use of technology. It is therefore logical to suggest that attention needs to be paid to the nature of this resource and its management as this will impact on human resource behaviour and performance and consequently the performance of the organisation. Indeed Boxall and Steneveld (1999) argue that there is no need to prove the relationship between firm performance and labour management as it is self-evident that the quality of human resource management is a critical influence on the performance of the firm. It is not, therefore, surprising that the rhetoric of strategic human resource management has been readily adopted, especially as a strategic approach is considered to be one of the characteristics of HRM as opposed to personnel management, which is seen as operational. HR needs to be a strategic player and the role of business strategist will be a key role for HR specialists in the future (Cleland *et al*. 2000).

In this chapter we first discuss some basic issues in relation to the nature of human resource strategy and strategic human resource management, we then explore three different theoretical perspectives on strategic human resource management and conclude by considering the role of HR specialists in strategic HRM.

Strategic human resource management and human resource strategy

Our understanding of HR strategy has changed considerably since strategy first became the subject of great attention. We have moved from viewing strategy as a physical document to strategy as an incremental process, affected by political influences and generating learning. Tyson's (1995) definition of human resource strategy is a useful starting point, although somewhat limited, as will be seen from our later discussion:

> **the intentions of the corporation both explicit and covert, toward the management of its employees, expressed through philosophies, policies and practices.**
> (Tyson 1995)

This definition is helpful because research on human resource strategy in the early 1980s tended to focus on seeking an HR strategy document in order to determine whether there was a strategic approach to HR and what that approach was. This was rather like searching for the Holy Grail. Not surprisingly few complete HR strategies were found and HR specialists berated themselves for having failed in this critical area. Gradually the thinking changed to encompass a view that HR strategy need not be written on a piece of paper or need not indeed, be explicit, as the Tyson quotation illustrates. Further developments in thinking began to take on board the idea that strategies are neither finished, nor complete, but rather incremental and piecemeal. There is compelling evidence to suggest that strategic HR tends to be issue based rather than the formulation of a complete and integrated strategy (for example Grundy 1998; Hall and Torrington 1998). Strategic thinking, strategic decision making and a strategic orientation (for example, Hunt and Boxall 1998) were gradually understood as much more realistic expectations.

In parallel with this thinking there were developments in the general strategy literature which viewed strategy as a process which was not necessarily rational and top down, but a political and evolutionary process (see, for example, Mintzberg 1994). Mintzberg argues that strategy is 'formed' rather than 'formulated' and that any intended strategy is changed by events, opportunities, the actions of employees and so on – so that the realised strategy is different from the initial vision. Strategy, Mintzberg argues, can only be identified in retrospect. Wrapped up in this view is also the idea that strategy is not necessarily determined by top management, alone, but can be influenced, 'bottom up' as ideas are tried and tested in one part of the organisation, and gradually adopted in a wholesale manner if they are seen to be applicable and successful.

This leads on to the concept of strategy as learning both in content and process (see, for example, Senge 1990; Pedler *et al.* 1991) which is supported by the notion of strategy as a process of change (see, for example, Hendry and Pettigrew 1992). Literature draws out the need to sense changes in the environment, develop a resultant strategy and turn this strategy into action. While the HR function has often found itself excluded from the strategy formation process, HR strategy has more often been seen in terms of the implementation of organisational strategies. However implementation of HR strategy has been weak, at best. Among the qualities of the most successful organisations is the ability to turn strategy into action quickly (Ulrich 1998), in other words to implement the chosen strategy (Grensing-Pophel 1999), and Guest (1987) maintained that the capability to implement strategic plans is an important feature of successful HRM. However a lack of attention to the implementation of HR strategy has been identified (Beaumont 1992; Lundy and Cowling 1996; Skinner and Mabey 1997), and the information that does exist suggests that this is a problematic area. Legge (1995) maintained that the evidence of implementation of HR strategies was patchy and sometimes contradictory, and Skinner and Mabey (1997) found that responsibility for implementation was unclear with only 54 per cent of respondents, in organisations with an HR Director, perceiving that the HR function played a major part in implementation. In their research Kane and Palmer (1995) found that the existence of an HR strategy was only a minor influence on the HR policies and procedures that were used.

This brings us to the final issue in this introduction – that of the link between organisational strategy and HR strategy. Figure 3.1 is a simple model that is useful in visualising these relationships and has relevance for the newer conceptions of strategy based on the resource-based view of the firm, as well as earlier conceptions.

In the *separation model* (A) there is no relationship at all, if indeed organisational and human resource strategy *does* exist in an explicit form in the organisation. This is a typical picture of twenty years ago, but it still exists today, particularly in smaller organisations.

The *fit model* (B) represents a growing recognition of the importance of people in the achievement of organisational strategy. Employees are seen as key in the implementation of the declared organisational strategy, and human resource strategy is designed to fit with this. Some of the early formal models of human resource strategy, particularly that proposed by Fombrun *et al.* (1984), concentrate on how the human resource strategy can be designed to ensure a close fit, and the same approach is used in the Schuler and Jackson example in Table 3.1.

This whole approach depends on a view of strategy formulation as a logical rational process, which remains a widely held view. The relationship in the fit model is exemplified by organisations which cascade their business objectives down from the senior management team through functions, through depart-

Figure 3.1 Potential relationships between organisational strategy and HR strategy

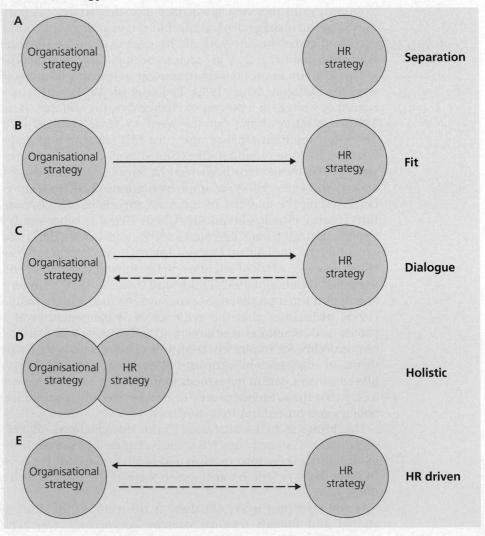

ments, through teams and so on. Functions, for example, have to propose a functional strategy which enables the organisational strategy to be achieved. Departments have to propose a strategy which enables the functional strategy to be achieved, and so on. In this way the HR function (as with any other) is required to respond to organisational strategy by defining a strategy which meets organisational demands.

The *dialogue model* (C) takes the relationship one step further, as it recognises the need for two-way communication and some debate. What is demanded in the organisation's strategy may not be viewed as feasible and alternative possibilities need to be reviewed. The debate, however, is often limited, as shown in the example in the Window on Practice which follows.

WINDOW ON PRACTICE

In one large, multinational organisation an objectives-setting cascade was put in place. This cascade allowed for a dialogue between the planned organisation strategy and the response of each function. In the organisation strategy there was some emphasis on people growth and development and job fulfilment. The HR Department's response included among other things an emphasis on line management involvement in these areas, which would be supported by consultancy help from the HR Department.

The top management team replied to this by asking the HR Department to add a strategic objective about employee welfare and support. The HR Department strongly argued that this was a line management responsibility, along with coaching, development and so on. The HR Function saw its customers as the managers of the organisation, not the employees. The result of the debate was that the HR Function added the strategic objective about employee welfare.

Although the approach in this case appeared two-way, the stronger of the parties was the management team, and they were determined that their vision was the one that would be implemented!

The holistic model and the HR-driven model (D and E) show a much closer involvement between organisational and human resource strategy.

The *holistic model* (D) represents the people of the organisation being recognised as the key to competitive advantage rather than just the way of implementing organisational strategy. In other words HR strategy is not just the means for achieving business strategy (the ends), but an end in itself. Human resource strategy therefore becomes critical and, as Baird *et al.* (1983) argued, there can be no strategy without human resource strategy. Boxall (1996) develops this idea in relation to the resource-based firm, and argues convincingly that business strategy can usefully be interpreted as more broad than a competitive strategy (or positioning in the marketplace). In this case business strategy can encompass a variety of other strategies including HRM, and he describes these strategies as the pieces of a jigsaw. This suggests mutual development and some form of integration, rather than a slavish response to a predetermined business strategy.

The *HR-driven model* (E) offers a more extreme form, which places human resource strategy in prime position. The argument here is that if people are the key to competitive advantage, then we need to build on our people strengths. Logically, then, as the potential of our employees will undoubtedly affect the achievement of any planned strategy, it would be sensible to take account of this in developing our strategic direction. Again this model is a reflection of a resource-based strategic HRM perspective. Butler (1988/89) identifies this model as a shift from human resources as the implementors of strategy to human resources as a driving force in the formulation of the strategy.

Activity 3.1

■ Which of these approaches to human resource strategy most closely fits your organisation? (If you are a full-time student read one or two relevant cases in *People Management* and interpret these as 'your organisation'.)

■ Why did you come to this decision?

■ What are the advantages and disadvantages of the approach used?

Theoretical perspectives of strategic human resource management

Three theoretical approaches to strategic HRM can be identified. The first is founded on the concept that there is 'one best way' of managing human resources in order to improve business performance. The second focuses on the need to align employment policies and practice with the requirements of business strategy in order that the latter will be achieved and the business will be successful. This second approach is based on the assumption that different types of HR strategies will be suitable for different types of business strategies. Third, a more recent approach to strategic HRM is derived from the resource-based view of the firm. This view focuses on the quality of the human resources available to the organisation and their ability to learn and adapt more quickly than their competitors. Supporters of this perspective challenge the need to secure a mechanistic fit with business strategy and focus instead on long-term sustainability and survival of the organisation via the pool of human capital.

Universalist approach

The perspective of the universalist approach is derived from the conception of human resource management as 'best practice', as we discussed in Chapter 1. In other words it is based on the premise that one model of labour management – a high-commitment model – is related to high organisational performance in all contexts, irrespective of the particular competitive strategy of the organisation. An expression of this approach can be seen in Guest's theory of HRM, which is a prescriptive model based on four HR policy goals: strategic integration, commitment, flexibility and quality. These policy goals are related to HRM policies which are expected to produce desirable organisational outcomes as shown in Figure 3.2.

Guest (1989b) describes the four policy goals as follows:

■ **Strategic integration** – ensuring that HRM is fully integrated into strategic planning, that HRM policies are coherent, that line managers use HRM practices as part of their everyday work.
■ **Commitment** – ensuring that employees feel bound to the organisation and are committed to high performance via their behaviour.
■ **Flexibility** – ensuring an adaptable organisation structure, and functional flexibility based on multiskilling.
■ **Quality** – ensuring a high quality of goods and services through high-quality, flexible employees.

Guest sees these goals as a package – all need to be achieved to create the desired organisational outcomes.

Figure 3.2 A theory of HRM

HRM policies ⟷	Human resource outcomes ⟷	Organisational outcomes
Organisational/ job design		*High* Job performance
Management of change	Strategic integration	*High* Problem-solving Change Innovation
Recruitment Selection Socialisation	Commitment	
Appraisal training development	Flexibility/adaptability	*High* Cost effectiveness
Reward systems		
Communication	Quality	*Low* Turnover Absence Grievances

Leadership/culture/strategy

Source: D. Guest (1989b) 'Personnel and HRM: can you tell the difference?' in *Personnel Management*, January, p. 49. Reproduced with the permission of the author.

Clarity of goals gives a certain attractiveness to this model – but this is where the problems also lie. Whipp (1992) questions the extent to which such a shift is possible, and Purcell (1991) sees the goals as unattainable. The goals are also an expression of human resource management, as opposed to personnel management, and as such bring us back to the debate about what human resource management really is and the inherent contradictions in the approach (Legge 1991, 1995). Ogbonna and Whipp (1999) argue that internal consistency within such a model is extremely difficult to achieve because of such contradictions (for example the tension between flexibility and commitment). Because the prescriptive approach brings with it a set of values, it suggests that there is only one best way and this is it. Although Guest (1987) has argued that there is no best practice, he also encourages the use of the above approach as the route to survival of UK businesses.

Pfeffer (1994) and Becker and Gerhart (1996) are well-known exponents of this view. While there is some support for this perspective, which we consider in more depth in Chapter 16 on Strategic Aspects of Performance, there remains some debate as to which particular human resource practices will stimulate high commitment. The following Window on Practice gives an example of one interpretation of a high-commitment, high-performance approach to human resource management strategy.

Falling somewhere between the universalist approach and the fit approach is the Harvard model of HRM. This model, produced by Beer, Spector, Lawrence, Quinn Mills and Walton (1984), is analytical rather than prescriptive. The model, shown in Figure 3.3, recognises the different stakeholder interests that impact on employee behaviour and performance, and also gives greater emphasis to factors

WINDOW ON PRACTICE

High performance teams at Digital, Ayr

In an extremely competitive market the Ayr plant had to demonstrate that they could manufacture specified computer systems at a 'landed cost' competitive with other Digital plants, especially those in the Far East. To do this management had to rapidly introduce a package of changes. They had a strategic focus and a clear vision of the changes (both technical and organisational) required to promote success and they 'sold' this to the employees and corporate management. The high-performance team concept they sold had two great advantages – inbuilt quality and flexibility.

Supportive policies were put in place – such as a new skills-based pay system.

Employment policies in terms of career planning, training and development and other reward policies were also designed to be consistent with and reinforce the initiative. Management introduced unsupervised autonomous groups called 'high performance teams' with around a dozen members with full 'back to front' responsibility for product assembly, testing, fault finding, and problem solving, as well as some equipment maintenance. They used flexitime without time clocks and organised their own team discipline. Individuals were encouraged to develop a range of skills and help others in developing their capability. The ten key characteristics of the teams were as follows:

■ self-managing, self-organising, self-regulating;
■ front-to-back responsibility for core process;
■ negotiated production targets;
■ multiskilling – no job titles;
■ share skills, knowledge, experience and problems;
■ skills-based payment system;
■ peer selection, peer review;
■ open layout, open communications;
■ support staff on the spot;
■ commitment to high standards and performance.

Management had to learn to stand back and let the groups reach their own decisions – an approach that eventually released considerable management time. A great deal of attention was given to how the transition was managed and this was seen as critical to the success of the approach. Time was taken to ensure maximum formal and informal communication and consultation, and there was a critical mass of key individuals prepared to devote themselves to ensure success. Employees were involved to the fullest extent so they eventually felt they owned the concepts and techniques which they used. Training covered job skills, problem-solving techniques and 'attitude training' in the concepts of high-performance organisational design.

Source: Adapted from D.A. Buchanan (1992) 'High performance: new boundaries of acceptability in worker control', in G. Salaman *et al.* (eds), *Human Resource Strategies*. California: Sage.

in the environment that will help to shape human resource strategic choices – identified in the **Situational factors** box. Poole (1990) also notes that the model has potential for international or other comparative analysis, as it takes into account different sets of philosophies and assumptions which may be operating.

Although Beer *et al.*'s model is primarily analytical, there are prescriptive elements leading to some potential confusion. The prescription in Beer *et al.*'s model is found in the **HR outcomes** box, where specific outcomes are identified as universally desirable.

Fit or contingency approach

The fit or contingency approach is based on two critical forms of fit. The first is

Figure 3.3 The Harvard framework for human resource management

Stakeholder interests
Shareholders
Management
Employee groups
Government
Community
Unions

Situational factors
Work force
  characteristics
Business strategy
  and conditions
Management
  philosophy
Labour market
Unions
Task technology
Laws and
  societal values

HRM policy choices
Employee
  influence
Human resource
  flow
Reward systems
Work systems

HR outcomes
Commitment
Competence
Congruence
Cost
  effectiveness

Long-term consequences
Individual
  well-being
Organisational
  effectiveness
Societal
  well-being

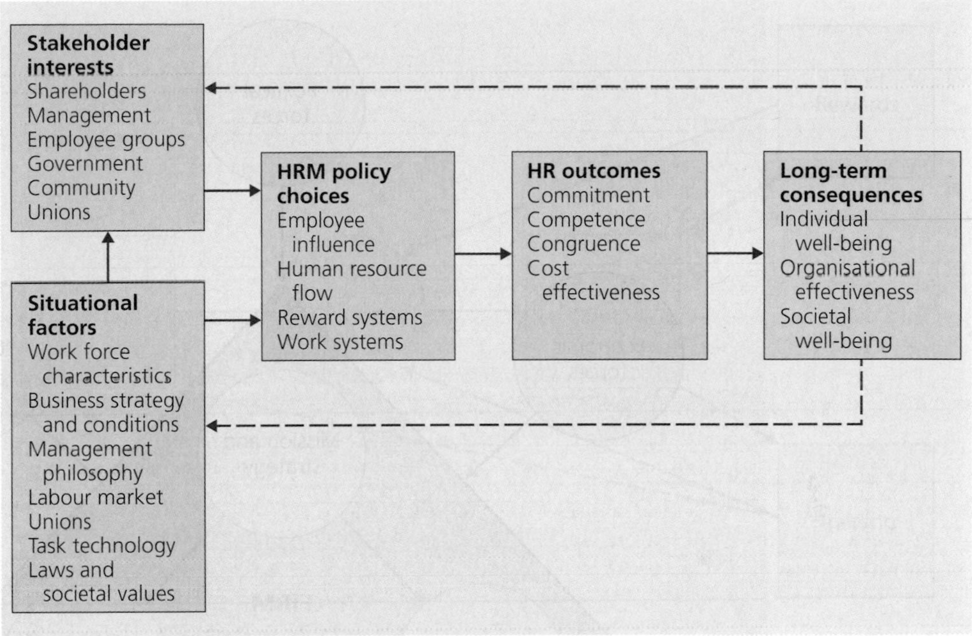

Source: Adapted with permission of The Free Press, a Division of Simon & Schuster, Inc., from *Managing Human Assets* by Michael Beer, Bert Spector, Paul R. Lawrence, D. Quinn Mills, Richard E. Walton. New York: The Free Press. Copyright © 1984 by The Free Press.

external fit – that HR strategy fits with the demands of business strategy; the second is internal fit – that all HR policies and activities fit together so that they make a coherent whole, are mutually reinforcing and one applied consistently. One of the foundations of this approach is found in Fombrun *et al.* (1984), who proposed a basic framework for strategic human resource management, shown in Figures 3.4 and 3.5. Figure 3.4 represents the location of human resource management in relation to organisational strategy, and you should be able to note how the Fit Model (B) is used. Figure 3.5 shows how activities within human resource management can be unified and designed in order to support the organisation's strategy.

The strength of this model is that it provides a simple framework to show how selection, appraisal, development and reward can be mutually geared to produce the required type of employee performance. For example, if an organisation required co-operative team behaviour with mutual sharing of information and support, the broad implications would be:

■ **Selection**: successful experience of team work and sociable, co-operative personality; rather than an independent thinker who likes working alone.
■ **Appraisal**: based on contribution to the team, and support of others; rather than individual outstanding performance.
■ **Reward**: based on team performance and contribution; rather than individual performance and individual effort.

There is little doubt that this type of internal fit is valuable. However, questions have been raised over the model's simplistic response to organisation strategy.

Part I
Case study problem

You have just been appointed to replace the personnel manager in an organisation where members of the Board felt that personnel practice had become overpreoccupied with 'fads and gimmicks' rather than with the needs of the business and the people who worked there. They have asked you to:

1 Review the ways in which human resource management is being conducted across the entire business, within the line as well as by the HR specialists.
2 Identify aspects of best practice currently being employed by leading-edge HR practitioners.
3 Draft proposals for a programme of strategic initiatives to enhance human resource management throughout the business.

On investigation you find:

1 Moves towards a single union agreement have foundered because of implacable resistance from two unions with members in the organisation whose representatives were excluded from discussions about the proposals.
2 The concept of performance management has been introduced at the same time as moves to empower line managers. Many line managers feel that empowerment means no more than taking the blame for things that go wrong, and many of their subordinates feel that they are now cut off from the centralised, expert services of the HR function.
3 A case for the Investors in People award was turned down because practice failed to match the policy.
4 Members of the HR function say that they have lost credibility and job satisfaction by a series of grandiose schemes that were not fully developed and which could not be fully implemented in a short time.

Required

Produce outline, costed proposals, with a timetable, for the Board to consider, setting out what you would do in the first six months and in the next twelve months to deal with this situation.

Locate the organisation in whatever industry you prefer.

Part I
Examination questions

Undergraduate introductory

1 Summarise the stages in development of personnel management and human resource management.
2 Examine some likely future trends in Human Resource Management. Which developments do you expect to be prevalent, and why?

Undergraduate finals

3 Explain the problems of integrating HR strategy with corporate strategy. How can these problems be addressed?
4 'The employment relationship is not just an economic transaction; it also has social and moral connotations.' Discuss the arguments for and against this view and the implications for HRM practice.

Masters

5 Analyse the links between business strategy and HRM, using examples to support your answer.
6 Tom Keenoy (1990) claims:

Far from indicating a new era of humane people-oriented employment management, the primary purpose of the rhetoric of HRM might be to provide a legitimatory managerial ideology to facilitate the intensification of work.

(*Personnel Review*, Vol. 19, No. 2)

Discuss this proposition in the light of both your studies and your working experience.

Professional

7 In May 1993 Fortune magazine set out 'six trends that will re-shape the workplace':
  (a) The average organisation will become smaller, employing fewer people.
  (b) The traditional hierarchical organisation will give way to a variety of forms, foremost being the network of specialists.
  (c) Technicians will replace manufacturing operatives as the worker elite.
  (d) The vertical division of labour will be replaced by a horizontal division.
  (e) The paradigm of doing business will shift from making a product to providing a service.
  (f) Work will be redefined towards constant learning, more higher-order thinking, less nine to five.
  How far do you see these trends exemplified in (a) the economy generally and (b) your own organisation?

8 'In my business my colleagues and I undertake a number of strategic initiatives, but it is unrealistic to claim that we have a human resource strategy, as that would bring us into futile conflict with our managerial colleagues.'
  Discuss that comment, by an HR Director, in the light of your own experience.

ORGANISATION

The management of people takes place in, or in relation to, some organisation and co-ordination of their activities. This produces synergy: working together to produce a result that is greater than the sum of the individual parts. That co-ordination spreads beyond the employees of the business along the supply chain, or value chain, to include suppliers and customers.

The processes of organisation are concerned with communication and information. We all need to know who does what, where we can find the information we need and who needs information from us so that they can do their jobs. One of the main instruments in organisation is planning requirements before then working out how those requirements can be met, and one of the main methods of co-ordination is organisation structure and culture. The structure describes the bare bones of the various working relationships between the people in the business, while the culture is a collection of values and attitudes that the people of the business have in common to energise them and get them working effectively together. People working together frequently need to meet. Where more than two or three are meeting, someone has to run the meeting and make it effective.

Chapter 4   Strategic aspects of organisation

Personnel managers have always been involved in the organisation of the business in their operational role. This is why there was the development phase, described in Chapter 1, of the humane bureaucrat, as businesses grew bigger and became more specialised. The interest in organisation development provided a further twist to the tale. In this part of the book we examine several aspects of personnel activities which are linked in to the organisation-as-entity and organisation-as-process. Structure and culture are largely concerned with the entity; planning, information, communication and presentation are all to do with organisaton as a process.

Strategic aspects of organisation are grounded in the simple proposition of Alfred Chandler (1962) that 'structure follows strategy'. Whatever strategy for growth a business pursued, the structure of the business followed and reflected the demands of that strategy. He was, of course, writing at a time when the idea of growth was universally accepted as an automatic objective for any business, but his analysis remains a central feature of understanding business organisations.

Chandler's three stages of business development

After examining the growth of 70 large American businesses, Chandler concluded that they all pass through three stages of development: unit, functional and multi-divisional.

Any business begins by being on a single location, with a single product and a single decision maker. It may be Rolls and Royce or Hewlett and Packard, rather than Eddie Land or Clive Sinclair but it is still a single decision-making function with two or three people working very closely together and doing almost everything. The first stage of development into the *unit firm* involves the process of vertical integration, with specialist functions being set up and other people employed as there is increasing turnover, the beginning of hierarchy and attempts to achieve some economies of scale. One further feature of this is to expand forwards or backwards in the operating chain, by acquiring other business, such as a supplier or raw materials or a retail outlet.

Evolving into a *functional organisation* introduces specialisation as departments are established to deal with different functions, such as marketing, personnel and finance. If the business expands still further and diversifies into different industries and products, there is then the final stage of turning into *a multi-divisional firm*. Chandler observed that the process of transition was usually delayed and often very dissatisfying to the original entrepreneur. His explanation for this was that the entrepreneur/founder was typically brilliant at strategy (otherwise there would not be a continuing business) but rarely interested in, or skilful at, structuring a business, especially as the structuring process put power and decision into other hands.

Chandler's thesis has been examined by a number of researchers in the period since it was first propounded. Three slight modifications are worth mentioning here, particularly in relation to the evolution of the multi-divisional form. First, Rumelt (1982) showed that the likelihood of a firm having a multi-divisional structure increased as it diversified. Miles and Snow (1984) carried out extensive studies to examine what they called 'strategic fit': the match between strategy, structure and internal management processes. They demonstrate that businesses need organisation structures and management processes that are appropriate to their strategy, or there is a likelihood that their strategy will fail. Both of these may seem unsurprising, even obvious, conclusions: their value is to confirm the enduring potency of Chandler's ideas. A more significant modification comes from Waterman and Peters (1980), who suggested that businesses could make temporary structural changes to cope with the more rapidly changing contemporary environment without abandoning their overall structure.

Having a structure that matches the strategy is thus crucial to the success of strategy, and structure (organisation-as-entity) interrelates closely with the management processes (organisation-as-process).

WINDOW ON PRACTICE

One of the most remarkable entrepreneurs and technological innovators of the 1970s was Clive Sinclair. The dramatic success of the first pocket calculator was quickly followed by the digital watch and the first home computers, ZX81 and Spectrum. An admiring prime minister gave him a knighthood and it seemed that he could do no wrong, but there was no appropriate structure to sustain the strategy. There was a shortage of management skills, especially in marketing and distribution, so there was a retreat. Sir Clive re-established his company to undertake only research and invention. Everything else was sub-contracted, while the handful of people who made up Sinclair Research concentrated on the next technological breakthrough: the electric car. Technically ingenious, the product was a flop. There had been no authoritative marketing guidance to demonstrate that the product would never sell. The strategy could not succeed without the appropriate structure and management processes.

Centralisation and decentralisation

One of the popular ideas of the 1980s was the strategic business unit, which was a method of empowerment, except that it was not an individual manager being empowered, but a complete operating unit of the business. The management of a particular unit was given an agreed budget and an agreed set of targets for the forthcoming period. Thereafter they had freedom to manage themselves in whatever way they thought fit, provided that they first submitted regular reports and, second, met the targets and complied with the budget expectations.

This was a form of decentralisation, and many managers in strategic business units made the wry comment that the one thing that was not decentralised was the strategy!

What is to be decentralised and what is to remain central or drawn into the centre? Chris Hendry (1990, p. 93) makes the interesting observation that in the process of a business decentralising its operations, personnel often remains one of the last centralising forces. He attributes this to the beliefs of personnel people and Chief Executives about issues such as equity, order, consistency and control. The personnel function will relinquish these only reluctantly as they see great risks in, for instance, methods of payment being set up on different principles in separate parts of the business. What about coercive comparisons? What about equal value claims if we do not monitor closely from the centre?

The focus of this concern is changing. Control of collective bargaining and pay structures – the traditional strongholds of the Personnel Director – are being gradually abandoned and decentralised in favour of new power bases, such as group contracts, succession planning, management development and graduate recruitment (ibid., p. 99).

There is, however, a different dimension to the centralisation/decentralisation question. In writing about international companies Kobrin (1988) has demonstrated that managers have to centralise and decentralise at the same time. It does not need the international dimension to make this comment valid. Each component of the business has to have its strengths and knowledge developed and exploited to the full if it is to be effective, and this requires a greater degree of empowerment than most advocates of budget-driven strategic business units acknowledge. At the same time the individual operating unit has to maximise its contribution to group objectives, and that will inevitably lead to occasional profound conflict between unit and group objectives. The strategic role for the personnel people here is not simply to cope with the conflict when it breaks out, but somehow to develop a culture that succeeds in delivering the apparently irreconcilable requirements: enough autonomy for people to really deploy their skills, enthusiasm and commitment, but enough control for group-wide considerations

WINDOW ON PRACTICE

Henry was the Managing Director of a growing business with six operating subsidiaries. Fiona was the Financial Director, who had just joined from a rather larger company. One of the six operating subsidiaries was in difficulties and it appeared to Henry, Fiona and their Board colleagues that it would need to be closed. Fiona said she would work out the numbers over the week-end.

On Monday Fiona showed her proposals to Henry, including the cost of severance for all employed at the subsidiary, including Barry, the General Manager. She sighed and said she supposed he would like her to go down and get it done with. Henry asked if she had consulted with the Personnel Director, George. She had not, so George was asked in and a different strategy was agreed: Barry would be called up to Head Office.

Barry came, clearly having a shrewd idea of what was afoot. Henry explained the situation and said there really seemed no alternative but to close the plant, but Barry was not to worry; he would be looked after. Barry replied that the plant would only close over his dead body and that they did not know what they were talking about. Fiona produced her analysis and was closely questioned by Barry and strongly challenged on certain of her assumptions. After three hours of vigorous argument Henry called a halt by asking Barry to come back within a week with counter-proposals. Henry still felt that Fiona's analysis was correct and that the plant should close, but if Barry could produce watertight, convincing alternatives, they would be listened to. Fiona complained that her professional judgement was being doubted, but George shepherded Barry out of the room.

Five days later Barry was back with a plan that he had discussed with the General Managers of two other subsidiaries and which they said they could make work by slight variations in the way they worked together. The plan involved a drastic reduction in the workforce, but Barry's plant would remain open, targets would be met and they would be back within budget in six months' time. Now it was the turn of Henry and Fiona to question Barry closely, but eventually they agreed that his proposal was a better strategy for the group as a whole.

ultimately to prevail, when they have been tested in the furnace of unit-wide aggressive interrogation. The last part is vital.

Personnel people increasingly have as a part of their role those aspects of co-ordination that go beyond budgetary and planning controls. There are two particular suggestions.

The first is *evangelisation*, the process of winning the acceptance throughout the business of a common mission and a shared purpose. This idea of needing to win hearts and minds has been a common thread in management thinking for most of the twentieth century, and a specialised example is provided later in this chapter from the work of Hopfl (1993). It takes on particular significance in the decentralised business and it is indeed a remarkable management team that will be able to commit themselves with enthusiasm to closing down their local operation on the grounds that the business as a whole will benefit if an operation elsewhere is developed.

Co-ordination through evangelisation works through **shared belief**. The beliefs may be interpreted in different ways and may produce varied behaviours, but there is the attempt to promulgate relatively simple doctrines to which members of the organisation subscribe and through which they are energised. Some readers of this book will have learned their catechism as children, or will have studied the thirty-nine articles defining the doctrinal position of the Church of England. Although this may seem inappropriate to the business world, in the 1970s a British company, Vitafoam, was established by a man who required his senior executives to copy out his annual policy statement by hand, three times, before handing it back to him. It is now commonplace for companies to have mission statements, which come close to being unifying articles of faith.

> At the top is the mission statement, a broad goal based on the organization's planning premises, basic assumptions about the organization's purpose, its values, its distinctive competencies, and its place in the world. A mission statement is a relatively permanent part of an organization's identity and can do much to unify and motivate its members. (Stoner and Freeman 1992, p. 188)

Evangelisation also works through **parables**. Ed Schein (1985, p. 239) identified 'stories and legends' as one of the key mechanisms for articulating and reinforcing the organisation's culture.

The company house magazine helps in circulating the good news about heroic deeds in all parts of the company network. Better are the word-of-mouth exchanges and accounts of personal experience. Evangelisation can use **apostles** – ambassadors sent out to preach the faith. These are the people – usually in senior positions – who move round the company a great deal. They know the business well and can describe one component to another, explaining company policy, justifying particular decisions and countering parochial thinking. They can also move ideas around ('In Seoul they are wondering about ... what do think?') and help in the development of individual networks ('Try getting in touch with Oscar Jennings in Pittsburgh ... he had similar problems a few weeks ago'). At times of crisis, apostles are likely to be especially busy, countering rumour and strengthening resolve. It may be important that most of the apostles come from headquarters and have personally met, and can tell stories about, the founder. Anita Roddick's Body Shop is an organisation that grew rapidly on the basis of working in a way that was markedly different from the conventions of the cosmetics industry that it was challenging. Its growth seemed to need people in all parts to identify closely with the vision and personality of the founder:

> The inductresses' eyes seem to light up whenever Anita's name is mentioned. We are told, in semi-joyous terms, the great tale concerning that first humble little shop in Brighton. And . . . one of our inductresses uses the phrase, 'And Anita saw what she had done, and it was good'.
>
> (Keily 1991, p. 3)

Co-ordination can be improved by the development and promulgation of *standards and norms*. Many companies have sought the accreditation of BS 5750, the British Standard for quality; others claim to be equal opportunity employers. Thinking companies will wish to set standards for many aspects of their operation, especially in personnel matters. The Human Resources Section at Shell Centre is charged with developing and maintaining standards relating to alcohol and drug abuse. If standards are adopted throughout a company, they become a form of co-ordination. Furthermore, it is not necessary for all of them to be developed at the centre. Decentralised standard formulation can enable different parts of the business to take a lead as a preliminary to universal adoption of the standard they have formulated: an excellent method of integration.

Planning

Just as the concept of strategy has somewhat overwhelmed the use of policy as a management instrument, it has also shaded out the use of planning. Planning had its heyday in management thinking during the 1960s, when the clever ideas of operations research were seen as a means whereby future activities could be forecast with confidence so that plans could then be made to deliver that future, 'the past is history . . . the future is planning'. The attraction of planning was that you could make the future happen instead of waiting for it to happen to you. To be a reactive manager was almost as bad as having a communicable disease.

The trouble was that the future rarely turned out as expected; some completely unforeseen event scuppered the plans. The great example was the use of Programme Evaluation Review Technique (PERT) in planning the development and production of the Polaris missile system. Sapolsky (1972, p. 246) studied its application and decided that as a planning technique it was as effective as rain dancing, and that its obvious success was due not to its technical efficiency but to the mystique of infallibility that its managers were able to promote.

As enthusiasm for change took over from a commitment to planning among managers, there was a tendency to think that all action needed to be spontaneous. Particularly in Britain, the predilection for short-term thinking received an unfortunate boost, with the concomitant difficulties of a reluctance to invest and an unwillingness to make provision – through training, for instance – to a future that might not happen. Tom Peters appeared to dismiss planning altogether, producing less than two pages devoted to the topic in a 560-page tome:

> The long-range strategic plan, of voluminous length, is less useful than before. But a strategic 'mind-set', which focuses on skill/capability building (e.g. adding value to the work force via training to prepare it to respond more flexibly and be more quality-conscious) is more important than ever.
>
> (Peters 1989, p. 394)

There we have another clue to the future orientation of personnel management, as we think of organisation as process rather than entity. Peters sees little scope for the strategic plan of the type beloved by the marketing specialists and the MBA graduate, but calls instead for some forward-looking, creative personnel work. This echoes the Japanese concern with the longer term. Holden (1994, p. 125) gives the example of a Japanese computer company with a development plan for all employees that takes 42 years to complete!

As will be seen in the next few chapters, personnel work requires an approach to planning that is rather more flexible and imaginative – soft as well as hard – than that of the manpower planning textbooks of the 1970s.

Information and communication

Information is a prerequisite for all decision making, and the handling of information is crucial to all personnel work: aggregated data on numbers, ages, skills, hours, rates of pay and so on and information relating to invididuals.

Communication is a varied process whereby information of the above, specific type is merged with other types of data, understanding, feeling and image to create the process whereby the organisation functions. This requires care with organisational structure, for what is an organisation chart except a statement about responsibilities, status, channels of communication and job titles? It requires an appreciation of organisational culture, an effective set of systems, procedures and drills, and it requires personal competence in members of the organisation, especially managers.

One of the main strategic aspects of communication is communicating across national and cultural boundaries, where feedback is especially important both to monitor what is happening and to develop understanding between the operations. Those in country A will inevitably have limited understanding about the situation of those in country B, to say nothing of the cultural and linguistic uncertainties that feedback can help clear up.

Recently, business expansion has frequently been by acquisition rather than simple growth of what Alfred Chandler described as the unit firm. This produces a particularly intense communications problem. Employees in the acquired company will feel a greater sense of community with each other than with those who have acquired them. They will see corporate affairs from their own standpoint and will tend to be cautious in their behaviour and suspicious in their interpretation of what they hear from their new owners. Personnel people can have a crucial part to play in managing the requisite communications and information flow.

When the expansion is by acquisition of businesses in a different country, with a different set of cultural norms, the problems are intensified. Even when initial suspicion begins to unwind, there are still difficulties. For example, there are the problems of rivalry, distorted perceptions and resource allocation.

Rivalry

Whatever is done to develop a shared sense of purpose and a common identity, companies in different countries tend to take pride in their own accomplishments and to disparage the accomplishments of other nationality groups. As long

ering the line manager is a theme to which there is frequent reference in this book. This empowerment goes both ways, as managers from other backgrounds bring their perspective more intrusively into what personnel specialists have liked to regard as their own preserve. The public relations approach is a clear example, with many businesses running communications with employees along similar lines to communications with customers. Often privately derided as 'hard-sell gimmicks,' these methods are not always popular in the personnel community. Perhaps the best-known of these activities was a series of commitment-raising projects in British Airways. Heather Hopfl describes the opening of a three-day workshop, 'Visioning the Future':

> This event requires a level of stage management that would not be unfamiliar to a touring rock band. . . . One of the trainers stands at the door to ensure that no-one gets in early to 'spoil' the experience. Nine o'clock. The doors to the conference room are opened . . . the opening music from 'Also Sprach Zarathustra' . . . blasts out a triumphal welcome. . . . The lights dim and the corporate logo appears before them. Three days of management development have begun.   (Hopfl 1993, p. 120)

Although this is alien to many personnel people, they soon realised that people are so used to slick presentation in all departments of their lives, that presentation of information at work needs to use contemporary techniques if it is to have impact.

Summary propositions

4.1 Organisational strategy is inextricably linked with the structure of the business; one cannot be changed without changing, or requiring change, in the other.

4.2 One common strategic initiative is to decentralise, using the strategic business unit as the locus of business activity. This requires specific measures to co-ordinate the decentralised fragments.

4.3 The international, or global, business can have considerable problems in co-ordination. Ways of dealing with them include evangelisation, the development of standards and norms and planning.

4.4 Communication in any business confirms the holistic nature of the enterprise.

References

Brandt, W.K. and Hulbert, J.M. (1976) 'Patterns of communication in the multinational company', *Journal of International Business Studies* (Spring), pp. 57–64.

Chandler, A.D. (1962) *Strategy and Structure*. Cambridge, Mass: MIT Press.

Foulds, J. and Mallet, L. (1989) 'The European and international dimension', in T. Wilkinson (ed.), *The Communications Challenge*. London: IPM.

Hendry, C. (1990) 'Corporate management of human resources under conditions of decentralisation', *British Journal of Management*, Vol. 1, No. 2, pp. 91–103.

Holden, N.J. (1994) 'International HRM with vision', in D.P. Torrington, *International Human Resource Management*. Hemel Hempstead: Prentice Hall International.

Hopfl, H. (1993) 'Culture and commitment: British Airways', in D. Gowler, K. Legge and C. Clegg (eds), *Case Studies in Organizational Behaviour*, 2nd edn. London: Paul Chapman Publishing.

Keily, D. (1991) 'Body Shop blues', *The Sunday Times*, 8 December, p. 3.

Kobrin, S.J. (1988) 'Expatriate reduction and strategic control in American multi-national corporations', *Human Resource Management*, Vol. 27, No. 1, pp. 63–75.

Miles, R.E. and Snow, C.E. (1984) 'Fit, failure and the hall of fame', *California Management Review*, Vol. 26, No. 3, pp. 10–28.

Pascale, R.T. (1978) 'Communication and decision making across cultures: Japanese and American comparisons', *Administrative Science Quarterly*, March, pp. 91–110.

Peters, T.J. (1989) *Thriving on Chaos*. London: Pan Books.

Richards-Carpenter, C. (1994) 'Why the CPIS is a Disappointment', *Personnel Management*, Vol. 26, No. 5, pp. 63–4.

Rumelt, R.P. (1982) 'Diversification strategy and profitability', *Strategic Management Journal*, Vol. 3, pp. 359–69.

Sapolsky, H. (1972) *The Polaris System Development*. Cambridge, Mass: Harvard University Press.

Schein, E.H. (1985) *Organizational Culture and Leadership*. San Francisco: Jossey-Bass.

Stoner, J.A.F. and Freeman, R.E. (1992) *Management*, 5th edn. Englewood Cliffs, NJ: Prentice Hall Inc.

Waterman, R.H. and Peters, T.J. (1980) 'Structure is not organisation', *Business Horizons*, June.

General discussion topics

1 How do you understand the ideas of evangelisation, parables, apostles and standards and norms? What are the advantages and drawbacks of using religious imagery in this context?

2 What lessons should Henry, Fiona and Barry learn from their discussions?

3 What is the difference between information and communication?

Chapter 5   Planning: jobs and people

Planning for human resources has experienced a chequered history. In the 1960s and 1970s it was heralded as a critical tool for business success, as planning to get the right people in the right place at the right time was seen to be essential to achieving rapidly growing production. In the 1980s and 1990s planning was viewed as a suitable tool for managing downsizing and redundancies. On the other hand it has been argued that planning, which has always been accused of having feasibility and implementation problems, is no longer meaningful in an era of discontinuous change; and increasing attention to a broader and more flexible strategic approach appeared to put planning in the shadows. As Mintzberg (1994) put it, 'the most successful strategies are visions, not plans'. In spite of this planning remains alive and well. The emphasis and scope has changed and broadened but there is a strong lobby maintaining its importance in supporting strategic HRM rather than being substituted by it.

In this chapter we will first consider the contribution and feasibility of HR planning and then go on to explore a broad integrated model of HR planning. Throughout the explanation of the model we refer to the appropriate parts of an associated exercise which is located on the website.

The contribution and feasibility of HR planning

A useful starting point is to consider the different contributions that strategy and planning make to the organisation. A common view has been that they are virtually one and the same – hence the term 'strategic planning'. In an article in the *Harvard Business Review* (February 1994, p. 108), Henry Mintzberg gives us his view. He distinguishes between strategic thinking, which is about involving synthesis, intuition, and creativity to produce a not-too-precisely articulated vision of direction, and strategic planning, which is about collecting the relevant information to stimulate the visioning process and also programming the vision into what needs to be done to get there. It is helpful to look at human resource planning in the same way, which is demonstrated in Figure 5.1. In more detail he suggests:

■ **Planning as strategic programming** – planning cannot generate strategies, but it can make them operational by clarifying them; working out the consequences of them; and identifying what must be done to achieve each strategy.
■ **Planning as tools to communicate and control** – planning can ensure co-ordination and encourage everyone to pull in the same direction; planners can assist in finding successful experimental strategies which may be operating in just a small part of the organisation.

Figure 5.1 Human resource strategic visioning and strategic planning

Strategic planning	Strategic visioning	Strategic planning
Providing HR data, ideas Asking difficult questions	Defining a vision of the future (organisational and HR)	Programme the vision – HR objectives targets action plans

Source: After Mintzberg 1994.

■ **Planners as analysts** – planners need to analyse hard data, both external and internal, which managers can then use in the strategy development process.
■ **Planners as catalysts** – raising difficult questions and challenging the conventional wisdom which may stimulate managers into thinking in more creative ways.

Planners, therefore, whether organisational planners or human resource planners, make an essential contribution to strategic visioning. Walker (1992a) maintains that planning is necessary to support strategy and Sisson and Storey (2000) identify HR planning as 'one of the basic building blocks of a more strategic approach'. Lam and Schaubroeck (1998) identify three specific ways in which HR planning is critical to strategy, as it can be used to identify:

■ gaps in capabilities which would prevent the strategy being implemented successfully – in other words lack of sufficient skills, people, knowledge and so on in the organisation;
■ surpluses in capabilities that may provide opportunities for efficiencies and responsiveness – in other words the skills, people and knowledge that may be underused, so the organisation could consider new opportunities and ventures that would capitalise on these human resources – in other words to influence or shape the strategy;
■ poor utilisation of people in the organisation – suggesting inappropriate human resource practices which could be reviewed and altered.

If you turn back to Chapter 3 and have another look at the resource-based view of the firm you will see how these three areas are critical to underpinning the value of human resources as sustained competitive advantage.

While there may be some strong arguments identifying the potential value of HR planning, concerns have always been raised about its feasibility. These focus on the nature of the human resource, the nature of the planning in an uncertain environment and the difficulty of implementing plans. Hussey (1982, 1999), in books about corporate planning, argues that the human resource is far more complex to plan for than the financial resource. He comments on the critical differences between people, the difficulty of moving them around, the costs of overstaffing and the importance of treating people as people and not as an inanimate resource. In addition, individuals have their personal set of values and motivations, and these need to be accounted for in the potential achievement of identified plans.

The balance between visioning and planning will be different depending on the environment. In a highly uncertain environment the emphasis needs to be more on the visioning process. Where things are slightly less chaotic planning has a greater contribution to make. Even so, plans need to be viewed as flexible and be reviewed regularly, rather than being seen as an end point in the process. Planning is not an isolated event, but something that has to be continuously monitored, refined and updated. Bell (1989) argues that while there may be an annual cycle of planning, this should represent a review activity that goes on throughout the year; and that each cycle should feed into the next.

Implementation issues are tied up with the weight that line managers attach to human resource plans. They are more likely to be supportive if they have been involved in the human resource planning process and if the analyses used are simple rather than complex. Walker (1992b) comments that human resource plans are becoming more flexible and shorter term, with a clearer focus on human resource issues, simpler data analysis and an emphasis on action planning and implementation. There is continued strong support for these views, which suggest that the output of the planning process needs to be user friendly, and owned by line management rather than the personnel function (see, for example, Greer *et al.* 1989). Ulrich (1989) points to the need for human resource plans to be seen as the means to an end (achieving the vision), rather than an end in themselves.

WINDOW ON PRACTICE	Tony, the Personnel Manager, shouted at Ian, the Chief Executive: 'What do you mean, it wasn't agreed?'

'I mean it's the first I've heard that you need £22k for a new apprentice scheme.'
'Well, it was in the plan.'
    'What plan?'
'The manpower plan, what other f*****g plan would I mean!'
'You didn't ask me for the money.'
'I asked you in the plan, and you didn't come back and say we couldn't have it.'
'I didn't come back and say you could – now let's start at the beginning – tell me why we need to spend it and what will happen if we don't.'
The conversation continued and finally Tony and Ian began to talk about the real issues. Ian never told Tony that he had filed the manpower plan unread, but he did tell him that he wanted next year's plan to be five pages of interpretation and recommendations and not 85 pages of figures.

There is considerable support for simple issues-based planning, and this fits well with the growing trends in strategic HRM. In Chapter 3 we found that HR strategy was originally conceptualised as holistic, where everything in HR was accounted for in one exercise, but that in practice HR strategy tends to respond on an issue-by-issue basis to business strategy and demands. There is a similar recognition in the HR planning literature – while a comprehensive plan may remain the ideal, it may only be practical to plan on an issue-by-issue basis (see, for example, Schuler and Walker 1990).

So far we have identified the value and contribution of HR planning, recognised some of the limitations to carrying it out practice and reviewed some of the ways in which it can be made more feasible, practical and relevant. We now go on to explore how the scope of HR planning has developed to respond to the needs of today's organisations, and this brings us to models of HR planning.

Models of human resource planning

Traditionally human resource planning, generally termed manpower planning, was concerned with the numbers of employees and skill levels and types in the organisation. A typical model of traditional manpower planning is shown in Figure 5.2. In this model the emphasis is on balancing the projected demand for and supply of labour, in order to have the right number of the right employees in the right place at the right time. The demand for manpower is influenced by corporate strategies and objectives, the environment and the way that staff are utilised within the business. The supply of manpower is projected from current employees (via calculations about expected leavers, retirements, promotions, etc.) and from the availability of the required skills in the labour market. Anticipated demand and supply are then reconciled by considering a range of options, and plans to achieve a feasible balance are designed.

As the world has moved on this model has been viewed as too narrow, being heavily reliant on calculations of employee numbers or potential employee numbers. It has also been criticised for giving insufficient attention to skills (Hendry 1994; Taylor 1998). In addition there has been an increasing recognition of the need to plan for the softer (rather than hard numbers) issues of employee behaviour, organisation culture and systems, which have been identified as having a key impact on business success in the current environment. Bramham (1989) in his first book entitled *Human Resource Planning* (after earlier editions entitled *Manpower Planning*), explains the differences between the old and new approaches:

Figure 5.2 A model of traditional manpower planning

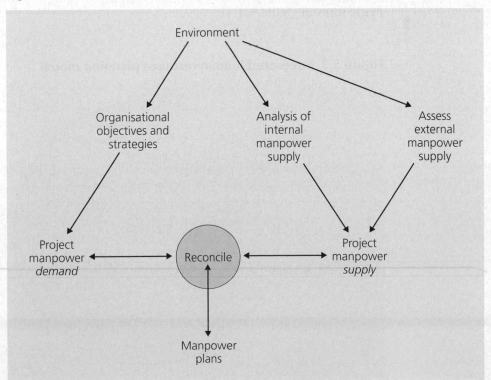

> There are particularly important differences in terms of process and purpose. In human resource planning the manager is concerned with motivating people – a process in which costs, numbers, control and systems interact to play a part. In manpower planning the manager is concerned with the numerical elements of forecasting, supply-demand matching and control, in which people are a part. There are therefore important areas of overlap and interconnection but there is a fundamental difference in underlying approach.   (Bramham 1989, p. 147)

Whether we see current HR planning as a different approach, as Bramham does, or as an expanded version of manpower planning (as, for example, do Marchington and Wilkinson 1996), it is clear that HR planning encompasses a much broader perspective than previously.

Increasingly there is a need for organisations to integrate the process of planning for numbers and skills or employees; employee behaviour and organisational culture; organisation design and the make-up of individual jobs; and formal and informal systems. These aspects are all critical in terms of programming and achieving the vision. Each of these aspects interrelates with the others. However, reality has always been recognised as a long way from identified best practice. Undoubtedly different organisations will place different emphases on each of these factors, and may well plan each separately or plan some and not others (particularly in the light of current issues-based approaches).

The model we shall use in this chapter attempts to bring all aspects of planning together, incorporating the more traditional model of 'manpower planning', but going beyond this to include behaviour, culture, systems and so on. Our model identifies 'where we want to be', translated from response to the strategic vision; 'where we are now'; and 'what we need to do to make the transition' – all operating within the organisation's environment. The model is shown in diagrammatic form in Figure 5.3.

Figure 5.3 Integrated human resource planning model

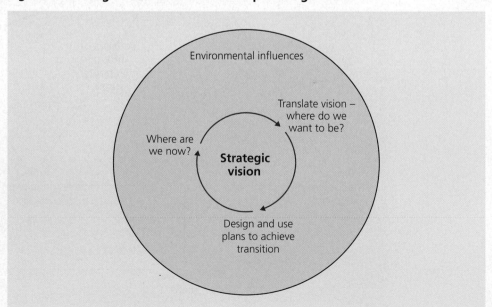

We shall now look in more depth at each of these four areas. It is important to remember that although the steps may logically follow on in the way that they are presented, in reality they may be carried out in parallel, and/or in an informal fashion, and each area may well be revisited a number of times.

Analysing the environment

In this chapter we refer to the environment broadly as the context of the organisation, and this is clearly critical in the impact that it has on both organisational and human resource strategy. Much strategy is based on a response to the environment – for example, what our customers now want or what competitors are now offering – or a proactive effort to guess what customers will want or to persuade them what they will need. In human resource terms we need to identify, for example, how difficult or easy it will be to find employees with scarce skills and what these employees will expect from an employer so that we can attract them. (See HRP exercise, note 1, on the website (as explained on p. xxiv of the Preface).) We shall be concerned with legislation which will limit or widen the conditions of employment that we offer, with what competitors are offering and with what training schemes are available locally or nationally.

Table 5.1 Sources of information on environment trends

Trend area	Possible sources
Social	Census information CIPD journals News media *Social Trends* *General Household Survey* *Employment Gazette* Local papers
Demographics	*Labour Market Quarterly* Census information *Employment Gazette* Local Council, TEC
Political and legislative	News media *Proceedings of European Parliament* *Proceedings of British Parliament* Hansard *Industrial Relations Review and Report* *Industrial Law Journal* *IDS Brief*
Industrial and technological	*Employment Digest* Journals specifically for the industry *Financial Times* Employers' association Trade association
Competitors	Annual reports Talk to them!

Data on relevant trends can be collected from current literature, company annual reports, conferences/courses and from contacts and networking. Table 5.1 gives examples of the many possible sources against each major area.

Once one has acquired and constantly updated data on the environment, one of the most common ways of analysing this is to produce a map of the environment, represented as a wheel. The map represents a time in the future, say three years out. In the centre of the wheel can be written the core purpose of the organisation as it relates to people, or potential future strategies or goals. Each spoke of the wheel can then be filled in to represent a factor of the external environment, for example, potential employees, a specific local competitor, competitors generally, regulatory bodies, customers, government. From all the spokes the six or seven regarded as most important need to be selected.

Figure 5.4 Mapping the environment

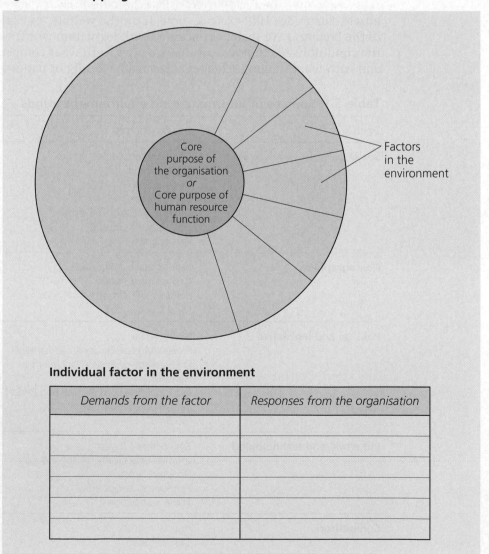

Core
purpose of
the organisation
or
Core purpose of
human resource
function

Factors
in the
environment

Individual factor in the environment

Demands from the factor	Responses from the organisation

These can then be worked on further by asking what demands each will make of the organisation, and how the organisation will need to respond in order to achieve its goals. From these responses can be derived the implications for human resource activities. For example, the demands of potential employees may be predicted as:

- We need a career not just a job.
- We need flexibility to help with childrearing.
- We want to be treated as people and not machines.
- We need a picture of what the organisation has in store for us.
- We want to be better trained.

And so on.

Managers then consider what the organisation would need to offer to meet these needs – in order to meet a declared organisational goal or strategy. It is a good way of identifying human resource issues which need to be addressed. The analysis can also be fed back into identifying and clarifying the future vision or goals in human resource terms. Figure 5.4 gives an outline for the whole process. (For a worked example see HRP Exercise, note 2 on the website.)

Activity 5.1

Draw a map of the external environment, for any organisation in which you are involved, for three to five years ahead. Individually or as a group, brainstorm all the spokes in the wheel and select the six most important ones. Draw up a demands and responses list for each. Write a one-side of A4 summary of what you think your organisation's priorities should be in the people area over the next 3–5 years.

Defining the future in human resource terms

Organisation, behaviour and culture

There is little specific literature on the methods used to translate the strategic objectives of the organisation and environmental influences into qualitative or soft human resource goals. In general terms, they can be summed up as the use of managerial judgement. If the activity is seen as vital to the organisation, then senior managers will be involved in the processes and it will be more likely to be identified as part of the strategic visioning rather than a planning activity. Brainstorming, combined with the use of structured checklists or matrices, can encourage a more thorough analysis. Organisation change literature and corporate planning literature are helpful as a source of ideas in this area. Three simple techniques are a human resource implications checklist (see Figure 5.5), a strategic brainstorming exercise (Figure 5.6) and a behavioural expectation chart (HRP Exercise, note 3 on the website).

Employee numbers and skills (demand forecasting)

There is far more literature in the more traditional area of forecasting employee number demand based on the organisation's strategic objectives. Both objective and subjective approaches can be employed.

Figure 5.5 The beginnings of a human resource implications checklist

Corporate goal	Human resource implications in respect of:	Methods of achieving this
	New tasks? For whom? What competencies needed? Relative importance of team/individual behaviour Deleted tasks? How will managers need to manage?	

Figure 5.6 Strategic brainstorming exercise

Managers write a corporate goal in the centre and brainstorm changes
that need to take place in each of the four areas, one area at a time

Objective methods

Statistical methods

Some statistical methods depend on the assumption that the future situation will display some continuity from the past. Past trends are projected into the future to simulate or 'model' what would happen if they continued – for example, historical trends of employee numbers could be projected into the future. These methods are rarely used in the present climate as they are inappropriate in a context of rapid and often discontinuous change.

Other statistical models relate employee number demand to more specific organisational and environmental circumstances. These models are used to calculate people demand as a result of, usually, organisational activities. Models can take account of determining factors, such as production, sales, passenger miles, level of service. These factors can be used separately or in combination with other determining factors. A simple model might relate people demand to production, using a constant relationship, without making any assumptions about economies of scale. In this model if output is to be doubled, then employees would also need to be doubled. (See HRP Exercise, note 4, on the website.)

More complicated equations can be formulated, which describe the way that a combination of independent factors has affected the dependent employee demand. By inserting new values of the independent factors, such as new projected sales figures, the demand for employees can be worked out from the equation. The equations can also be represented as graphs, making the relationships clear to see. These models can be adapted to take account of projected changes in utilisation, owing to factors such as the introduction of new technology, or alternative organisational forms, such as high performance teams.

Work study

The work-study method is based on time study and a thorough analysis of the work done to arrive at the person-hours needed per unit of output. Standards are developed for the numbers and levels of employees that are needed to do the work tasks. These standards may be developed within the organisation or elsewhere and are most useful when studying production work. It is important that the standards are checked regularly to make sure they are still appropriate. Work study is usually classified as an objective measure; however it is often accepted that since the development of standards and the grouping of tasks is partly dependent on human judgement, it should be considered as a subjective method.

Subjective methods

Managerial judgement

Sometimes called executive judgement, managerial opinion or inductive method, it can also include the judgements of other operational and technical staff, as well as all levels of managers. This method is based on managers' estimates of manpower demand based on past experience and on corporate plans. Managerial judgements can be collected from the 'bottom up' with lower-level managers providing estimates to go up the hierarchy for discussion and redrafting. Alternatively, a 'top-down' approach can be used with estimates made by the highest level of management to go down the hierarchy for discussion and redrafting. When using this method it is difficult to cope with changes that are very different from past experiences. It is also less precise than statistical methods, but it is more comprehensive. Managerial judgement is a simple method, which can be applied fairly quickly and is not restricted by lack of data, particularly historical data, as are statistical techniques. However, managerial judgement is important even when statistical techniques are used. (See HRP Exercise, note 5, on the website.)

Delphi technique

The Delphi technique is a specialised procedure for the collection of managerial opinions based on the idea of the oracle at Delphi. A group of managers anonymously and independently answer questions about anticipated manpower demand. A compilation of the answers is fed back to each individual, and the process is repeated until all the answers converge. Empirical data suggest that this technique is little used at present, although it is often referred to as a common method.

Taking account of changing employee utilisation

The emphasis on employee utilisation varies considerably between authors – some see it as the most critical issue, whereas others give it only passing attention. There is a vast range of ways to change the way that employees are used:

1 Introducing new materials or equipment, particularly new technology.
2 Introducing changes in work organisation, such as:
   (a) quality circles;
   (b) job rotation;
   (c) job enlargement;
   (d) job enrichment;
   (e) autonomous work-groups;
   (f) high-performance teams;
   (g) participation.
3 Organisation development.
4 Introducing changes in organisation structure, such as:
   (a) centralisation/decentralisation;
   (b) new departmental boundaries;
   (c) relocation of parts of the organisation;
   (d) flexible project structures.
5 Introducing productivity schemes, bonus schemes or other incentive schemes.
6 Encouraging greater staff flexibility and work interchangeability.
7 Altering times and periods of work.
8 Training and appraisal of staff.
9 Developing managers and use of performance management.

Some of these methods are interrelated or overlap and would therefore be used in combination. (See HRP Exercise, note 6, on the website.) Interconnections between most of these areas and soft human resources planning are also apparent.

Analysing the current situation

Organisation, behaviour and culture

It is in this area that more choice of techniques is available, and the possibilities include the use of questionnaires to staff (HRP Exercise, note 7, on the website), interviews with staff and managerial judgement. Focus groups are an increasingly popular technique where, preferably, the Chief Executive meets with, say, 20 representative staff from each department to discuss their views of the strengths and weaknesses of the organisation, and what can be done to improve. These approaches can be used to provide information on, for example:

- Motivation of employees.
- Job satisfaction.
- Organisational culture.
- The way that people are managed.
- Attitude to minority groups and equality of opportunity.
- Commitment to the organisation and reasons for this.

- Clarity of business objectives.
- Goal-focused and other behaviour.
- Organisational issues and problems.
- What can be done to improve.
- Organisational strengths to build on.

WINDOW ON PRACTICE

Jennifer Hadley is the Chief Executive of Dynamo Castings, a long-established organisation which had experienced rapid growth and healthy profits until the past three years. Around 800 staff were employed mostly in production, but significant numbers were also employed in marketing/sales and research/development. Poor performance over the last three years was largely the result of the competition who were able to deliver a quality product at a competitive price more quickly. Dynamo retained the edge in developing new designs, but this consumed a high level of resources and was a lengthy process from research to eventual production. Most employees had been with the company for a large part of their working lives and the culture was still appropriate to the times of high profit where life had been fairly easy and laid back. Messages about difficult times, belt tightening and higher productivity with fewer people had been filtered down to employees – who did not change their behaviour but did feel threatened.

It was with some trepidation that Jennifer decided to meet personally with a cross-section of each department to talk through company and departmental issues. The first meeting was with research/development. As expected, the meeting began with a flood of concerns about job security. No promises could be given. However the mid-point of the meeting was quite fruitful, and the following, among other, points became clear:

- that development time could be reduced to one year from two if some production staff were involved in the development process from the very beginning;
- that many development staff felt their career prospects were very limited and a number expressed the wish to be able to move into marketing – they felt this would have an advantage also when it came to marketing new products;
- that staff felt fairly paid and would be prepared to forgo salary rises for a year or two if this would mean job security; they liked working for Dynamo and didn't want to move;
- that staff were aware of the difficult position the company was in but they really didn't know what to do to make it any better;
- development staff wanted to know why Dynamo didn't collaborate with Castem Ltd on areas of mutual interest (Jennifer didn't know the answer to this one).

The meeting not only gave Jennifer a better understanding of what employees felt, but also some good ideas to explore. Departmental staff knew their problems had not been wiped away, but did feel that Jennifer had at least taken the trouble to listen to them.

Turnover figures, performance data, recruitment and promotion trends and characteristics of employees may also shed some light on these issues.

Data relating to current formal and informal systems, together with data on the structure of the organisation, also need to be collected, and the effectiveness, efficiency and other implications of these need to be carefully considered. Most data will be collected from within the organisation, but data may also be collected from significant others, such as customers, who may be part of the environment.

Current and projected employee numbers and skills (employee supply)

Current employee supply can be analysed in both individual and overall statistical terms.

Analysis may be made for any of the following factors, either singly or in combination: number of employees classified by function, department, occupation job title, skills, qualifications, training, age, length of service, performance appraisal results. (See HRP Exercise, note 8, on the website.)

Forecasting of employee supply is concerned with predicting how the current supply of manpower will change over time, primarily in respect of how many will leave, but also how many will be internally promoted or transferred. These changes are forecast by analysing what has happened in the past, in terms of staff retention and/or movement, and projecting this into the future to see what would happen if the same trends continued. Bell (1989) provides an extremely thorough coverage of possible analyses, on which this section is based. However, although statistical analyses are most well developed for the forecasting of employee supply, behavioural aspects are also important. These include investigating the reasons why staff leave and criteria that affect promotions and transfers. Changes in working conditions and in personnel policy would be relevant here. Statistical techniques fall broadly into two categories: analyses of staff leaving the organisation, and analyses of internal movements.

Analyses of staff leaving the organisation

Annual labour turnover index

The annual labour turnover index is sometimes called the percentage wastage rate, or the conventional turnover index. This is the simplest formula for wastage and looks at the number of staff leaving during the year as a percentage of the total number employed who could have left.

$$\frac{\text{Leavers in year}}{\substack{\text{Average number of staff} \\ \text{in post during year}}} \times 100 = \text{per cent wastage rate}$$

(See HRP Exercise, note 9, on the website.)

This measure has been criticised because it gives only a limited amount of information. If, for example, there were 25 leavers over the year, it would not be possible to determine whether 25 different jobs had been left by 25 different people, or whether 25 different people had tried and left the same job. Length of service is not taken into account with this measure, yet length of service has been shown to have a considerable influence on leaving patterns – such as the high number of leavers at the time of induction.

Stability index

The stability index is based on the number of staff who could have stayed throughout the period. Usually, staff with a full year's service are expressed as a percentage of staff in post one year ago.

$$\frac{\substack{\text{Number of staff with one year's} \\ \text{service at date}}}{\substack{\text{Number of staff employed exactly} \\ \text{one year before}}} \times 100 = \text{per cent stability}$$

(See HRP Exercise, note 10, on the website.)

This index, however, ignores joiners throughout the year and takes little account of length of service.

Bowey's Stability Index (Bowey 1974) attempts to take account of the length of service of employees.

Cohort analysis

A cohort is defined as a homogeneous group of people. Cohort analysis involves the tracking of what happens, in terms of leavers, to a group of people with very similar characteristics who join the organisation at the same time. Graduates are an appropriate group for this type of analysis. A graph can be produced to show what happens to the group. The graph can be in the form of a survival curve or a log-normal wastage curve, which can be plotted as a straight line and can be used to make predictions. The disadvantage of this method of analysis is that it cannot be used for groups other than the specific type of group for which it was originally prepared. The information has also to be collected over a long time-period, which gives rise to problems of availability of data and their validity.

Half-life

The half-life is a figure which expresses the time taken for half the cohort to leave the organisation. The figure does not give as much information as a survival curve, but it is useful as a summary and as a method of comparing different groups.

Census method

The census method is an analysis of leavers over a reasonably short period of time – often over a year. The length of completed service of leavers is summarised by using a histogram, as shown in Figure 5.7. (See HRP Exercise, note 11, on the website.)

Figure 5.7 Census analysis: percentage of leavers with differing length of service

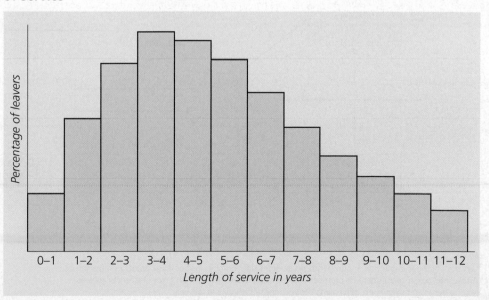

Percentage of leavers

0–1 1–2 2–3 3–4 4–5 5–6 6–7 7–8 8–9 9–10 10–11 11–12

Length of service in years

Retention profile

Staff retained, that is those who remain with the organisation, are allocated to groups depending on the year they joined. The number in each year group is translated into a percentage of the total number of individuals who joined during that year.

Analyses of internal movements

Techniques of analysing internal movements tend to be more sophisticated than those dealing with the analysis of wastage.

Age and length of service distributions can be helpful to indicate problems that

Figure 5.8 Stocks and flows: current establishment and staff in post, with movements over the last year

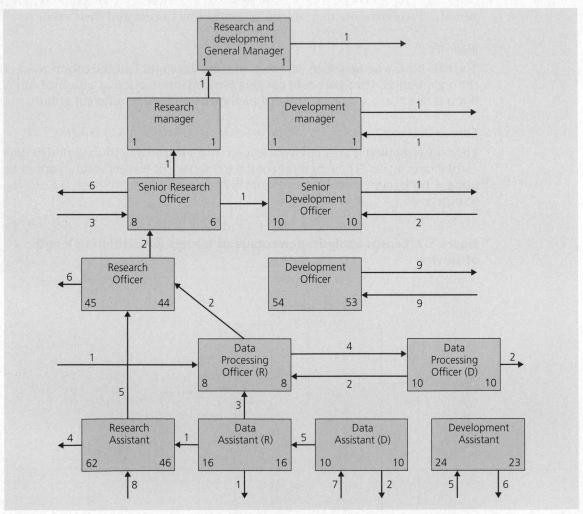

Note:
Left side: number inside box = number of posts. Right side: number inside box = actual number in post.
Arrow into box = recruitment or promotion or sideways move. Arrow from box = leavers or movers.
No line between boxes = no movement between those positions in last year.

may arise in the future, such as promotion blocks. They need to be used in conjunction with an analysis of previous promotion patterns in the organisation. (See HRP Exercise, note 12, on the website.) More sophisticated tools such as the Markov chain and renewal models are rarely used.

A simpler and more popular technique is a stocks and flows analysis of the whole organisation or a part of it, such as a department. The model is constructed to show the hierarchy of positions and the numbers employed in each. Numbers moving between positions, and in and out of the organisation over any time-period, can be displayed. An example of a stocks and flows analysis is given in Figure 5.8. The model is a visual way of displaying promotion and lateral move channels in operation, and shows what happens in reality to compare with the espoused approach.

Individual analysis

Similar information to the above can be collected on an individual basis to facilitate succession, career, redundancy and relocation planning. Replacement planning and succession planning are increasingly used and often represented in the form of charts, as shown in Figure 5.9.

Succession planning is usually only carried out for a select group in the organisation – those who are identified as having high potential – and generally

Figure 5.9 Two formats for succession planning

Post	Current post holder	Ready now	Ready soon	Ready future
Marketing Manager	D. Peters	F. Davis	F. Heald	B. Baker
Development Manager	R. Trice	D. Peters	M. Marks	B. Baker L. Brice
Research Manager	J. Moore		J. Old	C. Chane F. Davis
Data Manager	T. Totter	D. Peters	K. James J. Old	C. Churcher

Candidate	Present	Probable	Possible	Future	Development/ experience needed for each role
D. Peters	Marketing manager	Development manager	Data manager	Marketing manager	
F. Davis	Unit leader	Marketing manager		Research manager	
M. Marks	Development team leader		Development manager		

centres on the most senior jobs. The emphasis is on organisation needs – identifying who will be equipped to fill the most senior positions and over what timescale. It is usually a closed process, so that an individual is not likely to know whether they are on a succession list or chart. In these ways succession is very different from career planning, which we look at in detail in Chapter 27. Walker (1992a) examines the difference between succession planning and replacement planning. He identifies the characteristics of replacement planning as:

■ it is an informal approach, often based on personal knowledge of possible candidates;
■ it is often lacking in a thorough analysis of the challenges within the jobs, usually short term;
■ it concentrates on vertical moves with little consideration of lateral or diagonal moves.

Walker describes succession planning as overcoming these weaknesses, being more systematic and longer term, with a thorough analysis of the demands of future jobs and of the strengths, weaknesses and experiences of key employees. The emphasis is on developing individuals for the potential challenges ahead of them.

Activity 5.2

1 Why do employees leave organisations?
2 What are the determinants of promotion in your organisation? Are they made explicit? Do staff understand what the determinants are?
3 What would be your criteria for promotion in your organisation?

Reconciliation, decisions and plans

We have already said that, in reality, there is a process of continuous feedback between the different stages of human resource planning activities, as they are all interdependent. On the soft side (organisation, behaviour and culture) there is a dynamic relationship between the future vision, environmental trends and the current position. Key factors to take into account during reconciliation and deciding on action plans are the acceptability of the plans to both senior managers and other employees, the priority of each plan, key players who will need to be influenced and the factors that will encourage or be a barrier to successful implementation. Piercy (1989), in relation to strategic planning generally, offers a series of tools to help managers work through these issues.

On the hard side feasibility may centre on the situation where the supply forecast is less than the demand forecast. Here, the possibilities are to:

1 Alter the demand forecast by considering the effect of changes in the utilisation of employees, such as training and productivity deals, or high-performance teams.
2 Alter the demand forecast by considering using different types of employees to meet the corporate objectives, such as employing a smaller number of staff with higher level skills, or employing staff with insufficient skills and training them immediately.
3 Change the company objectives, as lack of manpower will prevent them from

being achieved in any case. Realistic objectives may need to be based on the manpower that is, and is forecast to be, available.

When the demand forecast is less than the internal supply forecast in some areas, the possibilities are to:

1 Consider and calculate the costs of overemployment over various timespans.
2 Consider the methods and cost of losing staff.
3 Consider changes in utilisation: work out the feasibility and costs of retraining, redeployment, and so on.
4 Consider whether it is possible for the company objectives to be changed. Could the company diversify, move into new markets, etc.?

We have also noted the interrelationship between the soft and the hard aspects of planning. For example, the creation of high-performance teams may have implications for different staffing numbers, a different distribution of skills, alternative approaches to reward and a different management style. The relocation of supplier's staff on to customer premises, in order to get really close to the customer, could have implications for relocation, recruitment, skills required and culture encouraged. The development of a learning organisation may have implications for turnover and absence levels, training and development provision, culture encouraged and approach to reward.

Once all alternatives have been considered and feasible solutions decided upon, specific action plans can be designed covering all appropriate areas of human resource management activity. For example:

1 **Human resource supply plans**: Plans may need to be made concerning the timing and approach to recruitment or downsizing. For example, it may have been decided that in order to recruit sufficient staff, a public relations campaign is needed to promote a particular company image. Promotion, transfer and redeployment and redundancy plans would also be relevant here.
2 **Organisation and structure plans**: These plans may concern departmental existence, remit and structure and the relationships between departments. They may also be concerned with the layers of hierarchy within departments and the level at which tasks are done, and the organisational groups within which they are done. Changes to organisation and structure will usually result in changes in employee utilisation.
3 **Employee utilisation plans**: Any changes in utilisation that affect human resource demand will need to be planned. Some changes will result in a sudden difference in the tasks that employees do and the numbers needed; others will result in a gradual movement over time. Managers need to work out new tasks to be done, old ones to be dropped and the timescale by which they need the right number of people fully operational. Other plans may involve the distribution of hours worked, for example the use of annual hours contracts; or the use of functional flexibility where employees develop and use a wider range of skills. There are implications for communications plans as the employees involved will need to be consulted about the changes and be prepared and trained for what will happen. There will be interconnections with supply plans here: for example, if fewer employees will be needed, what criteria will be used to determine who should be made redundant and who should be redeployed and retrained, and in which areas.

4 **Training and management development plans**: There will be training implications from both the manpower supply and manpower utilisation plans. The timing of the training can be a critical aspect. For example, training for specific new technology skills loses most of its impact if it is done six months before the equipment arrives. If the organisation wishes to increase recruitment by promoting the excellent development and training that it provides for employees, then clear programmes of what will be offered need to be finalised and resourced so that these can then be used to entice candidates into the organisation. If the organisation is stressing customer service or total quality, then appropriate training will need to be developed to enable employees to achieve this.

5 **Performance plans**: Performance plans directly address performance issues, for example the introduction of an objective-setting and performance-management system; setting performance and quality standards; or culture change programmes aimed at encouraging specified behaviour and performance.

6 **Appraisal plans**: The organisation needs to make sure that it is assessing the things that are important to it. If customer service is paramount, then employees need to be assessed on aspects of customer service relevant to their job, in addition to other factors. This serves the purpose of reinforcing the importance of customer service, and also provides a mechanism for improving performance in this area, and rewarding this where appraisal is to be linked to pay.

7 **Reward plans**: It is often said that what gets rewarded gets done, and it is key that rewards reflect what the organisation sees as important. For example, if quantity of output is most important for production workers, bonuses may relate to number of items produced. If quality is most important, then bonuses may reflect reject rate, or customer complaint rate. If managers are only rewarded for meeting their individual objectives there may be problems if the organisation is heavily dependent on teamwork.

8 **Employee relations plans**: These plans may involve unions, employee representatives or all employees. They would include any matters which need to be negotiated or areas where there is the opportunity for employee involvement and participation.

9 **Communications plans**: The way that planned changes are communicated to employees is critical. Plans need to include not only methods for informing employees what managers expect of them, but also methods to enable employees to express their concerns and needs for successful implementation. Communications plans will also be important if, for example, managers wish to generate greater employee commitment by keeping employees better informed about the progress of the organisation.

Once the plans have been made and put into action, the planning process still continues. It is important that the plans be monitored to see if they are being achieved and if they are producing the expected results. Plans will also need to be reconsidered on a continuing basis in order to cope with changing circumstances.

Summary propositions

5.1 Human resource planning activities are all interdependent.

5.2 Human resource planning methods range from sophisticated statistical techniques to simple diagnostic tools to analyse judgemental data.

5.3 As human resource planning deals with people, planners need to plan for what is acceptable as well as what is feasible.

5.4 Human resource planning is a continuous process rather than a one-off activity.

5.5 Human resource plans cover areas such as people supply, communications, training/development, appraisal, organisation and pay.

References

Bell, D.J. (1989) *Planning Corporate Manpower*. London: Longman.

Bowey, A. (1974) *A Guide to Manpower Planning*. London: Macmillan.

Bramham, J. (1989) *Human Resource Planning*. London: IPM.

Greer, C.R., Jackson, D.L. and Fiorito, J. (1989) 'Adapting human resources planning in a changing business environment', *Human Resource Management*, Vol. 28, No. 1 (Spring).

Hussey, D. (1982) *Corporate Planning: Theory and practice*, 2nd edn. Oxford: Pergamon.

Hussey, D. (1999) *Strategy and Planning: a manager's guide*. Chichester: John Wiley and Sons.

Hendry, C. (1994) *Human Resource Strategies for International Growth*. London: Routledge.

Lam, S.S. and Schaubroeck, J. (1998) 'Integrating HR planning and organizational strategy', *Human Resource Management Journal*, Vol. 8, No. 3, pp. 5–19.

Marchington, M. and Wilkinson, A. (1996) *Core Personnel and Development*. London: IPD.

Mintzberg, H. (1994) 'The fall and rise of strategic planning', *Harvard Business Review* (Jan./Feb.).

Piercy, N. (1989) 'Diagnosing and solving implementation problems in strategic planning', *Journal of General Management*, Vol. 15, No. 1, pp. 19–38.

Schuler, R.S. and Walker, J.W. (1990) 'Human resources strategy: focusing on issues and actions', *Organisational Dynamics* (Summer).

Sisson, K. and Storey, J. (2000) *The Realities of Human Resource Management*. Buckingham: Open University Press.

Taylor, S. (1998) *Employee Resourcing*. London: IPD.

Ulrich, D. (1989) 'Strategic human resource planning: why and how?', *Human Resource Planning*, Vol. 10, No. 1.

Walker, J.W. (1992a) *Human Resource Strategy*. Maidenhead: McGraw Hill.

Walker, J.W. (1992b) 'Human resource planning, 1990s-style', *Human Resource Planning*, Vol. 13, No. 4.

General discussion topics

1 Discuss the proposition that traditional (numbers) human resource planning is only of interest to organisations in periods of growth when unemployment levels are low.

2 'It is worthwhile planning even if you have no strategy.' For what reasons might you agree or disagree with this statement?

Chapter 6   Organisational design

Organisations have both a structure and a culture. The structure is a framework that can be described and altered at will. The culture is much more difficult to grasp and understand; it is also much more difficult to change. There are theories of organisational design that are directed towards the structure; no one has yet claimed to design a culture. Yet structure and culture are as interdependent as lungs and oxygen in providing the business with life and purpose.

Gradually attitudes towards structure are altering. Few people now see the design of an organisation as a single act of creation, deploying power and wisdom to put people in a constructive working relationship with each other: the moment comes and the organisation is created in an instantaneous 'big bang'. However attractive this idea may be, it is the minority of managers who find themselves in that situation. For most people the organisation is in a steady state of being not right: a pattern of working relationships bedevilled by inefficiency, frustration and obsolescence. For them, organisation design is a process of tinkering, pushing and shoving, getting bits and pieces of improvement where possible and occasionally coping with a cataclysm – like a need to shed half the workforce – that seems to leave the worst possible combination of human resources in its wake.

Changing the structure is easy – it can be done almost literally by the stroke of a pen – but ensuring appropriate culture change as well is much harder. Pursuing the lungs and oxygen analogy, there is no point in repairing a damaged lung if there is no oxygen to inflate it. Too often involvement is in sorting out a mess rather than in finding ways of avoiding the mess.

Whether one is creating the single grand design, coping with the steady state or trying to change the structure, it is necessary first to understand the process of organising, and the alternative main forms of organisation, before proceeding to consider methods of intervention and the significance of culture.

The fundamentals of the organising process

Organising requires both **differentiation** and **integration**. The process of differentiation is setting up the arrangements for an individual job or task to be undertaken effectively, while integration is co-ordinating the work of individuals so that the whole task is completed satisfactorily. There is no one best way of doing either. The organising of the individual job will vary according to the degree of predictability in what has to be done, so that the organising of manufacturing jobs tends to emphasise sticking to a routine of clearly defined tasks and much specialisation. Jobs that have constantly fresh problems and unpredictable requirements, like marketing and social work, produce frequent redefinitions of job boundaries, a tendency to flexible networks of working relationships rather than a clear hierarchy and a greater degree of individual autonomy. The greater the differentiation, the harder will be the task of co-ordination.

We can now see how differentiation and integration are put into action in the face of uncertainty to produce a working organisation. There are two fundamentals: task identity/job definition and structure.

Task identity and job definition

A job holder has a label or title which provides the basic identity, content and boundaries of what the job holder does. Some titles are explicit and understood well enough to meet most organisational requirements. Hearing that someone's job is marketing director, office cleaner, commissionaire, plumber, photographic model or train driver provides you with a good initial understanding of that person's role in the business. Other titles are imprecise or confusing. A single issue of a national newspaper includes the following among the advertised vacancies: clerical assistant, jazz assistant administrator, plastics executive, administrator, information specialist, third party products manager, sub titler and editorial services controller. Some of these are general titles, which are widely used to cover jobs without highly specific content; others probably are precisely understood by those with experience in a particular industry or business, even though they puzzle those of us without that insider knowledge.

There are still many questions to be answered so that other members of the business can understand the job holder's status, power, expertise, scope of responsibility and reliability. These questions are especially important where jobs adjoin each other. Where does A's responsibility finish and B's begin? Do areas of responsibility overlap? Are there matters for which no one appears to be responsible? Precise definition can be a nightmare, as there is as much definition of what **not** to do as on what to do. Some analysts believe that task definition stifles potential and frustrates people's contribution, so they advocate terms like 'key result areas' or 'responsibilities'.

> Job duties tell you what you have to do. Responsibilities tell you what you have to **accomplish**. Objectives are **targets**. Key result areas are areas in which **results** are expected. These differences are part and parcel of the whole move away from jobs. The twin brother of TIM-J ('That isn't my job') is IDM-J, or 'I've done my job (So don't expect anything else out of me)!' You can do your job and still fail to achieve the results your job was originally meant to serve. It's like the operation that was a success – although the patient died.   (Bridges 1995, p. 155)

Activity 6.1 Write down job titles in your organisation that you do not understand, or which you regard as confusing. How would you change them so that they become more effective labels? How many job titles include words like 'senior', 'principal' or 'manager' which have no significance other than to confer status on the job holder?

Although the standard device for clarifying task identity and job definition is the job description, it is frequently seen as the epitome of stifling, irrelevant bureaucracy, as well as being lost in a filing cabinet. There is always the risk that it becomes a straitjacket rather than a framework.

In stable organisations the job description is probably an acceptable mechanism for clarifying the boundaries and content of jobs. In businesses where uncertainty is the only thing that is certain, job descriptions will be less acceptable and appropriate, but identifying the task and defining the job remain fundamentals of the organising process.

Structure

People work together, even though the extent to which jobs interlock will vary, so the organisation designer has to decide how identified tasks should be grouped together. There are four common bases for such groupings. First is grouping according to **function**, so that the sales personnel are put together in one group, public relations in another group, research in another and so on. The logic here is that the group members share an expertise and can therefore understand each other, offering valid criticism, leadership and mutual support.

A second principle is to group people on the basis of **territory**, with employees of different and complementary skills being co-ordinated in a particular locality. This is usually where there is a satellite separated geographically from the main body of the organisation, like the Glasgow office of a nationwide business having a handful of people based in Glasgow covering duties such as sales, service and maintenance, warehousing, invoicing and stock control. The best-known example is the department store or the high street branch of a national bank.

A third alternative is to group on the basis of **product**, so that varied skills and expertise are again brought together with a common objective; not this time a group of customers in a particular territory, but a product that depends on the interplay of skill variety. For example some of the products of Virgin would be record stores; trains; financial services; in a hospital, medical, nursing, clerical and technical personnel are deployed in groups specialising with such 'products' or activities as maternity, paediatrics and accidents.

The fourth alternative grouping logic is by **time-period**, a form which is dictated by operating circumstances. Where a limited number of people work together at unusual times, like a night shift, then that time-period will be the group boundary for organisational purposes, and group members would probably identify first with the group and may feel estranged from the rest of the organisation.

Alternative forms of organisation structure

Charles Handy (1985, 1993) drew on earlier work by Roger Harrison (1972) to produce a fourfold classification of organisations, which has caught the imagination of most managers who have read it. Here we present a slightly different explanation, but acknowledge the source of the main ideas. There is no single ideal organisational form:

> organizations are as different and varied as the nations and societies of the world. They have differing cultures – sets of values and norms and beliefs – reflected in different structures and systems. And the cultures are affected by the events of the past and by the climate of the present, by the technology of the type of work, by their aims and the kind of people that work in them. (Handy 1993, p. 180)

Despite this variety, three broad types of structure are found most often and a fourth type is becoming more common.

The entrepreneurial form

The entrepreneurial form emphasises central power. It is like the spider's web, with one person or group so dominant that all power stems from the centre, all decisions are made and all behaviour reflects expectations of the centre (Figure 6.1). There are few collective decisions and much reliance on individuals, and actions stem from obtaining the approval of key figures. It is frequently found in businesses where decisions must be made quickly and with flair and judgement rather than careful deliberation. Newspaper editing has an entrepreneurial form of organisation and most of the performing arts have strong centralised direction.

This is the form of most small and growing organisations as they owe their existence to the expertise or initiative of one or two people, and it is only by reflecting accurately that originality that the business can survive. As the business expands this type of structure can become unwieldy because too many peripheral decisions cannot be made without approval from the centre, which then becomes overloaded. It is also difficult to maintain if the spider leaves the centre. A successor may not have the same degree of dominance. In some instances the problem of increasing size has been dealt with by maintaining entrepreneurial structure at the core of the enterprise and giving considerable independence to satellite organisations, provided that overall performance targets are met.

The bureaucratic form

The bureaucratic form, rooted in the recommendations of Weber (translated into English in 1947), emphasises the distribution rather than centralisation of power and responsibility. It has been the conventional means of enabling an organis-

Figure 6.1 Entrepreneurial organisation structure

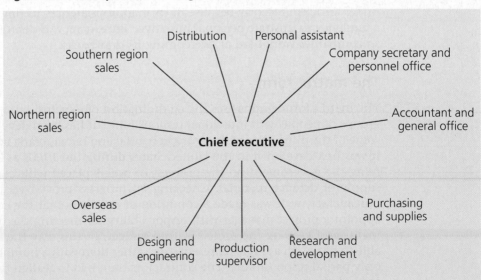

Figure 6.2 Typical bureaucratic organisation structure

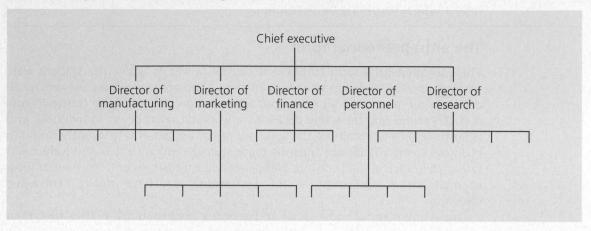

ation to grow beyond the entrepreneurial form to establish an existence that is not dependent on a single person or group of founders (Figure 6.2). Through an emphasis on role rather than flair, operational processes become more predictable and consistent, with procedure and committee replacing individual judgement. Responsibility is devolved through the structure and it is a method of organisation well suited to stable situations, making possible economies of scale and the benefits of specialisation. There is seldom the flexibility to deal with a volatile environment and a tendency to be self-sufficient. Rules and procedures are intended to provide predictability and fairness, but their inflexibility and time-consuming nature can become barriers to action. While superficially the model focuses on distributing decision making and responsibility across different areas (functional for example), there is no inbuilt emphasis on pushing decision making down the hierarchy.

Bureaucracy has been the standard form of structure for large organisations for thousands of years and remains the dominant form today. It has, however, come under criticism recently because of its inappropriateness in times of change and a tendency to frustrate personal initiative. 'Bureaucracy' is definitely a dirty word, so companies work hard at overcoming its drawbacks.

The matrix form

The matrix form emphasises the co-ordination of expertise into project-oriented groups of people with individual responsibility. It has been developed to counter some of the difficulties of the entrepreneurial and bureaucratic forms (Figure 6.3). It was first developed in the United States during the 1960s as a means of satisfying the government on the progress of orders placed with contractors for the supply of defence material. Checking on progress proved very difficult with a bureaucracy, so it was made a condition of contracts that the contractor should appoint a project manager with responsibility for meeting the delivery commitments and keeping the project within budget. In this way the government was able to deal with a single representative rather than with a number of people with only partial responsibility. The contractors then had to realign their organisation so that the project manager could exercise the degree of control necessary to

Figure 6.3 Typical matrix organisation structure

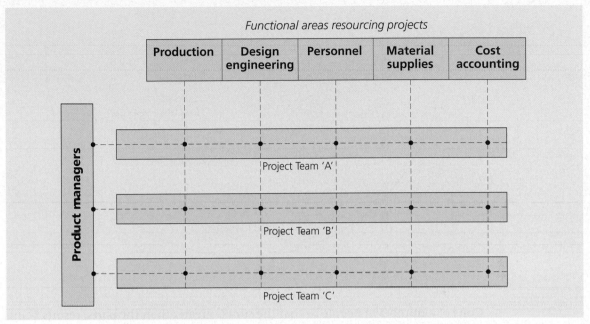

make the responsibility effective. This is done either by appointing a product manager with considerable status and power, or by creating product teams with specialists seconded from each functional area. The first method leaves the weight of authority with the functional hierarchy, while the product managers have a mainly co-ordinating, progress-chasing role as lone specialists. The second method shifts power towards the product managers, who then have their own teams of experts, with the functional areas being seen as a resource rather than the centre of action and decision. A third, but less common, situation is a permanent overlay of one set of hierarchical connections laid horizontally over a pre-existing conventional, vertical hierarchy. This brings the relative power distribution into approximate balance, but can also make decision making very slow as a result of that equilibrium.

Matrix is the form that appeals to many managers because it is theoretically based on expertise and provides scope for people at relatively humble levels of the organisation to deploy their skills and carry responsibility. It has, however, recently lost favour because it can generate expensive support systems for product managers needing additional secretaries, assistants and all the panoply of office, as well as the unwieldy administration referred to above.

One way in which matrix has found a new lease of life is in the increasing internationalisation of business, where the impracticability of bureaucracy is most obvious. International business tends to run on matrix lines with complex patterns of working relationship and a greater emphasis on developing agreement than on telling people what to do.

The independence form

The independence form emphasises the individual and is almost a form of non-organisation. The other three are all methods of putting together the contribu-

Figure 6.4 The independence form of organisation

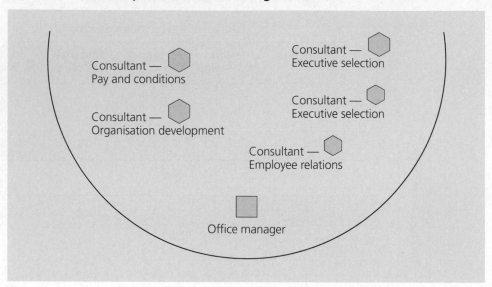

tions of a number of people so that the sum is greater than the parts, results being achieved by the co-ordination of effort. The independence form is a method of providing a support system so that individuals can perform, with the co-ordination of individual effort being either subsidiary or absent (Figure 6.4).

Barristers' chambers and doctors' clinics work in this way and it is a form of organisation attractive to those of independent mind who are confident of their ability to be individually successful. Some firms of consultants and craft workshops operate similarly, with a background organisation to enable the specialists to operate independently. It has been regarded as unsuitable for most types of undertaking because of the lack of co-ordination and control, but there is growing interest in it with the increasing emphasis on individual responsibility and professional skill in business.

| Activity 6.2 | Which of the four forms of organisation would you regard as most important for the following? |

Which of the four forms of organisation would you regard as most important for the following?

(a) The operating theatre of a hospital (f) A primary school
(b) A kibbutz (g) A psychiatric ward
(c) A library (h) A hotel
(d) A university department (i) A fashion house
(e) A department store (j) A trade union

Summary of differentiated structures

This fourfold classification is a means of analysis rather than a description of four distinct types of organisation with any undertaking being clearly one of the four (Table 6.1). Bureaucracies will typically have matrix features at some points and few entrepreneurial structures are quite as 'pure' as described here. Probably any organisation you could name could be classified as having one of these four fea-

Table 6.1 Conditions favouring different organisational forms

Form	Conditions
Entrepreneurial	■ Dominance of single person or group at centre, due to ownership, expertise or the need of the operation for a strong controlling figure ■ Modest size, simple technology and single, dominant technical expertise ■ Uncertain or rapidly changing environment
Bureaucratic	■ Complex organisation with devolved power and expertise ■ Large size, complex technology and varied technical expertise ■ Stable environment
Matrix	■ Complex organisation with bureaucratic features and need to devolve responsibility and enhance responsiveness to clients
Independence	■ Simple organisation form to support independent activities of specialists, with little co-ordination ■ Professional rather than management orientation among specialists

tures dominant and in some there is one form dominant in one section of the business and another form dominant elsewhere. Large banks, for example, are bureaucratic in their retailing operations as consistency is of paramount importance and any changes need to be put into operation simultaneously by a large number of people while being comprehensible to a large number of customers. The same banks will, however, tend to an entrepreneurial emphasis in their merchant banking activities and to independence in currency dealings.

New forms of structure?

There is much discussion about new forms of organisation that will be needed in the future, based on an assessment of current and evolving pressures and developments (such as technology) that could make such new forms viable. There is a view that big is no longer always beautiful; that growth can be achieved through means other than internal expansion of existing activities; that organisations need to focus on the external relations such as customers and suppliers rather than dwell solely on their internal structures; and that control is more effective if it is performance based rather than task based. We will pick up on these perspectives in the following five sections which attempt to summarise the major current themes in organisational redesign.

Smaller size: downsizing, delayering and outsourcing

Belbin (1996) offers a useful distinction between downsizing and delayering when he characterises the first as random reductions in employee numbers, often based on those who offer themselves for voluntary redundancy; delayering, on the other hand, is characterised as a much more systematic process involving the removal of whole tiers of management in the hierarchy. Both activities remain a popular managerial pastime, with the rationale being to speed response times and make the operation more cost efficient and competitive. One of the implications of downsizing is often the increased workload of retained staff, with a consequent increase in stress levels, and one of the consequences of delayering is the empowerment of staff lower down the hierarchy.

Outsourcing is a further method which organisations employ to keep employee numbers down and to increase flexibility (see Chapter 9 on Strategic aspects of resourcing), and an increasing range of activities is outsourced – for example catering, training, security, legal services. An additional pressure is that running a business requires an increasing variety of skills and diverse expertise, so that management relies on people knowing what to do and being required to get on with it. Seldom is a single business big enough to employ all the experts it requires, so many skills have to be bought in on a temporary basis from consultants or contractors.

Activity 6.3	If you were running an airport, which of the following activities would you outsource and why?

1 Baggage handling	5 Airport information
2 The fire service	6 Car park attendance
3 Catering	7 Maintenance of premises and services
4 Newsagency	8 Cleaning

Growth: diversification, acquisitions, mergers, alliances and joint ventures

Most organisational structures evolved on an implicit assumption that the business would naturally expand, but this is no longer seen as the sole form of growth: diversification and change are equally interesting, and sometimes wiser, alternatives. Growth can be achieved more rapidly in expanding markets via acquisitions and mergers – buying in the expertise, infrastructure and customer base, instead of developing this internally.

WINDOW ON PRACTICE	Sainsbury's demonstrates how businesses can grow from within by diversifying – they have expanded from food retailing to banking including the supply of savings accounts, mortgages and credit cards. In this way Sainsbury's can grow business by building on their current customer base and offering them a wider range of serv-

ices. This 'cross marketing' is seen to be a key advantage of diversification.

Lloyds Bank have grown via business merger and takeover. They first merged with TSB to form LloydsTSB and acquired the Cheltenham and Gloucester Building Society and latterly Scottish Widows. The merger with TSB could be seen to provide economies of scale and new customers; and the acquisitions can be seen to provide the immediate expertise and capacity to generate mortgage and life assurance business and to expand their pensions business.

Such mergers and takeovers usually enable a reduction in employee numbers (compared with the staffing numbers of all the original businesses). Efficiency savings may be made via this and growth achieved through expanding the customer base and greater cross-marketing opportunities.

Activity 6.4	What are the different human resource implications from the two different growth strategies outlined in the Window on Practice, above?

No longer is business necessarily directed towards permanence. Until quite recently enterprises were established with the objective of continuing indefinitely, often with a semi-dynastic objective: 'All this will be yours one day, my lad'. There is now greater emphasis on terms like project and venture, setting up an enterprise that will run for a time and then be closed or sold on. Joint ventures and alliances provide the partner organisations with the necessary compatible expertise and knowledge base and infrastructure to achieve what neither could have done alone. These ventures may be short or longer term, and the partners will separate when it is in their mutual interest to do so.

Decentralisation and empowering teams and individuals

There has been a trend to decentralise decision making in larger organisations so that business units have a greater level of autonomy than previously (though not complete autonomy).

Consequently central headquarters have reduced levels of power over the business units. In some cases this strategy has worked well, but in other cases problems have emerged which have provoked recentralisation.

In terms of individuals and teams, empowerment involves pushing down authority to employees lower down in the hierarchy. For example Shackleton (1995) defines it as 'giving more responsibility and decision making authority to more junior people in the organisation'. Managers move from controlling employees to coaching them. It is a particularly popular technique in delayered organisations and is seen as a way of 'overcoming the problems of staid, bureaucratic and rigid organizations' (D'Annunzio-Green and Macandrew 1999). In addition the prescriptive literature suggests that empowerment saves management time and is a means of motivating employees and increasing their commitment. See the Window on Practice example of teamwork and empowerment at Digital, Ayr, in Chapter 3.

In retail organisations where decisions are pushed down to the location of the problem there is much more chance of a fast and appropriate decision and a happy customer feeling that their request or complaint has been dealt with effectively. For example a hotel receptionist may be empowered to reduce room charges, offer superior rooms at standard prices, include a free meal or offer additional non-standard services if they consider it appropriate. In making these decisions they do not have to check with higher management, as the decision-making authority is theirs.

However the term is very ambiguous (see Lashley 1999 and Collins 1999 for an in-depth discussion of this issue) and empowerment in one organisation may be completely different from that in another; the way empowerment is viewed by the empowered workers in an organisation may be very different from the management view in that same organisation. This is just one difficulty with the concept. There are many examples of empowerment not working in the way anticipated, and in some cases empowerment has been reintroduced. Other problems have been identified in its effective implementation:

■ Current structure, culture and HR systems may conflict with the empowerment message – see, for example, Procter *et al.* (1999).
■ The boundaries of empowerment are often not clear, leading to confusion.
■ Managers are sometimes not willing to give up their power, or decide to take it back when the going gets rough.

■ Employees may not want to be empowered – Wilkinson (1998) points out that empowerment is on the management agenda: they are giving away power, rather than employees taking it.

The how not the what: business process reengineering

The concept of business process reengineering was introduced by Hammer, a professor at MIT and Champy, and while it promised rapid and significant improvement in organisational performance, there are many examples of the approach failing to deliver. For example Hammer and Champy (1993) estimate a failure rate as high as 70 per cent. Some of the barriers to effective implementation are outlined by Attaran and Wood (1999), and they include problems such as misunderstanding and misapplying the concept, a lack of proper strategy, the failure of management to change and failure to understand the importance of people.

The term itself implies radical redesign of the organisation, starting with a blank sheet of paper rather than adapting what is already there. The work is then organised around the core process of the organisation rather than, say, areas of functional expertise. The focus is on how the work is done rather than what is being produced, and encourages a concentration on the customer and the outputs and makes the purpose of the organisation more visible. Some organisations do change their basic structure in order to operate around the core processes, while others overlay the process structure on top – in this way it may be viewed as a specific form of matrix structure. Many reengineering efforts involve the use of empowered cross-functional teams.

WINDOW ON PRACTICE

Hammer and Stanton (1999) report the experiences of Duke Power in the United States. Within the Customer Operations function they identify five core processes. These were:

■ Develop market strategies.
■ Acquire and maintain customers.
■ Provide reliability and integrity.
■ Deliver products and services.
■ Calculate and collect revenues.

Each process has a process owner who is responsible for setting targets, establishing budgets and distributing budgets to the regions. Although the regions still have authority over people, they are evaluated on how well they meet the targets set by the process owners. Duke Power found that influencing was the key skill required by managers. Managers cannot command and control; they have to co-ordinate and collaborate. Owners of the different processes had to come together, rather than work in isolation, to make sure all the processes were run effectively and that doing well at one was not compromising the success of another.

Redefining the boundaries

There are a number of different interpretations of organisational forms of the future which involve the minimisation of external and internal organisational boundaries, in particular: virtual organisations, networked organisations and boundaryless organisations. All these terms relate to a change in organisational boundaries, and below we will explore the underlying concepts rather than trying to define each of the terms differentially.

Turning, first, to the external organisational boundary, we have two complementary aspects. Supply-chain development is the process of expanding the activity of the business along the supply chain, by moving some activities to suppliers and moving some on towards the customer. The best-known example is probably Marks & Spencer underwear. Although marketed by Marks & Spencer, it is not made by them, but by their suppliers. In this instance the retailer has long controlled supply by maintaining a strict quality and price regime, but this approach has become a much more common feature of the flexibility of shifting an activity and all its attendant responsibilities to a supplier. The same sort of shift can be seen in the way manufacturers increase their control over agents and retailers. Most motor manufacturers control the price of servicing their vehicles as well as specifying the standards to which servicing should be carried out. Supply-chain development reduces the risk for the core business and integrates more closely the activities of several separate businesses.

Training may well be carried out in common with the core business and there are many examples of a supplier organisation locating some of its staff of the premises of the core business.

In some cases, of course, the customer is also involved in doing a part of the work. The concept of the supermarket started the trend of eliminating the need for sales staff to pick, weigh and wrap prior to cash. Various other elements of self-service extend this practice. A useful example is IKEA, who not only expect customers to serve themselves, by providing a catalogue delivered to the home for prior selection, but also expect the customer to assemble the piece of furniture that is collected.

There is a different sense in which the external boundaries of the organisation may become blurred, and this second aspect is where organisations work together opportunistically when it is in their mutual interest. Byrne and Brandt (1992) identify this as the virtual organisation, which they see as the 'new corporate model' similar to, and an expansion of joint ventures and strategic alliances – referred to above. They define virtual organisations as temporary networks of organisations which come together quickly to exploit a window of opportunity. In this way the partner organisations share costs, skills, access and so on. Byrne and Brandt identify the key attributes of such organisations as excellence (derived from the core competence of each organisation); technology (to speed linkage); opportunism in terms of low formalisation and temporary nature; trust; and lack of borders.

The boundaryless concept has also been applied internally to the lack of boundaries between jobs and departments, encouraging a greater collaboration in the achievement of organisational goals.

These five trends have been described separately but are often interlinked and some of the concepts clearly overlap. The terminology in this area is at present confusing.

Organisational culture

Organisational culture is an alternative way of describing the same thing as structure, but as the concept and the language are different, our approach and resultant methods are different as well. Here are some of the ways in which the approach differs:

- Structure is firm; culture is soft.
- Structure is clear; culture is intangible.
- Structure is about systems to which people have to adapt; culture is about people who have norms and values in common.
- Structure is about the distribution of authority; culture is about how people work together.

Organisational culture is the characteristic spirit and belief of an organisation, demonstrated, for example, in the norms and values that are generally held about how people should behave and treat each other, the nature of working relationships that should be developed and attitudes to change. These norms are deep, taken-for-granted assumptions which are not always expressed, and are often known without being understood.

Through the 1980s in particular there was great interest in organisational culture as the key to improved organisational effectiveness (for example, Deal and Kennedy 1982; Handy 1985) and this complemented the earlier preoccupation with organisational structure. Peters and Waterman (1982), for example, identified a strong culture as one of the characteristics of the 'excellent' organisations which they studied, and they argued that this acts as corporate glue. Organisation charts may be useful in clarifying reporting relations and subtleties of seniority, but the culture or ethos of the business is believed to be an equally important determinant of effectiveness. Just as most of the developments described earlier in this chapter have been attempts to reduce the rigidity of structure – particularly in bureaucracies – the interest in culture is an attempt to achieve the same objective, but by redefining the problem.

The history and traditions of an organisation reveal something of its culture because the cultural norms develop over a relatively long period, with layers and layers of practice both modifying and consolidating the norms and providing the framework of ritual and convention in which people feel secure, once they have internalised its elements. A debate rages as to whether culture is a variable of an organisation, that is, something which the organization 'has', or whether culture is a metaphor for what the organisation 'is'. The former perspective suggests that culture can be manipulated at will, the latter suggests that culture is more complex than this.

There has been a wealth of writers aiming to provide an analytical framework for understanding organisational culture. Perhaps the most influential of these is Schein (1984), who postulated three levels of organisational culture and their interaction. At the most superficial level are artifacts and creations, for example the technology and art of an organisation and visible patterns of behaviour. These include office layout, decoration, car parking, behaviour at meetings and so on. For example, do employees stop and converse in corridors, and interrupt the conversations of others to get a quickish answer to a question that must be resolved – or is dialogue much more structured via the use of appointments, meetings and the formalisation of proceedings? Schein identifies all these aspects of culture as visible but not very decipherable. In the last example the extended use of corridor meetings and conversations could reflect many different things about the organisation – such as 'action oriented, and problems are solved immediately'; or, for example, 'warm and friendly environment where interpersonal interaction is welcomed rather than avoided'. The next, deeper level down Schein identifies as values – these are widely espoused by organisations in the ubiquitous value statements which organisations are constantly publishing in order to demonstrate their corporate culture (which they have inevitably been trying to 'manage').

WINDOW ON PRACTICE	**KPMG: revitalising culture through values**

Jan Thornbury (1999) reports the process of changing the KPMG culture at the end of the 1990s. The result of this was a global values statement:

'We are passionate about working with our clients to deliver exceptional value: *which means*

- being passionate about client service
- robust, long lasting relationships
- being committed to adding value

Our people flourish and release their full potential: *which means*

- Respect, support and trust
- Adding value to our people by providing varied, challenging and rewarding work and planned career development
- Teamwork: self-fulfilment through working and growing together

We continuously extend the frontiers of our shared knowledge: *which means*

- Openness of mind and continuous learning
- Treating knowledge as a highly valued asset
- Everyone in the firm has a right and an obligation to access our knowledge base, and the responsibility to contribute to it.'

Source: Thornbury, J. (1999) 'KPMG revitalising culture through values', *Business Strategy Review,* Vol. 10, No. 4, pp. 1–15.

The problem with these espoused values is that they may not reflect what really goes on in the organisation, but instead are just part of the rhetoric and the promotion of image. They may be 'genuine' in that the organisation is trying to promote and instil these values, and some managers may convince themselves that this is the way they operate, where again the reality may be different. The third and deepest level of culture, which Schein describes as taken-for-granted, invisible and preconscious, he labels 'basic assumptions', and these are broadly similar to those identified by other writers on culture. Schein lists five, which are:

1 The organisation's relationship to its environment.
2 The nature of reality and truth.
3 The nature of human nature.
4 The nature of human activity.
5 The nature of human relationships.

To take a very simple example: the nature of human nature is about whether mankind is basically good, evil or neutral; and about whether theory '*x*' or theory '*y*' (McGregor 1960) better describes human beings. (Theory '*x*' identifies human nature as characterised by work avoidance, only putting in effort when pushed and monitored; theory '*y*' on the other hand identifies humans as enjoying satisfaction from work, and as being naturally committed and motivated by doing a good job.) You can see that an organisation which has a basic assumption of theory '*x*' will unconsciously have the view that employees need to be closely supervised and checked on, perhaps relating pay to output as a means of getting people to put in effort. On the other hand an organisation with a basic assumption of theory '*y*' will tend to trust employees to get on with the job, will be prepared to delegate and reward via recognition of people's achievements.

So far we have assumed that an organisation has 'one' culture, but Schein does acknowledge that there may be sub-cultures in an organisation and his frequently quoted definition of organisational culture can be interpreted in this way:

> Corporate culture is the pattern of basic assumptions that a given group has invented, discovered, or developed in learning to cope with its problems of external adaptation and integration, and that have worked well enough to be considered valid, and, therefore, to be taught to new members as the correct way to perceive, think and feel in relation to those problems.   (Schein 1984, p. 262)

Meyerson and Martin in 1994 produced a very perceptive analytical framework of organisational culture which develops our understanding in relation to this issue of an organisation not necessarily having one single unified culture. They propose three different ways of understanding organisational culture: integration, differentiation and ambiguity.

The integration perspective is the popular conception that an organisation will have a single uniform culture, and will focus on the organisational leaders as the culture creators. From this perspective culture is the key to organisational control. Culture is seen a variable of an organisation and can be changed by management at will – it is therefore not surprising that it is this perspective that the many consultants in the culture field will use.

The second perspective, differentiation, is where inconsistencies, lack of consensus and non-leader sources of culture change are recognised. In this view overlapping sub-cultures are identified, such as departmental groups, professional specialism, gender, hierarchical levels and geographical location. Meyerson and Martin suggest that this is a smaller version of the integration perspective, because although sub-cultures overlap, each is seen to have a distinctive boundary, with consistency within the boundary.

The final perspective, ambiguity, views consistency and consensus as an illusion and embraces differences and paradoxes. From this perspective differences in meanings and values are immeasurable and irreconcilable. Culture is seen as a web with transient patterns coming to the fore at different times. The work of Meyerson and Martin is valuable as it enables us to stand back from the prescriptive literature on culture change and question the assumptions on which it is based. The reality of culture change has been questioned increasingly, for example by Ogbonna (1993) and Ogbonna and Harris (1998).

Further challenges to the prescriptive literature come from Woodall (1996). She argues that effective management does not necessarily involve the alignment of values; that values can not necessarily be easily changed; that changes in values can come from sources other than management; and that strong cultures do not necessarily result in successful organisations. In the same vein Hope and Hendry (1995) contend that culture change is less relevant to newer forms of jobs and organisation.

Although culture change may be of a problematic and possibly unhelpful nature, it is still important that those employed in an organisation should try to understand the culture they share. Managers in general, and HR managers in particular, have to understand the extent to which culture can be changed and how the changes can be made, even if the changes may be much harder and slower to make than most managers believe and most circumstances allow. As we have said, culture is often not expressed and may be known without being understood. It is none the less real and powerful, so that the enthusiasts who unwittingly work counter-culturally will find that there is a metaphorical but solid brick wall against which they are beating their heads. Enthusiasts who pause to work out the nature of the culture in which they are operating can at least begin the process of change and influence the direction of the cultural evolution, because culture can never be like a brick wall. It is living and growing, able to strengthen and support the efforts of those who use it, as surely as it will frustrate the efforts of those who ignore it.

Summary propositions

6.1 Organisation design is occasionally a process of creating an entire organisation from scratch, but for most people it is modifying bits of an existing organisation.

6.2 The fundamentals of organisation design are task identity/job definition and structure.

6.3 Alternative forms of structure are entrepreneurial, bureaucratic, matrix and independence.

6.4 New trends in organisational design are characterised by reducing headcount; growth by diversification, mergers, takeovers and alliances; decentralisation and empowerment of individuals and teams; recognition of the importance of business processes; and the redefinition of the organisational boundary.

6.5 The culture of an organisation is the characteristic spirit and belief of its members, demonstrated by the behavioural norms and values held by them in common.

6.6 Organisations do not have a single unified culture.

6.7 Corporate culture is a culture that those directing the organisation seek to create and foster in the interests of the organisation achieving its objectives.

6.8 Attempting to change the culture of the organisation is fraught with difficulties and may not even be desirable in terms of organisational effectiveness.

References

Attaran, M. and Wood, G. (1999) 'How to succeed at reengineering', *Management Decision*, Vol. 37, No. 10, pp. 752–7.

Belbin, M. (1996) *The Coming Shape of Organisation*. Oxford: Butterworth Heinemann.

Bridges, W. (1995) *Jobshift: How to prosper in a workplace without jobs*. London: Nicholas Brealey.

Buchanan, D. (1992) 'High Performance: new boundaries of acceptability in worker control', in G. Salaman *et al.* (eds), *Human Resource Strategies*. California: Sage.

Byrne, G. and Brandt, W. (1992) in W. Davidow and M. Malone (eds), *The Virtual Corporation*. New York: HarperCollins.

Collins, D. (1999) 'Born to fail? Empowerment, ambiguity and set overlap', *Personnel Review*, Vol. 28, No. 3, pp. 208–21.

D'Annunzio-Green, N. and Macandrew, J. (1999) 'Re-empowering the empowered – the ultimate challenge', *Personnel Review*, Vol. 28, No. 3, pp. 258–78.

Deal, T.E. and Kennedy, A.A. (1982) *Corporate Cultures: The rites and rituals of corporate life*. Reading, Mass: Addison-Wesley.

Hammer, M. and Champy, J. (1993) *Re-engineering the Corporation*. New York: Harper Business.

Hammer, M. and Stanton, S. (1999) 'How Process enterprises *really* work', *Harvard Business Review*, Nov.–Dec.

Handy, C.B. (1985 and 1993) *Understanding Organizations*, 3rd and 4th edns. Harmondsworth: Penguin Books.

Harrison, R. (1972) 'How to describe your organization', *Harvard Business Review*, Sept/Oct.

Hope, V. and Hendry, J. (1995) 'Corporate cultural change – is it relevant for the organisations of the 1990s?', *Human Resource Management Journal*, Vol. 5, No. 4.

Lashley, C. (1999) 'Employee empowerment in services: a framework for analysis', *Personnel Review*, Vol. 28, No. 3, pp. 169–91.

McGregor, D. (1960) *The Human Side of Enterprise*. New York: McGraw-Hill.

Meyerson, D. and Martin, J. (1994) 'Cultural change: an integration of three different views', in H. Tsoukas (ed.), *New Thinking in Organisational Behaviour*. Oxford: Butterworth Heinemann.

Ogbonna, S. (1993) 'Managing organisational culture: fantasy or reality?', *Human Resource Management Journal*, Vol. 3, No. 2.

Ogbonna, S. and Harris, L. (1998) 'Managing Organisational Culture: compliance or genuine change?', *British Journal of Management*, Vol. 9.

Peters, T. and Waterman, R. (1982) *In Search of Excellence*. New York: Random House.

Procter, S., Currie G. and Orme, H. (1999) 'The empowerment of middle managers in a community health trust; structure, responsibility and culture', *Personnel Review*, Vol. 28, No. 3, pp. 242–57.

Schein, E. (1984) 'Coming to a new awareness of organisational culture', *Sloan Management Review*, Winter, Vol. 25, No. 2.

Shackleton, V. (1995) *Business Leadership*. London: Routledge.

Thornbury, J. (1999) 'KPMG: Revitalising Culture through values', *Business Strategy Review*, Vol. 10, No. 4, pp. 1–15.

Weber, M. (trans 1947) *The Theory of Social and Economic Organization* (translated by M. Henderson and T. Parsons). New York: The Free Press.

Wilkinson, A. (1998) 'Empowerment: theory and practice', *Personnel Review*, Vol. 27, No. 1, pp. 40–56.

Woodall, J. (1996) 'Managing culture change, can it ever be ethical?', *Personnel Review*, Vol. 25, No. 6.

General discussion topics

1 What are the strengths and weaknesses of the bureaucratic form of organisation? Have downsizing and customer care made it obsolete?

2 Can organisational culture be changed at will?

3 What are the weaknesses of a strong organisational culture?

Chapter 7   Communication and information

In this chapter we look first at the scope of communicating in organisations, then consider in more detail the processes and the barriers to their effectiveness, before reviewing some well-used techniques and systems. Turning to information we will review a model of different types of HR information and then consider the implications of the 1998 Data Protection Act and other recent legislation.

Meaning and scope of communication

Communication involves both the giving out of messages from one person and the receiving and understanding of those messages by another or others. If a message has been given out by one person but has not been received or understood by another, then communication has not taken place. The methods of communicating in organisations include speech, non-verbal communication, writing, audio-visual and electronic means. These methods are considered in greater detail later in this chapter. The method used will depend on the precise message that needs to be passed on. In general, messages may contain factual information, opinion or emotion.

In organisations a wide variety of messages will need to be communicated. Some messages are individually specific – for example, a supervisor giving feedback on a completed task or expressing concern at continued lateness; or individuals explaining their future career plans. Others are team- or group-oriented, such as current group objectives; a change in team structure or office accommodation; or sharing action plans for the week. A third group of messages is concerned with all employees, examples being quarterly business results, new company image, revised payment system; or expressions of employee confusion over a new organisational change programme being introduced. In this chapter we concentrate on communication relevant to all or groups of employees. Individually specific communication is dealt with elsewhere in this book, in the chapters on performance management, appraisal, discipline and grievance.

From the above examples it is clear that organisational communication is not only top down, but also bottom up and lateral. All aspects are important and all are included. The key to success of many organisational communications systems is the extent to which they provide for two- or three-way communication, rather than just one-way traffic.

Within any organisation there are both formal and informal channels of communication. The formal channels are those that are officially acknowledged and approved, such as circulars, meetings, posters and so on. Informal channels of communication, those which are part of our social relationships at work, will have some impact on how formal communications are interpreted and understood.

Purposes of communication in organisations

Some purposes of communications are designed to be persuasive – for example, safety campaigns. Increasing attention is being given to disclosure of company information and to seeking employee views as a form of involvement and participation. Cully *et al.* (2000) report that information about the financial position of the workplace, the financial position of the organisation and, in particular, investment plans were being increasingly imparted to employees and their representatives over the period 1984–98. They report increasing use of suggestion schemes and regular meetings between management and the workforce.

Upwards communication is important for the following reasons:

1 It helps managers to understand employees' concerns.
2 It helps managers to keep more in touch with employees' attitudes and values.
3 It can alert managers to potential problems.
4 It can provide managers with workable solutions to problems.
5 It can provide managers with the information that they need for decision making.
6 It helps employees to feel that they are participating and contributing, and can encourage motivation and commitment to future courses of action.
7 It provides some feedback on the effectiveness of downwards communication, and ideas on how it may be improved.

ACAS (2000) suggests that good communications can improve organisational performance, improve management performance and decision making, improve employee performance and commitment, help develop greater trust and increase job satisfaction.

Activity 7.1	In your organisation, or any organisation with which you are familiar: 1 What formal channels of lateral communication are there? 2 How effective are these and why? 3 How could lateral communication be improved?

Organisational communication is directed at the outside world as well as at employees. Company newspapers, for example, are to inform employees of what is going on in the company, but also project an image to the outside world.

The process of communicating

A convenient and well-established method of approaching and understanding communication is to draw an analogy with telecommunications (see, for example, Torrington and Weightman 1991). From this perspective the sender has an idea of something they wish to communicate, and which they then translate into, for example, spoken words, pictures or email text. The words/pictures are consequently transmitted to the receiver, who attempts to translate the message in order to derive understanding and meaning.

Through these various stages of translation from the mind of one to the mind of the other there are various points at which error is possible, and even likely. It is almost impossible to know whether the abstract idea in the mind of one person has been transferred accurately to the mind of the other. One essential element in the whole process is feedback, which completes the circuit so that there is some indication from the listener that the message has been received and understood. It is probable that the feedback response will give some indication to the transmitter of the quality of the message that has been received. If the transmitter expects a reaction of pleasure and the feedback received is a frown, then it is immediately known that there is an inaccuracy in the picture that has been planted in the mind of the receiver, and the opportunity arises to identify and correct the inaccuracy.

A further element in the communication process is 'noise'. This is used as a generic term to describe anything that interferes in the transmission process: inaudibility, inattention, physical noise and so forth. The degree to which some noise element is present will impair the quality of both transmission and feedback.

WINDOW ON PRACTICE

Hirst (1999) explains how The Idea Group together with Birkbeck College London has recently carried out research into the experiences of middle managers communicating in a variety of situations, and to different audiences. From this they derived a model of best practice face-to-face communication in the form of a 'communication cycle'. (You will no doubt note how this concept fits well with the telecommunications analogy we have just discussed.)

The cycle they outline is this:

- Opening (starting the conversation).
- Transmitting (getting the message across).
- Receiving/sensing (listening to a response).
- Reflecting/responding (thinking and answering).
- Exiting (finishing the conversation).

They suggest that this can be used to enable individuals to consider their own communications performance and identify where improvements need to be made.

More recent analysis of the communication process has led to a greater understanding of the setting in which communication takes place, so that now perhaps we focus more on understanding the process and the activity of receiving and interpreting information than we do on the activities involved in transmitting information. Shoveller (1987) lists no fewer than 24 reasons why communications in organisations may fail. These range from people failing to accept the responsibility to communicate to lack of interest on behalf of the recipient.

Barriers to communicating

It is the listener or reader who will determine the extent to which the message is understood. What we hear, see or understand is shaped very largely by our own experience and background, and the interpretation of the world which we have constructed in our heads. Our way of interpreting the world will create a series of expectations when we communicate, so, for example, instead of hearing what people tell us, we hear what our minds tell us they have said – the two may be different. We shall look at some of the principal ways in which this operates.

The frame of reference

Few of us change our opinions alone. We are likely to be influenced by the opinions developed within the group with which we identify ourselves: the reference group. If a particular group of people hold certain values in common, individual members of that group will not easily modify their values unless and until there is a value shift in the group as a whole. This is perhaps most apparent in the relative intractability of opinions relating to political party allegiance. In the workplace employees' frame of reference is likely to be partly determined by the group of people with which they work, and they will have developed, to some extent, their own work culture, as we saw in Chapter 6. Managers frequently direct to an individual a message, request, instruction or rebuke which would find a more likely response if it were mediated through a representative of the group of employees rather than being directed at an individual. For example, trying to persuade an individual employee of the the importance of safe working practices is unlikely to work if this does not fit with group norms in this area. A more useful approach may be to negotiate a change of behaviour through group representatives.

Whenever a matter is being discussed, the people among whom it is being considered will view it from their particular personal frame of reference. Where the frames of reference of transmitter and receiver differ widely, there may be substantial difficulties in accurate transmission of messages and even greater difficulties in ensuring that the response of the receiver is that which the transmitter intended.

Cultural differences provide a frame of reference through which an individual interprets meaning, and you will find an example of how this can impact on the communications process on the website.

The stereotype

An extreme form of letting expectation determine communication content is stereotyping, where we expect a particular type of statement or particular type of attitude from a stereotype of a person. For example the Irish are talkative, the Scots are mean and the English fail to show emotion. People also have stereotypes of certain office holders. There is still a widespread stereotype of shop stewards which shows them as being militant, politically extreme in one, and only one, direction, unreasonable, unintelligent and obstructive. Equally, there are widespread stereotypes of different types of manager and for some people there is a stereotype of managers as a whole. One of the greatest difficulties in achieving equal opportunities at work is the challenging of deeply held stereotypes about men and women. Stereotypes about women include the view that they are unwilling to be away from home due to family commitments, that they do not want to rise too high in the hierarchy and that they will invariably leave to have children. Men, on the other hand, are often seen as career driven and intent on promotion. There are also stereotypes relating to age, such as an older person being seen as unable to stand the pace, no longer able to think quickly and unwilling to change.

The effect of these stereotypes in communication matters is that the person who encounters someone for whom they have a stereotype will begin hearing what the person says in the light of the stereotype held.

Cognitive dissonance

Another area of difficulty, which has been explored extensively by Festinger (1957) and others, is the extent to which people will cope successfully with information inputs that they find irreconcilable with their personally constructed view of the world. If someone receives information that is consistent with what they already believe, they are likely to understand it, believe it, remember it and take action upon it. If, however, they receive information that is inconsistent with their established beliefs, then they will have genuine difficulty in understanding, remembering and taking action. This is because one of the ways of dealing with the discomfort of dissonance is to distort the message so that what they hear is what they want to hear, what they expect to hear and can easily understand rather than the difficult, challenging information that is being put to them.

The halo or horns effect

A slightly different aspect of expectation determining communication content is the halo or horns effect, which causes the reaction of receivers of information to move to extremes of either acceptance or rejection. When we are listening to somebody in whom we have confidence and who has earned our trust we may be predisposed to agree with what they say because we have placed an imaginary halo around their head. Because of our experience of their trustworthiness and reliability we have an expectation that what they say will be trustworthy and reliable. On the other hand, if we have learned to distrust someone, then what we hear them say will be either ignored or treated with considerable caution. Perhaps the most common example in the HR field is that the initial reaction (whether positive or negative) of interviewers to candidates when they first see and speak to them is likely to affect their longer-term perceptions of that candidate, whatever that candidate subsequently goes on to say or do.

Semantics and jargon

One difficulty about transferring ideas from one person to another is that ideas cannot be transferred because meaning cannot be transferred – all the communicators can use as their vehicle is words or symbols, but unfortunately the same symbols may suggest different meanings to different people. The meanings are in the hearers rather than the speakers and certainly not in the words themselves. A simple example of this is 'quite ill' which could have a variety of weightings according to how it was heard and the circumstances in which the comment was made.

The problem of jargon is where a word or a phrase has a specialised meaning that is immediately understandable by the *cognoscenti*, but meaningless or misleading to those who do not share the specialised knowledge. The Maslovian hierarchy of human needs is by now well known in management circles. On one occasion a lecturer was describing the ideas that were implicit in this notion and was rather surprised some months later in an examination paper to see that one of the students had heard not 'hierarchy' but 'high Iraqi'. The unfamiliarity of the word 'hierarchy' had been completely misinterpreted by that particular receiver, who had imposed their own meaning on what they heard because of the need to make sense of what it was that they received.

Another interesting example was in a school of motoring, where for many years trainee drivers were given the instruction 'clutch out' or 'clutch in', which nearly always confused the trainee. Later the standard instruction was altered to 'clutch down' or 'clutch up'.

Activity 7.2

In your organisation, or any organisation with which you are familiar:
Consider any brief conversation, perhaps during a meeting, and write down all the words/terms/statements which an outsider, or new member of the organisation, would not be able to understand. Consider the impact that this has on any newcomer and suggest the most appropriate ways in which they can be inducted into your 'organisational language'.

Not paying attention and forgetting

The final combination of problems to consider here is, first, the extent to which people do not pay attention to what is being said or to what they see. There is a human predilection to be selective in attention. There are many examples of this, perhaps the most common being the way in which a listener can focus attention on a comment being made by one person in a general babble of sound by a group of people. This is complicated by the problem of noise, which we have already considered, but it has the effect of the listener trying very hard to suppress all signals other than the particular one that they are trying to pick up.

The rate at which we forget what we hear is considerable. We have probably forgotten half the substance of what we hear within a few hours of hearing it, and no more than 10 per cent will remain after two or three days. Figure 7.1 provides a summary of the main phases in communication and the barriers to effectiveness.

Activity 7.3

When a computer system is designed in-house, analysts from the computer services department will liaise with members of the user department. Why is the computer system that results from this rarely what the user department wanted?

WINDOW ON PRACTICE

Gill (1996) analysed a communications exercise within a medium-sized private sector company. The company was introducing gainsharing and implemented a communications and involvement programme to support the design and implementation of the scheme. Gill used group and individual interviews together with a questionnaire to find out to what extent employees understood the objectives of the new scheme, whether they considered the involvement and communications processes to have been effective and their desire to participate in the scheme.

She found that employees had a different understanding of the objectives of the scheme compared to senior management. To senior management the objectives were behavioural and in particular were to motivate employees, increase commitment, improve/develop team working and improve communications, with the anticipation that this would result in improved profitability.

Figure 7.1 The main barriers to effective communication

	Sender	Recipient	Social/environmental
Barriers in sending message	Unaware message needed Inadequate information in message Pre-judgements about message Pre-judgements about recipient		
Barriers to reception		Needs and anxieties Beliefs and values Attitudes and opinions Expectations Pre-judgements Attention to stimuli	Effects of other environmental stimuli
Barriers to understanding	Semantics and jargon Communication skills Length of communication Communication channel	Semantics problems Concentration Listening abilities Knowledge Pre-judgements Receptivity to new ideas	
Barriers to acceptance	Personal characteristics Dissonant behaviour Attitudes and opinions Beliefs and values	Attitudes, opinions and prejudices Beliefs and values Receptivity to new ideas Frame of reference Personal characteristics	Interpersonal conflict Emotional clashes Status differences Group frame of reference Previous experience of similar interactions
Barriers to action	Memory and retention Level of acceptance	Memory and attention Level of acceptance Flexibility for change of attitudes, behaviour, etc. Personal characteristics	Conflicting messages Actions of others Support/resources

Employees, on the other hand, considered that the two key objectives were to increase output and improve profits. Other objectives they identified were: to get people to work harder, improve the product, improve motivation, commitment and team working and increase employees' earnings. In terms of the effectiveness of the communications process 93 per cent of employees thought this to be ineffective and felt that their views had not been taken into account. Senior management felt that communications were better than they ever had been. They felt that they had sought employees' views and taken them on board, and could provide examples of this, although some also acknowledged that they could have done even better. However 90 per cent of employees did want to participate in the scheme.

In her analysis Gill identified recent company history and levels of trust between different levels of management and employees as critical factors in the effectiveness of the communications, in addition to the actual methods used.

Ways of communicating in organisations

As discussed at the beginning of this chapter, there are many communication media: speech (for example mass meetings, briefing groups, focus groups, presentations), writing (for example memos, newsletters, reports, emails, training handouts, notices) and audio-visual (for example video conferencing, power-point presentations, slides, posters). When speech and some audio-visual means are used non-verbal communication (for example gestures, posture, tone of voice, eye contact) will also have some impact on the communication. Some methods are appropriate only for downwards communication, such as films and posters, other methods are suitable for upwards communication only, such as suggestion schemes. Many methods, however, are suitable for both downwards and upwards communication as well as for lateral communication. The choice of communication method will depend not only on the direction of the communication, and the speed with which it needs to be delivered, but also on the specific nature of the message to be communicated. Notifying employees about a reorganisation which directly affects them would not be best communicated solely via a general email. Many messages, however, are best transmitted by the use of more than one communication medium. Company rules, for example, might most effectively be communicated verbally: communication on an induction course supported by a written summary for employees to take away, and on the company website for future reference. Company performance may well be written about in the company newspaper and sent out as a general email, but may also be displayed diagrammatically via a poster or on the noticeboard. As a general rule, messages are more successfully communicated if more than one communication medium is used.

If more than one medium is used it is imperative that each message reinforces the other, and that conflicting messages are avoided. Variety is another important factor when choosing a communication method. If any particular channel of communication is overloaded, this may result in escape, queuing, loss of quality, delegation or prioritising. If, for example, a company tries to communicate too many messages by means of posters, then employees may escape by ceasing to read any posters, or not read them properly and so on. If a communication channel is overused, it becomes less effective, and some authors have noted the danger of a general communications overload.

Cully *et al.* (2000) reporting the results of the 1998 Workplace Employee Relations Survey (WERSurvey) report that the most commonly used method of communicating with the workforce remained 'systematic use of the management chain', with 60 per cent of respondents using this, a similar percentage to 1984. Fifty per cent used regular newsletters distributed to all employees (compared with 34 per cent in 1984); 48 per cent used regular meetings between management and the total workforce (compared with 34 per cent in 1984) and 33 per cent used suggestion schemes (compared with 25 per cent in 1984). Focus groups are often used as a method of enabling the workforce to communicate their views to management, as are suggestion schemes. Chapter 29 on Strategic Aspects of Employee Relations discusses team briefing (one approach to systematic use of the management chain). With the development of the internet, email systems now operate very effectively on a worldwide basis, and many of us have become dependent on this method of communication which allows us to send reports on the date they need to be received, and obtain immediate feedback from colleagues who are never

Communicating change at Grants of St James

Grants of St James were embarking on a radical reorganisation, and recognised that communication was a critical factor in its success. They introduced a business briefing system and developed the capacity of managers to communicate and manage change. In supporting briefers Grants were open about why changes were required, allowed managers to question the strategy and also involved them in planning the communications needed and the implementation of change.

They produced a briefing pack for supervisors and managers which included a script and visual aids outlining the changes; answers to anticipated questions; an information pack for each employee; copies of all press releases and guidance on how to handle questions from the press; guidance on follow-up communications and how to handle disputes; a process for follow-up meetings.

As well as direct communications to employees, there were communications via union representatives, and also via the Communications Co-ordination Group. This group was set up to co-ordinate communications over 13 locations, and it liaised with line managers on each site, the Board and the Press Office. They provided a hot-line service to managers for the week immediately following the announcement of changes.

For a fuller explanation, see Withers and Hurley (1990).

available to pick up the telephone when we need them to. In spite of such efficiency improvements email has also impacted on our behaviour in other ways. For example there are reports of colleagues sitting within metres of one another in the office sending emails to each other rather than engaging in face-to-face communication, partly so that they have their activities 'on record'. Alternatively some employees only look at their emails every few weeks, and others on return from their holidays are so daunted by the long list of messages awaiting them that they delete them all. Email is a rapidly growing form of communication, and research in this area, although relatively thin until recently, is steadily growing. Initial research concentrated on email use in relation to the technology, and in particular on the barriers to individual email use, such as lack of user involvement, avoidance of change and difficulties in relation to user cognitive style. More recently collective level explanations have been explored (see, for example, Markus 1994), and these studies have considered cultural and situational factors and pressure from others. Another focus of early research was the characteristics that affected the adoption, use and successful implementation of email. There is a growing trend to consider the **impact** of email use on employee and organisational behaviour. Sproull and Kiesler (1991) argue that it has social features which distinguish it from other technologies and which can result in a democratising effect. For example, it has the potential to facilitate communication between those at the bottom of the organisation and those at the top, and to enable people at the periphery of the organisation to become more visible.

Activity 7.4

What do you think would be the most effective way(s) of communicating the following in a non-unionised organisation with 3,000 employees?

1 Instructions from the computer services department on how to use the new computer system.
2 Sales targets for the forthcoming year.
3 Plans to relocate to a new plant five miles away.
4 New absence and holiday reporting procedures.

WINDOW ON PRACTICE

Pliskin *et al.* (1997) studied a 2½ year long strike of academics in Israel where email was used as the medium of communication between the strikers. They found that it enabled unity to develop within the striker group as they were in constant communication, sharing information and jokes and boosting morale. It was also used to distribute offers of practical help, to debate issues and as a vehicle through which they consolidated their support of their leadership. In particular it also provided contact between the strike leaders and the strikers (where there is often a communication gap) so that the leaders did not become separate from the strikers. It also facilitated the negotiation process by involving everyone in the debate about what should be done next and what solutions to the strike were acceptable.

Brigham and Corbett (1997) in their study of email in a large UK organisation found that it had an impact on power relations in the organisation. Although some managers stated that it made their job easier, they also felt that it was a mechanism for monitoring their work. An example was given of opening email post – where the sender received not only confirmation of delivery, but of the post being opened and the time it was opened. Some felt inundated by information which they could not use.

HR information: a computer revolution?

Technology has provided the means for developments in information handling as well as communications and we turn now to information and the use of computers in the HR department. Implementing a new HR information system represents a major form of organisation change, and there has been little research from this perspective (Kossek *et al.* 1994).

WINDOW ON PRACTICE

Kossek *et al.* (1994), in North America, report on a longitudinal case study of the implementation of a new corporate HRIS specifically designed to enhance strategic and business decision making at 'Opco', a worldwide business. They were particularly concerned with the reactions of members of the HR department to the new corporate system. Four major themes emerged: that the new HRIS symbolised the wish of the HR department to become more of a strategic business partner; second, that the new HRIS will enable HR to perform new or enhanced roles of information brokers and decision enabler; and third, that the new HRIS is a catalyst for altering power dynamics and communications patterns between HR and other management functions. In comparison with these positive perspectives the fourth theme revealed that 'real' HR managers do not directly use the HRIS or do not view HRIS use as a critical competency. Alongside this it is interesting to note that as the implementation of the system progressed their expectations of the system remained high, but their intention to use the system significantly decreased.

Kossek *et al.* concluded that 'implementing a new HRIS requires new frames or socially constructed views and ways of thinking'. They argue that a sophisticated HRIS cannot just be bolted on, but requires organisational development. For effective organisational change to occur they also argue that there must be congruence between the capabilities of the innovation and employees' ideals and beliefs regarding the change. If HR specialists do not value HRIS skills or comprehend the significance of the new system then little change will happen and the use of the system will remain geared to administrative support rather than decision support.

Activity 7.5

How is the computer used in your HR department to meet the department's and the organisation's needs? What needs are not being met? Why not? What specific objectives would you set for a new or improved system?

If you are not employed in an organisation. For an organisation of 300 employees with a personnel department of three staff: what questions would you ask, of whom, in order to come to a recommendation about whether a computerised HRIS would be useful and the ways in which it could be best used?

In spite of the barriers identified above, HR professionals are certainly becoming more familiar with the computer's potential contribution to personnel information, and in writing the bulk of this chapter we have assumed such facilities as:

■ producing employee listings according to specified criteria,
■ producing a wide range of aggregate statistics in a variety of forms, including matrices, graphs and charts,
■ administrative/operational systems which produce required letters and provide residue data of transactions and timings.

The conference papers resulting from the annual Computers in Personnel Conferences are an excellent source of information and ideas. However Liff's article (1997) highlights the danger of assuming that data held in an HRIS are objectively accurate.

HR information: a model

The framework in Figure 7.2 shows different types of HR information that are helpful to the organisation. **Individual information** is an employee's individual record, which would include personal information and job and employment history. This information is helpful as a factual record of past events which can assist operational decisions in respect of the employee, such as a promotion decision based on employee performance and potential ratings, job experiences, qualifications, skills and abilities.

Individual information about each employee is the foundation of **aggregate employee information** which provides a basis for strategy and policy decisions which would apply across departments, functions or the whole organisation. Aggregate information can also be analysed against organisational information to identify the effectiveness of the workforce as a whole.

Information from **HR systems and activities** can also provide aggregate information about employees or potential employees, such as the ethnic breakdown of all applicants to the organisation. It can also provide information about the workload which has been undertaken and the speed and timing of different activities. An example would be the volume and pace of recruitment activity over a specified period. This information is helpful for staffing levels, and personnel standards and service agreements with different departments or the whole organisation. It can be helpful in identifying targets or benchmarks towards which the function can strive.

The **information on the HR function** is derived from data about HR systems, aggregate employee data and other organisational data. Together these provide

Figure 7.2 A framework for personnel information

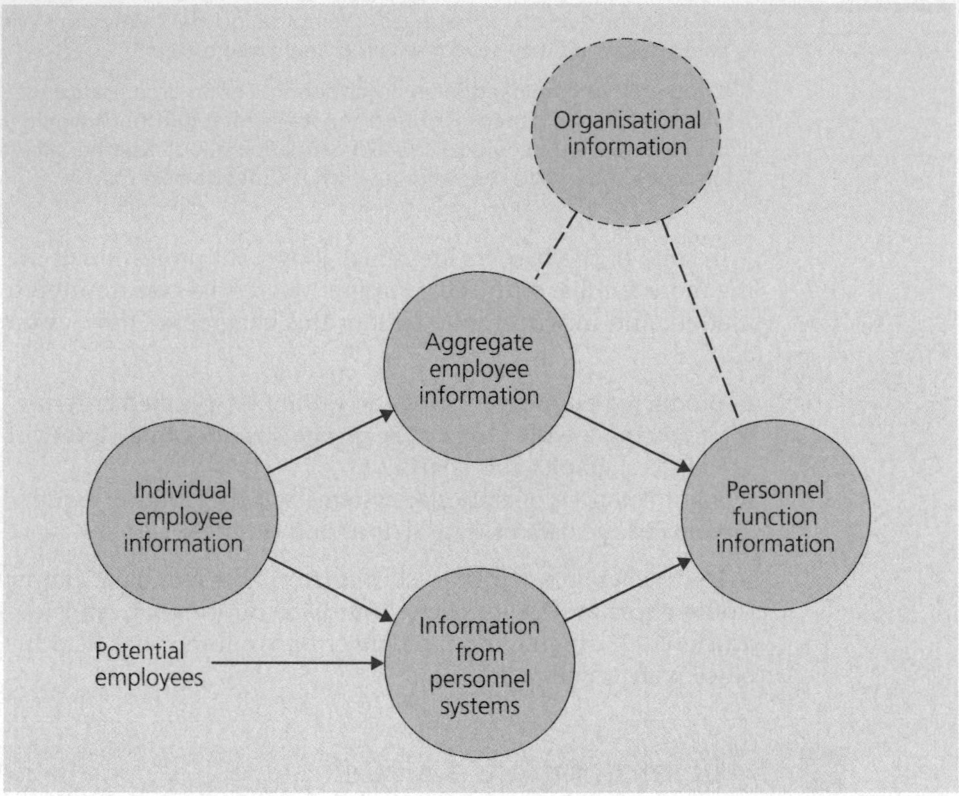

information about the function's efficiency, particularly in financial terms. An example here would be HR staffing ratios and cost–benefit analyses of training activity.

In addition there exists **external information** which can be used for comparative purposes.

We shall now take each one of these information areas and explore them in some more detail.

Individual employee information

Individual employee data chiefly comprise information gleaned from the application form together will employment history that has built up since the employee joined. Areas covered usually include:

- Basic personal and contract details.
- Training/development/education details.
- Appraisal details/career progression.
- Payment and pension details.
- Fringe benefits.
- Discipline/grievance details.
- Health/safety/welfare details.

- Absence details.
- Termination details, e.g. reason for leaving.

Information relating to these areas may be stored in varying amounts of depth depending on the needs of the particular department.

One of the chief users of this type of information is the individual's line manager, for example to check previous training courses attended before agreeing to a training course request, or checking absence history when an employee has had a recent spate of absences. Usually the line manager does not have easy access to this information, because it is on a computer system to which the line manager is unlikely to have access.

WINDOW ON PRACTICE

In a multinational business unit of around 3,500 employees the personnel function used a computer system which had been specified and designed for the Organisational Head Office HR Function. The system was helpful but not user friendly, and information was input by HR staff daily and updated into the records on-screen on a monthly basis. There was a large volume to input and only critical areas were updated, for example absence data, at the expense of training details. Many departments found that they were unable to get complete and accurate information from the system that could help them in managing their staff. One department dealt with this by buying their own PC and inputting and updating all the HR data that they required.

Activity 7.6

What are the respective roles of the HR function and line managers in your organisation in relation to individual employee data?

What are the reasons for this?

What are the advantages and disadvantages of the way that the roles are divided?

How would you recommend that this situation be changed, and why?

If you are not employed in an organisation. How should individual data be managed in an organisation of 150 staff with no personnel department and two payroll staff?

The organisation as a whole also has an interest in individual employee data, which can be used to select individuals for promotion or lateral moves, for relocation or a secondment. If the data are on a computer system it is relatively easy to produce a list of employees who have, for example, electronic engineering skills, French as a second language, a specified performance rating and have worked for the organisation for two years or more. Individual data of a similar nature can also be transferred into a succession planning system (described in more detail in Chapter 5). Lastly individual information can be used in redundancy situations to identify a list of individuals who meet the agreed redundancy criteria.

Aggregate employee information

Aggregate employee information describes the characteristics of the current workforce. It is used at a strategic level in the planning process as described in Chapter 5, and it is also used to inform policy and design changes to improve the current position. Typical areas of information that are analysed include:

- Skills profile.
- Length of service profile.
- Absence levels and costing.
- Turnover levels and costing.
- Age profile.
- Gender profile.
- Ethnic profile.
- Disability profile.
- Internal organisational movement.
- Salary and benefits costs.

In addition aggregate employee information can be used in conjunction with organisational data to gain measures of workforce effectiveness.

We shall look in more detail at some of the above analyses.

Absence analysis and costing

Huczynski and Fitzpatrick (1989) suggest three main approaches to analysing absence, which can be applied on an individual or an aggregate workforce basis. For aggregate analysis **absence rate** is the number of days of absence, that is, when attendance would have been expected, of all employees. **Absence percentage rate** is this figure divided by the total number of actual working days for all employees over the year, multiplied by 100. This simple percentage figure is the one most often used and enables the organisation's absence level to be compared with national figures, or other organisations in the same sector.

Absence frequency rate is the number of spells of absence over the period, usually a year. Comparing this and the absence percentage rate gives critical information about the type of absence problem that the organisation is experiencing.

Absence data, as well as enabling external comparisons, can be analysed by department, work group, occupation, grade and so on. In this way the analysis will throw up problem areas, and additional analysis can be used to try to identify the causes of differing levels of absence in different parts of the organisation. The data may be supplemented by information from questionnaires or interviews with employees or line managers.

The purpose of producing this information is to understand the causes and extent of absence in order to manage it effectively. So, for example, such analysis may result in a new absence policy, employee communications about the impact of absence, appropriate training for line managers, changes to specific groups of jobs and the introduction of a new type of attendance system such as flexitime. The information provides a base for future monitoring. Absence data can be analysed further to provide benchmarks of 'high', 'medium' and 'low' absence levels in the organisation, and assuming the organisation finds current absence levels acceptable, this analysis can be used to trigger specific management actions when an employee reaches different benchmark levels.

The costing of absence needs to have a wider focus than just the pay of the absent individual. Other costs include:

- line manager costs in finding a temporary replacement or rescheduling work;
- the actual costs of the temporary employee;
- costs of showing a temporary employee what to do;

■ costs associated with a slower work rate or more errors from a temporary employee;
■ costs of contracts not completed on time.

These costs can be calculated and provide the potential for productivity improvement.

Equal opportunities analysis

Equal opportunities analysis aims to provide an organisational profile of ethnic origin, gender, age and disability. The resulting percentages from this can be compared with national and local community figures to give an initial idea of how representative the organisation is. Further analyses break these figures down to compare them by department, job category and grade. It is in this type of analysis that startling differences are likely to be found, for example as shown in Figure 7.3.

Figure 7.3 Breakdown of senior manager staff group and administrative staff group

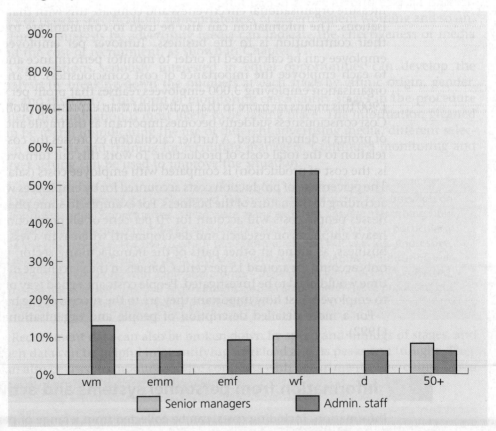

Key: wm, white males; emm, ethnic minority males; emf, ethnic minority females; wf, white females; d, disabled; 50+, aged over 50 years.
Note: Percentages of senior manager category and administrative category each add to over 100 per cent as there is some overlap between the groups into which they have been subdivided.

Information on the HR function

A range of figures is often calculated in relation to the size and effectiveness of the HR function. Probably the most common is the ratio between headcount in the HR function and total organisational headcount. One use of this is to control the number of HR staff linked to the size of the organisation, once a workable ratio has been identified. Typical ratios lie between 1:50 and 1:100. Other figures concentrate on the expenditure for which the HR function is responsible. So, for example, the operating budget of the HR function is added to HR staff salaries and on-costs. This figure will be monitored annually. Further analyses take this cost and divide it by the number of employees in the organisation, which gives HR costs per employee.

Another way of reviewing HR costs is to compare them with all other costs of the organisation, and this ratio can then be monitored for changes, and as a way of assessing the productivity of the function. Similarly costs can be compared against HR departments in other organisations. The value of the HR department can also be assessed in terms of satisfaction with its contribution.

Activity 7.8

Design a questionnaire to assess customer satisfaction with the personnel function in your organisation, or any organisation with which you are familiar.

Who are the customers you will approach?

Confidentiality, privacy and security

Concerns about confidentiality, privacy and security of personal information have always been present but have been highlighted by the growing use of computers.

Confidentiality

Confidentiality relates to information sought, obtained or held by an organisation, the disclosure of which might be detrimental to that organisation or to the third party that supplied it.

The guarantee given to the reference writer that everything they say will be treated in the strictest confidence is to protect the reference writer, the third party, rather than the person about whom the reference is written.

Privacy

Privacy relates to information sought, obtained or held by an organisation about a past, present or prospective employee, the use of which might be detrimental to that employee. For example the information may not be accurate, it may be accessed by people who do not need to have it or it may be used for a purpose other than originally intended.

Security

Appropriate security, for example the use of password protection, audit trails and back-ups, is necessary in order to protect both the individual and the employer.

The Data Protection Act 1998

The Data Protection Act 1998 attempts to regulate the above dangers, and provides a broader legislative framework than the 1984 Data Protection Act which it will eventually completely replace. The 1998 Data Protection Act came into force on 1 March 2000, although there are transitional arrangements for the way in which it is applied (see later). It differs from the 1984 Act in two major ways:

1 The legislation applies to all data regardless of how they are collected and stored. The previous Act excluded manual records but they are now included, as long as they are arranged in a recognisable order.
2 The legislation is now concerned with privacy as well as transparency – in other words there are now controls over the content of the information which can be held, as well as over proper ways of managing the information and making it available to data subjects (that is, the individuals on which the data are held). The regulations of privacy underpin the Human Rights Act 2000.

When does the Data Protection Act apply?

The Act applies to organisations holding personal data. Personal data have been defined as:

> data which relates to a living individual who can be identified from the information including an expression of opinion about an individual but not any indication of the intentions of the data user in respect of that individual.
>
> (Data Protection Act 1998, s. 1(3))

All organisations using personal data have annually to notify the Data Protection Commission of the data they are processing. This requirement replaces the one-off registration under the old Act. In the new Act the definition of processing has been widened to include 'obtaining, holding and disclosing' personal data.

Data protection principles

There are eight data protection principles. These are:

1 Personal data shall be processed fairly and lawfully.
2 Personal data shall be processed for intended purposes.
3 Personal data shall be adequate, relevant and not excessive in relation to purpose.
4 Personal data shall be accurate.
5 Personal data shall not be kept for longer than necessary.
6 Personal data shall be processed in accordance with the data subject's rights.
7 Personal data shall be secure.
8 Personal data shall not be transferred to other countries without adequate data protection.

The first five of these principles are very similar to the principles outlined in the 1984 Act, while the last three represent significant developments from 1984.

Sproull, L. and Kiesler, S. (1991) *Connections: New ways of working in networked organisations*. Cambridge, Mass: MIT Press.

Torrington, D. and Weightman, J. (1991) *Action Management*. London: IPM.

Withers, M. and Hurley, B. (1990) 'Grants grows its own grapevine', *Personnel Management*, November.

General discussion topics

1 We have used a rational approach to communication in this chapter, but in practice communication in organisations is affected by politics and individual agendas. What types of impact do politics and individual agendas have on organisational communications?

   (a) Should organisations seek to address these issues?

   (b) How might they do this, and is it feasible?

2 'Getting too involved in HRI systems is a dangerous step for the HR professional because it pulls them away from their area of core expertise (people and people systems) which they need to continuously develop and exploit.' Do you agree?

3 Discuss the notion that information is power, and apply this to the specialist personnel function.

Chapter 8 Interactive skill: chairing meetings

Meetings do not constitute management, although they take up a large part of the time of human resource managers, but they are an inescapable part of the management process and they are frequently less successful than they should be. Leading, or chairing, meetings is a challenging skill but a rewarding aspect of human resource management. Chairing meetings is also a position that is associated with authority. Company boards, benches of magistrates, Cabinet committees, employment tribunals, political parties, debating societies are among the many activities that are led by the person in the chair. Professors in universities are appointed to chairs, not because they are too weary to stand up, but because the chair represents authority.

WINDOW ON PRACTICE	In courts of law there is a standard opening to proceedings whereby everyone present stands for the entry of the judge or the magistrates. If there is more than one person on the bench, the chair for the central person usually has a higher back than the others to emphasise the authority of the office that person holds.

HR specialists have many meetings to chair, including selection panels, meetings with union officials, health and safety committees, job evaluation groups and many more. It is not sufficient just to know why a meeting is being held for it to be a success: the processes by which a meeting works have to be understood as well. In one of our research projects 433 meetings were observed, and many showed the chair to have such limited understanding of the basic mechanics of meetings that there was inadequate discussion, understanding and action about important matters. Poor meetings not only fail to achieve objectives; but also do harm, as members become frustrated about lack of progress or about not being able to get their point of view across. It is not just the fault of the person in charge: all participants have to learn meeting mechanics. The analogy of the orchestra is apt. The conductor is responsible for the final quality of the co-ordinated act, but every instrumentalist has to make a distinctive, but not individualistic, contribution that blends with all the others.

We have to pay careful attention to the details of running the meeting. Good intentions and the importance of the matter to be considered are not enough on their own. The person in charge of the meeting takes the blame for things not being right. Those who feel overlooked or outmanoeuvred are merciless with those who have overlooked them – however unintentionally. The person in charge may feel very uncomfortable and may lose respect in the eyes of colleagues, but something is still usually achieved: catharsis for group members and some information exchange.

The basic necessities are a clear format, purpose and preparation, with the leader being in control. Those attending the meeting can then concentrate on content rather than fretting about the way the meeting is being conducted. People will only attend and make a success of meetings they see as useful.

Preparation

Making effective arrangements for a meeting help it to be an effective meeting. It can help to run through a series of check questions.

Who should attend the meeting?

A large group will ensure that a wide range of interests is represented, so that there should be few problems of people complaining that they were excluded. It is usually appropriate when pressing matters of major importance are to be discussed and a large number of people have to be informed quickly. The problems are that the more people who attend, the more likely it is that the business will grind to a halt. Also the more people who attend, the less likely it is that there will be any useful discussion.

A small group makes discussion easier and more productive as there are fewer people competing to have their say and it is easier for the person in the chair to blend together a range of contributions in finding a consensus.

Ideally you want people either who have expertise in the matter being discussed or who have a stake in the matter. This ensures focus for the discussion and should help outcomes, as people will support that which they have helped to create. Observers or free-loaders can be a nuisance as they do not have the discipline of having to deliver on whatever is agreed and can therefore tend to get more concerned to make an impression as someone with bright ideas rather than thinking of practical solutions.

You may want a variety of personalities and styles to ensure a lively discussion. This is dealt with in Chapter 19 on team building.

What is the brief or terms of reference of the meeting?

Does this meeting have the power to take a decision, or to make a recommendation, or simply to exchange information? All of these are equally valid objectives for a meeting, but it helps to be clear on this basic question of objective.

Sometimes there is a limit to how wide the discussion can usefully range. Some aspects will be outside the competence of the meeting and such discussion could distract those present from dealing with the matter they should be discussing. An example is where a decision has already been made elsewhere that can not be changed. If it has been decided elsewhere that a plant should close, there will then be a number of other meetings to decide how that decision should be implemented. It is rarely appropriate for a management meeting to try and get that decision changed.

As well as explicit terms of reference that define the range of discussion, there may well be some conclusions that would be unacceptable. The chair needs to have sufficient nous to be aware of what these are and to whom they would not be acceptable, so that they can either be ruled out in discussion or questioned if suggested.

What should the agenda be?

There are two questions about the agenda, one more obvious than the other: what do we need to consider, and in what order?

The content of the agenda is usually drafted and proposed by the Chair or, in more formal meetings, the Chair in consultation with the Secretary. The topics for consideration need to be clearly described, so that members of the group can come to the meeting with a clear understanding of them and with a focus on the key issues. There is a risk in putting too many items on the agenda so that some are rushed, or put off to another occasion.

The sequence of items can be affected by the consideration of which chicken needs to come before which egg. Getting the right things early on the agenda can make it easier to resolve later matters provided they are in the right order; otherwise decisions are half made and then deferred 'until we have dealt with item x'.

With meetings where there are minutes to review, matters arising and any other business can take up a lot of time unless there is careful planning.

Activity 8.1

Reflect on a meeting you attended recently that you felt was not well organised and run. Were the terms of reference for the meeting clear to all attending? Was the sequence of items on the agenda conducive to a successful meeting? Would the meeting have been more effective if the sequence had been different?

What about the physical location and arrangements?

How often have you attended a meeting where one or more of the following occur:

- Two people do not come because they were not told about it (or so they say).
- Three people arrive late because they could not find the room.
- Two of the late arrivals immediately leave to try and borrow chairs from another room because there are not enough.
- Coffee arrives ten minutes after the meeting has started and is served (or distributed) by catering assistants who swap comments with each other in loud voices such as, 'One more down here, Flo'.
- Several people mutter that they had specifically asked for tea, whereupon Flo produces a docket and reads out what it says so as to clear Flo and her colleague of any responsibility for the fact that tea has not been provided.
- After half an hour a succession of people arrive for a completely different meeting, because the room has been double-booked (or so they say. Probably they forgot to book it. You're sure that you did book it, aren't you?).
- The room is noisy, too hot or too cold, the wrong shape or in the wrong place, and the loos are miles away.

Incidents like these can wreck a meeting, or at least send the Chair into convulsions, yet most of them can be avoided with good organisation, so that you merely have to contend with the people who have brought the wrong papers or do not know what is going on as they have not opened their email since last month.

What is the meeting for?

The person leading the meeting needs a clear view of what type of meeting it is going to be. This will affect the way it is run and the way in which those attending are asked to participate.

The meeting may be *to convey information*. Then the sole focus is on the Chair, who is passing on information, or analysis or news to a gathering of those who need to know. The only role for others attending the meeting is to listen, perhaps ask questions and probably mutter explanations and reiterations to each other to check their understanding. The reason for doing this in a meeting rather than distributing a memorandum is to give the opportunity for further clarification through questions, as well as the symbolic impact of information being passed on personally rather than impersonally. It is therefore usually for matters of weight and significance.

If a meeting is *to share information* the Chair is the co-ordinator rather than the fount of all wisdom. A case conference is a typical example and the Chair needs skill to elicit constructive participation, encourage a free flow of information at the same time as preventing such a free flow that the meeting becomes chaotic and loses any sense of direction.

A meeting *to make a decision* will have a different style again. The expertise needed to make the right decision is distributed among the members of the group, so that much of the time is spent sharing information, but there has to be joint ownership of, or support for, the decision that is eventually made. A board meeting is the obvious example and the actual dynamics of the encounter itself will vary according to the relative status and authority of those present. The Chair may be so dominant that the meeting is to win the support of members to a decision that is already made. In other situations it is necessary for a consensus to be identified as the discussion develops so that it can be articulated for everyone to accept or modify until it wins general acceptance and commitment.

Conduct of the meeting itself (the encounter)

How can contributions be stimulated and controlled?

For each item on the agenda, the Chair needs to consider:

■ Who has something to say?
■ How can I get them to say it?
■ How can I keep the long-winded brief?
■ When should I nudge the meeting towards a decision/the next item.

Few people are accustomed to expressing a point of view in a meeting, and most are likely to find it inhibiting. They speak best when asked to do so, and when speaking on something about which they are knowledgeable. Leaders of meetings get contributions by asking people to speak, picking up non-verbal cues of a desire to speak or reaction to what someone else has said. Statements of fact rather than expressions of opinion are the easiest way for people to make their first contribution. Experienced members of groups can help the less experienced by 'shaping' the clumsy or over-emotional comments of their colleagues and agreeing with them (for example: 'I would like to agree with what Hilary was saying and make the further point ...' NOT, 'I think Hilary was trying to say ...').

Inexperienced leaders of meetings sometimes show their worry about losing control by constantly emphasising the limited time available, but this makes it harder for people to make coherent contributions. People speak more effectively and come to the point more quickly when not under time pressure.

Curbing the excesses of the verbose is a true test of chairing skill. Making a succinct and focused contribution is a competence not found often among people attending meetings, so the Chair has to be skilled not only in eliciting contributions, but also in closing people down when they are running out of control. Here are some suggestions:

- Use eye contact with the speaker to indicate encouragement or discouragement. When you begin to lose interest, or become mildly irritated, the speaker will receive that silent message and respond to it.
- For those who will not respond, use more direct signals, such as looking away or looking anxiously at your watch.
- Use focus questions. The speaker will be rambling on and on, so you focus what is being said by interrupting with a question to focus the speaker and to elicit an answer that is likely to be brief. Examples are:
  - 'How long will it take for X's performance to improve?'
  - 'What will it cost?'
  - 'Have you got it cleared?'

Bringing people in

An aspect of control is finding ways to bring people in to the discussion at the time when their contribution is most appropriate. Ways to do it are like this:

- Pick out someone who you think should have a relevant or constructive comment to make and invite them: 'What is your view, Henry?' or 'I wonder if Sheila could help us with the exact figures ...'.Or ,'Well I know that Harry has direct experience of this sort of problem ...'.
- Pick out someone whose body language indicates a potential willingness to speak. This might be a raised hand, or an obviously angry reaction to a comment from someone else, a worried expression, a vigorous nod of agreement or a sudden change in someone's demeanour showing that they have just had a brainwave. The tricky thing is to decide who to bring in to the discussion when, bearing in mind that people raising their hands or looking angry will have to have their say eventually.

Keeping it going

A meeting is best chaired when the Chair takes part constantly in the discussion, not necessarily expressing an opinion (nor declining to do so) but watching the pattern develop and helping everyone to see the pattern and concentrate on it.

- Summarise sparingly, but summarise well. It is pointless to summarise every individual contribution, as the contributors will not see that their own, crystal-clear, succinct comments need any summarising from anyone else. Summarising is needed when there are a number of contributions that have to be pulled together and a pattern found.
- An exception to the last sentence is where someone has not expressed themselves at all well, and is prepared to acknowledge it: 'I have not put that very

clearly, but do you see what I am driving at?' Because you have been listening closely, you are able to move things forward by saying something like, 'Well what I got from that was . . . Have I got it right?' The person will then confirm that you got it right or will modify it. Either way they will be grateful to you. Do not say, 'I think what you were trying to say was . . .'. That shows you to be patronising and the other person to be inadequate.

■ Be ready to summarise where the discussion has reached, but do not summarise in search of a conclusion until you are confident that there is at least a partial consensus among all those present. Picking the right time is risky but unavoidable. If you go for a conclusion too quickly, you may not carry the meeting with you and you seriously undermine your necessary authority. Leaving it too late makes everyone fed up because things are dragging on. People grumble about meetings, but they rarely grumble about the (very few) meetings that are well run.

■ Where things are really difficult, try getting a series of partial solutions. This is trying to split up an issue into parts and identifying a part where there appears to be general agreement and confirming that with the rest of the group, even if it is conditional on some other problem being resolved later. This helps the group by giving everyone a sense of some agreement and progress. Once there are two or three small matters on which there is agreement, it is surprising how much more progress can be made.

And what about your own input?

The person chairing the meeting is not simply enabling everyone else to have their say, like the Speaker of the House of Commons. There is usually a strong personal contribution to be made, often a leading contribution. People will want to hear what you have to say, may be looking to you for a lead, but you still need to carry them with you.

There are basically two alternative approaches: playing the waiting game or leading from the front. Playing the waiting game is setting up the discussion of different points by a brief, summary introduction of the issue and eventually shaping the discussion with your own views and reaction. Leading from the front is setting out your position and then inviting suggestions. Neither is better than the other; they are simply different approaches that suit different situations and people.

Winding it up

Finally the Chair sums things up by reiterating the points upon which agreement has been reached and the nature of that agreement. There may well be further points of clarification and even argument, but the Chair has to nail down what people will accept and commit to. Equally important is to sum up the remaining points of disagreement, again with as much succinct clarity as possible. This is when you might just get your lucky break, because your summary might make someone realise that they really have been a bit petty and it is time for a magnanimous gesture. Also someone may have been doggedly hanging on to a position in the hope of movement elsewhere and is now prepared to shift because they are simply not going to win their argument. No one likes to be the reason for a group failing to agree.

Activity 8.2

On the basis of the suggestions in the last few pages formulate some forms of words that would be effective for your own personal style in various aspects of chairing a meeting, such as:

- Stimulating and controlling contributions.
- Curbing the verbose.
- Bringing people in.
- Keeping it going.
- Making your own input.

Members of the group need to disperse feeling that their time has been well spent and that they had their day, knowing what has been agreed and what is outstanding, and knowing what happens next.

Follow-up

When the meeting has finished, the leader of the meeting still has work to do.

Minutes or report of the meeting

Formal meetings have minutes. Less formal meetings have notes. Informal meetings may not have any agreed record at all, but people will still have made jottings in their diary, on a clipboard or in the margin of the agenda. You have no control over what notes people at the meeting make for their own use, but the way you run the meeting will, of course, affect what they write.

The more formal minutes or notes will be written by the Secretary (if there is one) or by the Chair. The purpose is to produce a stimulus to appropriate action, not to write historical analysis. Sometimes it is important to describe the discussion and issues, so that those not in attendance can understand not simply what was agreed but at least some of the reasoning. In other cases it is sufficient simply to list the action points and who is responsible for following them through.

Here is a framework of an administrative drill for a committee secretary to follow. To make this illustration concrete we are assuming a meeting once a month on Day 28.

Day	Phase One: MINUTES AND PRELIMINARIES
1, 2	Write draft of minutes for yesterday's meeting, including notes of action items.
5	Clear minutes with Chair and confirm date and time of next meeting.
6, 7	Type, copy and distribute minutes.
	1.0 Book room for next meeting.
	Phase Two: AGENDA
18	Ask committee members for items to be included on next agenda.
	2.1 Discuss order of agenda and inclusion/deferment of items with Chair.

▶

Suggested sequence:
(a) Announcements (apologies, introduction of new members, Chair's points).
(b) Minutes of previous meeting and matters arising, where matter involves brief report. Matters arising for further discussion to be separate agenda items.
(c) Items requiring decision but involving little controversy.
(d) Most difficult item.
   (possible break)
(e) Next most difficult item.
(f) Items requiring discussion but not decision.
(g) Easy items.
(h) Any other business.
(i) Provisional date of next meeting.

Phase Three: RUN-UP

22   Circulate agenda and other papers to members, with note of date, time and venue.

26   Check seating, catering, visual aids.

      Collate all papers, past minutes, apologies.

28   Attend meeting and take notes for minutes.

Implementation of proposals

The meeting will have ended with general understanding that various actions would follow. Some of these will follow at once, as people scurry away to make their phone calls or look up information. Other actions will be forgotten unless there is a reminder. This is where the circulation of the minutes can be useful. Other actions will probably need the Chair to push them along and pull together actions by different people as the situation changes in the days after the meeting.

Summary propositions

8.1   Chairing meetings is an aspect of management that is crucial to making and implementing management decisions.

8.2   Key aspects of preparing for a meeting are: who should attend, what is the brief, what is the agenda, what about physical location and arrangements, what is the meeting for: to convey information, to share information or to make a decision?

8.3   Key features of conducting the meeting itself are: how contributions can be stimulated and controlled, bringing people in, keeping it going, making your own input and winding it up.

8.4   An administrative drill for a meeting secretary deals with minutes and preliminaries, agenda and run-up.

General discussion topics

1 What advantages and drawbacks do you see in an arrangement where everyone takes it in turn to chair a meeting of a particular group?

2 Why do so many people complain about the amount of time they spend in meetings?

Part II
Case study problem

Setting up a call centre

Recently there has been a dramatic growth in the number of call centres. These are large groups of staff gathered together at a centre to deal with much, if not all, of the dealings between the business and its customers. This development is made possible by advances in telecommunications and is made necessary to overcome many of the inefficiencies and delays that come from having to rely mainly on communication by post. Typically the call centre is geographically remote from the rest of the business. Often this is to avoid the high labour costs of south-east England, but there is also a view that regional accents are more acceptable to customers than those from the south-east.

One of the earliest call centres was Direct Line Insurance, which sold policies by telephone, reducing the need for personal, face-to-face discussion with customers. This produces economies of scale and reduced charges, which generated very successful business. Another example was Littlewoods Mail Order, where the well-established routine was for agents to have a catalogue and sell to their friends from the catalogue and then send in a postal order form. The practice developed of the order being telephoned in, instead of posted. Both these developments, and the many others that have followed, required well-trained staff, who can deal with a wide range of enquiries and issues in a manner that will induce the uncertain customer to buy and persuade the dissatisfied customer that something will be done.

The majority of staff are female and it is increasingly an area of graduate employment as a preliminary to seeking greater responsibility.

You have to set up the staffing and organisation of a new call centre that is to operate on a seven-day week, open to telephone callers from 08.00 to 22.00 daily. The centre is to handle a new range of financial services products and the business plan calls for a minimum of 120 operators to be available at all times. From 10.00 to 17.00, 200 need to be available, and 350 are needed from 17.00 to 21.00.

The majority of the work will be selling in direct response to customer calls, where the operator will sell the product, but then arrange for the necessary follow-up: information and/or communication through the post, the raising of an invoice, a return call by someone with specialist expertise, checking of customer references prior to confirmation, a follow-up call in one week by the operator, and so on.

There will also be some cold calling by other staff, as well as the management and supervision of the administrative system and financial control.

Required

You now have to set up the centre, starting with the following questions:

1 What number of operative staff will you require to meet the staffing levels needed?

2 How will you organise the shift rotas for maximum effectiveness?

3 What mix of full-time and part-time staff will you aim for?

4 What type of organisational structure will you need to produce effective co-ordination of, and communication between, the numbers of staff you have identified in answer to questions 2 and 3?

5 How do you overcome the problems of communication that are likely to arise when people spend their working day in the 'blinkered' workplace of headset and computer terminal?

6 How will you develop an organisational culture to overcome the potential for this sort of work to become alienating in the same way as many mass-production operations in manufacturing?

Part II
Examination questions

Undergraduate introductory

1 Explain the thinking behind the statements by Alfred Chandler that structure follows strategy.

2 What are the consequences of deficient organisation structures and their capacity to change?

Undergraduate finals

3 Of the four organisational forms identified (Entrepreneurial, Bureaucratic, Matrix and Independence) what would be the problems facing a firm moving from one form to one of the other forms? Explain which change you are discussing.

4 Evaluate the typical problems facing HR managers in trying to organise effective communication in businesses. How can these problems be overcome?

Masters

5 'Consumption is more important than work for modern identity.' Discuss.

6 Critically appraise the current role of the personnel specialist in the area of HR planning and information systems.

Professional

7 'Giving feedback lies at the heart of coaching and mentoring, and it should also feature in all managers' informal day-to-day working contacts with their staff', writes Alan Fowler (*People Management*). Why is giving feedback so difficult? What do's and don'ts advice would you give to a manager who seeks your help on two matters: (a) the effective use of feedback as a motivational tool for the encouragement of good performers; (b) how feedback may be constructively deployed in remedial scenarios where poor performance is linked to abrasive and unco-operative behaviour?

8 What are the key criteria for assessing the effectiveness of a personnel information system?

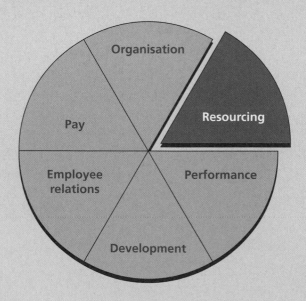

PART III

RESOURCING

The first major activity of the human resource specialist is to find and bring in the people that the business needs for its success. The people may not be employees – they may be consultants or subcontractors. They may be temporary, full-time, part time or occasional, and the working relationship between the business and its people is the contract, which sums up the features of that relationship so that both parties know where they stand. Nearly always there is a face-to-face meeting between the parties to agree terms before the relationship begins. The process of 'coming to terms' is one of mutual appraisal. Many prospective employees reject a prospective employer by deciding not to apply for a post, or by discontinuing their application. Employers always choose between many – and often feel there are too few applicants. Once recruited, people have to be retained within the business by a series of strategies that sustain their interest and motivation as well as keeping the focus of their activities within a changing organisational and business context. Contracts end as well as begin, and we have to be sure that the arrangements to end the contract are as sound as those for it to start.

Chapter 9 # Strategic aspects of resourcing

'Angela's leaving – quick, we must make sure to get the ad in this month's journal.'

'It's hopeless – they all leave just as soon as we've trained them. What's the point?'

'It's not my fault – we just can't get the staff. No wonder quality is so poor.'

'That's it. The results are so bad we'll have to let some of them go. Tony, draw up a shortlist of possibles and we'll try and get it sorted this week.'

All too often employee resourcing is a reactive activity, without any link to organisational strategy and without internal coherence. To bridge this gap we suggest a range of aspects which together can form the framework for a resourcing strategy to facilitate the future direction of the organisation. Each of these aspects offers choices. We begin by reviewing the major labour market trends of recent years and their implications for employers. We go on to identify the main ways in which individual labour markets vary, suggesting that different approaches are needed in each case. Finally we consider two areas in which organisations need to make strategic resourcing choices. The first concerns the extent to which different forms of flexible working are appropriate. The second relates to the relative merits of recruiting qualified staff or developing the required skills internally.

Responding to labour market trends

The starting point for all strategic activity in HRM is to understand the environment in which an organisation operates. It is only possible to formulate the most appropriate policies and practices once its key features have been identified and their importance grasped. In the field of employee resourcing the environment with which we are concerned is the labour market – the pool of available talent in which employers compete to recruit and subsequently retain staff. Later we look at different types of labour market and their implications for employers. Here we focus on three major trends in the UK labour market as a whole and look at how they are affecting decision making in organisations.

Demographic developments

In 2000 the UK's population numbered 59 million, of whom just under half (28.5 million) were either in work or actively seeking work. Both figures are projected to rise marginally during the first ten years of the new millennium. The overall population is increasing, despite falling birth rates, because of lengthening life expectancy. The number of people who are economically active is increasing largely because of women spending a greater proportion of their lives in paid work than has been the case historically. Over the longer term, however, the proportion of the population that is of working age will shrink in comparison with the total population as more and more people live longer after reaching retirement age. This process has already begun in countries such as Japan and Germany with significant implications for the provision of care and pensions for the growing number of elderly people. In the UK there are currently 21 people over the age of 65 for every 100 people of working age. The change is predicted to occur after 2010 when this number will start to rise significantly. By 2030 more than a quarter of the population will be over 65. The coming years will therefore see a substantial change in the age profile of the workforce, as the population as a whole gets older and a greater proportion of young people remain in full-time education for longer.

There are two major implications for employers. First, because their numbers will fall, it will be progressively harder to recruit and retain the more talented younger workers. Organisations that have sought to resource their organisations by recruiting and training new graduates or school leavers will either have to work a good deal harder at competing for them or have to bring in older people in their place. Second, there are implications for the capacity of the state to provide a reasonable level of pension for so many retired people. Increasingly, therefore, people are likely to look at the nature of occupational pension being provided by employers when deciding on their career options. Organisations offering good, well-communicated pension benefits will be better placed than others to attract and retain the employees they need.

Diversity

According to the most recent Workplace Employee Relations Survey (Cully *et al.* 1999, pp. 23–6), men now account for 52 per cent and women for 48 per cent of jobs in UK workplaces employing over 25 people. Increased female participation in the workforce has been one of the most significant social trends over recent decades. In 1980 the employment rate for women of working age was 59 per cent, by 1998 the figure had reached 68 per cent and it is expected to continue rising for some years. As a result there has been some decline in the number of workplaces where women are heavily outnumbered by men and an increase in the number where men are outnumbered by women. Although the vast majority of management posts are still held by men, we have also seen a substantial increase in the number of women occupying such positions – another trend that is going to continue in the years ahead. Despite these developments there remain many areas of work which are dominated by either men or women and a continued substantial gender gap in overall pay levels. A trend which has been identified in many surveys is the growth in the number of part-time workers in the UK. They now account for over a quarter of the total workforce and over 80 per cent of them are women. Representation of ethnic minorities has also increased over recent years. In the early 1980s around 4.5 per cent of employees came from ethnic minorities. Twenty years on the figure is 6.5 per cent. Whereas in 1980 two-thirds of workplaces employed no one from an ethnic minority, over half now do (Millward *et al.* 2000, p. 43). Increases in representation have occurred across the industrial sectors.

Taken together, these various trends mean that the workforce is steadily becoming more diverse in its make-up. While there remains a strong degree of segregation in terms of the types of work performed, the trend is towards heterogeneity at all organisational levels. There are a number of important implications for human resource managers:

■ In order to attract and retain the best employees it is necessary to take account of the needs of dual-career families. The law now requires employers to offer a measure of support with recent measures on parental leave and the right to time off for family emergencies, but there is a great deal more that can be done. Career-break entitlements, crèches and job-share schemes are the most common initiatives.

■ There is a heightened need for awareness of the possibility of discrimination against any group which is underrepresented in the workplace. The perception of inequity, however justifiable in practice, is all that is needed for staff turnover rates to increase and for an employer to gain a poor reputation in its labour markets.

■ Employers are required to pay more serious attention to the issue of sexual and racial harassment in a workplace characterised by diversity than in one which is less heterogeneous. It is advisable to have written policies covering such matters and to ensure that line managers are fully aware of the developing law on harassment.

Skills and qualifications

The third major development in the labour market is the changing occupational structure, leading to a greater demand for skilled staff. In recent decades the chief job growth areas have been in the managerial and professional occupations, and in service industries such as retailing, security and catering. By contrast there has been an ongoing decline in demand for people to work in the manufacturing and agricultural sectors (Morris and Willey 1996, pp. 88–9). While technical skills are not a requirement for all of the new jobs, social skills are necessary, as is the ability to work effectively without close supervision.

The past two decades have also seen a strong increase in demand for graduates. Over 400,000 now graduate from universities in the UK every year, including 260,000 with first degrees. Unemployment among this group is considerably lower than for the rest of the population whatever the economic conditions, indicating a capacity on the part of employers to absorb the growing numbers into their labour forces. However, despite the increasing numbers of people gaining formal qualifications at all levels (HMSO 1999), there remain skills shortages. When the economy is performing well these can be significant. The annual Skills Needs in Britain Survey for 1998 reported that 42 per cent of employers had had problems filling vacancies, while a survey of graduate recruiters found that over half were unable to find graduates for all their positions (Pearson *et al.* 1999, p. 48). There are still too few people with high-level IT and scientific qualifications entering the labour market and far too many people lacking basic numeracy and literacy skills. The government estimates that seven million adults in the UK are innumerate and unable to read beyond the most basic level (Office of National Statistics 1997).

Policy initiatives are in place to improve skills levels at both ends of the scale, but it will take a number of years before the effects are apparent in the labour market. Until then employers have to devise strategies to deal with skills shortages in key areas. One approach is simply to work harder at recruiting and retaining employees. Another is to find ways of reducing reliance on the hard-to-recruit groups by reorganising work and dividing tasks up differently so that people with particular skills spend 100 per cent of their time undertaking the duties for which only they are qualified. A third response is to look overseas for recruits interested in working in the UK. Where skills shortages are particularly acute there is also the possibility of relocating one or more organisational functions abroad. Finally, of course, it is possible to recruit people without the required skills and to provide the necessary training and development opportunities.

Analysing labour markets

While the general trends outlined above have significant implications for employers, more important for individual organisations are developments in the particular labour markets which have relevance to them. An understanding of what is going on in these can then form the basis of decision making across the employee resourcing field. There are several different ways in which labour markets vary.

Geographical differences

For most jobs in most organisations the relevant labour market is local. Pay rates and career opportunities are not so great as to attract people from outside the district in which the job is based. The market consists of people living in the 'travel to work area', meaning those who are able to commute within a reasonable period of time. In determining rates of pay and designing recruitment campaigns there is a need to compare activities with those of competitors in the local labour market and to respond accordingly. Skills shortages may be relieved by increases in the local population or as a result of rival firms contracting. New roads and improved public transport can increase the population in the travel to work area, with implications for recruitment budgets and the extent to which retention initiatives are necessary. For other jobs, usually but not always those which are better paid, the relevant labour market is national or even international. Here different approaches to recruitment are necessary and there is a need to keep a close eye on what a far larger number of rival employers are doing to compete for staff.

Tight v. loose

A tight labour market is one in which it is hard to recruit and retain staff. Where the labour market is loose, there are few problems finding people of the required calibre. Labour market conditions of this type clearly vary over time. The higher the rate of unemployment in an area, the looser the labour market will be. However, some labour markets always remain tight whatever the economic conditions simply because there are insufficient numbers of people willing or able to apply for the jobs concerned. In recent years, even at the depths of the recessions of the 1980s and 1990s, it has been difficult to find good IT staff and effective sales people.

A number of researchers have looked at the responses of employers faced with either loose or tight labour markets. Windolf (1986) identified four types of approach used in the UK and in Germany which varied depending not only on the tightness of the market, but also on the capacity of the organisation to respond intelligently to the situation. He found that many organisations with high market power (that is, faced with a relatively loose labour market) made little effort at all in the employee resourcing field. They simply took the opportunity to spend as little as possible on recruitment and selection and waited for people to come to them. When there was a vacancy it tended to be filled by a similar person to the one who had left, thus maintaining the status quo. According to Windolf, the more intelligent organisations took the opportunity afforded by favourable labour market conditions to seek out people with the capacity to innovate and who would develop their roles proactively. All available recruitment channels were used, leading to the development of a richly diverse and creative workforce. A similar dichotomy was identified in the case of tight labour markets. Here many organisations simply 'muddled through', finding people where they could, giving them training and hoping that they would stay long enough to give a decent return on the investment. By contrast, the more intelligent organisations were looking at restructuring their operations, introducing flexible working patterns and devising ways of reducing their reliance on people who were difficult to recruit.

Occupational structure

Labour markets also differ according to established behavioural norms among different occupational groups. The attitudes of people to their organisations and to their work vary considerably from profession to profession, with important implications for their employers. A useful model developed by Mahoney (1989) illustrates these differences. He identifies three distinct types of occupational structure: craft, organisation career and unstructured. In craft-oriented labour markets, people are more committed over the long term to their profession or occupation than they are to the organisation for which they work. In order to develop a career they perceive that it is necessary for them to move from employer to employer, building up a portfolio of experience on which to draw. Remaining in one organisation for too long is believed to damage or at least to slow down career prospects. Examples include teaching, where there is often a stronger loyalty to the profession as a whole than there is towards the employing institution. By contrast, an organisation-career occupation is one in which progress is primarily made by climbing a promotion ladder within an organisation. People still move from employer to employer, but less frequently and will tend to stay in one organisation for as long as their careers are advancing. Mahoney's third category, the unstructured market, consists of lower-skilled jobs for which little training is necessary. Opportunities for professional advancement are few, leading to a situation where people move in and out of jobs for reasons which are not primarily career related.

To an extent employers can seek to influence the culture prevailing among members of each type of occupational group. There is much to be gained in terms of employee retention, for example, by developing career structures which encourage craft-oriented workers to remain for longer than they otherwise would. However, a single employer can have limited influence of this kind. It is therefore necessary to acknowledge the constraints associated with each labour market and to manage within them. Different areas of HR activity have to be prioritised in each case. It is necessary to work harder at retaining people in craft-oriented labour markets than in those which are organisation oriented, because people will be more inclined to stay with one employer in the latter than in the former. Recruitment and selection will be different too. Where career advancement is generally achieved within organisations (as in banking or the civil service) there is a good case for giving a great deal of attention to graduate recruitment. It is worth spending large sums to ensure that a good cohort is employed and subsequently developed because there is likely to be a long period in which to recoup the investment. The case is a good deal weaker in craft-oriented labour markets where there is less likelihood of a long association with individual employees.

Generational differences

Employee resourcing practices should also be adapted to take account of variations in the age profile of those whom the organisation is seeking to employ. While it is clearly wrong to assert that everyone of a certain age shares the same attitudes and characteristics, broad differences between the generations can be identified. Research on generational differences from a management perspective remains underdeveloped, but a number of writers have put forward interesting ideas. Zemke *et al.* (2000), for example, identify four groups defined by their dates of birth. They go on to argue that each must be treated rather differently if they are to be successfully managed. The four categories are Veterans (born before and during the Second World War), Baby Boomers (late 1940s and 1950s), Generation X (1960s and 1970s) and a group labelled 'Nexters' (born after 1980). Some of the points made about each are as follows:

■ Veterans are attracted to workplaces which offer stability and which value experience.
■ Boomers place a high value on effective employee participation.
■ Xers enjoy ambiguity and are at ease with insecurity.
■ Nexters are wholly intolerant of all unfair discrimination.
■ Boomers do not object to working long hours.
■ Xers require a proper 'work-life balance'.
■ Veterans are loyal to their employers and are less likely to look elsewhere for employment opportunities than younger colleagues.
■ Xers are strongly resistant to tight control systems and set procedures.
■ Nexters, being serious-minded and principled, prefer to work for ethical employers.
■ Xers and nexters work more easily with new technology than veterans and boomers.

Where a workforce is dominated by a particular age group, it makes sense to manage the workers in a way with which they feel comfortable. Organisational performance as well as turnover rates improve as a result. Similarly, where a recruitment drive is aimed at a particular age group, it is important to give out appropriate messages about what the organisation is able to offer.

Activity 9.1

Zemke and his colleagues developed these theories of intergenerational difference in the context of labour markets in the USA. Their analysis is based on the idea that successive generations of Americans have been shaped by shared formative influences.

In what ways has the historical experience of these generational groups differed in the UK?

What implications might such differences have from an employer's perspective?

Flexible resourcing choices

Understanding the dynamics of the organisational environment is only one part of taking a strategic approach to employee resourcing. Having gained an understanding one must decide how the organisation can best interact with its environment to maximise its performance. One set of key choices concerns the extent to which the organisation can aspire to flexibility and in what ways this can be achieved. Three types of flexibility are often identified in the literature; numerical flexibility, temporal flexibility and functional flexibility. A fourth type, financial flexibility, is discussed in Chapter 36.

Numerical flexibility

Numerical flexibility allows the organisation to respond quickly to the environment in terms of the numbers of people employed. This is achieved by using alternatives to traditional full-time, permanent employees. The use of, for example, short-term contract staff, staff with rolling contracts, staff on short-term, government-supported training schemes, outworkers, and so on, enable the organisation to reduce or expand the workforce quickly and cheaply.

Atkinson is one of a number of commentators who has described the way in which firms may develop flexibility in their approach to employment, as shown in Figure 9.1. The flexible firm in this analysis has a variety of ways of meeting the need for human resources. First are core employees, who form the primary labour market. They are highly regarded by the employer, well paid and involved in those activities that are unique to the firm or give it a distinctive character. These employees have improved career prospects and offer the type of flexibility to the employer that is so prized in the skilled craftworker who does not adhere rigidly to customary protective working practices.

There are then two peripheral groups: first, those who have skills that are needed but not specific to the particular firm, like typing and word processing. The strategy for these posts is to rely on the external labour market to a much greater extent, to specify a narrow range of tasks without career prospects, so that the employee has a job but not a career. Some employees may be able to transfer to core posts, but generally limited scope is likely to maintain a fairly high turnover, so that adjustments to the vagaries of the product market are eased.

The second peripheral group is made up of those enjoying even less security, as they have contracts of employment that are limited, either to a short-term or to a part-time attachment. There may also be a few job sharers and many participants on government training schemes find themselves in this category. An alternative or additional means towards this flexibility is to contract out the work

Figure 9.1 Atkinson's model of the flexible firm

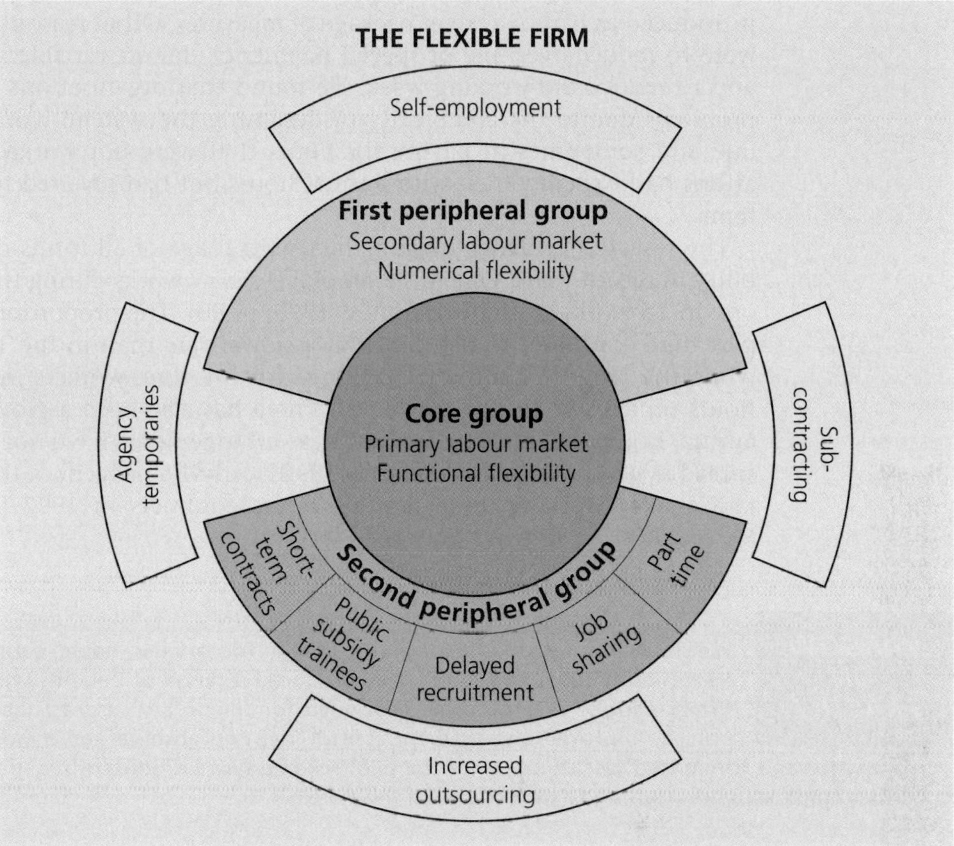

THE FLEXIBLE FIRM

Self-employment

First peripheral group
Secondary labour market
Numerical flexibility

Core group
Primary labour market
Functional flexibility

Agency
temporaries

Sub-
contracting

Second peripheral group

Short-
term
contracts

Public
subsidy
trainees

Delayed
recruitment

Job
sharing

Part
time

Increased
outsourcing

Source: J. Atkinson (1984) 'Manpower strategies for flexible organisations', *Personnel Management*, August. Used with the permission of the author.

that has to be done, either by employing temporary personnel from agencies or by subcontracting the entire operation.

As we saw in the chapter on organisation structure, a slightly different version of the peripheral workforce is the way in which the organisation boundary may be adjusted by redefining what is to be done in-house and what is to be contracted out to various suppliers.

Temporal flexibility

Temporal flexibility concerns varying the pattern of hours worked in order to respond to business demands and employee needs. Moves away from the 9–5, 38-hour week include the use of annual hours contracts, increased use of part-time work, job sharing and flexible working hours. For example, an organisation subject to peaks and troughs of demand (such as an ice cream manufacturer) could use annual hours contracts so that more employee hours are available at peak periods and less are used when business is slow. Flexitime systems can benefit the employer by providing employee cover outside the 9–5 day and over lunchtimes, and can also provide employee benefits by allowing personal demands to be fitted more easily around work demands.

Gall (1996) found in his research in 49 organisations that annual hours contracts were used most often to 'promote work practice changes', and were often introduced as part of a larger package of measures. Other reasons for introduction were to reduce overtime or special payments; due to variable/seasonal demand and to reduce the working week. He found that organisations had experienced problems due to the complexity of designing the system; working out the pay due and sometimes in paying for hours that were not worked. Some organisations had experimented with annual hours but had reverted to traditional systems.

The research evidence suggests increased usage of all forms of temporal flexibility in recent years. One in six employees now works during the evening, while one in 16 works at night (Harkness 1999, p. 90). The proportion of jobs that are part time continues to rise, albeit at a slower rate than in the 1970s and 1980s, while the length of the working week for full-time workers increased by three hours on average during the 1990s. There has also been a growth in the use of annual hours (IRS 2000, p. 6), but these arrangements have not become as widespread as was predicted in the early 1990s; only 4.5 per cent of the working population were working under annual hours contracts in 1997 (Arrowsmith and Sisson 2000, p. 300).

| WINDOW ON PRACTICE | Welsh Water introduced a pilot scheme for annual hours contracts in 1991 (Hutchinson 1993) and found they produced a range of benefits which included a firmer control over overtime, less need for temporary contract labour, increased output, improved management control, reduced absence and a more flexible, co-operative and committed workforce. Since the pilot scheme was introduced they have found that other employees are pressing to be included in the system. |

Functional flexibility

The term 'functional flexibility' refers to a process in which employees gain the capacity to undertake a variety of tasks rather than specialising in just one area. Advocates of such approaches have been influenced by studies of Japanese employment practices as well as by criticisms of monotonous assembly-line work. Horizontal flexibility involves each individual employee becoming multi-skilled so that they can be deployed as and where required at any time. It is often associated with shop-floor manufacturing work, but can be applied equally in other workplace settings. Vertical flexibility entails gaining the capacity to undertake work previously carried out by colleagues higher up or lower down the organisational hierarchy. It is thus related to the development of flatter organisational structures such as those discussed in Chapter 6.

The primary purpose of functional flexibility initiatives is to deploy human resources more efficiently. It should mean that employees are kept busy throughout their working day and that absence is more easily covered than in a workplace with rigidly defined demarcation between jobs. Another source of efficiency gains arises because employees are more stretched, fulfilled and thus productive than is the case in a workplace with narrowly defined jobs. Despite its potential advantages research suggests that employers in the UK have been less successful than competitors elsewhere in Europe at developing functional flexibility.

According to Blyton (1998, p. 748), this is primarily because of a reluctance to invest in the training necessary to support these new forms of working.

Debates about flexibility

The growth in flexible working arrangements combined with their promotion by governments since the 1990s has led to the development of robust debates about their desirability and usage in practice. As much controversy has centred on the Atkinson model of the flexible firm as on the rather different elements that go to make it up. There has been a continuing debate, for example, about whether the model of core and periphery is a description of trends or a prescription for the future. Two streams of research have flowed from these interpretations. The first concerns the extent to which the model has been adopted in practice, the second focuses on the advantages and disadvantages of the model as a blueprint for the future organisation of work.

Pollert (1991) and Atkinson and Meager (1986) found the use of such approaches to be ad hoc rather than strategic. Legge (1995) concluded that the empirical evidence suggests that flexibility is used in a pragmatic and opportunistic way rather than as a strategic HRM initiative. Hakim (1990) found few firms explicitly pursuing a core/periphery strategy, while Blyton and Turnbull (1992) suggested that empirical studies demonstrate a gap between the rhetoric and the reality of flexibility. In our recent research we found much evidence of numerical flexibility, which was generally adopted in a reactive and opportunistic way. Of the 20 interview respondents with whom we discussed flexibility, 17 were able to give examples of flexible resourcing, and the emphasis was on the use of short-term contract and temporary staff. There was no strategic view of the future intended shape of the organisation, and flexible practices were adopted due to operational demands such as cost cutting, the introduction of computerisation, seasonal business demands, no-redundancy policies and the inability to recruit the desired full-time permanent staff. Only a small amount of functional flexibility was reported and only two organisations had a strategic approach to this.

On the question of the desirability of flexibility a number of views have been expressed. The theoretical advantages for organisations arise from productivity gains. In different ways each type of flexibility aims to deploy employee time and effort more efficiently, so that staff are only at work when they need to be and are wholly focused on achieving organisational objectives throughout that time. However, the extent to which this is achieved in practice is not clear. Blyton (1993), for example, found that the introduction of formal multiskilling arrangements in a steel plant proved less effective than the informal approaches that were previously in place. There are also doubts about the extent to which employee commitment and motivation levels can be maintained when a large portion of a workforce is seen as being 'peripheral' and perhaps more dispensable than the 'core'. Sisson and Storey (2000, p. 83) make the further observation that too much 'hollowing out' can impair organisational learning and lead to the loss of expertise which is difficult to recover.

WINDOW ON PRACTICE

Tuselmann (1996) argues that a high degree of interdependence exists between the different forms of flexibility, that there are costs and benefits of each, and that organisations choose an optimal mix dependent on their market conditions and the country in which they operate. He suggests that a high degree of functional flexibility may be generally inconsistent with a high degree of numerical or financial flexibility. It has been argued that while Britain pursues numerical flexibility, in an unregulated and decentralised labour market, there is a greater emphasis in other parts of Europe on functional flexibility. In particular Germany has successfully followed this route within a high regulatory framework with a high degree of centralisation and industrial relations consensus. Tuselmann notes that this framework also constrains their pursuit of numerical, temporal and financial flexibility, and that as Germany experiences increasing competitive pressures, their model of labour flexibility is at a crossroads.

There are other balances in resourcing strategy that can be addressed, for example the balance between numbers of permanent staff employed and the hours that each employee works. In November 1993 Volkswagen in Germany announced that in their current poor financial situation they were employing too many people. In order to avoid redundancies they agreed with the workforce that hours would be reduced by 20 per cent so that they worked a four-day week, and that wages would be reduced by 10 per cent. There is a good deal of emphasis in Europe on reducing the working week to help reduce redundancies, unemployment and absence levels, and to improve family life.

Activity 9.2

What evidence can you find in your organisation to support a more flexible approach to resourcing? What were the driving forces behind these changes?

How have employees responded and why?

Ready-made or home-grown?

Organisations have a choice whether to depend extensively on the talent available in the external labour market or to invest heavily in training and development and career systems to exploit the potential in the internal labour market. Some organisations thrive on high levels of turnover, while others thrive on the development of employees who remain with the organisation in the long term. The emphasis on either approach, or a balance between the two, can be chosen to support organisational strategy.

Sonnenfield *et al.* (1992) propose a model which relates entry and exit of staff with promotion and development of staff in the organisation. One axis of the model is supply flow. They argue that, strategically, organisations that focus on internal supply tend to see people as assets with a long-term development value rather than costs in terms of annual expenditure. The other axis is labelled the assignment flow, which describes the basis on which individuals are assigned new tasks in the organisation. The criteria for allocation may be in terms of individual contribution to organisational performance, or on group contribution – which Sonnenfield *et al.* identify as factors such as loyalty, length of service and support of others. They argue that, strategically, organisations that emphasise individual contribution expect individuals to provide value on a continuous basis, whereas those that emphasise group contribution see employees as having intrinsic value.

The model proposed describes the combination of these two aspects of resourcing and results in four typical 'career systems' as shown in Figure 9.2. In each box alongside the career system label (academy, club, baseball team and fortress) Sonnenfield *et al.* identify the strategic organisation model and the competitive strategy which are most likely to drive each career system. They also identify the likely orientation of the human resource function. In this chapter we are concerned with the characteristics of the career systems, which are discussed below.

Academies

In academies there is a heavy emphasis on individual contribution, in terms of reward and promotion. They are characterised by stability and low turnover of staff, with many employees remaining until retirement. There is an emphasis on development and often competitions for promotion and barriers to leaving the organisation. Examples of typical industries where academies operate are pharmaceuticals and automobiles.

Clubs

Again there is a heavy emphasis on the internal labour market, but promotion in clubs is more likely to be based on loyalty, length of service, seniority and equality rather than individual contribution. There is an emphasis on staff retention. Sectors where this type of system is likely to operate include public bodies,

Figure 9.2 A typology of career systems

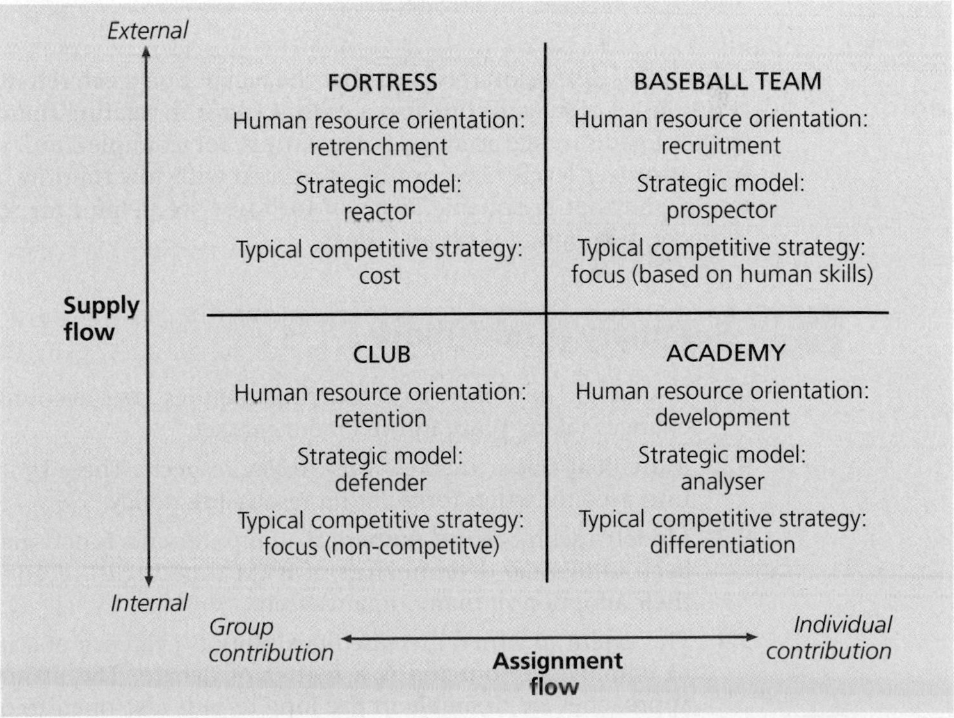

Source: J.A. Sonnenfield *et al.* (1992) 'Strategic determinants of managerial labour markets', *Human Resource Management*, Vol. 27, No. 4. Copyright © 1992 John Wiley and Sons, Inc. Reproduced with permission of John Wiley and Sons, Inc.

although the introduction of competitive forces will mean that a different career system may be appropriate.

Baseball teams

Organisations characterised as baseball teams use external labour sources at all levels to seek the highest contributors. There is an emphasis on recruitment to maintain staffing levels. Employees will tend to identify with their profession rather than the organisation, and examples given are advertising, accountancy and legal firms.

Fortresses

Fortress organisations are concerned with survival and cannot afford to be concerned with individuals, in terms of either reward or promotion. They are more likely to depend on external recruitment, often for generalists who meet the needs of a retrenchment or turnaround situation. Examples given are publishing, retailing and the hotel sector.

Activity 9.3	Which of the four career systems in the Sonnenfield *et al.* model typifies your organisation? What characteristics lead you to this conclusion?
	How does this career systems strategy fit with your organisational strategy and organisational mission (either explicitly stated or implicit)?

From this discussion it is clear that the balance between retention and turnover is not just a cost factor but also a critical factor in relating human resource strategy to organisational strategy. Some writers, for example Cann (1993), argue that high turnover levels need not be associated with low training and development levels, and that reasonable levels of turnover are helpful for some industries in terms of distributing skills and ideas.

Summary propositions

9.1 A strategic approach to resourcing requires that account is taken of the changes taking place in the labour market.

9.2 Individual labour markets vary in key respects. These too need to be taken into account when formulating resourcing policy.

9.3 Models incorporating numerical, temporal and functional flexibility have been influential determinants of HRM thinking in recent years, leading to their adoption in many organisations.

9.4 The extent to which increased flexibility is evidence of a strategic approach to employee resourcing is a matter of debate. The extent to which such approaches are desirable in the long term is also open to question.

9.5 Organisations have strategic choices concerning the use they make of their internal and external labour market.

References

Arrowsmith, J. and Sisson, K. (2000) 'Managing Working Time', in S. Bach and K. Sisson (eds), *Personnel Management: A Comprehensive Guide to Theory and Practice*, 3rd edn. Oxford: Blackwell.

Atkinson, J. (1984) 'Manpower strategies for flexible organisations', *Personnel Management*, August.

Atkinson, J. and Meager, N. (1986) *New Forms of Work Organisation*. IMS Report 121. Brighton: IMS.

Blyton, P. (1993) 'Steel', in A. Pendleton and J. Winterton (eds), *Public Enterprise in Transition*. London: Routledge.

Blyton, P. (1998) 'Flexibility', in M. Poole and M. Warner (eds), *The IEBM Handbook of Human Resource Management*. London: Thomson.

Blyton, P. and Turnbull, P. (1992) *Reassessing Human Resource Management*. London: Sage.

Cann, T. (1993) 'Why poaching is good practice', *Personnel Management*, October.

Cully, M., Woodland, S., O'Reilly, A. and Dix, G. (1999) *Britain at Work. As depicted by the 1998 Workplace Employee Relations Survey*. London: Routledge.

Gall, G. (1996) 'All year round: the growth of annual hours in Britain', *Personnel Review*, Vol. 25, No. 3, pp. 35–52.

Hakim, C. (1990) 'Core and periphery in employers' workforce strategies: evidence from 1987 ELUS survey', *Work Employment and Society*, Vol. 4, No. 2, pp. 157–88.

Harkness, S. (1999) 'Working 9–5?', in P. Gregg and J. Wadsworth (eds), *The State of Working Britain*. Manchester: Manchester University Press.

HMSO (1999) *Education and Training Statistics for the United Kingdom*, 1998 edn. London: The Stationery Office.

Hutchinson, S. (1993) 'The changing face of annual labour', *Personnel Management*, April.

IRS (2000) 'Working Time 2000', *Employment Trends 696* (January). Industrial Relations Services.

Legge, K. (1995) *Human Resource Management: Rhetorics and realities*. Basingstoke: Macmillan.

Mahoney, T.A. (1989) 'Employment Compensation Planning and Strategy', in L. Gomez-Mejia (ed.), *Compensation and Benefits*. Washington, DC: BNA.

Millward, N., Bryson, A. and Forth, J. (2000) *All Change at Work? British employment relations 1980–1998, as portrayed by the Workplace Industrial Relations Survey series*. London: Routledge.

Morris, H. and Willey, B. (1996) *The Corporate Environment: A Guide for Human Resource Managers*. London: Financial Times Management.

Office for National Statistics (1997) *Adult Literacy in Britain*. London: ONS.

Pearson, R., Perryman, S., Connor, H., Jagger, N. and Aston, J. (1999) *The IES Annual Graduate Review 1998–1999: the key facts*. Institute for Employment Studies Report 345. Brighton: IES.

Pollert, A. (1991) 'The Orthodoxy of Flexibility', in A. Pollert (ed.), *Farewell to Flexibility*. Oxford: Blackwell.

Sisson, K. and Storey, J. (2000) *The Realities of Human Resource Management: Managing the Employment Relationship*. Buckingham: Open University Press.

Sonnenfield, J.A. *et al*. (1992) 'Strategic determinants of managerial labour markets', in G. Salaman *et al*. (eds), *Human Resource Strategies*. London: Sage.

Tuselmann, H.-J. (1996) 'The path towards greater labour flexibility in Germany: hampered by past success?', *Employee Relations*, Vol. 18, No. 6, pp. 26–47.

Windolf, P. (1986) 'Recruitment, Selection and Internal Labour Markets in Britain and Germany', *Organizational Studies*, Vol. 7, No. 3, pp. 235–54.

Zemke, R., Raines, C. and Filipczak, B. (2000) *Generations at Work*. New York: AMACOM.

General discussion topics

1 In times of high unemployment, many employers still continue to experience skills shortages. What steps can *employers* take to alleviate this situation? What steps might the *government* take?

2 Discuss the claim that flexible resourcing strategies should be welcomed by the individual as they provide new areas of opportunity rather than a threat.

Chapter 10   Contracts, contractors and consultants

Although a great deal is written about 'psychological contracts' and 'contracts for performance', the association between employer and employee remains at base a legal relationship governed by 'a contract of employment'. In law the existence of such a contract confers on both parties important obligations as well as giving the employee access to significant legal rights which are not available to people who work under different contractual arrangements. In the first part of this chapter we set out the principles of the law as far as the contract of employment is concerned before looking at the different forms a contract of employment can take. We then turn to the most common other forms of contractual arrangement used by employers looking to meet their human resource needs. In particular we focus on issues relating to the employment of consultants, a group whose numbers have increased substantially over recent years.

Contracts of employment

As far as the law is concerned nearly 90 per cent of people who work in the UK are employees. This means that they have a contract of employment with their employer, with the duties and privileges that that implies. The employer may be an individual, as with most small businesses, or the contract may be with a large corporation. Throughout this book we use terms like 'organisation' and 'business' more or less interchangeably and 'employer' is the legal term to describe the dominant partner in the employment relationship. This derives from the old notion of a master and servant relationship and indicates that the employee (or servant) has obligations to the employer or master and vice versa. In contrast, those who are self-employed or subcontractors have greater autonomy, but no one standing between them and legal accountability for their actions.

The law makes an important distinction between the two groups, employees having access to a wider range of legal rights than non-employees. While some areas of employment law apply to all workers, others only apply to employees. The former are deemed to be working under 'a contract for services' rather than 'a contract of service' as is the case for employees. In 2001 the main statutory rights that applied to each were those shown in Table 10.1.

Table 10.1 Access to statutory employment rights

Employment rights which apply to all workers:	■ Equal pay for equal work ■ Non-discrimination on grounds of sex, race and disability ■ Right not to have unauthorised deductions from pay ■ Basic health and safety rights ■ Minimum wage ■ Working time regulations ■ Data protection rights ■ Time off to care for dependants ■ Part-time Workers Regulations
Employment rights which apply only to employees:	■ Right to a statement of terms and conditions of employment ■ Right to an itemised pay statement ■ Statutory Sick Pay ■ Time off for public duties ■ Eighteen weeks' maternity leave ■ Trade union rights ■ Minimum notice periods ■ Statutory Maternity Pay (after six months' service) ■ Extended maternity leave (after one year's service) ■ Unfair dismissal rights (after one year's service) ■ Parental leave (after one year's service)

In addition to the statutory rights conferred by Acts of Parliament, a range of common law duties are owed by employers to employees and vice versa which do not apply in the case of other forms of relationship. The major obligations are as follows:

1 *Owed by employers to employees*:
  ■ a general duty of care
  ■ a duty to pay agreed wages
  ■ a duty to provide work
  ■ a duty not to treat employees in an arbitrary or vindictive manner
  ■ a duty to provide support to employees
  ■ a duty to provide safe systems of work

2 *Owed by employees to employers:*
  ■ a duty to co-operate
  ■ a duty to obey reasonable/lawful instructions
  ■ a duty to exercise reasonable care and skill
  ■ a duty to act in good faith

3 *Owed by employers to employees and vice versa*:
  ■ to maintain a relationship of mutual trust and confidence

4 *Owed by employees and ex-employees*:
  ■ duty of fidelity

A contract of employment, contrary to common perception, need not exist in written form. It is much more satisfactory for both parties if there is documentary evidence of what terms and conditions have been offered and accepted, but a contract of employment exists whether agreed verbally on the telephone or sealed with no more than a handshake. Where there is any doubt about whether someone is an employee or not, the courts look at the evidence presented to them concerning the reality of the existing relationship between the two parties. If they consider, on balance, that it is governed by a 'contract of service' rather than a 'contract for services', they will consider the worker to be an employee and entitled to the full range of rights outlined above.

WINDOW ON PRACTICE

A recent case heard in the House of Lords illustrates the importance of employee status. Mrs Carmichael and a colleague were employed as tour guides at a power station run by National Power PLC. They started working for the company on a casual basis in 1989, undertaking about four hours work each week as and when they were needed. By 1995 they each were working around 25 hours a week, so they decided to ask for written particulars of their terms and conditions of employment. The company refused on the grounds that they were casual workers and not employees. The women won their case in the lower courts, but the company decided to appeal right up to the House of Lords. At this stage the women lost their case on the grounds that there was no mutuality of obligation. They could, and indeed had, turned down requests to work without suffering any disciplinary action. They were therefore not employees and not entitled to the rights associated with full employment status.

An employment contract comes into existence when an unambiguous offer of employment is made and is unconditionally accepted. Once agreed neither side can alter the terms and conditions which govern their relationship without the agreement of the other. An employer can not therefore unilaterally cut employees' pay, lengthen their hours of work, reduce their holiday entitlement, change their place of work or move them to another kind of work. To do so the employer either has to secure the employees' agreement (by offering some kind of sweetener payment) or has to ensure that the right to make adjustments to terms and conditions is written into the contract by means of flexibility clauses. Table 10.2 provides a checklist for preparing a contract of employment.

Table 10.2 Checklist for preparing a contract of employment

1 Name of employer; name of employee.
2 Date on which employment began.
3 Job title.
4 Rate of pay, period and method of payment.
5 Normal hours of work and related conditions, such as meal-breaks.
6 Arrangements for holidays and holiday pay, including means whereby both can be calculated precisely.
7 Terms and conditions relating to sickness, injury and sick pay.
8 Terms and conditions of pension arrangements, including a note about whether or not the employment is contracted out under the provisions of the Social Security Pensions Act 1975.
9 Length of notice due to and from employee.
10 Disciplinary rules and procedure.
11 Arrangements for handling employee grievances.
12 (Where applicable) Conditions of employment relating to trade union membership.

Contracts of limited duration

Contracts of employment vary in all manner of ways. One of the most important distinctions relates to their length. Here it is possible to identify three basic forms:

- **Permanent**: This is open-ended and without a date of expiry.
- **Fixed-term**: This has a fixed start and finish date, although it may have provision for notice before the agreed finish date.
- **Temporary**: Temporary contracts are for people employed explicitly for a limited period, but with the expiry date not precisely specified. A common situation is where a job ends when a defined source of funding comes to an end. Another is where someone is employed to carry out a specified task, so that the expiry date is when the task is complete. The employer is obliged to give temporary workers an indication in writing at the start of their employment of the expected duration of the job.

According to Cully *et al.* (1999, p. 35) 44 per cent of employers, including 72 per cent of public sector bodies, employ people on a fixed-term basis, while a further 28 per cent make use of agency temps. In 2000 a total of 1.7 million people worked under some form of non-permanent contract, which is 7.1 per cent of all employees (IDS 2000a, p. 2). This is appreciably more than the 5 per cent who were employed on such a basis in the 1980s. Only around half of temporary staff work in full-time jobs.

Some of the reasons for employing people on a temporary or fixed-term basis are obvious. Retail stores need more staff immediately before Christmas than in February and ice cream manufacturers need more people in July than November, so both types of business have seasonal fluctuations. Nowadays, however, there is the additional factor of flexibility in the face of uncertainty. Will the new line sell? Will there be sustained business after we have completed this particular contract?

Often temporary staff are needed to cover duties normally carried out by a permanent employee. This can be due to sickness absence or maternity leave, or it may occur when there is a gap between one person resigning and another taking up the post. Another common approach is to employ new starters on a probationary basis, confirming their appointments as permanent when the employer is satisfied that they will perform their jobs successfully.

Research suggests that there are a number of other ways in which managers find temporary workers to be an asset. Geary (1992), for example, found that the use of temporary contracts in the Republic of Ireland gave management a greater degree of control over labour. The temporary employee worked under the constant, unspoken threat of dismissal and felt the need to behave with total compliance to avoid this. Managers were uncomfortable about the working relationship, feeling that it was divisive and unfair, but maintained that the main reason for employing temporary staff was their motivation. They put a lot of effort into their work in the hope of being made permanent and were seldom absent. Their presence also improved control over permanent staff:

> Very often when temporary workers felt obliged to do overtime, for instance, so did their permanent counterparts. A shop steward who had worked in the plant for eight years told me of the frustration by many permanent employees, 'People complain to me about the level of overtime. But what can you do when you have 20

temps and 5 permanent people on a line? Temps feel obliged to come in at the weekend and so do permanent people as a result.' (Geary 1992, p. 56)

Unpublished research by Curtis (1996) in the West Midlands largely supports Geary's conclusions, but adds the fear by managers of having to go through the trauma of redundancies. Having had to make large proportions of the workforce redundant in previous years, they were anxious to avoid a repetition of that at all costs.

The law on the employment of fixed-term workers changed in October 1999. Prior to that it was possible to employ staff on fixed-term contracts which contained clauses waiving the right to claim unfair dismissal. This meant that the employer could terminate the relationship by failing to renew the contract whether or not there was a good reason for doing so. It was thus possible substantially to avoid liability for claims of unfair dismissal by employing people on a succession of short contracts. For fixed-term contracts entered into after October 1999 waiver clauses no longer apply. Henceforth employers who do not renew a fixed-term contract will have to be able justify their decision just as they do with any other dismissal, if they want to avoid court action. Temporary and fixed-term workers also gain a number of further rights under recent European law designed to ensure that they enjoy the same terms and conditions as permanent employees undertaking equivalent roles. Employers are now obliged to inform temporary staff of permanent vacancies and to allow them access to training opportunities.

A special type of contract is that for apprenticeship. Although this is not to be seen as a contract of employment for the purpose of accumulating employment rights, it is a form of legally binding working relationship that pre-dates all current legislative rights in employment, and the apprentice therefore has additional rights at common law relating to training. An employer cannot lawfully terminate an apprentice's contract before the agreed period of training is complete, unless there is closure or a fundamental change of activity in the business to justify redundancy.

Part-time contracts

At one time part-time working was relatively unusual and was scarcely economic for the employer as the national insurance costs of the part-time employee were disproportionate to those of the full-timer. The part-time contract was regarded as an indulgence for the employee and only a second-best alternative to the employment of someone full time. This view was endorsed by lower rates of pay, little or no security of employment and exclusion from such benefits as sick pay, holiday pay and pension entitlement. How things have changed!

In the last thirty years the proportion of the employed workforce on part-time contracts has increased dramatically. In 1971 15 per cent of employees were employed on a part-time basis. By 1991 the figure had reached 22 per cent and in March 2000 it stood at 28.5 per cent (Labour Market Trends 2000, p. S23). Table 10.3 shows that this proportion is greater than that in most other EU countries, although there is some difficulty of definition. What is part time? At the moment the British method of calculation classifies anything less than the normal weekly hours at the place of work to be part time, so a part-timer could be working 6 hours a week or 35.

Table 10.3 Proportion of the total workforce working part time in EU countries (1998)

Country	Per cent
Greece	6.0
Italy	7.3
Spain	8.1
Luxembourg	8.8
Portugal	11.1
Finland	11.7
Ireland*	12.3
Belgium	15.7
Austria	15.8
France	17.3
Germany	18.3
Denmark	22.3
Sweden	23.9
UK	24.9
Netherlands	38.8
EU Average	17.4

*The Irish figure relates to data collected in 1997.
Source: European Commission, *Employment in Europe* 1999.

Over three-quarters of part-time workers are women. The rise in their numbers has coincided with campaigns to enhance the employment opportunities of women, with the Equal Opportunities Commission advocating the development of job sharing. A leavening of part-time posts provides flexibility to the management in staffing the operation and employment opportunities for those who do not seek full-time work. However, too many part-time posts can destabilise the staffing of the operation by increasing training and administration costs. Although there has been some increase in part-time working for men, it has grown rapidly among women. This is partly because many women wish to work only part-time (for example when they have young children) and partly because the sectors in which part-time work has grown most have tended to be those which are less male dominated.

WINDOW ON PRACTICE	*The Times* (14 June 1994, p. 29) reported that Marks & Spencer is the blue-chip operator of part-time working, with forty years' experience and frequently sought out by other businesses to find out how it is done. They now feel that some stores are using too many part-timers and are aiming to reduce the part-time workforce from 80 per cent to 70 per cent.

Many part-timers work short shifts and sometimes two will share a full working day. Others will be in positions for which only a few hours within the normal day are required or a few hours at particular times of the week. Retailing is an occupation that has considerable scope for the part-timer, as there is obviously a greater need for counter personnel on Saturday mornings than on Monday mornings. Also many shops are now open for longer periods than would be normal hours for a full-time employee, so that the part-timer helps to fill the gaps and provide the extra staffing at peak periods. Catering is another example, as is market research interviewing, office cleaning, clerical work and some posts in education.

Most discrimination against part-time workers has effectively been outlawed in the UK since 1994 when it was held by the courts, potentially, to amount to indirect discrimination on grounds of sex. Since 2000, however, statute has required that all part-timers and full-timers are treated equally. In most respects the Part-time Workers (Prevention of Less Favourable Treatment) Regulations apply to all workers, whether or not they are employees. First, they provide that part-time workers are to be given the same pay per hour and the same terms and conditions of employment as full-time colleagues undertaking the same or similar work. All benefits must also be provided to part-timers on a pro-rata basis. Second, the regulations state that employers cannot subject workers to a detriment of any kind simply because they work part time. This means, for example, that both part-time and full-time workers must be given equal access to training. It also means that the fact that an employee works part time should not be taken into account when deciding who is to be made redundant. Unlike other forms of direct discrimination, however, in the case of part-timers employers can seek to justify their actions on objective grounds.

Working patterns

Aside from payment arrangements, for full-time workers the pattern of hours which they are expected to work is the most important contractual issue. The total number of hours worked by the average full-time worker in the UK fell substantially for much of the past 150 years, but has recently begun to rise. In 1850 the normal working week was established as 60 hours spread over six days of 10 hours each. The average number of hours worked in 1998, including paid and unpaid overtime, was 47 hours for men and 43 hours for women (Harkness 1999, pp. 92–3). This represents a rise from 45 hours and 40 hours respectively during the previous decade.

According to Bienefeld (1972, p. 224), hours have come down in the past at periods when economic conditions were favourable, unemployment low and union bargaining power high (see Table 10.4). Employers agreed to reduce hours when they were confident that doing so would not have a negative effect on productivity. In some cases they were persuaded by the argument that staff would be able to work harder if they were less tired, in others concessions on hours were made in exchange for changes in working practices which enhanced productivity levels.

Table 10.4 Percentage reduction in British working hours between 1850 and the early 1960s

Period	Weekly hours' reduction	Percentage fall
1850–75	60–50	10%
1896–1920	54–48	11%
Late 1940s	48–44	8%
Early 1960s	44–40	9%

In recent years governments have legislated to reduce hours. The European Union's Working Time Directive was introduced into UK law in 1998 as a health and safety initiative (see Chapter 31). Among other measures, it seeks to ensure that no one is required to work more than an average of 48 hours a week against their will. In some countries legislation limiting working hours is primarily seen as a tool for reducing unemployment. In France, for example, the recent 'loi Aubry' was introduced limiting people to an average working week of only 35 hours (EIRR:1998).

Activity 10.1

Would you like to see legislation passed in the UK limiting the number of hours a week each person can work to 35?

What would be the main arguments for and against the introduction of such legislation?

In addition to working more hours, the past two decades have seen some increase in the proportion of the working population engaged in shiftworking. This is nothing new in the manufacturing sector where the presence of three eight-hour shifts has permitted plants to work round the clock for many years. Recently, however, there has been a substantial rise in the number of service-sector workers who are employed to work shifts. They, unlike most factory-based staff, are not generally paid additional shift payments to reward them for working unsocial hours. According to IDS (2000b), the change has come about because of moves towards 'a 24-hour society' on the back of globalisation, the emergence of e-commerce and consumer demand. Each year more and more people are reported to be watching TV and making phone calls in the early hours of the morning, while late night shopping has become the norm for a third of adults in the UK. Banks, shops, airports and public houses are now round-the-clock operations. The result is a steadily increasing demand for employees to work outside the standard hours of 9–5, Monday to Friday – a trend long established in the USA where fewer than a third of people work the standard weekday/day-time shift (IDS 2000b, p. 1).

While some people remain attached to the 'normal' working week and would avoid working 'unsocial hours' wherever possible, others like the flexibility it gives them, especially where they are rewarded with shift premia for doing so. Shiftworking particularly appeals to people with family responsibilities as it permits at least one parent to be present at home throughout the day. Several types of distinct shift pattern can be identified, each of which brings with it a slightly different set of problems and opportunities.

Part-timer shifts require employees to come to work for a few hours each day. The most common groups are catering and retail workers employed to help cover the busiest periods of the day (such as a restaurant at lunchtime) and office cleaners employed to work early in the morning or after-hours in the evening. This form of working is convenient for many and clearly meets a need for employers seeking people to come in for short spells of work.

Permanent night shifts create a special category of employee who is set apart from everyone else. They work full time, but often have little contact with other staff who leave before they arrive and return after they have left. Apart from 24-hour operations, the major categories are maintenance specialists employed to carry out work when machinery is idle or when roads are quiet, and security staff. There are particular problems from an HR perspective as they are out of touch with company activities and may be harder to motivate and keep committed as a result. Some people enjoy night work and maintain this rhythm throughout their working lives, but for most it will be undertaken either reluctantly or for relatively short periods. Night working is now heavily regulated under the Working Time Regulations 1998.

Double day shifts involve half the workforce coming in from early in the morning until early afternoon (an early shift), while the other half work from early afternoon until 10.00 or 11.00 at night (a late shift). A handover period occurs between the two shifts when everyone is present, enabling the organisation to operate smoothly for 16–18 hours a day. Such approaches are common in organisations such as hospitals and hotels which are busy throughout the day and evening but which require relatively few people to work overnight. Rotation between early and late shifts permits employees to take a 24-hour break every other day.

Three-shift working is a well-established approach in manufacturing industry and in service sector organisations which operate around the clock. Common patterns are 6–2, 2–10 and 10–6 or 8–4, 4–12 and 12–8. A further distinction can be made between discontinuous three-shift working, where the plant stops operating for the weekend, and continuous three-shift working, where work never stops. Typically the workforce rotates between each shift on a weekly basis, but in doing so suffer the consequences of a 'dead fortnight' when normal evening social activities are not possible. This is avoided by accelerating the rotation with a 'continental' shift pattern, whereby a team spends no more than three consecutive days on the same shift.

Split shifts involve employees coming into work for two short periods twice in a day. They thus work on a full-time basis, but are employed on part-timer shifts to cover busy periods. They are most commonly used in the catering industry so that chefs and waiting staff are present during meal times and not during the mornings and afternoons when there is little for them to do. Drawbacks include the need to commute back and forth from home to work twice and relatively short rest-periods in between shifts in which staff can wind down. For these reasons split shifts are unpopular and are best used in workplaces which provide live-in accommodation for staff.

Compressed hours shifts are a method of reducing the working week by extending the working day, so that people work the same number of hours but on fewer days. An alternative method is to make the working day more concentrated by reducing the length of the midday meal-break. The now commonplace four-night week on the night shift in engineering was introduced in Coventry as a result of absenteeism on the fifth night being so high that it was uneconomic to operate.

Flexible working hours

Another way of dealing with longer operating hours and unpredictable workloads is to abandon regular, fixed hours of working altogether. This allows an organisation to move towards the 'temporal flexibility' we discussed in Chapter 9. The aim is to ensure that employees are present only when they are needed and are not paid for being there during slack periods. However, there are also advantages for employees. Three types of arrangement are reasonably common in the UK: flexitime, annual hours and zero hours contracts.

Flexitime

A flexitime system allows employees to start and finish the working day at different times. Most systems identify core hours when everyone has to be present (for example 10–12 and 2–4) but permit flexibility outside those times. Staff can then decide for themselves when they start and finish each day and for how long they are absent at lunchtime. Some systems require a set number of hours to be worked every day, while others allow people to work varying lengths of time on different days provided they complete the quota appropriate for the week or month or whatever other settlement period is agreed. This means that someone can take a half-day or full day off from time to time when they have built up a sufficient bank of hours.

There are great advantages for employees working under flexitime. Aside from the need formally to record time worked or to clock in, the system allows them considerable control over their own hours of work. They can avoid peak travel times, maximise the amount of time they spend with their families and take days off from time to time without using up holiday entitlement. From an employer's perspective flexitime should reduce the amount of time wasted at work. In particular, it tends to eliminate the frozen 20-minute periods at the beginning and end of the day when nothing much happens. If the process of individual start-up and slow down is spread over a longer period, the organisation is operational for longer. Moreover, provided choice is limited to a degree, the system encourages staff to work longer hours at busy times in exchange for free time during slack periods.

Annual hours

Annual hours schemes involve an extension of the flexitime principle to cover a whole year. They offer organisations the opportunity to reduce costs and improve performance by providing a better match between working hours and a business's operating profile. Unlike flexitime, however, annual hours systems tend to afford less choice for employees.

Central to each annual hours agreement is that the period of time within which full-time employees must work their contractual hours is defined over a whole year. All normal working hours contracts can be converted to annual hours; for example, an average 38-hour week becomes 1,732 annual hours, assuming five weeks' holiday entitlement. The principal advantage of annual hours in manufacturing sectors, which need to maximise the utilisation of expensive assets, comes from the ability to separate employee working time from the operating hours of the plant and equipment. Thus we have seen the growth of five-crew systems, in particular in the continuous process industries. Such systems are capable of delivering 168 hours of production a week by rotating five crews. In 365 days there are 8,760 hours to be covered, requiring 1,752 annual hours from each shift crew, averaging just over 38 hours for 46 weeks. All holidays can be rostered into 'off' weeks, and 50 or more weeks of production can be planned in any one year without resorting to overtime. Further variations can be incorporated to deal with fluctuating levels of seasonal demand.

The move to annual hours is an important step for a company to take and should not be undertaken without careful consideration and planning. Managers need to be aware of all the consequences. The tangible savings include all those things that are not only measurable but capable of being measured before the scheme is put in. Some savings, such as reduced absenteeism, are quantifiable only after the scheme has been running and therefore cannot be counted as part of the cost justification. A less tangible issue for both parties is the distance that is introduced between employer and employee, who becomes less a part of the business and more like a subcontractor. Another problem can be the carrying forward of assumptions from the previous working regime to the new. One agreement is being superseded by another and, as every industrial relations practitioner knows, anything that happened before which is not specifically excluded from a new agreement then becomes a precedent.

Zero hours

A zero hours contract is one in which individuals are effectively employed on a casual basis and are not guaranteed any hours of work at all. Instead they are called in as and when there is a need. This has long been the practice in some areas of employment, such as nursing agencies and the acting profession, but it has recently been used to some extent in other areas, such as retailing, to deal with emergencies or unforeseen circumstances. Such contracts allow employers to cope with unpredictable patterns of business, but they make life rather more unpredictable for the individuals involved. The lack of security associated with such arrangements makes them an unattractive prospect for many.

Activity 10.2

What types of job would you regard as most appropriate for the following variations of the conventional 9-to-5 working pattern?

1 Shift working.

2 Part-time working.

3 Job sharing.

4 Flexible hours.

5 Compressed hours.

6 Annual hours.

What types of job would not be suitable for each of these?

Distance working and subcontracting

In the quest for greater flexibility many employers are beginning to explore new ways of getting work done which do not involve individuals working full time on their premises. Working overseas, selling in the field and home-working are the most obvious types of distance working. Other forms include teleworking, working on far-flung sites, or off-site as subcontractors and consultants. Contractually, 'distant' or 'peripheral' working can include anything that is different from the traditional full-time contract even though employees may be geographically present for part or all of the time; for example, part-time working and job sharing, temporary and short-term working, on-site subcontracting and consultancy.

There is increasing interest in the concepts of teleworking and tele-cottaging. *Tele* is from the Greek for distant, and is familiar to us in terms like telegram and television. A more specific definition is provided by Incomes Data Services from a survey by Huws (1996) which puts it in two categories:

> The first is the individualised form of teleworking which involves work completed away from the employer's premises, such as home-based teleworking or multi-locational working. The second category is a collective form of teleworking which covers work completed on non-domestic premises and managed by the employer or third party. This includes call centres and tele-cottages. (IDS 1996, p. 22)

The number of people engaged in distance working or teleworking is difficult to estimate, as there are so many people who have always worked in this way, such as sales representatives, and by no means all fall into the stereotype category of someone sitting at a remote computer terminal. The total number is small, but it is certainly growing, despite some of the drawbacks mentioned in the last chapter. The main advantage, for both the employer and the employee, is the flexibility it provides, but the employer also benefits from reduced office accommodation costs and an increase in productivity.

Between 1986 and 2000 the number of self-employed people in Britain increased from 2,566,000 to 3,412,000, moving from 11 per cent to just over 12 per cent of the working population (Central Statistical Office 1994, p. 58; Labour Market Trends 2000, p. S22). Rothwell (1987) has identified several issues relating to the employment of distance workers. These are considered next.

Finding the right people

One source may be existing staff who would prefer more flexible working arrangements, or those who have left employment for family reasons, travel, redundancy or early retirement. Subcontractors whose businesses have been set up as a result of company hive-offs or buy-outs are another potential source. Information regarding the relevant public and private agencies, subcontractors and consultants may well be something which more managers need to acquire. More effective relationships can be established by taking time to classify needs and developing longer-term arrangements with public/private agencies and with subcontractors.

Job specification and selection

Job specification is important in all selection processes but is critical in most forms of geographically and contractually distant working, particularly in subcontracted work. It is important to set out clearly defined parameters of action, criteria for decisions and issues which need reference back. Person specifications are also crucial since in much distance working there is less scope for employees to be trained or socialised on the job. In addition, 'small business' skills are likely to be needed by teleworkers, networkers, consultants and subcontractors.

Communication and control

Attention needs to be given to the initial stages of settling in these distance workers. Those off-site need to know the pattern of regular links and contacts to be followed. Those newly recruited to the company need the same induction information as regular employees. In fact, those working independently with less supervision may need additional material, particularly on health and safety. Heightened team-building skills will also be needed to encompass staff who are working on a variety of different contracts and at different locations.

Pay and performance

A key aspect of the employment of distance workers is the close link between pay and performance. Managers must be able to specify job targets and requirements accurately and to clarify and agree these with the employees or contractors concerned. Where a fee rather than a salary is paid, the onus is on the manager to ensure the work has been completed satisfactorily. Others (consultants, teleworkers, networkers) may be paid on the basis of time, and it is for the supervisor to ensure the right level and quality of output for that payment.

It is doubtful whether pay levels of peripheral staff can be related to existing job-evaluated systems or salary structures. Indeed, one advantage of extending the variety of peripheral workers is the ability to move outside those constraints, which may no longer be appropriate. Concepts of the total compensation package may need to be examined more closely in relation to distance workers – will financial services (e.g. low interest loans) and provision of home computers become more important?

Employing consultants

The Bertie Ramsbottom Ballad below incorporates nearly all the nightmares about consultants. Although the ballad is directed at external consultants, whose services are bought in, many of the reservations also apply to much personnel work, which is advisory and seeking to bring about change in the attitudes and practices of managerial colleagues.

One is entitled to some scepticism about the value of using external consultants:

> The naive might have imagined that as management disciplines matured and executives increasingly mastered them, the need for outside advisers would fade. Think again ... the global consultancy market is now worth around $40 billion ... and employs upwards of 100,000 of the most highly-qualified people in the world.
>
> (Caulkin 1997, p. 33)

Daily fees for consultants frequently are £3,000 per person-day, with some of the superstars asking five times that amount. The odd thing is the rare occasion when anyone says it was worth every penny. The typical comment is exactly the opposite. Simon Caulkin quotes Lord Weinstock and Anita Roddick:

> [Lord Weinstock] Consultants are invariably a waste of money. There has been the occasional instance where a useful idea has come up, but the input we have received has usually been banal and unoriginal, wrapped up in impressive sounding but irrelevant rhetoric.

> Anita Roddick says that having consultants tramping through the Body Shop was the most uncomfortable period in its history.   (Caulkin 1997, p. 34)

WINDOW ON PRACTICE

The Preying Mantis

Of all the businesses, by far,
Consultancy's the most bizarre.
For, to the penetrating eye,
There's no apparent reason why,
With no more assets than a pen,
This group of personable men
Can sell to clients more than twice
The same ridiculous advice,
Or find, in such a rich profusion,
Problems to fit their own solution.
The strategy that they pursue –
To give advice instead of do –
Keeps their fingers on the pulses
Without recourse to stomach ulcers,
And brings them monetary gain,
Without a modicum of pain.
The wretched object of their quest,
Reduced to cardiac arrest,
Is left alone to implement
The asinine report they've sent.
Meanwhile the analysts have gone
Back to client number one,
Who desperately needs their aid
To tidy up the mess they made.
And on and on – ad infinitum –
The masochistic clients invite 'em.
Until the merciful reliever
Invokes the company receiver.
No one really seems to know
The rate at which consultants grow.
By some amoeba-like division?
Or chemobiologic fission?
They clone themselves without an end
Along their exponential trend.
The paradox is each adviser,
If he makes his client wiser,
Inadvertently destroys
The basis of his future joys.
So does anybody know
Where latter-day consultants go?

Source: Ralph Windle (1985) from *The Bottom Line* by Bertie Ramsbottom, published by Hutchinson. Reprinted by permission of the Random House Group Ltd.

Some personnel activities are undoubtedly best undertaken by consultants. An example is the use of personnel tests in selection. These have been available for many years as a means of making selection more systematic and objective, yet their use remains limited and is sometimes misguided. Few employing organisations are big enough to have a scale of recruitment *for similar posts* which produces a large enough set of results for analysis and comparison to be fruitful. The Royal Air Force selects trainee pilots using a battery of tests developed over many years. There is also a wealth of evidence from tests and subsequent performance, for the ability to fly an aircraft to be predicted with reasonable accuracy from test results alone.

Few other employers can accumulate enough evidence to make comparable predictions, but specialist firms of consultants can, at least theoretically, produce occupational norms to provide useful performance indicators from test results.

Duncan Wood (1985, p. 41) asked senior representatives of 14 well-established consultancies to rank seven reasons for their use in personnel work. The result was:

- First: To provide specialist expertise and wider knowledge not available within the client organisation.
- Second: To provide an independent view.
- Third: To act as a catalyst.
- Fourth: To provide extra resources to meet temporary requirements.
- Fifth: To help develop a consensus when there are divided views about proposed changes.
- Sixth: To demonstrate to employees the impartiality/objectivity of personnel changes or decisions.
- Seventh: To justify potentially unpleasant decisions.

In further research it was found that confident and competent personnel managers can call on the services of outside experts without fear of jeopardising their own position and being able to specify closely what they require (Torrington and Mackay 1986).

Where the HR function is under-resourced, or where the HR manager lacks professional expertise, then consultants will be used reluctantly, with a poor specification of requirements and the likelihood of an unsatisfactory outcome for both client and consultant. In deciding whether or not outside consultants should be used for a specific assignment we suggest the following approach.

Activity 10.3

What personnel problems currently facing your organisation do you think might best be approached by using outside consultants? Why? How would you specify the requirements?

What personnel problems currently facing your organisation would you not remit to outside consultants? Why not?

Describe the problem

What is the problem about which you might seek external advice? This may not be obvious, as worrying away at an issue can show that the real matter needing to be addressed is not what is immediately apparent. If, for example, the marketing manager leaves abruptly – as they often seem to do – the immediate problem will present itself as: 'We must find a replacement'. So you begin to think of ringing up the executive search consultant you used when you needed someone for the Middle East in a hurry. Working at finding a correct description of the problem could suggest that the presenting cause is easy to deal with because young X has been waiting for just such an opportunity for months and all the

Question	Company A	Company B
1 Do you understand the new scheme?	87%	44%
2 Have you had targets set?	77%	29%
3 Have you had management feedback?	87%	41%
4 Have you had the training?	53%	24%
5 Do you understand the pay plan?	44%	38%

There can be all sorts of explanation for the variable response, but there is at least a very strong indication indeed that the internal management of the initiative had a great bearing on the apparently different level of effectiveness. There is a great irony in the fact that both companies are outstandingly successful in their respective fields, by almost every conceivable criterion.

Summary propositions

10.1 The law distinguishes between 'employees' and 'workers', the former enjoying a wider range of statutory and contractual rights than the latter.

10.2 Once a contract is established its terms can not be broken by either party without the consent of the other.

10.3 In recent years we have seen a growth in the number of 'atypical contracts' such as those which provide work on a temporary or fixed-term basis.

10.4 Patterns of work vary considerably. The traditional Monday to Friday, 9–5 pattern is increasingly giving way to new shift patterns and contractual arrangements.

10.5 New technologies allow a greater proportion of people to work from home. This development brings all manner of new challenges for HR managers.

10.6 The use of outside consultants to undertake HR activities is rising.

References

Bienefeld, M.A. (1972) *Working Hours in British Industry: An economic history*. London: Weidenfeld & Nicolson.

Caulkin, S. (1997) 'The great consultancy cop-out', *Management Today*, February, pp. 32–8.

Central Statistical Office (1994) *Social Trends 24*. London: HMSO.

Cully, M., Woodland, S., O'Reilly, A. and Dix, G. (1999) *Britain at Work As depicted by the 1998 Workplace Employee Relations Survey*. London: Routledge.

Curtis, S. (1996) 'Differences in Conditions of Employment between Temporary and Permanent Shopfloor Workers in Three Manufacturing Companies', unpublished M.Sc. Dissertation, UMIST.

European Industrial Relations Review (EIRR) (1998) 'Making way for the 35-hour working week', *EIRR 294*. London: Eclipse Group Ltd.

European Commission (1999) *Employment in Europe 1999*. Brussels: EU.

Geary, J.F. (1992) 'Employment flexibility and human resource management: the case of three electronics plants', *Work, Employment and Society*, Vol. 4, No. 2, pp. 157–88.

Harkness, S. (1999) 'Working 9–5?', in P. Gregg and J. Wadsworth (eds), *The State of Working Britain*. Manchester: Manchester University Press.

Huws, U. (1996) *Teleworking: An Overview of the Research*. London: HMSO.

IDS (1996) *Teleworking*, IDS Study 616. London: Incomes Data Services Ltd.

IDS (2000a) *Temporary Workers*, IDS Study 689. London: Incomes Data Services Ltd.

IDS (2000b) *24-hour society*, IDS Focus 93. London: Incomes Data Services Ltd.

Labour Market Trends (2000) 'Employment: Workforce Jobs', *Labour Market Trends*. London: HMSO.

Priestley, P., McGuire, J., Flegg, D., Hemsley, V. and Welham, D. (1978) *Social Skills and Personal Problem Solving*. London: Tavistock.

Rothwell, S. (1987) 'How to manage from a distance', *Personnel Management*, September, pp. 22–6.

Torrington, D.P. and Mackay, L.E. (1986) 'Will consultants take over the personnel function?', *Personnel Management*, February, pp. 34–7.

Windle, R. (1985) *The Bottom Line*. London: Century-Hutchinson.

Wood, D. (1985) 'The uses and abuses of personnel consultants', *Personnel Management*, October, pp. 40–7.

General discussion topics

1 What are the advantages and disadvantages of part-time working for the employer and for the employee? In what ways do the age and domestic situation of the employee alter the answer?

2 The chapter indicates some of the problems in employing consultants. How can these be overcome?

3 What is the future for teleworking?

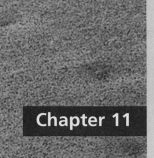

Chapter 11   Recruitment

There is always a need for replacement employees and those with unfamiliar skills that business growth makes necessary. Recruitment is also an area in which there are important social and legal implications, but perhaps most important is the significant part played in the lives of individual men and women by their personal experience of recruitment and the failure to be recruited. Virtually everyone reading these pages will know how significant those experiences have been in their own lives.

Over three million people are recruited by employers in the UK each year. It can be a costly and difficult process when skills are in short supply and labour markets are tight. In such circumstances the employer needs to 'sell' its jobs to potential employees so as to ensure that it can generate an adequate pool of applicants. According to Barber (1998) it is important that employers do not consider the recruitment process to be finished at this point. It continues during the shortlisting and interviewing stages and is only complete when an offer is made and accepted. Until that time there is an ongoing need to ensure that a favourable impression of the organisation as an employer is maintained in the minds of those whose services it wishes to secure.

In this chapter we shall consider various aspects of an employer's recruitment strategy; determining the vacancy, the range of recruitment methods available, recruitment advertising, and several features of recruitment method, including employee documentation and shortlisting.

Determining the vacancy

Is there a vacancy? Is it to be filled by a newly recruited employee? These are the first questions to be answered in recruitment. Potential vacancies occur either through someone leaving or as a result of expansion. When a person leaves, there is no more than a prima facie case for filling the vacancy thus caused. There may be other ways of filling the gap. Vacancies caused by expansion may be real or imagined. The desperately pressing need of an executive for an assistant may be a plea more for recognition than for assistance. The creation of a new post to deal with a specialist activity may be more appropriately handled by contracting that activity out to a supplier. Recruiting a new employee may be the most obvious tactic when a vacancy occurs, but it is not necessarily the most appropriate. Listed below are some of the options.

■ **Reorganise the work**: Jobs may be rearranged so that the total amount of work to be done in a section is done by the remaining employees without replacement of the leaver. One clue to the likelihood of this being the right move lies in the reasons for leaving. If the person has left because there was not enough to do, or because the other employees formed a tight-knit group that was difficult to break into, then there may be grounds for considering this strategy. It can also work between departments, with people redundant in one area being redeployed elsewhere.

■ **Use overtime**: Extra output can be achieved by using overtime, although there is always the possibility that the work to be done is simply expanded to fill the greater amount of time available for its completion. Few personnel managers like the extensive use of overtime, and it lacks logic at a time of high unemployment, but it may be the best way of dealing with a short-term problem where, for instance, one employee leaves a month before another is due back from maternity leave.

■ **Mechanise the work**: There are all sorts of ways in which the work of a departing member of staff can be mechanised, though it is seldom feasible to mechanise, automate or robotise on the basis of a single, casual vacancy. However, the non-replacement of a departing member of staff is often used to justify the expense of introducing new equipment.

■ **Stagger the hours**: As we saw in Chapter 10, there can be staffing economies in introducing shifts, staggering hours or trying flexible working hours. It is again rarely practicable to take these steps when there is a single vacancy, although sometimes staggering hours can work in that sort of situation.

■ **Make the job part time**: Replacing full-time jobs with part-time jobs has become widespread and has the attraction of making marginal reductions more possible at the same time as providing the possibility of marginally increasing the amount of staff time available in the future by redefining the job as full time. It also provides potential flexibility by making it possible to turn one full-time job into two part-time posts located in two separate places.

■ **Subcontract the work**: By this means the employer avoids ongoing costs and obligations of employing people by transferring those obligations to another employer. It is simpler to do this when the work can be easily moved elsewhere, like some features of computer programming, than when the work has to be done on your own premises, with the comparisons of terms and conditions that inevitably take place. Also, the advantages of avoiding employment costs and obligations have to be offset against the disadvantages of less direct control and probably higher overall costs in the medium term.

■ **Use an agency:** A similar strategy is to use an agency to provide temporary personnel, who again do not come onto the company payroll.

Activity 11.1   Can you think of further ways of avoiding filling a vacancy by recruiting a new employee? What are the advantages and disadvantages of the methods you have thought of? For what types of job with which you are familiar would each of your methods, and those listed above, be most appropriate?

If your decision is that you are going to recruit, there are four questions to determine the vacancy:

1 What does the job consist of?
2 In what way is it to be different from the job done by the previous incumbent?
3 What are the aspects of the job that specify the type of candidate?
4 What are the key aspects of the job that the ideal candidate wants to know before deciding to apply?

The conventional HR approach to these questions is to produce job descriptions and personnel specifications. Methods of doing this are well established. Good accounts are in Ungerson (1983) and Pearn and Kandola (1988). The approach involves breaking the job down into its component parts, working out what its chief objectives will be and then recording this on paper. A person specification listing the key attributes required to undertake the role can then be derived from the job description and used in recruiting the new person. An example of a job description is given in Table 11.1.

An alternative approach which allows for more flexibility is to dispense with the job description and to draw up a person specification using other criteria. One way of achieving this is to focus on the characteristics or competences of current job holders who are judged to be excellent performers. Instead of asking 'What attributes are necessary to undertake this role?', this second method involves asking 'What attributes are shared by the people who have performed best in the role?'. According to some (for example Whiddett and Kandola 2000), the disadvantage of the latter approach is that it tends to produce employees who are very similar to one another and who address problems with the same basic mindset. Where innovation and creativity are wanted it helps to recruit people with more diverse characteristics.

Methods of recruitment

Once an employer has decided that external recruitment is necessary, a cost-effective and appropriate method of recruitment must be selected. There are a number of distinct approaches to choose from, each of which is more or less appropriate in different circumstances. As a result most employers use a wide variety of different recruitment methods at different times. In many situations there is also a good case for using different methods in combination when looking to fill the same vacancy. Table 11.2 sets out the usage of different methods reported in a recent IRS survey of 280 larger UK employers.

Table 11.1 Job description for senior sales assistant

Job title: SENIOR SALES ASSISTANT

Context

The job is in one of the thirteen high-technology shops owned by 'Computext'

Location: Leeds

Supervised by, and reports directly to, the Shop Manager

Responsible for one direct subordinate: Sales Assistant

Job summary

To assist and advise customers in the selection of computer hardware and software, and to arrange delivery and finance where appropriate.

Objective is to sell as much as possible, and for customer and potential customers to see 'Computext' staff as helpful and efficient.

Job content

Most frequent duties in order of importance

1 Advise customers about hardware and software.
2 Demonstrate the equipment and software.
3 Organise delivery of equipment by liaising with distribution department.
4 Answer all after-sales queries from customers.
5 Contact each customer two weeks after delivery to see if they need help.
6 Advise customers about the variety of payment methods.
7 Develop and keep up to date a computerised stock control system.

Occasional duties in order of importance

1 Arrange for faulty equipment to be replaced.
2 Monitor performance of junior sales assistant as defined in job description.
3 Advise and guide, train and assess junior sales assistant where necessary.

Working conditions

Pleasant, 'business-like' environment in new purpose-built shop premises in the city centre. There are two other members of staff and regular contact is also required with the Delivery Department and Head Office. Salary is £18,000 p.a. plus a twice-yearly bonus, depending on sales. Five weeks' holiday per year plus statutory holidays. A six-day week is worked.

Other information

There is the eventual possibility of promotion to shop manager in another location depending on performance and opportunities.

Performance standards

There are two critically important areas:

1 Sales volume. Minimum sales to the value of £700,000 over each six-month accounting period.
2 Relations with customers:
   – Customers' queries answered immediately.
   – Customers always given a demonstration when they request one.
   – Delivery times arranged to meet both customer's and delivery department's needs.
   – Complaints investigated immediately.
   – Customers assured that problem will be resolved as soon as possible.
   – Customers never blamed.
   – Problems that cannot be dealt with referred immediately to Manager.

Table 11.2 Usage of various methods of recruitment by 280 organisations in 1999

Advertisements in local press	93%	Headhunters	50%
Advertisements in specialist press	92%	Careers fairs and open days	46%
Advertisements in national press	81%	Internet	44%
Employment agencies	78%	Networking / word of mouth	43%
Notices inside employer premises	78%	Notices outside employer premises	20%
Job centres	77%	Vacancy directories	19%
Education liaison	62%	Local radio	12%
Unsolicited applications	62%	Leaflet distribution	5%
Careers Service	49%		

Source: IRS (1999).

It is interesting to compare these figures with those reported in surveys of how people actually find their jobs in practice. These repeatedly show that informal methods (such as word of mouth and making unsolicited applications) are as common as, if not more common than, formal methods such as recruitment advertising. In 1999, the Labour Force Survey asked over a million people how they had obtained their current job. The results were as follows:

	Men	Women
Hearing from someone who worked there	33%	28%
Reply to an advertisement	21%	30%
Direct application	16%	16%
Private employment agency	10%	10%
Job centre	8%	7%
Other	12%	9%

Source: Labour Market Trends (2000).

The recruitment methods compared

All the various methods of recruitment have benefits and drawbacks, and the choice of a method has to be made in relation to the particular vacancy and the type of labour market in which the job falls. A general review of advantages and drawbacks is given in Table 11.3.

Activity 11.2

We have seen the significance of informal methods of recruitment whereby new employees come as a result of hearing about a vacancy from friends, or putting their names down for consideration when a vacancy occurs. Employees starting employment in this way present the employer with certain advantages as they come knowing that they were not wooed by the employer: the initiative was theirs. Also they will probably have some contacts in the company already that will help them to settle and cope with the induction crisis.

What are the drawbacks of this type of arrangement?

Table 11.3 Advantages and drawbacks of different methods of recruitment

Job centres

Advantages: (a) Applicants can be selected from nationwide sources with convenient, local availability of computer-based data.

(b) Socially responsible and secure.

(c) Can produce applicants very quickly.

(d) Free service for employers.

Drawbacks: (a) Registers are mainly of the unemployed rather than of the employed seeking a change.

(b) Produces people for interview who are not genuinely interested in undertaking the job.

Commercial employment agencies and recruitment consultancies

Advantages: (a) Established as the normal method for filling certain vacancies, e.g. secretaries in London.

(b) Little administrative chore for the employer.

Drawbacks: (a) Can produce staff who are likely to stay only a short time.

(b) Widely distrusted by employers (Knollys 1983, p. 234).

(c) Can be very expensive.

Management selection consultants

Advantages: (a) Opportunity to elicit applicants anonymously.

(b) Opportunity to use expertise of consultant in an area where employer will not be regularly in the market.

Drawbacks: (a) Internal applicants may feel, or be, excluded.

(b) Cost.

Executive search consultants ('headhunters')

Advantages: (a) Known individuals can be approached directly.

(b) Useful if employer has no previous experience in specialist field.

(c) Recruiting from, or for, an overseas location.

Drawbacks: (a) Cost.

(b) Potential candidates outside the headhunter's network are excluded.

(c) The recruit may remain on the consultant's list and be hunted again.

Visiting universities

Advantages: (a) The main source of new graduates from universities.

(b) Rated by students as the most popular method.

Drawbacks: (a) Need to differentiate presentations from those of other employers.

(b) Time taken to visit a number of universities (i.e. labour intensive).

Schools and the Careers Service

Advantages: (a) Can produce a regular annual flow of interested enquirers.

(b) Very appropriate for the recruitment of school-leavers, who seldom look further than the immediate locality for their first employment.

Drawbacks: (a) Schools and the advisers are more interested in occupations than organisations.

(b) Taps into a limited potential applicant pool.

Recruitment advertising

In order to assist them in drafting advertisements and placing them in suitable media, many employers deal with a recruitment advertising agency. The basic service such an agency will provide is considerable:

> only one copy of the text need be supplied no matter how many publications are to be used; the agency will book space; prepare the layout and typography; read and correct proofs; verify that the right advertisement has appeared in the right publications at the right time; and only one cheque has to be raised to settle the agency's monthly account. (Plumbley 1985, p. 55)

These basic technical services are of great value to the personnel manager and are 'free' in that the agency derives its income from the commission paid by the journals on the value of the advertising space sold. Moreover, the bigger agencies are able to negotiate substantial discounts because of the amount of business they place with the newspapers and trade journals. A portion of this saving is then passed on to the employer so that it can easily be cheaper *and* a great deal more effective to work with an agent providing this kind of service. The HR manager placing, say, £50,000 of business annually with an agency will appreciate that the agency's income from that will be between £5,000 and £7,500, and will expect a good standard of service. The important questions relate to the experience of the agency in dealing with recruitment, as compared with other types of advertising, the quality of the advice they can offer about media choice and the quality of response that their advertisements produce.

In choosing where to place a recruitment advertisement the aim is to attract as many people as possible with the required skills and qualifications. You also want to reach people who are either actively looking for a new job or thinking about doing so. The need is therefore to place the advertisement where job seekers who are qualified to take on the role are most likely to look. Except in very tight labour markets, where large numbers of staff are required at the same time, there is no point in placing a recruitment advertisement outside a newspaper or journal's recruitment pages. In some situations newspaper readership figures are helpful when deciding where to advertise. An example would be where there are two or more established trade journals or local newspapers competing with one another, both of which carry extensive numbers of recruitment advertisements. Otherwise readership figures are unimportant because people tend to buy different newspapers when job searching than they do the rest of the time. It is often more helpful to look at the share of different recruitment advertising markets achieved by the various publications, as this gives an indication of where particular types of job are mostly advertised. In the UK in recent years the *Guardian* newspaper has gained and sustained a 40 per cent market share of national recruitment advertising. For many jobs in the media, education and the public sector it is now established as the first port of call for job seekers. This has been achieved by cutting rates to less than half those charged by other national newspapers. For the more senior private sector jobs, however, the established market leaders are the *Daily Telegraph*, *The Sunday Times* and the *Financial Times*. While recruitment advertising agents are well placed to advise on these issues, it is straightforward to get hold of information about rates charged by

Table 11.4 The advantages and drawbacks of various methods of job advertising

Internal advertisement

Advantages: (a) Maximum information to all employees, who might then act as recruiters.

(b) Opportunity for all internal pretenders to apply.

(c) If an internal candidate is appointed, there is a shorter induction period.

(d) Speed.

(e) Cost.

Drawbacks: (a) Limit to number of applicants.

(b) Internal candidates not matched against those from outside.

(c) May be unlawful if indirect discrimination. (See Chapter 21.)

Vacancy lists outside premises

Advantage: (a) Economical way of advertising, particularly if premises are near a busy thoroughfare.

Drawbacks: (a) Vacancy list likely to be seen by few people.

(b) Usually possible to put only barest information, like the job title, or even just 'Vacancies'.

Advertising in the national press

Advantages: (a) Advertisement reaches large numbers.

(b) Some national newspapers are the accepted medium for search by those seeking particular posts.

Drawbacks: (a) Cost.

(b) Much of the cost 'wasted' in reaching inappropriate people.

Advertising in the local press

Advantages: (a) Recruitment advertisements more likely to be read by those seeking local employment.

(b) Little 'wasted' circulation.

Drawback: (a) Local newspapers appear not to be used by professional and technical people seeking vacancies.

Advertising in the technical press

Advantage: (a) Reaches a specific population with minimum waste.

Drawbacks: (a) Relatively infrequent publication may require advertising copy six weeks before appearance of advertisement.

(b) Inappropriate when a non-specialist is needed, or where the specialism has a choice of professional publications.

Internet

Advantages: (a) Information about a vacancy reaches many people.

(b) Inexpensive once a website has been constructed.

(c) Speed with which applications are sent in.

(d) Facilitates online shortlisting.

Drawbacks: (a) Can produce thousands of unsuitable applications.

(b) Worries about confidentiality may deter good applications.

different publications and their respective market shares. Good starting points are the websites of British Rate and Data (www.brad.co.uk), which carries up-to-date information about thousands of publications, and the National Readership Survey (www.nrs.co.uk) which provides details of readership levels among different population groups.

Drafting the advertisement

The decision on what to include in a recruitment advertisement is important because of the high cost of space and the need to attract attention; both factors will encourage the use of the fewest number of words. Where agencies are used they will be able to advise on this, as they will on the way the advertisement should be worded, but the following is a short checklist of items that must be included.

Name and brief details of employing organisation

The recruiter seeking anonymity will usually eschew press advertising in favour of some other medium. The advertisement that conceals the identity of the advertiser will be suspected by readers, not least for fear that they might be applying to their present organisation. If the advertisement conceals the name but gives clues to the identity of the organisation ('our expanding high-precision engineering company in the pleasant suburbs of —') then there is the danger that the reader will guess . . . wrongly. The brief details will fill in some of the uncertainty about what exactly the organisation is and does. The better known the employer, the less important the details.

Job and duties

The potential applicant will want to know what the job is. The title will give some idea, including a subjective assessment of its status, but rarely will this be sufficient. Particularly for knowledge workers some detail of duties will be sought. Potential candidates are increasingly interested in the training and development that will be available. If space permits, this should also be included.

Key points of the personnel specification or competency profile

If you really believe that the only candidates who will be considered are those with a specific qualification, then this may be included in the advertisement. Not only do you preclude other applicants who would be wasting your time and theirs, you also bring the vacancy into sharper focus for those you are seeking. But do you want to limit your search to that extent? If, for instance, you ask for 'full, clean driving licence', do you really wish to exclude all those who have ever had any sort of endorsement, or only those who have current endorsements? Do you really mean a *clean* driving licence or a valid licence? Other typical key points are further qualifications and experience, as long as these can be expressed clearly. 'Highly qualified' and 'considerable experience' are valueless in an advertisement.

Salary

Many employers are coy about declaring the salary that will accompany the advertised post. Sometimes this is reasonable as the salary scales are well known and inflexible, as in much public sector employment. Elsewhere the coyness is due either to the fact that the employer has a general secrecy policy about salaries and does not want to publicise the salary of a position to be filled for fear of dissatisfying holders of other posts, or does not know what to offer and is waiting to see 'what the mail brings'. All research evidence, however, suggests that a good indication of the salary is essential if the employer is to attract a useful number of appropriate replies (see De Witte 1989). Table 11.5 lists the phrases about salary used in a single issue of one quality paper. These include some of the common jargon terms: '*c.*' is an abbreviation of the Latin *circa*, meaning 'about', 'k' means 1,000, as in kilometre, 'neg' is short for negotiable, and 'OTE' stands for on-target earnings.

The other common feature of phrases about salary is to include words that are meaningless. The advertisements containing the phrases shown in Table 11.5 include 'attractive', 'competitive', 'excellent', 'exceptional', 'significant' and 'substantial' as explanations of the income level. It is very difficult indeed to argue that these terms mean anything that would cause an applicant to apply for one job rather than another.

Activity 11.3

Table 11.5 contains phrases about the value in pay terms of 12 different jobs. Try putting them in rank order of actual cash value to the recipient. Then ask a friend to do the same thing and compare your lists.

What to do

Finally, the advertisement tells potential applicants what to do. This will vary according to the nature of the post. It is conventional for manual employees to call at the personnel department, while managerial employees will be more disposed to write. Applicants who obey the instruction 'write with full details to . . .' will be understandably discouraged if the response to their letter is an application form to be completed, giving roughly the same information in a different way. Application forms are now generally accepted, but applicants not only feel it is unnecessary to be asked for the same information twice, they also develop reservations about the administrative efficiency of the organisation that they had been thinking of joining.

Table 11.5 Phrases from a quality newspaper about salary

1 *c.*£60,000 + bonus + car + benefits
2 from *c.*£35k
3 £30,000–£40,000 + substantial bonus + car
4 You will already be on a basic annual salary of not less than £40,000
5 Six-figure remuneration + profit share + benefits
6 *c.*£60,000 package
7 Attractive package
8 Substantial package
9 £50,000 OTE, plus car and substantial benefits
10 £ excellent + benefits
11 £ Neg.
12 *c.*£60k package + banking benefits

E-recruitment

The use of the internet for recruitment purposes is undoubtedly the most significant contemporary development in the field. Around 50 per cent of employers were advertising jobs on the web in 2000 (Finn 2000, p. 38), principally management, professional and graduate posts (IRS 1999, p. 13). It is clear that e-recruitment will increase substantially as more people gain access to the internet – a trend that has led some to argue that it will soon become the norm and replace established methods altogether. Internet recruitment takes two basic forms. The first is centred on the employer's own website, jobs being advertised alongside information about the products and services offered by the organisation. The second approach makes use of the growing number of cyber-agencies which combine the roles traditionally played by both newspapers and employment agents. They advertise the job and undertake shortlisting before sending on a selection of suitable CVs to the employer.

For employers the principal attraction is the way that the internet allows jobs to be advertised inexpensively to a potential audience of millions. According to Frankland (2000) the cost of setting up a good website is roughly equivalent to that associated with advertising a single high-profile job in a national newspaper. Huge savings can also be made by dispensing with the need to print glossy recruitment brochures and other documents to send to potential candidates. The other big advantage is speed. People can respond within seconds of reading about an opportunity by e-mailing their CV to the employer. Shortlisting can also be undertaken quickly with the use of CV-matching software or online application forms.

In principle e-recruitment thus has a great deal to offer. In practice, however, there are major problems which may take some years to iron out. A key drawback is the way that employers advertising jobs tend to get bombarded with hundreds of applications. This occurs because of the large number of people who read the advertisement and because it takes so little effort to email a copy of a pre-prepared CV to the employer concerned. In order to prevent 'spamming' of this kind it is necessary to make use of online shortlisting software which is able to screen out unsuitable applications. Such technologies, however, are not wholly satisfactory. Those which work by looking for key words in CVs inevitably have a 'hit and miss' character and can be criticised for being inherently unfair. The possibility that good candidates may not be considered simply because they have not chosen a particular word or phrase is strong. The alternative is to require candidates to apply online by completing an application form or pschyometric test. This approach has the advantage of deterring candidates who are not prepared to invest the time and effort required to complete the forms, but is unreliable in important respects – there is no guarantee that the test is in fact being completed by the candidate, nor is it completed within a standard, pre-determined time limit. Other problems concern fears about security and confidentiality which serve to deter people from submitting personal details over the web:

> Everybody should be familiar with the fear of using a credit card on-line even though good e-commerce sites have secure servers that enable these transactions to take place safely. The job-seeker's equivalent of this is 'how safe is it to put my CV on-line?' Although the figures prove that plenty of people have overcome this fear

(there are an estimated 4.5 million CVs on-line), horror stories of candidates' CVs ending up on their employer's desktop aren't entirely without foundation.

(Weekes 2000, p. 35)

Criticisms have also been made about poor standards of ethicality on the part of cyber-agencies. Like conventional employment agents there are a number who employ sharp practices such as posting fictional vacancies and falsely inflating advertised pay rates in order to build up a bank of CVs which can be circulated to employers on an unsolicited basis. Some cyber-agencies also copy CVs from competitors' sites and send them on to employers without authorisation. Over time, as the industry grows, professional standards will be established and a regulatory regime established, but for the time being such problems remain.

The fact that there are so many drawbacks alongside the advantages explains why so many employers appear to use the internet for recruitment while rating it relatively poorly. When asked to rank recruitment methods in terms of their effectiveness very few employers indeed place the internet at the top of the list (IRS 1998 and 1999). Established approaches such as newspaper advertising and education liaison are much more highly rated and are thus unlikely to be replaced by e-recruitment in the near future. Over the longer term, technological developments and increased web usage should improve the effectiveness of e-recruitment considerably:

In the future, the standard for Web sites will be high graphic content that is interactive, user friendly, fast working and fun to visit. To design, develop and maintain such a site will take a huge amount of capital – much more than was needed several years ago for start-up job ad sites ... What will emerge is a handful of well-funded job sites that have high amounts of traffic and dozens of smaller sites with extremely valuable targeted traffic. All will process excellent graphic content, be user-friendly and offer the job seeker a well-rounded array of jobs that keeps them coming back.

(Schreyer and McCarter 1998, p. 222)

WINDOW ON PRACTICE

In 2000 an unemployed 53-year-old electronics manager called David Hall took part in a project commissioned by Wynnwith, an established recruitment company. He spent three months unsuccessfully looking for a job using the services of twelve well-known cyber-agencies. He registered with each, giving full details of his background and skills. At the end of the period he concluded that 'these sites appear to offer little more than pretty coloured graphics and empty promises about job opportunities'. He was offered one interview during the twelve weeks, for a role that was unsuitable given his experience. Of the hundreds of job opportunities e-mailed to him, he reckoned that only 5% matched his capabilities. Among his criticisms were the following:

- the same jobs were advertised week after week
- very little information was provided about most vacancies
- salary levels were inflated to make jobs more appealing
- he received no feedback on applications that failed
- he was concerned that his CV was being circulated without his consent
- his emails were often not acknowledged

Source: 'Online Recruitment Study' at www.wynnwith.com.

Control and evaluation

The HR manager needs to monitor the effectiveness of advertising and all other methods of recruitment, first to ensure value for money, and second, to ensure that the pool of applicants produced by the various methods is suitable. Jenkins (1983, p. 259) provides a useful example of monitoring the effectiveness of advertising for management trainees in retailing.

Table 11.6 reveals a number of interesting points, the first being that employment decisions are mainly taken by applicants rather than by employers. Of the 370 originally expressing interest, over half eliminated themselves by not returning the application form. Of the 23 to whom jobs were offered over a third did not take up the offer. An important part of the whole employment process is making sure that inappropriate people eliminate themselves from consideration, and they can only do this when given sufficient information. Table 11.6 also provides information on approximately what number of initial applications is needed to produce a specific number of accepting candidates and what it costs to fill the vacancies by this means. We would suggest this type of simple, clear way of recording developments is the most useful method of building up a stock of control data from which to develop a recruitment advertising strategy.

How effective is the recruiting you undertake? It is an expensive, time-consuming process with legal pitfalls, so you need some process to monitor its effectiveness. One method is that illustrated in Table 11.6. Wright and Storey (1994, p. 209) suggest four numbers to collect:

1 Number of initial enquiries received which resulted in completed application forms.
2 Number of candidates at various stages in the recruitment and selection process, especially those shortlisted.
3 Number of candidates recruited.
4 Number of candidates retained in organisation after six months.

There is also a good case for monitoring the numbers of men and women who are successful at each stage of the process and the numbers of people from dif-

Table 11.6 Monitoring the effectiveness of advertising for management trainees in retailing

Medium	National press
Size of advertisement	60 column cm
Initial response	370
Booklet and application form sent out to	321
Application form returned from	127
Selection board attended by	95
Job offered to	23
Jobs accepted by	19
Employment actually started by	15
Total cost	£1,440
Cost per starter	£96

Source: J.F. Jenkins (1983) 'Management trainees in retailing', in B. Ungerson (ed.), *Recruitment Handbook*, 3rd edn. Aldershot: Gower, p. 259.

ferent ethnic minorities. Where an imbalance becomes apparent the organisation can then take remedial action.

There needs, however, to be more than this in order to get to the more intangible questions, such as 'Did the best candidate not even apply?' The most important source of information about the quality of the recruitment process is the people involved in it. Do telephonists and receptionists know how to handle the tentative employment enquiry? What did they hear from applicants in the original enquiries that showed the nature of their reaction to the advertisement? Is it made simple for enquirers to check key points by telephone or personal visit? Is there an unnecessary emphasis on written applications before anything at all can be done? Useful information can also be obtained from both successful and unsuccessful applicants. Those who have been successful will obviously believe that recruitment was well done, while the unsuccessful may have good reason to believe that it was flawed. However, those who are unsuccessful sometimes ask for feedback on the reasons. If a recruiter is able to do that, it is also a simple development to ask the applicant for comment on the recruitment process.

Employment documentation

Table 11.6 shows the importance of one type of documentation – the booklet sent out to applicants – as a means of focusing the minds of recruits on whether the job will suit them or not. We must also remember the significance of informal recruitment and the need to have information available to the casual enquirer, as well as documents for reference. Documents that are commonly provided for applicants are as follows:

- a copy of the relevant job description and personnel specification;
- a copy of the advertisement for reference purposes;
- a copy of any general recruitment brochure produced by the organisation;
- the staff handbook or details of a collective agreement;
- details of any occupational pension arrangements;
- general information about the organisation (e.g. a mission statement, annual report or publicity brochures).

Correspondence

It is essential to have some method of tracking recruitment, either manually or by computer, so that an immediate and helpful response can be given to applicants enquiring about the stage their application has reached. It is also necessary to ensure that all applicants are informed about the outcome of their application. This will reduce the number of enquiries that have to be handled, but it is also an important aspect of public relations, as the organisation dealing with job applicants may also be dealing with prospective customers. Many people have the experience of applying for a post and then not hearing anything at all. Particularly when the application is unsolicited, personnel managers may feel that there is no obligation to reply, but this could be bad business as well as disconcerting for the applicant. Standard letters ('I regret to inform you that there were many applications and yours was not successful ...') are better than nothing, but letters containing actual information ('out of the seventy-two appli-

Activity 11.4

Recruiters are interested in the job to be done, so that they concentrate on how the vacancy fits into the overall structure of the organisation and on the type of person to be sought. Applicants are interested in the work to be done, as they want to know what they will be doing and what the work will offer to them. Think of your own job and list both types of feature.

The job to be done

1 ....

2 ....

3 ....

4 ....

5 ....

The work that is offered

1 ....

2 ....

3 ....

4 ....

5 ....

How does your listing of features in the second list alter the wording of advertisements and other employment documentation?

cations, we included yours in our first shortlist of fifteen, but not in our final shortlist of eight') are better. Best of all are the letters that make practical suggestions, such as applying again in six months' time, asking if the applicant would like to be considered for another post elsewhere in the organisation, or pointing out the difficulty of applying for a post that calls for greater experience or qualifications than the applicant at that stage is able to present.

Shortlisting

Shortlisting of candidates can be difficult in some instances because of small numbers of applicants and in other instances because of extremely large numbers of applicants. Such difficulties can arise unintentionally when there is inadequate specification of the criteria required or intentionally in large-scale recruitment exercises such as those associated with an annual intake of graduates.

In such circumstances it is tempting for the HR department to use some form of arbitrary method to reduce the numbers to a more manageable level. Examples include screening people out because of their age, because of their handwriting style or because their work history is perceived as being unconventional in some way. No doubt there are other whimsical criteria adopted by managers appalled at making sense of 100 or so application forms and assorted curricula vitae. Apart from those that are unlawful, these criteria are grossly unfair to applicants if not mentioned in the advertisement, and are a thoroughly unsatisfactory way of recruiting the most appropriate person.

It is far more satisfactory to have in place a fair and objective system for short-listing candidates which produces the best group of alternative candidates to move forward to the interview stage. This can be achieved in one of two basic ways – either used separately or in combination. The first involves using a panel of managers to undertake shortlisting, reducing the likelihood that individual prejudices will influence the process. A number of distinct stages can be identified:

- **Stage 1:** Panel members agree essential criteria for those to be placed on the shortlist.
- **Stage 2:** Using those criteria, selectors individually produce personal lists of, say, ten candidates. An operating principle throughout is to concentrate on who can be included rather than who can be excluded, so that the process is positive, looking for strengths rather than shortcomings.
- **Stage 3:** Selectors reveal their lists and find their consensus. If stages 1 and 2 have been done properly the degree of consensus should be quite high and probably sufficient to constitute a shortlist for interview. If it is still not clear, they continue to:
- **Stage 4:** Discuss those candidates preferred by some but not all in order to clarify and reduce the areas of disagreement. A possible tactic is to classify candidates as 'strong', 'possible' or 'maverick'.
- **Stage 5:** Selectors produce a final shortlist by discussion, guarding against including compromise candidates: not strong, but offensive to no one.

The second approach involves employing a scoring system as advocated by Roberts (1997) and Wood and Payne (1998). As with the panel method, the key shortlisting criteria are defined at the start of the process (e.g. three years' management experience, a degree in a certain discipline, current salary in the range of £20,000–£30,000, evidence of an ability to drive change, etc.). The shortlister then scores each CV or application form received against these criteria awarding an A grade (or high mark) where clear evidence is provided that the candidate matches the criteria, a B grade where there is some evidence or where the candidate partially meets the criteria and a C grade where no convincing evidence is provided. Where a structured application form has been completed by the candidates, this process can be undertaken quickly (two or three minutes per application) because a candidate can be screened out whenever, for example, more than one C grade has been awarded.

A third approach involves making use of the software systems on the market which shortlist candidates electronically. The different types of system and some of the drawbacks were described above in the section on e-recruitment. Despite the problems, such systems can be useful where the criteria are very clearly and tightly defined, and where an online application form is completed which makes use of multiple-choice answers. Such forms can be scored speedily and objectively, the candidate being given feedback on whether or not they have been successful. Only those who make the 'right' choices when completing the online questionnaire are then invited to participate in the next stage of the recruitment process.

Summary propositions

11.1 Alternatives to filling a vacancy include reorganising the work; using overtime; mechanising the work; staggering the hours; making the job part time; subcontracting the work; using an employment agency.

11.2 Recent trends indicate a greater use by employers of recruitment agencies and executive consultants, open days, recruitment fairs, etc. Relocation constraints have also prompted a move towards the use of regional as opposed to national recruitment advertising.

11.3 Advertising agencies and specialist publications provide a wealth of information to ensure that advertisements reach the appropriate readership.

11.4 The most significant recent development is the growth of e-recruitment. This provides great potential advantages for employers but is not seen as being especially effective at present.

11.5 Increasing the amount of information provided to potential applicants reduces the number of inappropriate applications.

11.6 The most important feature of candidate decision making in recruitment is finding an answer to the question, 'How much will I get paid?' Advertisements are frequently misleading on this.

11.7 Care with shortlisting increases the chances of being fair to all applicants and lessens the likelihood of calling inappropriate people for interview.

References

Barber, A.E. (1998) *Recruiting Employees: Individual and Organizational Perspectives*. Thousand Oaks, Cal.: Sage.

De Witte, K. (1989) 'Recruiting and Advertising', in P. Herriott (ed.), *Assessment and Selection in Organisations*. Chichester: Wiley.

Finn, W. (2000) 'Screen Test', *People Management*, 22 June, pp. 38–43.

Frankland, G. (2000) 'If you build it, they will come', *People Management*, 16 March, p. 45.

Howard, S. (2000) 'Pressing Ahead. Annual Review of the Recruitment Advertising Industry 2000', People Management, July.

IRS (1998) *Graduate Recruitment and Sponsorship: The 1998 IRS Survey of employer Practice*. Employee Development Bulletin 107, November.

IRS (1999) *Cost-effective recruitment: an IRS survey of employers' experience*. Employee Development Bulletin 115, June.

Labour Market Trends (2000) 'Labour market spotlight', *Labour Market Trends*, January.

Jenkins, J.F. (1983) 'Management trainees in retailing', in B. Ungerson (ed.), *Recruitment Handbook*, 3rd edn. Aldershot: Gower.

Knollys, J.G. (1983) 'Sales Staff', in B. Ungerson (ed.), *Recruitment Handbook*, 3rd edn. Aldershot: Gower.

Pearn, M. and Kandola, R. (1988) *Job Analysis: A practical guide for managers*. London: IPM.

Plumbley, P.R. (1985) *Recruitment and Selection*, 4th edn. London: IPM.

Roberts, G. (1997) *Recruitment and Selection*. London: IPD.

Schreyer, R. and McCarter, J. (1998) *The Employer's Guide to Recruiting on the Internet*. Manassas Park USA: Impact.

Ungerson, B. (1983) *How to Write a Job Description*. London: IPM.

Weekes, S. (2000) 'Hire on the wire', *Personnel Today*, 2 May, pp. 31–5.

Whiddett, S. and Kandola, B. (2000) 'Fit for the job?' *People Management*, 25 May, pp. 30–4.

Wood, R. and Payne, T. (1998) *Competency Based Recruitment and Selection: A Practical Guide*. Chichester: Wiley.

Wright, M. and Storey, J. (1994) 'Recruitment', in I. Beardwell and L. Holden (eds), *Human Resource Management*. London: Pitman.

General discussion topics

1 What are the advantages and disadvantages of graduate recruitment fairs?

2 In June 2000 an article in the *People Management* annual review of the Recruitment Advertising Industry by Simon Howard confirmed the long-term trend whereby the quality press continues to grow while the mid-market and popular press is becoming increasingly irrelevant in recruitment terms. Why do you think this is?

3 Can you improve on the suggestions for shortlisting that the chapter contains?

Chapter 12   Selection methods and decisions

While the search for the perfect method of selection continues, in its absence personnel and line managers continue to use a variety of imperfect methods to aid the task of predicting which applicant will be most successful in meeting the demands of the job. Selection is increasingly important as more attention is paid to the costs of poor selection, in a very competitive market for talent.

Legislation promoting equality of opportunity has underlined the importance of using well-validated selection procedures, and there is increasing emphasis on ensuring that the selection process discriminates fairly, and not unfairly, between applicants.

In this chapter we first consider the role of HR management in selection, and selection as a two-way process. Next we look at selection criteria and choosing appropriate selection methods. Various methods are then considered, including application forms, testing, group selection and assessment centres, references, use of consultants and some less traditional methods, such as graphology. We conclude by looking at selection decision making, the validation of selection procedures, and selection and the law. Interviews, the most popular selection method, are covered in depth in Chapter 15.

The role of HR management in selection

HR managers still have a key role in the selection process, although in many organisations this is becoming less direct, as indicated in Chapter 9. From an emphasis on direct involvement in shortlisting, interviewing and control of administrative procedures, the nature of involvement is shifting towards provision of specialist advice, guidance and training, and evaluation of selection effectiveness.

HR managers are able to draw on their expertise to recommend the most effective selection methods for each particular job or group of jobs. They are also in a position to encourage the development and use of personnel specifications as an aid to selection. A member of the HR department will normally be the organisation's expert on test use and have the British Psychological Society (BPS) certificate of competence. In an organisation where tests are particularly appropriate selection methods, that person will advise managers on the most suitable tests to use, although test administration may be devolved to department level. In a more general sense HR managers can act as an advice centre on selection methods for line managers, and they are usually involved in formal and informal training in selection skills, particularly interviewing skills. 'How to do it' packs are often produced by the HR department so that line managers have specialist information about selection activities at their fingertips. HR departments still frequently play a co-ordinating role in selection activities in many organisations.

In our recent research we found that HR managers remained heavily involved in selection interviewing, particularly for managers, with over three-quarters (77 per cent) of establishments reporting this. Lower levels of involvement were identified in selection and vacancy decision making (less than one-third of establishments identifying HR involvement for any employee group in these areas). In all cases the personnel function was involved with managerial and non-manual employment to a greater extent than with manual employment. The nature of the HR role will vary considerably depending on the specific organisation, and presence at interview is not necessarily the critical factor, and should not be confused with influence.

WINDOW ON PRACTICE

Lupton (2000) investigated the HR role in medical staffing in the NHS and found that although HR staff were normally present at interviews for doctors, their 'weak' role in the organisation meant that their contribution was limited to administrative arrangements, accommodation enquiries and 'passing the coffee'. These individuals did not have a significant impact on either the selection decision or the structure of the process. Lupton argues that their weak organisational position is linked to the continuance of haphazard and informal selection processes.

Selection as a two-way process

The various stages of the selection process provide information for decisions by both the employer and the potential employee. While employment decisions have long been regarded as a management prerogative there is considerable evidence that the two-way nature of the process is now being widely acknowledged (see, for example, Wanous 1992; Papadopoulou *et al.* 1996). The management prerogative perspective, however, is likely to persist in many organisations for various reasons:

1 It is attractive to managers because it underlines their authority, and they frequently feel that the ability to choose their subordinates is a key to their own effectiveness.
2 It is supported by much academic research. Psychologists have studied individual differences, intelligence and motivation extensively and have produced a number of prescriptions for those managing selection procedures on how to make sound judgements about candidates.
3 Candidates are convinced of their helplessness in selection, which they see as being absolutely controlled by the recruiting organisation.

Despite these features of the situation, we continue to advocate a more reciprocal approach to employment decision making in the belief that managers will be more effective in staffing their organisations if they can bring about some shift of stance in that direction. We must be concerned not only with the job to be done, but also with the work that is offered.

Throughout the selection process applicants choose between organisations by evaluating the developing relationship between themselves and the prospect.

This takes place in the correspondence from potential employers; in their experience of the selection methods used by the employer; and in the information they gain on interview. Applicants will decide not to pursue some applications. Either they will have accepted another offer, or they will find something in their correspondence with the organisation that discourages them and they withdraw. When large numbers of candidates withdraw it may be because the information provided by the organisation was sufficiently detailed, accurate and realistic that they were able to make a wise decision that they were not suited to the organisation and that time would be wasted by continuing. On the other hand, it might be that potentially admirable recruits were lost because of the way in which information was presented, lack of information, or the interpretation that was put on the 'flavour' of the correspondence.

If candidates get as far as interview they will also be influenced by recruiter behaviours in deciding whether to accept a job offer, if one is made. Papadopoulou *et al.*, for example, demonstrated that candidates were influenced by the recruiter's ability to supply adequate and accurate information, as this is what they had expected from the interview. In addition they were influenced by the way the recruiter managed the interaction, as well as the content, so the recruiter's control of the interaction, their listening ability and in particular their ability/willingness to allow the candidate to present themselves effectively are all important.

The frame of reference for the applicant is so different from that of the manager in the organisation that the difference is frequently forgotten. It would not be unrealistic to suggest that the majority of applicants have a mental picture of their letter of application being received through the letterbox of the company and immediately being closely scrutinised and discussed by powerful figures. The fact that the application is one element in a varied routine for the recipient is incomprehensible to some and unacceptable to many. The thought that one person's dream is another's routine is something the applicant cannot cope with.

If they have posted an application with high enthusiasm about the fresh prospects that the new job would bring, they are in no mood for delay and they may quickly start convincing themselves that they are not interested, because their initial euphoria has not been sustained. They are also likely to react unfavourably to the mechanical response that appears to have been produced on a photocopier that was due for the scrapheap. Again there is a marked dissonance between the paramount importance of the application to the applicant and its apparent unimportance to the organisation. Some of the points that seem to be useful about correspondence and interaction with the candidate are:

1 Reply, meaningfully, fast. The printed postcard of acknowledgement is not a reply, neither is the personal letter which says nothing more than that the application has been received.
2 Conduct correspondence in terms of what the applicants want to know. How long will they have to wait for an answer? If you ask them in for interview, how long will it take, what will it involve, do you defray expenses, can they park their car, how do you find you, etc.?
3 Interviewers should be trained to ensure that they not only have full knowledge of the relevant information, but also have the skills to manage the interaction effectively.

Selection criteria and the person specification

Unless the criteria against which applicants will be measured are made explicit, it is impossible to make credible selection decisions. It will be difficult to select the most appropriate selection procedure and approach, and it will be difficult to validate the selection process. Selection criteria are normally presented in the form of a person specification representing the ideal candidate. There is a wide range of formats for this purpose: the two most widely known are Alec Rodger's Seven Point plan and John Munro Fraser's fivefold framework. Both are shown in Table 12.1.

Lewis (1985) suggests that selection criteria can be understood in terms of three aspects: organisational criteria, departmental or functional criteria and individual job criteria.

Organisational criteria

The organisational criteria are those attributes that an organisation considers valuable in its employees and that affect judgements about a candidate's potential to be successful within an organisation. For example, the organisation may be expanding and innovating and require employees who are particularly flexible and adaptable. Previously, these organisational criteria were rarely made explicit and they were often used at an intuitive level. However, Townley (1991) argues that organisations are increasingly likely to focus on more general attitudes and values rather than narrow task-based criteria. Barclay (1999) explains how fit with the organisation is often expressed in terms of personality, attitudes, flexibility, commitment and goals, rather than the ability to do the specific job for which they are being recruited. Such organisational criteria are important in a context of rapid change where the job for which a person is initially recruited may change within weeks of their being appointed. There are also some groups who are recruited into the organisation rather than into specific jobs or even a specific function – new/recent graduates, for example, and, here again, organisation criteria are important.

Functional/departmental criteria

Between the generality of the organisational criteria and the preciseness of job criteria there are departmental criteria, such as the definition of appropriate interpersonal skills for all members of the HR department.

Table 12.1 Two well-used human attribute classification systems: Rodger's seven point plan and Fraser's fivefold grading

Rodger's seven point plan	*Fraser's fivefold grading*
■ Physical make-up	■ Impact on others
■ Attainments	■ Qualifications or acquired knowledge
■ General intelligence	■ Innate abilities
■ Special aptitudes	■ Motivation
■ Interests	■ Adjustment or emotional balance
■ Disposition	
■ Circumstances	

Individual job criteria

Individual job criteria contained in job descriptions and person specifications are derived from the process of job analysis. It is these criteria, derived from the tasks to be completed, that are most often used in the selection process. A sample person specification drawn up on this basis can be found in Table 12.2.

Although it is reasonably easy to specify the factors that should influence the personnel specification, the process by which the specification is formed is more difficult to describe. Van Zwanenberg and Wilkinson (1993) offer a dual perspective. They describe 'job first – person later' and 'person first – job later' approaches. The first starts with analysing the task to be done, presenting this in the form of a job description and from this deriving the personal qualities and attributes or competencies that are necessary to do the task. The difficulty here is in the translation process and the constant change of job demands and tasks. The alternative approach suggested by van Zwanenberg and Wilkinson starts with identifying which individuals are successful in a certain job and then describing their characteristics. The authors note that the difficulty here is choosing which attributes are key and need to be specified. Wilkinson and van Zwanenberg (1994) also report on the development of a computer-based expert system which can be used to guide line managers through the development of a person specification for managerial jobs.

In addition to, or sometimes instead of, a person specification, many organisations are increasingly developing a competency profile as a means of setting the criteria against which to select. Competencies have been defined as underlying

Table 12.2 Person specification for the job of senior sales assistant using Rodger's seven point plan

Physical make-up
Essential: Tidy, and dressed in a business-like manner.

Attainment
Preferred: GCSE Maths grade A; English grade B
Essential: Maths grade D–E; English grade D–E
Preferred: Previous attendance at a programming course, in or out of school; or demonstrate some self-taught knowledge of programming
Essential: Good keyboard skills – 40 wpm. Preferred 20 wpm with a willingness to improve to 40 wpm

General intelligence
Essential: Above-average and quick to grasp the meaning of problems

Special aptitudes
Essential: Ability to relate to people – to be outgoing and form relationships quickly

Interests
Essential: Interested in both computer hardware and software

Disposition
Essential: Patience

Circumstances
Essential: Circumstances that enable attendance at work every Saturday

characteristics of a person which result in effective or superior performance; they include personal skills, knowledge, motives, traits, self-image and social role (see Boyatzis 1982). The advantage of competencies is that they can be used in an integrated way for selection, development, appraisal and reward activities; and also that from them behavioural indicators can be derived against which assessment can take place. For a fuller discussion of the nature and role of competencies, see Chapter 25. Woodruffe (1992) and Whiddett and Hollyforde (1999) are useful practical sources of information on how to use competencies in the selection process. It should be noted, however, that using competencies as the only selection criteria is considered to be limiting and unhelpful (see, for example, Brittain and Ryder (1999) and Whiddett and Kandola (2000)).

Choosing selection methods

It is unusual for one selection method to be used alone. A combination of two or more methods is generally used, and the choice of these is dependent upon a number of factors:

1 **Selection criteria for the post to be filled**: for example, group selection methods and assessment centre activities would be most useful for certain types of job, such as managerial, professional, supervisory and those who will be part of self-managing teams.
2 **Acceptability and appropriateness of the methods**: for the candidates involved, or likely to be involved, in the selection. The use, for example, of intelligence tests may be seen as insulting to applicants already occupying senior posts.
3 **Abilities of the staff involved in the selection process**: this applies particularly in the use of tests and assessment centres. Only those staff who are appropriately qualified by academic qualification and/or attendance on a recognised course may administer psychological tests.
4 **Administrative ease**: for administrative purposes it may be much simpler, say, to arrange one or two individual interviews for a prospective candidate rather than organise a panel consisting of four members, all needing to make themselves available at the same time.
5 **Time factors**: sometimes a position needs to be filled very quickly, and time may be saved by organising individual interviews rather than group selection methods, which would mean waiting for a day when all candidates are available.
6 **Accuracy**: accuracy in selection generally increases in relation to the number of appropriate selection methods used.
7 **Cost**: tests may cost a lot to set up but once the initial outlay has been made they are reasonably cheap to administer. Assessment centres would involve an even greater outlay and continue to be fairly expensive to administer. Interviews, on the other hand, cost only a moderate amount to set up in terms of interviewer training and are fairly cheap to administer. For the costlier methods great care needs to be taken in deciding whether the improvement in selection decision making would justify such costs.

Selection methods

Application forms

Growing use is being made of the application form as a basis for employment decisions, and IRS (1997) found that they were used in some way by 93 per cent of the organisations they surveyed. For a long time the application form was not suitable for use in that way; it was a personal details form, which was intended to form the nucleus of the personnel record for the individual when they began work. It asked for some information that was difficult to supply, like national insurance number, and some that seemed irrelevant, like the identity of the family doctor and next of kin. It was largely disregarded in the employment process, which was based on an informal and unstructured 'chat'. As reservations grew about the validity of interviews for employment purposes, the more productive use of the application form was one of the avenues explored for improving the quality of decisions.

Forms were considered to act as a useful preliminary to employment interviews and decisions, either to present more information that was relevant to such deliberations, or to arrange such information in a standard way rather than the inevitably idiosyncratic display found in letters of application. This made sorting of applications and shortlisting easier and enabled interviewers to use the form as the basis for the interview itself, with each piece of information on the form being taken and developed in the interview. While there is heavy use of CVs for managerial and professional posts, many organisations, especially in the public sector, require both – off-putting to the applicant but helpful to the organisation in eliciting comparable data from all applicants.

More recently the application form has been extended by some organisations to take a more significant part in the employment process. One form of extension is to ask for very much more, and more detailed, information from the candidate.

Another extension of application form usage has been in weighting, or biodata. Biodata have been defined by Anderson and Shackleton (1990) as 'historical and verifiable pieces of information about an individual in a selection context usually reported on application forms'. Biodata are perhaps of most use for large organisations filling fairly large numbers of posts for which they receive extremely high numbers of applications. This method is an attempt to relate the characteristics of applicants to characteristics of successful job holders. The method is to take a large population of job holders and categorise them as good, average or poor performers, usually on the evaluation of a supervisor. Common characteristics are sought out among the good and poor performers. The degree of correlation is then translated into a weighting for evaluating that characteristic when it appears on the application form, or the additional biodata form. The obvious drawbacks of this procedure are, first, the time that is involved and the size of sample needed, so that it is only feasible where there are many job holders in a particular type of position. Second, it smacks of witchcraft to the applicants who might find it difficult to believe that success in a position correlates with being, *inter alia*, the first born in one's family. However, Robertson and Makin (1986) report that biodata were being used by 8 per cent of major British companies at the time of their survey and we found 12 per cent of organisations in our study in 1994 were using this method. However, in 1997 the IRS report biodata being used by only 5 per cent of the organizations they surveyed. This wavering interest is not surprising, given – as Taylor (1998) notes – its controversial nature and high development costs. In addition the 1998 Data Protection Act prohibits the use of an automated selection process (which biodata invariably is) as the *only* process used at any stage in the procedure.

Generally, application forms are used as a straightforward way of giving a standardised synopsis of the applicant's history. This helps applicants present their case by providing them with a predetermined structure, it speeds the sorting and shortlisting of applications and it guides the interviewers as well as providing the starting point for personnel records. In application form design the following points are worth checking:

1 Handwriting is usually larger than typescript. Do the boxes on the form provide enough room for the applicant to complete their information?
2 Forms that take too long to complete run the risk of being completed perfunctorily, or not being completed at all. Is the time the form takes to complete appropriate to the information needs of the employment decision?
3 Some questions are illegal, some are offensive, others are unnecessary. Does the form call only for information that is appropriate to employment decision making?
4 Allan (1990) suggests that in the age of word processors there is no excuse for failing to produce separate application forms for each vacancy advertised, or for not personalising forms and making them more user-friendly. One way of increasing user-friendliness is to use introductory paragraphs explaining why the information in each section is being sought.
5 Given our increasing technological sophistication many candidates would also appreciate an electronic version of the application form. This encourages candidates to respond; facilitates higher standards of presentation; and eliminates the problem of the application form designer in determining how much space to leave for each section of the form.

Activity 12.1	Design an application form for the sales assistant post we have used in previous examples, maximising critical information, but asking only for information that is strictly relevant.

Self-assessment

There is increasing interest in providing more information to applicants concerning the job. This may involve a video, an informal discussion with job holders or further information sent with the application form. This is often termed giving the prospective candidate a 'realistic job preview' (Wanous 1992), enabling them to assess their own suitability to a much greater extent. Another way of achieving this is by asking the candidates to do some form of pre-work. This may also involve asking them questions regarding their previous work experiences which would relate to the job for which they are applying.

Arthur Andersen Consulting (now Accenture) has produced a very different type of graduate prospectus. It contains all the usual material about different types of work available, the varied development on offer, and makes a consultant's career sound very exciting. However it also contains some very realistic work scenarios. In these the job is portrayed as far from glamorous; instead there is a picture of gruelling hard work, heavy demands on the individual and extreme tiredness.

This approach has two advantages. It will (presumably) enable some individuals to withdraw, as they realise 'that is not the life for me', so they will not waste their own or the organisation's time. Furthermore, those that continue with the process from this stage are at least doing so in the knowledge of what is involved in the job, and will have a more accurate picture of what they may take on rather than the usual 'rose-tinted' one. If they are appointed they will, hopefully, adapt to the reality of the job more quickly.

Telephone screening

Telephone screening can be used instead of an application form if speed is particularly important, and if geographical distance is an issue, as interviews with appropriate candidates can be arranged immediately. This method works best where a checklist of critical questions has been prepared so that each candidate is being asked for standardised information. There are, however, problems with this method. Because the organisational response to prospective employees is immediate, the decision can be haphazard unless pre-set standards are agreed in advance. The difficulty with setting standards in advance is that these may turn out to be inappropriate in selecting either too many or too few candidates to interview. The standards can, of course, be changed as enquiries are coming in, but the best candidate, who may have called early, might not be invited to interview if the standards were initially too high. Also, since organisational response has to be immediate there is no time for reflection, or discussion with others, and little opportunity to be flexible.

Other, more recent approaches to telephone interviews often form part of a structured selection procedure.

One large employer requests CVs from applicants, and, on the basis of these, invites a selected number to take part in a telephone interview. A date and time are given and an idea of the questions that will be asked so that the candidate can prepare. The interview takes about 15–20 minutes, and time is allowed for the candidate to ask questions of the interviewer as well. Candidates are also told in advance of the telephone interview that if they are successful at this stage they will be invited to a one-day assessment centre on a specified date. After the telephone interview candidates are notified in writing whether or not they will move on to the assessment centre stage of the selection procedure.

Activity 12.2

What are the advantages of using telephone interviews of the type described in the box? For what types of job would you use this approach to selection?

Testing

The use of tests in employment procedures is surrounded by strong feelings for and against, and a lively debate on the value of personality tests is found in Fletcher and others (1990). Those in favour of testing in general point to the unreliability of the interview as a predictor of performance and the greater potential accuracy and objectivity of test data. Tests can be seen as giving credibility to selection decisions. Those against them either dislike the objectivity that testing implies or have difficulty in incorporating test evidence into the rest of the evidence that is collected. Questions have been raised as to the relevance of the tests to the job applied for and the possibility of unfair discrimination and bias. Also, some candidates feel that they can improve their prospects by a good interview performance and that the degree to which they are in control of their own destiny is being reduced by a dispassionate routine.

The use of tests for employment selection is, however, increasing – IRS reported in 1997 that 75 per cent of organisations studied used ability tests and 60 per cent used personality tests. Newell and Shackleton (1994) report that testing is more likely to be used for management and graduate jobs than for administrative, secretarial or manual jobs.

Tests are chosen on the basis that test scores relate, or correlate, to subsequent job performance, so that a high test score would predict high job performance and a low test score would predict low job performance.

Critical features of test use

Validity

Different types of validity can be applied to psychological tests. Personnel managers are most concerned with predictive validity, which is the extent to which the test can predict subsequent job performance. Predictive validity is measured by relating the test scores to measures of future performance, such as error rate, production rate, appraisal scores, absence rate or whatever criteria are important to the organisation. Sometimes performance is defined as the level of the organisation to which the individual has been promoted – so the criteria here are organisational rather than job specific. If test scores relate highly to future performance, however defined, then the test is a good predictor.

Reliability

The reliability of a test is the degree to which the test measures consistently whatever it does measure. If a test is highly reliable, then it is possible to put greater weight on the scores that individuals receive on the test. However, a highly reliable test is of no value in the employment situation unless it also has high validity.

Use and interpretation

Tests need to be used and interpreted by trained or qualified testers. Test results, especially personality tests, require very careful interpretation as some aspects of personality will be measured that are irrelevant to the job. Wills (1990) reports concerns that tests are carried out by unqualified testers. The British Psychological Society (BPS) has now introduced a certificate of competence for occupational testing at levels A and B. Both the BPS and the Chartered Institute of Personnel and Development (CIPD) have produced codes of practice for occupational test use. It is recommended that tests are not used in a judgemental, final way, but to stimulate discussion with the candidate based on the test results. Research by Newell and Shackleton (1994) suggests, unfortunately, that tests are not used as the basis for discussion. Feedback to those tested is also identified as a key issue, yet again Newell and Shackleton found that this is not always given. In addition it is recommended in the CIPD code that test data alone should not be used to make a selection decision (which could contravene the 1998 Data Protection Act), but should always be used as part of a wider process where inferences from test results can be backed up by other sources. Norm tables and the edition date of a test are also important features to check. For example Ceci and Williams (2000) warn that intelligence is a relative concept and that the norm tables change over time – so using an old test with old norm tables may be misleading.

Context of tests

Test scores need to be evaluated in the context of other information about individuals. Selection decisions need to be made up of a number of different pieces of information. Test results cannot be seen as having a simple relationship with job performance, as, for example, there are many relevant aspects of an individual which a test cannot measure.

Problems with using tests

A number of problems can be incurred when using tests.

1 In the last section we commented that a test score that was highly related to performance criteria has good validity. The relationship between test scores and performance criteria is usually expressed as a correlation coefficient (r). If $r = 1$ then test scores and performance would be perfectly related; if $r = 0$ there is no relationship whatsoever. A correlation coefficient of $r = 0.4$ is comparatively good in the testing world and this level of relationship between test scores and performance is generally seen as acceptable. Tests are, therefore, not outstanding predictors of future performance. Robertson and Smith (1989) carried out a meta-analysis of research on the validity of test results. They found that correlations for cognitive tests were between 0.25 and 0.45, and that those for personality tests were between 0.15 and 0.10.

2 Validation procedures are very time consuming, but are essential to the effective use of tests.

3 The criteria that are used to define good job performance in developing the test are often inadequate. They are subjective and may account to some extent for the mediocre correlations between test results and job performance.

4 Tests are often job specific. If the job for which the test is used changes, then the test can no longer be assumed to relate to job performance in the same way. Also, personality tests only measure how individuals see themselves at a certain time and cannot therefore be reliably reused at a later time.

5 Tests may not be fair as there may be a social, sexual or racial bias in the questions and scoring system. People from some cultures may, for example, be

unused to 'working against the clock'. Wood and Barron (1992) provide some further examples of how tests may discriminate in an unlawful or unhelpful way.

6 Increasingly organisations are using competencies as a tool to identify and develop the characteristics of high performance. However, as Fletcher (1996) has pointed out it is difficult to relate these readily to psychological tests. Rogers (1999) reports research which suggests the two approaches are compatible – but there is little evidence to support this so far.

WINDOW ON PRACTICE

Wood and Barron (1992) describe how in 1991 some guards at Paddington Station took British Rail to an industrial tribunal. These guards maintained that the selection processes that British Rail used for train drivers discriminated unfairly against ethnic minorities. As part of the settlement British Rail promised to improve the situation. One action was to run workshops on test taking. They found that the ethnic minority guards were not used to a test-taking culture and so they produced an open learning pack which gave them helpful hints on taking tests and gave them material to practise with. As a result five of the seven guards passed the selection test which enabled them to train as train drivers.

Activity 12.3

In what ways could you measure job performance for the following?

■ A mobile telephone engineer
■ A clerk
■ A supervisor

Types of test for occupational use

Aptitude tests

People differ in their performance of tasks, and tests of aptitude measure an individual's potential to develop in either specific or general terms. This is in contrast to attainment tests, which measure the skills an individual has already acquired. For the purposes of this chapter we shall use aptitude and ability interchangeably (although some authors do identify a difference between them), and as something quite separate from attainment. When considering the results from aptitude tests it is important to remember that a simple relationship does not exist between a high level of aptitude and a high level of job performance, as other factors, such as motivation, also contribute to job performance.

Aptitude tests can be grouped into two categories. Those measuring general mental ability or general intelligence, and those measuring specific abilities or aptitudes.

General intelligence tests

Intelligence tests, sometimes called mental ability tests, are designed to give an indication of overall mental capacity. A variety of questions are included in such tests, including vocabulary, analogies, similarities, opposites, arithmetic, number extension and general information. Ability to score highly on such tests correlates with the capacity to retain new knowledge, to pass examinations and to succeed at work. However the intelligence test used would still need to be carefully validated in terms of the job for which the candidate was applying. And Ceci and Williams (2000) note that intelligence is to some extent determined by the context – so an individual's test score may not reflect capacity to act intelligently. Indeed practical intelligence, associated with success in organisations, may be different from the nature of intelligence as measured by tests (Williams and Sternberg 2001). Examples of general intelligence tests are found in IDS (2000).

Special aptitude tests

There are special tests that measure specific abilities or aptitudes, such as spatial abilities, perceptual abilities, verbal ability, numerical ability, motor ability (manual dexterity), and so on. There is some debate over the way that general intelligence and special abilities are related. In the United Kingdom the design of ability or aptitude tests has been much influenced by Vernon's (1961) model of the structure of abilities. Vernon suggested a hierarchical model of abilities with general intelligence at the top and abilities becoming more specific and finely divided lower down in the hierarchy. Here an individual's potential ability to perform a task is the result of a combination of the specific appropriate ability and general intelligence. In the United States abilities are generally seen as more distinct (Thurstone 1938), and less emphasis is put on general intelligence as a contributing factor. The development of tests of specific aptitudes is obviously influenced by the model of intelligence and ability that is used. One test of special abilities is the Critical Reasoning Test developed by Smith and Whetton (see IDS 2000).

Trainability tests

Trainability tests are used to measure a potential employee's ability to be trained, usually for craft-type work. The test consists of the applicants doing a practical task that they have not done before, after having been shown or 'trained' how to do it. The test measures how well they respond to the 'training' and how their performance on the task improves. Because it is performance at a task that is being measured, these tests are sometimes confused with attainment tests; however, they are more concerned with potential ability to do the task and response to training.

Attainment tests

Whereas aptitude tests measure an individual's potential, attainment or achievement tests measure skills that have already been acquired. There is much less resistance to such tests of skills. Few candidates for a typing post would refuse to take a typing test before interview. The candidates are sufficiently confident of their skills to welcome the opportunity to display them and be approved. Furthermore, they know what they are doing and will know whether they have done well or badly. They are in control, while they feel that the tester is in control of intelligence and personality tests as the candidates do not understand the evaluation rationale. Attainment tests are often devised by the employer.

Personality tests

The debate still rages as to the importance of personality for success in some jobs and organisations. The need for personality assessment may be high but there is even more resistance to tests of personality than to tests of aptitude, partly because of the reluctance to see personality as in any way measurable. There is much evidence to suggest that personality is also context dependent, and Iles and Salaman (1995) also argue that personality changes over time. Both of these factors further complicate the issue. In spite of this there has been a marked increase in personality test use (Fletcher 1993), although IRS (1997) found that personality test use stabilised during the 1990s at around 60 per cent of the organisations they surveyed. Personality tests are mainly used for management, professional and graduate jobs, although there is evidence of their use when high-performance teams are developed.

Theories of human personality vary as much as theories of human intelligence. The psychiatrist Karl Jung was content to divide personalities into extroverts and introverts; subsequently Eysenck and Eysenck (1963) regarded the factors of neuroticism and extroversion as being sufficient. The most extensive work was done by Cattell (1965), who identified 16 factors. Amongst them he identified: reserved/outgoing; affected by feelings/emotionally stable; submissive/dominant; tough-minded/sensitive; group dependent/self-sufficient and trusting/suspicious. Based on research to date Cooper and Robertson (1995) argue that it is now possible to state that there are five basic building blocks of personality: extroversion/introversion; emotional stability; agreeableness; conscientiousness and openness to new experiences.

It is dangerous to assume that there is a standard profile of 'the ideal employee' (although this may fit nicely with theories of culture change) or the ideal personality for a particular job, as the same objectives may be satisfactorily achieved in different ways by different people. Another problem with the use of personality tests is that they rely on an individual's willingness to be honest, as the socially acceptable answer or the one best in terms of the job are often easy to pick out (Lewis 1985), although 'lie detector' questions are usually built in. Ipsative* tests may seek to avoid the social desirability problem by using a different test structure – but different problems arise from this approach. There is a further problem that some traits measured by the test will not be relevant in terms of performance on the job.

An example of a personality test is Cattell's 16PF (see IDS 2000).

Group selection methods and assessment centres

Group methods

The use of group tasks to select candidates is not new – the method dates back to the Second World War – but such measures have gained greater attention through their use in assessment centres. Plumbley (1985) describes the purpose of group selection methods as being to provide evidence about the candidate's ability to:

■ get on with others;
■ influence others and the way they do this;
■ express themselves verbally;
■ think clearly and logically;
■ argue from past experience and apply themselves to a new problem;
■ identify the type of role they play in group situations.

---

* Ipsative tests require the candidate to make a *choice*, usually between two statements or adjectives, rather than allowing the candidate to answer, for example, 'true' or 'false' against every statement.

schemes in the same organisation. For some jobs, such as photographers and artists, a sample of work in the form of a portfolio is expected to be presented at the time of interview. Kanter (1989) suggests that managers and professionals should also be developing portfolios of their work experiences and achievements as one way of enhancing their employability.

References

One way of informing the judgement of managers who have to make employment offers to selected individuals is the use of references. Candidates provide the names of previous employers or others with appropriate credentials and then prospective employers request them to provide information. There are two types: the factual check and the character reference.

The factual check

The factual check is fairly straightforward as it is no more than a confirmation of facts that the candidate has presented. It will normally follow the employment interview and decision to offer a post. It does no more than confirm that the facts are accurate. The knowledge that such a check will be made – or may be made – will help focus the mind of candidates so that they resist the temptation to embroider their story.

The character reference

The character references is a very different matter. Here the prospective employer asks for an opinion about the candidate before the interview so that the information gained can be used in the decision-making phases. The logic of this strategy is impeccable: who knows the working performance of the candidate better than the previous employer? The wisdom of the strategy is less sound, as it depends on the writers of references being excellent judges of working performance, faultless communicators and – most difficult of all – disinterested. The potential inaccuracies of decisions influenced by character references begin when the candidate decides who to cite. They will have some freedom of choice and will clearly choose someone from whom they expect favourable comment, perhaps massaging the critical faculties with such comments as: 'I think references are going to be very important for this job' or 'You will do your best for me, won't you?'

Other methods

A number of other less conventional methods such as physiognomy, phrenology, body language, palmistry, graphology and astrology have been suggested as possible selection methods. While these are fascinating to read about there is little evidence to suggest that they could be used effectively. Thatcher (1997) suggests that the use of graphology is around 10 per cent in Holland and Germany and regularly used in France – in the UK he found nine per cent of small firms (less than 100 employees), one per cent of medium-sized firms (100–499 employees) and five per cent of larger firms used graphology as a selection method. In 1991 Fowler suggested that the extent of use of graphology is much higher in the UK than reported figures indicate, as there is some reluctance on the part of organisations to admit that they are using graphology for selection purposes. There are also concerns about the quality of graphologists – who can indeed set themselves up with no training whatsoever. The two main bodies in this field in the UK are the British Institute of Graphology and the International Graphology Association and both these organisations require members to gain qualifications before they can practice.

WINDOW ON PRACTICE

It is interesting to contrast different approaches to selection in different countries. Bulois and Shackleton (1996) note that interviews are the cornerstone of selection activity in both Britain and France, but that they are consciously used in different ways. In Britain they argue that interviews are increasingly structured and criterion referenced, whereas in France the approach tends to be deliberately unstructured and informal. They note that in France the premise is that 'the more at ease the candidates are, the higher the quality of their answer', whereas in Britain they characterise the premise as 'the more information you get about an individual, the better you know him/her and the more valid and reliable your judgement is' (p. 129). Tixier (1996), in a survey covering the EU (but excluding France), Switzerland, Sweden and Austria, found that structured interviews were favoured in the UK, Scandinavia, Germany and Austria. This contrasted with Italy, Portugal, Luxembourg and Switzerland where unstructured styles were preferred.

Bulois and Shackleton identify selectors in Britain as more aware of the limitations of interviews and as attempting to reduce the subjectivity by also carrying out assessment centres and psychological tests; whereas in France these methods were identified as unnatural, tedious and frustrating. Interviews are much more likely to be supplemented by handwriting analysis in France – both methods being identified as valuable, flexible and cheap sources of information. Shackleton and Newell (1991) report that handwriting analysis was used in 77 per cent of the organisations that they surveyed in France compared with 2.6 per cent of the organisations they surveyed in the UK.

Both culture and employment legislation clearly have an influence on the selection methods adopted in any country and the way in which they are used.

Using consultants

Consultants are increasingly involved in the recruitment and selection process and will in some cases directly apply a variety of the selection methods outlined above, although it is very rare that they would make the final selection decision.

The problem with using consultants is that organisations may have difficulty in communicating their exact requirements to the consultants and that some criteria – for example, ability to fit into the organisation and be successful in it – are best judged directly by a member of the organisation rather than by an intermediary. In addition aligning the expectations of the recruitment and selection process between candidates, consultants and the client organisation is clearly an issue, as outlined by Ball, Britton and Wright (1999).

Final selection decision making

The selection decision involves measuring each candidate against the selection criteria defined in the person specification, and not against each other. A useful tool to achieve this is the matrix in Figure 12.2. This is a good method of ensuring that every candidate is assessed against each selection criterion and in each

12.5 Assessment centres have the advantage of providing a full range of selection methods, and are increasingly used. They have been found to be more valid than other approaches to selection.

12.6 Selection methods should be validated. A simple system is better than no system at all.

References

Allan, J. (1990) 'How to recruit the best people', *Management Accounting*, February.

Anderson, N. and Shackleton, V. (1990) 'Staff selection decision making into the 1990s', *Management Decision*, Vol. 28, No. 1.

Ball, D., Britton, C. and Wright, M. (1999) 'Talking Heads', *People Management*, 14 January.

Barclay, J. (1999) 'Employee Selection: a question of structure', *Personnel Review*, Vol. 28, No. 1/2, pp. 134–51.

Bartram, D. (1991) 'Addressing the abuse of psychological tests', *Personnel Management*, April.

Boyatzis, R. (1982) *The Competent Manager*. Chichester: John Wiley.

Brittain, S. and Ryder, P. (1999) 'Get complex', *People Management*, 25 November, pp. 48–51.

Bulois, N. and Shackleton, V. (1996) 'A qualitative study of recruitment and selection in France and Britain: the attitudes of recruiters in multinationals', in I. Beardwell (chair), *Contemporary Developments in Human Resource Management*. Paris: Editions ESKA, pp. 125–35.

Cattell, R.B. (1965) *The Scientific Analysis of Personality*. Harmondsworth: Penguin Books.

Ceci, S. and Williams, W. (2000) 'Smart Bomb', *People Management*, 24 August, pp. 32–6.

Cooper, D. and Robertson, I. (1995) *The Psychology of Personnel Selection*. London: Routledge.

Eysenck, H.J. and Eysenck, S.B.G. (1963) *The Eysenck Personality Inventory*. London: University of London Press.

Fletcher, C. (1993) 'Testing times for the world of psychometrics', *Personnel Management*, December, pp. 46–93.

Fletcher, C. (1996) 'Mix and match fails to work on competencies', *People Management*, September.

Fletcher, C. *et al.* (1990) 'Personality tests: the great debate', *Personnel Management*, September.

Fowler, A. (1990) 'The writing on the wall', *Local Government Chronicle*, 26 January, pp. 20–8.

Iles, P. (1992) 'Centres of excellence? Assessment and development centres, managerial competence and human resource strategies', *British Journal of Management*, Vol. 3, pp. 79–90.

Iles, P. and Salaman, G. (1995) 'Recruitment, selection and assessment' in J. Storey (ed.) *Human Resource Management: A critical text*. London: Routledge.

Incomes Data Services (IDS) (2000) *IDS Study Plus: Psychological Tests*, Spring.

Industrial Relations Services (IRS) (1997) 'The state of selection: an IRS survey', *Employee Development Bulletin* 85 (Jan.).

Kanter, R.M. (1989) *When Giants Learn to Dance*. New York: Simon and Schuster.

Lewis, C. (1985) *Employee Selection*. London: Hutchinson.

Lupton, B. (2000) 'Pouring the coffee? Personnel's role in the selection of doctors', *Personnel Review*, Vol. 29, No. 1, pp. 48–64.

Mabey, B. (1989) 'The majority of large companies use occupational tests', *Guidance and Assessment Review*, Vol. 5, No. 3, pp. 1–4.

Newell, S. and Shackleton, V. (1994) 'The use (and abuse) of psychometric tests in British industry and commerce', *Human Resource Management Journal*, Vol. 4, No. 1.

Papadopoulou, A., Ineson, E. and Williams, D. (1996) 'The graduate management trainee preselection interview', *Personnel Review*, Vol. 25, No. 4, pp. 21–37.

Plumbley, P.R. (1985) *Recruitment and Selection*, 4th edn. London: Institute of Personnel Management.

Robertson, I.T. and Makin, P.J. (1986) 'Management selection in Britain: a survey and critique', *Journal of Occupational Psychology*, Vol. 59, pp. 45–57.

Robertson, I. and Smith, M. (eds) (1989) *Personnel Selection Methods: Advances in selection and assessment*. Chichester: John Wiley.

Rogers, G. (1999) 'All round vision', *People Management*, 2 July.

Shackleton, V. and Newell, S. (1991) 'Management selection: a comparative survey of methods used in top British and French companies', *Journal of Occupational Psychology*, Vol. 64, pp. 23–36.

Taylor, S. (1998) *Employee Resourcing*. London: IPD.

Thatcher, M. (1997) 'A test of character', *People Management*, 15 May.

Thurstone, L.L. (1938) 'Primary mental abilities', *Psychometric Monographs*, No. 1. Chicago: University of Chicago Press.

Tixier, M. (1996) 'Employers' recruitment tools across Europe', *Employee Relations*, Vol. 18, No. 6, pp. 67–78.

Townley, B. (1991) 'Selection and appraisal: reconstituting social relations?', in J. Storey (ed.), *New Perspectives in Human Resource Management*. London: Routledge.

van Zwanenberg, N. and Wilkinson, L.J. (1993) 'The person specification – a problem masquerading as a solution?', *Personnel Review*, Vol. 22, No. 7, pp. 54–65.

Vernon, P. (1961) *The Structure of Human Abilities*, 2nd edn. London: Methuen.

Wanous, J.P. (1992) *Organisational Entry: Recruitment, Selection, Orientation and Socialisation of newcomers*. Reading, Mass.: Addison-Wesley.

Whiddett, S. and Hollyforde, S. (1999) *The competencies handbook*. London: IPD.

Whiddett, S. and Kandola, B. (2000) 'Fit for the job?', *People Management*, 25 May.

Wilkinson, L.J. and van Zwanenberg, N. (1994) 'Development of a person specification system for managerial jobs', *Personnel Review*, Vol. 23, No. 1, pp. 25–36.

Williams, W. and Sternberg, R. (2001) *Success for Managers*. London: Lawrence Erlbaum Associates.

Willis, Q. (1984) 'Managerial research and management development', *Journal of Management Development*, Vol. 3, No. 1.

Wills, J. (1990) 'Cracking the nut', *Local Government Chronicle*, 26 January, pp. 22–3.

Wood, R. and Barron, H. (1992) 'Psychological testing free from prejudice', *Personnel Management*, December.

Woodruffe, C. (1992) *Assessment Centres*. London: IPD.

General discussion topics

1 It could be argued that the selection process identifies candidates who are competent in the selection process rather than candidates who are most competent to perform the job on offer. Discuss this in relation to all forms of selection.

2 'It is unethical and bad for business to make candidates undergo a selection assessment centre without providing detailed feedback and support.' Discuss.

Chapter 13   Staff retention

The last three chapters focused on the processes used to mobilise a workforce: activities which are often expensive and time consuming. It is estimated that the costs associated with recruiting and training a new employee average between half and one and a half times the annual salary for the post in question, depending on the approaches used (Thompson 2000). In this chapter we consider the most important way in which human resource managers seek to reduce the time and money spent on these activities, namely by trying to ensure that people choose not to leave an organisation voluntarily in the first place.

The extent of interest in employee retention issues varies over time as labour markets become successively tighter and looser depending on economic conditions. In recent years, as unemployment has fallen, making it harder to recruit staff with the necessary skills and attitudes, the subject has again moved up the human resource management agenda. This has led to the publication of several new books and articles exploring how organisations can ensure that they have the best chance of retaining the people they employ. The authors tend to take one of two distinct perspectives on the subject. The first focuses on the organisation as a whole, tracking staff turnover rates over time, benchmarking the figures against industry or regional averages and developing organisational policy aimed at improving retention generally. The second, illustrated in recent work by Hiltrop (1999), Woodruffe (1999), Williams (2000) and Cappelli (2000), concentrates primarily on retaining high-performing key players. Each of these authors uses the expression 'the war for talent' to illustrate the significance and difficulty faced by those competing for the services of individuals who have the capacity to make a real difference to an organisation's competitive position. While the methods put forward to reduce turnover are similar in each case, the second group advocate more sophisticated retention practices aimed specifically at those whose talents are the most scarce.

Activity 13.1

Employee retention becomes an important item on the HRM agenda when organisations are faced with skills shortages. When labour is in reasonably good supply leavers can easily be replaced by new starters.

Aside from working harder at retaining staff, what alternative approaches could be adopted to help staff an organisation when the skills it requires are in short supply?

Here we start by examining recent trends in job tenure in the UK. We look at the arguments for and against investing in measures which reduce employee turnover. We go on to consider the different reasons people have for leaving jobs and at ways of computing the cost of turnover in particular organisations. Finally we take a look at some of the more significant initiatives employers adopt as a means of improving retention rates among their employees.

Turnover rates and trends

For much of the 1990s there has been a mismatch between the rhetoric about job tenure and the reality. Much mileage continues to be made by some consultants, academics and management gurus out of the claim that 'there are no longer any jobs for life', suggesting that the length of time we spend working for organisations has fallen substantially in recent years. In fact this is a misleading claim. Detailed analyses of data from the New Earnings Survey, the General Household Survey and the British Labour Force Survey show that relatively little actually changed in terms of employee retention during the 1980s and 1990s (see IDS 1995; Gregg and Wadsworth 1999; Medows 1999). Table 13.1 shows that average job tenure in the UK fluctuated up and down over this period, people remaining somewhat longer in their jobs during recessions than periods of low unemployment. The only discernible long-term trends are a marginal decline in male job tenure and an increase in that of female workers. Gregg and Wadsworth (1999, p. 116) show that the biggest increase has been among women with children. In 1975, on average, they remained in a job for 20 months; the figure in 1998 was 46 months. Job turnover rates have principally increased among people in the 18 to 24 age group and among older men. Between the ages of 25 and 50 we continue to average between three and four jobs, as was the case twenty years ago, while the proportion of the working population who have been with their current employers for ten years or more hardly changed between the 1960s and 1990s (IDS 1995, p. 5). The truth is that 'jobs for life' have always been a relative rarity.

The overall figures mask substantial differences between tenure and turnover rates in different industries. Studies undertaken annually by the Chartered Institute of Personnel and Development persistently show retailing and catering to be the sectors with the highest turnover levels, with rates averaging over 40 per cent in the late 1990s. By contrast the most stable workforces are to be found in the police and fire services, where reported annual turnover rates are only 6 or 7 per cent (IRS 1999, p. 15). Rates also vary from region to region and over time, being highest when and where average pay levels are highest and unemployment

Table 13.1 Job tenure in the UK since 1975

Year	Male job tenure	Female job tenure	Average tenure
1975	6 years, 6 months	3 years, 7 months	4 years, 9 months
1985	7 years, 2 months	3 years, 10 months	5 years, 6 months
1990	6 years	3 years, 9 months	4 years, 4 months
1995	6 years, 10 months	4 years, 6 months	5 years, 7 months
1998	5 years, 9 months	4 years, 4 months	4 years, 10 months

Source: Adapted from P. Gregg and J. Wadsworth (1999) 'Job tenure, 1975–98', in P. Gregg and J. Wadsworth (eds), *The State of Working Britain*. Manchester: Manchester University Press, p. 115.

Table 13.2 Average turnover figures for 1995–1999 by region (per cent)

Region	1995/6	1996/7	1997/8	1998/9
London	19	21	24	22
South West	14	22	22	26
West Midlands	12	20	22	17
North West	13	19	21	20
Scotland	15	19	21	–
South East	16	25	21	21
East Midlands	13	19	20	17
Eastern	12	25	20	18
Wales	12	21	19	–
Yorks/Humberside	16	20	19	15
North East	10	18	17	22
Merseyside	12	18	15	–

Adapted from *Skill Needs in Britain Surveys* 1997–2000. IFF Research, Oxford.

is low (see Table 13.2). The more opportunities there are to switch jobs, the more likely people are to do so.

Activity 13.2 Why do you think staff turnover rates are so much higher in some industries than others? Make a list of the different factors you consider may account for variations.

The impact of staff turnover

There is some debate about the level which staff turnover rates have to reach in order to inflict measurable damage on an employer. The answer varies from organisation to organisation. In some industries it is possible to sustain highly successful businesses with turnover rates that would make it impossible to function in other sectors. Some chains of fast food restaurants, for example, are widely reported as managing with turnover rates in excess of 300 per cent. This means that the average tenure for each employee is only four months (Ritzer 1996, p. 130; Cappelli 2000, p. 106), yet the companies concerned are some of the most successful in the world. By contrast, in a professional services organisation, where the personal relationships established between employees and clients are central to ongoing success, a turnover rate in excess of 10 per cent is likely to cause damage to the business.

There are sound arguments that can be made in favour of a certain amount of staff turnover. First, it is fair to say that organisations need to be rejuvenated with 'fresh blood' from time to time if they are to avoid becoming stale and stunted. This is particularly true at senior levels, where new leadership is often required periodically to drive change forward. More generally, however, new faces bring new ideas and experiences which help make organisations more dynamic. Second, it is possible to argue that a degree of turnover helps managers to keep firmer control over labour costs than would otherwise be the case. This is particularly true of organisations which are subject to regular and unpredictable changes in business levels. When income falls it is possible to hold back from replacing leavers until such time as it begins to pick up again. In this way organisations are able to minimise staffing budgets while maintaining profit levels during leaner periods. Redundancy bills are also lower in organisations with relatively high staff turnover because they are able to use natural wastage as the main means of reducing their workforce before compulsory lay-offs are needed. Third, it can be plausibly argued that some employee turnover is 'functional' rather than 'dysfunctional' because it results in the loss of poor performers and their replacement with more effective employees.

The arguments against staff turnover are equally persuasive. First are the sheer costs associated with replacing people who have left, ranging from the cost of placing a recruitment advertisement, through the time spent administering and conducting the selection process, to expenses required in inducting and training new employees. On top of these there are less easily measurable losses sustained as a result of poorer performance on the part of less experienced employees. For larger organisations employing specialist recruiters these costs can add up to millions of pounds a year, with substantial dividends to be claimed from a reduction in staff turnover levels by a few percentage points. The second major argument in favour of improving staff retention results from a straightforward recognition that people who leave represent a lost resource in whom the organisation has invested time and money. The damage is all the greater when good people, trained and developed at the organisation's expense, subsequently choose to work for competitors. Finally, it is argued that high turnover rates are symptomatic of a poorly managed organisation. They suggest that people are dissatisfied with their jobs or with their employer and would prefer to work elsewhere. It thus sends a negative message to customers and helps create a poor image in the labour market, making it progressively harder to recruit good performers in the future.

We can thus conclude that the case for seeking to reduce staff turnover varies from organisation to organisation. Where replacement employees are in plentiful supply, where new starters can be trained up quickly and where business levels are subject to regular fluctuation it is possible to manage effectively with a relatively high level of turnover. Indeed, it may make good business sense to do so if the expenditure required to increase employee retention is greater than the savings that would be gained as a result. In other situations the case for taking action on turnover rates is persuasive, particularly where substantial investment in training is required before new starters are able to operate at maximum effectiveness. Companies which achieve turnover rates below their industry average are thus likely to enjoy greater competitive advantage than those whose rates are relatively high.

Turnover analysis and costing

There is little that an organisation can do to manage turnover unless there is an understanding of the reasons for it. Information about these reasons is notoriously difficult to collect. Most commentators recommend exit interviews (that is, interviews with leavers about their reasons for resigning), but the problem here is whether the individual will feel able to tell the truth, and this will depend on the culture of the organisation, the specific reasons for leaving and support that the individual will need from the organisation in the future in the form of refer-

| WINDOW ON PRACTICE | It is very easy for an organisation to get itself into a vicious circle of turnover if it does not act to stem a retention problem. Modest turnover rates can rapidly increase as the pressures on remaining staff become greater, leading to serious operational difficulties. As soon as more than one or two people leave an estab- |

lished team, more is demanded of those left to carry the burden. First, there may be a sizeable time gap between leavers resigning and new starters coming into post. Then there is the period when the new people are learning their jobs, taking more time to accomplish tasks and needing assistance from more established employees. The problem can be compounded with additional pressure being placed on managers and HR specialists faced with the need to recruit people quickly, leading to the selection of people who are not wholly suited to the jobs in question. The result is greater turnover as people respond by looking for less pressured job opportunities elsewhere.

Problems of this kind were faced by the Japanese engineering company, Makita. It addressed the issue by increasing its induction programme from half a day to four weeks and by taking a good deal more care over its recruitment and selection processes. The result was a reduction in turnover levels from 97 per cent in 1997 to 38 per cent in 1999.

Source: IDS 2000, pp. 14–17.

ences. Despite their disadvantages, exit interviews may be helpful if handled sensitively and confidentially – perhaps by the HR department rather than the line manager. In addition, analyses of turnover rates between different departments and different job groups may well shed some light on causes of turnover. Attitude surveys can also provide relevant information.

People leave jobs for a variety of different reasons, many of which are wholly outside the power of the organisation to influence. One very common reason for leaving, for example, is retirement. It can be brought forward or pushed back for a few years, but ultimately it affects everyone. In many cases people leave for a mixture of reasons, certain factors weighing more highly in their minds than others. The following is one approach to categorising the main reasons people have for voluntarily leaving a job, each requiring a different kind of response from the organisation.

Outside factors

Outside factors relate to situations in which someone leaves for reasons that are largely unrelated to their work. The most common instances involve people moving away when a spouse or partner is relocated. Others include the wish to fulfil a long-term ambition to travel, pressures associated with juggling the needs of work and family and illness. To an extent such turnover is unavoidable, although it is possible to reduce it somewhat through the provision of career breaks, forms of flexible working and/or childcare facilities.

Functional turnover

The functional turnover category includes all resignations which are welcomed by both employer and employee alike. The major examples are those which stem from an individual's poor work performance or failure to fit in comfortably with an organisational or departmental culture. While such resignations are less damaging than others from an organisation's point of view they should still be regarded as lost opportunities and as an unnecessary cost. The main solution to the reduction of functional turnover lies in improving recruitment and selection procedures so that fewer people in the category are appointed in the first place. However, some poorly engineered change management schemes are also sometimes to blame, especially where they result in new work pressures or workplace ethics.

Push factors

With push factors the problem is dissatisfaction with work or the organisation, leading to unwanted turnover. A wide range of issues can be cited to explain such resignations. Insufficient development opportunities, boredom, ineffective supervision, poor levels of employee involvement and straightforward personality clashes are the most common precipitating factors. Organisations can readily address all of these issues. The main reason that so many fail to do so is the absence of mechanisms for picking up signs of dissatisfaction. If there is no opportunity to voice concerns, employees who are unhappy will inevitably start looking elsewhere.

Pull factors

The opposite side of the coin is the attraction of rival employers. Salary levels are often a factor here, employees leaving in order to improve their living standards. In addition there are broader notions of career development, the wish to move into new areas of work for which there are better opportunities elsewhere, the chance to work with particular people, and more practical questions such as commuting time. For the employer losing people as a result of such factors there are two main lines of attack. First, there is a need to be aware of what other employers are offering and to ensure that as far as possible this is matched – or at least that a broadly comparable package of pay and opportunities is offered. The second requirement involves trying to ensure that employees appreciate what they are currently being given. The emphasis here is on effective communication of any 'unique selling points' and of the extent to which opportunities comparable to those offered elsewhere are given.

Activity 13.3	Think about jobs that you or members of your family have left in recent years. What were the key factors that led to the decision to leave? Was there one major factor or did several act together in combination?

When deciding what kind of measures to put in place in order to improve staff retention generally or the retention of particular individuals, organisations need to balance the costs involved against those that are incurred as a direct result of voluntary resignations. Although it is difficult to cost turnover accurately, it is possible to reach a fair estimate by taking into account the range of expenses involved in replacing one individual with another. Once a figure has been calculated for a job, it is relatively straightforward to compute the savings to be gained from a given percentage reduction in annual turnover rates. Figure 13.1 shows the approach to turnover costing recommended by Hugo Fair (1992).

Figure 13.1 A sample form for costing labour turnover

Enter number of employees	_____ (a),
Enter average weekly wage	£ _____ (b),
Multiply (a) x (b)	£ _____ (c),
Multiply (c) x 52	£ _____ (d) = *Total paybill*
Enter current turnover rate	_____ % (e),
Multiply (e) x (a)	_____ (f) = *Staff loss p.a.*
Enter average number of days to replace	_____ (g),
Multiplier rate for overtime/temps.	_____ (h),
Multiply (b) x (h)	£ _____ (i),
Multiply (f) x (g) x [(i)/5]	£ _____ (j) = Immediate cover costs
Preparation and interview time per applicant (days)	_____ (k),
Shortlisted applicants per position	_____ (l),
Enter average manager weekly wage	£ _____ (m),
Multiply (f) x (k) x (l) x [(m)/5]	£ _____ (n) = Interview time costs
Enter average recruitment fees	_____ % (o),
Multiply (d) x (e) x (o)	£ _____ (p) = Recruitment fee costs
Length of induction training (days)	_____ (q),
Frequency of this training (p.a.)	_____ (r),
Multiply [(b)/5] x (q) x [(f)+(r)]	£ _____ (s) = Induction training cost
Duration of learning curve (months)	_____ (t),
Enter non-productive element	_____ % (u),
Multiply (d) x (e) x [(t)/12] x (u)	£ _____ (v) = Non-productive costs
Multiply (t) x (u) (months)	£ _____ (w),
Multiply (d) x (e) x (h) x [(w)/12]	£ _____ (x) = Continuing cover costs
Multiply (g) x [(b)/5] x (f)	£ _____ (y) = Salary savings
Add (j) + (n) + (p) + (s) + (v) + (x) – (y)	£ _____ (z) = *Turnover cost p.a.*

Potential cost saving

Enter expected turnover reduction	_____ % (1),
Multiply (z) x [(1)/(e)]	£ _____ (2) = Labour turnover savings
Enter reduction in replacement time	_____ % (3),
Multiply (j) x (3)	£ _____ (4) = Added cover savings
Add (2) + (4)	£ _____ (5) = *Total savings p.a.*

Source: H. Fair (1992) *Personnel and Profit: The pay-off from people*, p. 41. London: IPM. Used with permission of CIPD Publications.

Staff retention strategies

The straightforward answer to the question of how best to retain staff is to provide them with a better deal, in the broadest sense, than they perceive they could get by working for alternative employers. Terms and conditions play a significant role, but other factors are often more important. For example, there is a need to provide jobs which are satisfying, along with career development opportunities, as much autonomy as is practicable and, above all, competent line management. Indeed, at one level, most of the practices of effective human resource management described in this book can play a part in reducing turnover. Organisations which make use of them will enjoy lower rates than competitors who do not. Below we look at five measures that have been shown to have a positive effect on employee retention, focusing particularly on those practices which are not covered in any great depth elsewhere in the book.

Pay

There is some debate in the retention literature about the extent to which raising pay levels reduces staff turnover. On the one hand there is evidence to show that, on average, employers who offer the most attractive reward packages have lower attrition rates than those who pay poorly (Gomez-Mejia and Balkin 1992, pp. 292–4), an assumption which leads many organisations to use pay rates as their prime weapon in retaining staff (Cappelli 2000, pp. 105–6; IRS 2000a, p. 10; IRS 2000b, p. 9). On the other, there is questionnaire-based evidence which suggests that pay is a good deal less important than other factors in a decision to quit one's job (Bevan *et al.* 1997, p. 25; Hiltrop 1999, p. 424). The consensus among researchers specialising in retention issues is that pay has a role to play as a satisfier, but that it will not usually have an effect when other factors are pushing an individual towards quitting. Raising pay levels may thus result in greater job satisfaction where people are already happy with their work, but it will not deter unhappy employees from leaving. Sturges and Guest (1999), in their study of leaving decisions in the field of graduate employment, summed up their findings as follows:

> As far as they are concerned, while challenging work will compensate for pay, pay will never compensate for having to do boring, unstimulating work.
>
> (Sturges and Guest 1999, p. 19)

Recent research findings thus appear to confirm the views expressed by Herzberg (1966) that pay is a 'hygiene factor' rather than a motivator. This means that it can be a cause of dissatisfaction at work, but not of positive job satisfaction. People may be motivated to leave an employer who is perceived as paying badly, but once they are satisfied with their pay additional increases have little effect.

The other problem with the use of pay increases to retain staff is that it is an approach that is very easily matched by competitors. This is particularly true of 'golden handcuff' arrangements which seek to tie senior staff to an organisation for a number of years by paying substantial bonuses at a defined future date. As Cappelli (2000, p. 106) argues, in a buoyant job market, recruiters simply 'unlock the handcuffs' by offering equivalent signing-on bonuses to people they wish to employ.

It is important that employees do not perceive their employers to be treating them inequitably. Provided pay levels are not considerably lower than those paid by an organisation's labour market competitors, other factors will usually be more important contributors towards high turnover levels. Where the salaries that are paid are already broadly competitive, little purpose is served by increasing them further. The organisation may well make itself more attractive in recruitment terms, but the effect on staff retention will be limited. Moreover, of course, wage costs will increase.

There is potentially more to be gained from enhancing benefits packages, because these are less easily imitated or matched by competitors. Where particular benefits, such as staff discounts, holiday entitlements or private health care

There is no 'right' length for an induction programme. In some jobs it can be accomplished effectively in a few days, for others there is a need for some form of input over a number of weeks. What is important is that individuals are properly introduced both to the organisation and to their particular role within it. These introductons are usually best handled by different people. Organisational induction, because it is given to all new starters, is normally handled centrally by the HR department and takes place in a single place over one or two days. Job-based induction takes longer, will be overseen by the individual's own line manager and will usually involve shadowing colleagues. The former largely takes the form of a presentation, while the latter involves the use of a wider variety of training methods. IRS (2000c, pp. 10–12) draw attention to the recent development of web-based training packages which allow new employees to learn about their organisations and their jobs at their own pace, when they get the opportunity.

WINDOW ON PRACTICE

IRS (2000c, p. 11) describes an original approach taken to the induction of staff at a large Novotel Hotel in London. Unusually for the hotel industry the induction programme here lasts for three weeks. It includes some job shadowing of experienced staff, but also consists of several days spent in a training room learning about the hotel's main services and learning how to deal with difficult customers. A variety of training techniques are used including quizzes, games, discussion forums and role play exercises. The management saw their retention rates increase by 12 per cent after the introduction of the new programme.

Family-friendly HR practices

Labour Force Survey statistics show that between 5 per cent and 10 per cent of employees leave their jobs for 'family or personal reasons' (IRS 1999, p. 6), while Hom and Griffeth (1995, p. 252) quote American research indicating that 33 per cent of women quit jobs to devote more time to their families – a response given by only 1 per cent of men. To these figures can be added those quoted by Gregg and Wadsworth (1999, p. 116) which show average job tenure among women with children in the UK to be over a year shorter than that of women without children and almost two years shorter than that of men. These statistics suggest that one of the more significant reasons for voluntary resignations from jobs is the inability to juggle the demands of a job with those of the family. They indicate that there is a good business case, particularly where staff retention is high on the agenda, for considering ways in which employment can be made more family friendly.

As a result of legislation under the Working Time Regulations 1998 and the Employment Relations Act 1999, UK employers are now obliged by law to provide the following as a minimum floor of rights:

■ 18 weeks' maternity leave for all employees with more than six months' service paid according to a formula set out in the Act;
■ additional unpaid maternity leave (to the twenty-ninth week of a new child's life) for employees with over a year's service;
■ reasonable paid time off for pregnant employees to attend ante-natal clinics;
■ specific health and safety measures for workers who are pregnant or have recently given birth;

- four weeks' paid holiday each year;
- a total of three months' unpaid parental leave for mothers and fathers on the birth or adoption of a child;
- reasonable unpaid time off for employees to deal with family emergencies such as the sickness of a child or dependent relative.

Many employers, however, have decided to go a good deal further down this road than is required by law. The most common example is the provision of more paid maternity leave and the right, where possible, for mothers to return to work on a part time or job-share basis if they so wish. Crèche provision is common in larger workplaces, while others offer childcare vouchers instead. Career breaks are offered by many public sector employers, allowing people to take a few months off without pay and subsequently to return to a similar job with the same organisation. Flexi-time systems such as those described in Chapter 10 are also useful to people with families and may thus serve as a retention tool in some cases. In the USA the literature indicates growing interest in 'elder care' arrangements (Lambert 2000) aimed specifically at providing assistance to those seeking to combine work with responsibility for the care of elderly relatives. An example in the UK is the 'granny crèche' established by Peugeot for employees at its plant in Coventry.

Training and development

There are two widely expressed, but wholly opposed, perspectives on the link between training interventions and employee turnover. On the one hand is the argument that training opportunities enhance commitment to an employer on the part of individual employees making them less likely to leave voluntarily than they would if no training were offered. The alternative view holds that training makes people more employable and hence more likely to leave in order to develop their careers elsewhere. The view is thus put that money spent on training is money wasted because it ultimately benefits other employers.

In a recent article, Green *et al.* (2000, pp. 267–72) report research on perceptions of 1,539 employees on different kinds of training. They found that the overall effect is neutral, 19 per cent of employees saying that training was 'more likely to make them actively look for another job' and 18 per cent saying it was less likely to do so. However, they also found the type of training and the source of sponsorship to be a significant variable. Training which is paid for by the employer is a good deal less likely to raise job mobility than that paid for by the employee or the government. Firm-specific training is also shown in the study to be associated with lower turnover than training which leads to the acquisition of transferable skills. The point is made, however, that whatever the form of training an employer can develop a workforce which is both 'capable and committed' by combining training interventions with other forms of retention initiative.

The most expensive types of training intervention involve long-term courses of study such as an MBA, CIPD or accountancy qualification. In financing such courses, employers are sending a very clear signal to the employees concerned that their contribution is valued and that they can look forward to substantial career advancement if they opt to stay. The fact that leaving will also mean an end to the funding for the course provides a more direct incentive to remain with the sponsoring employer.

WINDOW ON PRACTICE

An interesting approach to improving retention is reported by Cappelli (2000, p. 108) as being used at a computer company in the USA. It is believed to have played a major role in keeping turnover rates among software engineers to 7 per cent – unusually low for computer workers.

The aim has been to work hard at creating a sense of community among employees so that 'leaving the company means leaving your social network of company-sponsored activities'. Strong social ties are fostered by organising all manner of out-of-work activities including sports teams and investment clubs. In addition to this, the company tries to place employees in closely knit teams when they are at work. Because team members rely so much on one another, it makes people think twice about resigning and abandoning their team-mates.

Summary propositions

13.1 Staff turnover tends to decrease in recessions and increase during economic booms. Contrary to much popular perception, average job tenure has not reduced substantially over the past thirty years.

13.2 Retention rates vary very considerably between industries and between different regions.

13.3 While there are arguments that can be deployed in favour of modest staff turnover, it is generally agreed that too great a rate is damaging for an organisation.

13.4 In planning retention initiatives it is important both to analyse the causes of turnover and to calculate the current costs associated with each voluntary resignation.

13.5 Specific programmes which lead to improved retention include flexible benefits, better induction, the effective management of expectations, family-friendly initiatives and training opportunities.

References

Bevan, S., Barber, L. and Robinson, D. (1997) *Keeping the Best: a practical guide to retaining key employees.* Brighton: Institute for Employment Research.

Cappelli, P. (2000) 'A market-driven approach to retaining talent', *Harvard Business Review*, January/February, pp. 103–11.

Carroll, M., Marchington, M., Earnshaw, J. and Taylor, S. (1999) 'Recruitment in small firms: processes, methods and problems', *Employee Relations*, Vol. 21, No. 3, pp. 236–50.

Fair, H. (1992) *Personnel and Profit: The pay-off from people.* London: IPM.

Gomez-Mejia, L. and Balkin, D. (1992) *Compensation, Organizational Strategy and Firm Performance.* Cincinnati: South Western College Publishing.

Green, F., Felstead, A., Mayhew, K. and Pick, A. (2000) 'The impact of training on labour mobility: individual and firm-level evidence from Britain', *British Journal of Industrial Relations*, Vol. 38, No. 2.

Gregg, P. and Wadsworth, J. (1999) 'Job tenure, 1975–98', in P. Gregg and J. Wadsworth (eds), *The State of Working Britain.* Manchester: Manchester University Press.

Herzberg, F. (1966) *Work and the Nature of Man.* Cleveland, Ohio: World Publishing.

Hiltrop, J.-M. (1999) 'The quest for the best: human resource practices to attract and retain talent', *European Management Journal*, Vol. 17, No. 4, pp. 423–31.

Hom, P. and Griffeth, R. (1995) *Employee Turnover*. Cincinnati: South Western College Publishing.

IDS (1995) 'The Jobs Mythology', *IDS Focus 74*, March.

IDS (2000) 'Improving Staff Retention', *IDS Study 692*, July.

IRS (1999) 'Benchmarking labour turnover: annual guide 1999/2000', *Employee Development Bulletin 118*, October.

IRS (2000a) 'Employee Retention 1 – the tools and techniques', *Employee Development Bulletin 128*, pp. 6–10, August.

IRS (2000b) 'Retention 2 – effective methods', *Employee Development Bulletin 129*, pp. 6–16, September.

IRS (2000c) 'Improving retention and performance through induction', *Employee Development Bulletin 130*, pp. 10–16, October.

Jenner, S and Taylor, S. (2000) *Recruiting, Developing and Retaining Graduate Talent*. London: Financial Times/Prentice Hall.

Lambert, S. (2000) 'Added benefits: The link between work-life benefits and organizational citizen behavior', *Academy of Management Journal*, Vol. 43, No. 5, pp. 801–15.

Medows, P. (1999) *The Flexible Labour Market: Implications for Pensions Provision*. London: National Association of Pension Funds.

Ritzer, G. (1996) *The Macdonaldisation of Society: an investigation into the changing character of contemporary social life*, Revised edition. Thousand Oaks, Cal.: Pine Forge.

Sturges, J. and Guest, D. (1999) *Shall I Stay or Should I go?* Warwick: Association of Graduate Recruiters.

Taylor, S. (2000) 'Occupational pensions and employee retention: debate and evidence', *Employee Relations*, Vol. 22, No. 3, pp. 246–59.

Thompson, H. (2000) 'If you leave me now . . .', *Daily Telegraph*, 2 November 2000.

Wanous, J.P. (1992) *Recruitment, Selection, Orientation and Socialization of Newcomers*. Reading, Mass.: Addison Wesley.

Williams, M. (2000) *The War for Talent*. London: CIPD.

Woodruffe, C. (1999) *Winning the Talent War*. Chichester: Wiley.

General discussion topics

1 What are the main reasons for the trends in job tenure illustrated in Table 13.1?

2 Staff turnover is generally low during recessions, but it increases substantially in firms which get into financial difficulty. What factors account for this phenomenon?

3 Think about your own experiences at work or those of close friends and family. What were the key factors that affected decisions to leave a particular job? What, if anything, could the employer have done to ensure that no resignation took place?

Chapter 14 Ending the contract

In the last chapter we looked at situations in which employees decide to end their contracts of employment by giving their employers notice. Here we focus on circumstances when the contract is brought to an end by the employer through a dismissal of one kind or another – something that over a million employees experience in the UK each year (DTI 1999). In some cases employees are happy to leave (or at least not unhappy) such as when they are retiring or when they are due to receive a large redundancy payment. More common, however, are situations where the dismissee is distinctly unhappy about the contract being brought to an end. When someone feels that they have been treated unfairly in terms of the reason for or the manner of their dismissal they can take their case to an employment tribunal. In practice, between 5 per cent and 10 per cent of all dismissed workers who qualify do bring such claims (DTI 1999). If someone wins their case they may ask to be reinstated, but will usually settle for a compensation payment. The size of such awards is not generally substantial (around £3,000 on average), but occasionally people are awarded large sums. Whatever the final outcome there are often additional legal costs for the employer to bear, not to mention the loss of a great deal of management time. An organisation's reputation as a good employer can also be damaged by adverse publicity arising from such cases. Employers generally take careful account of the requirements of the law when dismissing employees. The alternative is to run the risk of being summoned to an employment tribunal and possibly losing the case.

In the UK there are three forms of dismissal claim that can be brought to a tribunal. Rights associated with the law of **wrongful dismissal** are the longest established. A person who claims wrongful dismissal complains that the way that they were dismissed breached the terms of their contract of employment. **Constructive dismissal** occurs when someone feels forced to resign as a direct result of their employer's actions. In this area the law aims to deter employers from seeking to avoid dismissing people by pushing them into resignation. The third category, **unfair dismissal**, is by far the most common. It is best defined as a dismissal which falls short of the expectations of the law as laid down in the Employment Rights Act 1996. We return to wrongful and constructive dismissals later in the chapter; we start by reviewing the principles that govern the law of unfair dismissal.

Unfair dismissal

The law of unfair dismissal dates from 1971 since when it has been amended a number of times. Although new additions and the outcomes of leading cases have made it more complex than it was originally, the basic principles have stood the test of time and remain in place.

In most circumstances the right to bring a claim of unfair dismissal applies to employees who have completed a year's continuous service with their employer on the date their contract was terminated. This allows the employer a period of 12 months to assess whether or not an individual employee is suitable before the freedom to dismiss is restricted. For a number of years until 1999 the time limit was two years. In reducing the period, the government brought an additional 2.8 million more people within the scope of unfair dismissal law (DTI 1999).

At the time of writing (early 2001) the right not to be unfairly dismissed was not available for people who were over the age of 65 or 'the normal retiring age' in a particular employment. It seems likely, however, that the latter provision will soon be removed from the statutes as a result of new measures outlawing age discrimination. These restrictions on qualification apply except where the reason for the dismissal is one of those listed below which are classed as 'automatically unfair' or 'inadmissible'. A further requirement is that the claim form is lodged at the tribunal office before three months have elapsed from the date of dismissal. Unless there are exceptional circumstances justifying the failure to submit a claim before the deadline, applications received after three months are ruled out of time.

Before a case comes to tribunal, officers of the Advisory, Conciliation and Arbitration Service (ACAS) will often try to help the parties reach a settlement. The papers of all cases lodged with the employment tribunals' offices are sent to ACAS with a view to conciliation taking place ahead of a tribunal hearing. As a result the majority of cases either get settled or are withdrawn without the need for the parties to attend a full hearing.

When faced with a claim of unfair dismissal, an employment tribunal asks two separate questions:

1 Was the reason for the dismissal one which is classed by the law as legitimate?
2 Did the employer act reasonably in carrying out the dismissal?

Where the answer to the first question is 'no', there is no need to ask the second because the dismissed employee will already have won his/her case. Interestingly the burden of proof shifts as the tribunal moves from considering the first to the second question. It is for the employer to satisfy the tribunal that it dismissed the employee for a legitimate reason. The burden of proof then becomes neutral when the question of reasonableness is addressed.

Activity 14.1

Consider the working activities of some of your colleagues (and perhaps your own working activities). What examples are there of behaviour that you feel justify dismissal? Make a list of your ideas and check them when you have finished this chapter and see how many might be classified by a tribunal as unfair dismissals.

Automatically unfair reasons

Certain reasons for dismissal are declared in law to be inadmissable or automatically unfair. Where the tribunal finds that one of these was the principal reason for the dismissal, they find in favour of the applicant (i.e. the ex-employee) whatever the circumstances of the case. In practice, therefore, there is no defence that an employer can make to explain its actions that will be acceptable to the tribunal. Some of these relate to other areas of employment law such as non-discrimination, working time and the minimum wage, which are discussed in more detail elsewhere in this book. The list of automatically unfair reasons for dismissal has grown steadily in recent years as new employment rights have come on to the statute book; in 2000 it was as follows:

■ on grounds of sex, marital status or gender reassignment;
■ on racial grounds;
■ on grounds of disability (unless objectively justified);
■ on grounds of having commited a criminal offence where the conviction is spent;
■ on grounds of religion or political belief (in Northern Ireland only);
■ on grounds of pregnancy or maternity;
■ on grounds of being a part-time worker;
■ for exercising the right to parental leave or time off for dependants;
■ for carrying out duties as a safety representative;
■ for carrying out duties as a pension fund trustee;
■ for refusing to work on a Sunday (retail workers only);
■ for taking part, or proposing to take part in lawful trade union activity;
■ for joining or refusing to join a trade union;
■ for taking part in official industrial action (i.e. organised and approved by a trade union executive) during the first eight weeks that the action takes place;
■ for asserting a statutory right.

This last provision relates to the various other employment protection rights set out in statute. It is designed to ensure that no one is victimised by being dismissed (unfairly or constructively) simply because they sought to exercise their rights under employment law.

The following are the principal Acts covered:

■ Trade Union and Labour Relations (Consolidation) Act 1992;
■ Employment Rights Act 1996;
■ Working Time Regulations 1998;
■ Public Interest Disclosure Act 1998 (often known as the 'Whistleblowers' Act);
■ National Minimum Wage Act 1998;
■ Tax Credits Act 1999;
■ Employment Relations Act 1999.

A further situation which is classed as automatically unfair is a dismissal which occurs directly as a result of a business changing hands (known as a Transfer of Undertakings case). Dismissals for this reason will be judged as unfair by employment tribunals unless it can be shown that the dismissals were for economic, technical or organisational reasons. Unlike the other automatically unfair dismissals, transfer of undertakings cases can only be brought by ex-employees who have completed a year's continuous service and are under the 'normal' age of retirement at the time of their dismissal.

Potentially fair reasons

From an employer's perspective it is important to be able to satisfy the tribunal that the true reason for the dismissal was one of those reasons classed as potentially fair in unfair dismissal law. Only once this has been achieved can the second question (the issue of reasonableness) be addressed. The potentially fair grounds for dismissal are as follows:

■ **Lack of capability or qualifications**: If an employee lacks the skill, aptitude or physical health to carry out the job, then there is a potentially fair ground for dismissal.
■ **Misconduct**: This category covers the range of behaviours that we examine in considering the grievance and discipline processes: disobedience, absence, insubordination and criminal acts. It can also include taking industrial action.
■ **Redundancy:** Where an employee's job ceases to exist, it is potentially fair to dismiss the employee for redundancy.
■ **Statutory bar:** When employees cannot continue to discharge their duties without breaking the law, they can be fairly dismissed. Most cases of this kind follow disqualification of drivers following convictions for speeding, drunk or dangerous driving. Other common cases involve foreign nationals whose work permits have been terminated.
■ **Some other substantial reason**: This most intangible category is introduced in order to cater for genuinely fair dismissals for reasons so diverse that they could not realistically be listed. Examples have been security of commercial information (where an employee's husband set up a rival company) or employee refusal to accept altered working conditions.

Determining reasonableness

Having decided that potentially fair grounds for the dismissal exist, the tribunal then proceeds to consider whether the dismissal is fair in the circumstances. There are two questions: was the decision reasonable in the circumstances, and was the dismissal carried out in line with the procedure? The second is the easier question to answer as procedural actions are straightforward, and the dismissal should be procedurally fair if the procedure has been carefully followed without any short cuts. When considering the first, tribunal members pay particular attention to consistency of treatment, seeking to satisfy themselves that the dismissed employee has not been treated more severely than others have been in similar circumstances. They are also required to have regard to the size and resources of the employer concerned. Higher standards are thus expected of a large PLC with a well-staffed HR department than of a small owner-managed business employing a handful of people. The former, for example, might be expected to give two or three warnings and additional training before dismissing someone on grounds of incapability. One simple warning might suffice in a small business which relied heavily on an acceptable level of performance from the individual concerned.

The importance of procedure was reaffirmed by the House of Lords in the leading case of *Polkey* v. *AE Dayton Services* (1987). This particular case concerned the fairness of a redundancy when the employer had failed to consult the employee and had also failed to give proper notice. In giving judgment Lord Mackay ruled that the fact that consultation would have made no difference to the final outcome did not render the dismissal fair.

The extent to which employers find themselves in difficulty because of not following procedure can be considerable. Jill Earnshaw (1997) carried out research for the DTI on the part played by procedural defects in unfair dismissal claims. In 40 per cent of the cases reviewed the finding went in favour of the ex-employee. The typical failings were:

- no chance given to the applicants to give an explanation;
- dismissal without any prior disciplinary hearing;
- no procedure in cases involving senior staff;
- the procedure used did not comply with the respondent's own rules;
- unwillingness to have a procedure because of disliking formality; and
- no chance for the applicant to rectify their shortcomings.

The standard used by the tribunal in reaching decisions about the fairness of a dismissal is that of the reasonable employer. Tribunal members are not required to judge cases on the basis of what they would have done in the circumstances or what the best employers would have done. Instead they have to ask themselves whether what the employer did in the circumstances of the time fell within a possible band of reasonable responses. In practice this means that the employer wins the case if it can show that the decision to dismiss was one that a reasonable employer *might* conceivably have taken.

In this book we have separated the consideration of discipline from the consideration of dismissal in order to concentrate on the practical aspects of discipline (putting things right) rather than the negative aspects (getting rid of the problem). The two cannot, however, be separated in practice and the question of dismissal needs to be reviewed in the light of the material in Chapter 32.

WINDOW ON PRACTICE

In 1999 the Employment Appeal Tribunal made a landmark decision in the case of *Haddon* v. *Van den Bergh Foods* only to be overturned a few months later in another case. Mr Haddon was dismissed in extraordinary circumstances when he failed to return to work after having attended a ceremony at which he had been presented with a long service award. Rather than completing the last few hours of his shift, he decided to take the time off. This was contrary to the workplace rules; so he was fired. When the case came to an employment tribunal Mr Haddon lost on the grounds that the employer's decision, though harsh, fell within the band of reasonable responses open to an employer in the circumstances. He appealed to the EAT, who took the opportunity not only to overturn the original decision, but also to hold that the long-established 'band of reasonable responses' test was unhelpful. Instead, they suggested that tribunals should simply make a general judgment about whether or not an employer had acted reasonably, taking into account their own opinion about what is appropriate.

For a few months the new ruling stood and tribunals began to use it in order to find in favour of ex-employees in many more cases than had been their practice previously. In March 2000, the EAT (with a new chairman) overturned its own decision in Haddon's case, putting back the band of reasonable responses test in the case of *Midland Bank* v. *Madden* (IRS 2000a). It argued that only a higher court, such as the Court of Appeal or the House of Lords, could discard the test, so it must remain until this occurs.

Lack of capability or qualifications

The first aspect of capability relates to skill or aptitude. Although employers have the right and opportunity to test an applicant's suitability for a particular post before that individual is engaged, or before promotion, the law recognises that mistakes may be made so that dismissal can be an appropriate remedy for the error, if the unsuitability is gross and beyond redemption. In order for such a dismissal to be fair and reasonable at least one warning has to be given and a reasonable opportunity to improve before the dismissal is implemented.

Where an employee is going through a period of probation at the time of termination, the following are appropriate check questions:

1 Has the employer shown that reasonable steps were taken to maintain the appraisal of the probationer through the period of probation?
2 Was there guidance by advice or warning when it would have been useful or fair to provide it?
3 Did an appropriate person make an honest effort to determine whether the probationer came up to the required standard, after reviewing the appraisals made by supervisors and other facts recorded about the probationer?

The employer will always need to demonstrate the employee's unsuitability to the satisfaction of the tribunal by producing evidence of that unsuitability. This evidence must not be undermined by, for instance, giving the employee a glowing testimonial at the time of dismissal or by the presence of positive appraisal reports on the individual's personal file. Lack of skill or aptitude is a fair ground when the lack can be demonstrated and where the employer has not contributed to it by, for instance, ignoring it for a long period. Normally there must be the chance to state a case and/or improve before the dismissal will be procedurally fair. Redeployment to a more suitable job is also an option employers are expected to consider before taking the decision to dismiss.

The second aspect of capability is qualifications: the degree, diploma or other paper qualification needed to qualify the individual to do the work for which employed. The simple cases are those of misrepresentation, where an employee claims qualifications he or she does not have. More difficult are the situations where the employee cannot acquire the necessary qualifications.

WINDOW ON PRACTICE

Dr Al-Tikriti was a senior registrar employed by the South Western Regional Health Authority. The practice of the authority was to allow registrars three attempts at passing the examination of the Royal College of Pathologists. Dr Al-Tikriti failed on the third attempt and was subsequently dismissed. He claimed that the dismissal was unfair on the grounds that he had had insufficient training to pass the exams. The tribunal, having heard evidence from the Royal College, decided that the training had been adequate and found the dismissal to have been fair (*Al-Tikriti* v. *South Western RHA* (1986)).

The third aspect of employee capability is health. It is potentially fair to dismiss someone on the grounds of ill health which renders the employee incapable of discharging the contract of employment. Even the most distressing dismissal can be legally admissible, provided that it is not too hasty and that there is consideration of alternative employment. Employers are expected, however, to take account of any medical advice available to them before dismissing someone on grounds of ill health. Companies with occupational health services are well placed to obtain detailed medical reports to help in such judgements but the decision to terminate someone's employment is ultimately for the manager to take and, if necessary, to justify at a tribunal. Medical evidence will be sought and has to be carefully considered but dismissal remains an employer's decision, not a medical decision.

Normally, absences through sickness have to be frequent or prolonged in order for dismissal on the grounds of such absence to be judged fair, although absence which seriously interferes with the running of a business may be judged fair even if it is neither frequent nor prolonged. In all cases the employee must be consulted before being dismissed.

Drawing on the judgment of the EAT in the leading case of *Egg Stores* v. *Leibovici* in 1977, Selwyn lists nine questions that have to be asked to determine the potential fairness of dismissing someone after long-term sickness:

> (a) how long has the employment lasted (b) how long had it been expected the employment would continue (c) what is the nature of the job (d) what was the nature, effect and length of the illness (e) what is the need of the employer for the work to be done, and to engage a replacement to do it (f) if the employer takes no action, will he incur obligations in respect of redundancy payments or compensation for unfair dismissal (g) are wages continuing to be paid (h) why has the employer dismissed (or failed to do so) and (i) in all the circumstances, could a reasonable employer have been expected to wait any longer?   (Selwyn 1985, p. 241)

This case was of frustration of contract, and there is always an emphasis in all tribunal hearings that the decision should be based on the facts of the particular situation of the dismissal that is being considered, rather than on specific precedents. For this reason the nine questions are no more than useful guidelines for managers to consider: they do not constitute 'the law' on the matter.

A different situation is where an employee is frequently absent for short spells. Here too it is potentially reasonable to dismiss, but only after proper consideration of the illnesses and after warning the employee of the consequences if their attendance record does not improve. As is made clear by Duggan (1999, pp. 140–1) each case has to be decided on its own merits. Medical evidence must be sought and a judgement reached about how likely it is that high levels of absence will continue in the future. The fact that an employee is wholly fit at the time of his/her dismissal does not mean that it is necessarily unfair. What matters is the overall attendance record and its impact on the organisation.

In another leading case, that of *International Sports Ltd* v. *Thomson* (1980), the employer dismissed an employee who had been frequently absent with a series of minor ailments ranging from althrugia of one knee, anxiety and nerves to bronchitis, cystitis, dizzy spells, dyspepsia and flatulence. All of these were covered by medical notes. (While pondering the medical note for flatulence, you will be interested to know that althrugia is water on the knee.) The employer issued a series of warnings and the company dismissed the employee after consulting its medical adviser, who saw no reason to examine the employee as the illnesses had no connecting medical theme and were not chronic. The Employment Appeals Tribunal held that this dismissal was fair because proper warning had been given and because the attendance record was deemed so poor as not to be acceptable to a reasonable employer.

The law on ill-health dismissals described above is well established. In recent years, however, a major change has occurred which employers must take account of – the passing of the Disability Discrimination Act 1995 which came into operation in 1997. In Chapter 21 we look at this important piece of legislation in detail. Here it is simply necessary to state that dismissing someone who is disabled according to the definition given in the Act, without first considering whether adjustments to working practices or the working environment would allow them to continue working, is now unlawful. Reasonable adjustments might well include tolerance of a relatively high level of absence, especially where the employer is large enough to be able to cope perfectly well in the circumstances. Employers are well advised to pay particular attention to disability discrimination issues when dismissing people on grounds of ill health because the level of compensation that can be awarded by tribunals in such cases is considerably higher than it is for unfair dismissal.

WINDOW ON PRACTICE

In 1998 Mr Kirker, a man with a visual impairment, was selected for redundancy by managers at British Sugar PLC. The selection criteria included assessments of competence and potential, on both of which measures he scored poorly because of his disability. He took his case to an employment tribunal and won. It was ruled that in dismissing him, the employer had unlawfully discriminated on grounds of disability. Had it not been for the visual impairment, he would have been retained.

There are no limits on the amount of compensation that can be awarded in disability discrimination cases, so the tribunal can make an award based on their estimate of the true level of financial loss suffered by the individual concerned. In Mr Kirker's case the figure was £103,146. British Sugar subsequently lost their appeal to the Employment Appeal Tribunal.

Source: *British Sugar* v. *Kirker* [1998] IRLR 624.

Misconduct

The law expects employers to make a distinction between two classes of misconduct when dismissing employees or considering doing so.

1 **Gross misconduct**. This occurs when an employee commits an offence which is sufficiently serious to justify summary dismissal. To qualify, the employee must have acted in such a way as to have breached either an express term of their contract or one of the common law duties owed by an employee to an employer (see Chapter 10).
2 **Ordinary misconduct**. This involves lesser transgressions, such as minor breaches of rules and relatively insignificant acts of disobedience, insubordination, lateness, forgetfulness or rudeness. In such cases the employer is deemed by the courts to be acting unreasonably if it dismisses as a result of a first offence. The dismissal would only be fair if, having been formally warned at least once, the employee failed to improve his/her conduct.

Employers have a wide degree of discretion when it comes to deciding what exactly does and does not constitute gross misconduct, and this will vary from workplace to workplace. For example, a distinction can be made between smoking in an office where there is a no-smoking policy (ordinary misconduct) and smoking on the factory floor near to combustible materials (gross misconduct). While much depends on the circumstances, the tribunals also look carefully at an employer's established policies on matters of conduct:

> Where the disciplinary rules spell out clearly the type of conduct that will warrant dismissal then a dismissal for this reason may be fair. Conversely, if the rules are silent or ambiguous as to whether particular conduct warrants dismissal, a dismissal for a first offence may be unfair. (Duggan 1999, p. 178)

It is important, therefore, for employers to set out in writing what standards of conduct they expect, to make clear what will be regarded as 'sackable misconduct', and to ensure that everyone is aware of these rules.

The second key principle in misconduct cases concerns procedure. Whether the individual is dismissed summarily for gross misconduct or after a number of warnings for ordinary misconduct, the tribunals are only able to judge the dismissal fair if a reasonable procedure has been used. We look in more detail at disciplinary procedures in Chapter 32. Here it is necessary to note the main questions that an employment tribunal asks when faced with such cases:

1 Was the accusation thoroughly, promptly and properly investigated by managers before the decision was made to dismiss or issue a formal warning?
2 Was a formal hearing held at which the accused employee was given the opportunity to state their case and challenge evidence brought forward by managers?
3 Was the employee concerned permitted to be accompanied at the hearing by a colleague or trade union representative?
4 Was the employee treated consistently when compared with other employees who had committed similar acts of misconduct in the past?

Only if the answers to all these questions is 'yes' will a tribunal find a dismissal fair. They do not, however, expect employers to adhere to very high standards of evidence gathering such as those employed by the police in criminal investigations. Here, as throughout employment law, the requirement is for the employer to act reasonably in all the circumstances, conforming to the principles of natural justice and doing what it thought to be right at the time, given the available facts.

Conversely, if an employee is found guilty by court proceedings, this does not automatically justify fair dismissal; it must still be procedurally fair and reasonable. A theft committed off duty and away from the workforce is not necessarily grounds for dismissal; it all depends on the nature of the work carried out by the employee concerned. For example, it might well be reasonable to dismiss members of staff with responsibility for cash if they commit an offence of dishonesty while off duty.

On the other hand, evidence that would not be sufficient to bring a prosecution may be sufficient to sustain a fair dismissal. Clocking-in offences will normally merit dismissal. Convictions for other offences like drug handling or indecency will only justify dismissal if the nature of the offence will have some bearing on the work done by the employee. For someone like an instructor of apprentices it might justify summary dismissal, but in other types of employment it would be unfair, just as it would be unfair to dismiss an employee for a driving offence when there was no need for driving in the course of normal duties and there were other means of transport for getting to work.

WINDOW ON PRACTICE

In the past few years employment tribunals have had to come to grips with a new type of dismissal case – situations in which people are fired for downloading and storing pornographic images from the internet. Tribunals have had to consider whether or not such actions constitute gross misconduct (leading to summary dismissal without notice), or whether they should be considered as ordinary misconduct, in which case summary dismissal for a first offence would be regarded as being unfair.

Cases have been decided in different ways depending on the clarity of established rules and procedural matters. In *Parr* v. *Derwentside District Council* (1998), Mr Parr was summarily dismissed having been caught by his employers accessing pornography from his computer while at work. He claimed that he had visited the site concerned by accident, had got himself stuck in it and had subsequently 'revisited it only because he was disturbed by the prospect that entry could easily be made by children'. His claim for unfair dismissal failed because the employers had used a fair procedure and because they were able to show that Mr Parr had broken established codes of conduct.

By contrast, in *Dunn* v. *IBM UK Ltd* (1998), a summary dismissal occurring in similar circumstances was found to fall outside the 'band of reasonable responses'. In this case the employers were found not to have investigated the matter properly and not to have convened a fair disciplinary hearing – the whole matter was handled far too hastily. Moreover, there was no company policy on internet usage for Mr Dunn to have broken and he was unaware that he had done anything that would be construed as gross misconduct. He won his case, but had his compensation reduced by 50 per cent on the grounds that he was partly responsible for his own dismissal.

In a third case, *Humphries* v. *VH Barnett & Co* (1998), a tribunal stated that in normal circumstances the act of accessing pornography from the internet while at work should not be construed as gross misconduct unless such a policy was made clear to employees and established as a workplace rule. However, in this case, the tribunal decided that the pictures downloaded were so obscene that Mr Humphries could be legitimately treated as having commited an act of gross misconduct.

Source: IDS (1999).

Redundancy

Dismissal for redundancy is protected by compensation for unfair redundancy, compensation for genuine redundancy and the right to consultation before the redundancy takes place:

> An employee who is dismissed shall be taken to be dismissed by reason of redundancy if the dismissal is attributable wholly or mainly to:
> (a) the fact that his employer has ceased, or intends to cease, to carry on the business for the purposes of which the employee was employed by him, or has ceased, or intends to cease, to carry on that business in the place where the employee was so employed, or
> (b) the fact that the requirements of that business for employees to carry out work of a particular kind, or for employees to carry out work of a particular kind in the place where he was so employed, have ceased or are expected to cease or diminish. (Employment Rights Act 1996, s. 139(1))

Apart from certain specialised groups of employees, anyone who has been continuously employed for two years or more is guaranteed a compensation payment from an employer, if dismissed for redundancy. The compensation is assessed on a sliding scale relating to length of service, age and rate of pay per week. If the employer wishes to escape the obligation to compensate, then it is necessary to show that the reason for dismissal was something other than redundancy.

Although the legal rights relating to redundancy have not altered for 35 years, there have been persistent problems of interpretation, different courts reaching different decisions when faced with similar sets of circumstances (see IRS 2000b). In 1999 the House of Lords provided some long-needed clarification of key issues in the cases of *Murray et al* v. *Foyle Meats Ltd*, where it was decided that tribunals should look at the actual facts of someone's working situation rather than at their written contractual terms when deciding whether or not their jobs were redundant. In so doing it confirmed that the practice of 'bumping', where the employer dismisses a person whose job is remaining to retain the services of another employee whose job is disappearing, is acceptable under the statutory definition. The questions laid out by the Employment Appeals Tribunal (EAT) in *Safeway* v. *Burrell* (1997) are thus now confirmed as those that tribunals should ask when considering these cases:

1 Has the employee been dismissed?
2 Has there been an actual or prospective cessation or diminution in the requirements for employees to carry out work of a particular kind?
3 Is the dismissal wholly or mainly attributable to the state of affairs?

The employer has to consult with the individual employee before dismissal takes place, but there is also a separate legal obligation to consult with recognised trade unions or some other body of employee representatives where no union is recognised. If 20 or more employees are to be made redundant, then the employer must give written notice of intention to any recognised unions concerned and the Department of Trade and Industry at least 30 days before the first dismissal. If it is proposed to make more than 100 employees redundant within a three-month period, then 90 days' advance notice must be given. Having done this, the employer has a legal duty to consult on the redundancies. There is no obligation to negotiate with employees, merely to explain, listen to comments and reply with reasons. Employees also have the right to reasonable time off with pay during their redundancy notice so that they can seek other work.

One of the most difficult aspects of redundancy for the employer is the selection of who should go. The traditional approach provides that people should leave on a last-in-first-out basis, or LIFO, as this provides a rough-and-ready justice with which it is difficult to argue. In recent years, however, an increasing number of employers are using a mix of other criteria, including skill, competence and attendance record. A third approach involves drawing up a new post-redundancy organisation structure and inviting everyone to apply for the jobs that will remain. In principle all are acceptable as far as the law is concerned provided they are carried out objectively and consistently.

Increasingly, employers are trying to avoid enforced redundancy by a range of strategies, such as not replacing people who leave, early retirement and voluntary redundancy. The large scale of redundancies in recent years has produced a variety of managerial initiatives to mitigate the effects. One of the most constructive has been a redundancy counselling or outplacement service. Sometimes this is administered by the HR department, but many organisations use external services. Contrary to some popular perception there is no legal requirement to offer such services or to ask for volunteers before carrying through a programme of compulsory redundancies.

Some other substantial reason

As the law of unfair dismissal has evolved since 1971 the most controversial area has been the category of potentially fair dismissals known as 'some other substantial reason'. Many commentators see this as a catch-all or dustbin category which enables employers to dismiss virtually anyone provided a satisfactory business case can be made. All manner of cases have been successfully defended under this heading including the following: dismissals resulting from personality clashes, pressure to dismiss from subordinates or customers, disclosure of damaging information, the dismissal of a man whose wife worked for a rival firm, and the dismissal of a landlord's wife following her husband's dismissal on grounds of capability.

The majority of cases brought under this heading, however, result from business reorganisations where there is no redundancy. These often occur when the employer seeks to alter terms and conditions of employment and cannot secure the employee's agreement. Such circumstances can result in the dismissal of the employee together with an offer of re-employment on new contractual terms. Such dismissals are judged fair provided a sound business reason exists to justify the changes envisaged. It will usually be necessary to consult prior to the reorganisation but the tribunal will not base its judgment on whether the employee acted reasonably in refusing new terms and conditions. The test laid down in *Hollister* v. *The National Farmers' Union* (1979) by the Court of Appeal merely requires the employer to demonstrate that the change would bring clear organisational advantage. According to the barrister John Bowers:

> A review of the re-organisation case law shows that the EAT and Court of Appeal appear to accept as wholly valid employers' claims that to compete effectively in a free market they must be allowed latitude to trim and make efficient their workforce and work methods without being hampered by laws protecting their workers.
>
> (Bowers 1990)

Written statement of reasons

The Employment Rights Act 1996 (s. 92) gives employees the right to obtain from their employer a written statement of the reasons for their dismissal, if they are dismissed after completing a year's continuous service. If asked, the employer must provide the statement within 14 days. If it is not provided, the employee can complain to an employment tribunal that the statement has been refused and the tribunal will award the employee two weeks' pay if they find the complaint justified. The same right applies where a fixed-term contract is not renewed after having expired. The employee can also complain, and receive the same award, if the employer's reasons are untrue or inadequate – provided, again, that the tribunal agrees.

Such an award is in addition to anything the tribunal may decide about the unfairness of the dismissal, if the employee complains about that. The main purpose of this provision is to enable the employee to test whether there is a reasonable case for an unfair dismissal complaint or not. Although the statement is admissible as evidence in tribunal proceedings, the tribunal will not necessarily be bound by what the statement contains. If the tribunal members were to decide that the reasons for dismissal were other than stated, then the management case would be jeopardised.

Constructive dismissal

When the behaviour of the management causes the employee to resign, the ex-employee may still be able to claim dismissal on the grounds that the behaviour of the employer constituted a repudiation of the contract, leaving the employee with no alternative but to resign. The employee may then be able to claim that the dismissal was unfair. It is not sufficient for the employer simply to be awkward or whimsical; the employer's conduct must amount to a significant breach, going to the root of the contract, such as physical assault, demotion, reduction in pay, change in location of work or significant change in duties. The breach must, however, be significant, so that a slight lateness in paying wages would not involve a breach, neither would a temporary change in place of work.

Some of the more interesting constructive dismissal cases concern claims that implied terms of contract have been breached, such as the employer's duty to maintain safe systems of working or mutual trust and confidence.

WINDOW ON PRACTICE

In 1994 a former manager of an off-licence called Mrs Gullyes won a case of constructive dismissal. She argued successfully that her employer had breached an implied term of her contract and that this had led directly to her resignation.

At the time of her resignation, Mrs Gullyes had been employed as a branch manager for four years – a job she carried out with conspicuous success. As a result she had been promoted into a manager's role in a larger branch with severe staffing problems. She accepted the new post with some reluctance after agreeing with the company that she could transfer again if things did not work out.

She found the new job hard from the start, finding herself working 76 hours a week and gaining insufficient help from other members of staff. After a few months she went away on holiday, returning to find that two of her staff had been transferred to other branches in her absence. At this point she requested a transfer herself and was refused. She resigned and brought a claim of constructive dismissal.

Mrs Gullyes won her case by arguing that the company had breached its common law duty to provide adequate support to her in the new job. The case was appealed to the EAT, where she won again.

Source: L. Macdonald (1998) 'Termination of Employment: Breach of contract, constructive dismissal and wrongful dismissal', *Personnel Manager's Fact Finder*. London: Gee Publishing. *Whitbread/Thresher* v. *Gullyes* (1994).

Constructive dismissal, like unfair dismissal, dates from 1971. It too only applies to employees who have completed a year's continuous service. The cases are harder for employees to win and easier for employers to defend because of the need to establish that a dismissal has taken place, before issues of reasonableness in the circumstances are addressed. The burden of proof is on the employee to show that they were forced into resigning as a result of a repudiatory breach on the part of the employer.

Compensation for dismissal

Having found in favour of the applicant in cases of unfair or constructive dismissal, the tribunal can make two types of decision: either they can order that the ex-employee be re-employed or they can award some financial compensation from the ex-employer for the loss that the employee has suffered. Originally it was intended that re-employment should be the main remedy, although this was not previously available under earlier legislation. In practice, however, the vast majority of ex-employees (over 95 per cent) want compensation.

Tribunals will not order re-employment unless the dismissed employee wants it, and tribunals can choose between reinstatement or re-engagement. In reinstatement the old job is given back to the employee under the same terms and conditions, plus any increments, etc., to which the individual would have become entitled had the dismissal not occurred, plus any arrears of payment that would have been received. The situation is just as it would have been, including all rights deriving from length of service, if the dismissal had not taken place. The alternative of re-engagement will be that the employee is employed afresh in a job comparable to the last one (usually in a different department), but without continuity of employment. The decision as to which of the two to order will depend on assessment of the practicability of the alternatives, the wishes of the unfairly dismissed employee and the natural justice of the award taking account of the ex-employee's behaviour.

Tribunals calculate the level of compensation under a series of headings. First is the **basic award** which is based on the employee's age and length of service. It is calculated in the same way as statutory redundancy payments;

■ half a week's pay for every year of service below the age of 22;
■ one week's pay for every year of service between the ages of 22 and 41;
■ one and a half weeks' pay for every year of service over the age of 41.

The basic award is limited, however, because tribunals can only take into account a maximum of 20 years' service when calculating the figure to be awarded. A maximum weekly salary figure is also imposed by the Treasury. This was £230 in 2001. The maximum basic award that can be ordered is therefore £6,900. In many cases, of course, where the employee has only a few years' service the figure will be far lower. In addition a tribunal can also order compensation under the following headings:

■ **Compensatory awards** take account of loss of earnings, pension rights, future earnings loss, etc. The maximum level in 2001 was £50,000.
■ **Additional awards** are used in cases of sex and race discrimination and also when an employer fails to comply with an order of reinstatement or re-engagement. In the former case the maximum award is 52 weeks' pay, in the latter 26 weeks' pay.
■ **Special awards** are made when unfair dismissal relates to trade union activity or membership. They can also be used when the dismissal was for health and safety reasons.

A tribunal can reduce the total level of compensation if it judges the individual concerned to have contributed to his or her own dismissal. For example, a dismissal on grounds of poor work performance may be found unfair because no procedure was followed and consequently no warnings given. This does not automatically entitle the ex-employee concerned to compensation based on the above formulae. If the tribunal judges them to have been 60 per cent responsible for their own dismissal the compensation will be reduced by 60 per cent. Reductions are also made if an ex-employee is judged not to have taken reasonable steps to mitigate his or her loss.

References

Bowers, J. (1990) *Bowers on Employment Law*. London: Blackstone.

Disney, R. (1999) 'Why have older men stopped working?', in P. Gregg and J. Wadsworth (eds), *The State of Working Britain*. Manchester: Manchester University Press.

DTI (1999) *The Unfair Dismissal and Statement of Reasons for Dismissal (variation of qualifying period) Order 1999 – regulatory impact assessment*. London: Department of Trade and Industry.

Duggan, M. (1999) *Unfair Dismissal: Law, practice & guidance*. Welwyn Garden City: CLT Professional Publishing.

Earnshaw, J.M. (1997) 'Tribunals and tribulations', *People Management*, May, pp. 34–6.

IDS (1999) 'Downloading pornography', *IDS Brief 637*, May.

IRS (2000a) 'Range of reasonable responses test is not wrong', *Industrial Relations Law Bulletin 638*, April.

IRS (2000b) 'The (re)definition of redundancy', *Industrial Relations Law Bulletin 633*, January.

Macdonald, L. (1998) 'Termination of Employment: Breach of contract, constructive dismissal and wrongful dismissal', *Personnel Manager's Fact Finder*. London: Gee Publishing.

Selwyn, N. (1985) *Law of Employment*, 5th edn. London: Butterworth.

Legal cases

Al-Tikriti v. *South Western RHA* 1986.

British Sugar v. *Kirker* [1998] IRLR 624.

Dunn v. *IBM UK Ltd* (1998) IDS Brief 637, May 1999.

Egg Stores v. *Leibovici* [1977] ICR 260.

Haddon v. *Van den Bergh Foods* [1999] IRLR 672, EAT.

Hollister v. *The National Farmers' Union* [1979] ICR 542.

Humphries v. *VH Barnett & Co* (1998) IDS Brief 637, May 1999.

International Sports Ltd v. *Thomson* [1980] IRLR 340.

Midland Bank v. *Madden* [2000] IRLR 288.

Murray et al. v. *Foyle Meats Ltd* [1999] IRLR 562.

Parr v. *Derwentside District Council* (1998) IDS Brief 637, May 1999.

Polkey v. *AE Dayton Services* [1987] ICR 142.

Safeway v. *Burrell* [1997] IRLR 200.

Whitbread PLC/Thresher v. *Gullyes* [1994] EAT 478/92.

General discussion topics

1 If you were dismissed in circumstances that you regarded as legally unfair, would you prefer to seek satisfaction through ACAS conciliation or through a tribunal hearing? Why?

2 In some countries a dismissal cannot be made until *after* a tribunal hearing, so that its 'fairness' is decided before it takes effect. What do you see as the benefits and drawbacks of that system?

3 What changes would you make in the criteria for dismissal on the grounds of misconduct?

Chapter 15 | Interactive skill: selection interviewing

We now discuss one of the most familiar and forbidding encounters of organisational life – the selection interview. Most people have had at least one experience of being interviewed as a preliminary to employment and few reflect with pleasure on the experience. Personnel specialists have a critical role in selection interviewing, carrying out many of the interviews and encouraging good interviewing practice in others by example, support and training.

In this chapter we review the varieties of selection interview and the criticism that has been made of the interview, in spite of its importance as a selection tool. Interview strategy and the number of interviews and interviewers are then considered, and this discussion is followed by sections on preparation and conduct of the interview.

Varieties of interview

There is a wide variety of practice in selection interviewing. At one extreme we read of men seeking work in the docks of Victorian London and generally being treated as if they were in a cattle market. They had to queue up in a series of gangways, similar to those used today to corral cattle at market, and had to vie with each other for the attention of the foreman hiring labourers for the day. Some of the older men apparently used to dye their hair in a pathetic attempt to catch the foreman's eye as being younger and fitter than they were in reality.

There is a neat spectrum of employee participation in the employment process which correlates with social class and type of work. While the London docks situation of the 1890s is not found today, there are working situations where the degree of discussion between the parties is limited to perfunctory exchanges about trade union membership, hours of work and rates of pay: labourers on building sites and extras on film sets being two examples. As interviews move up the organisational hierarchy there is growing equilibrium with the interviewer becoming more courteous and responsive to questions from the applicant, who will probably be described as a 'candidate' or someone who 'might be interested in the position'. For the most senior positions it is unlikely that people will be invited to respond to vacancies advertised in the press. Individuals will be approached, either directly or through consultants, and there will be an elaborate pavane in which each party seeks to persuade the other to declare an interest first.

Another indication of the variety of employment practice is in the titles used. The humblest of applicants seek 'jobs' or 'vacancies', while the more ambitious are looking for 'places', 'posts', 'positions', 'openings' or 'opportunities'. The really high-flyers seem to need somewhere to sit down, as they are offered 'seats on the board', 'professorial chairs' or 'places on the front bench'.

The purpose of the selection interview

An interview is a controlled conversation with a purpose. There are more exchanges in a shorter period related to a specific purpose than in an ordinary conversation. In the selection interview the purposes are:

1 To collect information in order to predict how well the applicants would perform in the job for which they have applied, by measuring them against predetermined criteria.
2 To provide the candidate with full details of the job and organisation to facilitate their decision making.
3 To conduct the interview in such a manner that candidates feel that they have been given a fair hearing.

Criticism of the selection interview

The selection interview has been extensively criticised as being unreliable, invalid and subjective, although such criticism is directed towards the decisions made and ignores the importance of the interview as a ritual in the employment process. A recent comprehensive analysis of selection interview effectiveness is in McDaniel *et al.* (1994).

The most perceptive original criticism is by Webster (1964), summarising extensive research. The main conclusions were:

1 Interviewers decided to accept or reject a candidate within the first three or four minutes of the interview and then spent the remainder of the interview time seeking evidence to confirm that their first impression was right.
2 Interviews seldom altered the tentative opinion formed by the interviewer seeing the application form and the appearance of the candidate.
3 Interviewers place more weight on evidence that is unfavourable than on evidence that is favourable.
4 When interviewers have made up their minds very early in the interview, their behaviour betrays their decision to the candidate.

However much this criticism is justified, it does not solve the problem, it only identifies it. All the complaints and denunciations boil down to the simple fact that the interviewer and not the interview is at the heart of the problem. The world is full of poor interviewers, as your own personal experience will probably confirm, but the selection interview is of paramount importance in the employment process. The world is also full of poor drivers, but that does not devalue the motor car.

Anderson and Shackleton summarise the research conclusions:

Utilized properly, depending upon its exact purpose, the interview emerges as a valid and reliable tool in candidate assessment. Moreover, its flexibility to act as a medium for mutual preview or as a final-stage forum for negotiation between the

parties, renders the interview more useful in selection than narrowly focused definitions of validity and reliability can convey.

(Anderson and Shackleton 1993, p. 68)

A key skill for personnel and other managers is how to handle this most crucial
of encounters, as the interview provides a number of important advantages
which cannot be provided by any other means.

The importance of the selection interview

The selection interview cannot be bettered as a means of exchanging information
and meeting the human and ritual aspects of the employment process.

Exchanging information

The interview is a flexible and speedy means of exchanging information, over a
broad range of topics. The employer has the opportunity to sell the company and
explain job details in depth. Applicants have the chance to ask questions about
the job and the company in order to collect the information they require for
their own selection decision. The interview is also the logical culmination of the
employment process, as information from a variety of sources, such as application forms, tests and references, can be discussed together.

Human and ritual aspects

In an interview some assessment can be made of matters that cannot be
approached any other way, like the potential compatibility of two people who
will have to work together. Both parties need to meet before the contract begins,
to 'tune in' to each other and begin the process of induction. The interview is
valuable in that way to both potential employee and potential employer. It gives
interviewees the feeling that they matter as another person is devoting time to
them and they are not being considered by a computer. Also, giving applicants a
chance to ask questions underlines their decision-making role, making them feel
less helpless in the hands of the all-powerful interviewer. Selection interviewing
has powerful ritual elements, as the applicant is seeking either to enter, or to rise
within, a social system. This requires the display of deferential behaviours:

> upward mobility involves the presentation of proper performances and . . . efforts
> to move upward . . . are expressed in terms of sacrifices made for the maintenance
> of front. (Goffman 1974, p. 45)

At the same time those who are already inside and above display their superiority and security, even unconsciously, in contrast with the behaviour of someone
so obviously anxious to share the same privileged position.

Reason tells us that this is inappropriate at the beginning of the twenty-first
century as it produces an unreasonable degree of dependency in the applicant;
and the books are full of advice to interviewers not to brandish their social superiority, but to put applicants at their ease and to reduce the status differentials.
This, however, still acknowledges their superiority as they are the ones who take
the initiative; applicants are not expected to help the interviewer relax and feel
less apprehensive. Also the reality of the situation is usually that of applicant

anxious to get in and selector choosing among several. Status differentials cannot simply be set aside. The selection interview is at least partly an initiation rite, not as elaborate as entry to commissioned rank in the armed forces, nor as whimsical as finding one's way into the Brownie ring, but still a process of going through hoops and being found worthy in a process where other people make all the rules.

Activity 15.1

For a selection interview in which you recently participated, either as selector or as applicant, consider the following:

1 What were the ritual features?
2 Were any useful ritual features missing?
3 Could ritual have been, in any way, *helpfully* reduced?

No matter what other means of making employment decisions there may be, the interview is crucial, and when worries are expressed about its reliability, this is not a reason for doing away with it: it is a reason for conducting it properly.

Interview strategy

The approach to selection interviewing varies considerably from the amiable chat in a bar to the highly organised, multi-person panel.

Frank and friendly strategy

By far the most common is the approach which Hackett (1978) described as frank and friendly. Here the interviewer is concerned to establish and maintain the rapport. This is done in the belief that if interviewees do not feel threatened, and are relaxed, they will be more forthcoming in the information that they offer. It is straightforward for both interviewer and interviewee and has the potential advantage that the interviewees will leave with a favourable impression of the business.

Problem-solving strategy

A variation of the frank and friendly strategy is the problem-solving approach. It is the method of presenting the candidate with a hypothetical problem and evaluating his or her answer, like the king in the fairy tale who offered the hand of the princess in marriage to the first suitor who could answer three riddles.

These are sometimes called situational interviews. The questions asked are derived from the job description and candidates are required to imagine themselves as the job holder and describe what they would do in a variety of hypothetical situations. This method is most applicable to testing elementary knowledge, like the colour coding of wires in electric cables or maximum dosages of specified drugs. It is less effective to test understanding and ability.

WINDOW ON PRACTICE	The following intriguing poser was put to a candidate for the position of security officer at a large department store:

'If you were alone in the building and decided to inspect the roof, what would you do if the only door out on to the roof banged itself shut behind you and the building caught fire?'

The retired police superintendent to whom that question was posed asked, very earnestly and politely, for six pieces of additional information, like the location of telephones, time of day, height of building, fire escapes. The replies became progressively more uncertain and the interviewer hastily shifted the ground of the interview to something else.

There is no guarantee that the candidate would actually behave in the way suggested. The quick thinker will score at the expense of the person who can take action more effectively than they can answer riddles. A useful analysis and commentary on situational interviews is in Latham *et al.* (1980).

Biographical strategy

Similar to the problem-solving strategy is the biographical method. The focus is on the candidate's past behaviour and performance, which is a more reliable way of predicting future performance than asking interviewees what they would do in a certain situation. Candidates are requested to describe the background to a situation and explain what they did and why; what their options were; how they decided what to do; and the anticipated and real results of their action. The success of this method is critically dependent on in-depth job analysis, and preferably competency analysis, in order to frame the best questions.

Stress strategy

In the stress approach the interviewer becomes aggressive, disparages the candidates, puts them on the defensive or disconcerts them by strange behaviour. The Office of Strategic Services in the United States used this method in the Second World War to select men for espionage work, and subsequently the idea was used by some business organisations on the premise that executive life was stressful, so a simulation of the stress would determine whether or not the candidate could cope.

The advantage of the method is that it may demonstrate a necessary strength or a disqualifying weakness that would not be apparent through other methods. The disadvantages are that evaluating the behaviour under stress is problematic, and those who are not selected will think badly of the employer.

The likely value of stress interviewing is so limited that it is hardly worth mentioning, except that it has spurious appeal to many managers, who are attracted by the idea of injecting at least some stress into the interview 'to see what they are made of', 'to put them on their mettle' or some similar bluster. Most candidates feel that the procedures are stressful enough, without adding to them.

Number of interviews and interviewers

There are two broad traditions governing the number of interviewers. One tradition says that effective, frank discussion can only take place on a one-to-one basis, so candidates meet one interviewer, or several interviewers, one at a time. The other tradition is that fair play must be demonstrated and nepotism prevented so the interview must be carried out, and the decision made, by a panel of interviewers. Within this dichotomy there are various options.

The individual interview

The individual interview gives the greatest chance of establishing rapport, developing mutual trust and the most efficient deployment of time in the face-to-face encounter, as each participant has to compete with only one other speaker. It is usually also the most satisfactory method for the candidate, who has to tune in only to one other person instead of needing constantly to adjust to different interlocutors. The candidate can more readily ask questions, as it is difficult to ask a panel of six people to explain the workings of the pension scheme, and it is the least formal type of interview.

The disadvantages lie in the dependence the organisation places on the judgement of one of its representatives – although this can be mitigated by a series of individual interviews – and the ritual element is largely missing. Candidates may not feel they have been 'done' properly. A sole interview with the line manager is very popular in the selection of blue-collar staff, being used in over one-third of cases. It is much less popular for white-collar and management staff.

Sequential interviews

Sequential interviews take the form of a series of individual interviews. The series most often consists of just two interviews for blue- and white-collar staff, but more than two for managerial staff. The most frequent combination is an interview with the line manager and an interview with a representative of the HR department. For managerial posts this will be extended to interviews with other departmental managers, top managers and significant prospective colleagues. Sequential interviews are useful as they can give the employer a broader picture of the candidate and they also allow the applicant to have contact with a greater number of potential colleagues. However, the advantages of sequential interviews need to be based on effective organisation and the holding of all interviews on the same day. It is important that all interviewers meet beforehand to agree on the requirements of the post and to decide how each will contribute to the overall theme. Immediately following the interviews a further meeting needs to take place so that the candidates can be jointly evaluated. One disadvantage of the method is the organisation and time that it takes from both the employer's and the candidate's point of view. It requires considerable commitment from the candidate who may have to keep repeating similar information and whose performance may deteriorate throughout the course of the interviews due to fatigue.

Panel interviews

The panel interview method has the specious appeal of sharing judgement and may appear to be a way of saving time in interviewing as all panel members are operating at once. It is also possible to legitimise a quick decision, always popular with candidates, and there can be no doubt about the ritual requirements being satisfied. Panel interviews are useful in reducing the likelihood of personal bias in interviewing, particularly in guarding against possible infringements of legal requirements. They can also ensure the candidate is acceptable to the whole organisation, and allow the candidate to get a good feel for the the business and its organisation.

The drawbacks lie in the tribunal nature of the panel. They are not having a conversation with the candidates; they are sitting in judgement upon them and assessing the evidence they are able to present in response to their requests. There is little prospect of building rapport and developing discussion, and there is likely to be as much interplay between members of the panel as there is between the panel and the candidate.

Panel interviews tend to over-rigidity and give ironic point to the phrase 'it is only a formality'. They are ritualistically superb, but dubious as a useful preliminary to employment. However, the benefits of the panel interview can be increased, and the disadvantages reduced, if the interviewers are properly trained and the interview well organised, thoroughly planned and made part of a structured selection process.

Activity 15.2	In your organisation how many interviews and interviewers are used? How effective is this approach and why? In what ways could the approach be improved?

The selection interview sequence

Preparation

We assume that the preliminaries of job analysis, recruitment and shortlisting are complete and the interview is now to take place. The first step in preparation is for the interviewers to brief themselves. They will collect and study a job description or similar details of the post to be filled, a candidate specification or statement of required competencies and the application forms or curricula vitae of the candidates.

If there are several people to be interviewed the interview timetable needs greater planning than it usually receives. The time required for each interview can be determined beforehand only approximately. A rigid timetable will weigh heavily on both parties, who will feel frustrated if the interview is closed arbitrarily at a predetermined time and uncomfortable if an interview that has 'finished' is drawn out to complete its allotted span. However, the disadvantages of keeping people waiting are considerable and underrated.

The experience of Barbara Trevithick reflects the thinking of some selectors that candidates are supplicants waiting on interviewers' pleasure, they have no competing calls on their time and a short period of waiting demonstrates who is

WINDOW ON PRACTICE

Barbara Trevithick applied for a post as personnel officer at a hospital and was invited for interview at 2.00 p.m. On arrival she was ushered into a small, window-less room where four other people were waiting. At 2.20 a secretary came in and asked Mr Brown to come with her. At 3.00 Mr Jones was called for. At 3.45 the remaining three candidates went out in search of the secretary to ask what the remaining timetable for the day was to be. The secretary replied that she did not know but the panel members had just gone to the canteen for a cup of coffee. By now Barbara had figured out that her surname was the last in alphabetical order. Miss Mellhuish was called for interview at 4.10 and Miss Roberts left because her last train home to Scotland was due in 20 minutes. Barbara Trevithick went in for interview at 4.45 to find that two members of the panel 'had had to leave', so she was interviewed by the two surviving members: a personnel officer and a nursing officer. At the close of the interview she asked when the decision would be made and was told that the two interviewers would have to consult with their two absent colleagues in the morning. Three weeks later Barbara rang to ask the outcome, as she had not received a letter, to be told that Mr Brown had been appointed and 'I'm surprised they didn't tell you, as it was offered to him that afternoon, after the coffee break'.

in charge. There are flaws in this reasoning. Most candidates will have competing calls on their time, as they will have taken time off to attend and have earmarked the anticipated interview time to fit in a busy schedule. Some may have other interviews to go to. An open-ended waiting period can be worrying, enervating and a poor preliminary to an interview. If the dentist keeps you waiting you may get distressed, but when the waiting is over you are simply a passive participant and the dentist does not have the success of the operation jeopardised. The interview candidate has, in a real sense, to perform when the period of waiting is over and the success of the interaction could well be jeopardised.

The most satisfactory timetable is the one that guarantees a break after all but the most voluble candidates. If candidates are asked to attend at hourly intervals, for example, this would be consistent with interviews lasting between 40 and 60 minutes. This would mean that each interview began at the scheduled time and that the interviewers had the opportunity to review and update their notes in the intervals.

Reception

Candidates arrive on the premises of their prospective employer on the lookout for every scrap of evidence they can obtain about the business – what it looks like, what the people look like and what people say. Candidates will make judgements as quickly as interviewers, and we have already seen the risk of interviewers making their decision within a few minutes and then using the rest of the time to confirm it. A candidate is likely to meet at least one and possibly two people before meeting the interviewer. First will be the commissionaire or receptionist. There is frequently also an emissary from the HR department to shepherd them from the gate to the waiting-room. Both are valuable sources of information, and interviewers may wish to prime such people so that they can see their role in the employment process and can be cheerful, informative and helpful.

The candidate will most want to meet the interviewer, the unknown but powerful figure on whom so much depends. Interviewers easily forget that they know much more about the candidates than the candidates know about them, because the candidates have provided a personal profile in the application form.

Interviewers do not reciprocate. To bridge this gap it can be very useful for interviewers to introduce themselves to the candidate in the waiting-room, so that contact is made quickly, unexpectedly and on neutral territory. This makes the opening of the interview itself rather easier.

Candidates wait to be interviewed. Although there are snags about extended, open-ended waiting periods, some time is inevitable and necessary to enable candidates to compose themselves. It is a useful time to deal with travelling expenses and provide some relevant background reading about the employing organisation.

The appropriate setting for an interview has to be right for the ritual and right from the point of view of enabling a full and frank exchange of information. It is difficult to combine the two. Many of the interview horror stories relate to the setting in which it took place. A candidate for a post as Deputy Clerk of Works was interviewed on a stage while the panel of 17 sat in the front row of the stalls, and a candidate for a Headteacher post came in to meet the interview panel and actually moved the chair on which he was to sit. He only moved it two or three inches because the sun was in his eyes, but there was an audible frisson and sharp intake of breath from the members of the panel.

Remaining with our model of the individual interviewer, here are some simple suggestions about the setting.

1 The room should be suitable for a private conversation.
2 If the interview takes place across a desk, as is common, the interviewer may wish to reduce the extent to which the desk acts as a barrier, inhibiting free flow of communication.
3 All visitors and telephone calls should be avoided, as they do not simply interrupt: they intrude and impede the likelihood of frankness.
4 It should be clear to the candidates where they are to sit.

Interview structure

There are several important reasons why the employment interview should be structured, making use of the application or CV:

1 The candidate expects the proceedings to be decided and controlled by the interviewer and will anticipate a structure within which to operate.
2 It helps the interviewer to make sure that they cover all relevant areas and avoid irrelevancies.
3 It looks professional. Structure can be used to guide the interview and ensure that it makes sense.
4 It assists the interviewer in using the time available in the most effective way.
5 The application form can be used as a memory aid by the interviewer when making notes directly after the interview.
6 It can make it easier to compare candidates.

The selection interview

There are several different ways to structure the interview. We recommend the form set out in Table 15.1. This divides activities and objectives into three interview stages: opening, middle and closing. While there are few, if any, alternative satisfactory ways for conducting the beginning and the end of the interview, the middle can be approached from a number of different angles, depending on the circumstances.

The interviewer needs to work systematically through the structure that has been planned but the structure does not have to be adhered to rigidly. Interviewers should abandon their own route whenever the candidate chooses one that seems more promising.

The opening of the interview is the time for mutual preliminary assessment and tuning in to each other. A useful feature of this phase is for the interviewer to sketch out the plan or procedure for the interview and how it fits in with the total employment decision process. It is also likely that the application form will provide an easy, non-controversial topic for these opening behaviours.

One objective is for the two parties to exchange words so that they can adjust their receiving mechanism to be mutually intelligible. It also provides an opportunity for both to feel comfortable in the presence of the other. Interviewers able to achieve these two objectives may then succeed in developing a relationship in which candidates trust the interviewer's ability and motives so that they will speak openly and fully. This is known as 'rapport' and the interviewer's effectiveness will greatly depend on being skilled at this process.

For the middle of the interview the biographical approach is the most straightforward. It works on the basis that candidates at the time of the interview are the product of everything in their lives that has gone before. To understand the candidate the interviewer must understand the past and will talk to the candidate about the episodes of his or her earlier life, education, previous employment, etc.

The advantage of this is that the objectives are clear to both interviewer and interviewee, there is no deviousness or 'magic'. Furthermore, the development can be logical and so aid the candidate's recall of events. Candidates who reply to enquiries about their choice of A level subjects will be subconsciously triggering their recollection of contemporaneous events, like the university course they took, which are likely to come next in the interview. The biographical approach

Table 15.1 Interview structure: a recommended pattern

Stage	Objectives	Activities
Opening	To put the candidate at ease, develop rapport and set the scene	Greet candidate by name Introduce yourself Explain interview purpose Outline how purpose will be achieved Obtain candidate assent to outline
Middle	To collect and provide information	Asking questions within a structure that makes sense to the candidate, such as biographical, areas of the application form, or competencies identified for the job Listening Answering questions
Closing	To close the interview and confirm future action	Summarise interview Check candidate has no more questions Indicate what happens next and when

is the simplest for the inexperienced interviewer to use as discussion can develop from the information provided by the candidate on the application form.

Some version of sequential categories, like employment, education and training, seems the most generally useful, but it will need the addition of at least two other categories: the work offered and the organisational context in which it is to be done. The middle of the interview can be structured by systematically working through items of the job description or the person specification. Increasingly, where competencies have been identified for the job, these are used as the basis of the structure.

In the preparatory stage of briefing the interviewer will also prepare notes on two elements to incorporate in their plan: key issues and checkpoints.

Key issues will be the two or three main issues that stand out from the application form for clarification or elaboration. This might be the nature of the responsibilities carried in a particular earlier post, the content of a training course, the reaction to a period of employment in a significant industry or whatever else strikes the interviewer as being productive of useful additional evidence.

Checkpoints are matters of detail that require further information: grades in an examination, dates of an appointment, rates of pay, and so forth.

At the close of the interview the explanation of the next step needs especial attention. The result of the interview is of great importance to the candidates and they will await the outcome with anxiety. Even if they do not want the position they will probably hope to have it offered. This may strengthen their hand in dealings with another prospective employer – or their present employer – and will certainly be a boost to their morale. The great merit of convention in the public sector is that the chosen candidate is told before the contenders disperse: the great demerit is that they are asked to say yes or no to the offer at once.

In the private sector it is unusual for an employment offer to be made at the time of the interview, so there is a delay during which the candidates will chafe. Their frustration will be greater if the delay is longer than expected and they may start to tell themselves that they are not going to receive an offer, in which case they will also start convincing themselves that they did not want the job either! It is important for the interviewer to say as precisely as possible when the offer will be made, but ensuring that the candidates hear earlier rather than later than they expect, if there is to be any deviation.

The interviewer will need to call into play at least five key aspects of method.

1 Some data can be collected by simple observation of the candidate. Notes can be made about dress, appearance, voice, height and weight, if these are going to be relevant, and the interviewer can also gauge the candidate's mood and the appropriate response to it by the non-verbal cues that are provided. The study of body language has achieved great popularity in the last twenty years, largely because of its alleged potential for interpreting the thoughts and intentions of members of the opposite sex in social situations. Although the available books are designed for a popular market, they are usually sound and contain useful advice for the selection interviewer. Glass (1992) is a good example of this genre and demonstrates the dangers of interpreting body language without reference to a person's gender, ethnic and social background.

2 The remainder of the evidence will come from listening to what is said, so the interviewer has to be very attentive throughout; not only listening to the answers to questions, but also listening for changes in inflection and pace, nuances and

overtones that provide clues on what to pursue further. The amount of time that the two spend talking is important, as an imbalance in one direction or the other will mean that either the candidate or the interviewer is not having enough opportunity to hear information. Inclining the body towards the other person is a signal of attentiveness, so we need to remember our *posture*, which should be inclined forward and facing the other squarely with an open posture: folded arms can be inhibiting.

Eye contact is crucial to good listening, but is a subtle art:

> Effective eye contact expresses interest and a desire to listen. It involves focusing one's eyes softly on the speaker and occasionally shifting the gaze . . . to a gesturing hand, for example, and then back to the face and then to eye contact once again.
>
> (Bolton 1987, p. 36)

The distinction between 'focusing one's eyes softly' and staring is vital, though difficult to describe, and competence in eye contact is never easy to establish. It is one of the most intimate ways of relating to a person and many managers fear that the relationship may become too close. Even if you are happy with it, you may find that the other person is uncomfortable with you looking through the 'window' of their eyes.

We have to avoid distracting the other person by physical behaviour that is unrelated to what is being said; fiddling with a pen, playing with car keys, scrutinising your fingernails, wringing your hands, brushing specks of dust off your sleeves are a few typical behaviours that indicate inattention. Skilled listeners not only suppress these, they also develop minor gestures and posture variants that are directly responsive to what the other person is saying.

Being silent and deliberately leaving verbal lulls in face-to-face situations provide the opportunity for the other person to say more – perhaps more than was initially intended. Silence still has to be attentive and the longer the silence, the harder it is to be attentive.

3 In order to have something to hear, the interviewer will have to direct the candidate. This, of course, is done by questioning, encouraging and enabling the candidate to talk, so that the interviewer can learn. The art of doing this depends on the personality and style of the interviewer who will develop a personal technique through a sensitive awareness of what is taking place in the interviews.

It is helpful to distinguish between different types of question in selection interviewing. Closed questions are used when we want precise, factual information. We close the question to control the answer ('Is it Clarke with an e, or without?'). These are useful at the point in the interview where you want clear, straightforward data.

Open-ended questions are quite different as they avoid terse replies, inviting candidates to express their opinions and to explain things in their own words and emphasis. The question does little more than introduce a topic to talk about ('What does your present job entail?'). The main purpose is to obtain the type of deeper information that the closed question misses, as the shape of the answer is not predetermined by the questioner. You are informed not simply by the content of the answers, but by what is selected and emphasised.

Probes are forms of questioning to obtain information that the respondent is trying to conceal. When this happens the questioner has to make an important, and perhaps difficult decision: do you respect the candidate's unwillingness and

WINDOW ON PRACTICE

Reflection

The effectiveness of listening can be aided by reflection – the listener picks up and restates the content of what has just been said. It indicates that you are attending to what the other person is saying, have understood it and you are providing the opportunity for any misunderstanding to be pointed out. The standard method is *paraphrasing*, by which the listener states the essence of what has been said. This is done concisely and gives the speaker a chance to review what has been said.

An example of how this would be done is in the following exchange:

Respondent: 'Seniority does not count for as much as it should in my present company.'
Reflection: 'You feel there is not enough acknowledgement of loyalty and long service?'

Alternative reactions would have a different effect, for example:

'You sound like someone who has been passed over for promotion', or
'Oh, I don't know about that.'

Both push the respondent on the defensive, expecting a justification of what has been said. Another alternative:

'Well, I think seniority is sometimes over-emphasised'

stifles the opinion before it has been fully expressed. The diffident candidate will not develop the feeling further, so the matter cannot be resolved. There is also the danger that any one of these evaluative reactions could evoke a comeback from the respondent which complies with the view suggested by the interviewer. This is the same problem as that of the leading question.

let the matter rest, or do you persist with the enquiry? Reluctance is quite common in selection interviews where there may be an aspect of the recent employment history that the candidate wishes to gloss over. The most common sequence for the probe takes the following form: (a) Direct questions, replacing the more comfortable open-ended approach ('What were you doing in the first six months of 1999?'). Careful phrasing may avoid a defensive reply, but those skilled at avoiding unwelcome enquiry may still deflect the question, leading to (b) Supplementaries, which reiterate the first question with different phrasing ('Yes, I understand about that period. It's the first part of 1999 that I'm trying to get clear: after you came back from Belgium and before you started with Amalgamated Widgets'). Eventually this should produce the information you need. (c) Closing. If the information has been wrenched out like a bad tooth and the interviewer looks horrified or sits in stunned silence, then the candidate will feel put down beyond redemption. The interviewer needs to make the divulged secret less awful than the candidate had feared, so that the interview can proceed with reasonable confidence ('Yes, well you must be glad to have that behind you'). It may be that the interviewer will feel able to develop the probe by developing the answer by a further question such as, 'and how did that make you feel?' or 'and how did you react to that? It must have been a terrible blow?' It is only reasonable to do this if the resultant exchange adds something useful to your understanding of the client: simple nosiness is not appropriate!

Some common lines of questioning should be avoided because they can produce an effect that is different from what is intended. *Leading questions* ('Would you agree with me that ...?') will not necessarily produce an answer that is informative, but an answer in line with the lead that has been given. *Multiple*

References

Anderson, N. and Shackleton, V. (1993) *Successful Selection Interviewing*. Oxford: Blackwell.

Bolton, R. (1987) *People Skills*. Sydney: Simon & Schuster.

Glass, L. (1992) *He Says, She Says*. London: Piatkus.

Goffman, E. (1974) *The Presentation of Self in Everyday Life*. London: Penguin Books.

Hackett, P. (1978) *Interview Skills Training: Role Play Exercises*. London: Institute of Personnel Management.

Latham, G., Saari, L.M., Pursell, E.D. and Campion, M.A. (1980) 'The Situational Interview', *Journal of Applied Psychology*, Vol. 65, No. 4, pp. 422–7.

McDaniel, M.A., Whetzel, D.A., Schmidt, F.L., Maurer, S.D. (1994) 'The validity of the employment interview', *Journal of Applied Psychology*, Vol. 79, No. 19, pp. 599–616.

Webster, E.C. (1964) *Decision Making in the Employment Interview*. Toronto: Industrial Relations Centre, McGill University, Canada.

Practical exercise in selection interviewing

For this exercise you need a co-operative, interested relative, or a very close friend, who would welcome interview practice.

1 Follow the sequence suggested in Table 15.1 to give your partner practice in being interviewed for a job, and giving yourself practice in interviewing and note taking.

2 After the interview, discuss your mutual feelings about the process around questions such as:

Selector   Did you ever feel you were being misled? When? Why?

Did you feel the interview got out of your control? When? Why?

How could you have avoided the problem?

How was your note-taking?

What, if anything, made you bored or cross?

What did you find most difficult?

How comprehensive is the data you have collected?

Candidate   Were you put at your ease?

Were you at any time inhibited by the selector?

Did you ever mislead the selector? When? How?

Did the selector ever fail to follow up important points? When? Which?

Were you in any way disconcerted by the note taking?

Has the selector got a comprehensive set of data about you, so that you could feel any decision made about you would be soundly based?

What did you think of the interview experience?

3 Now swap roles.

Part III
Case study problem

You are the Human Resources Manager for a large insurance company with 2,000 employees based in a large city in the north of England and your company has just taken over another insurance company in the south of England which currently employs 1,100 staff. Both firms have a long history and to some extent cover the same insurance markets, although the company in the south of England covers two fairly large specialist areas which are not covered in the north. This was one of the reasons for the takeover, as such specialist staff require a long training and need to acquire high levels of expertise. There are 300 staff in the south who are dedicated to these specialist insurance services.

The takeover did not go smoothly as there was resistance from the southern company, and now it is complete there is considerable uneasiness. Only three years ago the southern company was party to a merger with another local firm and as a result 20 per cent of staff were made redundant. There had been promises of a bright future after these difficult times.

For financial and pragmatic reasons it has been decided that the southern office will close almost immediately and all staff will be located in newly built offices 15 miles out of the northern city. Many of the southern staff are alarmed at the idea of moving and equally alarmed that they may not be invited to move due to another round of redundancies. This especially applies to those who are over 50. The northern staff are divided in their views about the move out of the city centre. Those who live on the western side of the city where the new offices are located are generally delighted to be able to work near to home in an exclusive part of the county. Staff who live on the other side of the city are concerned – some are not happy to travel long distances each day, and for a variety of reasons do not want to move to the other side of the city. Some would like to move, but find that the difference in house prices is too great. Many are disappointed that they will no longer work in the city centre, which is something they had valued. Redundancy is not a possibility which was seriously considered by the northern staff.

The required profile is broadly as set out in the following table:

A. Senior and middle management	35
B. Professional/junior management	1,700 (to include 300 specialist staff)
C. Clerical/administrative	600
D. Manual/ancillary	65

Current staffing

	Northern	Southern	Total
A.	30	20	50
B.	1,400	700	2,100

(there are no specialist professional staff in the north and 300 in the south)

C.	540	370	910
D.	30	10	40

In terms of staffing demand it has been estimated that a total staffing of 2,400 is required for the next three-year period with hopes of some increase after this period, based on growth.

The reduction in the number of professional/junior management staff required reflects a general reduction of all types of professional staff due to the economies of scale and more sophisticated IT use. The only professional staff group to increase in size is the IT group.

The reduction in clerical/administrative staff is due largely to the use of more sophisticated IT systems.

The increase in the number of manual/ancillary staff is due to the move to a much larger site with substantial grounds, including a range of on-site facilities due to a non-city centre location.

You are informed that staffing levels and the move should be complete in six months' time and that, as HR Manager, you are to have a high profile role. You have initially been asked for a recommended strategy and plan to achieve the target resourcing figures with the least possible disruption and damage to morale.

Required

1 What information would you gather before putting your proposal together?

2 What issues would you address in the proposal?

3 What options are there for achieving the target, what impact might each have, and which would you recommend and why?

Part III
Examination questions

Undergraduate introductory

1 Where does the calculation of labour turnover fit with the human resource planning process as a whole?

2 Outline the advantages and disadvantages of (a) panel interviews, and (b) serial interviews. In which circumstances would you recommend each approach?

Undergraduate finals

3 What techniques can managers adopt to improve their recruiting and interviewing practices?

4 Describe and explain the management practices necessary to avoid a claim at a tribunal for unfair dismissal.

Masters

5 Outline the major factors that influence the use of part-time work in Britain, and discuss the implications of part-time work for part-time workers.

6 Under what conditions may annualised hours systems provide employers with the 'flexibility they require'?

Professional

7 Wanous (1992) in his book on organisational entry talks about the idea of 'realistic recruitment'. Design a recruitment and selection process with this in mind for a sales team manager in the software business. Explain how your choice of recruitment and selection activities would achieve this objective.

8 Your organisation is about to embark on a major recruitment campaign, for the first time in a number of years. Twelve of the first line managers will be involved in the recruitment interviewing. Their interviewing skills are weak, either because they have not been involved in the interview process before, or because they have had no opportunity to use them for a long time.

   As the Training Officer, you have been asked to provide the training for the first line managers. Outline the course that you propose, giving objectives, content, methods and timing.

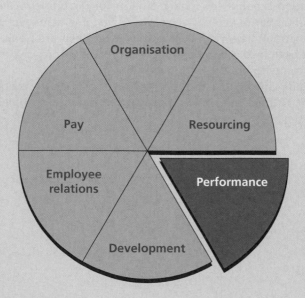

PART IV

PERFORMANCE

It is no good having all the right people all in the right place, but not delivering the goods. It was suggested in the opening chapter of this book that there is a general move away from the contract *of* employment towards a contract *for* performance. We all have to perform effectively.

A large part of achieving effective performance is getting the organisational processes right, but within the organisational framework there are the teams, groups and individuals who do the work. Also within that framework we have to understand what it is that motivates people to perform and deploy leadership skills that match those motivations.

Performance management is an idea that has been developed to co-ordinate several features – targets, training, appraisal and payment – to deliver effectiveness. Within that sequence is the hardest type of meeting most managers ever have to handle: the appraisal interview. Also included here is the management of diversity, an approach which starts from the premise that the people working for the business have a very wide range of capacities and that management has to make the most of everyone, moving beyond the idea that some may be only able to make a limited contribution because of their gender, race, disability, age or sexuality.

Chapter 16   Strategic aspects of performance

In our opening chapters we described the shift in emphasis away from the contract of employment towards the contract for performance. Even before the development of Taylor's Scientific Management methods a century ago, getting the most out of the workforce has always been a predominant management preoccupation, and the management literature is full of studies on the topic. Psychologists have studied motivation and leadership, ergonomists have dismantled and reconstructed every aspect of the physical environment in which people work, industrial relations specialists have pondered power relationships and reward, while sociologists discussed the design of organisations and their social structure, and operations experts have looked for ways to engineer process improvements.

In this chapter we review some major influences on our current thinking about performance. From this we explore in more detail some views on which human resource policies and practices result in high performance and then focus on understanding how this comes about. We shall conclude by briefly reviewing a range of popular strategic performance initiatives. The following three chapters look in more detail at organisational, individual and team performance.

A change in perspective: from employment to performance

The traditional human resource management approach to enhancing individual performance has centred on the assessment of past performance and the allocation of reward (Walker 1992). The secret was seen to lie in the interplay between individual skill or capacity and motivation. There has also been a pattern of thinking which set reward as separate from performance: rewards were provided in exchange for performance. This has been powerfully influenced by the industrial relations history, as trade unions have developed the process of collective bargaining and negotiation.

The prime purpose of trade unions has always been to improve the terms and working conditions of their members, although there may be other objectives in addition to this. With that objective, the union has only one thing to offer in exchange for improvements in terms and conditions, that is, some opportunity for improvement in productivity or performance. With the steadily increasing influence of unions in most industrial countries through most of the twentieth century, it was inevitable that performance improvement was something of direct interest only to management. Performance therefore became stereotyped as something of no intrinsic interest to the person doing the work.

The influence of trade unions has altered and collective bargaining does not dominate the management agenda as much as it used to. This is the most significant feature in the general change in attitudes about what we go to work for. Managements are gradually waking up to this fact and realising that there is now scope for integration in a way that was previously unrealistic. Not only is it possible to say, 'Performance is rewarded', one can now begin to say, 'Performance *is* a reward.' The long-standing motivational ideas of job enlargement, job enrichment, and so forth, become more cogent when those at work are able to look for the satisfaction of their needs not only in the job, but in their performance in it.

WINDOW ON PRACTICE	Mavis has worked in a retail store for eighteen years and has recently attended a training course in customer care.

'I always regarded the customer as some sort of enemy; we all did. In our coffee breaks we chatted away about the customer from hell, who was never satisfied, or who always put you down. Also I used to feel that I had to grin and bear it in trying to be nice to these enemies in order to earn commission.

Since the course I feel much more in control and have more self-respect. I really feel that most customers will respond positively if I approach them in the right way. It is my performance that largely affects how they behave. I actually enjoy what I am doing most of the time (and I never thought I'd say that!), because I can see myself doing a bit of good as well as selling more than I used to.'

Although it may seem like playing with words, this subtle shift of emphasis is fundamental to understanding the strategic approach to performance.

Influences on our understanding of performance

The Japanese influence

The success of Japanese companies and the decline of Western organisations has encouraged an exploration and adoption of Japanese management ideas and practices in order to improve performance. Thurley (1982) described the objectives of personnel policies in Japan as performance, motivation, flexibility and mobility. Delbridge and Turnbull (1992) described type 'J' organisations (based on Japanese thinking) as characterised by commitment, effort and company loyalty. A key theme in Japanese thinking appears to be people development and continuous improvement, or 'kaizen'.

Much of this thinking and the specific management techniques used in Japan, such as JIT (just in time), have been adopted into UK organisations, often in an uncritical way and without due regard for the cultural differences between the two nations. It is only where the initiatives are developed *and modified* for their location that they appear to succeed.

The American literature

Key writers from the American 'excellence' school, Peters and Waterman (1982), identified eight characteristics that they found to be associated with excellent companies – all American. These companies were chosen as excellent on the basis of their innovativeness and on a set of financial indicators, compared on an industry-wide basis. The characteristics they identified were:

- a bias for action – rather than an emphasis on bureaucracy or analysis;
- close to the customer – concern for customer wishes;
- autonomy and entrepreneurship – the company is split into small operational units where innovation and initiative are encouraged;
- productivity through people – employees are seen as the key resource, and the value of the employees' contribution is reinforced;
- hands-on, value-driven – strong corporate culture promoted from the top;
- stick to the knitting – pursuing the core business rather than becoming conglomerates;
- simple form, lean staff – simple organisation structure and small HQ staffing;
- simultaneous loose and tight properties – company values strongly emphasised, but within these considerable freedom and errors tolerated.

Peters and Waterman identified a shift from the importance of strategy and structural factors to style, systems, staff and skills (from the hard 's's to the soft 's's). In a follow-on book Peters and Austin (1985) identify four key factors related to excellence as concern for customers, innovation, attention to people and leadership.

Guest (1992) analyses why this excellence literature has had such an impact and identifies a range of methodological and analytical problems associated with the research, which question its validity. For example, he points out that no comparison was made with companies not considered to be excellent. We do not, therefore, know whether these principles were applied to a greater extent in excellent organisations. Hitt and Ireland (1987) go so far as to say that 'the data call into question whether these excellent principles are related to performance'. In addition, a number of the companies quoted have experienced severe problems since the research was carried out, and there remains the problem of the extent to which we can apply the results to UK organisations.

Whatever the reservations, the influence of the text on strategic thinking about performance remains profound. Even the use of the term 'excellence' means that there is a change of emphasis away from deadpan, objective terms like profitability, effectiveness, value-added and competitive advantage towards an idea that may trigger a feeling of enthusiasm and achievement. 'Try your best' becomes 'Go for it'.

More recently there has been considerable work in the USA that aims to identify HR practices which lead to high organisational performance, for example Huselid (1995) and Pfeffer (1998). The predominant method used to identify such relationships is quantitative analysis of large sets of statistical data. This type of approach is typical in research in the USA, but in the UK we tend to use a much greater mix of methods. However, the last few years have seen an increase in the use of quantitative methods in the UK, to attempt to establish the HR practices which are related to high performance, in other words to identify what are termed 'high performance work practices' in US terminology and 'high commitment work practices' in UK terminology.

HRM and the strategy literature

The HRM strategy literature provides different ways to understand the contribution of HR policies and practices to organisational performance. We noted in Chapter 3 that three distinct approaches to HR strategy can be identified. The universalist or best practice approach presupposes that certain HR policies and practices will always result in high performance, and the question is to identify exactly what these are. The contingency or fit approach suggests that different HR policies and practices will be needed to produce high performance in different firms depending on their business strategy and environment. However, it is usually considered possible to categorise different business strategies and environmental influences, and, on the basis of these, to identify the HR policies and practices that will result in high performance. Finally the resource-based view of the firm suggests that neither of these approaches is sufficient, but that every organisation and its employees should be considered as unique and that the set of HR policies and practices that will result in high performance will also be unique to that firm. From this perspective no formula can be applied, and the way that people processes contribute to organisational performance can only be understood within the context of the particular firm. These three perspectives have resulted in different investigational approaches to understanding the impact of people management on organisational performance, as will become clear in the following section.

Do people-management processes contribute to high performance?

The investigations to date have had a dual purpose, the first being to seek to establish a link between people-management practices and organisational performance. In other words, does the way that people are managed affect the bottom line? The second one follows logically from this, and is: 'If the answer to the first question is yes, then which particular policies and practices result in high performance?' Both these questions are usually investigated in parallel. A variety of different definitions of performance have been used in these studies. These range from bottom line financial performance (profitability), through productivity measures, to measurement of outcomes such as wastage, quality and labour turnover (which are sometimes referred to as internal performance outcomes). Sometimes the respondent's view of performance is used, on the basis that bottom line figures can be influenced by management accounting procedures. The studies have generally used large datasets and complex statistical analysis to determine relationships.

Much of the research has been carried out from the assumption of the universalist, or best practice approach to HR strategy. Reviewing the academic literature Richardson and Thompson (1999) come to the conclusion that the evidence indicates a positive relationship between innovative and sophisticated people-management practices and better business performance. Some researchers argue that the performance effects of HR policies and practices are multiplicative rather than additive, and this is often termed the 'bundles' approach (see, for example, MacDuffie 1995). In other words, a particular set of mutually reinforcing practices is likely to have more impact on performance than applying one or just some of these in isolation. Pfeffer (1998), for example, identifies seven critical people-management policies: emphasising employment security; recruiting the 'right' people; extensive use of self-managed teams and decentralisation; high wages solidly linked to organisational performance; high spending on training; reducing status differentials; and sharing information; and he suggests that these policies will benefit *every* organisation. In the UK the Sheffield Enterprise Programme (Patterson *et al.* 1997) has studied 100 manufacturing organisations over 10 years (1991–2001) and has used statistical techniques to identify which factors affect profitability and productivity. It has been reported that aspects of culture, supervisory support, concern for employee welfare, employee responsibility, training, job satisfaction and organisational commitment were all important variables in relation to organisational performance. It is worth noting that here variables associated with employee attitudes are included, that is, job satisfaction and commitment, in addition to the variables which comprise policies or practices. We will consider this mix in the following section. Also in the UK, Wood and de Menezes (1998) identify a bundle of HR practices which they term high-commitment management, and these comprise recruitment and selection processes geared to selecting flexible and highly committed individuals; processes which reward commitment and training by promotion and job security; and the use of direct communication and teamwork.

This avenue of work has a very optimistic flavour, suggesting that not only are people-management practices related to high organisational performance, but that we can identify the innovative and sophisticated practices that will work best in combination. On a practical level there are problems because different researchers identify different practices or 'bundles' associated with high performance (see, for example, Becker and Gerhard 1996). There have been many criticisms of this approach, partly based on the methods used – which involve, for example, the view of a single respondent as to which practices are in place, with no account taken of how the practices are implemented. A further problem is causality. It could be that profitable firms use best practice people-management methods, because they can afford to since they are profitable, rather than that such methods lead to profitability. A further issue concerns the conflict between different aspects of the bundle, along the lines of Legge's (1989) criticism of Guest's model of strategic HRM. Such contradictions are, for example, between individualism and teamwork and between a strong culture and adaptability. These contradictions can also be seen in some of the performance variables and strategic performance initiatives discussed below. Lastly, this approach ignores the business strategy of the organisation. Guest (2000) and particularly Purcell (1999) provide detailed expositions of the problems with this approach. While they recognise the value of the work they also see it as limited.

MacDuffie (1995) suggests that the best bundle is dependent on the logic of the organisation, and other researchers such as Wright and Snell (1998), have pursued the link between HR and organisational performance from the contingency, or fit, perspective. While this approach does bring the integration with business strategy to the fore, it fails to provide a more useful way forward. Attempting to model all the different factors that influence the appropriate set of HR policies and practices that lead to high performance is an extremely complex, if not impossible task. In addition to this Purcell *et al.* (2000) argue that the speed of change poses a real problem for the fit approach, and Purcell (1999) suggests that a more useful approach is to focus on the resource-based view of the firm, which is the third perspective on HR strategy that we considered in Chapter 3.

Becker and Gerhart suggest that it is more likely to be the architecture of the system, not just a group of HR practices, that results in high performance, and Purcell suggests that it is how practices are implemented and change is managed that makes the difference. The resource-based view would indicate that competencies in the implementation and management of change could form part of the basis of sustained competitive advantage. Hutchinson *et al.* (2000) term this 'idiosyncratic fit'. Part of the CIPD's major research project on investigating the link of HR to performance will involve longitudinal case studies that may shed some light on this issue.

How do HR policies and practices affect performance?

On the basis that we have sufficient evidence to claim that HR policies and practices do affect company performance (although it should be noted that some studies do not support this, for example Lahteenmaki and Storey 1998), we need to understand better the processes which link these HR practices to business performance. As Purcell *et al.* (2000) point out, 'what remains unclear is what is actually happening in successful organisations to make this connection' (p. 30). The results from one part of the CIPD study, referred to above, should help us understand how, why and where certain HR policies and practices result in high performance. Currently our interpretation focuses on the central importance of commitment in mediating the impact of HR policies and practices on business performance, and we shall consider this in more detail.

Commitment

Historically, some writers have identified commitment as resulting in higher performance. Commitment has been described as:

- **Attitudinal commitment** – that is, loyalty and support for the organisation, strength of identification with the organisation (Porter 1985), a belief in its values and goals and a readiness to put in effort for the organisation.
- **Behavioural commitment** – actually remaining with the company and continuing to pursue its objectives.

Walton (1985) notes that commitment is **thought** to result in better quality, lower turnover, a greater capacity for innovation and more flexible employees. In turn these are seen to enhance the ability of the organisation to achieve competitive advantage. Iles, Mabey and Robertson (1990) add that some of the outcomes of commitment have been identified as the industrial relations climate, absence levels, turnover levels and individual performance. Pfeffer (1998) and Wood and Albanese (1995) argue that commitment is a core variable, and Guest (1998, p. 42) suggests that:

> The concept of organizational commitment lies at the heart of any analysis of HRM. Indeed the whole rationale for introducing HRM policies is to increase levels of commitment so that other positive outcomes can ensue.

Hence we see the adoption of the terms 'high commitment work practices' and 'high commitment management' and their linkage with high performance. Meyer and Allen (1997) argue that there is not a great deal of **evidence** to link high commitment and high levels of organisational performance. Guest (2000) reports analyses of the Workplace Employment Relations Survey (WERS) data and the Future of Work Survey data to show some support for the model that HR practices have an impact on employee attitudes and satisfaction, which in turn

Figure 16.1 A simple model of HRM and performance

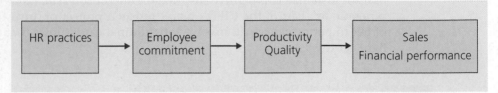

Source: D. Guest (2000) 'Human resource management, employee well-being and organizational performance'. Paper presented to the CIPD Professional Standards Conference, 11 July. Reproduced with the permission of the author.

has an impact on internal performance outcomes. He is, however, cautious about identifying causal links.

In this context Guest uses commitment as shorthand for employee attitudes and values, as shown in his model in Figure 16.1.

Some authors, however, have argued that high commitment could indeed reduce organisational performance. Cooper and Hartley (1991) suggest that commitment might decrease flexibility and inhibit creative problem solving. If commitment reduces staff turnover, this may result in fewer new ideas coming into the organisation. Staff who would like to leave the organisation but who are committed to it in other ways, for example through high pay and benefits, may stay, but may not produce high levels of performance.

As well as the debate on the value of commitment to organisational performance, there is also the debate on the extent to which commitment can be managed, and how it can be managed. Guest (1992) suggests that commitment is affected by:

■ personal characteristics;

WINDOW ON PRACTICE

Rebecca Johnson (1999) reports on performance initiatives at the Holiday Inn, Mayfair. Through a 'back to the floor' experience senior managers realised that front line staff did not have sufficient authority and autonomy to solve routine customer problems and that this was having an adverse impact on customer perceptions. A range of initiatives were thus implemented:

■ training to equip front line staff to take greater responsibility in solving customer problems;
■ new recruitment and selection strategies to help identify potential employees who are 'focused on going the extra mile', rather than those who have technical skills, which can be learned on appointment. Processes include 'auditions' to identify favourable attitudes;
■ demonstrating a genuine commitment to employees. Initiatives included attitude surveys, continued IIP recognition, a training resource centre and a network of mentors and 'buddies';
■ encouraging a sense of fun and openness;
■ a performance appraisal system which is also geared towards career development, and internal promotions where possible;
■ measuring customer feedback through a 'guest tracking system'.

Johnson reports that all these policies are paying off as profits have been increasing steadily for the last five years. She also reports the views of a recently appointed corporate sales executive who claims to have joined the organisation, partly because of the training programme, and who noted that 'the commitment is very strong'.

Source: Adapted from a case study by R. Johnson (1999) 'Case 2: Holiday Inn Mayfair', in A. Baron and R. Collard 'Realising our assets', *People Management*, 14 October.

- experiences in job role;
- work experiences;
- structural factors; and
- personnel policies.

Morris, Lydka and O'Creevy (1992/3) also identify that personnel policies have an effect on commitment. In particular they found career prospects as the most important factor in their research on graduates. This brings us to the link between commitment and the psychological contract and the role that trust and job security have on the experience of commitment.

One of the difficulties with the concept of commitment, as Singh and Vinnicombe (1998) suggest, is whether it is defined in the same way by employees and the organisation, and whether or not our general understanding of the term needs to be reviewed in the light of a different organisational environment which rarely allows for organisations to invest in the long-term careers of employees. They use a definition of commitment in their article which encompasses commitment, not only to the organisation, but to one's career.

Lastly, it is important to consider whether using commitment as a shorthand for attitudes and satisfaction is sufficient, and whether there are other important dimensions which may be lost, by focusing on commitment alone.

Major performance initiatives

We have previously considered some HR policies and practices that have been identified as related to high performance, and have noted the idea of using practices in bundles. Many of the popular performance initiatives that companies have adopted represent similar (but not the same) bundles of HR policies and practices, and we now turn to these. There are many small initiatives every day that help to improve performance, but we are concentrating here on major strategic initiatives, 'big ideas', as described by Connock (1992). A big idea with the same label may, of course, mean different things in practice in different organisatons. Mueller and Purcell (1992, p. 28) reach the heart of the issue when they say:

> It is the integration of change initiatives with other aspects of organisational life which is the key to success. It is very rare for a single initiative, however well designed to generate significant or lasting benefit.

Moving to a performance culture is an all-or-nothing change in the way the business is run. This brings us to the concern that too many initiatives in the same organisation will give conflicting messages to employees, particularly when they are introduced by different parts of the business. There may, for example, be contradictions between the messages of Total Quality Management (TQM) and those of the learning organisation type of approach. We will explore these further in Chapter 17.

Table 16.1 lists some of the major performance initiatives. They are divided according to their primary focus: organisational, individual or team. Some of them partly cover the same ground, and it would be surprising to find them in the same business at the same time.

Table 16.1 **Some major performance initiatives**

Organisational focus	Learning organisation
	Investors in people
	Total quality management (TQM)
	Performance culture
	Lean production
	Business Process Reengineering
	Just in Time (JIT)
	Standards: BS5750
	ISO9000
	Customer care/orientation
Individual focus	Performance management
	Performance-related pay
	Self-development/continuous development
Team focus	High-performance teams
	Cross-functional teams
	Self-regulating teams

Activity 16.1

1 Identify the main performance initiatives in your organisation.

2 What/who is the source of each initiative?

3 In what ways do they mutually support each other, and in what ways do they conflict?

Things that go wrong

The level of satisfaction with performance initiatives is typically low (Jacobs 1993; Antonioni 1994), so we close this chapter with a summary of the problems most often reported.

The process/people balance

Schemes rarely strike the right balance between a people emphasis and a process emphasis. Concentrating on being brilliant at talking to the people, getting them going and talking them down gently if they don't quite make it will not suffice if there is not a clear, disciplined process that brings in the essential features of consistency and defining sensible goals. Getting the goals and measures right is a waste of time if there is not the necessary input to changing attitudes, developing skills and winning consent.

Getting the measures right

On the basis of what gets measured gets done, it is critical that the organisation selects the most useful measure of performance for the organisaton as a whole and for the individuals within it. Single measures are unlikely to be sufficiently robust. Kaplan and Norton (1992) argue convincingly that the mix of measures which an organisation should use to assess its performance should be based around four different perspectives:

- **Financial measures** – such as sales growth, profits, cash flow and increased market share.
- **Customer measures** – that is, the customer perspective, which looks at, for example, delivery time, service quality, product quality.
- **Internal business measures** – cycle time, productivity, employee skills, labour turnover.
- **Innovation and learning perspective** – including such elements as ability to innovate and improve.

The focus must be on what is achieved: results are what count. At an individual level a focus on behaviour rather than results achieved can be unhelpful, leading to personality clashes, and misleading. Doing things in the right way is no substitute for doing the right things.

Management losing interest

A constant axiom with any initiative is the need for endorsement from senior management. With a performance initiative there is the need to go a great deal further. First, senior managers have to accept that the initiative is something in which they have to participate continuously and thoroughly. They cannot introduce it, say how important it is and then go off to find other games to play:

> studies have shown that in organisations that utilise performance management, 90 per cent of senior managers have not received performance reviews in the last two years. Clearly the problem here is that PM is not used, modelled and visibly supported at the top of the organisation. Sooner or later people at lower levels catch on and no longer feel compelled to take the time to make PM work.
>
> (Sparrow and Hiltrop 1994, p. 565)

The second aspect is indicated in that quotation. Performance initiatives will not work unless people at all levels either believe in them or are prepared to give them a try with the hope that they will be convinced by the practice.

The team/individual balance

Individuals can rarely perform entirely on their own merits; they are part of a department or team of people whose activities interact in innumerable ways. Trevor Macdonald may read the television news with a clarity and sureness that is outstanding, but it would be of little value if the lights did not work or the script contained errors. Most working people, no matter how eminent, are not solo performers to that extent. Somehow the performance initiative has to stimulate both individual and team performance, working together within the envelope of organisational objectives.

> Historically the individual has been the basis of performance management strategies. However, this may be problematic in that performance variation tends to be falsely attributed to individuals, and the enhancement of individual performance does not necessarily coincide with the enhancement of the greater unit or work system.
>
> (Waldman 1994, p. 41)

Activity 16.2 Think of situations in your own experience outside working life, where there has been a potential clash between individual performance and team performance. Examples might be:

(a) the opening batsman more concerned with his batting average than with the team winning the match;

(b) the person playing the lead in the amateur operatic society's production of *The Merry Widow* who ignores the chorus; or

(c) the local councillor more concerned with doing what is needed to earn an MBE than with supporting the collective view of the council.

How was the potential clash avoided, or not? How could it have been managed more effectively to harmonise individual and team performance?

Leaving out the development part

A key feature of managing performance is developing people so that they *can* perform. This is the feature that is most often not delivered. It is often the lack of follow-up on development needs that is the least satisfactory aspect of performance management systems.

Implementing and managing the change

If, as Purcell (1999) identifies, 'our concern should be less about the precise policy mix in the 'bundle' and more about how and when organisations manage the HR side of change', then the way that large and small performance initiatives are implemented and managed is critical. While this is well-trodden ground, there is considerable evidence of attempted changes which have failed for a wide range of reasons including: trust is low; change is seen as a management fad which will go away; change has been poorly communicated and understood; change is just a way to get us to work harder for the same money.

Getting it right

Here are four suggestions for running a successful performance initiative:

1 Develop and promulgate a clear vision for the business as a framework for individual/team goals and targets.

2 In consultation, develop and agree individual goals and targets with three characteristics: (a) what to do to achieve the target; (b) how to satisfy the customer rather than pleasing the boss; (c) targets that are precise, difficult and challenging, but attainable, *with feedback*.

3 Do not begin until you are sure of: (a) unwavering commitment from the top; (b) an approach that is driven by the line and bought into and owned by middle and first-line managers; (c) a system that is run, monitored and updated by HR specialists; (d) an agreement that every development commitment or pay commitment is honoured, or a swift, full explanation is given of why not.

4 Train all participants.

Summary propositions

16.1 Central to understanding management interest in performance is understanding the subtle change in attitudes: not only is performance rewarded, performance is also a reward.

16.2 In the UK our views of performance improvement have been influenced by the US literature, the Japanese experience and the HRM strategy literature.

16.3 There has been considerable research effort devoted to investigating the link between a bundle of people management practices and organisational performance, and some would argue that the link has been successfully demonstrated.

16.4 Much less clear are the processes by which the link is made, for example how, why and in what context? So far we see commitment as the moderating variable between HR practices and organisational performance.

16.5 Things that typically go wrong with performance initiatives are getting the people/process balance wrong, not selecting the right performance measures, management losing interest and getting the team/individual balance wrong.

16.6 Factors likely to produce success relate to a clear, understood vision, effective target setting, full management commitment, training and honouring commitments.

References

Antonioni, D. (1994) 'Improve the performance management process before discontinuing performance appraisals', *Compensation and Benefits Review*, Vol. 26, No. 2, pp. 29–37.

Becker, B. and Gerhard, B. (1996) 'The impact of human resource management on organizational progress and prospects', *Academy of Management Journal*, Vol. 39, No. 4, pp. 779–801.

Connock, S. (1992) 'The importance of big ideas to HR managers', *Personnel Managers*, June.

Cooper, J. and Hartley, J. (1991) 'Reconsidering the case for organisational commitment', *Human Resource Management Journal*, Vol. 3, Spring, pp. 18–32.

Delbridge, R. and Turnbull, P. (1992) 'Human resource maximisation: The management of labour under just-in-time manufacturing systems', in P. Blyton and P. Turnbull (eds), *Reassessing Human Resource Management*. Beverly Hills: Sage.

Guest, D. (1992) 'Right enough to be dangerously wrong; an analysis of the "In search of excellence" phenomenon', in G. Salaman *et al.* (eds), *Human Resource Strategies*. London: Sage.

Guest, D. (1998) 'Beyond HRM: Commitment and the contract culture', in P. Sparrow and M. Marchington (eds), *Human Resource Management: The New Agenda*. London: Financial Times Pitman Publishing.

Guest, D. (2000) 'Human Resource Management, employee well-being and organizational performance'. Paper presented at the CIPD Professional Standards Conference, 11 July.

Hitt, M. and Ireland, D. (1987) 'Peters and Waterman revisited; the unending quest for excellence', *Academy of Management Executive*, Vol. 1, No. 2, pp. 91–8.

Huselid, M. (1995) 'The impact of human resource management practices on turnover, productivity and corporate financial performance', *Academy of Management Journal*, Vol. 38, No. 3, pp. 635–73.

In comparing your HR department against others:

(a) Which other HR departments would you choose to compare yourselves with and why?

(b) What quality measures or indicators would you use for the comparison and why?

or

Think of any organisation in which you are involved in any capacity:

(a) Which other organisations would you compare this organisation with and why?

(b) What quality measures or indicators would you use for the comparison and why?

WINDOW ON PRACTICE

Mohrman *et al.* (1995) identify 13 practices which they regard as commonly included in the practices of companies which regard themselves as operating TQM. The practices, in three groups, are as follows:

Core practices

■ quality improvement teams;
■ quality councils;
■ cross-functional planning;
■ process reengineering;
■ work simplification;
■ customer satisfaction monitoring;
■ direct employee exposure to customers.

Production-oriented practices

■ self-inspection;
■ statistical control method used by front line employees;
■ just-in-time deliveries;
■ work cells or manufacturing units.

Other

■ cost of quality monitoring;
■ collaboration with suppliers in quality efforts.

Mohrman *et al.* surveyed the 1992 Fortune 1000 listing in the United States which comprises the largest 500 manufacturers and the largest 500 service organisations. They found that 73 per cent of the organisations that responded to the survey had a quality initiative in place which covered an average of 50 per cent of employees in the organisation. The two most frequently used practices of the 13 listed above were customer satisfaction monitoring and quality improvement teams, with 56 per cent and 59 per cent of organisations, respectively, covering 50 per cent or more of their employees in these practices. Self-inspection, collaboration with suppliers and exposure to customers are slightly less frequently used, but still within the 35–40 per cent range. The least used practice was that of work cell organisation.

Source: Summarised from Mohrman, S., Tenkas, R., Lawler, E. and Ledford, G. (1995) 'Total Quality Management – practice and outcomes in the largest US firms', *Employee Relations*, Vol. 17, No. 3.

What happens in practice?

In an ideal world organisations implementing TQM would follow the above steps on a continuous basis and quality improvements would ensue. While there are reports of organisational successes, research increasingly suggests that it is not as simple as this for most. The IPM survey referred to above (reported in Marchington *et al.* 1993) identifies four out of five organisations experiencing people problems in implementing quality initiatives. These problems centred on commitment to the aims of quality initiatives. Dale and Cooper identified middle managers as a block to implementation. This is sometimes because these managers see TQM as representing a greater workload for them without any immediate payoff, or alternatively they fear delegating responsibility and being left with no job or no power. Wilkinson *et al.* (1992) found that rather than TQM uniting middle managers behind a common cause, it actually became a source of competition. Wilkinson *et al.* (1994), reporting on an Institute of Management study, found that managers felt TQM placed a greater emphasis on teamwork, made greater demands on their time and made management jobs more demanding in terms of both technical and people skills needed. Many managers acknowledged that it placed them under greater scrutiny from senior managers, and also that there was greater pressure from employees below them. These same managers reported the need for further training in a variety of areas relevant to TQM, especially in the area of TQM tools and techniques (54 per cent) followed by TQM philosophy (33 per cent) and project management skills (32 per cent).

Schein (1991) also identifies the most commonly cited failure of TQM as the failure of upper and middle management to commit themselves to it, and Glover (2000) found that the failure of TQM in her research organisation was due to the failure of management to implement and maintain it effectively, rather than to workforce resistance. Managers often lack the passion and enthusiasm that TQM requires, and top management all too often delegate their involvement. Miller and Cargemi (1993) remind us that quality needs to be an obsession with everyone in the organisation. This requires a common understanding and a common language at all levels of the organisation. Prest (1995), in a case study of one organisation, found that senior managers were satisfied with the way that TQM was being developed within the organisation, yet first-line employees had a very different understanding of what TQM was about, the implications it had for them and the rationale for implementing it. Despite a considerable amount of training a common understanding and language had not developed and senior managers were unaware of this. Many employees were also frustrated because they were unable, for a variety of reasons, to put their new learning into practice. Employee interpretations must be critical to success, but perhaps the lack of consensus in the above study was at least partly due to the TQM programme being less than one year old, and it is recognised that TQM is not a quick fix, needing several years to become fully established (see, for example, Hill and Wilkinson 1995).

A further difficulty for managers is in wrestling with the concepts of TQM. TQM requires an environment where mistakes are seen as learning opportunities. How do managers reconcile this with 'zero defect' and 'right first time' and avoid using mistakes as punishment opportunities? Political barriers are clearly another force to reckon with, for example the impact of the unions. While Mohrman *et al.* (1995) found that the unions had not been a problem in a US context, one interpretation of their data is that the unions influence the way that TQM is implemented (Hill and Wilkinson 1995).

Wilkinson *et al.* (1992) from their research identified some further issues related to difficulties in sustaining TQM:

Review

The HR function is well placed to identify some of the effects and issues in implementing TQM. Attitude and opinion surveys are one popular way of identifying these. Working closely with departments as a consultant is another, and in this way richer information can be gathered giving a more in-depth understanding of issues and problems.

Learning organisations

The interest in learning organisations has been stimulated by the need to be competitive, as learning is considered to be the only way of obtaining and keeping a competitive edge. Edmonson and Moingeon (1998, p. 9) put it very well when they say:

> To remain viable in an environment characterized by uncertainty and change, organizations and individuals alike depend upon an ability to learn.

While the concept of organisational learning has been explored for some time, the concept of the learning organisation is a recent notion reflected in the literature since the late 1980s. Pedler *et al.* (1989) suggested that the concept of the learning organisation was a response to poor organisational performance. In other words they saw it as a way of overcoming

> sluggishness, an excess of bureaucracy and over-control, of organisations as straitjackets frustrating the self-development efforts of individual members and failing to capitalise upon their potential.

In 1987 Pedler, Boydell and Burgoyne carried out a project entitled 'Developing the Learning Company' and interviewed staff in organisations which were pursuing learning company strategies. They asked why these strategies had been adopted, and found such reasons as the need to improve quality; the wish to become more people oriented in relation to both staff and customers; the need to encourage 'active experimentation' and generally to cope with competitive pressures in order to survive. They defined the learning organisation, which they identify as a 'dream' rather than a description of current practice, as:

> an organisation which facilitates the learning of all its members and continually transforms itself.

By the year 2000 there was still little empirical evidence of organisations that have transformed themselves like this, and in 1999 Sloman suggested that the concept of the learning organisation was in terminal decline. Part of the problem, he argues, is that there is such confusion over the concept. While Burgoyne (1999), and many others, such as Popper and Lipshitz (2000) concur with the extent of confusion, Burgoyne claims that there is still considerable interest in the idea from both organisations and academics, and that our understanding of the concept needs to be developed. He recognises that much of the early thinking about the learning organisation was naïve, and suggests that, as the concept is developed, organisations will have more success with it. In particular, he describes the idea of becoming a learning organisation as one grand project, as 'utopian and unrealistic', and he recognises the value of a more incremental approach.

Easterby-Smith and Araujo (1999) note that a number of different disciplines have made a contribution to the debate on organisational learning and learning organisations, producing a plurality of perspectives. Part of the confusion, though, lies in the practices adopted by organisations under the banner of a learning organisation, rather than in the fundamental ideas. Academics and theorists may place different emphases on different aspects, but these are mutually supportive rather than conflicting. There is a common thread of a holistic approach and that organisational learning is greater than the sum of individual learning in the organisation. Different organisations appear to have been inspired by some aspects of this approach, and having adopted these, they see themselves as learning organisations. In essence they have taken some steps towards their goal, and have certainly improved the level of learning going on in the organisation, but have taken a partial rather than a holistic approach. A further confusion is the difference between the nature of organisational learning and the learning organisation, which we consider in the following section.

Organisational learning and the learning organisation

The study of *organisational learning* is based on the detached observation of individual and collective learning processes in the organisation. The approach is critical and academic, and the focus is the nature and processes of learning, whereas Easterby-Smith and Araujo (1999) suggest that the study of *learning organisations* is focused on 'normative models for creating change in the direction of improved learning processes'. Much of the research on learning organisations has been produced by consultants and organisations that are involved in the process. In other words the data come from an action learning perspective and are produced by interested parties, giving, inevitably, a positive spin to what is produced. This is not to say that the learning organisation perspective is devoid of theory (Easterby-Smith and Araujo 1999). The study of learning organisations often focuses on organisational learning mechanisms, and these can be seen as a way of making the concept of organisational learning more concrete, and thus linking the two perspectives. Popper and Lipshitz (1998) describe organisational learning mechanisms as the structural and procedural arrangements that allow organisations to learn, in other words:

> that is to collect, analyse, store, disseminate and use systematically information that is relevant to their and their members' performance.

These issues are well reflected in Pedler *et al.*'s (1991) model of the learning organisation, which we will describe, shortly. Easterby-Smith and Araujo (1999) argue that the literature on the learning organisation draws heavily on the concepts of organisational learning, from a utilitarian perspective, and there is some commonality in the literature – as Argyris and Schon (1996) suggest. It is generally agreed that there is a lack of critical research from both perspectives.

Organisational and individual learning

Although some pragmatic definitions of learning organisations centre on more and more individual learning, learning support and self-development, organisational learning is more than just the sum of individual learning in the organisation. It is only when an individual's learning has an impact on and interrelates with others that organisation members learn together and gradually begin to change the way things are done.

Figure 17.3 Blueprint of a learning company

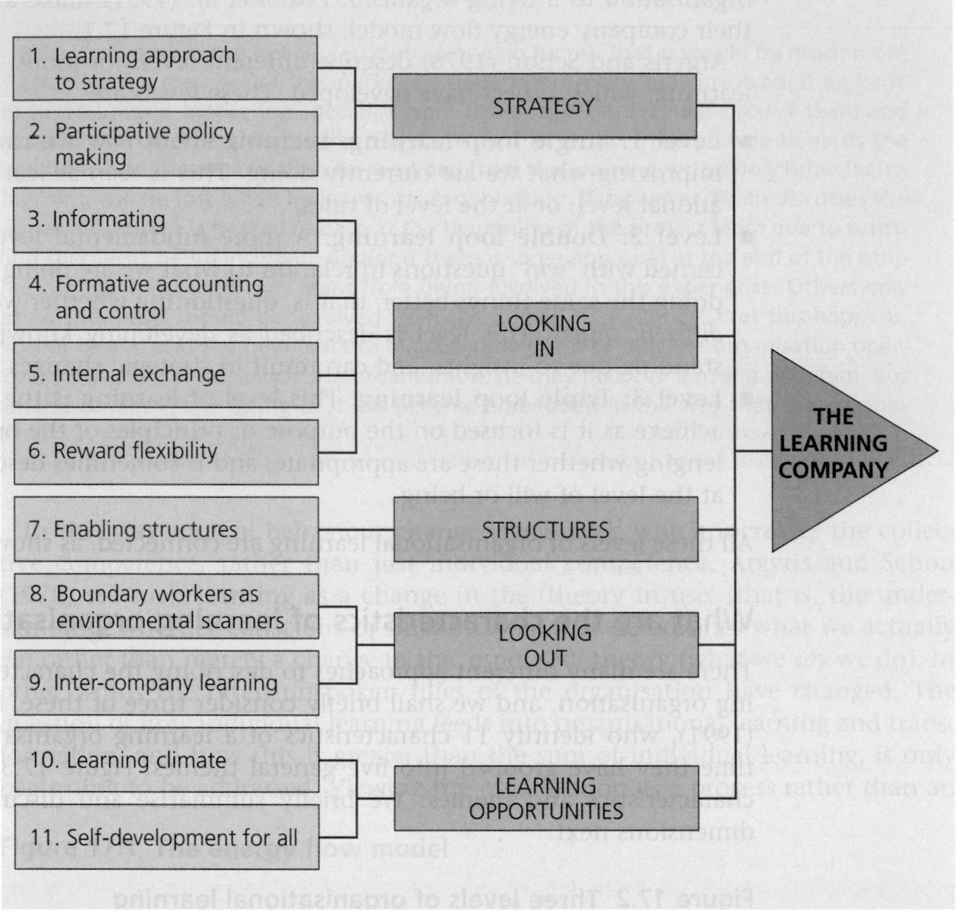

Source: M. Pedler, J. Burgoyne and T. Boydell (1991) *The Learning Company*. Maidenhead: McGraw-Hill. Copyright © 1991 McGraw-Hill Europe. Reproduced with the permission of McGraw-Hill Book Company, Europe.

A learning approach to strategy

Strategy formation, implementation, evaluation and improvement are deliberately structured as learning experiences. Explicit feedback loops are built into the process so that there can be continuous improvement in the light of experience. This approach is very close to Mintzberg's ideas of strategy formation (see, for example, Mintzberg 1987).

Participative policy making

Policy making is shared with all in the organisation, and even further, suppliers, customers and the total community have some involvement. The aim of the policy is to 'delight customers', and the differences of opinion and values that are revealed in the participative process are seen as productive tensions. A closeness to the principles of total quality management can be seen here. Nonaka and Johansson (1985) note how extensive internal consultations are carried out in Japanese organisations before major decisions are taken.

Informating

Technology is used to empower and inform employees, and is made widely available. They note that such information should be used to understand what is going on in the company, and so stimulate learning, rather than used to reward, punish or control. There are some clear difficulties here with the practical example we described, of information use in a total quality environment. Easterby-Smith (1989) makes the point that good news, such as sales achieved, is often reported, rather than the information that would be of more value – why some orders were lost. He also notes the importance of systems that are future oriented rather than past oriented.

Formative accounting and control

Pedler *et al.* (1991) see formative accounting and control as a particular application of informating where accounting, budgeting and reporting systems are designed to assist learning. They also identify a purpose here of delighting the internal customer.

Internal exchange

Internal exchange involves the general idea of all internal units seeing themselves as customers and suppliers of each other, but causing them to operate in a collaborative rather than a competitive way. This is, of course, also a key theme in TQM.

Reward flexibility

While Pedler *et al.* (1991) note that money is not seen as the sole reward, they also consider that the question of why some receive more money than others is a debate to be brought out into the open. They recommend that alternatives are discussed and tried out, but recognise that this is the most difficult of the 11 characteristics to put into practice.

Enabling structures

Structures are enabling if roles are loosely structured in line with the needs of internal customers and suppliers, and in a way that allows for personal growth and experimentation. Internal boundaries can be flexible. Easterby-Smith (1989) reports on some research with managers from different organisations. They were asked whether they had learned and developed through their past work experiences, and the results indicated that managers in different organisations differed greatly in the extent to which they had done this. One of the key characteristics which distinguished organisations where individuals had learned and those where they had not was the use of project groups and transient structures, and individual encouragement to try new ways of working. These structures help to break down barriers between units, provide mechanisms for spreading new ideas and encourage the idea of change.

Boundary workers as environmental scanners

The concept of boundary workers as environmental scanners relates to the need to collect data from outside the organisation. It is seen as part of the role of all workers who have contact with suppliers, customers and neighbours of the organisation to participate in collection.

Inter-company learning

Inter-company learning entails joining with customers and suppliers in training experiences, research and development and job exchanges. Pedler *et al.* (1991) also note the possibility of learning with competitors. They also suggest that benchmarking can be used to learn from other companies.

Learning climate

A learning climate is one that primarily encourages experimentation and learning from experience. To achieve this current ideas, attitudes and actions need to be questioned and new ideas tried out. Mistakes are allowed because not all new ideas will work. The importance of continuous improvement is underlined – that it is always possible to do it better. The involvement of customers, suppliers and neighbours in experimentation is suggested. A learning climate suggests that feedback from others is continually requested, is made available and is acted upon.

Self-development opportunities for all

Resources and facilities for self-development must be available to employees at all levels in the organisation, and coaching, mentoring, peer support, counselling, feedback, and so on must be available to support individuals in their learning.

Activity 17.3	Which of the 11 dimensions identified by Pedler *et al.* (1991) are currently being pursued in your organisation, or any organisation with which you are familiar? How is this being done?
	Which of the 11 would be the most difficult for this organisation to pursue? What are the barriers, and how might they be overcome?

Peter Senge (1990) takes a slightly different perspective. In his book about the art and practice of a learning organisation he identified five vital dimensions in building organisations which can learn, which he refers to as disciplines:

1 **Systems thinking**: This is an understanding of the interrelatedness between things, seeing the whole rather than just a part, and concentrating on processes. In terms of organisational actions it suggests that connections need to be constantly made and that there must be consideration of the implications that every action has elsewhere in the organisation.
2 **Personal mastery**: This underlines the need for continuous development and individual self-development.
3 **Mental models**: This is about the need to expose the 'theories in use' in the organisation. These can block change and the adoption of new ideas, and can only be confronted, challenged and changed if they are brought to the surface rather than remaining unconscious.
4 **Shared visions**: This is expressing the need for a common purpose or vision which can inspire members of the organisation and break down barriers and mistrust. Senge argues that such a vision plus an accurate view of the present state results in a creative tension which is helpful for learning and change.
5 **Team learning**: Teams are seen as important in that they are microcosms of the organisation, and the place where different views and perspectives come together, which Senge sees as a productive process.

Senge acknowledges that he presents a very positive vision of what organisations can do, and recognises that without the appropriate leadership this will not happen. He goes on to identify three critical leadership roles: designer, teacher and steward. As designer the leader needs to engage employees at all levels in designing the vision, core purpose and values of the organisation: design processes for strategic thinking and effective learning processes. As teacher the leader needs to help all organisation members gain more insight into the organisational reality, to coach, guide and facilitate, and help others bring their theories into use. As steward the leader needs to demonstrate a sense of personal commitment to the organisation's mission and take responsibility for the impact of leadership on others.

Bob Garratt (1990) concentrates on the role that the directors of an organisation have in encouraging a learning organisation and in overcoming learning blocks. He suggests:

- the top team concentrate on strategy and policy and hold back from day-to-day operational issues;
- thinking time is needed for the top team to relate changes in the external environment to the internal working of the organisation;
- the creation of a top team, involving the development and deployment of the strengths of each member;
- the delegation of problem solving to staff close to the operation;
- acceptance that learning occurs at all levels of the organisation, and that directors need to create a climate where this learning freely flows.

Clearly, a learning organisation is not something that can be developed overnight and has to be viewed as a long-term strategy.

Easterby-Smith (1989) makes some key points about encouraging experimentation in organisations in relation to flexible structures, information, people and reward. We have discussed flexibility and information in some detail. In respect of people he argues that organisations will seek to select those who are similar to current organisation members. The problem here is that such a strategy, in reinforcing homogeneity and reducing diversity, restrains the production of innovative and creative ideas. He sees diversity as a positive stimulant and concludes that organisations should therefore select some employees who would not normally fit their criteria, and especially those who would be likely to experiment and be able to tolerate ambiguity. In relation to the reward system he notes the need to reinforce rather than punish risk taking and innovation.

Critique

The initial idealism of the learning organisation concept has been tempered by experiences over the past 10 years, and more pragmatic material is gradually being developed. For example Burgoyne (1999) has drawn up a series of nine things that need to happen for continuous learning to become a reality, and Popper and Lipshitz (2000) have identified four conditions under which organisational learning is likely to be productive. These are in situations where there is:

1 **Valid information** – that is, complete, undistorted and verifiable information.
2 **Transparency** – where individuals are prepared to hold themselves open to inspection in order to receive valid feedback. This reduces self-deception, and helps to resist pressures to distort information.

3 **Issues orientation rather than a personal orientation** – that is, where information is judged on its merits and relevance to the issue at hand, rather than on the status or attributes of the individual who provides the information.
4 **Accountability** – that is, 'holding oneself responsible for one's own actions and their consequences and for learning from these consequences'.

However, there remain a wide range of concerns regarding the concept of the learning organisation. Hawkins (1994) notes the evangelistic fervour with which learning organisations and total quality management are recommended to the uninitiated. His concern with the commercialisation of these ideas is that they thereby become superficial. He argues that an assumption may be made that all learning is good whatever is being learned whereas the value of learning is where it is taking us. Learning, then, is the means rather than the end in itself. Learning to be more efficient at what is being done does not necessarily make one more effective – it depends on the appropriateness of the activity itself. Nor does the literature cover adequately the barriers to becoming a learning organisation – for example, the role of politics within the organisation. If learning requires sharing of information, and information is power, then how can individuals be encouraged to let go of the power they have? In particular, both Senge (1990) and Garratt (1990) have high expectations of the leaders of organisations. To what extent are these expectations realistic, and how might they be achieved? The literature of learning organisations has a clear unitarist perspective – the question of whether employees desire to be involved in or united by a vision of the organisation needs to be addressed. For a useful critique of the assumptions behind learning organisations, see Coopey (1995). In addition, the full complexity of the ideas implicit in the words 'learning organisation' requires more explanation.

Organisational development

Organisational development (OD) has been, and remains, a key approach to developing performance in some organisations. French and Bell (1984) have described OD as an approach to organisational improvement using behavioural science techniques. Hawkins (1994) sees the learning organisation as an umbrella for OD activities, while recognising there is value in the slightly different perspectives of each. Other writers have argued that the learning organisation is enabling individuals to do collectively what OD sets out to do, but that they are doing it by themselves without external help.

Typically, OD has involved an internal or external consultant/facilitator using behavioural science principles in working on organisational problem solving. Currently, OD practitioners may be particularly involved in the introduction of change, whether it be technical, cultural or organisational. OD's method of operation centres not only on objectives and aims, but on interpersonal behaviour, attitudes and values in the organisation. There is usually an emphasis on openness between colleagues, improved conflict-resolution methods, more effective team management and the collaborative diagnosis and solution of problems. OD does not necessarily include formalised training and development, although it is most likely that this will be incorporated.

Any training strategy typically centres on groups of managers, or directly on organisational processes with the assistance of the change agent or consultant, who helps the participants to perceive, face up to and resolve the behavioural problems experienced. OD is a 'macro' approach to development, as contrasted with individual training and development, which is primarily a 'micro' approach.

Specific issues that OD practitioners may be involved with include:

- developing processes for bringing about and implementing change;
- assessing organisational effectiveness and developing improvement plans;
- organisation structure and design;
- bringing about cultural change;
- designing effective communication processes;
- building effective work-groups and multidisciplinary teams;
- managing the implementation and organisational implications of new technology;
- effective work practices, such as clarification of roles and responsibilities in complex situations, work-group objective setting;
- stimulating innovation and creativity;
- problem solving and effective decision-making processes;
- managing interpersonal and inter-group conflict.

(Adapted from Purves 1989)

Van Eynde and Bledsoe (1990) found in their research that OD practitioners were more likely to be working with client managers on more task-focused issues directly related to organisational effectiveness, and less on improvement of inter-personal relationships, than they were in the 1980s. Team dynamics, for example, would now be dealt with inside the framework of helping a team to resolve a critical issue. Increasingly, OD consultants are involved in helping organisations to envisage the future. The researchers also found that there are increasing opportunities for OD practitioners to work with the highest levels in the organisation on changes that impact on the whole organisation.

It is through these types of intervention, and from their experiences of the processes used, that managers develop further and are more able successfully to work through similar issues in the future. Buchanan *et al.* (1999) surveyed the state of OD and change management with representatives of 61 public and private organisations in 1997. They that found that almost all these organisations identified change management as central to the performance of their organisation, but less than a third employed a full-time change specialist and only 40 per cent found external help to be useful. In most cases change management responsibilities were 'bolted on' to line manager jobs, and most were painfully aware that they did not have the number of people they needed with change management experience. The authors came to the conclusion that the role of change agent was poorly defined and understood in these organisations and that change agents were poorly recognised and rewarded.

Summary propositions

17.1 There is an increasing emphasis on organisational performance and the factors that affect it.

17.2 Systems, structures, processes, resources and culture will all have an impact on organisational performance, as well as on individual motivation and ability.

17.3 Total quality management and learning organisations are two important philosophies for improving organisational performance.

17.4 Both of these approaches require a long-term perspective and are more complex than the way in which they are often presented.

17.5 Total quality management has a statistical, 'hard' strand and a people-centred 'soft' strand. Difficulties experienced in adopting TQM have mainly focused on people issues.

References

Argyris, C. and Schon, D.A. (1978) *Organisational Learning*. Reading, Mass.: Addison-Wesley.

Argyris and Schon (1996) *Organisation Learning II: Theory, Method and Practice*, Reading, MA: Addison-Wesley.

Baldridge National Quality Programme (1999) 'Criteria for Performance Excellence', *Baldridge National Quality Programme*. Gaithersburg, Md.: Baldridge National Quality Programme.

Buchanan, D., Claydon, T. and Doyle, M. (1999) 'Organisation development and change: the legacy of the nineties', *Human Resource Management Journal*, Vol. 9, No. 2, pp. 20–37.

Burgoyne, J. (1999) 'Design of the times', *People Management*, 3 June, pp. 38–44.

Coopey, J. (1995) 'The learning organisation, power, politics and ideology', *Management Learning*, Vol. 26, No. 2, pp. 193–213.

Crosby, P.B. (1979) *Quality is Free*. Maidenhead: McGraw-Hill.

Dale, B. and Cooper, C. (1992) *Total Quality and Human Resources: An executive guide*. Oxford: Blackwell.

Deming, W.E. (1986) *Out of the Crisis*. Cambridge, Mass.: MIT Institute for Advanced Engineering Study.

Easterby-Smith, M. (1989) 'Creating a learning organisation', *Personnel Review*.

Easterby-Smith, M. and Araujo, L. (1999) 'Organisational Learning: Current debates and opportunities', in M. Easterby-Smith, J. Burgoyne and L. Araujo (eds), *Organisational Learning and the Learning Organisation*. London: Sage.

Edmonson, A. and Moingeon, B. (1998) 'From organizational learning to the Learning Organisation', *Management Learning*, Vol. 29, pp. 5–20.

Forrester, P. (2000) 'BPR and TQM: Bedfellows or Aliens'. Seminar given at Manchester Metropolitan University, 6 December.

French, W.L. and Bell, C.H. (1984) *Organisation Development: Behavioural science intervention for organisational improvement*, 4th edn. Hemel Hempstead: Prentice Hall.

Garratt, B. (1990) *Creating a Learning Organisation*. Hemel Hempstead: Director Books.

Glover, L. (2000) 'Neither poison nor panacea: shopfloor responses to TQM', *Employee Relations*, Vol. 22, No. 2.

Harari, O. (1993) 'Ten reasons why TQM doesn't work', *Management Review*, Vol. 82, No. 1, January.

Hawkins, P. (1994) 'Organisational learning; Taking stock and facing the challenge', *Management Learning*, Vol. 25, No. 1.

Hill, S. and Wilkinson, A. (1995) 'In search of TQM', *Employee Relations*, Vol. 17, No. 3.

Honeycutt, A. (1993) 'Total quality management at RTW', *Journal of Management Development*, Vol. 12, No. 5.

Jeffery, J.R. (1992) 'Making quality managers: redefining management's role', *Quality*, Vol. 31, No. 5, May.

Lee, R.A. and Lazarus, H. (1993) 'Uses and criticisms of total quality management', *Journal of Management Development*, Vol. 12, No. 7, pp. 5–10.

Marchington, M., Dale, B. and Wilkinson, A. (1993) 'Who is really taking the lead on quality?', *Personnel Management*, April.

Mendelowitz, A.I. (1991) *Management Practices – US companies improve performance through quality efforts.* United States General Account Office (GAO/NSIAD–91–190).

Miller, R.L. and Cargemi, J.P. (1993) 'Why total quality management fails: perspective of top management', *Journal of Management Development*, Vol. 12, No. 7.

Mintzberg, H. (1987) 'Crafting strategy', *Harvard Business Review*, July/August, pp. 66–75.

Mohrman, S.A., Tenkas, R.V., Lawler, E.E. III and Ledford, G.E. (1995) 'Total quality management – practice and outcomes in the largest US firms', *Employee Relations*, Vol. 17, No. 3.

Nonaka, I. and Johansson, J. (1985) 'Japanese management: what about the "hard skills"?', *Academy of Management Review*, Vol. 10, No. 2, pp. 181–91.

Pedler, M., Boydell, T. and Burgoyne, J. (1989) 'Towards the learning company', *Management Education and Development*, Vol. 20, Pt 1.

Pedler, M., Burgoyne, J. and Boydell, T. (1991) *The Learning Company.* Maidenhead: McGraw-Hill.

Popper, M. and Lipshitz, R. (2000) 'Organisational Learning', *Management Learning*, Vol. 31, No. 2, pp. 181–96.

Popper, M. and Lipshitz, R. (1998) 'Organisational Learning mechanisms: A cultural and structural approach to organizational learning', *Journal of Applied Behavioural Science*, Vol. 34, pp. 161–78.

Prest, A. (1995) 'Perspectives of Total Quality Management', unpublished MA thesis.

Purves, S. (1989) 'Organisation and process consultancy', unpublished paper.

Rees, C. (1999) 'Teamworking and service quality: the limits of employee involvement', *Personnel Review*, Vol. 28, No. 5/6.

Schein, L. (1991) 'Communicating quality in the service sector', in B.H. Peters and J.L. Peters (eds), *Maintaining Total Quality Advantage.* New York: The Conference Board, pp. 40–2.

Senge, P. (1990) *The Fifth Discipline: The art and practice of the learning organisation.* London: Century Business, Random House.

Sewell, G. and Wilkinson, B. (1992) 'Empowerment or emasculation? Shopfloor surveillance in a total quality organisation', in P. Blyton and P. Turnbull (eds), *Reassessing Human Resource Management.* London: Sage.

Sloman, M. (1999) 'Seize the Day', *People Management*, 20 May.

Storey, J. (1992) *Developments in the Management of Human Resources.* Oxford: Blackwell.

Swieringa, J. and Wierdsma, A. (1992) *Becoming a Learning Organisation.* Wokingham: Addison-Wesley.

Valentine, R. and Knights, D. (1997) 'TQM and BRP – can you spot the difference?', *Personnel Review*, Vol. 27, No 1, pp. 78–85.

van Eynde, D.F. and Bledsoe, J.A. (1990) 'The changing practice of organisation development', *Leadership and Organisation Development Journal*, Vol. 11, No. 2, pp. 25–33.

Walker, V. (1993) 'Kaizen – the art of continual improvement', *Personnel Management*, August.

Wilkinson, A., Marchington, M., Goodman, J. and Ackers, P. (1992) 'Total quality management and employee involvement', *Human Resource Management Journal*, Vol. 2, No. 4, pp. 1–20.

Wilkinson, A., Redman, T. and Snape, E. (1994) 'Quality management and the manager: a research note on findings from an Institute of Management study', *Employee Relations*, Vol. 16, No. 1, pp. 62–70.

Wilkinson, A., Godfrey, G. and Marchington, M. (1997) 'Bouquets, brickbats and blinkers: total quality management and employee involvement', *Organisation Studies*, Vol. 118, No. 5, pp. 799–819.

Wilkinson, A., Redman, T., Snape, E. and Machington, M. (1998) *Managing with Total Quality Management.* Basingstoke: Macmillan Business.

General discussion topics

1 Is quality management a threat to or an opportunity for the personnel function?

2 'Learning organisations are dreams which can never come true.' Discuss why you agree or disagree with this statement.

Chapter 18 # Managing individual performance

The treatment of individual performance in organisations has traditionally centred on the assessment of performance and the allocation of reward. Walker (1992) notes that this is partly due to these processes being institutionalised through the use of specific systems and procedures. Performance was typically seen as the result of the interaction between individual ability and motivation.

Increasingly, organisations recognise that planning and enabling performance have a critical effect on individual performance. So, for example, clarity of performance goals and standards, appropriate resources, guidance and support from the individual's manager all become central.

In this chapter we start with the fundamental steps for managing individual performance, review performance appraisal systems, discuss the nature and use of 360-degree feedback, and then explore how performance management systems attempt to integrate both enabling and assessing individual performance.

The performance cycle

The performance cycle identifies three key aspects of effective performance, as shown in Figure 18.1. These aspects can be used as stepping stones in managing employee performance.

Planning performance

Planning performance recognises the importance of a shared view of expected performance between manager and employee. The shared view can be expressed in a variety of ways, such as a traditional job description, key accountabilities, performance standards, specific objectives or targets and essential competencies.

In most cases a combination of approaches is necessary. There is a very clear trend to use specific objectives with a timescale for completion in addition to the generic tasks, with no beginning and no end, which tend to appear on traditional job descriptions. Such objectives give individuals a much clearer idea of performance expectations and enable them to focus on the priorities when they have to make choices about what they do. There is a long history of research demonstrating how clarity of goals improves employee performance.

The critical point about a *shared* view of performance suggests that handing out a job description or list of objectives to the employee is not adequate. Performance expectations need to be understood and, where possible, to involve a contribution from the employee. For example, although key accountabilities may be fixed by the manager, they will need to be discussed. Specific

Figure 18.1 Three key aspects of effective performance

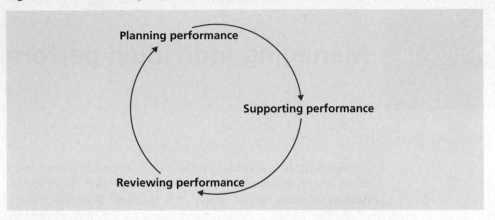

objectives allow for and benefit from a greater degree of employee input as employees will have a valid view of barriers to overcome, the effort involved and feasibility. Expressing objectives as a 'what' statement rather than a 'how' statement gives employees the power to decide the appropriate approach once they begin to work on the issue. Incorporating employee input and using 'what' statements are likely to generate a higher degree of employee ownership and commitment.

Planning the training, development and resources necessary for employees to achieve their objectives is imperative. Without this support it is unlikely that even the most determined employees will achieve the performance required.

Supporting performance

While the employee is working to achieve the performance agreed, the manager retains a key enabling role. Organising the resources and off-job training is clearly essential. So too is being accessible. There may well be unforeseen barriers to the agreed performance which it falls within the manager's remit to address, and sometimes the situation will demand that the expected performance needs to be revised. The employee may want to sound out possible courses of action on the manager before proceeding, or may require further information. Sharing 'inside' information that will affect the employee's performance is often a key need, although it is also something that managers find difficult, especially with sensitive information. Managers can identify information sources and other people who may be helpful.

Ongoing coaching during the task is especially important. Managers can guide employees through discussion and by giving constructive feedback. They are in a position to provide practical job experiences to develop the critical skills and competencies that the employee needs, and can provide job-related opportunities for practice. Managers can identify potential role models to employees, and help to explain how high achievers perform so well.

Although it is the employee's responsibility to achieve the performance agreed, the manager has a continuous role in providing support and guidance, and in oiling the organisational wheels.

Activity 18.1

Do managers actively support employee performance in your organisation? If they do, by what means do they do this and how effective is it? If they do not, why not, and what is the impact of this?

or

Think of any organisation in which you have had some involvement:

■ How has individual performance been supported?

■ How effective was/is this?

■ How would you improve the way in which performance was/is supported?

Ongoing review

Ongoing review is an important activity for employees to carry out in order to plan their work and priorities and also to highlight to the manager well in advance if the agreed performance will not be delivered by the agreed dates. Joint employee/manager review is essential so that information is shared. For example, a manager needs to be kept up to date on employee progress, while the employee needs to be kept up to date on organisational changes that have an impact on the agreed objectives. Both need to share perceptions of how the other is doing in their role, and what they could do that would be more helpful.

These reviews are normally informal in nature, although a few notes may be taken of progress made and actions agreed. They need not be part of any formal system and therefore can take place when the job or the individuals involved demand, and not according to a pre-set schedule. The purpose of the review is to facilitate future employee performance, and provide an opportunity for the manager to confirm that the employee is 'on the right track', or redirect him or her if necessary. They thus provide a forum for employee reward in terms of recognition of progress. A 'well done' or an objective signed off as completed can enhance the motivation to perform well in the future.

Using the performance cycle

The performance cycle describes effective day-to-day management of performance. As such it was often used as the reason why no formal appraisal system was in place – 'because performance is appraised informally on a continuous basis'. In reality performance was usually managed on a *dis*continuous basis, with very little action unless there was a performance problem which needed sorting out! Even then the problem was often avoided until it had become so severe that someone would begin to talk of disciplinary procedures.

The performance cycle, as we have described above, is intended to be viewed as a positive management tool to enhance employee performance and to support whatever formal appraisal or performance management system is in place.

Appraisal systems

Appraisal systems formalise the review part of the performance cycle. They are typically designed on a central basis, usually by the HR function, and require that each line manager appraise the performance of their staff on an annual, six-monthly or even quarterly basis. Elaborate forms are often designed to be completed as a formal record of the process.

Appraisal has traditionally been seen as most applicable to those in management and supervisory positions, but increasingly clerical and secretarial staff are being included in the process. Manual staff, particularly those who are skilled or have technical duties, are also subject to appraisal, although to a lesser extent than the other groups. Long (1986) noted that there has been a substantial increase in performance reviews for non-managerial staff. It has been argued that this increase reflects the increase in individual discretion and autonomy amongst employees which makes direct monitoring more difficult (Townley 1993). Some organisations have a flexible approach whereby individuals in certain grades – for example, secretarial and clerical – can elect whether or not to be included in the appraisal system. Other organisations allow those over a certain age to opt out of the system if they so wish.

Why have an appraisal system?

The different purposes of appraisal systems frequently conflict. Appraisal can be used to improve current performance, provide feedback, increase motivation, identify training needs, identify potential, let individuals know what is expected of them, focus on career development, award salary increases and solve job problems. It can be used to set out job objectives, provide information for human resource planning and career succession, assess the effectiveness of the selection process, and as a reward or punishment in itself. Fletcher and Williams (1985) have suggested two conflicting roles of judge and helper, which the appraiser may be called upon to play, depending on the purpose of the appraisal process. If a single appraisal system was intended to improve current performance and to act as the basis for salary awards, the appraiser would be called on to play both judge and helper at the same time. This makes it difficult for the appraiser to be impartial. It is also difficult for the appraisee, who may wish to discuss job-related problems, but is very cautious about what she or he says because of not wanting to jeopardise a possible pay rise. Randell *et al.* (1984) suggest that the uses of appraisal can be divided into three broad categories, and that an appraisal system should attempt to satisfy only one of these. The categories they suggest are reward reviews, potential reviews and performance reviews. This implies that HR managers need to think more carefully about the primary purpose of their appraisal system, and make sure that procedures, training and individual expectations of the system do not conflict.

Given that there is a choice about the way the appraisal system will be used, Randell *et al.* believe that the greatest advantages will be gained by the use of performance reviews. Such reviews include appraisal of past performance, meeting objectives, identification of training needs, problems preventing better performance, and so on. This poses a great problem, particularly for the private sector, but increasingly in the public sector, where there is a predilection to link pay directly to performance. Do these organisations settle just for reward reviews and forgo the advantages of performance reviews? Do they have two different appraisal systems – one for reward and one for performance at two distinctly different times of the year? Do they forget about linking performance and pay? These are key questions in relation to performance management systems, and are discussed later in this chapter.

Activity 18.2	What are the key purposes of performance appraisal in your organisation, or any organisation with which you are familiar?
	What conflicts does this create?
	How might these conflicts be resolved?

What is appraised?

Appraisal systems can measure a variety of things. They are sometimes designed to measure personality, sometimes behaviour or performance, and sometimes achievement of goals. These areas may be measured either quantitively or qualitatively. Qualitative appraisal often involves the writing of an unstructured narrative on the general performance of the appraisee. Alternatively, some guidance may be given as to the areas on which the appraiser should comment. The problem with qualitative appraisals is that they may leave important areas unappraised, and that they are not suitable for comparison purposes. Coates (1994) argues that what is actually measured in performance appraisal is the extent to which the individual conforms to the organisation.

When the areas for appraisal are measured quantitively some form of scale is used, often comprising five categories of measurement from 'excellent', or 'always exceeds requirements' at one end to 'inadequate' at the other, with the mid-point being seen as acceptable. Scales are, however, not always constructed according to this plan. Sometimes on a five-point scale there will be four degrees of acceptable behaviour and only one that is unacceptable. Sometimes an even-numbered (usually six-point) scale is used to prevent the central tendency. There is a tendency for raters to settle on the mid-point of the scale, either through lack of knowledge of the appraisee, lack of ability to discriminate, lack of confidence or through a desire not to be too hard on appraisees. Rating other people is not an easy task, but it can be structured so that it is made as objective as possible. If performance appraisal is related to pay, then some form of final scale is normally used. A typical approach is for there to be forced distributions on this scale – so, for example, only a specified proportion of staff fall into the highest, middle and lowest categories.

Avoidance of personality measures

Much traditional appraisal was based on measures of personality traits that were felt to be important to the job. These included traits such as resourcefulness, enthusiasm, drive, application and other traits such as intelligence. One difficulty with these is that everyone defines them differently, and the traits that are used are not always mutually exclusive. Raters, therefore, are often unsure of what they are rating. Ill-defined scales like these are more susceptible to bias and prejudice. Another problem is that since the same scales are often used for many different jobs, traits that are irrelevant to an appraisee's job may still be measured. One helpful approach is to concentrate on the job rather than the person. In an attempt to do this some organisations call their annual appraisal activity the 'job appraisal review'. The requirements of the job and the way that it is performed are considered, and the interview concentrates on problems in job performance which are recognised as not always being the 'fault' of the person performing the job. Difficulties in performance may be due to departmental structure or the equipment being used, rather than the ability or motivation of the employee. Other approaches concentrate on linking ratings to behaviour and performance on the job.

Behaviourally anchored rating scales

One way of linking ratings with behaviour at work is to use behaviourally anchored rating scales (BARS). These can be produced in a large organisation by asking a sample group of raters independently to suggest examples of behaviour for each point on the scale in order to collect a wide variety of behavioural examples. These examples are then collated and returned to the sample raters without any indication of the scale point for which they were suggested. Sample raters allocate a scale point to each example, and those examples that are consistently located at the same point on the scale are selected to be used as behavioural examples for that point on the scale. Future raters then have some guidance as to the type of behaviour that would be expected at each point. BARS can be used in conjunction with personality scales, but are most helpful when used with scales that relate more clearly to work behaviour. Table 18.1 shows an example of a BARS in relation to 'relations with clients' – for the sake of clarity just one behavioural example is given at each point on the scale, whereas in a fully developed scale there may be several at each point. Another advantage of the development of BARS is that appraisers have been involved in the process and this can increase their commitment to the outcome.

Behavioural observation scales

Behavioural observation scales (BOS) provide an alternative way of linking behaviour and ratings. Fletcher and Williams (1985) comment that these scales are developed by lengthy procedures, and are similar in some ways to BARS. They indicate a number of dimensions of performance with behavioural statements for

Table 18.1 An example of a behaviourally anchored rating scale: relations with clients

Behavioural example	Points of the rating scale
Often makes telephone calls on behalf of the client to find the correct office for him/her to go to even though this is not part of the job	A
Will often spend an hour with a client in order to get to the root of a very complex problem	B
Usually remains calm when dealing with an irate client	C
If the answer to the client's problem is not immediately to hand s/he often tells them s/he has not got the information	D
Sometimes ignores clients waiting at the reception desk for up to 10 minutes even when s/he is not busy with other work	E
Regularly keeps clients waiting for 10 minutes or more and responds to their questions with comments such as 'I can't be expected to know that' and 'You're not in the right place for that'	F

each. They give the example of leadership/staff supervision as a dimension of performance, and then flesh this out with five or six behavioural statements, such as 'praises staff for doing things well' and 'passes important information to subordinates'. A five-point scale ranging from 'almost never' to 'almost always' is provided so that the appraiser can rate the extent to which each behaviour is displayed.

Meeting objectives

Another method of making appraisal more objective is to use the process to set job objectives over the coming year and, a year later, to measure the extent to which these objectives have been met. The extent to which the appraisee is involved in setting these objectives varies considerably. One of the biggest problems with appraisal on the basis of meeting objectives is that factors beyond the employee's control may make the objectives more difficult than anticipated, or even impossible. We discuss other problems with the 'meeting objectives' approach in the last section of this chapter, on performance management systems, as the process of implementing performance management invariably involves setting and meeting objectives.

Performance against job description

Some systems require the manager to appraise performance against each task specified in the job description or against each key accountability. The appraisal in this case may be in the form of narrative statements and/or a performance rating.

Performance against job competencies

When a competency profile has been identified for a particular job, it is then possible to use this in the appraisal of performance. Many appraisal systems combine competency assessment with assessment against objectives or job accountabilities.

Surveillance of actual performance

Performance appraisal need not only be centred on opinions and reactions reported back by an appraisal interview, as there are increasing opportunities for collecting primary data via various forms of electronic surveillance system. There

---

WINDOW ON PRACTICE

Dick Grote (2000), President of Grote Consulting in Dallas, reports on how the City of Irving in Texas has identified 23 competencies that are considered critical to success. For each of the competencies the designers of the appraisal system wrote dozens of examples reflecting different levels of performance in each competency – ranging from totally ineffective to excellent. Grote points out that the system took a long time to develop, but that in the long run it is much more efficient as 'all the appraiser has to do is to pick the ones that best describe how the employee behaves'.

Note: While it could be argued that much will be lost if appraisal is limited to such a reductionist approach, the use of such scales (similar to BARS and BOS) can focus and stimulate thinking and can be a *useful part* of the appraisal process.

Source: Adapted from D. Grote (2000) 'Performance Appraisal reappraised', *Harvard Business Review,* Jan.–Feb., p. 21.

are increasing examples of how activity rates of computer operators can be recorded and analysed, and how the calls made by telephone sales staff can be overheard and analysed. Sewell and Wilkinson (1992) describe a Japanese electronics plant where the final electronic test on a piece of equipment can indicate not only faults but the individual operator responsible for them. On another level some companies test the performance of their sales staff by sending in assessors acting in the role of customer (Newton and Findlay 1996), often termed 'mystery shoppers'.

Who contributes to the appraisal process?

The direct line manager is most often the key or only source of feedback and assessment and is the most likely person to carry out the appraisal interview (see Chapter 23 for further details). The advantage of this is that the immediate supervisor usually has the most intimate knowledge of the tasks that an individual has been carrying out and how well they have been done. The annual appraisal is also the logical conclusion of ongoing management of performance that should have been taking place throughout the year between the supervisor and the appraisee. However, contributions may be made by a variety of others. For example the level of authority above the immediate manager can be involved in the appraisal process in one of two ways. First, they may be called upon to countersign the manager's appraisal of the employee in order to give a 'seal of approval' to indicate that the process has been fairly and properly carried out. Second, the manager's manager may directly carry out the appraisal. This is known as the 'grandfather' approach to appraisal. This is more likely to happen when the appraisal process is particularly concerned with making comparisons between individuals and identifying potential for promotion. It helps to overcome the problem that managers will all appraise by different standards, and minimises the possibility that appraisees will be penalised due to the fact that their manager has very high standards and is a 'hard marker'. Grandfather appraisal is often used to demonstrate fair play. Much less frequently an employee will be appraised by a member of the HR department. This may happen when there is no obvious ongoing immediate manager, for example, in a matrix organisation. This type of appraisal can be tricky to organise and much depends on the skills of the co-ordinator in the HR department.

Self-appraisal has become a familiar concept of late, and Fletcher (1993b) argues that there is little doubt that people are capable of rating themselves, but the question is, are they willing to do this? Fletcher notes that one of the most fruitful ways for individuals to rate themselves is by rating different aspects of their performance relative to other aspects, rather than relative to the performances of other people. He comments that by approaching self-appraisal in this way, individuals are more discriminating.

Self-appraisal is unlikely to be used alone, however, and individuals carry out an element of self-appraisal in some of the more traditional appraisal schemes. Self-appraisal forms part of 360-degree feedback, which we consider in the following section. Some organisations encourage individuals to prepare for the appraisal interview by filling out some form of appraisal on themselves. The differences between the individual's own appraisal and the manager's appraisal can then be a useful starting point for the appraisal interview. The difference between this and self-appraisal is that it is still the superior's appraisal that officially counts, although in the light of the subordinate's comments they might amend some of the ratings that they have given. In many schemes appraisees are asked to sign the completed appraisal form to show that they agree with its conclusions. In the event of disagreement a space is provided for details of controversial items. At the other end of the scale there are 'closed' schemes which not only eschew any form of contribution from the appraisees, but also prevent the appraisees from knowing the ratings that they have been given by their appraiser. There is a current trend to encourage employee participation in the appraisal process (see, for example, Newton and Findlay 1996).

Peers and subordinates may be invited informally by the line manager to contribute to an individual's appraisal, but again these sources are unlikely to be used alone. Although most appraisal systems focus on appraisal by the direct manager, Fisher (1994) identifies two distinct emphases – hierarchical appraisal (by the management system) and peer appraisal (which he found in some educational institutions and private professional practice firms). Redman and Snape (1992) argue that asking for this type of information from subordinates facilitates empowerment. Fletcher (1993a) comments that upward appraisal is only likely to be used as an occasional and additional activity rather than as an integral part of the appraisal process. Recent examples of upward appraisal include the Post Office (Cockburn 1993) and W.H. Smith (Fletcher 1993a). Further research by Redman and Snape (1992) revealed that only 13 per cent of their sample of 280 respondents were subject to a formal system of upward appraisal. In general their respondents (whether subject to such a system or not) found upward appraisal less acceptable than the conventional approach, and those who did receive it were reluctant to share upward appraisal data with others.

An increasingly useful source of appraisal information is from internal and external customers. This information can be collected directly by the direct manager from internal customers – for example, the training manager may collect information from a department on the support given to them by their specified training officer. Collecting information from external customers is a bit more tricky, but can be done in a positive manner, framed in terms of improving customer services, and designed to be not too time-consuming.

Activity 18.3

Almost all organisation members will have contact with a variety of internal customers. Identify your internal customers, or those of another member of staff, and design a short questionnaire to collect feedback that would be important in an appraisal situation.

What difficulties might you encounter in collecting and using this information?

Note: You can use any organisation with which you are familiar, and any role played by yourself or another person whose role you know about.

Assessment centres can be used in the appraisal of potential supervisors and managers. The advantage of assessment centres for this purpose is that ratings of potential can be assessed on the basis of factors other than current performance. It is well accepted that high performance in a current job does not mean that an individual will be a high performer if promoted to a higher level. It is also increasingly recognised that a moderate performer at one level may perform much better at a higher level. Assessment centres use tests, group exercises and interviews to appraise potential.

Effectiveness of appraisal systems

The effectiveness of appraisal systems hinges on a range of different factors and recent research by Longenecker (1997) in the USA sheds some light on this. In a large-scale survey and focus groups he found that the three most common reasons for failure of an appraisal system were: unclear performance criteria or an ineffective rating instrument (83 per cent); poor working relationships with the boss (79 per cent) and that the appraiser lacks information on the manager's actual performance (75 per cent). Other problems experienced were a lack of ongoing performance feedback (67 per cent) and a lack of focus on management development/improvement (50 per cent). Smaller numbers identified problems with the process, such as lack of appraisal skills (33 per cent) and the review process lacking structure or substance (29 per cent).

We would add that ownership of the system is also important – if it was designed and imposed by the HR function there may be little ownership of the system by line managers. Similarly, if paperwork has to be returned to the HR function the system may well be seen as a form-filling exercise for someone else's benefit and with no practical value to performance within the job. More fundamentally Egan (1995) argues that the problem with appraisal not only relates to poor design or implementation, but is rooted deeply in the basic reaction of organisational members to such a concept. Fletcher (1993a) makes the interesting comment that all systems have a shelf-life – maybe changes are required to the system to renew interest and energy. In any case, as Fletcher also notes, organisations have changed so much, and continue to do so, that it is inevitable that the nature of the appraisal process will change too (see Fletcher 1993b). There is an increasing body of critical literature addressing the role and theory of appraisal. These debates centre on the underlying reasons for appraisal (see, for example, Barlow 1989, Townley 1989, 1993; Newton and Findlay 1996) and the social construction of appraisal (see, for example, Grint 1993). This literature throws some light on the use and effectiveness of performance appraisal in organisations.

360-degree feedback

Our previous discussion of who contributes to the appraisal process, and the reasons why such a process may fail, leads us nicely into defining the nature and use of 360-degree feedback, which is a very specific term used to refer to what was previously termed multi-rater feedback.

The nature of 360-degree feedback

This approach to feedback refers to use of the whole range of sources from which feedback can be collected about any individual. Thus feedback is collected from every angle on the way that the individual carries out their job: from immediate line manager; peers; subordinates; more senior managers; internal customers; external customers; and from themselves. It is argued that this breadth of feedback provides superior feedback to feedback from the line manager's perspective only, since the latter will only be able to observe the individual in a limited range of situations. Hogetts *et al.* (1999) report that more than 70 per cent of United

Parcels Service employees found that feedback from multiple sources was more useful in developing self-insight than feedback from a single source. Individuals, it is argued, will find feedback from peers and subordinates compelling and more valid (see, for example, Borman 1998), and Edwards and Ewen (1996, p. 4) maintain that:

> No organizational action has more power for motivating employee behaviour change than feedback from credible work associates.

Such all-round feedback enables the individual to understand how they may be seen differently (or similarly) by different organisational groups, and how this may contrast with their own views of their strengths and weaknesses. This provides powerful information for the development of self-awareness. While 360-degree feedback may be collected using informal methods, as shown in the Window on Practice box on Humberside Tec, the term itself is a registered trade mark, and refers to a very specific method of feedback collection and analysis which was devised in the United States (see Edwards and Ewen 1996, p. 19), and they suggest that 'simplistic, informal approaches to multi-source assessment are likely to multiply rather than reduce error'. However, informal approaches to 360-degree feedback are sometimes used (as an alternative to a survey questionnaire and statistical analysis) quite successfully.

The formal process is a survey approach which involves the use of a carefully constructed questionnaire that is used with all the contributors of feedback. This questionnaire may be bought off the peg, providing a well-tested tool, or may be developed internally, providing a tool which is more precisely matched to the needs of the organisation. Whichever form is used, the essence is that it is based on behavioural competencies (for a more detailed explanation of these see Chapter 25), and their associated behaviours. Contributors will be asked to score, on a given scale, the extent to which the individual displays these behaviours.

WINDOW ON PRACTICE	**Using an informal approach to 360-degree feedback at Humberside Tec**

Storr (2000) reports on a 360-degree feedback process which is quite different from the survey approach. It is a process which has gradually been built up from upward appraisal for team leaders, has been piloted, and has gradually become standard. The process is owned by the appraisees, and is different because it is carried out face to face rather than using a paper system, and by all raters at the same time in a group-based approach for 90 per cent of individuals. It is a dialogue rather than a survey, and the only rule is that every individual must carry out at least one per year. The purpose of the sytem is to 'improve performance and enable people to learn and grow' (p. 38). Each group has a trained facilitator who supports both appraisers and appraisees. Different individuals have reacted differently to the approach, as might be expected: one individual said that they see it as empowerment, and many found that there was a great advantage in seeing the world from other people's point of view. Storr reports on one individual who received similar feedback from the group to that which she had received previously, from her manager, but hearing it from the six members of the group had a much stronger effect on her. Individuals often used their first experience of the process in a general way to ask the group what they should start doing, stop doing, continue doing, or do differently. Over time, however, individuals began to ask more specific questions.

Source: Summarised from F. Storr (2000) 'This is not a circular', *People Management*, 11 May, pp. 38–40.

Using a well-designed questionnaire, distributed to a sufficient number of contributors and appropriate sophisticated analysis, for example specifically designed computer packages which are set up to detect and moderate collusion and bias on behalf of the contributors, should provide reliable and valid data for the individual. The feedback is usually presented to the individual in the form of graphs, or bar charts showing comparative scores from different feedback groups, such as peers, subordinates, customers, where the average will be provided for each group, and single scores from line manager and self. In most cases the individual will have been able to choose the composition of the contributors in each group, for example which seven subordinates, out of a team of 10, will be asked to complete the feedback questionnaire. But beyond this the feedback will be anonymous as only averages for each group of contributors will be reported back, except of course for the line manager's score. The feedback will need to be interpreted by an internal or external facilitator, and done via a face-to-face meeting. It is generally recommended that the individual will need some training in the nature of the system and how to receive feedback, and the contributors will need some training on how to provide feedback. The principle behind the idea of feedback is that individuals can then use this information to change their behaviours and to improve performance, by setting and meeting development goals and an action plan.

Reported benefits include a stronger ownership of development goals, a climate of constructive feedback, improved communication over time and an organisation which is more capable of change as continuous feedback and improvement have become part of the way people work (Cook and Macauley 1997). Useful texts on designing and implementing a system include Edwards and Ewen (1996) from the US perspective and Ward (1998) from the UK perspective. A brief 'how to do it guide' is Goodge and Watts (2000).

Difficulties and dilemmas

As with all processes and systems there needs to be clarity about the purpose. Most authors distinguish between developmental uses, which they identify as fairly safe and a good way of introducing such a system, and other uses such as to determine pay awards. There seems to be an almost universal view that using these data for pay purposes is not advisable, and in the literature from the United States there is clearly a concern about the legal ramifications of doing this. Ward (1998) provides a useful framework for considering the different applications of this type of feedback, and reviews in some detail other applications such as using 360-degree feedback as part of a training course to focus attention for each individual on what they need to get out of the course. Other applications he suggests include using 360-degree feedback as an approach to team building, as a method of performance appraisal/management, for organisation development purposes and to evaluate training and development. Edwards and Ewen (1996) suggest that it can be used for nearly all HR systems, using selection, training and development, recognition and the allocation of job assignments as examples.

As well as clarity of purpose, confidentiality of raters is very important with most approaches to 360-degree feedback, and this can be difficult to maintain with a small team, as Hurley (1998) suggests. Thus raters may feel uncomfortable about being open and honest. The dangers of collusion and bias need to be eliminated, and it suggested that the appropriate software systems can achieve this,

Jacob and Flood (1995) report on how 360-degree feedback was used as part of a senior management development programme in a French agrochemicals company – Rhône-Poulenc. This approach was felt to be more accurate than an assessment centre because it collected data directly from on-the-job performance rather than from a substitute environment. The questionnaire was designed around a strategically developed competency framework – bosses, peers and subordinates took part in the process as well as the manager themselves. The identity of all contributors was anonymous, except for the immediate boss. The questionnaire took around 20 minutes to complete and was administered prior to the development programme, and at a later date after the programme. As part of the process, individual managers had to present what they had learned about themselves to others in a team setting. Despite this, Jacob and Flood state that 'most participants have suggested that they have never experienced such powerful and apparently insightful feedback about their performance'.

In the United States, where 360-degree feedback appears to have originated, Edwards and Ewen (1996) provide an example of how this process was used to improve customer satisfaction. At Chemetals when sales staff complete a client call they leave the client with a computer disk containing an assessment questionnaire. The client is asked to complete this and mail it on to another party for analysis. Analyses at July 1993, December 1993 and July 1994 demonstrate improvements on a number of aspects of customer satisfaction, particularly in communication and responsiveness. The authors maintain that there was no training, or other initiatives, in the intervening period, and while they cannot exclude some influence from other factors, it appears that the 360-degree feedback was a major cause of the improved job performance.

but they are of course expensive, as are well-validated off-the-peg systems. Follow-up is critical and if the experience of 360-degree feedback is not built on via the construction of development goals and the support and resources to fulfil these, the process may be viewed negatively and may be demotivational. London *et al.* (1997) report concerns about the way systems are implemented, and that nearly one-third of respondents they surveyed experienced negative effects. 360-degree appraisal clearly needs to be handled carefully and sensitively and in the context of an appropriate organisational climate so that it is not experienced as a threat.

Performance management systems

Performance management systems are increasingly seen as the way to manage employee performance rather than relying on appraisal alone. Bevan and Thompson (1992), for example, found that 20 per cent of the organisations they surveyed had introduced a performance management system. In 1997 Armstrong and Baron (1998a) report that 69 per cent of the organisations they surveyed said that they operated a formal process to measure manager performance. Such systems offer the advantage of being tied closely into the objectives of the organisation, and therefore the resulting performance is more likely to meet organisational needs. The systems also represent a more holistic view of performance. Performance appraisal is almost always a key part of the system, but is integrated with ensuring that employee effort is directed towards organisational priorities, that appropriate training and development is carried out to enable employee effort to be successful, and that successful performance is rewarded and reinforced. Given that there is such an emphasis on a link into the organisation's objectives it is somewhat disappointing that Bevan and Thompson found no correlation between the existence of a performance management system and organisational performance in the private sector. Similarly, Armstrong and Baron (1998a) report from their survey that no such correlation was found. They do report, however, that 77 per cent of organisations surveyed regarded their systems as effective (to some degree) – so performance management, like HR systems and processes, still remains an act of faith.

As with appraisal systems, some performance management systems are development driven and some are reward driven. A good example of a development-driven system, which does include an element of reward, is Sheard (1992) reporting on performance management at Zeneca Pharmaceuticals. Whereas in the 1992 IPD survey 85 per cent of organisations claimed to link performance management to pay, Armstrong and Baron found that only 43 per cent of survey respondents reported such a link. However, 82 per cent of the organisations that they visited had some form of performance related pay (PRP) or competency based pay, so the picture is a little confusing. What does seem to be emerging, Armstrong and Baron (1998b) suggest, is a view of performance management which centres on 'dialogue', 'shared understanding', 'agreement' and 'mutual commitment', rather than rating for pay purposes.

There are many different definitions of performance management and some have identified it as 'management by objectives' under another name. There are, however, some key differences here. Management by objectives was primarily an off-the-peg system which organisations bought in, and generally involved objectives being imposed on managers from above. Performance management tends to be tailor-made and produced in-house (that's why there are so many different versions), and there is an emphasis on mutual objective setting and on ongoing performance support and review. The term, therefore, remains ambiguous, and rightly so as it is argued that it is critical that the system adopted fits with the culture and context of the organisation (see, for example, Armstrong and Baron 1998b; Hendry *et al.* 2000).

Figure 18.2 shows a typical system, including both development and reward aspects, the main stages of which are:

Figure 18.2 Four stages of a typical performance management system

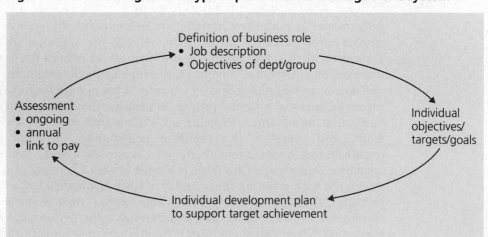

1 **A written and agreed job description, reviewed regularly**. There must be objectives for the work-group which have been cascaded down from the organisation's strategic objectives. Bevan and Thompson (1992) found that performance management organisations were more likely to have an organisational mission statement and to communicate this to employees.

2 **Individual objectives** derived from the above, which are jointly devised by appraiser and appraisee. These objectives are results rather than task oriented, are tightly defined and include measures to be assessed. The objectives are designed to stretch the individual, and offer potential development as well as meeting business needs. Many organisations use the 'SMART' acronym for describing individual objectives or targets:

- Specific
- Measurable
- Appropriate
- Relevant
- Timed

It is clearly easier for some parts of the organisation than others to set targets. There is often a tendency for those in technical jobs, for example, computer systems development, to identify purely technical targets – reflecting heavy task emphasis – they see in their jobs. Moving staff to a different view of how their personal objectives contribute to team and organisational objectives is an important part of the performance management process. An objective for a team leader in systems development could be:

> To complete development interviews with all team members by end-July 2002.
> (written March 2002)

Clearly, the timescale for each objective will need to reflect the content of the objective and not timescales set into the performance management system. As objectives are met, managers and their staff need to have a brief review meeting to look at progress in all objectives and decide what other objectives should be added. Five or six ongoing objectives are generally sufficient for one individual to work on at any time.

3 **A development plan** devised by the manager and the individual detailing development goals and activities designed to enable the individual to meet the objectives. The emphasis here is on managerial support and coaching, very much as described in the performance support phase of managing individual performance (see the discussion of the performance cycle earlier in this chapter). Those organisations with a development-driven performance management system may well have development objectives alongside performance objectives to ensure that this part of the system is given proper attention.

4 **Assessment of objectives**. Ongoing formal reviews on a regular basis are needed. These are designed to motivate the appraisee and concentrate on developmental issues. Also, an annual assessment is needed, which affects pay received, which in turn depends on performance in achievement of objectives. Many systems still include this link with pay, but Fletcher and Williams (1992b) point to some difficulties experienced. Some organisations (both public and private) found that the merit element of pay was too small to motivate staff, and indeed was sometimes found to be insulting. Although performance management organisations were more likely to have merit or performance-related pay (Bevan and Thompson 1992), some organisations

have regretted its inclusion. Armstrong and Baron (1998a) report that staff almost universally disliked the link with pay, and one manager from one of their case study companies reported that 'the whole process is an absolute nightmare' (p. 172).

Implementation and critique of performance management

Performance management needs to be line driven rather than HR driven (see, for example, Fletcher 1993b), and therefore mechanisms need to be found to make this happen. The incorporation of line managers alongside HR managers in a working party to develop the system is clearly important. This not only ensures that the needs of the line are taken into account in the system design, but also demonstrates that the system is line led. Training in the introduction and use of the system is also ideally line led, and Fletcher and Williams (1992b) give us an excellent example of an organisation where line managers were trained as 'performance management coaches' who were involved in departmental training and support for the new system. However, some researchers have found that line managers are the weak link in the system (see, for example, Hendry *et al.* 1997).

WINDOW ON PRACTICE

The scheme was introduced by training a series of nominated line manager coaches from each department. They had then to take the message back to their colleagues and train them, tailoring the material to their department (Personnel/Training providing the back-up documentation). These were serving line managers who had to give up their time to do the job. Many of them were high-flyers, and they have been important opinion leaders and influencers – though they themselves had to be convinced first. Their bosses could refuse to nominate high-quality staff for this role if they wished, but they would subsequently be answerable to the Chief Executive. This approach was taken because it fits with the philosophy of performance management (i.e. high line-management participation), and because it was probably the only way to train all the departmental managers in the timescale envisaged).

Source: C. Fletcher and R. Williams (1992b) *Performance Management in the UK: Organisational Experience.* London: IPM, p. 133.

Bevan and Thompson (1992) found incomplete take-up of performance management, with some aspects being adopted and not others. They noted that there was a general lack of integration of activities. This is rather unfortunate as one of the key advantages of performance management is the capacity for integration of activities concerned with the management of individual performance. This problem is still apparent. Hendry *et al.* (1997) reported the comments of Phil Wills from GrandMet, who suggests that there is still a lack of understanding of what we mean by an integrated approach to performance management, and that while alignment is critical, some organisations do not understand whether their HR processes are aligned or pulling in different directions.

It appears, not surprisingly, that performance management suffers from the same problems as traditional appraisal systems. Armstrong and Baron (1998a) report, for example, that over half the respondents to their survey feel that managers give their best ratings to people that they like (p. 202), and over half the managers surveyed felt that they had not received sufficient training in performance management processes (p. 203). They also report (1998b) that the use of ratings was consistently derided by staff and seen as subjective and inconsistent.

In terms of individual objective setting linked to organisational performance objectives, Rose (2000) reports on a range of problems. In particular he notes how SMART targets can be problematic, if they are not constantly reviewed and updated – a time-consuming process. He goes on to argue that pre-set objectives can be a constraining factor in such a rapidly changing business context, and reminds us of the trap of setting measurable targets, precisely because they are measurable and satisfy the system, rather than because they are most important to the organisation. He argues that a broader approach which assesses the employee's accomplishments as a whole and their contribution to the organisation is more helpful than concentrating on pre-set objectives. There is a further concern with SMART targets, which is that they are inevitably time constrained and have a short-term focus.

There is a very strong argument that what is most important to the organisation are developments which are complex and longer term, and hence are very difficult to pin down to short-term targets (see, for example, Hendry *et al.* 1997). Armstrong and Baron (1998b) do note that a more rounded view of performance is gradually being adopted, which involves the 'how' as well as the 'what', and inputs such as the development of competencies. There is, however, a long way to go to adequately describe performance and define what is really required for organisational success.

Summary propositions

18.1 Effective management of individual performance rests on managing the performance cycle – ongoing performance planning, support and review.

18.2 Appraisal is most often carried out by the immediate manager, but is enhanced by information from other parties.

18.3 There is a conflict in many appraisal systems in the role of the manager – as judge and as helper.

18.4 360-degree feedback is increasingly being used to provide individuals with a basis for changing behaviour and improving performance.

18.5 Performance management systems incorporate appraisal activity, but include other aspects such as a link to organisational objectives and a more holistic view of performance.

18.6 So far performance management has generally been adopted in a piecemeal way with a lack of integration between performance activities. There are, however, some good examples of carefully thought through and implemented systems.

References

Armstrong, M. and Baron, A. (1998a) *Performance Management – The New Realities*. London: IPD.

Armstrong, M. and Baron, A. (1998b) 'Out of the Tick Box', *People Management*, 23 July, pp. 38–41.

Barlow, G. (1989) 'Deficiencies and the perpetuation of power: latent functions in management appraisal', *Journal of Management Studies*, Vol. 26, No. 5, pp. 499–518.

Bevan, S. and Thompson, M. (1992) 'An overview of policy and practice', in *Personnel Management in the UK: an anaylsis of the issues*. London: IPM.

Borman, W. (1998) '360 ratings: an analysis of assumptions and a research agenda for evaluating their validity', *Human Resource Management Review*, Vol. 7, pp. 299–315.

Coates, G. (1994) 'Performance appraisal as icon: Oscar winning performance or dressing to impress?', *International Journal of Human Resource Management*, No. 1, February.

Cockburn, B. (1993) 'How I see the personnel function', *Personnel Management*, November.

Cook, S. and Macauley, S. (1997) 'How colleagues and customers can help improve team performance', *Team Performance Management*, Vol. 3, No. 1.

Edwards, M.R. and Ewen, A.J. (1996) *360 Degree Feedback*. New York: Amacom, American Management Association.

Egan, G. (1995) 'A clear path of peak performance', *People Management*, 18 May, pp. 34–7.

Fisher, C.M. (1994) 'The differences between appraisal schemes: variation and acceptability – Part 1', *Personnel Review*, Vol. 23, No. 8, pp. 33–48.

Fletcher, C. (1993a) *Appraisal: Routes to improved performance*. London: IPM.

Fletcher, C. (1993b) 'Appraisal: an idea whose time has gone?', *Personnel Management*, September.

Fletcher, C. and Williams, R. (1985) *Performance Appraisal and Career Development*. London: Hutchinson.

Fletcher, C. and Williams, R. (1992a) 'The route to performance management', *Personnel Management*, October.

Fletcher, C. and Williams, R. (1992b) *Performance Management in the UK: Organisational experience*. London: IPM.

Goodge, P. and Watts, P. (2000) 'How to manage 360° feedback', *People Management*, 17 February, pp. 50–2.

Grint, K. (1993) 'What's wrong with performance appraisals? – a critique and a suggestion', *Human Resource Management Journal*, Vol. 3, No. 3, pp. 61–77.

Grote, D. (2000) 'Performance Appraisal Reappraised', *Harvard Business Review*, Jan.–Feb., p. 21.

Hendry, C., Bradley, P. and Perkins, S. (1997) 'Missed a motivator?', *People Management*, 15 May, pp. 20–5.

Hendry, C., Woodward, S., Bradley, P. and Perkins, S. (2000) 'Performance and rewards: cleaning out the stables', *Human Resource Management Journal*, Vol. 10, No. 3, pp. 46–62.

Hogetts, R., Luthans, F. and Slocum, J. (1999) 'Strategy and HRM initiatives for the '00s: environment redefining roles and boundaries, linking competencies and resources', *Organizational Dynamics*, Autumn, p. 7.

Hurley, S. (1998) 'Application of team-based 360° feedback systems', *Team Performance Management*, Vol. 4, No. 5.

Jacob, R. and Flood, M. (1995) 'A bumper crop of insights', *People Management*, 9 February.

London, M., Smither, J. and Adsit, D. (1997) 'Accountability: the achilles heel of multi-source feedback', *Group and Organizational Dynamics*, Vol. 22, No. 2, pp. 162–84.

Long, P. (1986) *Performance Appraisal Revisited*. London: IPM.

Longenecker, C. (1997) 'Why managerial performance appraisals are ineffective: causes and lessons', *Career Development International*, Vol. 2, No. 5.

Newton, T. and Findlay, P. (1996) 'Playing God? – the performance of appraisal', *Human Resource Management Journal*, Vol. 6, No. 3, pp. 42–58.

Randell, G., Packard, P. and Slater, I. (1984) *Staff Appraisal*. London: IPM.

Redman, T. and Snape, E. (1992) 'Upward and onward: can staff appraise their managers?', *Personnel Review*, Vol. 21, pp. 32–46.

Rose, M. (2000) 'Target Practice', *People Management*, 23 November, pp. 44–5.

Sewell, G. and Wilkinson, B. (1992) 'Someone to watch over me: surveillance, discipline and the just-in-time process', *Sociology*, Vol. 26, pp. 271–89.

Sheard, A. (1992) 'Learning to improve performance', *Personnel Management*, September.

Storr, F. (2000) 'This is not a circular', *People Management*, 11 May, pp. 38–40.

Townley, B. (1989) 'Selection and appraisal: reconstituting social relations', in J. Storey (ed.), *New Perspectives on Human Resource Management*. London: Routledge.

Townley, B. (1993) 'Performance appraisal and the emergence of management', *Journal of Management Studies*, Vol. 30, No. 2, pp. 27–44.

Walker, J.W. (1992) *Human Resource Strategy*. Maidenhead: McGraw-Hill.

Ward, P. (1995) 'A 360 degree turn for the better', *People Management*, 9 February.

Ward, P. (1998) *360-degree Feedback*. London: IPD.

General discussion topics

1 In what ways is the concept of performance management different from the way in which management has been traditionally practised? What are the advantages and disadvantages for employees and employers?

2 360-degree appraisal may have many advantages, but there is the argument that it can never really work because of the built-in biases, such as marking a boss well because you're due for a pay rise; marking yourself low so that you can be happily surprised by others' evaluations; marking peers down to make oneself look better.

   Discuss as many built-in biases as you can think of, and suggest how they might be tackled and whether substantive improvements could be made.

Chapter 19   Team performance

The appointments pages of *Personnel Management* in the early 1990s were littered with advertisements looking for 'an effective team player' to 'join an established HR team', where one of the 'key organisational issues is team working' so that they can 'add value to the European HR team', 'enhance the skills of the management team', and 'facilitate effective team development'. In *People Management* in 1997 the trend continued, with, perhaps a little more focus, as organisations were seeking 'proactive', 'natural', 'enthusiastic', 'genuine' and 'effective' team players, who 'enjoy' or 'have a preference for' working in a team environment, and who are 'committed' to team working. In 2001, team-related criteria will still be evident, but not quite so prominent.

While few would argue that the 1990s was the age of the team and teamwork, the twenty-first century has brought with it a much more sceptical attitude to teamwork. In spite of a more critical perspective, teamwork is still used and introduced as a way of empowering employees and facilitating the development of their full potential in order to enhance organisational performance. A heavy emphasis on teamwork usually corresponds with flatter organisations which have diminished status differentials. Teamwork, of course, is not a recent idea, and the autonomous working groups of the 1960s and 1970s are clear forerunners. The similarities are increasing responsibility, authority and a sense of achievement among group members. The protagonists of autonomous working groups were also intent on improving the quality of working life of employees by providing a wider range of tasks to work on (job enrichment) and a social environment in which to carry them out. The emphasis currently is quite different – performance is the unvarying aim. Higher performance is expected due to increased flexibility and communication within teams, increased ownership of the task and commitment to team goals. Some of the most famous autonomous working groups at Volvo in Sweden have now been disbanded because their production levels were too low compared with other forms of production. Current teams are designed to outperform other production methods, and Natale *et al.* (1998), for example, argue that they are fundamental to continuous corporate improvement. They are also seen as critical in the development of a learning organisation (see, for example, Senge 1990).

While there remain many strong supporters of teamwork and many organisations committed to this approach, it is in the achievement of improved performance where teamwork has often fallen short. Butcher and Bailey (2000), for example, note that teamwork has not always achieved the desired result, and Attaran and Nguyen (2000) note that flexible structures, such as teamwork, have sometimes been abandoned in favour of returning to more traditional approaches. Not only have organisations begun to consider whether teamwork will produce the expected productivity gains, employees who have experienced teamwork have sometimes viewed it as unsuccessful and feel less optimistic about it than previously (Proehl 1997). Part of the problem may also be unrealistic expectations. Very often performance dips when teamwork is introduced, and the performance improvements only come later on. Teamwork is not a 'quick fix', as has been noted by many of those who have been involved (see, for example, Scott and Harrison 1997; Arkin 1999). Part of the problem may also be that, as Church (1998) notes, there has been a tendency to think that teamwork is a solution for all our problems. Thus teamwork has undoubtedly been used in some situations where it was inappropriate, or where there was insufficient support to make it effective

So, what is a team? How does it differ from all the other groups in organisations? A team can be described as more than the sum of the individual members. In other words, a team demands collaborative, not competitive, effort, where each member takes responsibility for the performance of the team rather than just their own individual performance. The team comes first, the individual comes second, and everything the individual member does is geared to the fulfilment of the team's goals rather than their individual agenda. If you think of a football team, a surgical team or an orchestra, it is easier to see how each member is assigned a specific role depending on their skills and how individuals use their skills for the benefit of the team performance rather than selectively using them for personal achievement. In a football game, for example, a player making a run

WINDOW ON PRACTICE

Mueller (1992) compares and contrasts German and Japanese approaches to flexible teamwork in the European automobile industry. The German approach, influenced by a long-term system of apprenticeships, relies on the heavy use of qualified and skilled production workers in their production teams. Mueller argues that the usefulness of skilled workers depends on the number of skilled tasks required to be done, and found that in the German situation a large number of skilled tasks were carried out, including quality checks, machine supervision and checking, minor maintenance and machine adjustments. However they found substantial differences between the jobs of team members, depending on whether they were skilled or not. For unskilled employees jobs are limited and routine, compared with the job enrichment for skilled workers. The unskilled with limited roles were often demotivated. The skilled workers were highly valued and some plants were considering reconstituting teams with 100 per cent of skilled workers. Mueller argues that there may be potential problems with the heavy use of skilled workers, as they may be top craftsmen but not necessarily good teamworkers. He also suggests that the current system might create demarcations and distinctions within the production team which are alien to the new employee relations. Even for skilled workers, for example electricians, he identifies demotivation as a problem when not enough is demanded of them.

Mueller compares this with the Japanese approach at Honda where qualifications are seen as less important and on-the-job learning is seen as vital. The emphasis here is on attitude, teamworking and openness to change, which can be justified in relation to the accelerating pace of change and a need for a fast response to customers. There was a complete absence of job descriptions, and everyone in the team was paid the same rate. Although team leaders sometimes received a higher rate they also operated as team members as well as leaders. Everyone was considered to be skilled because on-the-job training is continuous (and in the hands of the line manager, not the training department).

The essential elements of good teamwork were seen to be single status, good communication, participation, togetherness, self-development, fairness, competitive working conditions and flexibility. Production teams were given much more autonomy.

Source: Adapted from Mueller, F. (1992) 'Designing flexible teamwork: comparing German and Japanese approaches', *Employee Relations*, Vol 14, No. 1, pp. 5–16.

towards the goal would pass to another player in a better position to score rather than risk trying to score themselves for the sake of personal glory.

Moxon (1993) defines a team as having a common purpose; agreed norms and values which regulate behaviour; members with interdependent functions and a recognition of team identity. Katzenbach and Smith (1993) and Katzenbach (1997) have also described the differences that they see between teams and work-groups, and identify teams as comprising individuals with complementary skills, shared leadership roles, mutual accountability and a specific team purpose, amongst other attributes. In organisations this dedication only happens when individuals are fully committed to the team's goals. This commitment derives from an involvement in defining how the goals will be met and having the power to make decisions within teams rather than being dependent on the agreement of external management. These are particularly characteristics of self-managing teams.

Organisational teams differ, though, in terms of their temporary or permanent nature, the interchangeability of individual members and tasks and the breadth of tasks or functions held within the team:

- **Timespan**: Some teams are set up to solve a specific problem, and when this has been solved the team disbands. Other teams may be longer term and project based, and may disband when the project is complete. Some teams will be relatively permanent fixtures, such as production teams, where the task is ongoing.
- **Interchangeability**: Teams differ in the range of specific skills that are required and the expectation of all members learning all skills. In some production teams interchangeability of skills is key, and all members will have the potential and will be expected to learn all skills eventually. In other types of teams, for example cross-functional teams (surgical teams, product development

Figure 19.1 Different types of team

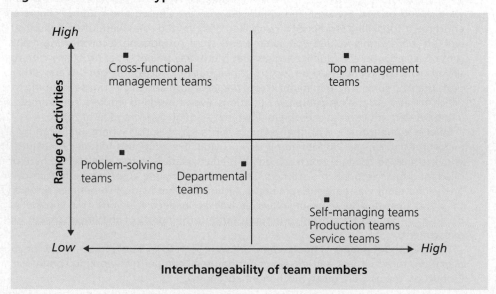

Note: High range of activities indicates activities over a broad range of functions; low range of activities indicates activities within a function and within a single task.

teams), each member is expected to bring their specialist skills to use for the benefit of the team, and they are not expected to be able to learn all the skills of each other member.

■ **Task and functional range**: Many production teams will often be designed to cover a whole task and within this there will be a wide range of activities. This clearly differs from the traditional line form of production where the tasks are broken down and segmented. Other teams will span a range of functions – for example cross-functional teams involving, say, research, development, marketing and production staff.

Figure 19.1 shows how different types of teams can be represented on a framework representing interchangeability and task/functional spread.

In this chapter we shall go on to look at the characteristics of four broad types of teams: production or service teams; cross-functional management teams; problem-solving teams; and departmental teams. We then look at what factors affect teams' performance and what can be done to improve team effectiveness, as these matters are currently of critical concern.

Activity 19.1

Think of the different types of teams in your organisation, or any organisation in which you have been involved (such as school, university, sports clubs, etc.) and plot them on the framework given in Figure 19.1.

What does this tell you about:

(a) your organisation's approach to teamwork?

(b) the different purposes of the different types of teams?

Broad team types

Production and service teams

It is producton and service teams that are often referred to as **self-managing teams**, **self-managing work teams**, or **self-directed teams**. They are typically given the authority to submit a team budget, order resources as necessary within budget, organise training required, select new team members, plan production to meet predefined goals, schedule holidays and absence cover, and deploy staff within the team. There is a clear emphasis on taking on managerial tasks that would previously have been done by a member of the managerial hierarchy. These managerial tasks are delegated to the lowest possible organisational level in the belief that these tasks will be carried out in a responsible manner for the benefit of the team and the organisation. The payoff from this self-management has been shown in Monsanto, for example, to be a 47 per cent increase in productivity and quality over four years (Attaran and Nguyen 2000). These teams are often used in such areas as car production and the production of electrical and electronic equipment. Teams will be based around a complete task so that they perform a whole chunk of the production process and in this way have something clear to manage. For example, the team will normally include people with maintenance skills, specific technical skills and different types of assembly skills so that they are self-sufficient and not dependent on waiting for support from other parts of the organisation. The ultimate aim is usually for all members to have all the skills needed within the team. Self-managing teams may also be found in the service arena as well as the manufacturing one. We referred to the high performance teams at Digital in Chapter 3 (Buchanan 1992) and you may wish to turn back to this example. Other examples of well-known companies using teams are Coca-Cola, Motorola, Procter & Gamble and Federal Express (Piczak and Hause 1996). Although used initially in the manufacturing sector such teams have increasingly been used in the service sector too.

WINDOW ON PRACTICE

Vesuvius

Arkin (1999) reports how Vesuvius, an isolated Scottish outpost of a large international conglomerate, used self-managed teams throughout the production process, and how this, together with an emphasis on employee development, has driven rapid company growth. Vesuvius introduced self-managed teams in a careful manner and built upon a period of gradual, negotiated (with the union) change in working practices where the job and wage structure was changed, and where production workers were given training so that they could do all jobs within the new teams. There were suspicions to begin with and some resistance, and the new teams were slow to start operating effectively. Inevitable concerns were about job losses, but management tried to develop trust by taking out the time clocks so there was no more checking in and out. Teams became responsible 'for the tasks they carried out, the materials they used and the problems they encountered'. Foremen were extensively developed in their new role as facilitators to the teams, and began to focus on safety, quality and training. In addition every employee had a personal development plan. Opinion surveys show that the workforce is more enthusiastic, the number of customer complaints has decreased and the company has made cost savings of £500,000 a year. While it is not possible to attribute these satisfactory outcomes purely to the introduction of self-managed teams, it is reasonable to conclude that these have contributed.

Source: Summarised from Arkin, A. (1999) 'Peak practice', *People Management*, 11 November.

Nationwide

In a very different setting the Nationwide Building Society decided to introduce self-managed team-working into the administrative centre at Northampton as an approach which would further develop multiskilling in a flatter structure (Scott and Harrison 1997). Teams were introduced into the mortgage and insurance customer service department, based on previous work-groups, and were accompanied by increased training and support for decision making, conflict management and team-building skills. Each team has between nine and 18 members, and the leader's role is defined as a coaching rather than a directing role. The team allocates work as it comes in, depending on skills and workloads. Gradually teams took on the responsibility of liaising with branches to improve mutual understanding and develop better ways to work together. The results of each team are charted in a variety of league tables and there is a conscious competitive element between teams. This spurred teams to manage absence levels, amongst other performance criteria. At first there were concerns that self-managed teams were a way to get greater work out of the employees with no more pay, and some team leaders feared a loss of control. There was a temporary dip in performance after the teams were initially set up, but eventually performance improved and absence declined. The approach is now being spread to other locations, although the presence of other initiatives means that it is difficult to tie improvements to the introduction of self-managed teams.

Source: Summarised from Scott, W. and Harrison, H. (1997) 'Full team ahead', *People Management*, 9 October.

In some teams a leader is appointed from the outset, but in others a leader is left to emerge. Whatever process is used, the leader is the same level of employee as other members and is as fully involved in the task of the team. They are therefore not part of the traditional managerial hierarchy, and yet they will need to take on managerial tasks such as planning, organising, supporting individuals, presenting information and representing the team to the rest of the organisation. The way that the leader carries out these activities and involves others in them will clearly have an impact on the effectiveness of the team. In some teams the leadership may vary according to the nature of task, resting with whoever has the most appropriate skills to offer. Where leadership is static the leader's role is often defined in terms of a coaching rather than a directing role.

WINDOW ON PRACTICE

The British company Whitbread have established a small, upmarket chain of restaurants called 'Thank God it's Friday', which is abbreviated to 'Friday's' or TGIF. The marketing is directed towards the relatively young and affluent and a part of this strategy has been to avoid the traditional hierarchy of the good-food restaurant – maître d'hôtel, chef de rang, commis waiter and so forth – by empowering the person with whom the customer deals directly: the waiter. This person can take decisions on such matters as complimentary drinks without reference to anyone else. There is no manager, but each restaurant has a team leader known as the Coach.

The nature of self-management also has an impact on the role of managers outside the team. Traditionally these managers would carry out the tasks described above and would monitor and control the performance of the team. If these tasks are no longer appropriate, what is the role of the manager – is there a role at all? It will come as no surprise that the formation of self-managed teams is seen as a threat to some managers. However, Casey (1993) comments that 'self-managed teams do not deny the role of manager, they redefine it'. He also notes that the management of the team is a balance between responsibility within the team and management without, rather than an all-or-nothing situation. He suggests a move towards 90 per cent within the team in a self-management situation rather than nearer 30 per cent in a traditional management situation.

Where there are self-managed teams the role of the traditional manager outside the team changes to adviser and coach, as they have now delegated most of their responsibilities for directly managing the team. These managers become a resource to be called on when needed in order to enable the team to solve their own problems. Salem, Lazarus and Cullen (1992) comment that:

> The SMT approach requires a conscious effort on the part of the management to encourage and reinforce both the individual members and the team as a whole. Management's tools are stimulating questions designed to motivate the individual to examine himself or herself in relation to the attainment of the group's objectives.

Oliva (1992) draws a helpful framework for understanding the respective managerial roles of traditional managers and teams in a team environment, shown in Figure 19.2.

The self-managing team concept has much to offer in terms of increasing employee ownership and control and thereby releasing their commitment, creativity and potential. There are, of course, potential problems with this approach too. Salem, Lazarus and Cullen (1992) identify the difficulty of returning to traditional systems once employees have experienced greater autonomy; resistance from other parts of the organisation; and peer pressure and its consequences. We would also add resistance from team members too. Let us look at some of these in more detail.

Figure 19.2 Teamwork relationships in the 1990s

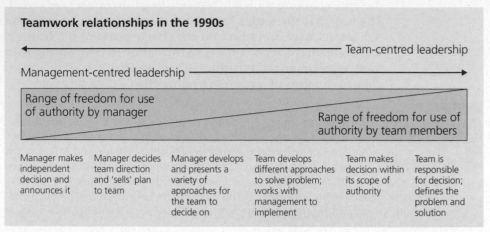

Teamwork relationships in the 1990s

← Team-centred leadership

Management-centred leadership →

Range of freedom for use of authority by manager

Range of freedom for use of authority by team members

| Manager makes independent decision and announces it | Manager decides team direction and 'sells' plan to team | Manager develops and presents a variety of approaches for the team to decide on | Team develops different approaches to solve problem; works with management to implement | Team makes decision within its scope of authority | Team is responsible for decision; defines the problem and solution |

Source: L.M. Oliva (1992) *Partners not Competitors*, p. 76. London: Idea Group Publishing. Reproduced with the permission of Idea Group Publishing.

Resistance from other parts of the organisation

As self-managing teams have clear knock-on effects for other parts of the organisation these other parts will react. If traditional managers do not give direction and control over to the team an immediate conflict is set up as to who makes the decisions around here; if they fail to support and coach, the team may feel abandoned and insecure. In general, the climate of the organisation needs to be supportive in terms of the value placed on individual autonomy and learning. There are situations also where the rhetoric of the organisation is about delegating responsibility to the team, but where management fail to give up ownership of the task (see the Window on Practice box in Chapter 17 that presents an example adapted from Sewell and Wilkinson 1992).

Resistance within the team

Individuals who have spent many years being told what to do may need some time to take this responsibility for themselves. It is clear that operating self-managed teams will be easier on a greenfield site. However, for locations which want to make the transition, the importance of team selection of newcomers and of selecting skills relevant to a team environment as well as essential technical skills will be key. Salem, Lazarus and Cullen (1992) note that the most often cited individual characteristics for a team environment are 'interpersonal skills, self-motivation, ability to cope with peer pressure, level of technical/administrative experience, communication skills and the ability to cope with stress'. Other characteristics that have been noted elsewhere include the ability to deal with ambiguous situations and cope with conflict in a constructive way.

Peer pressure

The byproducts of peer pressure have been identified as lower absence levels, due to an awareness that colleagues have to cover for them; and a higher production rate so as not to let colleagues down. However, intense peer pressure can lead to stress and destroy many of the perceived benefits of team involvement from the employees' perspective. Some of the destructive aspects of peer pressure can also be seen in the Sewell and Wilkinson example in Chapter 17. Banner, Kulisch and Peery (1992) also note issues about the limits of peer involvement when they ask whether team members should exercise discipline over one another, and whether they should be responsible for the performance appraisal process.

Cross-functional management teams

Cross-functional management teams are very different from the teams described above, and members are more likely to retain other roles in the organisation. Typically they will see themselves as members of their function, whether it be marketing, research, sales, development and members of a specific project team as well. In fact the term 'project' (for example as in 'projects for change') rather than 'team' is being used increasingly to minimise any negative connotations of the word 'team' (see, for example, Proehl 1997; Butcher and Bailey 2000). Very often the project team will surround the development of a particular product from creation to sales – for example, a new computer package, a drug, a piece of electrical equipment. Members may be allocated to the team by their home function for all or part of their time. In fact many cross-functional teams are virtual teams, and although they may work closely together, they are rarely physically together. Henry and Hartzler (1998) defines virtual teams as 'groups of people who work closely together even though they are geographically separated and may reside in different time zones in different parts of the world'. It is in this context that technology comes into its own – video conferencing, for example. However, Bal and Grundy (1999) argue that all too often it is the technology that is concentrated upon, rather than the all-important human processes.

The thinking behind a cross-functional team is that each member brings with them the expertise in their own function and the dedication to the team task around a certain product or project. By bringing individuals together as a team the project gains through the commitment of team members to a task that they feel that they own. Bringing these individuals together enables the development of a common language and the overcoming of departmental boundaries. For a further discussion of the matrix form of organisation in which cross-functional teams are a key feature, see Chapter 6.

WINDOW ON PRACTICE

At one Ford manufacturing plant multifunctional teams were used to improve product quality. Team members were trained to collect and analyse data so that they could solve their own quality problems.

Quality engineers had also been appointed in order to assist the teams. The divisional management then asked the engineers for a divisional quality report, and in order to complete this the engineers asked the teams for the data that they had collected, and they summarised these.

As time went on the teams began to wait for the engineers to collect and analyse their raw data before they made any decisions regarding quality. They even began to wait for directions from the engineers before taking action. Problems that the teams had previously solved were now being solved with the help of the engineers, who began to ask for more engineers to support this process.

The intention had been to empower the teams, but the teams did not act as though they were empowered as management had still remained in control by asking for the quality reports from the engineers.

Source: Adapted from C. Meyer (1994) 'How the right measures help teams excel', *Harvard Business Review*, May–June, pp. 95–103.

Meyer (1994) expresses the importance of measures of performance for cross-functional teams, and sees process measures as key rather than just measures of achievements. His argument is that process measures help the team to gauge their progress, and identify and rectify problems. It follows from this that the performance measures used need to be designed by the team and not imposed on them from senior management, as the team will know best what measures will help them to do their job. Inevitably these measures will need to be designed against a strategic context set by higher management. Meyer describes a good example of the problems that can result if managers try and control the performance measurement process rather than empowering team members.

The process of agreeing their own performance measures will also enable the team to identify different assumptions and perceptions that each team member holds, and generate discussion on the exact goals of the team. All this is helpful in bringing the team together, generating a common language and ensuring that everyone is pulling in the same direction.

One special form of cross-functional management team is the top management team of the organisation – the directors. Clearly, this team is different in that it is permanent and not project based, but the need to work as a team rather than a collection of individuals is key. Katzenbach and Smith (1993) note that it is more difficult to get this group to work together as a team as they are more likely to be individualists. Directors often still see themselves as representatives of their function rather than members of a team, and thus will be more likely to defend their position and attempt to influence each other rather than pulling together. Katzenbach (1997) suggests that strong executive leadership and true teamwork require different, but equally important disciplines, which need to be integrated rather than being seen as alternatives. Garratt (1990) asks three key questions of top teams to assess whether they are truly direction-giving teams. He asks about regular processes, outside formal meetings, to discuss what is going on in the organisation and what possibilities exist; to what extent the team involve themselves in unstructured visioning before grappling with the practical matters of plans and budgets; and to what extent they assess individual contributions and the skills and resources owned within the team. Garratt explains that he usually gets little evidence of any of these activities taking place.

Functional teams

Functional teams, as the name implies, are made up of individuals within a function. For example, the training section of the HR department may well be referred to as the training team – different groups of nurses on a specific ward are sometimes divided into, say, the 'red' team and the 'blue' team. Sales staff for a particular product or region may refer to themselves as the 'games software sales

---

Activity 19.2

Think of some functional teams that you either belong to or have belonged to, or have had some contact with.

To what extent, and why, is each truly a team, or just a group of individuals with the title 'team'?

Use the ideas presented in this chapter and Figure 19.1 to to help you with this assessment.

team' or the 'north west sales team'. Some of the rationale behind this is to give the customer, internal or external, an identified set of individuals to liaise with. Given that these will be a smaller set than those in the whole department, they will be able to gain a much closer knowledge of particular customers and a better understanding of customer needs. The extent to which these are really teams as opposed to groups of individuals will vary enormously.

Problem-solving teams

Problem-solving teams may be within a function or cross functional. Within-function teams may typically be in the form of quality circles where employees voluntarily come together to tackle production and quality issues affecting their work. Unfortunately, many of these teams have had little clout and rec-ommended changes and improvements have not been possible to implement, owing to the retention of management control. Other within-function teams may consist of specially selected individuals who will be involved in the implementation of a major development within the function or department. For example, the implementation of performance management may be supported by specific coaches in each department who carry out related training, offer coun-selling and advice and who tailor organisation policy so that it meets department needs. These coaches may become the departmental performance management team.

Cross-functional teams may be brought together to solve an identified and specific organisational problem, and will remain together for a short period until that problem has been solved. They differ from cross-functional management teams as their role is not to manage anything, but rather to collect and analyse data and perspectives and develop an understanding of the nature of the prob-lem. From this they will make recommendations on how to solve the problem which are then passed on to higher management. Usually their remit ends here, and they have little or no involvement in implementation. Team members will retain their normal work role at the same time as being a team member.

Activity 19.3
If you have belonged to, or observed, a problem-solving team:
(a) What were the barriers to team formation?
(b) In what ways did team members support the team?
(c) In what ways did team members concentrate on themselves as individuals?

Team effectiveness

For a team to be effective they need a clear and agreed vision, objectives and set of rules by which they will work together. Proehl (1997), for example, identifies the need for a clear project purpose, which members agree is worthy. In addition, he found, clear project boundaries, deadlines, and specific follow-up activities by a designated co-ordinator were all important to team effectiveness.

Team members will need to feel able to be open and honest with each other and be prepared to confront difficulties and differences. It is also important for members to be able to tolerate conflict and be able to use this in a collaborative way in the achievement of the team's objectives. Some researchers have commented upon the size of the team and suggest it should be small enough, say no more than 20, for communications to be feasible. Others have suggested that proximity is important in maintaining communications and team spirit.

We have previously mentioned support from management as being critical to team success. And Edwards and Wright (1998) note from their case study the problems caused by managers who interfere with team autonomy. Next we explore the key issues of selection, training and development, assessment and reward in relation to team effectiveness.

Selecting team members

The effectiveness of any team depends to a large extent on the appropriateness of the team members. For self-managing teams there is a strong lobby for newcomers to be appointed by the team themselves, and indeed some would argue that unless this happens the team is not truly self-managing (see, for example, Banner *et al.* 1992). Other case studies suggest that team members, whether selected by the team or by others, are chosen very carefully in the likeness of the team and with the 'right attitudes'. For all teamwork Katzenbach and Smith (1993) identify three critical selection criteria: technical or functional expertise, problem-solving and decision-making skills and interpersonal skills.

Another approach to selection of team members is to gain an understanding of the team roles that they are best able to play, so that the team is endowed with a full range of the roles that it will need to be effective. Meredith Belbin (1993a), through extensive research and the evolution of his original ideas, has identified nine team roles which are important to a team and which individuals may have as strengths or weaknesses. The absence of some or many of these roles can cause problems in team effectiveness. Too many individuals playing the same type of role can cause undue friction in the team and again damage effectiveness. The key is achieving a balance. These team roles are as follows:

1 **Co-ordinator**: This person will have a clear view of the team objectives and will be skilled at inviting the contribution of team members in achieving these, rather than just pushing his or her own view. The co-ordinator (or chairperson) is self-disciplined and applies this discipline to the team. They are confident and mature, and will summarise the view of the group and will be prepared to take a decision on the basis of this.
2 **Shaper**: The shaper is full of drive to make things happen and get things going. In doing this they are quite happy to push their own views forward, do not mind being challenged and are always ready to challenge others. The shaper looks for the pattern in discussions and tries to pull things together into something feasible which the team can then get to work on.
3 **Plant**: This member is the one who is most likely to come out with original ideas and challenge the traditional way of thinking about things. Sometimes they become so imaginative and creative that the team cannot see the relevance of what they are saying. However, without the plant to scatter the seeds of new ideas the team will often find it difficult to make any headway. The plant's strength is in major new insights and changes in direction and not in contributing to the detail of what needs to be done.
4 **Resource investigator**: The resource investigator is the group member with

the strongest contacts and networks, and is excellent at bringing in information and support from the outside. This member can be very enthusiastic in pursuit of the team's goals, but cannot always sustain this enthusiasm.

5 **Implementer**: The individual who is a company worker is well organised and effective at turning big ideas into manageable tasks and plans that can be achieved. Such individuals are both logical and disciplined in their approach. They are hardworking and methodical but may have some difficulty in being flexible.

6 **Team worker**: The team worker is the one who is most aware of the others in the team, their needs and their concerns. They are sensitive and supportive of other people's efforts, and try to promote harmony and reduce conflict. Team workers are particularly important when the team is experiencing a stressful or difficult period.

7 **Completer**: As the title suggests, the completer is the one who drives the deadlines and makes sure they are achieved. The completer usually communicates a sense of urgency which galvanises other team members into action. They are conscientious and effective at checking the details, which is a vital contribution, but sometimes get 'bogged down' in them.

8 **Monitor evaluator**: The monitor evaluator is good at seeing all the options. They have a strategic perspective and can judge situations accurately. The monitor evaluator can be overcritical and is not usually good at inspiring and encouraging others.

9 **Specialist**: This person provides specialist skills and knowledge and has a dedicated and single-minded approach. They can adopt a very narrow perspective and sometimes fail to see the whole picture.

Activity 19.4

Think of a team situation in which you have been involved, in either a work or a social/family setting:

(a) Which roles were present and which were absent?

(b) What was the effect of this balance?

An individual's potential team roles can be interpreted from some of the psychometric tests used in the normal selection procedure (for example, Cattell's 16PF). They can also be assessed in a different way. Belbin designed a specific questionnaire to identify the individual's perceived current team role strengths (that is, the roles they have developed and are actually playing). This is particularly helpful for development within the current team, but may be less useful for selection purposes. Although helpful, current team role strengths may not be automatically transferred into another team situation.

The psychometric properties of the Belbin Team Roles Self-perception Inventory (BTRSPI) have been assessed by Furnham *et al.* (1993), whose work has cast doubt on the ability of the BTRSPI to be a reliable measure of team role preference. Further research by Fisher *et al.* (1996) confirms these doubts and also questions the extent to which team role preferences identified by the BTRSPI correlate with those identified by the 16PF. Fisher *et al.* note that although they found both tests to be imperfect, the evidence available supports the 16PF rather than the BTRSPI. Belbin (1993b) maintains that the BTRSPI was never intended to be a formal psychometric test, and Fisher *et al.* conclude that, despite questions over its reliability, and since the Belbin *model* itself has intuitive appeal and some empirical support, it would be a pity to disregard it. They recommend further research. Using the 16PF, Fisher *et al.* (2000) found in a study of almost 1,800 managers that some roles were more scarce than others. Although co-ordinators and resource investigators were plentiful, there were few completers, monitor evaluators, plants and shapers. They suggest that selection preferences may be causing this pattern and recommend that managers consider wider selection criteria if they wish to broaden their base of employees to adequately represent all team roles.

Team leader and manager training

Both team leaders and senior managers begin to play new roles in team situations. Team leaders suddenly find themselves with a host of new responsibilities for the support of team members and the planning and organising of team activities – responsibilities for which they have little experience and often no training. Similarly managers will need some training support in moving from a directive, controlling role to a coaching and counselling role. Training needs to encompass not only new skills but an opportunity to discuss the changing philosophy of the organisation and to encourage attitude change. Support in understanding the nature of involvement, empowerment and participation will also be relevant.

Team member training

Whether or not the team has an appointed leader all team members will need some training support in working in a different environment with different rules about what they should and should not be doing. Being more involved and taking on more responsibility, and sometimes leading activities, will require some initial training support. Attaran and Nguyen (2000) suggest that training in problem solving, communications and time management is important. In particular, training in conflict management is recommended by Applebaum *et al.* (1999). Further training in new technical skills can often be handled within the team once at least one member has the required knowledge and has gained some training skills themselves.

Team development

Teams can be developed in many different ways, and perhaps one of the most critical early on is development through the task itself. For example, teams can develop by jointly describing the core purpose of the team, visualising the future position that they are aiming to achieve, developing the rules and procedures they will use, performance measures, and so on. If the team are given some support to do this, perhaps a facilitator from the HR function or externally, they can not only develop vital guidelines but also gain an understanding of a way of working things out together, a process, which they can use by themselves in the future.

Teams can also develop by looking at the way they have been working together since they came together. One way of doing this is by completing a team roles questionnaire to identify the strengths and weaknesses of each member. This will help to promote a better understanding of why things happen as they do, and also pave the way for some changes. On this basis some individuals can develop their potential in team roles that they are not presently using, but for which they have some preference, and in this way a better balance may be struck, making the team more effective. Another process is to review what the team as a whole are good at and bad at, what different individuals can do to enable others to carry out their tasks more effectively, and what improvements can be made in the way that the team organises itself. Simple suggestions can be surprisingly effective such as: 'It would really help me if you gave me a list of telephone numbers where I can leave a message for you when I need to get hold of you urgently' (cross-functional team); and 'I don't understand why we need to lay the figures out in this way and it really gets my back up – will someone take some time out to explain it to me?' Irwin, Plovnick and Fry (1974) identified four major problem areas in relation to group effectiveness – goals, roles, processes and relationships – and these four can be used to provide a framework for team development activities.

Other less direct methods of development involve working through simulated exercises as a team – for example, building a tower out of pieces of paper – and learning from this how the team operate and what they could do to operate better. Outdoor training is also used to good effect in team situations, where the team tackle new, and perhaps dangerous, activities in the outdoors. Typically, some activities involve learning to trust and to depend on each other in a real and risky situation, and the learning from this, and the trust developed, can then be transferred back into the work situation.

The approach taken to team building needs to be appropriate to the stage of development of the team. Tuckman (1965) identified four stages of team development – forming, storming, norming and performing. Forming centres on team members working out what they are supposed to be doing, and trying to feel part of it. At this stage they are quite likely to be wary of each other and hide their feelings. Storming is the stage where members are prepared to express strongly held views, where there is conflict and competition and where some push for power while others withdraw. The norming stage is characterised by a desire to begin to organise themselves. Members actually begin to listen to each other, become more open and see problems as belonging to the whole group. Performing is where a sense of group loyalty has developed and where all contribute in an atmosphere of openness and trust. Proehl (1997) identifies the importance of mutual respect, and Ingram and Descombe (1999) found in their research that camaraderie was very important in getting the work done.

Two very useful and practical texts for managers and facilitators on team building are Pearn (1998) and Moxon (1993).

Recognition and reward

Like individuals, teams need some form of recognition and reward for their efforts. Recognition may be in the form of articles in company newsletters or local papers about team successes, inscribing the team name on the product or monetary rewards. A sense of team identity is often encouraged by the use of team T-shirts, coffee mugs and other usable items. It is most important that other reward systems in the organisation, say based on individual contribution, do not cut across the reinforcement for team performance. In addition for those teams where the longer-term objective is for all members to acquire the whole range of skills then a payment system, which pays for skills gained rather than job done, will be important.

Are teams always the right answer?

Team-based work seems set to increase – on the premise that it will improve organisational commitment and performance. The three difficult issues that will need to be tackled are that not all employees will feel comfortable or perform their best in a team-based situation; that teamwork is not always the best approach; and that not all teams are effective teams. Critics of a team environment suggest that it can have a downward levelling effect, that it stunts creativity and is generally limiting (Stott and Walker 1995). The difficulty of generating the essential openness, trust and commitment is also a potential difficulty, and decision making can become a lengthy process. Where teams have been introduced inappropriately the result has been lower productivity, poorer decisions and increased dissatisfaction, as noted by Applebaum *et al.* (1999), and this finding conflicts with all the case examples of performance improvement due to the use of teams. These contradictory reports may be explained, as Edwards and Wright (1998) suggested, by the many different types of teams that are set up, and by the impact of different organisational environments.

Implications for the HR function

Team-based working gives rise to a number of implications for the HR function:

■ There will need to be increasing emphasis on training the trainers so that teams can do as much of their own training as possible.
■ Training in selection techniques will need to be made available if teams are to select members without ongoing assistance from the HR function.
■ The HR function will probably find it useful to produce guidance manuals for teams, giving a framework for those HR activities which will be carried out within the team, and which back up any training given.
■ There will be an increased demand, especially early on, for facilitation skills – a member of the personnel function will need to work with teams in reviewing their effectiveness and working out ways to improve.
■ There will also probably be an increased demand for HR consultancy skills and online advice.
■ Members of the HR function may well find they spend more time coaching senior managers in changing their role from directing to coaching.
■ The HR function may well become involved in efforts to change the culture of the organisation so that it is supportive of teamwork. The HR function may be involved in supporting the changes in senior managers' roles and in helping them view problems as learning opportunities.

Summary propositions

19.1 Team-based working has been increasing, due to a belief that this empowers employees, encourages them to use their full potential and results in better performance, although these aspirations are not always achieved in practice, or take some time to be achieved.

19.2 Three key variables in different types of teams are timespan of the team, interchangeability of team members and range of activities and functions involved.

19.3 There are four broad team types – production/service teams; cross-functional management teams; departmental teams; and problem-solving teams.

19.4 Team effectiveness is dependent on the team having agreed goals and methods of working, and a climate where team members can be open and honest and use conflict in a constructive way.

19.5 Selection of team members is key and it is important to have a well-balanced team in terms of the team roles described by Belbin.

19.6 Team-based work has an impact on the HR role – resulting in increased consultancy and facilitation, coaching of managers, training team trainers and producing team guides.

References

Applebaum, S., Abdallah, C. and Shapiro, B. (1999) 'The self-directed team: A conflict resolution analysis', *Team Performance Management*, Vol. 5, No. 2.

Arkin, A. (1999) 'Peak Practice', *People Management*, 11 November.

Attaran, M. and Nguyen, T. (2000) 'Creating the right structural fit for self-directed teams', *Team Performance Management*, Vol. 6, No. 1/2.

Bal, J. and Grundy, J. (1999) 'Virtual Teaming in the automotive supply chain', *Team Performance Management*, Vol. 5, No. 6.

Banner, D.K., Kulisch, W.A. and Peery, N.S. (1992) 'Self-managing work teams (SMWT) and the human resource function', *Management Decision*, Vol. 30, No. 3, pp. 40–5.

Belbin, M. (1993a) *Team Roles at Work*. London: Butterworth Heinemann.

Belbin, R.M. (1993b) 'A reply to the Belbin team role self-report inventory by Furnham, Steele and Pendleton', *Journal of Occupational and Organisational Psychology*, Vol. 66, pp. 259–60.

Buchanan, D. (1992) 'High performance: new boundaries of acceptability in worker control', in G. Salaman *et al.* (eds), *Human Resources Strategies*. London: Sage.

Butcher, D. and Bailey, C. (2000) 'Crewed awakenings', *People Management*, 3 August.

Casey, D. (1993) *Managing Learning in Organisations*. Milton Keynes: Open University Press, p. 60.

Church, A. (1998) 'From both sides now: the power of teamwork – fact or fiction?', *Team Performance Management*, Vol 4, No. 2.

Edwards, P. and Wright, M. (1998) 'HRM and commitment: a case study of teamworking', in P. Sparrow and M. Marchington (eds) *Human Resource Management:. The New Agenda*. London: Financial Times Pitman Publishing.

Fisher, S.G., Macrosson, W.D.K. and Sharp, G. (1996) 'Further evidence concerning the Belbin Team role self-perception inventory', *Personnel Review*, Vol. 25, No. 2, pp. 61–7.

Fisher, S., Hunter, T. and Macrosson, W.D.K. (2000) 'The distribution of Belbin team roles among UK managers', *Team Performance Management*, Vol. 29, No. 2.

Furnham, A., Steele, H. and Pendleton, D. (1993) 'A psychometric assessment of the Belbin team role self-perception Inventory', *Journal of Occupational and Organisational Psychology*, pp. 245–57.

Garratt, B. (1990) *Creating a Learning Organisation*. Hemel Hempstead: Director Books.

Henry, J. and Hartzler, M. (1998) *Tools for Virtual Teams – A Team Fitness Companion*. Milwaukee, WI: ASQ Quality Press.

Ingram, H. and Descombe, T. (1999) 'Teamwork: comparing academic and practitioners' perceptions', *Team Performance Management*, Vol. 5, No. 1.

Katzenbach, J. (1997) 'The myth of the Top Management Team', *Harvard Business Review*, November–December.

Katzenbach, J.R. and Smith, D.K. (1993) 'The discipline of teams', *Harvard Business Review*, March–April.

Meyer, C. (1994) 'How the right measures help teams excel', *Harvard Business Review*, May–June, pp. 95–103.

Moxon, P. (1993) *Building a Better Team*. Aldershot: Gower in association with ITD.

Mueller, F. (1992) 'Designing flexible teamwork: comparing German and Japanese approaches', *Employee Relations*, Vol. 14, No. 1, pp. 5–16.

Natale, S., Libertella, A. and Edwards, B. (1998) 'Team management: Developing concerns', *Team Performance Management*, Vol. 4, No. 8.

Oliva, L.M. (1992) *Partners not Competitors*. London: Idea Group Publishing.

Pearn, M. (1998) *Empowering Team Learning*. London: IPD.

Piczak, M. and Hause, R. (1996) 'SDWTs: a guide to implementation', *Quality Progress*, May.

Proehl, R. (1997) 'Enhancing the effectiveness of cross-functional teams', *Team Performance Management*, Vol. 3, No. 3.

Salem, M., Lazarus, H. and Cullen, J. (1992) 'Developing self-managing teams: structure and performance', *Journal of Management Development*, Vol. 11, No. 3, pp. 24–32.

Scott, W. and Harrison, H. (1997) 'Full team ahead', *People Management*, 9 October.

Senge, P. (1990) *The Fifth Discipline: The art and practice of the learning organisation*. London: Century Business, Random House.

Stott, K. and Walker, A. (1995) *Teams, Teamwork and Teambuilding*. Hemel Hempstead: Prentice Hall.

Tuckman, B.W. (1965) 'Development Sequences in Small Groups', *Psychological Bulletin*, Vol. 63, pp. 384–99.

General discussion topics

1 In an organisation which is moving into teamwork the supervisor's role will change from direct supervision to team facilitation and development. What problems are these supervisors likely to experience in their change of role, and what forms of training and development would help them?

2 The need to work as a team depends on the kinds of work that are carried out. Discuss.

Chapter 20   Leadership and motivation

Leadership and motivation are two of the most loaded and misunderstood words in management. Individual managers are often seduced by concepts of leadership that show them to be knights in shining armour with superhuman qualities and (this is the really dangerous bit) adoring followers. The followers rarely have that view of their managers. Motivation is often constructed in the same way, 'How can I motivate the members of my team?', although this ignores the mainsprings of motivation, which are in the performer rather than in the manager of the performer.

We must not, however, underestimate the importance of leadership, motivation *and the link between the two*. In this chapter we review the various studies of leadership and see that there are indeed sometimes needs for individual leaders who have outstanding personal qualities and who achieve extraordinary change in their business. On the other hand there are infinitely more roles which call on different and more modest leadership skills, which can be learned and which are equally important, even if they do not merit shining armour and a white charger.

We then look at the studies of motivation, as leaders and the rest of us need to understand how different people are motivated differently. This helps all of us to get through the working day, keep out of trouble, get good service at the supermarket, pull our weight in the football team and, perhaps, understand ourselves a little bit better. We start with some definitions.

Leadership and management

Northouse (1997) suggests that there are four components that characterise leadership: that leadership is a process; it involves influence; it occurs within a group context; and it involves goal attainment. This corresponds with Shackleton's (1995) definition, which we shall use as a working definition for the remainder of the chapter:

> **Leadership is the process in which an individual influences other group members towards the attainment of group or organizational goals.**   (Shackleton, 1995, p. 2)

This definition is useful as it leaves open the question of whether leadership is exercised in a commanding or a facilitative manner. It does suggest, however, that the leader in some way motivates others to act in such a way as to achieve group goals.

The definition also makes no assumptions about who is the leader – it may or may not be the nominal head of the group. Managers, therefore, may or may not be leaders, and leaders may or may not be managers. Some authors distinguish very clearly between the nature of management and the nature of leadership but this draws on a particular perspective, that of the transformational leader, and we will consider this in the section on whether the organisation needs heroes. This is a school of thought that concentrates on the one leader at the top of the organisation, which is very different from organisations and individuals who use the terms manager and leader interchangeably with nothing more than a vague notion that managers should be leaders. Indeed, any individual may act as a manager one day and a leader the next, depending on the situation.

In the following three sections we will look at three questions which underlie virtually all the work on leadership. First, what are the traits of a leader, or an effective leader? Second, what is the 'best' leadership style or behaviour? Third, if different styles are appropriate at different times, what factors influence the desired style?

What are the traits of leaders and effective leaders?

Trait approaches, which were earliest to be employed, seek to identify the traits of leaders – in other words what characterises leaders as opposed to those who are not leaders. These approaches rest on the assumption that some people were born to lead due to their personal qualities, while others are not. It suggests that leadership is only available to the chosen few and not accessible to all. These approaches have been discredited for this reason and for the fact that there has been little consistency in the lists of traits that research has uncovered. However, this perspective is frequently resurrected.

Kilpatrick and Locke (1991), in a meta-analysis, did seem to find some consistency around the following traits: drive to achieve; the motivation to lead; honesty and integrity; self-confidence, including the ability to withstand setbacks, standing firm and being emotionally resilient; cognitive ability; and knowledge of the business. They also note the importance of managing the perceptions of others in relation to these characteristics. Northouse (1997) provides a useful historical comparison of the lists of traits uncovered in other studies. Perhaps the most well-known expression of the trait approach is the work relating to charismatic leadership. House (1976), for example, describes charismatic leaders as being dominant, having a strong desire to influence, being self-confident and having a strong sense of their own moral values. We will pick up on this concept of leadership in the later section on heroes.

In a slightly different vein Goleman (1998) carried out a meta-analysis of leadership competency frameworks in 188 different companies. These frameworks represented the competencies related to outstanding leadership performance. Goleman analysed the competencies into three groups: technical, cognitive and emotional, and found that, in terms of the ratios between each group, emotional competencies 'proved to be twice as important as the others'. Goleman goes on to describe five components of emotional intelligence:

■ **Self-awareness**: this he defines as a deep understanding of one's strengths, weaknesses, needs, values and goals. Self-aware managers are aware of their own limitations.
■ **Self-regulation**: the control of feelings, the ability to channel them in constructive ways. The ability to feel comfortable with ambiguity and not panic.

- **Motivation**: the desire to achieve beyond expectations, being driven by internal rather than external factors, and to be involved in a continuous striving for improvement.
- **Empathy**: considering employees' feelings alongside other factors when decision making.
- **Social skill**: friendliness with a purpose, being good at finding common ground and building rapport. Individuals with this competency are good persuaders, collaborative managers and natural networkers.

Goleman's research is slightly different from previous work on the trait approach, as here we are considering what makes an effective leader rather than what makes a leader (irrespective of whether they are effective or not). It is also different in that Goleman refers to competencies rather than traits. For an in-depth discussion of competencies see Chapter 25, but suffice it to say, for now, that competencies include a combination of traits and abilities, amongst other things. There is some debate over whether competencies can be developed in people – the general feeling is that some can and some cannot. Goleman maintains that the five aspects of emotional intelligence can be learned and provides an example in his article of one such individual. In spite of his argument we feel that it is still a matter for debate, and as many of the terms used by Goleman are similar to those of the previous trait models of leadership, we have categorised his model as an extension of the trait perspective. To some extent his work sits between the trait approach and the style approach which follows.

Rajan and van Eupen (1997) also consider that leaders are strong on emotional intelligence, and that this involves the traits of self-awareness, zeal, resilience and the ability to read emotions in others. They argue that these traits are particularly important in the development and deployment of people skills. Heifetz and Laurie (1997) similarly identify that in order for leaders to regulate emotional distress in the organisation, which is inevitable in change situations, the leader has to have 'the emotional capacity to tolerate uncertainty, frustration and pain' (p. 128).

| **Activity 20.1** | Think of different leaders you have encountered – in particular those that were especially effective or ineffective: |

1 What differences can you identify in terms of their traits (personal characteristics)?

2 What differences can you identify in terms of their behaviour?

3 Are the trait and behaviour lists connected in any way? If so how?

4 Which of these two approaches – trait or behaviour – do you find more helpful in helping you to understand the nature of effective leadership?

What is the 'best way to lead'? leadership styles and behaviours

Dissatisfaction with research on leadership that saw leadership as a set of permanent personal characteristics that describe the leader led to further studies that emphasised the nature of the leadership process – the interaction between leader and follower – and sought to understand how the leaders *behave* rather than what they *are*. The first such studies sought to find the 'best' leadership style; from this perspective leadership comprises an ideal set of behaviours that can be learned. Fulop *et al.* (1999) suggest that Douglas McGregor's (1960) work, *The Human Side of Enterprise*, can be understood from this perspective. McGregor argued that American corporations managed their employees as if they were work-shy, and needed constant direction, monitoring and control (theory 'x'), rather than as if they were responsible individuals who were willing and able to take on responsibility and organise their own work (theory 'y'). McGregor argued that the underlying assumptions of the manager determined the way they managed their employees and this in turn determined how the employees would react. Thus if employees were managed as if they operated on theory 'x' then they would act in a theory 'x' manner; conversely if employees were managed as if they operated on theory 'y' then they would respond as theory 'y' employees would respond. The message was that management style should reinforce theory 'y' and thus employees would take on responsibility, be motivated by what they were doing and work hard. Although the original book was written forty years ago, this approach is being revisited (see, for example, Heil *et al.* 2000) and it fits well with the empowering or post-heroic approach to leadership that we discuss later in the chapter. Another piece of research from the style approach is that by Blake and Mouton (1964), who developed the famous 'Managerial Grid'. The grid is based on two aspects of leadership behaviour. One is concern for production, that is, task-oriented behaviours such as clarifying roles, scheduling work, measuring outputs; the second is concern for people, that is people-centred behaviour such as building trust, camaraderie, a friendly atmosphere. These two dimensions are at the heart of many models of leadership. Blake and Mouton proposed that individual leaders could be measured on a nine-point scale in each of these two aspects, and by combining them in grid form they identified the four leadership styles presented in Table 20.1.

Such studies, which are well substantiated by evidence, suggest that leadership is accessible for all people and that it is more a matter of learning leadership behaviour than it is of personality characteristics. Many leadership development courses have therefore been based around this model. However, as Northouse (1997) argues, there is an assumption in the model that the team management style (high concern for people and high concern for production; sometimes termed 9,9 management) is the ideal style; and yet this claim is not substantiated by the research. This approach also fails to take account of the characteristics of the situation and the nature of the followers.

Table 20.1 Blake and Mouton's four leadership styles

High concern for people Low concern for production **Country Club management**	High concern for people High concern for production **Team management**
Low concern for people Low concern for production **Impoverished management**	Low concern for people High concern for production **Authority-compliance management**

Source: Adapted from R.R. Blake and J.S. Mouton (1964) *The Managerial Grid*. Houston, Texas: Gulf Publishing.

> **WINDOW ON PRACTICE**
>
> A large organisation adopted the Managerial Grid as the framework for its leadership development programme. The programme was generally well accepted and successful application of the team management style was seen to be connected to future promotions. Most managers, on leaving the programme, set out to display 9,9 leadership behaviours. However this had unexpected and undesirable consequences. Not only were team members daunted by their managers suddenly displaying a different style, but sometimes the 9,9 style was not appropriate in the circumstances in which it was used. The organisation eventually discontinued the programme due to the damage that it was causing.

Much of the recent work on the notion of transformational/heroic leadership, and empowering/post-heroic leadership, similarly assumes that what is being discussed is the one best way for a leader to lead, and we return to this leadership debate later on.

Do leaders need different styles for different situations?

> **WINDOW ON PRACTICE**
>
> Mintzberg (1998) spent some time observing the conductor of an orchestra, Bramwell Tovey, to see whether this could help managers understand a different perspective on leadership. He found what he called covert as opposed to overt leadership, and proposed that this leadership approach was more appropriate for professionals and knowledge workers rather than a traditional approach. He argued that such employees respond better to inspiration than supervision, as they do not need to be told what to do, but rather to have their expertise co-ordinated. Mintzberg also makes the important point that such professionals need the support and protection of their leader in respect of dealings at the boundary of the organisation (in this case the orchestra).

A variety of models, sometimes termed contingency models, have been developed to address the importance of context in terms of the leadership process, and as a consequence these models become more complex. Many, however, retain the concepts of production-centred and people-centred behaviour as ways of describing leadership behaviour, but use them in a different way. Hersey and Blanchard (1988) developed a model which identified that the appropriate leadership style in a situation should be dependent on their diagnosis of the 'readiness', that is developmental level or maturity, of their followers. The model is sometimes referred to as 'situational leadership', and works on the premise that leaders can 'adapt their leadership style to meet the demands of their environment (Hersey and Blanchard 1988, p. 169). Readiness of followers is defined in terms of ability and willingness. Level of ability includes the experience, knowledge and skills that an individual possesses in relation to the particular task at hand; and level of willingness encompasses the extent to which the individual has the motivation and commitment, or the self-confidence, to carry out the task. Having diagnosed the developmental level of the followers, Hersey and Blanchard suggest that the leader then adapts their behaviour to fit. They identify two dimensions of leader behaviour; task behaviour, which is sometimes termed 'directive'; and

Table 20.2 Hersey and Blanchard's four styles of leadership

High relationship behaviour Low task behaviour Followers are able, but unwilling or insecure **Supportive (participating) style (3)**	High relationship behaviour High task behaviour Followers are unable, but willing or confident **Coaching (selling) style (2)**
Low relationship behaviour Low task behaviour Followers are both able and willing or confident **Delegation style (4)**	Low relationship behaviour High task behaviour Followers are unable and unwilling or insecure **Directing (telling) style (1)**

Source: Adapted from P. Hersey and K.H. Blanchard (1988) *Managerial Organizational Behavior: Utilising Human Resources*, 5th edn. © Copyright material, adapted reprinted with the permission of Center for Leadership Studies, Escondido, CA92025.

relationship behaviour, which is sometimes termed 'supportive'. Task behaviour is the extent to which leaders spell out what has to be done. This includes 'telling people what to do, how to do it, when to do it, where to do it, and who is to do it' (Hersey 1985, p. 19). On the other hand relationship behaviour is defined as 'the extent to which the leader engages in two-way or multi-way communication. The behaviours include listening, facilitating and supporting behaviours' (ibid.). The extent to which the leader emphasises each of these two types of behaviour results in the usual two-by-two matrix. The four resulting styles are identified, as shown in Table 20.2.

There is an assumption that the development path for any individual and required behaviour for the leader is to work through boxex 1, 2, 3 and then 4 in the matrix. Hersey and Blanchard produced questionnaires to help managers diagnose the readiness of their followers.

Other well-known contingency models include Fielder's (1967) contingency model where leadership behaviour is matched to three factors in the situation: the nature of the relationship between the leader and members, the extent to which tasks

WINDOW ON PRACTICE

Hilary Walmsley (1999) reports some of her work as a consultant with BUPA. One of the aims of the exercise she was involved in was to:

> raise individuals' awareness of their own management styles and encourage them to stop and think about which approach to adopt rather than automatically respond to every challenge in a similar way. (p. 48)

She recounts the experiences of Brian Atkins, General Manager of BUPA's Gatwick Park and Redwood Hospitals, as an illustration of this learning process. On joining the hospital group, which was undergoing a critical phase of change, in 1990, Atkins consciously used an authoritative leadership style, at the directive and controlling end of the spectrum. Once the hospital was soundly on course for recovery he began to use a more empowering and facilitative style. Atkins describes modern managers as 'style travellers', and suggests that they need to be skilled at using different styles, even though they may naturally prefer one approach. Walmsley notes that managers are tempted to use the same styles out of habit, and are often unaware of alternative styles they could use.

Table 20.3 Six leadership styles reported by Goleman

Coercive style	Leader demands immediate compliance
Authoritative style	Leader mobilises people towards a vision
Affiliative style	Leader creates emotional bonds and harmony
Democratic style	Leaders use participation to build consensus
Pacesetting style	Leader expects excellence and self-direction from followers
Coaching style	Leader develops people for the future

Source: Reprinted by permission of *Harvard Business Review*. Adapted from 'Leadership that gets results', by D. Goleman, March–April, pp. 80 and 82–3. Copyright © 2000 by the Harvard Business School Publishing Corporation; all rights reserved.

are highly structured and the position power of the leader. The appropriate leader behaviour (that is, whether it should be task oriented or relationship oriented) depends on the combination of these three aspects in any situation. Fielder's model is considered to be well supported by the evidence – the research was based on the relationship between style and performance in existing organisations in different contexts. For a very useful comparison of contingency models see Fulop *et al.* (1999).

Goleman (2000) reports the results of some research carried out by Hay/McBer who sampled almost 20 per cent of a database of 20,000 executives. The results were analysed to identify six different leadership styles, which are shown in Table 20.3, but most importantly Goleman reports that 'leaders with the best results do not rely on only one leadership style' (p. 78).

Goleman goes on to consider the appropriate context and impact of each style, and argues that the more styles the leader uses the better. We have already reported Goleman's work on emotional intelligence, and he links this with the six styles by suggesting that leaders need to understand how the styles relate back to the different competencies of emotional intelligence so that they can identify where they need to focus their leadership development.

Activity 20.2

For each of Goleman's six styles think of a leader you have worked with, or know of. For each of these individuals write a list of the *behaviours* that they use. Then consider the impact that these behaviours have on followers.

Do the behaviours have the same impact on all followers? If not, why not?

One of the differences between the contingency models we have just discussed and the 'best' style models is the implications for development. The Blake and Mouton model suggests leaders can be developed to lead in the one best way. The Hersey and Blanchard model, and most other contingency models, stress the flexibility of the leader – to learn to lead differently with different employees depending on their needs; hence the leader should learn many styles and learn to diagnose the needs of their employees. Fielder's model, however, emphasises matching the leader to the context (a selection decision), rather than developing leaders in the context.

Do we really need heroes?

A different approach to understanding leadership is transformational leadership, which focuses on the leader's role at a strategic level, so there is a concentration on the one leader at the top of the organisaton. There is a wide range of literature in this vein, most of it written in the 1980s. Since that time the academic literature may have moved on but there is considerable evidence to suggest that the image of the transformational leader still remains widely attractive. While this is a different approach it links back to our original three questions about leadership. Transformational leadership shows elements of the trait approach, as leaders are seen to 'have' charisma, which sets them apart as extraordinary and exceptional, and they are also seen to use a set of 'ideal' behaviours, with the assumption in many writings that this is the 'best' approach.

The leader is usually characterised as a hero, although Steyrer (1998) proposes that there are other charismatic types such as the father figure, the saviour and the king. Such leaders appear to know exactly what they are doing and how to 'save' the organisation from its present predicament (and consequently such leadership is found more often when organisations are in trouble). Leaders involve followers by generating a high level of commitment, partly due to such leaders focusing on the needs of followers and expressing their vision in such a way that it satisfies these needs. They communicate high expectations to followers and also the firm belief that followers will be able to achieve these goals. In this way the leader promotes self-confidence in the followers and they are motivated to achieve more than they ordinarily expect to achieve. In terms of behaviours, perhaps the most important is the vision of the future that the leader offers and that they communicate this and dramatise this to the followers. Such leaders are able to help the followers make sense of what is going on and why as well as what needs to be done in the future. It is from this perspective that the distinction between management and leadership is often made. Bennis and Nanus (1985), for example, suggest leadership is path finding while management is path following; and that leadership is about doing the right thing whereas management is about doing things right. Kotter (1990) identified leaders as establishing a direction (whereas managers plan and budget); leaders align people with the vision (whereas managers organise things); leaders motivate and inspire (whereas managers control and solve problems); and leaders encourage change (whereas managers encourage order and predictability). Other writers analysing leadership from this perspective include Tichy and Devanna (1986) and Bass (1985), and there is a wide research base to support the findings. The approach does have a great strength in taking followers' needs into account and seeking to promote their self-confidence and potential, and the idea of the knight in shining armour is very attractive and potentially exciting – Tichy and Devanna, for example, present the process of such leadership as a three act drama. However, in spite of the emphasis on process there is also an emphasis on leadership characteristics which harks back to the trait approach to leadership, and as such has been characterised as elitist. There is also the ethical concern of one person wielding such power over others.

Maybe we should ask whether organisations really require such leaders? A very different conception of leadership is now offered as an alternative, partly a reaction to the previous approach, and partly a response to a changing environment. This is termed empowering or post-heroic leadership, and could be described as the currently favoured ideal way to lead.

WINDOW ON PRACTICE

Arkin (1997) reports on the leadership experiences of Percy Barnevik who was Chief Executive of the engineering company ABB. Arkin explains how this charismatic leader transformed ABB into a 'competitive fighting force across the globe' (p. 27). Ten years later, on leaving the role of Chief Executive, Barnevik is reported to have said, 'Ten years after our big merger, we have come a long way from the large dependence on one man at the top' (p. 28).

Source: Summarised from A. Arkin (1997) 'The secret of his success', *People Management*, 23 October, pp. 27–8.

Fulop *et al.* (1999) identify factors in a rapidly changing turbulent environment which by the 1990s dilute the appropriateness of concentrating on the one leader at the top of the organisation. These factors include: globalisation making centralisation more difficult; technology enabling better sharing of information; and change being seen as a responsibility of all levels of the organisation – not just the top. They also note a dissatisfaction with corporate failures, identified few transformational leaders as positive role models, suggest that such a model of male authoritarian leadership is less relevant, and in particular that the macho leader with all the answers does not necessarily fit well with the encouragement of creativity and innovation. In addition they suggest increasing teamwork and an increasing emphasis on knowledge workers means that employees will be less responsive to a transformational leader. The emphasis therefore has moved away from understanding the traits and style of the one leader at the top of the organisation who knows how to solve all the organisation's problems, to how empowering or post-heroic leaders can facilitate many members of the organisation in taking on leadership roles.

The leader becomes a developer who can help others identify problems as opportunities for learning, and who can harness the collective intelligence of the organisation, and Fulop *et al.* (1999) note that this means in practice that they encourage the development of a learning organisation. Senge (1990), who is a protagonist of the learning organisation (see Chapter 17 for further details) sees the leader's new roles in encouraging a learning organisation as designer, teacher and steward, rather than a traditional charismatic decision maker. He suggests that leaders should *design* the organisation in terms of vision, purpose, core values, and the structures by which these ideas can be translated into business decisions. However, he also suggests that the leader should involve people at all levels in this design task. It is the role of the leader not to identify the right strategy, but to encourage strategic thinking in the organisation, and to design effective learning processes to make this happen. The leader's role as a *teacher* is not to teach people the correct view of reality, but to help employees gain more insight into the current reality. The leader therefore coaches, guides and facilitates. As a *steward* the leader acts as a servant in taking responsibility for the impact of their leadership on others, and in the sense that they override their own self-interest by personal commitment to the organisation's larger mission. To play this role effectively Senge suggests that the leader will need many new skills, in particular vision-making skills – a never-ending sharing of ideas and asking for feedback. Skills that will encourage employees to express and test their views of the world are also key. These involve actively seeking others' views, experimenting, encouraging enquiry and distinguishing 'the way things are done' from 'the way we think things are done'.

WINDOW ON PRACTICE

The role that leaders play in the organisation in the twenty-first century is seen by some as very different from the hero roles of the past, and leaders are no longer expected to always know the solutions to problems.

Williams (2000), who talks about enabling and empowering leadership, suggests that 'twenty first century leaders are not expected to be all-knowing gurus and peddlers of panaceas' (p. 113). However they are expected to know the right questions to ask, as Heifetz and Laurie (1997) suggest: 'leaders do not need to know all the answers. They do need to know the right questions' (p. 124).

Building on this a speaker from Henley Management College (Radio 4, 25 February 2001) argued that leaders need to be able to admit that they do not know all the answers, and that there was a paradox in leadership, as leaders need to display both boldness and humility.

Taking this one step further Anne Atkinson (Radio 4, 29 November 2000), speaking in relation to the tussle over who won the American presidential election, described the leader as a servant, arguing that the best leaders are unwilling leaders and do not seek power, but instead have a desire to benefit the people they lead.

These ideas take us some way from the charismatic and transformational view of the leader.

This changing perspective on leadership is well demonstrated by a survey on leadership skills reported by Rajan and van Eupen (1997). The research is based on interviews with 49 top business leaders, 50 HR directors and a postal questionnaire of 375 companies in the service sector. They asked what were the most important leadership skills during the period 1995–7 and compared the results with those of a similar survey conducted in the late 1980s. The change in skills base shown in Table 20.4 reflects very well the change in the idealised leadership role and the increasing importance of facilitative people-related skills. They also note the prediction that the future will require an equal balance of traditionally masculine and feminine personality traits.

From a slightly different perspective Heifetz and Laurie (1997) propose six guiding principles of post-heroic leadership, and they conclude that leadership is about learning and that the idea of having a vision and aligning people to this is bankrupt. The idea of one leader at the top creating major changes in order to solve a one-off challenge is no longer appropriate, as organisations now face a

Table 20.4 Leadership skills compared

	Top five skills in order of importance
1995–7	1 Ability to inspire trust and motivation
	2 Visioning
	3 Ability, willingness and self-discipline to listen
	4 Strategic thinking
	5 Interpersonal communication skills
Late 1980s	1 Strategic thinking
	2 Entrepreneurial skills
	3 Originality
	4 Flair
	5 Problem-solving skills

Source: Adapted from A. Rajan and P. van Eupen (1997) 'Take it from the top', *People Management*, 23 October, pp. 26 and 28.

constant stream of adaptive challenges, and leadership is required of many in the organisation, not just one person at the top. They argue that employees should be allowed to identify and solve problems themselves and learn to take responsibility. The role of the leader is to develop collective self-confidence.

These visions of leadership are very attractive but they do require a dramatic change in thinking for both leaders and followers. For leaders there is the risk of giving away power, learning to trust employees, developing new skills, developing a different perspective of their role and overriding self-interest. For followers there is the challenge of taking responsibility – which some may welcome, but others shun. Yet, if sustained competitive advantage is based on human capital and collective intelligence, it is difficult to relegate this perspective to 'just an ideal'.

While empowering leaders have been shown to fit with the current climate we may sometimes need heroic leaders. We conclude with the thought that there is no one best way – different leaders and different leader behaviours are needed at different times.

Leadership and motivation

All leadership models are based on the assumption that one person can motivate another to act, and we have looked at different explanations of how leaders may do this – based on their traits, their employment of the one best leadership style or their use of a style which matches (in some ways) the needs of their followers, and is responsive (in some ways) to the context. We have also explained how the leader may be reconceptualised as heroic (transformational leader) and as empowering or post-heroic.

Some interconnections can be made between these theories and motivation theories. It is not our purpose here to recount any motivation theories in details (for this see texts such as Buchanan and Huczynski 1997; Mullins 1999; or Fulop and Linstead 1999). Below we identify some of the key concepts addressed in motivation theories and suggest which leadership perspectives tap into these concepts:

- **Expectancy has an impact on motivation.** We have already mentioned McGregor's (1960) model and his argument that if you treat people as responsible and self-motivated then they will act in a responsible and motivated manner. In addition Vroom's (1964) expectancy theory of motivation recognises that in the process of motivation the extent to which the individual feels they can realistically achieve the target will have an influence on whether they are motivated even to try. In respect of transformational leadership it is argued that followers can be inspired to achieve beyond the normal, partly because the leader has high expectations of the followers and in addition expresses the belief that the followers are capable of achieving these great things. From a different perspective the post-heroic leader concept is based on trusting organisation members to play their part, trusting them with information and expecting them to use this wisely for the good of the organisation.
- **Social needs are important.** Maslow (1943), Mayo (1953) and McClelland (1971), amongst others, highlight the need for affiliation as a motivational factor. Some leadership models specifically respond to this, for example Blake and Mouton (1964) ('one best style' theory), Hersey and Blanchard (1988) and

Fielder (1967) (contingency theory) all use 'concern for people' in some form as one of the key aspects of their leadership models. The concept of post-heroic leadership concerns involving those who may previously have been excluded, and in being concerned about the impact of their leadership on individuals. In addition this perspective concentrates on the importance of learning and acting collectively.

■ **Importance of the work itself.** Maslow (1943), Herzberg (1968), and Hackman and Oldham (1976), for example, all underline the way in which individuals are motivated to seek and may achieve satisfaction through their jobs. Herzberg, for example, identifies how opportunities for achievement, recognition, responsibility, autonomy, challenging tasks and opportunities for development may all be motivational. In some ways, Hersey and Blanchard's (1988) model addresses these needs in their 'delegation' style. In the post-heroic model many people in the organisation need to be involved in meeting adaptive challenges, in working out solutions and in contributing to vision building and many need to take on the responsibility of leadership. This is very different from the transformational leadership model in which the leader at the top of the organisation is seen to have all the responsibility.

■ **Recognising different people are motivated by different things.** Expectancy theory, previously mentioned, also identifies that different individuals value different things and hence have different motivational needs. In the process of motivation, only those things that the individual values will spur them to act. Contingency models of leadership take this on board to some extent. From a different perspective the transformational leader develops an interpretation of the world, or narrative, that plays to the followers' needs. However, while post-heroic leadership identifies that different people may play a different part, there is an assumption that all will be prepared to be involved, to share information and to develop themselves in line with the needs of the organisation.

■ **Social influences on motivation.** Recent work in the area of motivation suggests that motivations are socially or culturally determined, and to a limited extent the transformational leader ties into this as they reinterpret the world for their followers.

In spite of the links between leadership and motivation theories, there are many aspects of motivation that the leadership theories ignore. For example some people have less internal energy and drive than others and less need for growth. Also individuals with high levels of energy and drive may satisfy these outside of the work environment. While we may try and motivate people externally the greatest power for motivation comes from within and is therefore under the control of the individual rather than another. The best we can say is that leaders can enhance followers' motivation by the way they treat them, and at worst leaders may neutralise the motivational energy in their followers. There will always be some factors on which leaders have no impact whatsoever.

Summary propositions

20.1 Leadership is a process where one person influences a group of others to achieve group or organisational goals – leadership is thus about motivation.

20.2 The trait model of leadership, although often discredited, continues to play a part in our understanding of leadership.

20.3 Behavioural models are more helpful as they concentrate on what leaders do rather than on what they are.

20.4 Some behavioural models offer a 'one best way' of leadership, but more sophisticated models take account of contingency factors such as maturity of followers and the nature of the task.

20.5 Models of transformational leadership treat the leader as a hero who can (singlehandedly) turn the organisation around and deliver it from a crisis.

20.6 Empowering and post-heroic leadership models conceptualise the leader as teacher and facilitator, who involves many in the leadership task.

20.7 While there are many ways in which leadership theories tap into concepts of motivation, at best leaders may enhance the motivation of their followers and at worst they may neutralise it.

References

Arkin, A. (1997) 'The secret of his success', *People Management*, 23 October, pp. 27–8.

Bass, B.M. (1985) 'Leadership: Good, Better, Best', *Organisational Dynamics*, Winter, pp. 26–40.

Bennis, W.G. and Nanus, B. (1985) *Leaders: the strategies for taking charge*. New York: Harper and Row.

Blake, R.R. and Mouton, J.S. (1964) *The Managerial Grid*. Houston, Texas: Gulf Publishing.

Buchanan, D. and Huczynski, A. (1997) *Organisational Behaviour*. London: Prentice Hall.

Conner, D.R. (1998) *Leading at the Edge of Chaos: How to Create the Nimble Organisation*. New York: John Wiley and Sons, Inc.

Fielder, F.E. (1967) *A Theory of Leadership Effectiveness*. New York: McGraw-Hill.

Fulop, L. and Linstead, S. (1999) *Management. A Critical Text*. South Yarra: Macmillan Business.

Fulop, L., Linstead, S. and Dunford, R. (1999) 'Leading and managing', in L. Fulop and S. Linstead, *Management. A Critical Text*. South Yarra: Macmillan Business.

Goleman, D. (1998) 'What makes . . . a leader?', *Harvard Business Review*, Nov.–Dec., pp. 93–102.

Goleman, D. (2000) 'Leadership that gets results', *Harvard Business Review*, March–April, pp. 78–90.

Hackman, J. and Oldham, G. (1976) 'Motivation through the design of work; test of a theory', *Organisational Behaviour and Human Performance*, Vol. 16, pp. 250–79.

Heifetz, R. and Laurie, D. (1997) 'The work of leadership', *Harvard Business Review*, Jan.–Feb., pp. 124–34.

Heil, G., Bennis, W. and Stephens, D.C. (2000) Douglas McGregor, revisited: managing the human side of the enterprise. New York: Wiley.

Hersey, P. (1985) *Situational Selling*. Escondido, Calif.: Centre for Leadership Studies.

Hersey, P. and Blanchard, K.H. (1988) *Management of Organizational Behavior: Utilizing Human Resources*, 5th edn. Englewood Cliffs, NJ: Prentice Hall International.

Herzberg, F. (1968) 'One more time. How do you motivate employees?', *Harvard Business Review*, Vol. 46, pp. 53–62.

House, R. (1976) 'A 1976 theory of charismatic leadership', in J. Hunt and L. Larson (eds), *Leadership: the Cutting Edge*. Carbondale: Southern Illinois University Press.

Kilpatrick, S. and Locke, E. (1991) 'Leadership: Do Traits Matter?', *Academy of Management Executive*, Vol. 5, No. 2, pp. 48–60.

Kotter, J. (1990) *A Force for change: How leadership differs from management*. New York: Free Press.

McClelland, D.C. (1971) *Motivational Trends in Society*. Morristown, NJ: General Learning Press.

McGregor, D. (1960) *The Human Side of Enterprise*.

Maslow, A. (1943) 'A theory of human motivation', *Psychological Review*, Vol. 50, pp. 370–96.

Mayo, E. (1953) *The problems with an industrialized civilization*. New York: Macmillan.

Mintzberg, H. (1998) 'Covert leadership: Notes on managing professionals', *Harvard Business Review*, Nov.–Dec., pp. 140–7.

Mullins, L. (1999) *Management and Organisational Behaviour*, 5th edn. Harlow: Financial Times Pitman Publishing.

Northouse, P. (1997) *Leadership – Theory and Practice*. California: Sage.

Rajan, A. and van Eupen, P. (1997) 'Take it from the top', *People Management*, 23 October, pp. 26–9.

Senge, P. (1990) *The Fifth Discipline: The art and practice of the learning organisation*. London: Century Business, Random House.

Shackleton, V. (1995) *Business Leadership*. London: Routledge.

Steyrer, J. (1998) 'Charisma and the Archetypes of leadership', *Organisation Studies*, Vol. 19, No. 5, pp. 807–28.

Tichy, N. and Devanna, M. (1986) *The Transformational Leader*. New York: Wiley.

Vroom, V. (1964) *Work and Motivation*. Chichester: John Wiley.

Walmsley, H. (1999) 'A suitable ploy', *People Management*, 8 April, pp. 48–50.

Williams, M. (2000) *The war for talent: Getting the best from the best*. London: CIPD.

General discussion topics

1 Do we need leaders at all? Discuss what alternatives there might be.

2 Consider the four types of charismatic leader identified by Styrer (1998): hero, father figure, missionary and saviour. Discuss the ways in which the types of leader are similar or different.

Chapter 21   Diversity: the legal framework

An important part of employment law in the UK is concerned with deterring employers from discriminating unfairly at any stage in their relationship with an individual worker. It is an area of law which is well established but which is also developing fast in new directions. As we write there are specific statutes making it unlawful to discriminate on the following grounds:

- sex;
- marital status;
- race;
- national origin;
- ethnicity;
- disability;
- union membership or non-membership;
- that individuals are part-time workers;
- that individuals are ex-offenders whose convictions are spent.

Wider protection is in the process of being established, principally as a result of European Union directives. Soon it will also become unlawful to discriminate against workers employed on fixed-term contracts, or on the grounds of their age or their religious or political beliefs. The position on sexual orientation remains unclear. Recent case law (notably *MacDonald* v. *Ministry of Defence* 2000) suggests that discrimination on grounds of sexual orientation is a form of unlawful sex discrimination. However, similar past rulings have subsequently been overturned by the appeal courts, so it cannot yet be stated with certainty that employers are acting unlawfully when discriminating against gays and lesbians.

Discrimination law operates rather differently in the case of each of the above grounds, providing a rather greater degree of protection to those discriminated against on the grounds of sex or race than to union members or ex-offenders. In this chapter we review the legal position in each area, establishing the core principles of discrimination law and using illustrative examples from tribunal cases. In the following chapter we look more generally at employment policy on equality issues and at the practices associated with the effective management of diversity.

| **Activity 21.1** | What other grounds, aside from those currently covered by the law, would you consider should be covered by discrimination law? Are there any that are currently covered that you think should not be? |

Discrimination on grounds of sex or marital status

The two major Acts of Parliament that govern sex discrimination matters in the UK are the Equal Pay Act 1970 and the Sex Discrimination Act 1975. Although both came into effect over 25 years ago they have been subsequently amended in important ways. Sex discrimination is an area of law in which there is EU competence, so appeals can be made to the European Court of Justice. UK law can also be challenged in the European courts if it is considered that it fails to comply in some way with Article 141 of the Treaty of Amsterdam (formerly Article 119 of the Treaty of Rome) or with EU directives in the sex discrimination field.

Employer actions are policed to some extent by the Equal Opportunities Commission (EOC) which is required to keep the legislation under review, to conduct formal investigations into employer actions where it has reason to suspect there has been a contravention of the law, to issue codes of practice and to provide legal assistance to employees who consider themselves to be victims of unfair discrimination. On many occasions the EOC has itself represented employees before employment tribunals. It also brings its own test cases in a bid to push back the frontiers of sex discrimination law.

The Equal Pay Act 1970

The Equal Pay Act 1970 was the first legislation promoting equality at work between men and women. Although passed in 1970, it only came into force in December 1975. It was subsequently amended, and its scope extended, by the Equal Pay (Amendment) Regulations 1983 and by the Sex Discrimination Act 1986. The Act is solely concerned with eliminating unjustifiable differences between the treatment of men and women in terms of their rates of pay and other conditions of employment. It is thus the vehicle that is used to bring a case to tribunal when there is inequality between a man's contract of employment and that of a woman. In practice the majority of cases are brought by women and concern discriminatory rates of payment, although there have been some important cases brought by men focusing on aspects of pension provision.

The Act, as amended in 1983, specifies three types of claim that can be brought. These effectively define the circumstances in which pay and other conditions between men and women should be equal:

1 **Like work:** where a woman and a man are doing work which is the same or broadly similar – for example where a woman assembly worker sits next to a male assembly worker, carrying out the same range of duties.
2 **Work rated as equivalent:** where a man and a woman are carrying out work which, while of a different nature, has been rated as equivalent under a job evaluation scheme. We cover this aspect of equal pay in greater detail in Chapter 35.
3 **Work of equal value:** where a man and a woman are performing different tasks but where it can be shown that the two jobs are equal in terms of their demands, for example in terms of skill, effort and type of decision making.

In order to bring a case the applicant must be able to point to a comparator of the opposite gender with whom he or she wishes to be compared. The comparator must be employed by the same employer and at an establishment covered by the same terms and conditions. When an equal value claim is brought which an employment tribunal considers to be well founded, an 'independent expert' is appointed to carry out a job evaluation exercise in order to establish whether or not the two jobs being compared are equal in terms of the demands they make.

Employers can employ two defences when faced with a claim under the Equal Pay Act. First they can seek to show that a job evaluation exercise has been carried out which indicates that the two jobs are not like, rated as equivalent or of equal value. To succeed the job evaluation scheme in use must be both analytical and free of sex bias (see Chapter 35). Second, the employer can claim that the difference in pay is justified by 'a genuine material factor not of sex'. For this to succeed, the employer has to convince the court that there is a good business reason for the unequal treatment and that there has thus been no sex discrimination. Examples of genuine material factors that have proved acceptable to the courts are as follows:

- different qualifications (e.g.where a man has a degree and a woman does not);
- performance (e.g. where a man is paid a higher rate than a woman because he works faster or has received a higher appraisal rating);
- seniority (where the man is paid more because he has been employed for several years longer than the woman);
- regional allowances (where a man is paid a London weighting, taking his pay to a higher rate than that of a woman performing the same job in the Manchester branch).

The courts have ruled that differences in pay explained by the fact that the man and woman concerned are in separate bargaining groups, by the fact that they asked for different salaries on appointment or because of an administrative error are not acceptable genuine material factor defences. It is possible to argue that a difference in pay is explained by market forces, but evidence has to be produced to satisfy the court that going rates for the types of work concerned are genuinely different and that it is therefore genuinely necessary to pay the comparator at a higher rate.

Where someone wins an equal pay claim they are entitled to receive up to six years' back pay to make up the difference between their salary and that of their comparator. Until 1999 there was a limit of only two years, but this was successfully challenged in the European Court of Justice in the case of *Levez* v. *T.H. Jennings (Harlow Pools) Ltd*. At the time of writing the six-year limit is itself the subject of legal challenge and may thus be removed in the near future.

WINDOW ON PRACTICE

Ms Smith was taken on to work for a company as a stockroom manager at a salary of £50 a week. After a few months she discovered that her predecessor (a man) had been paid £60 a week for doing the same job. As there was no suitable male comparator currently employed by the firm, she decided to bring an equal pay case using her predecessor as her male comparator. The European Court of Justice decided that this was acceptable under the terms of Article 119 of the Treaty of Rome. Ms Smith thus won her case.

In a more recent case, a woman who had been employed in a senior role resigned and was subsequently replaced by a man who was paid a considerably higher salary. She brought an equal pay claim against her former employer citing her successor as the male comparator. This too was ruled acceptable under the terms of the European Treaties.

Sources: *Macarthy's Ltd* v. *Smith* (1980), *Diocese of Hallam Trustees* v. *Connaughton* (1995).

The Sex Discrimination Act 1975

The Sex Discrimination Act also came into force in December 1975 and was designed to complement the Equal Pay Act 1970 by dealing primarily with non-contractual forms of sex discrimination such as employee selection, the provision of training opportunities, promotion, access to benefits and facilities and dismissal. It also applies outside the workplace, so case law that relates to events which have nothing at all to do with employment can be the source of important precedents. The Act covers all workers whether or not they serve under contracts of employment or are employed and all job applicants. The only groups excluded are ministers of religion, soldiers who may serve in front-line duties and people employed to work abroad. It thus remains permissible for firms recruiting employees to work in Saudi Arabia exclusively to select men. The Act applies equally to men and women, and also protects people from unfair discrimination on the grounds that they are married.

There are three headings under which claims are brought; direct discrimination, indirect discrimination and victimisation, the way the law works in each case being rather different.

Direct discrimination is straightforward. It occurs simply when an employer treats someone unfavourably and when sex or marital status is an important factor in this decision. In judging claims the courts use the 'but for' test, asking whether the woman would have received the same treatment as a man (or vice versa) but for her sex. Examples of direct sex discrimination include advertising for a man to do a job which could equally well be done by a woman, failing to promote a woman because she is pregnant or dismissing a married woman rather than her single colleague because she is known to have a working husband.

If an employer is found to have discriminated *directly* on grounds of sex or marital status, except in one type of situation, there is no defence. The courts cannot, therefore, take into account any mitigating circumstances or make a judgment based on the view that the employer acted reasonably. Once it has been established that direct discrimination has occurred, proceedings end with a victory for the applicant. The one exception operates in the area of recruitment, where it is possible to argue that certain jobs have to be reserved for either women or men. For this to be acceptable the employer must convince a court that it is a job for which there is a 'genuine occupational qualification'. The main headings under which such claims are made are as follows:

- **authenticity** (e.g. acting or modelling jobs);
- **decency** (e.g. lavatory or changing room attendants);
- **personal** services (e.g. a counsellor engaged to work in a rape crisis centre).

Direct discrimination on grounds of pregnancy or maternity is assumed automatically to constitute unlawful sex discrimination. This means that there is no defence of reasonableness whatever the individual circumstances. It is thus unlawful to turn down a job application from a well-qualified woman who is eight months pregnant, irrespective of her intentions as regards the taking of maternity leave.

Indirect discrimination is harder to grasp, not least because it can quite easily occur unintentionally. It occurs when a 'requirement or condition' is set which has the effect, in practice, of disadvantaging a significantly larger proportion of one sex than the other. In other words, if substantially fewer women than men can comply with the condition, even if it is applied in exactly the same way to both men and women, it is potentially unlawful. A straightforward example is a job advertisement which specifies that applicants should be taller than 5 feet 10 inches. This is indirectly discriminatory because a substantially smaller proportion of women are able to comply than men. The same rule applies in the case of discrimination on grounds of marital status, an example being that of an employer who offers promotion on the basis that the employee must be prepared to be away from home for considerable spells of time, when in reality such absence was never or rarely required.

Indirect discrimination differs from direct discrimination in that there are defences that an employer can deploy. For example, an employer can justify the condition or requirement they have set 'on grounds other than sex', in which case it may be lawful. An example might be a job for which a key requirement is the ability to lift heavy loads. It is reasonable in such circumstances for the employer to restrict recruitment to people who are physically able to comply, for example by including a test of strength in selection procedures. The fact that more men than women will be able to do so does not make the practice unlawful, provided the lifting requirement is wholly genuine.

In the USA the 'four-fifths rule' applies in judging cases of indirect discrimination, meaning that a practice is unlawful where the proportion of one sex that can comply with the condition is fewer than 80 per cent of the other. At present there is no such convention in the UK, meaning that it is for individual tribunals to decide what exactly constitutes 'a substantially smaller proportion' of men or women when judging these cases.

> **WINDOW ON PRACTICE**
>
> A leading case in indirect sex discrimination law is *Price* v. *Civil Service Commission* (1977). This concerned a requirement set by the Civil Service that applicants for posts of executive officer level should be between the ages of 17 and 28. Mrs Price, who was 36, claimed that an advertisement for an executive officer was indirectly discriminatory against women on the grounds that a substantially greater proportion of men could in practice comply with the age requirement. Her case was based on the contention that many women were outside the labour market during these ages bringing up children. The Employment Appeals Tribunal agreed with her and declared the age limitation to be unreasonable.

In the field of sex discrimination the term 'victimisation' means the same as it does in other areas of employment law. An employer victimises workers if it disadvantages them in any way simply because they have sought to exercise their legal rights or have assisted others in doing so. An employee would thus bring a claim of victimisation to a tribunal if they had been overlooked for promotion having recently successfully settled an equal pay claim. Importantly victimisation covers situations in which someone threatens to bring an action or plans to do so even if no case is ultimately brought.

Positive discrimination

Positive sex discrimination involves directly or indirectly discriminating in favour of women in situations where they are underrepresented – usually at senior levels in an organisation or in occupational groups which are male dominated. Such practices are unlawful under UK discrimination law when they involve actively discriminating against men who are better qualified to fill the positions concerned. However, it is lawful to take positive action aimed at encouraging and supporting women provided it stops short of actually discriminating in their favour. It is thus acceptable to include an equal opportunities statement in a job advertisement as a means of indicating that the organisation welcomes applications from women. Similarly employers can design and offer training courses tailored specifically for women. As long as men are not prevented from participating, such action is lawful.

Dress codes

In relation to dress codes, a tribunal will only find valid a claim of sex discrimination if the applicant or applicants can be shown to have suffered a detriment as a result of the condition being imposed. Merely treating members of the two sexes differently is not in itself sufficient to constitute unlawful indirect discrimination. For this reason it is acceptable in principle for employers to impose different dress codes on male and female staff, provided the same broad 'standard of conventionality' is applied.

It is thus lawful, as far as sex discrimination law is concerned, to insist that male employees wear business suits at work while permitting women more choice about their attire. Over the years, however, tribunals have adapted their interpretation of the term 'standards of conventionality' to reflect changing social norms. As a result sex discrimination claims have been successfully won by men who wish to retain their long hair tied in a pony-tail and women who wish to wear trousers at work.

Transsexuals

Whereas homosexuals have had great difficulty over the years in persuading the courts that they have rights under sex discrimination law, transsexuals are protected. It is therefore unlawful to discriminate against someone on the grounds that he or she is a medically defined transsexual. The rights of people undergoing gender reassignment are now specifically protected by the Sex Discrimination (Gender Reassignment) Regulations 1999.

Sexual harassment

While the area of sexual harassment is not specifically covered in the Sex

Activity 21.2

In making its judgment in *Rewcastle* v. *Safeway* (1989), a case that concerned the dismissal of a man who refused to cut his hair to a conventional male length, the tribunal made the following remark about the law on dress codes:

> Whilst we naturally accept the employer's right to determine standards of appearance and dress for its employees ... we question whether a policy which is designed to mirror 'conventional' differences between the sexes can be reconciled with the underlying rationale of the sex discrimination legislation which is to challenge traditional assumptions about sexes.

To what extent do you agree with these sentiments?

Source: IRS (1993, p. 11).

Discrimination Act 1975, the courts have accepted for some years that allowing someone to be subjected to acts of harassment which have a sexual dimension amounts to unlawful sex discrimination. Although the law applies equally to men and women, the vast majority of cases are brought by women as a result of acts perpetrated by men:

> Any unfavourable treatment to which a woman is subjected that includes a significant sexual element to which a man would not be vulnerable is to be regarded as unfavourable treatment on grounds of the woman's sex and is therefore directly discriminatory within the meaning of the Act. Since such treatment will inevitably comprise a 'detriment', it is rendered unlawful by Section 6(2)(b), which stipulates that it is unlawful for an employer to discriminate against a woman by 'dismissing her, or subjecting her to any other detriment'.
>
> (IDS 1998, p. 222)

The employer's liability in harassment cases arises from the application of the doctrine of **vicarious liability**, under which employers are held responsible for the commitment of civil wrongs by employees when they are at work. The doctrine also plays an important role in health and safety law, as we will see in Chapter 31.

Sexual harassment is defined in a European Union code of practice dating from 1991. It establishes the following:

(a) that it consists of unwanted conduct of a sexual nature or based on sex, which affects the dignity of men and women at work;
(b) that sexual harassment can be physical or verbal in nature;
(c) that the conduct *either* leads to material detriment (i.e. it affects promotion, pay, access to training, etc.) *or* creates an intimidating or humiliating work environment.

In judging cases the courts focus on the reaction of the victim and do not apply any general definitions of what types of conduct do and do not amount to unlawful harassment. Hence conduct which may not offend one person in the slightest can be found to constitute sexual harassment when directed at someone else who is deeply offended.

For an employer the only valid defences relate to the notion of vicarious liability. An employer can, for example, claim ignorance of the incident of which the victim is complaining or can claim that vicarious liability does not apply because it occurred away from the workplace and outside office hours. Finally the employer can defend itself by showing that all reasonable steps were taken to prevent the harassment from occurring or continuing. In order to succeed here, the employer needs to produce evidence to show that initial complaints were promptly acted upon and that appropriate action, such as disciplining the perpetrators or moving them to other work, was taken.

Race discrimination

UK race discrimination law is governed by the Race Relations Act 1976. Under the terms of the European Union Directive on Race Discrimination, agreed in 2000, this area of law will become one of European competence at some stage before 2003. As matters stand, the principles established in the 1976 Act are very similar to those set out in the Sex Discrimination Act described above. The law applies to all workers except those recruited to work overseas or in private households. The 'direct' and 'indirect' forms of discrimination are defined in the same way as in sex discrimination law, as are the terms 'victimisation', 'positive discrimination' and 'harassment'. Moreover, the Commission for Racial Equality plays a similar facilitating role to that played by the Equal Opportunities Commission in the field of sex discrimination. Precedents from the sex discrimination arena can apply in that of race discrimination and vice versa. There is, however, no equivalent law to that contained in the Equal Pay Act operating in the field of race discrimination.

Importantly the Act extends beyond discrimination on grounds of race to embrace the notions of nationality and ethnic and national origin. It is thus as unlawful for an employer to discriminate against someone because they are French or American as it is to treat someone less favourably because of their racial origins. According to Deakin and Morris (1998, pp. 598–9), the term 'ethnicity' was defined by Lord Fraser in the case of *Mandla* v. *Lee* (1983) as applying to a distinct group within the population sharing the following essential characteristics:

■ a long history of which the group is conscious as distinguishing it from other groups, and the memory of which keeps it alive;
■ a cultural tradition of its own, often but not necessarily associated with religious observance;
■ a common geographical origin, or descent from a small number of common ancestors;
■ a common language, not necessarily peculiar to the group;
■ a common literature peculiar to the group;
■ a common religion different from that of neighbouring groups or from the general community surrounding it;
■ being a minority or being an oppressed or a dominant group within a larger community.

According to this definition, merely practising a minority religion is an insufficient basis to constitute being of distinct ethnic origin. There also has to be a shared and long history of distinctiveness. This is why in *Dawkins* v. *Department of the Environment* (1993), Rastafarians were found not to be an ethnic group for the purposes of discrimination law.

Genuine occupational qualifications, as in sex discrimination law, permit discrimination on grounds of race at the recruitment stage for one or two kinds of job. The main grounds are authenticity and the provision of personal services to members of a particular racial community. In the case of race discrimination the defence of authenticity extends to employers of people to work in ethnic restaurants.

Most cases involving indirect discrimination under the Race Relations Act concern requirements being set for a high standard of English or for specific UK-based qualifications. As in sex discrimination law, it is necessary to be able to show objectively that these are necessary for the jobs in question. The courts will not allow employers to set conditions such as these unless it can be shown that there really is a *need* for such a condition. For example, in the case of *Hampson* v. *Department of Education and Science* (1990) a teacher was able to show that the requirement to have completed a three-year training course before being appointed to a teaching post in the UK unfairly discriminated against people of

Chinese origin who had qualified in Hong Kong. She was successful because she was able to convince the Court of Appeal that her two-year qualification followed by eight years' classroom experience made her well qualified to teach in Britain.

A fine line has to be trodden when recruiting people from overseas countries because there is a need to stay on the right side of both the Race Relations Act 1976 and the more recent Asylum and Immigration Act 1996. The former makes it unlawful to treat an overseas application unfavourably in any way, while the latter makes it a criminal offence to employ someone who does not have the right of residence in the UK or a valid work permit. Great care is thus called for in handling such matters.

WINDOW ON PRACTICE

A race discrimination case with important implications was brought by two women in 1996.

This case concerned the appearance at a private function of Mr Bernard Manning in the guise of a comedian. The audience consisted of 400 men who were treated to a routine consisting in large part of racially and sexually offensive jokes. Two of the waitresses employed by the hotel at the function were black. Bernard Manning noticed them and made a number of remarks directed at them during his routine.

The two women sued the hotel group which employed them on the grounds that it was vicariously liable and that they had been allowed to suffer racial harassment. The employer contested this, saying that it could not be vicariously liable for offensive remarks made by someone who was not an employee – indeed was not even a guest in the hotel and thus had no contractual relationship with it at all.

The women won their claim, successfully arguing that the hotel's management had failed to take action to prevent the harassment from occurring by removing them from the function at the earliest possible time. The employer was therefore vicariously liable and was required to pay compensation.

Source: *Burton* v. *De Vere Hotels* Ltd (1996).

Disability discrimination

The Disability Discrimination Act (1995) came into force in December 1996, since when several thousand cases have been lodged with employment tribunals. It replaced the Disabled Persons (Employment) Act 1944, which was widely criticised for being ineffective, only eight successful prosecutions having been brought during its fifty-year existence. From April 2000 the Disability Rights Commission has been in operation, with a remit in respect of discrimination against disabled people which is very similar to that of the Equal Opportunities Commission and the Commission for Racial Equality in their respective fields.

The new Act applies to all workers and to all organisations employing more than 15 people. While it shares some features in common with established legislation on sex and race discrimination, there are important differences. Of these, the most significant is the restriction of protection to direct discrimination and victimisation. There are no provisions equivalent to those on indirect discrimination in the Sex Discrimination and Race Relations Acts. The key words are as follows:

> An employer discriminates against a disabled person if for a reason which relates to the disabled person's disability, he treats him less favourably than he treats or would treat others to whom that reason does not or would not apply.

(Disability Discrimination Act 1995, s. 5.1)

The Act is thus concerned with preventing an employer from discriminating directly against an individual worker or job applicant who suffers from a disability. There is no specific prohibition on the setting of requirements for use in recruitment or promotion processes which might be held to discriminate against disabled people in general. It is thus lawful to list 'good record of health' as a desirable characteristic in a person specification – that alone cannot constitute discrimination under the terms of the Act. Employers only invite tribunal claims at the point that they actually discriminate against an individual.

However, this does not mean that employers can safely use language in job advertisements which is off-putting to disabled people, because the advertisement can later be used by a rejected applicant as evidence in support of a disability discrimination claim. Newspapers and employment agencies which knowingly publish advertisements which are discriminatory may also face fines of up to £5,000 if successfully prosecuted.

The other important difference between direct discrimination on grounds of disability and that on grounds of sex or race is the existence of defences which an employer can employ. Essentially, 'less favourable treatment' is permitted if it is for a good reason. An example of this might be a typist who is required to type at a certain speed due to valid job demands. If a person with arthritis in their hands, who could only type at a much lower speed, applied for this job, they could lawfully be rejected on the grounds of their disability provided the potential employer had first explored whether any adjustment in the working environment could be made to overcome the mismatch. Discrimination is thus permitted if no 'reasonable adjustment' can be made to allow the person concerned to perform the job satisfactorily.

There are two key issues which the courts are required to rule on when determining cases brought under the Disability Discrimination Act:

1 What does and what does not constitute a disability for the purposes of the Act.
2 What is and what is not 'a reasonable adjustment' for an employer to make in order to accommodate the needs of a disabled person.

The first issue is decided with reference to the words used in the Act. These define someone as disabled if they have 'a physical or mental impairment which has a substantial and long term adverse affect on their ability to carry out normal day to day activities'. The term 'impairment' is taken by the courts to mean any kind of a loss of a key bodily function such as the ability to hear, see, walk or write. It also covers conditions involving loss of memory and incontinence. An impairment is 'substantial' if it is more than minor or trivial, while 'long term' is defined as a condition which has lasted or *might reasonably* be expected to last for 12 months or more.

The words 'normal day to day activities' have been the source of much confusion and litigation. This is because the courts have taken the phrase very much at face value. It is thus the case that someone is not disabled – and is thus not protected by the Act – if their condition stops them from climbing mountains or playing football, as these are not considered to be 'normal day to day activities'. It has to be an impairment which severely restricts someone's ability to carry out basic, commonplace tasks in the household or workplace.

However, provided the symptoms are serious in their impact, virtually all medical conditions can potentially be accepted as 'disabilities' for the purposes of the Disability Discrimination Act. This includes mental illnesses as well as those with

In 1997 a Mr Quinlan was dismissed from his job as an assistant working at a garden centre after seven days because he refused to carry out the heavy lifting work that formed a part of the job. He would not do this because he had had open heart surgery some ten years previously and had been told that lifting heavy weights might injure his health. He brought a claim to a tribunal under the Disability Discrimination Act arguing that it would have been reasonable for the employer to omit from his work the requirement to lift heavy weights, and that his dismissal was thus unlawful.

He lost his case on the grounds that he was not disabled under the terms of the Act. This was because lifting heavy weights was not found to constitute 'a normal day to day activity'. He could only have succeeded had his illness not allowed him to lift everyday objects. There was no consideration given to questions of reasonable adjustment, because the Disability Discrimination Act was found not to apply to Mr Quinlan in the first place.

(*Quinlan* v. *B&Q plc* (1997) Employment Appeals Tribunal 1386/97).

Source: L. Macdonald (1998) 'Discrimination', *Personnel Manager's Factfinder*. London: Gee Publishing.

physical symptoms. Hence the definition of disability in the Act has been found by the courts to encompass severe depression, bulimia and ME, as well as asthma, speech impairments and severe back pain. Severe facial disfigurement is also included as a relevant condition. The only exceptions are a few conditions with socially undesirable symptoms which have specifically been excluded. These include alcoholism, drug addiction, exhibitionism, kleptomania and pyromania. Hay fever is also excluded. Importantly it is irrelevant whether or not an individual has recovered from their disability. Discriminating against someone on the grounds that they have suffered from a condition in the past amounts to unlawful discrimination, provided the discrimination met the definition set out in the Act. The fact that someone can live and work normally because they are receiving treatment for their condition, for example in the form of drugs or psychiatric counselling, does not mean that they have ceased to be disabled under the terms of the Act. It is thus unlawful to discriminate against them on these grounds without an objectively justifiable reason.

The burden of proof in disability discrimination cases passes to the employer to satisfy the tribunal that no reasonable adjustments could be made to accommodate the needs of a disabled person. The courts thus assume that adjustments are possible unless the employer can show that it would be unreasonable to expect them to be made. There are no general rules here, because the courts are obliged in reaching their judgments to take account of the size and resources of the employer concerned. The large PLC is thus expected to make bigger adjustments in response to the demands of the Act than the owner of a small corner shop.

It is expected that employers consider making adjustments to the physical working environment, working arrangements and working conditions. Minor building alterations are clearly covered; so unless the employer is very small and is unable to afford to make them, it would be expected that disabled toilets and/or wheelchair ramps would be installed to accommodate a disabled person. Other examples would include changing taps to make them easier to switch on, altering lighting for people with restricted vision, and allocating specific parking spaces. However, the concept of 'reasonable adjustment' goes a great deal further, encompassing changes in all kinds of working practices. It is thus expected that employers re-organise duties, allocate ground-floor offices to wheelchair users, adjust working hours for a disabled person or allow someone to work from home if these changes would allow an individual disabled person to be employed. Of particular importance is the requirement to permit disabled people a greater amount of sick leave than other employees. Hence, as was shown in Chapter 14, it is no longer possible to dismiss a chronically ill employee on grounds of incapability, without first considering whether reasonable adjustments could be made to allow them to continue working. The courts expect to see evidence that the employer has given serious consideration to a request for adjustments and that no request is turned down without a proper investigation having first taken place.

When applicants win their cases at tribunal, there are three possible outcomes:

1 The tribunal issues a declaration affirming the complainant's rights (e.g. preventing an employer from making someone redundant).
2 The tribunal makes a recommendation (e.g. requiring a doorway to be widened to accommodate a wheelchair).
3 The tribunal makes a compensatory award.

In the case of the third outcome, there are no statutory limits on the compensation that can be paid, allowing the courts to fully recompense people for any past or estimated future losses they may have incurred.

Trade union discrimination

The freedom to join a trade union and take part in its lawful activities is generally regarded as a fundamental human right. It is included in both the European Convention on Human Rights and the founding conventions of the International Labour Organisation. Although this freedom is not couched in the language of positive rights, it is in practice difficult for a UK employer lawfully to discriminate against people simply because they have joined a union or have taken part in union activities. These rights are long established, but are now found in the Trade Union and Labour Relations (Consolidation) Act 1992. In 1990, equivalent rights were extended to people who do not wish to join a union or become involved in its activities. There are three basic rights:

(a) the right not to be dismissed for a trade union reason;
(b) the right not to suffer action short of dismissal for a trade union reason;
(c) the right not to be refused a job on trade union grounds.

The first two of these protect people who take part (or refuse to take part) 'in the activities of an independent trade union at an appropriate time'. The protection, however, only extends to employees (i.e. people working under a contract of service) and does not apply in the police and armed services. In the case of dismissals, because trade union reasons are regarded as 'automatically unfair', there is no qualifying period of service. Full rights thus apply from the first day someone is employed at a particular establishment.

In order to gain the protection of the law in this area the organisation an individual joins or becomes involved with must be one which has been listed as an independent trade union by the Certification Officer. Moreover the activities which they engage in must be authorised by the trade union concerned and must, if they take place during work time, be carried out with the consent of the employer. Industrial action is not included in the definition of 'the activities of an independent trade union at an appropriate time', but is the subject of other protective legislation.

Discrimination against prospective employees at the recruitment stage simply because they are or are not union members has been an unlawful practice since 1990. In the Employment Relations Act 1999 rights in this area were extended to cover any discrimination occurring as a result of an individual's past involvement in trade union activity. The aim was to prevent groups of employers from maintaining black-lists of individuals perceived to be union troublemakers.

Part-time workers

Discriminating against a female part-time worker has long been taken by the courts to constitute indirect sex discrimination because the vast majority of part-time workers are female. Since 2000, however, it has not been necessary for part-time workers (of either gender) to use sex discrimination law to protect themselves. The Part-time Workers (Prevention of Less Favourable Treatment) Regulations 2000 were introduced to ensure that the UK complied with the EU's Part-Time Workers Directive. They now seek to ensure that part-time workers (not just employees) are treated equally with full-time workers in all aspects of work, the key features being as follows:

1 Part-time workers who believe that they are being treated less favourably than a comparable full-time colleague can write to their employers asking for an explanation. This must be given in writing within 14 days.
2 Where the explanation given by the employer is considered unsatisfactory, the part-time worker may ask an employment tribunal to require the employer to affirm the right to equal treatment.
3 Employers are required under the regulations to review their terms and conditions and to give part-timers pro rata rights with those of comparable full-timers.
4 There is a right not to be victimised on account of enforcing rights under the Part-time Workers Regulations.

Any term or condition of employment is covered by the regulations, as is any detriment caused as a result of failure to be promoted or given access to training. It is also now unlawful to select someone for redundancy simply because they work part-time.

There are a number of problems with the new regulations, including the absence of a statutory authority to enforce the third of the above points. One of the more complex issues involves how the term 'part-time worker' should be defined, because it is used differently in different workplaces. In some organisations someone working 35 hours a week is employed on a 'part-time contract' because full-time hours are 40 per week. Elsewhere, where everyone works 35 hours, such a worker would be regarded as a full-timer. The regulations simply state that a worker is part-time if they work fewer hours in a week than are worked by recognised full-timers. This obviously poses difficulties for organisations which do not employ people to work a set number of hours a week, or for whom patterns of hours vary considerably over the course of a year. There is also a need for part-time workers who consider themselves to have been less favourably treated to name a comparator employed in a broadly similar job who is employed on a full-time basis in the same employment. Where none exists it is effectively impossible to bring a claim.

Ex-offenders

Another group who are given some measure of legal protection from discrimination at work are ex-offenders whose convictions have been 'spent'. The relevant legislation is contained in the Rehabilitation of Offenders Act 1974 which sets out after how many years different types of criminal conviction become spent and need not be acknowledged by the perpetrator. In the field of employment, protection from discrimination extends to dismissal, exclusion from a position and 'prejudicing' someone in any way in their employment. In other words, employers cannot dismiss someone, fail to recruit them or hold them back in their occupations simply because they are known or discovered to have a former conviction. Failing to disclose the conviction can also be no grounds for discrimination. Moreover, no one (the individual concerned or anyone else) is under any obligation to tell anyone else about the conviction once it has been spent. Effectively, the slate is wiped clean, allowing the ex-offender to live and work as if no conviction had been received.

The rehabilitation periods set out in the Act vary depending on the type of sentence that has been received. The tariff is as follows:

imprisonment over 30 months:	never spent
imprisonment 6 to 30 months:	ten years
less than 6 months' imprisonment:	seven years
fine or community service order:	five years
detention in a detention centre:	three years
conditional discharge:	one year
absolute discharge:	six months

The time runs from the date of the conviction, the times being cut in half for those who are under the age of 18 at this time. It is the sentence imposed that is relevant to the Act and not the sentence actually served.

Numerous jobs and occupations are excluded from the terms of the Act. Organisations which employ people to work in these positions are entitled to know about spent convictions and can lawfully discriminate against individuals on these grounds. The list includes all jobs which involve the provision of services to minors, employment in the social services, nursing homes and courts, as well as employment in the legal, medical and accountancy professions.

Summary propositions

21.1 Discrimination law is growing rapidly. The coming years will see its extension into new areas including discrimination on grounds of age, religion and political belief.

21.2 Equal pay law requires men and women to be paid the same wage for doing work which is the same or which can be shown to be of equal value unless the employer can justify a difference on grounds other than sex.

21.3 In sex and race discrimination legislation an important distinction is made between direct and indirect discrimination. The latter relates to the setting of a requirement by an employer with which more of one sex than of the other can comply.

21.4 Sexual and racial harassment claims can be brought against any employer who allows a worker to be subjected to treatment which intimidates or humiliates the victim and is sexual or racial in nature.

21.5 The Disability Discrimination Act 1995 requires employers to consider making reasonable adjustments to working conditions to accommodate the needs of a disabled person before dismissing them or failing to offer them a job.

21.6 Limited protection from discrimination is given in law to trade union members, employees who do not engage in union activity, part-time workers and ex-offenders whose convictions are spent.

References

Deakin, S. and Morris, G. (1998) *Labour Law*, 2nd edn. London: Butterworth.

Incomes Data Services (1998) *Sex Discrimination and Equal Pay*. Employment Law Handbook. London: IDS.

Industrial Relations Services (1993) 'Dress and Personal Appearance at Work', *IRS Law Bulletin* 469, pp. 2–13.

Macdonald, L. (1998) 'Discrimination', *Personnel Manager's Factfinder*. London: Gee Publishing.

Legal cases

Burton v. *De Vere Hotels Ltd* [1996] IRLR 596.
Dawkins v. *Department of the Environment* [1979] IRLR 170.
Diocese of Hallam Trustees v. *Connaughton* (1995) (EAT 1128/95).
Hampson v. *Department of Education and Science* [1990] IRLR 302.
Levez v. *T.H. Jennings (Harlow Pools) Ltd* [1999] IRLR 3.
Macarthy's Ltd v. *Smith* [1980] IRLR 209–210.
MacDonald v. *Ministry of Defence* (2000) (EAT 121/00).
Mandla et al. v. *Lee et al.* [1983] IRLR 209.
Price v. *Civil Service Commission* [1977] IRLR 291.
Quinlan v. *B&Q plc* (1997) (EAT 1386/97).
Rewcastle v. *Safeway plc* (1989) (EAT 22482/89).

General discussion topics

1 Which groups who are not currently protected would you like to see covered by anti-discrimination law? What arguments could be advanced for and against your proposition from an employer perspective?

2 How far do you think that our discrimination law is effective in achieving its aims? What could be done to make it more effective?

| Chapter 22 | # Equality: equal opportunities and diversity |

Legislation, voluntary codes of practice and equality initiatives have resulted in some progress towards equality of treatment for minority groups, but there remains inescapable evidence of continuing discrimination. More recent approaches under the banner of management of diversity include the economic and business case for equality, the valuing and managing of diversity in organisations, culture change and the mainstreaming of equality initiatives. These approaches are partly a response to the insufficient progress made so far, yet there is only limited evidence that they have made a difference. They offer some useful perspectives and practices, although the underlying concepts also raise some issues and concerns.

We begin this chapter with a review of the current employment experiences of the members of socially defined minority groups, and then review the differing approaches to achieving equality for those groups, in particular contrasting the more traditional equal opportunities approach with the management of diversity approach. We then consider the implications which managing diversity has for organisations.

Current employment experiences of socially defined minority groups

For the purposes of this section we will consider the experiences of five socially defined minority groups: women, racial/ethnic minorities, disabled people, older people and individuals who are lesbian, gay or bisexual. In choosing these groups we have followed Kirton and Greene (2000), although others, such as British Telecom, have identified as many as 12 aspects of difference between employees (Liff 1999).

Women

If **participation** in the labour force is an indication of decreasing discrimination then recent figures are encouraging. From 1971 to 1998 the female participation rate in employment increased from 56.8 per cent to 72.5 per cent, compared with the male participation rate which is slowly falling, and these trends are predicted to continue (Skills and Enterprise Network 2000). Much of this increase has been due to the replacement of full-time jobs with part-time jobs. Indeed Hakim (1993) puts forward the strong argument, based on an alternative analysis of the census and employment data, that the increasing participation of women in employment between the 1950s and the late 1980s is a myth, although a real increase does appear to have taken place since the late 1980s. Her analysis shows that 'the much trumpeted rise in women's employment in Britain consisted entirely of the substitution of part-time for full-time jobs from 1951 to the late 1980s' (p. 102). Hakim concludes from the research that only an increase in full-time employment is likely to have a wider impact on women's opportunities at work and elsewhere.

Some of the more obvious signs of discrimination, such as in recruitment advertising, may have disappeared, and there is some evidence to suggest that women are beginning to enter some previously male-dominated occupations. For example, women have now been ordained as priests in the Church of England but not without deep and continuing debate. Similarly men are beginning to enter some previously female-only occupations, such as midwifery. However, there remains a high degree of subtle (for example, access to training and support for development and promotion) and not-so-subtle discrimination (for example, continued **gender segregation** in terms of both type and level of work undertaken (EOC 1994)). There are still few women in higher levels of management and not many male secretaries. The Labour Force Survey, 1998, reveals that 68 per cent of managers and administrators are men (Thair and Risdon 1999). Most women remain in three occupational groups: clerical and secretarial (where 74 per cent of employees are women); personal and protective services, for example catering, caring, cleaning (where 67 per cent of employees are women) and selling occupations (where women comprise 63 per cent of employees) (Thair and Risden 1999). These occupations are often characterised by part-time work, and are in a mainly narrow range of industrial sectors.

Dickens and Colling (1990) explain how continued job segregation in respect of both role and hours/arrangements is one of the influencing factors which results in discriminatory agreements between employers and unions. A large proportion of women still work part time (often from choice), to the extent that Thair and Risden report that 44 per cent of women work part time and that 80 per cent of all people working part time are women. Part-time workers are often described as part of the secondary labour market with pay, conditions and employment rights being vastly inferior to those of full-time permanent workers, although legislation now provides for some equalisation.

Pay differentials between men and women have changed very little except for a hike of women's pay upwards when the Equal Pay Act 1970 came into force in 1975. Women's full-time hourly pay was 82 per cent of full-time male earnings in 2000 (New Earnings Survey 2000), having increased from 65.8 per cent prior to the Equal Pay Act. However, if weekly earnings are compared the percentage reduces to 74.5 per cent, as this takes account of the greater number of hours worked by men. The same report states that in annual terms women who are full-time earn, on average, £17,556 compared with £24,298 for men. The same survey found that across all occupations women earned 60–70 per cent of male earnings in the same occupational group. Dickens and Colling highlight the problem of job evaluation schemes which perpetuate old values and hence discourage rather than encourage equality of pay, and they are also subject to managerial manipulation (McColgon 1994). In addition, the TUC (1995), amongst others, reports that part-timers (mostly women) shoulder the burden of low pay.

While some progress has been made towards equal pay, these factors still remain as barriers to be overcome. The abolition of the Wages Councils has not helped in this respect, but the minimum wage has provided some limited support.

Liff and Cameron (1997) argue that, so far, conventional equality measures have made a limited impact on women's position in the workforce.

Racial and ethnic groups

In spite of the legislation evidence of discrimination continues to exist. The TUC (2000) reports that the level of unemployment for black and Asian communities is 13 per cent compared with that for the white population of 6 per cent. This picture of **comparative level of unemployment** has barely changed over the last 15 years, and the gap appears to be widening rather than narrowing (TUC), although there are differences between the different ethnic groups. In addition, there is continued **segregation in the labour market**, with ethnic minority male employees being employed in the hotel, catering and repairs and distribution sectors, and manufacturing industry, to a much greater extent than their white counterparts. But for construction the reverse is true. Segregation also occurs vertically. Using comparative 1992/9 Labour Force Survey data, the TUC reports that in 1992 30 per cent of white people were classified as managers, compared with 25.4 per cent of black people, while in 1999 30.4 per cent of white people were classified as managers compared with 24.7 per cent of black people. Again the gap appears to be widening rather than narrowing. Other evidence of vertical segregation has been found by the Runnymede Trust (2000) when surveying the FTSE 100 companies. They found that 5.4 per cent of employees were from ethnic minority groups, compared with the representation of ethnic minorities in the general population of 6.4 per cent, but that this proportion fell sharply at higher grades, with 3.2 per cent of junior managers from ethnic minorities and 1 per cent of senior managers. Yet all of these companies believed that they did not unfairly discriminate. Samir Sharma OBE, Chair of the Runnymede Trust, commented that 'there is still a sea of white faces in the boardrooms of Europe' (Equal Opportunities Review (EOR) 2000).

In terms of **pay**, non-white workers are also comparatively disadvantaged, for example, on the basis of the Autumn 1994 Labour Force Survey, the Department for Education and Employment (1995) reports that black workers are paid, on average, almost 10 per cent less than white workers.

WINDOW ON PRACTICE

The *Guardian* (4 November 2000) contained the following report:
The IT industry is often considered to be one which is more open to the employment of different racial groups. But while the workforce may look more diverse the top jobs are still mostly filled by white people. The article goes on to report the experiences of two non-white IT directors. The first, Rene Carayol, is Chief Executive of an e-business consultancy, and comments that he is shocked by the racial prejudice that he encounters. For example when Rene and the team are visiting new offices, people who have not met them before look around the team for the white faces to work out who is the boss. He comments that it takes some time for people to get used to working with him, and feels that it took him longer to rise to his present position due to his race.

The second, Sarabjit Ubhey, Head of Operational Control at BUPA, identifies the glass ceiling above which there are few senior non-white IT people. She feels that the fundamental problem is awareness, pointing out, for example, that when social/networking events are held at a pub Muslims cannot be present. This, in addition to making them feel excluded, hinders their career progression.

Source: Adapted from R. Woolnough R. (2000) 'Racism reinforces the glass ceiling', *Guardian*, 4 November, p. 31.

Disabled people

Woodhams and Danieli (2000) point out that people who have a disability face common barriers to full integration into society and yet are a very varied group in that impairments can vary in severity, stability and type. The are 6.7 million people in the UK who have a current long-term health problem or disability which has a substantial adverse impact on their day-to-day activities and affects the work they can do (Bruyere 2000). People with a disability comprise nearly one-fifth of the working age population and yet comprise only about one-eighth of those in employment. In other words, people with a disability are more likely to be unemployed than their able-bodied counterparts, and once unemployed they are likely to remain so a longer period (Skills and Enterprise Network 2000).

Their choice of job is often restricted, and where they do find work it is likely to be in low-paid, less attractive jobs. People with a disability are overrepresented in plant and machine operative jobs and in the personal and protective services, and are underrepresented in professional and managerial jobs (Skills and Enterprise Network 2000). Periods of high general unemployment exacerbate these problems.

Employers traditionally have had a wide range of concerns regarding the employment of disabled people, including worries about general standards of attendance and health, safety at work, eligibility for pension schemes and possible requirements for alterations to premises and equipment.

Older people

A recent survey (EOR 1998), found that a range of employers specified age limits in 7.7 per cent of job advertisements, compared with 35 per cent in a similar survey in 1992–3, and 29 per cent in 1988–9, so the Code of Practice on Age Discrimination does appear to be having an impact. There is some evidence that the private and public sectors act differently in this respect. For example Itzin and Phillipson (1993), in their study of local authorities, note some improvements in terms of fewer upper age limits being applied, and Worsley (1996) reporting on research by the Carnegie Third Age Programme found that the voluntary and public sector organisations they studied did not specify age limits. However Itzin and Phillipson did find that the wording of some advertisements deters older workers from applying. Words like 'innovative', 'dynamic' and 'forward thinking' suggest a younger applicant. The Equal Opportunities Review (1998) also found that employers used coded language to indicate that they were looking for a specific age group, and found phrases such as 'young', 'articulate youngsters', 'second jobber', and 'young dynamic environment'. Itzin and Phillipson also identified discrimination at both the shortlisting and interview stage, with line managers having negative perceptions of older workers – seeing them as less able to cope with change, training or technology and less interested in their careers.

From January 1996 onwards *People Management* refused to accept job advertisements which specified numerical age limits, and MacLachlan *et al.* (1996) declared that they were:

> unwilling to play any part in prolonging misguided attitudes and patterns of behaviour among a minority of employers and agencies based on faulty assumptions and outdated recruitment practice.   (MacLachlan *et al.* 1996, p. 22)

In December 1996 MacLachlan *et al.* reported that this policy caused no damage to advertising revenue and from January 1997 they extended the ban to include the use of the words 'young' and 'old'.

However DfEE (1999) in a survey of 500 British residents between 50 and 69 years of age found that 85 per cent believed that employers discriminate against older workers. In particular discrimination was viewed to occur in relation to recruitment, selecting staff for promotion, redundancy, training and deciding the age of retirement. In a complementary study of employers the DfEE found that only 29 per cent were aware of the Code of Practice on Age (60 per cent in larger organisations), and only 23 per cent had seen a copy.

Respondents to a survey of IPM members (Warr) did identify some ways in which younger employees were preferred, but also a number of ways in which older workers were preferred. Workers over 40 were seen to be more loyal and conscientious, to have better interpersonal skills and to be more efficient in the job. The Equal Opportunities Review (1993), when reviewing research about older workers, concluded that experience in the job counteracts any age-related factors lowering productivity; that older workers are generally more satisfied with their jobs and have fewer accidents and a better absence record; and that in any case there is considerable variation within individuals.

Lesbian, gay and bisexual people

Of all the minority groups we are discussing this group is the most difficult to identify due to the fact that group membership is more easily concealed, usually due to the anticipation of discrimination. It is therefore difficult to quantify the extent to which these groups experience active discrimination.

Wilson (2000) in an article reporting three case studies found that in two of the three organisations sexuality other than the heterosexual norm was not considered acceptable in the culture. In one engineering company, the researcher was told that you would have to be very discreet if you were gay, and that one gay person, who had not 'come out', had left the organisation. In the second, a professional partnership, the researcher was told that sexuality was 'under wraps'. Only in the third, a media organisation, were different sexual orientations considered acceptable.

In a TUC survey carried out at the end of 1998 (EOR 1999b), 44 per cent of the 440 gay, lesbian and bisexual respondents said they had experienced discrimination at work due to their sexuality. Forms of discrimination reported ranged from verbal abuse to dismissal. Even in jobs where employees feel sufficiently comfortable to disclose their sexuality, there is considerable discrimination in the terms and benefits they receive. For example most pensions schemes only allow a spouse or heterosexual partner to receive dependant's benefits. Other areas such as concessions, for example travel concessions for partners, may exclude those with a same-sex partner.

Different approaches to equality

There has been a continuing debate concerning the action that should be taken to alleviate the disadvantages that minority groups encounter. One school of thought supports legislative action, which we considered in detail in the previous chapter, and this approach is generally referred to as the equal opportunities, or liberal approach. The other argues that this will not be effective and that the only way to change fundamentally is to alter the attitudes and preconceptions that are held about these groups. This second perspective is embodied in the managing diversity approaches. The initial emphasis on legislative action was adopted in the hope that this would eventually affect attitudes. A third, more extreme, radical and less supported approach comes from those who advocate legislation to promote positive or reverse discrimination to compensate for a history of discrimination against specified groups and to redress the balance more immediately. The arguments for and against such an approach are fully discussed by Singer (1993). In the UK legislation provides for positive action, such as special support and encouragement, for disadvantaged groups, but not positive or reverse discrimination (discriminating in their favour), although positive discrimination is legal in the USA. For a comparison of UK and US approaches to equality see Ford (1996).

The labels 'equal opportunities' and 'management of diversity' are used inconsistently, and to complicate this there are different perspectives on the meaning of managing diversity, so we shall draw out the key differences which typify each of these approaches, and offer some critique of their conceptual foundations and efficacy.

Equal opportunities approach

The equal opportunities approach seeks to influence behaviour through legislation so that discrimination is prevented. It has been characterised by a moral and ethical stance promoting the rights of *all* members of society. The approach, sometimes referred to as the liberal tradition (Jewson and Mason 1986), concentrates on the equality of opportunity rather than the equality of outcome found in more radical approaches. The approach is based on the understanding that some individuals are discriminated against, for example in the selection process, due to irrelevant criteria. These irrelevant criteria arise from assumptions based on the stereotypical characteristics attributed to them as members of a socially defined group, for example women will not be prepared to work away from home due to family commitments; a person with a disability will have more time off sick. As these assumptions are not supported by any evidence, in respect of any individual, they are regarded as irrelevant. The equal opportunities approach therefore seeks to formalise procedures so that relevant, job-based criteria are used (using job descriptions and person specifications), rather than irrelevant assumptions. The equal opportunities legislation provides a foundation for this formalisation of procedures, and hence procedural justice. As Liff (1999) points out, the use of systematic rules in employment matters which can be monitored for compliance is 'felt fair'. In line with the moral argument, and emphasis on systematic procedures, equal opportunities is often characterised as a responsibility of the HR Department.

The rationale, therefore, is to provide a 'level playing field' on which all can compete on equal terms. Positive action, not positive discrimination, is allowable in order that some may reach the level at which they can compete equally. An example is the illustration used in Chapter 12 on Selection where minority groups were given extra coaching and practice in a selection test for train drivers, as test taking was not part of their culture so that, when required to take a test, they were at a disadvantage.

Equal opportunities approaches stress disadvantaged groups, and the need, for example, to set targets for those groups to ensure that their representation in the workplace reflects their representation in wider society in occupations where they are underrepresented, such as the small numbers of ethnic minorities employed as firefighters and police officers, or the small numbers of women in senior management roles. These targets are not enforceable by legislation, as in the United States, but organisations have been encouraged to commit themselves voluntarily to improvement goals, and to support this by putting in place measures to support disadvantaged groups such as special training courses and flexible employment policies.

Differences between socially defined groups are glossed over, and the approach is generally regarded as one of 'sameness'. That is, members of disadvantaged groups should be treated in the same way as the traditional employee (white, male, young, able-bodied and heterosexual), and not treated differently due to their group membership, unless for the purpose of providing the 'level playing field'.

Problems with the equal opportunities approach

There is an assumption in the equal opportunities approach that equality of outcome will be achieved if fair procedures are used and monitored. In other words this will enable any minority groups to achieve a fair share of what employment has to offer. Once such minority groups become full participating members in employment, the old stereotypical attitudes on which discrimination against particular social groups is based will gradually change, as the stereotypes will be shown to be unhelpful.

The assumption that fair procedures or procedural justice will lead to fair outcomes has not been borne out in practice, as we have shown. In addition there has been criticism of the assumption that once members of minority groups have demonstrated their ability to perform in the organisation this will change attitudes and beliefs in the organisation. This is a naïve assumption, and the approach has been regarded as simplistic. Liff (1999) argues that attitudes and beliefs have been left untouched. Other criticisms pick up on the fact that the legislation does not protect all minority groups, and that there is a general lack of support within the organisation, partly due to the fact that equality objectives are not linked to business objectives (Shapiro and Austin 1996). Shapiro and Austin, amongst others, argue that equal opportunities has often been the concern of the HR function, and Kirton and Greene (2000) argue that a weak HR function has not helped. The focus of equal opportunities is on formal processes and yet it is it not possible to formalise everything in the organisation. Recent research suggests that this approach alienated large sections of the workforce (those not identified as disadvantaged groups) who felt that there was no benefit for themselves, and indeed that their opportunities were damaged. Others felt that equal opportunities initiatives had resulted in the lowering of entry standards, as in the London Fire and Civil Defence Authority (EOR 1996). Shapiro and Austin argue that this creates divisions in the workforce. Lastly, it is the individual who is expected to adjust to the organisation, and as Liff (1999) points out, 'traditional equal opportunities strategies encourage a view that women (and other groups) have a problem and need help' (p. 70).

In summary the equal opportunities approach is considered simplistic and to be attempting to treat the symptoms rather than the causes of unfair discrimination.

Management of diversity approach

The management of diversity approach concentrates on individuals rather than groups, and includes the improvement of opportunities for *all* individuals and not just those in minority groups. Hence managing diversity involves everyone and benefits everyone, which is an attractive message to employers and employees alike. Thus separate groups are not singled out for specific treatment. Kandola and Fullerton (1994, p. 47), who are generally regarded as the main UK supporters of a managing diversity approach, express it this way:

> Managing diversity is about the realisation of the potential of all employees . . . certain group based equal opportunities policies need to be seriously questioned, in particular positive action and targets.

In the second edition of their book (1998, p. 11) they contest, in addition, that:

> if managing diversity is about an individual and their contribution . . . rather than about groups it is contradictory to provide training and other opportunities based solely on people's perceived group membership.

Further differences from an equal opportunities approach are highlighted in the following definition from the USA, where managing diversity is described as:

> the challenge of meeting the needs of a culturally diverse workforce and of sensitising workers and managers to differences associated with gender, race, age and nationality in an attempt to maximise the potential productivity of all employees.
> (Ellis and Sonnenfield 1994, p. 82)

Ignoring for a moment the fact that some groups are specifically excluded from this definition, we will focus, amongst other themes, on two key issues that this quotation raises: recognition of difference and culture. Recognition of difference is also demonstrated by the IPD (1997) when they say that 'people have different abilities to contribute to organizational goals and performance' (pp. 1–2). Whereas the equal opportunities approach minimised difference, the managing diversity approach treats difference as a positive asset. Liff (1996), for example, notes that from this perspective organisations should recognise rather than dilute differences, as differences are positive rather than negative.

This brings us to a further difference between the equal opportunities approach and the managing diversity approach which is that the managing diversity approach is based on the economic and business case for recognising and valuing difference, rather than the moral case for treating people equally. Rather than being purely a cost, equal treatment offers benefits and advantages for the employer if they invest in ensuring that everyone in the organisation is valued and given the opportunities to develop their potential and make a maximum contribution. The practical arguments supporting the equalisation of employment opportunities are thus highlighted. Thompson and DiTomaso (reported by Ellis and Sonnenfield 1994) put it very well:

> Multicultural management perspective fosters more innovative and creative decision making, satisfying work environments, and better products because all people who have a contribution to make are encouraged to be involved in a mean-

ingful way ... More information, more points of view, more ideas and reservations are better than fewer.

A company that discriminates, directly or indirectly, against older or disabled people, women, ethnic minorities or people with different sexual orientations, will be curtailing the potential of available talent, and employers are not well known for their complaints about the surplus of talent. The financial benefits of retaining staff who might otherwise leave due to lack of career development or due to the desire to combine a career with family are stressed, as is the image of the organisation as a 'good' employer and hence its attractiveness to all members of society as its customers. A relationship between a positive diversity climate and job satisfaction and commitment to the organisation has also been found (Hicks-Clarke and Iles 2000). Although the impact on performance is more difficult to assess, it is reasonable to assume that more satisfied and committed employees will lead to reduced absence and turnover levels. In addition, the value of different employee perspectives and different types of contribution is seen as providing added value to the organisation, particularly when organisational members increasingly reflect the diverse customer base of the organisation. This provides a way in which organisations can better understand and therefore meet their customer needs. The business case argument is likely to have more support from managers as it is less likely to threaten the bottom line. (Policies that do pose such a threat can be unpopular with managers – see for example, Humphries and Rubery 1995.)

We return for a moment to the Ellis and Sonnenfeld quotation: managing diversity highlights the importance of culture. The roots of discrimination go very deep, and in relation to women, Simmons (1989) talks about challenging a system of institutional discrimination and anti-female conditioning in the prevailing culture. Culture is important in two ways in managing diversity – first, in respect of the whole range of approaches to managing diversity, organisational culture is a determinant of the way that organisations treat individuals from different groups. Equal opportunity approaches tended to concentrate on behaviour and, to a small extent, attitudes, whereas management of diversity approaches recognise a need to go beneath this. So changing the culture to one which treats individuals as individuals and supports them in developing their potential is critical, although the difficulties of culture change make this a very difficult task.

Second, depending on the approach to the management of diversity, the culture of different groups within the organisation comes into play. Recognising that men and women present different cultures at work and that this diversity needs to be managed, is key to promoting a positive environment of equal opportunity, which goes beyond merely fulfilling the demands of the statutory codes. Masreliez-Steen (1989) explains how men and women have different perceptions, interpretations of reality, languages and ways of solving problems, which, if properly used, can be a benefit to the whole organisation, as they are complementary. She describes women as having a collectivist culture where they form groups, avoid the spotlight, see rank as unimportant and have few but close contacts. Alternatively, men are described as having an individualistic culture, where they form teams, 'develop a profile', enjoy competition and have many superficial contacts. The result is that men and women behave in different ways, often fail to understand each other and experience 'culture clash'. However, the difference is about how things are done and not what is achieved.

The fact that women have a different culture, with different strengths and weaknesses, means that women need managing and developing in a different way, needing different forms of support and coaching. Women more often need help to understand the value of making wider contacts and how to make them. In order to manage such diversity, key management competencies for the future would be: concern with image, process awareness, interpersonal awareness/sensitivity, developing subordinates and gaining commitment. Attending to the organisation's culture suggests a move away from seeing the individual as the problem, and requiring that the individual needs to change because they do not fit the culture. Rather, it is the organisation that needs to change so that traditional assumptions of how jobs are constructed and how they should be carried out are questioned, and looked at afresh. As Liff (1999) comments, the sociology of work literature shows how structure, cultures and practices of organisations advantage those from the dominant group by adapting to their skills and lifestyles. This is the very heart of institutional discrimination, and so difficult to address as these are matters which are taken for granted and largely unconscious. The trick, as Thomas (1992) spells out, is to identify 'requirements as opposed to preferences, conveniences or traditions'. This view of organisational transformation rather than individual transformation is similar to Cockburn's (1989) 'long agenda' for equality, as she discusses changing cultures, systems and structures.

Finally managing diversity is considered to be a more integrated approach to implementing equality. Whereas equal opportunities approaches were driven by the HR function, managing diversity is seen to be the responsibility of all

Table 22.1 Major differences between 'equal opportunities' approaches and 'management of diversity' approaches

Aspect	Equal opportunities	Managing diversity
Purpose	Reduce discrimination	Utilise employee potential to maximum advantage
Case argued	Moral and ethical	Business case – improve profitability
Whose responsibility	HR/personnel department	All managers
Focuses on	Groups	Individuals
Perspective	Dealing with different needs of different groups	Integrated
Benefits for employees	Opportunities improved for disadvantaged groups, primarily through setting targets	Opportunities improved for all employees
Focus on management activity	Recruitment	Managing
Remedies	Changing systems and practices	Changing the culture

managers. And, as there are business reasons for managing diversity it is argued that equality should not be dealt with as a separate issue, as with equal opportunities approaches, but integrated strategically into every aspect of what the organisation does; this is often called mainstreaming.

Table 22.1 summarises the key differences between equal opportunities and managing diversity.

Problems with the managing diversity approach

While the management of diversity approach was seen by many as revitalising the equal opportunities agenda, and as a strategy for making more progress on the equality front, this progress has been slow to materialise. In reality, there remains the question of the extent to which approaches have really changed in organisations. Redefining equal opportunities in the language of the enterprise culture (Miller 1996) may just be a way of making it more palatable in today's climate, and Liff (1996) suggests that retitling may be used to revitalise the equal opportunities agenda.

It has been pointed out by Kirton and Greene (2000) that only a small number of organisations are ever quoted as management of diversity exemplars, and EOR (1999b) notes that even organisations which claim to be managing diversity do not appear to have a more diverse workforce than others, and neither have they employed more minority groups over the past five years.

Apart from this there are some fundamental problems with the management of diversity approach. The first of these is its complexity, as there are differing interpretations, which we have so far ignored, and which focus on the prominence of groups or individuals. Miller (1996) highlights two different approaches to the management of diversity. The first is where individual differences are identified and celebrated, and where prejudices are exposed and challenged via training. The second, more orthodox, approach is where the organisation seeks to develop the capacity of all. This debate between group and individual identity is a fundamental issue:

> Can people's achievements be explained by their individual talents or are they better explained as an outcome of their gender, ethnicity, class and age? Can anything meaningful be said about the collective experience of all women or are any generalisations undermined by other cross-cutting ideas? (Liff 1997, p. 11)

The most common approach to the management of diversity is based on individual contribution, as we have explained above, rather than group identity, although Liff (1997) identifies different approaches with different emphases. The *individualism* approach is based on dissolving differences. In other words, differences are not seen as being distributed systematically according to membership of a social group, but rather as random differences. Groups are not highlighted, but all should be treated fairly and encouraged to develop their potential. The advantage of this approach is that it is inclusive and involves all members of the organisation. An alternative emphasis in the management of diversity is that of *valuing differences* based on the membership of different social groups. Following this approach would mean recognising and highlighting differences, and being prepared to give special training to groups who may be disadvantaged and lack self-confidence, so that all in the organisation feel comfortable. Two further emphases are *accommodating* and *utilising* differences, which she argues are most similar to equal opportunity approaches where specific initiatives are available to aid identified groups, but also where these are also genuinely open for all other members of the organisation. In these approaches talent is recognised and used in spite of social differences, and this is done, for example, by recognising different patterns of qualifications and different roles in and out of paid work. Liff's conclusion is that group differences cannot be ignored, because it is these very differences which hold people back.

There is a further argument that if concentration on the individual is the key feature, then this may reduce our awareness of social-group-based disadvantage (Liff 1999) and may also weaken the argument for affirmative action (Liff 1996). The attractive idea of business advantage and benefits for all may divert attention from disadvantaged groups and result in no change to the status quo (see, for example, Ouseley 1996). Young (1990) argues that if differences are not recognised (as in the individualist approach), then the norms and standards of the dominant group are not questioned.

On the other hand a management of diversity approach may reinforce group-based stereotypes, when group-based characteristics are identified and used as a source of advantage to the organisation. For example Liff (1993) argues, in respect of women, that as these differences were treated previously as a form of disadvantage, women may be uncomfortable using them to argue the basis for equality. Others argue that a greater recognition of perceived differences will continue to provide a rationale for disadvantageous treatment.

In addition to this dilemma within managing diversity approaches, the literature provides a strong criticism of the business case argument, which has been identified as contingent and variable (Dickens 1999). Thus the business case is unreliable because it will only work in certain contexts. For example, where skills are easily available there is less pressure on the organisation to promote and encourage the employment of minority groups. Not every employee interacts with customers so if image and customer contact are part of the business case this will only apply to some jobs and not others. Also some groups may be excluded. For example, there is no systematic evidence to suggest that disabled customers are attracted by an organisation which employs disabled people. UK managers are also driven by short-term budgets and the economic benefits of equality may only be reaped in the longer term. Indeed as Kirton and Greene (2000) conclude, the business case is potentially detrimental to equality, when, for example, a cost–benefit analysis indicates that pursuing equality is not an economic benefit.

In addition there are concerns about whether diversity management, which originated in the USA, will travel effectively to the UK where the context is different – for example in terms of the demographics and the history of equality initiatives. Furthermore, there are concerns about whether diversity can be managed at all, as Lorbiecki and Jack (2000) note:

> the belief that diversity management is do-able rests on a fantasy that it is possible to imagine a clean slate on which memories of privilege and subordination leave no mark
> (p. 528)

and they go on to say that the theories do not take account of existing power differentials.

Lastly, managing diversity can be seen as introspective as it deals with people already in the organisation, rather than with getting people into the organisation – managing rather than expanding diversity (Donaldson 1993). Because of this

Thomas (1990) suggests that it is not possible to *manage* diversity until you actually have it.

Equal opportunities or managing diversity?

The first question to be addressed is whether equal opportunities and managing diversity are completely different things; the second is, if so, whether one approach is preferable to the other. For the sake of clarity, earlier in this chapter we characterised a distinct approach to managing diversity which suggests that it is different from equal opportunities. Miller (1996) identifies a parallel move from the collective to the individual in the changing emphasis in personnel management as opposed to HRM. However, as we have seen, managing diversity covers a range of approaches and emphases, some closer to equal opportunities, some very different.

Putting on one side the question of the extent of change, much of the management of diversity literature is written in such a way that it suggests that it is a superior approach to equal opportunities, and one that is not compatible with the latter (see Kandola *et al.* 1996). There is much support for equal opportunities and managing diversity to be viewed as mutually supportive and for this interaction to be seen as necessary for progress (see Ford 1996), although Newman and Williams (1995) argue that we are some way from a model which can incorporate difference and diversity in its individualised and collective sense. To see equal opportunities and management of diversity as *alternatives* threatens to sever the link between organisational strategy and the realities of internal and external labour market disadvantage.

Implications for organisations

Conceptual models of organisational responses to equal opportunities and managing diversity

A conceptual model of organisational responses to achieving equality, concentrating on perceived rationale and the differing contributions of equality of opportunity and managing diversity has been developed by LaFasto (1992). This is shown in Figure 22.1.

An alternative framework is proposed by Jackson *et al.* (1992) who, concentrating on culture, identify a series of stages and levels that organisations go through in becoming a multicultural organisation.

Level 1, stage 1: the exclusionary organisation

The exclusionary organisation maintains the power of dominant groups in the organisation, and excludes others.

Level 1, stage 2: the club

The club still excludes people but in a less explicit way. Some members of minority groups are allowed to join as long as they conform to predefined norms.

Level 2, stage 3: the compliance organisation

The compliance organisation recognises that there are other perspectives, but

Figure 22.1 Conceptual model of diversity

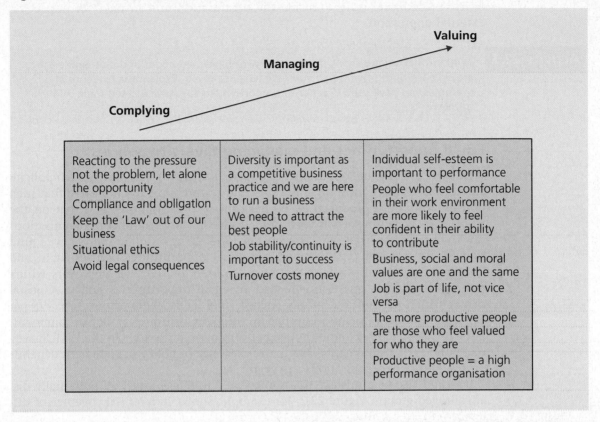

Reacting to the pressure not the problem, let alone the opportunity Compliance and obligation Keep the 'Law' out of our business Situational ethics Avoid legal consequences	Diversity is important as a competitive business practice and we are here to run a business We need to attract the best people Job stability/continuity is important to success Turnover costs money	Individual self-esteem is important to performance People who feel comfortable in their work environment are more likely to feel confident in their ability to contribute Business, social and moral values are one and the same Job is part of life, not vice versa The more productive people are those who feel valued for who they are Productive people = a high performance organisation

Complying → Managing → Valuing

Source: F. LaFasto (1992) 'Baxter Healthcare Organisation', in B.W. Jackson, F. LaFasto, H.G. Schultz and D. Kelly, 'Diversity', *Human Resource Management*, Vol. 31, Nos 1 and 2, Spring/Summer, p. 28. Reproduced with permission of John Wiley and Sons, Inc. Copyright © 1992 John Wiley and Sons, Inc.

does not want to do anything to 'rock the boat'. It may actively recruit minority groups at the bottom of the organisation and make some token appointments.

Level 2, stage 4: the affirmative action organisation

The affirmative action organisation is committed to eliminating discrimination and encourages employees to examine their attitudes and think differently. There is strong support for the development of new employees from minority groups.

Level 3, stage 5: the redefining organisation

The redefining organisation is not satisfied with being anti-racist and so examines all it does and its culture to see the impact of these on its diverse multicultural workforce. It develops and implements policies to distribute power among all groups.

Level 3, stage 6: the multicultural organisation

The multicultural organisation reflects the contribution and interests of all its diverse members in everything it does and espouses. All members are full participants of the organisation and there is recognition of a broader social responsibility – to educate others outside the organisation and to have an impact on external oppression.

Activity 22.1

Think of five organisations that you know or have read about and plot where they are on each of the two frameworks we have reviewed. Explain the evidence and examples you have used in order to support where you have located them in the frameworks.

Equal opportunities and managing diversity policies

While the use of equal opportunities policies has grown very slowly such policies are now a feature of most organisations. Our research in 1984 indicated that such policies were only produced by 60 per cent of organisations, and that on the whole they were not seen as very useful. Indeed, a large number of organisations saw their policy as irrelevant. However in 1994, using a similar sample, we found that 89 per cent of organisations had equal opportunities policies. Itzin and Phillipson (1993) also found that three-quarters of the 221 employers which responded to their questionnaire had an equal opportunities policy. A postal survey which was sent out in July–August 1999 (EOR 1999b) showed that 95 per cent of respondent organisations had an equal opportunities policy or statement, but Cully *et al.* (1999) found that 66 per cent of organisations in the WER Survey had policies or a statement. Clearly the existence of policy or statement depends on the nature of organisations surveyed.

It would also be a mistake to assume that all policies cover all potentially disadvantaged groups. Figure 22.2, for example, shows differential coverage of different minority groups in the 1999 EOR Survey.

It is interesting that EOR reported that organisations tended to have equal opportunities policies rather than managing diversity policies, and equal oppor-

Figure 22.2 Areas covered by equal opportunities policies

Area of equality	Percentage of sample covering this area of equality
Race	95
Gender	95
Disability	93
Religion	86
Sexuality	81
Age	76
HIV/Aids	64
Transsexuals	38
Marital status	13
Union activities	7
Political beliefs	6
Social and economic status	4
Caring responsibilities	4

Source: Adapted from EOR (1999b) 'Equal Opportunities Policies: An EOR survey of employers', *Equal Opportunities Review*, No. 87, September–October, pp. 14–23.

tunities and managing diversity appeared to be viewed as complementary means of achieving equality rather than different concepts.

However, despite the prevalence of policies there is always the concern that having a policy is more about projecting the right image than about reflecting how the organisation operates. For example Hoque and Noon (1999) found that having an equal opportunities statement made no difference to the treatment of speculative applications from individuals who were either white or from an ethnic minority group and that 'companies with ethnic minority statements were more likely to discriminate *against* the ethnic minority applicant'.

A process for managing diversity

Ross and Schneider (1992) advocate a strategic approach to managing diversity that is based on their conception of the difference between seeking equal opportunity and managing diversity. The difference, as they see it, is that diversity approaches are:

■ internally driven, not externally imposed;
■ focused on individuals rather than groups;
■ focused on the total culture of the organisation rather than just the systems used;
■ the responsibility of all in the organisation and not just the personnel function.

Their process involves the following steps:

1 Diagnosis of the current situation in terms of statistics, policy and culture, and looking at both issues and causes.
2 Setting aims which involve the business case for equal opportunities, identifying the critical role of commitment from the top of the organisation, and a vision of what the organisation would look like if it successfully managed diversity.
3 Spreading the ownership. This is a critical stage in which awareness needs to be raised, via a process of encouraging people to question their attitudes and preconceptions. Awareness needs to be raised in all employees at all levels, especially managers, and it needs to be clear that diversity is not something owned by the personnel function.
4 Policy development comes after awareness raising as it enables a contribution to be made from all in the organisation – new systems need to be changed via involvement and not through imposition on the unwilling.
5 Managing the transition needs to involve a range of training initiatives. Positive action programmes, specifically designed for minority groups, may be used to help them understand the culture of the organisation and acquire essential skills; policy implementation programmes, particularly focusing on selection, appraisal, development and coaching; further awareness training and training to identify cultural diversity and manage different cultures and across different cultures.
6 Managing the programme to sustain momentum. This involves a champion, not necessarily from the HR function, but someone who continues in his or her previous organisation role in addition. Also the continued involvement of senior managers is important, together with trade unions. Harnessing initiatives that come up through departments and organising support networks for

disadvantaged groups are key at this stage. Ross and Schneider also recommend measuring achievements in terms of business benefit – better relationships with customers, improvements in productivity and profitability, for example – which need to be communicated to all employees.

Ellis and Sonnenfield (1994) make the point that training for diversity needs to be far more than a one-day event. They recommend a series of workshops which allow time for individuals to think, check their assumptions and reassess between training sessions. Key issues that need tackling in arranging training are ensuring that the facilitator has the appropriate skills; carefully considering participant mix; deciding whether the training should be voluntary or mandatory; being prepared to cope with any backlash for previously advantaged groups who now feel threatened; and being prepared for the fact that the training may reinforce stereotypes. They argue that training has enormous potential benefits, but that there are risks involved.

WINDOW ON PRACTICE

Ethnic minorities in the police service

The current employment of ethnic minorities in the police force is not representative of their presence in the labour market. In England and Wales only 1.7 per cent of the police force are from ethnic minority groups, whereas ethnic minorities comprise 5.2 per cent of the economically active population. Percentages for Scotland are 0.2 per cent and 1 per cent respectively. In addition in England and Wales only 10 per cent of ethnic minorities are in the ranks above constable compared with 23 per cent for all other police staff.

In 1995 Her Majesty's Inspectorate of Constabulary (HMIC) stressed the business case for improving the current position:

All organisations need to exploit the talents and abilities of all their members. This cannot be done without a culture which welcomes, uses and manages diversity in the workplace … A workforce which reflects the society it serves provides an unrivalled source of accurate, unbiased management information and helps make policing the community more responsive and appropriate.

The EOR (1996) reports on steps being taken by some forces to overcome the barriers to recruitment and retention of ethnic minorities – which come within the areas of recruitment, promotion and culture.

Recruitment

Evidence suggested that the PIR (Police Initial Recruitment) test was found to be adversely affecting ethnic minority groups. In addition, it was found that ethnic minority groups were deterred from applying – for Asian groups it was viewed as a less suitable career than law or accountancy, and among Afro-Caribbean groups those who joined the police were seen as traitors.

To tackle these issues advertising campaigns were designed which went beyond equal opportunity statements to address specific barriers and attitudes. In addition, familiarisation courses were provided on the premise that ethnic minorities were less likely already to know someone who had joined the force. Strathclyde and other forces run pre-selection access courses which provide support and training for passing the PIR test. The Met. have Positive Action Teams which provide guidance for ethnic minority applicants in how to prepare for the selection procedure. Other forces support outreach work where there is police involvement with community relations officers, community leaders, and careers staff.

Promotion

The HMIC identified problems in the appraisal process in terms of poor training for appraisers, no routine auditing of performance appraisal and a lack of in-depth monitoring to check for bias. The lack of ethnic minorities in CID and specialist positions was noted. Although this may be partly explained by length of service, this was not a sufficient explanation. Some forces have now set up formal mentoring programmes, assertiveness courses and special support networks.

Culture

A prevalence of racial harassment was identified and many forces now have formal policies relating to harassment. In Leicester a confidential survey found that 26 per cent of ethnic minority staff had experienced harassment over the previous two years. In West Yorkshire on promotion to sergeant one of the skills tested is concerned with equal opportunities, on the premise that officers need to be able to confront and manage complaints of unacceptable behaviour. They say that this is 'sending a powerful and public message on the Force position'. Once appointed, sergeants undergo training with a significant input on equal opportunities, discrimination law, harassment and community and race relations.

Source: Based on EOR (1997) 'Ethnic minorities in the police service', *Equal Opportunities Review*, No. 73.

Activity 22.2

The Police Service example illustrates some aspects of a management of diversity approach (as well as some aspects of an equal opportunities approach).

Explain what steps you would recommend to extend the management of diversity approach that has begun.

WINDOW ON PRACTICE

BT – Championing women in a man's world

BT is often used as an exemplar of an organisation which has taken significant steps to encouraging women in a male-dominated engineering environment and the *Equal Opportunities Review* (1999a) reports on how BT has gone about this.

First, BT has top-level strategic support to increase the proportion of women at all levels in the organisation, and has also identified the need for line managers to be convinced of the economic value of such policies.

The initiatives introduced involve the appointment of a gender champion, assessing the HR director, partly on objectives relating to gender issues, and running a one-day workshop for all 5,000 managers to stress the business case and attempt to change attitudes.

In terms of access to employment BT has targeted universities with a higher proportion of women students, revised job titles and specifications and considered ways of developing eligibility criteria for jobs. BT has set improvement targets, and encouraged 'take your daughters to work' days.

In respect of existing employees BT has: produced a women's development portfolio and a women's management development programme, developed strategic skills for senior women managers, a women's network and website and raised the issues of life/work balance and childcare.

Source: Summarised from EOR (1999a) 'BT: Championing women in a man's world', *Equal Opportunities Review*, No. 84, March–April, pp. 14–20.

Activity 22.3

Prepare a strategy for managing diversity which would be appropriate for your organisation, or one with which you are familiar.

Summary propositions

22.1 The essence of much HR work is to discriminate between individuals. The essence of equality is to avoid unfair discrimination.

22.2 Unfair discrimination often results from people being treated on the basis of limited and prejudiced understanding of the groups to which they belong rather than on the basis of an assessment of them as individuals. People are not always aware when they are discriminating unfairly.

22.3 Organisations and their cultures, processes and structures are founded on the needs of the majority group and individuals from other groups are expected to adapt to this norm.

22.4 Equal opportunities approaches highlight the moral argument for equal treatment, whereas managing diversity highlights the business case.

22.5 Legislation can have only a limited effect in achieving equality, and does not change attitudes, beliefs and cultures.

22.6 Actual changes in practice relating to equalising opportunity are taking place very slowly, and only long-term organisational transformation is likely to support equality.

22.7 Equal opportunities approaches and the management of diversity are best viewed, not as alternatives, but as complementary approaches which need to be interrelated.

References

Bruyere, S. (2000) 'Managing Disability in the workplace', *Equal Opportunities Review*, No. 92, July–August.

Cockburn, C. (1989) 'Equal Opportunities: the long and short agenda', *Industrial Relations Journal*, Vol. 20, No. 3, pp. 213–25.

Cully, M., Woodland, S., O'Reilly, A. and Dix, G. (1999) *Britain at Work: As depicted by the 1998 Workplace Employee Relations Survey*. London: Routledge.

Department for Education and Employment (1999) *Evaluation of the Code of Practice on Age Diversity in Employment: interim survey for wave 2*. Sheffield: DfEE.

Department for Education and Employment (1995) *Labour Force Survey*.

Dickens, L. (1999) 'Beyond the business case: a three pronged approach to equality action', *Human Resource Management Journal*, Vol. 9, No. 1, pp. 9–19.

Dickens, L. and Colling, T. (1990) 'Why equality won't appear on the bargaining agenda', *Personnel Management*, April, pp. 48–53.

Donaldson, L. (1993) 'The recession: a barrier to equal opportunities?', *Equal Opportunities Review*, No. 50, July/August.

Ellis, C. and Sonnenfield, J.A. (1994) 'Diverse approaches to managing diversity', *Human Resource Management*, Spring, Vol. 33, No. 1, pp. 79–109.

Equal Opportunities Commission (1994) 'The Inequality Gap', *Equal Opportunities Review*, No. 41, pp. 20–6.

Equal Opportunities Review (1993) 'Age discrimination – no change', *Equal Opportunities Review*, No. 48, March/April, pp. 21–5.

Equal Opportunities Review (1994) 'Statistics: ethnic minorities in the labour market', *Equal Opportunities Review*, No. 56.

Equal Opportunities Review (1996) 'Ethnic minorities in the police service', *Equal Opportunities Review*, No. 68, July–August.

Equal Opportunities Review (1997) 'Ethnic minorities in the police service', *Equal Opportunities Review*, No. 73.

Equal Opportunities Review (1998) 'Tackling Age bias: code or law?', *Equal Opportunities Review*, No. 80, July–August.

Equal Opportunities Review (1999a) 'BT: Championing women in a man's world', *Equal Opportunities Review*, No. 84, March–April, pp. 14–20.

Equal Opportunities Review (1999b) 'Equal Opportunities Policies: An EOR survey of employers', *Equal Opportunities Review*, No. 87, September–October.

Equal Opportunities Review (2000) 'Businesses urged to shape up on race', *Equal Opportunities Review*, No. 90, March–April.

Ford, V. (1996) 'Partnership is the secret of success', *People Management*, 8 February, pp. 34–6.

Hakim, C. (1993) 'The myth of rising female employment', *Work Employment and Society*, Vol. 7, No. 1, March, pp. 121–33.

Hicks-Clarke, D. and Iles, P. (2000) 'Climate for diversity and its effects on career and organizational attitudes and perceptions', *Personnel Review*, Vol. 29, No. 3.

Hoque, K. and Noon, M. (1999) 'Racial discrimination in speculative applications: new optimism six years on?', *Human Resource Management Journal*, Vol. 9, No. 3, pp. 71–82.

Humphries, J. and Rubery, J. (1995) *Research Summary of the Economics of Equal Opportunity*. Manchester: EOC.

Institute of Personnel and Development (1997) *Managing Diversity: A Position paper*. London: IPD.

Itzin, C. and Phillipson, C. (1993) *Age Barriers at Work: Maximising the potential of mature and older people*. London: Metropolitan Authorities Recruitment Agency.

Jackson, B.W., LaFasto, F., Schultz, H.G. and Kelly, D. (1993) 'Diversity', *Human Resource Management*, Vol. 31, Nos 1 and 2, Spring/Summer, pp. 21–34.

Jewson, N. and Mason, D. (1986) 'The theory and practice of equal opportunities policies: liberal and radical approaches', *Sociological Review*, Vol. 34, No. 2, pp. 307–34.

Kandola, P. and Fullerton, J. (1994, 1998) *Managing the Mosaic*. London: IPD.

Kandola, R., Fullerton, J. and Mulroney, C. (1996) *1996 Pearn Kandola Survey of Diversity Practice Summary Report*. Oxford.

Kirton, G. and Greene, A. (2000) *The dynamics of managing diversity: a critical approach*. Oxford: Butterworth Heinemann.

LaFasto, F. (1992) 'Baxter Healthcare Organisation', in B.W. Jackson *et al.*, *Human Resource Management*, Vol. 31, Nos 1–2, Spring/Summer.

Liff, S. (1989) 'Assessing equal opportunities policies', *Personnel Review*, Vol. 18, No. 1, pp. 27–34.

Liff, S. (1996) 'Managing diversity: new opportunities for women?', *Warwick Papers in Industrial Relations* No. 57. Coventry: IRU, Warwick University.

Liff, S. (1997) 'Two routes to managing diversity: individual differences or social group characteristics?', *Employee Relations*, Vol. 19, No. 1, pp. 11–26.

Liff, S. (1999) 'Diversity and Equal Opportunities: room for a constructive compromise?', *Human Resource Management Journal*, Vol. 9, No. 1, pp. 65–75.

Liff, S. and Cameron, I. (1997) 'Changing equality cultures to move beyond "women's problems"', *Gender, Work and Organisation*, Vol. 4, No. 1, January, pp. 35–46.

Lorbiecki, A. and Jack, G. (2000) 'Critical turns in the evolution of diversity management', *British Journal of Management*, Vol. 11, pp. S17–S31.

McColgan, A. (1994) 'Pay equity – just wages for women'. London: Institute of Employment Rights.

MacLachlan, R., Grant, B. and Smith, P. (1996) 'Standing up to be counted', *People Management*, 11 January, p. 22.

Masreliez-Steen, G. (1989) *Male and Female Management*. Sweden: Kontura Group.

Miller, D. (1996) 'Equality management – towards a materialist approach', *Gender, Work and Organisation*, Vol. 3, No. 4, pp. 202–14.

New Earnings Survey (2000) in IDS (2000) 'Analysis', IDS Report 821, November, pp. 10–11.

Newman, J. and Williams, F. (1995) 'Diversity and change, gender, welfare and organisational relations', in C. Itzin and J. Newman, *Gender, Culture and Organisational Change*. London: Routledge.

Ouseley, H. (1996) quoted in S. Overell, 'Ouseley in assault on diversity', *People Management*, 2 May, pp. 7–8.

Ross, R. and Schneider, R. (1992) *From Equality to Diversity – a business case for equal opportunities*. London: Pitman.

Runnymede Trust (2000) *Moving on up? Racial Equality and the Corporate Agenda, A Study of the FTSE 100 companies*. London: Central Books.

Shapiro, G. and Austin, S. (1996) 'Equality drives total quality', *Occasional Paper*. Brighton: Brighton Business School.

Simmons, M. (1989) 'Making equal opportunities training effective', *Journal of European Industrial Training*, Vol. 13, No. 8, pp. 19–24.

Singer, M. (1993) *Diversity-based Hiring*. Aldershot: Avebury.

Skills and Enterprise Network (2000) *Labour Market and Skills Trends*. Sheffield: DfEE.

Thair, T. and Risden, A. (1999) 'Women in the labour market: results from the Spring 1998 Labour Force Survey', *Labour Market Trends*, March.

Thomas, R.R. (1990) 'From affirmative action to affirming diversity', *Harvard Business Review*, March–April.

Thomas, R.R. (1992) 'Managing diversity: a conceptual framework', in S. Jackson (ed.) *Diversity in the Workplace*. New York: Guildford Press.

Trades Union Congress (1995) *Arguments for a Minimum Wage*. London: TUC.

Trades Union Congress (2000) *Qualifying for Racism*. London: TUC.

Wilson, E. (2000) 'Inclusion, exclusion and ambiguity – the role of organizational culture', *Personnel Review*, Vol. 29, No 3.

Woodhams, C. and Danieli, A. (2000) 'Disability and diversity – a difference too far?' *Personnel Review*, Vol. 29, No. 3.

Woolnough, R. (2000) 'Racism reinforces the glass ceiling', *Guardian,* 4 November, p. 31.

Worsley, R. (1996) 'Only prejudices are old and tired', *People Management*, 1 January, pp. 18–23.

Young, I.M. (1990) *Justice and the Politics of Difference*. Princeton, NJ: Princeton University Press.

General discussion topics

1 Discuss Liff's (1997) question:

> Can people's achievements be explained by their individual talents or are they better explained as an outcome of their gender, ethnicity, class and age? Can anything meaningful be said about the collective experience of all women or are any generalisations undermined by other cross-cutting ideas. (p. 11)

2 Which is preferable – the UK approach or the US approach to equal opportunities? What are the implications of each for all members of the organisation?

Chapter 23 | Interactive skill: the appraisal interview

Appraising performance is not a precise measurement but a subjective judgement. It has a long history of being damned for its ineffectiveness at the same time as being anxiously sought by people wanting to know how they are doing. It is difficult to do, it is frequently done badly with quite serious results, but on the rare occasions when it is done well it can be invaluable for the business, and literally life transforming for the appraisee. It is probably the most demanding and skilful activity for any manager to undertake:

> W. Edwards Deming has contended that performance appraisal is the number one American management problem. He says it takes the average employee (manager or non-manager) six months to recover from it. I think Dr Deming is about right, though I'd add the setting of objectives and job descriptions to the list of personnel control devices that are downright dangerous – as currently constituted.
>
> (Peters 1989, p. 495)

A selection of comments in recent examination scripts underlines the point:

1 Our scheme has been abandoned because of a lot of paperwork to be completed by the manager and the time-consuming nature of the preparation by both appraiser and appraisee. Assessment dragged on from week to week without any tangible outcome, there was no follow-up and few people understood the process. The interview was spent with managers talking generalities and appraisees having nothing to say (from a large engineering company).

2 We have had approximately one new scheme per year over the last six years. These have ranged from a blank piece of paper to multi-form exercises, complete with tick boxes and a sentence of near death if they were not complete by a specified date (from an international motor manufacturer).

3 Our scheme is not objective and has become a meaningless ritual. It is not a system of annual appraisal; it is an annual handicap (from a public corporation).

With reactions like this, it makes the appraisal interview sound even more suspect than the selection interview, as we saw in Chapter 15. If it is so difficult to get right, why does it survive? Why persist with something that Tom Peters regards as downright dangerous?

One might just as well ask why marriage survives despite its extensive failure and the innumerable personal tragedies it produces. Why do teachers grade students' work? Why do we all seek advice? Why do audiences applaud? Why do wives and husbands seek the views of their spouses on the prospective purchase of a new suit/dress/shirt/hat? The reason is simple: we all seek approval and confirmation that we are doing the right thing, and most of us yearn to advise or direct what other people should do.

At work these basic human drives are classified into activities including objective setting, counselling, coaching or feedback on performance. They all have in common the feature of one person meeting face to face with another for a discussion focused on the performance of only one of them.

There are appraisal schemes in all areas of employment. Once installed, schemes are frequently modified or abandoned, and there is widespread management frustration about their operation. Despite the problems, the potential advantages of appraisal are so great that organisations continue to introduce them and appraisal can produce stunning results. Here is another extract from the same set of examination answers referred to above:

> I have had annual appraisal for three years. Each time it has been a searching discussion of my objectives and my results. Each interview has set me new challenges and opened up fresh opportunities. Appraisal has given me a sense of achievement and purpose that I had never previously experienced in my working life.
>
> (from an insurance company)

Contrasting approaches to appraisal

There are two contrasting motivations that drive the appraisal interview: the motivation of management control and the motivation of self-development. These produce appraisal systems that show a mixture of both motivations, with the control approach still being the more common, especially when there is a link with performance-related pay, but the alternative development emphasis is gaining in popularity. Describing them as polar opposites helps to illustrate the key elements.

The management control approach starts with an expression of opinion by someone 'up there', representing the view of controlling, responsible authority, saying:

> We must stimulate effective performance and develop potential, set targets to be achieved, reward above-average achievement and ensure that promotion is based on sound criteria.

Despite the specious appeal of this most reasonable aspiration, that type of initiative is almost always resisted by people acting collectively, either by representation through union machinery or through passive resistance and grudging participation. This is because people whose performance will be appraised construe the message in a way that is not usually intended by the controlling authorities, like this:

> They will put pressure on poor performers so that they improve or leave. They will also make sure that people do what they're told and we will all be vulnerable to individual managerial whim and prejudice, losing a bit more control over our individual destinies.

It is the most natural human reaction to be apprehensive about judgements that will be made about you by other people, however good their intentions.

This approach is likely to engender:

1 Conflictual behaviour and attitudes within the organisation, including resistance by managers to the amount of administrative work involved in the process.

2 Negotiated modifications to schemes. These are 'concessions' made to ease the apprehension of people who feel vulnerable. These frequently make the schemes ineffective.

3 Tight bureaucratic controls to ensure consistency and fairness of reported judgements.

4 Bland, safe statements in the appraisal process.

5 Little impact on actual performance, except on that of a minority of self-assured high achievers at one extreme and disenchanted idlers at the other.

6 Reduced openness, trust and initiative.

This approach works best when there are clear and specific targets for people to reach, within an organisational culture that emphasises competition. There are considerable problems, like who sets the standards and who makes the judgements. How are the judgements, by different appraisers of different appraisees, made consistent? Despite its drawbacks, this approach is still potentially useful as a system of keeping records and providing a framework for career development that is an improvement on references and panel interviews. It is most appropriate in bureaucratic organisations. The emphasis is on form filling.

The development approach starts with the question in the mind of the individual job holder:

I am not sure whether I am doing a good job or not. I would like to find ways of doing the job better, if I can, and I would like to clarify and improve my career prospects.

This question is addressed by job holders *to themselves*. Not: 'Am I doing what you want?', but, 'Where can I find someone to talk through with me my progress, my hopes, my fears? Who can help me come to terms with my limitations and understand my mistakes? Where can I find someone with the experience and wisdom to discuss my performance with me so that I can shape it, building on my strengths to improve the fit between what I can contribute and what the organisation needs from me?'

Those in positions of authority tend to put a slightly different construction on this approach, which is something like:

This leads to people doing what they want to do rather than what they should be doing. There is no co-ordination, no comparison and no satisfactory management control.

This approach to appraisal:

1 Develops co-operative behaviour between appraisers and appraisees and encourages people to exercise self-discipline, accepting autonomous responsibility.

2 Confronts issues, seeking to resolve problems.

3 Does not work well with bureaucratic control.

4 Produces searching analysis directly affecting performance.

5 Requires high trust, engenders loyalty and stimulates initiative.

This approach works best with people who are professionally self-assured, so that they can generate constructive criticism in discussion with a peer; or in protégé/mentor situations, where there is high mutual respect. The emphasis is on *interviewing*, rather than on form filling. Despite the benefits of this approach, there are two problems: the first is the lack of the *systematic* reporting that is needed for attempts at management control of, and information about, the process; the second is the problem of everyone finding a paragon in whom they can trust.

Frances Storr describes an approach to performance appraisal that seeks to take out almost all the formality; it includes the appraisees choosing their own appraisers and usually the feedback is face to face, with virtually no form filling:

> its purpose is stated clearly: to improve performance and enable people to learn and grow. We emphasise that appraisal is as much about celebrating people's achievements, as it is about helping them to identify areas in which they can improve. Within that framework it is up to individuals to decide how they will carry out their own 360 degree appraisal. In more than 90 per cent of cases, feedback is given face to face, with people talking to their appraisers as a group. Any written material . . . belongs to the appraisee, with the result that the appraisal has become a dialogue rather than a survey. (Storr 2000, p. 39)

Activity 23.1	To what extent can the benefits of both approaches be created in a single scheme? Who should conduct the appraisal interview?

> Appraisal . . . requires a strong communications effort and a supportive skill-based training programme for appraisers and appraisees . . . complex systems requiring managers to complete large volumes of paperwork soon fall into disrepute. Care must be taken that simple user-friendly and useful systems remain so. However, the appraisal process should not be reduced to the mere ticking of meaningless boxes. (Snape *et al.* 1994, p. 66)

Appraisal is valueless unless the general experience of it is satisfactory. Appraisees have to find some value in the appraisal process itself and see tangible outcomes in follow-up. Appraisers have to find the appraisal process not too arduous and have to see constructive responses from appraisees. When general experience of appraisal is satisfactory, it becomes an integral part of managing the organisation and modifies the management process.

Who does the appraisal?

Individuals are appraised by a variety of people, including their immediate superior, their superior's superior, a member of the HR department, themselves, their peers or their subordinates. Sometimes, assessment centres are used to carry out the appraisal. You may find it helpful to refer back to Chapter 18 to remind yourself in more detail about these options.

There are, however, many problems for those carrying out the appraisal. For example:

- **Prejudice** – the appraiser may actually be prejudiced against the appraisee, or be anxious not to be prejudiced; either could distort the appraiser's judgement.
- **Insufficient knowledge of the appraisee** – appraisers often carry out appraisals because of their position in the hierarchy rather than because they have a good understanding of what the appraisee is doing.
- **The 'halo effect'** – the general likeability (or the opposite) of an appraisee can influence the assessment of the work that the appraisee is doing.

■ **The problem of context** – the difficulty of distinguishing the work of appraisees from the context in which they work, especially when there is an element of comparison with other appraisees.

Activity 23.2
Think of jobs where it is difficult to disentangle the performance of the individual from the context of the work. How would you focus on the individual's performance in these situations?

Problems for both the appraiser and the appraisee include:

■ **The paperwork** – documentation soon gets very cumbersome in the attempts made by scheme designers to ensure consistent reporting.
■ **The formality** – although appraisers are likely to try to avoid stiff formality, both participants in the interview realise that the encounter is relatively formal, with much hanging on it.

WINDOW ON PRACTICE
In 1997 the Secretary of State for Education issued guidance to schools and local education authorities about capability procedures to deal with the problem of school teachers who did not perform satisfactorily. This type of formality for dealing with performance is almost unheard of outside schools and produced major problems. Teachers who were 'put on procedure' found that so humiliating that they rarely improved and usually spent long periods of absence from school suffering from stress. Throughout the education system there was a preference for informal arrangements to deal with this very difficult issue.

Among the other common problems, which often cause appraisal schemes to fail, are:

■ **Outcomes are ignored** – follow-up action for management to take, although agreed in the interview, fails to take place.
■ **Everyone is 'just above average'** – most appraisees are looking for reassurance that all is well, and the easiest way for appraisers to deal with this is by stating or inferring that the appraiser is doing at least as well as most others, and better than a good many. It is much harder to deal with the situation of presenting someone with the opinion that they are average – who wants to be average?
■ **Appraising the wrong features** – sometimes behaviours other than real work are evaluated, such as time-keeping, looking busy and being pleasant, because they are easier to see.

The appraisal interview

The different styles of appraisal interview were succinctly described forty years ago by the American psychologist Norman Maier (1958). His threefold classification remains the most widely adopted means of identifying the way to tackle the interview. The *problem-solving* style has been summarised as:

The appraiser starts the interview by encouraging the employee to identify and discuss problem areas and then consider solutions. The employee therefore plays an active part in analysing problems and suggesting solutions, and the evaluation of performance emerges from the discussion at the appraisal interview, instead of being imposed by the appraiser upon the employee.   (Anderson 1993, p. 102)

This is certainly the most effective style, consistent with the development approach to appraisal set out at the opening of this chapter, provided that both the appraiser and appraisee have the skill and ability to handle this mode. This chapter is based on this style, but it is not the only style. Maier's alternatives included, first, *tell and sell*, where the appraiser acts as judge, using the interview to tell the appraisee the result of the appraisal and how to improve. This 'ski instructor' approach can be appropriate when the appraisees have little experience and have not developed enough self-confidence to analyse their own performance. *Tell and listen*, the second alternative, still casts the appraiser in the role of judge, passing on the outcome of an appraisal that has already been completed and listening to reactions. Both of these approaches could sometimes change the assessment, as well as enabling the two people to have a reasonably frank exchange.

A number of recent articles suggest *a contingency approach* to the personal interaction of the appraisal interview. George suggests that the effectiveness of the appraisal depends on the style not conflicting with the culture of the organisation. He goes on to suggest that the degree of openness required is 'unlikely to materialise without an atmosphere of mutual trust and respect – something which is conspicuously lacking in many employing organizations' (George 1986, p. 32).

George also comments on the links between the appraisal system and other personnel and organisational systems:

> An investment in a system must involve statements about certain desired organizational characteristics and about the treatment of people in an organization. It is very mistaken, therefore, to regard appraisal as merely a technique or a discrete process with an easily definable boundary. (ibid., p. 33)

Appraisal therefore needs to reflect the wider values of the business if it is to be properly integrated and survive in an effective form.

Other aspects of the contingency approach to appraisal include the appraiser's style in relation to their normal management style and to the needs and personality of the appraisee. Appraisers should aim for consistency between their normal day-to-day management style and the style that they adopt in appraisal interviews. People have few really open relationships at work and in the appraisal situation we may be expecting interactions of a nature and quality which are not evident in most relationships. Pryor (1985) offers a reappraisal of Maier's three styles, particularly the usefulness of tell and sell and tell and listen. He suggests that they can be effectively adapted to the needs of appraisees with little experience who require less participation in the appraisal interview.

It is tempting to identify the problem-solving approach as 'the best', because it appears to be the most civilised and searching, but not all appraisal situations call for this style, not all appraisees are ready for it and not all appraisers normally behave in this way.

The appraisal interview sequence

Certain aspects of the appraisal interview are the same as those of the selection interview discussed in Chapter 15. There is the inescapable fact that the appraiser determines the framework of the encounter, there is a need to open in a way that develops mutual confidence as far as possible and there is the use of closed and open-ended questions, reflection and summarising. It is also a difficult meeting for the two parties to handle:

> The appraisal interview is a major problem for both appraisers and appraisees. The appraiser has to have a degree of confidence and personal authority that few managers have in their relationship with all those who they have to appraise. The most contentious aspect of many appraisal schemes is the lack of choice that appraisees have in deciding who the appraiser should be. Interview respondents regularly cite the interview as something that they dread. (Torrington 1994, p. 149)

For the appraisee there are concerns about career progress, job security, the ongoing working relationship with the appraiser, and the basic anxieties relating to self-esteem and dealing with criticism.

The fundamental difference between selection and appraisal that every appraiser has to remember is that the objective is to reach an understanding that will have some impact on the future performance of the appraisee: it is not simply to formulate a judgement by collecting information, as in selection. A medical metaphor may help. A surgeon carrying out hip replacements will select patients for surgery on the basis of enquiring about their symptoms and careful consideration of the evidence. The surgeon asks the questions, makes the decision and implements that decision. A physician examining a patient who is overweight and short of breath may rapidly make the decision that the patient needs to lose weight and take more exercise. It is however not the physician but the patient who has to implement that decision. The physician can help with diet sheets, regular check-ups and terrifying advice; the real challenge is how to get the patient to respond.

The easy part of appraisal is sorting out the facts. The tricky bit is actually bringing about a change in performance. The interview, like the discussion in the physician's consulting rooms, is crucial in bringing about a change of attitude, fresh understanding and commitment to action.

Preparation

The appraiser should brief the appraisee on the form of the interview, possibly asking for a self-appraisal form to be completed in advance. To some extent this is establishing rapport, with the same objectives, and makes the opening of the eventual interview easier.

Asking for the self-appraisal form to be completed will only be appropriate if the scheme requires this. As we have seen, self-appraisal gives the appraisee some initiative, ensures that the discussion will be about matters which the appraisee can handle and on 'real stuff'.

The appraiser has to review all the available evidence on the appraisee's performance, including reports, records or other material regarding the period under review. Most important will be the previous appraisal and its outcomes.

Most of the points made in Chapter 15 about preparing for the selection interview apply to appraisal as well, especially the setting. Several research studies (e.g. Anderson and Barnett 1987) have shown the extremely positive response of appraisees who felt that the appraiser had taken time and trouble to ensure that the setting and supportive nature of the discussion was considerate of the appraisee's needs.

receives extra pay and status for making decisions, so why should the manager expect them to do his or her job as well? (Wright and Taylor 1984, p. 110)

These, however, are problems to be recognised and overcome: they are not reasons for not bothering to try.

Appraiser views can now be used in adding to the list of areas for improvement. In many instances there will be no additions to make, but usually there are improvement needs that the appraisee cannot, or will not, see. If they are put at this point in the interview, there is the best chance that they will be understood, accepted and acted upon. It is not possible to guarantee success. Demoralised collapse or bitter resentment is always a possibility, but this is the time to try, as the appraisee has developed a basis of reassurance and has come to terms with some shortcomings that he or she had already recognised.

The appraiser has to judge whether any further issues can be raised and if so, how many. None of us can cope with confronting all our shortcomings, all at the same time, and the appraiser's underlying management responsibility is that the appraisee is not made less competent by the appraisal interview. There is also a fundamental moral responsibility not to use a position of organisational power to damage the self-esteem and adjustment of another human being.

Problem solving is the process of talking out the areas for improvement that have been identified, so that the appraisee can cope with them. Underlying causes are uncovered through further discussion. Gradually huge problems come into clearer and less forbidding perspective, perhaps through being analysed and broken up into different components. Possibilities for action, by both appraiser and appraisee, become clear.

These central stages of the interview – factual exchange, appraisee views, appraiser views and problem solving – need to move in that sequence. Some may be brief, but none should be omitted and the sequence should not alter.

The final stage of the encounter is to agree what is to be done: **objective setting**. Actions need to be agreed and nailed down, so that they actually take place. One of the biggest causes of appraisal failure is with action not being taken, so the objectives set must be not only mutually acceptable, but also deliverable. It is likely that some action will be needed from the appraiser as well as some from the appraisee.

Making appraisal work

There are many reports of businesses installing an appraisal system only to find that they have to change it or completely abandon it after only a short time. Others battle on with their systems, but recognise that they are ineffective or inadequate or disliked. What can be done to encourage the system to work as effectively as possible?

Effectiveness will be greater if all involved are clear about what the system is for. The personnel manager and senior managers need to work out what they want the appraisal system to achieve and how it fits in with the other HR activities that feed into it and are fed by it, such as career planning, training and human resource planning. Those who have to operate the system also have to appreciate its objectives, otherwise they are just filling in forms to satisfy the irksome personnel people, as we saw at the opening of this chapter. Finally, those whose performance is to be appraised will answer questions and contribute ideas with much greater constructive candour if they understand and believe in the purposes of the scheme.

It is vital that the system is visibly owned by senior and line management in the business, and that it is not something that is done for the personnel department. This may mean, for example, that appraisal forms are kept and used within the department and only selected types of data are fed through to the personnel function or other departments. Ideally, the form itself should be a working document used by appraiser and appraisee throughout the year.

The more 'open' the appraisal system is, that is, the more feedback appraisees are given about their appraisal ratings, the more likely appraisees are to accept rather than reject the process. Similarly, the greater the extent to which appraisees participate in the system, the greater the chance of gaining their commitment, subject to the reservation already made: not all appraisees are ready and willing to participate, and not all organisational cultures support participative processes.

The involvement of both appraisers and appraisees in the identification of appraisal criteria has already been noted. Stewart and Stewart (1977) suggest that these criteria must be:

1 Genuinely related to success or failure in the job.
2 Amenable to objective, rather than subjective judgement, and helpful if they:
    (a) Are easy for the appraiser to administer.
    (b) Appear fair and relevant to the appraisee.
    (c) Strike a fair balance between catering for the requirements of the present job while at the same time being applicable to the wider organisation.

Appraisers need training in how to appraise and how to conduct appraisal interviews. Appraisees will also need some training if they have any significant involvement in the process. An excellent performance appraisal system is of no use at all if managers do not know how to use the system to best effect. Sims (1988) quotes an ineffective system which was sophisticated and well designed, but which line managers did not have the skills to use.

The appraisal system needs to be administered so that it causes as few problems as possible for both parties. Form filling should be kept to a minimum, and the time allocated for this activity should be sufficient for it to be done properly, but not so much that the task is seen as unimportant and low priority.

Appraisal systems need to be supported by follow-up action. Work plans agreed by appraiser and appraisee need to be monitored to ensure that they actually take place, or that they are modified in accordance with changed circumstances or priorities. Training needs should be identified and plans made to meet those needs. Other development plans may involve the personnel department in arranging temporary transfers or moves to another department when a vacancy arises. In order to do this, it is vital that appraisal forms are not just filed and forgotten. Peter Goodge and Philip Watts are consultants working in the field of 360-degree appraisal and one of their suggestions demonstrates the importance of follow-up:

> We suggest that organizations should spend 20 per cent of the project's budget on the assessment and 80 per cent on the subsequent development support.
>
> (Goodge and Watts 2000, p. 51)

Summary propositions

23.1 Performance appraisal has a poor track record, but it has considerable potential, when done well.

23.2 Among the problems of appraisal are prejudice, insufficient knowledge by the appraiser of the appraisee, the halo effect, the problem of context, the paperwork, the ignoring of outcomes, appraising the wrong features and the tendency for everyone to be just above average.

23.3 Three approaches to the appraisal interview are problem solving, tell and sell and tell and listen.

23.4 Features of the interview itself are the opening for preliminary mutual assessment; factual review; appraisee views on performance; appraiser views, to add perspective; problem solving; and objective setting.

23.5 Appraisers must follow up on interviews, making sure that all agreed action (especially that by the management) takes place.

23.6 Training in appraisal is essential for appraisers and for appraisees.

References

Anderson, G.C. (1993) *Managing Performance Appraisal Systems*. Oxford: Blackwell.

Anderson, G.C. and Barnett, J.G. (1987) 'The characteristics of effective appraisal interviews', *Personnel Review*, Vol. 16, No. 4.

Dainow, S. (1988) 'Goal-oriented appraisal', *Training Officer*, January, pp. 6–8.

Fletcher, C. (1984) 'What's new in performance appraisal?', *Personnel Management*, February.

George, J. (1986) 'Appraisal in the public sector: dispensing with the big stick', *Personnel Management*, May.

Goodge, P. and Watts, P. (2000) 'How to Manage 360 degree feedback', *People Management*, February, pp. 50–2.

Maier, N.R.F. (1958) *The Appraisal Interview: Objectives, methods and skills*. New York: John Wiley.

Peters, T. (1989) *Thriving on Chaos*. London: Pan Books.

Pryor, R. (1985) 'A fresh approach to performance appraisal', *Personnel Management*, June.

Sims, R.R. (1988) 'Training supervisors in employee performance appraisals', *European Journal of Industrial Training*, Vol. 12, No. 8, pp. 26–31.

Snape, E., Redman, T. and Bamber, G. (1994) *Managing Managers*. Oxford: Blackwell.

Stewart, V. and Stewart, A. (1977) *Practical Performance Appraisal*. Aldershot: Gower.

Storr, F. (2000) 'This is not a Circular', *People Management*, May, pp. 38–40.

Torrington, D.P. (1994) 'Sweets to the sweet: performance-related pay in Britain', *International Journal of Employment Studies*, Vol. 1, No. 2, pp. 149–64.

Wright, P.L. and Taylor, D.S. (1984) *Improving Leadership Performance*. Hemel Hempstead: Prentice Hall International.

Part IV
Case study problem

Bakersfield (new) University is in a process of change in order to promote more effective service delivery to their customers within tight budget constraints. Teaching staff have increasingly taken on higher teaching hours as the staff to student ratio has increased from 1:18 to 1:26 over the past eight years. The decrease in staff numbers has been managed through the non-replacement of leavers and a limited level of early retirement. In addition to taking on increased teaching loads staff have been exhorted to engage themselves in research to a much greater extent and to complete PhDs. The staff have increasingly felt under pressure, but have on the whole been dedicated workers. Those staff who were most seriously disillusioned by the changes taking place were generally those opting for early retirement, although this process also meant that much expertise was suddenly lost to many departments.

The pressure of work seems set to increase and the goodwill and relatively high performance of staff are increasingly at risk. In the current circumstances departments have found it difficult to recognise the good work of staff by promotion, which had been the traditional approach. Many department heads have tried to deal with this by holding out the hope of future promotion and by recognition of a good job done. Some department heads were more effective in this than others.

The University as a whole has decided to put two major schemes into place in relation to staff performance: first, a staff appraisal scheme, and second, an individual performance-related pay scheme. Standard forms were produced for all departments to use and guidelines were produced relating to the purpose and frequency of appraisal. All departments conformed in terms of carrying out the appraisals, but there were great differences in how this was handled in different departments. Those heads who had experience of successful systems elsewhere, or who were enthusiastic about this change, carried out the appraisals in a more thorough and committed way, and did try to integrate them into the running of the department and link them to departmental goals. Other heads failed to do this, and some were positively against the system as they saw it as impinging on academic freedom, and in any case had never seen themselves as true managers. The reaction of staff was mixed, often depending on their past employment experiences and length of time employed by the University.

There were similarly disparate reactions to the individual performance pay scheme. Department heads were each allocated a small pot of money to distribute as they saw fit between their staff. There were only two months between the announcement of the availability of this money and the date for distribution. Some department heads announced its availability and others never mentioned it. Some made allocations based on performance appraisal results and others made a separate judgement – perhaps allocating money only to someone who was highly valued and who had threatened to leave, but who was not necessarily the best performer. Others shared the money, in different amounts, between the top three high performers and one other shared the money out equally between all staff in the department. Most heads of department allocated the money without any consultation, indeed the heads never got together to talk about the new system and how to handle it. A small number of heads quickly formed a senior staff panel to judge the allocation and one head devised a peer assessment panel.

Staff reactions were mixed. Some were pleased that at last there was potential monetary recognition for the extra effort they had put in. But those who only found out about the system after the money had been allocated to others were angry. Some of the staff who had received the money were so embarrassed about it that they kept it secret. Union representatives complained about the 'shady' process in many departments. Only three heads announced the criteria which had been used to allocate the money. There were complaints about the timescale – but this was improved by the immediate announcement in the University's newsletter of a similar pot of money being made available for the following year. Many objected on principle, though, to the idea of individual performance pay and felt that it undermined the teamwork that was necessary for the department to run effectively. A number argued that if there was to be such pay next year, it should relate directly to the performance appraisal results, and hence became more concerned that these were carried out more thoughtfully.

Staff morale was damaged by these events and the University, which is aware that it mishandled these issues, is anxious to improve matters as quickly as possible.

Required

1 What were the main problems with the approach adopted by the University authorities?

2 What options does the University have for next year? What are the advantages and disadvantages of each?

3 Which option would you recommend, and how would you implement it?

Part IV
Examination questions

Undergraduate introductory

1 'Equal opportunities legislation is an unnecessary interference for business.' Discuss.

2 Outline the major implications of the Disability Discrimination Act 1995. Why was the Act seen as necessary?

Undergraduate finals

3 What is the business case for diversity management? How strong and persuasive do you regard this case to be?

4 Present arguments for and against linking pay to an assessment of individual performance. Having done this, explain whether or not you would like to be paid in this way, and why.

Masters

5 Discuss the reasons for the relative failure of women to move into the ranks of senior management in both private and public sector organisations.

6 Why is performance appraisal a process that frequently disappoints both appraisers and appraisees? How can these problems be overcome?

Professional

7 Given the models of best practice and the problems that have emerged in training for equal opportunities in the areas of both race and gender, suggest how these might influence equal opportunities training relating to the Disability Discrimination Act 1995.

8 As an HR consultant how would you evaluate client/customer satisfaction with your organisation's performance and why is it important to do so?

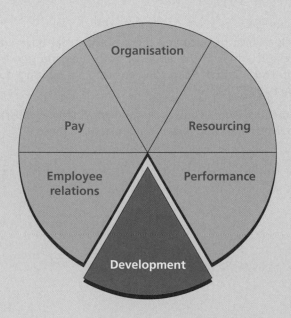

PART V

DEVELOPMENT

Having set up appropriate methods of organisation and systems to ensure performance, we now have to consider in more detail the ways in which people acquire skill and knowledge in order to develop their capacity to perform effectively.

One feature of development is the national framework within which vocational skills can be acquired. Here the individual employer relies on the provision of the education system and the arrangements of professional and other bodies, which specify the appropriate standards for vocational competence. This is then developed further within the business, especially in management development, where the skills and knowledge needed tend to be much more organisationally specific and the methods of development are geared to the ongoing processes of the business.

Individually we are all interested in our own careers. It is now unlikely that anyone will spend more than a few years with a single employer, especially at the start of their working life, so career development is something that we take on as our responsibility rather than the responsibility of our employer.

Central to all development is the teaching interaction, whether it be the instructor developing the capacity of someone else to acquire a practical skill, like driving a car or using a keyboard, or the mentor developing a protégé's self-confidence and effectiveness in social situations.

Chapter 24 Strategic aspects of development

First Monday of the month again – Board meeting. This was the opportunity I'd been waiting for – with some trepidation. My function had produced firm proposals on a new training and development strategy which I was to present to the Board. Development for all was the theme, with key competencies being identified at each level of the organisation and everyone being entitled to six days' off-job training per year, plus coaching on the job to meet individual development goals. A real step in the right direction at last. All I had to do was to get the Board's backing and we'd be off.

I began to present the scheme, complete with user-friendly overheads, information packs for employees and a manager guidance and support package. My colleagues listened intently, for about 5 minutes, then all hell broke loose.

'So what's going to happen to production when they're all off swanning around training – we're understaffed anyway?' – that was Gary, the Production Manager.

Brian from Marketing chipped in next: 'They'll be poached as soon as they're trained if word gets out about this – we'll be doing it for nothing'.

But worst of all was Karen, the MD: 'Why are you proposing this anyway? Granted we desperately need some skills training for those new machines and to encourage flexibility – but we didn't ask for all this. How will it improve business performance? What are we going to get out of all the money this is going to cost us?'

I had hoped more of Karen. She was usually very supportive when I came up with training proposals to solve business problems – well crises would be a better word – we did what I suggested and it usually worked.

This time my words fell on stony ground – no one was interested.

Where do we go from here??????

(Extract from the diary of Len Hodge, Human Resource Director)

Activity 24.1

Before you read on ...

- What went wrong in the Board meeting?
- Why do you think that the Directors reacted as they did?
- What could Len have done differently to improve his chances of success?
- Where does Len go from here?

Employee development has traditionally been seen as a cost rather than an investment in the UK, although this is certainly changing in some organisations. UK organisations give little support to training and development compared with our European partners (see, for example, Handy 1988; Constable and McCormick 1987). This lack of investment in training and development has been identified as a major factor in Britain's economic performance, and it has been argued that without such investment we will be trapped in a low wage, low skills economy (Rainbird 1994). Our national training framework is voluntarist, with the government's role limited to *encouraging* training rather than intervening, as in many other countries.

It is difficult to show a causal link between HR development and organisational performance, partly because such terms are difficult to define precisely, and partly because the payoff from development may not be seen in the short term. It is also difficult to tie down performance improvements to the development itself and to understand the nature of the link. For example, is performance better because of increased or different HR development, because the reward package has improved or because we have a clearer set of organisational and individual objectives? If there is a link with HR development initiatives, is it that employees have better skills, or that they are better motivated, or that they have been selected from a more able group of candidates attracted to the organisation as it offers a high level of development?

In spite of these difficulties it is important to identify the contribution of HR development to business success, and wider measures for assessing business success, beyond the standard financial indicators, make this more feasible, as, for example, suggested by Kaplan and Norton (1992) and discussed in Chapter 16. While the search for 'evidence' goes on, the current climate encourages high levels of attention to HR development, which is increasingly seen not only as a route to achieving business strategy, but also as a means of building core competence over the longer term to promote organisational growth and sustained competitive advantage. Global competition and a fast pace of change have emphasised the importance of the human capital in the organisation, and the speed and ways in which they learn. A Green Paper produced by the DfEE (1998) stated that 'investment in human capital will be the foundation of success in the 21st century'.

In addition, levels and sophistication of training and development have received considerable attention in the context of the 'new psychological contract' and the need to promote employability, which we discuss in more detail in Chapter 27. There is some evidence that employee demand for training and development is increasing and that unions are beginning to engage in bargaining for development. Opportunities for training and development may be a vital tool in recruitment and retention, and considered to be a reward when promotion or monetary rewards are less available.

For training and development to be effective in terms of business success there is a well-rehearsed argument that it should be linked up front with business strategy. McClelland's research (1994) is one of many studies that show that organisations generally do not consider development issues to be part of their competitive strategy formulation, although he found that those that do identified it to be of value in gaining as well as maintaining competitive advantage. Miller (1991), writing specifically of management development, points to a lack of fit between business strategy and development activity. Pettigrew and others (1988) did find, though, that development issues get a higher priority when they are linked to organisational needs and take a more strategic approach. Miller makes the point that although at the organisational level it is difficult to identify quantitatively the direct impact of strategic investment in development, this impact is well supported by anecdotal evidence and easily demonstrated at the macro-level.

It is in this context that we consider HR development strategy. In the first section of the chapter we consider the nature of the business strategy/HRD strategy link, and then look in more detail at specific aspects of strategic HRD, such as the external environment, integration with other aspects of HR strategy, training and development roles and evaluation. We conclude with a brief note on recent government initiatives and general trends in development. In the following chapter we look in more detail at government support for National Vocational Qualifications (NVQs) and the competence movement more generally.

Organisational strategy and HR development strategy

Those organisations that do consider HR development at a strategic level usually see it as a key to *implementing* business strategy in a reactive way. Luoma (2000) categorises this approach as a 'needs driven' approach, where the purpose of the HR development strategy is to identify and remedy skill deficiencies in relation to the organisational strategy. Luoma suggests that in many articles this is 'implicitly referred to as the only way of managing strategic HRD'. Miller, for example, has demonstrated how management development can be aligned with the strategic positioning of the firm, and this can be seen as coming within the

Table 24.1 Linking management development to strategic situations

	Environment condition			
	Stable	*Unstable growth*	*Unstable decline*	*Competitive*
Content	Environment scanning skills Understanding sources of stability (e.g. geographically isolated product market, state of technology) Defence strategies Industrial relations skills (but depends on source of stability)	Environment scanning skills Industry analysis skills Sales, marketing Financial control Creative thinking Team building Organisation structure skills Forecasting techniques	Stakeholder relations Executive retention skills Understanding competitor environment Negotiating skills Diversification skills (technology, human resources)	Competitive strategy development Competitor analysis Marketing/ cost control (dependent on competitive strategy) Industry analysis (dependent on competitive strategy)
Process	Slow pace but 'eventful' Modest emphasis on individual development Non-competitive but 'aggressive' Reactive	Fast-moving High pressure Intense Team-oriented Proactive	Medium pace Co-operative environment Reactive	High-pressure Competitive

Source: P. Miller (1991) 'A strategic look at management development', *Personnel Management*, August, p. 47. Reproduced with permission of the author.

broad remit of such approaches as a needs driven approach. He has produced a matrix demonstrating how development content and processes can reflect stable growth, unstable growth, unstable decline and competitive positions, as shown in Table 24.1. He offers the model as suggestive, only, of the 'possibilities in designing strategically-oriented management development programmes'.

Luoma, however, identifies a second approach to HR development strategy which is an 'opportunistic approach', where the impetus is external rather than internal. This would include applying leading ideas on development to the organisation in a more general way, rather than specifically in relation to meeting the current business objectives. Such ideas may be developed from benchmarking, case studies, networking and the academic and practitioner press. Such ideas could include content and method, for example the development of a corporate university, and the concept of developing non-employees who perhaps work for suppliers or who are contracted to the organisation. The abilities thus developed may indeed be relevant in achieving business objectives, but they may also be relevant in developing abilities and behaviours which may be the source of future competitiveness. Thus they may also be a means of achieving culture change and/or facilitating the strategy process itself by constructing it as a learning process. In this approach the learning potential of all employees will be emphasised, and the HR development strategy may meet reactive needs in implementation of business strategy, but may also be proactive in influencing the formation of future business strategy

The third approach to the strategy link suggested by Luoma is based on the concept, which we discussed in Chapter 3, of organisational capability as the key to sustained competitive advantage, the resource based view of the firm. This approach is proactive in that it focuses on the desired state of the organisation as defined in its future vision. Within this would come the interest in anticipatory learning, which has been attracting some interest, where future needs are predicated and development takes place in advance. The *Journal of Management Education and Development* (1994) devoted an entire issue to anticipatory learning, which included some ideas on how it might be identified and achieved.

Activity 24.2   How can future development needs, say five years out, be anticipated?

With a group of colleagues/students, brainstorm future needs for your own organisation, or the university/college which you attend.

Of paramount importance therefore is the ability to learn. Watkins (1987) suggests that development for strategic *capability*, rather than just targeting development on achieving business objectives, needs to reinforce an entrepreneurial and innovative culture in which learning is part of everyday work. He identifies the importance of acting successfully in novel and unpredictable circumstances and that employees acquire a 'habit of learning, the skills and learning and the desire to learn'. Within this same perspective Mayo (2000) suggests that intangible assets of the organisation are increasing in proportion to the value of tangible assets. He recognises that developing intellectual capital may be an 'act of faith', or one of budgetary allocation, and suggests that the most useful measures to track such investments are individual capability, individual motivation, the organisational climate and work-group effectiveness. While he recognises the value of competency frameworks in respect of individual development he does point out that these neglect such features as experience and the networks and range of personal contacts, both of which are key to the development of core organisational competencies which are key to developing uniqueness.

In a slightly different, but compatible approach McCracken and Wallace (2000) develop a redefinition of strategic HR development, based on an initial conception by Garavan (1991). They suggest nine characteristics of a strategic approach to HR development, which are that:

- HR development shapes the organisation's mission and goals, as well as having a role in strategy implementation.
- Top management are leaders rather than just supporters of HR development.
- Senior management, and not just HR development professionals, are involved in environmental scanning in relation to HR development.
- HR development strategies, policies and plans are developed, which relate to both the present and future direction of the organisation, and the top management team are involved in this.
- Line managers are not only committed and involved in HR development, but involved as strategic partners.
- There is strategic integration with other aspects of HRM.
- Trainers not only have an expanded role, including facilitation and acting as organisational change consultants, but also lead as well as facilitate change.
- HRD professionals have a role in influencing the organisational culture.
- There is an emphasis on future-oriented cost effectiveness and results, in terms of evaluation of HR development activity.

They suggest that each of these aspects needs to be interrelated in an open system. In the following sections we will address some of these characteristics in more detail.

Influence of the external labour market

The external availability of individuals with the skills and competencies required by the organisation will also have an impact on employee development strategy. If skilled individuals are plentiful, the organisation has the choice of whether, and to what extent it wishes, to develop staff internally. If skilled individuals are in short supply, then internal development invariably becomes a priority. Predicting demographic and social changes is critical in identifying the extent of internal development required and also who will be available to be developed. In-depth analysis may challenge traditionally held assumptions about who will be developed, how and to what extent. For example, the predicted shortage of younger age groups in the labour market, coupled with a shortage of specific skills, may result in a strategy to develop older rather than younger recruits. This poses potential problems about the need to develop older workers some of whom may learn more slowly. What is the best form of development programme for employees with a very varied base of skills and experiences? Another critical issue is that of redeployment of potentially redundant staff and their development to provide shortage skills.

Prediction of skills availability is critical, as for some jobs the training required will take years rather than months. Realising in January that the skills required in August by the organisation will not be available in the labour market is too late if the development needed takes three years!

The external labour market clearly has a big impact on employee development strategy, so it is important that there is effective integration between HR development strategy, other aspects of human resource strategy and overall organisational strategy.

Integration with other human resource strategy

Where there is a choice between recruiting required skills or developing them internally, given a strategic approach, the decision will reflect on the positioning of the organisation and its strategy. In Chapter 9 we looked at this balance in some depth and you may find it helpful to re-read this. A further issue is that of ensuring a consistency between the skills criteria used for recruitment and development.

From a slightly different perspective, the impact of the organisation's development strategy on recruitment and retention, either explicit or implicit, is often underestimated. There is increasing evidence to show that employees and potential employees are more interested in development opportunities, especially structured ones, than in improvements in financial rewards. Development activity can drive motivation and commitment, and can be used in a strategic way to contribute towards these. For these ends, publishing and marketing the strategy is key, as well as ensuring that the rhetoric is backed up by action. There is also the tricky question of access to and eligibility for development. If it is offered only very selectively, it can have the reverse of the intended impact.

However, not all employees see the need for, or the value of, development and this means that reward systems need to be supportive of the development strategy. If we want employees to learn new skills and become multiskilled, it is skills development we need to reward rather than the job that is currently done. If we wish employees to gain vocational qualifications, we need to reflect this in our recruitment criteria and reward systems. Harrison (1993) notes that these links are not very strong in most organisations.

Other forms of reward, for example promotions and career moves, also need to reflect the development strategy; for example, in providing appropriate, matrix, career pathways if the strategy is to encourage a multifunctional, creative perspective in the development of future general management. Not only do the pathways have to be available, they also have to be used, and this means encouraging current managers to use them for their staff. In Chapter 27 we explore such career issues more fully.

Finally, an organisation needs to reinforce the skills and competencies it wishes to develop by appraising *those* skills and competencies rather than something else. Developmentally based appraisal systems can clearly be of particular value here. Mabey and Iles (1993) note that a strategic approach to development differs from a tactical one in that a consistent approach to assessment and development is identified with a common skills language and skills criteria attached to overall business objectives. They also note the importance of a decreasing emphasis on subjective assessment. To this end many organisations have introduced a series of development centres, similar to the assessment centres discussed in Chapter 12, but with a clear outcome of individual development plans for each participant related to their current levels of competence and potential career moves, and key competencies required by the business.

Training and development roles

Salaman and Mabey (1995) identify a range of stakeholders in strategic training and development, each of which will have different interests in, influence over and ownership of training and development activities and outcomes. They identify senior managers as the *sponsors* of training and development, who will be influenced by professional, personal and political agendas; and business planners as the *clients* who are concerned about customers, competitors and shareholders. Third, they identify *line managers* who are responsible for performance, coaching and resources; and fourth, *participants* who are influenced by their career aspirations and other non-work parts of their lives. HRM staff are identified as *facilitators* who are concerned with best practice, budget credibility and other HR strategy. Lastly, training specialists are identified as *providers*, who are influenced by external networks, professional expertise and educational perspectives. The agendas of each of these groups will overlap on some issues and conflict on others. We have already noted how McCracken and Wallace (2000) have redefined the roles of top managers, line managers and HR professionals so that they are all more proactively involved in HRD strategy.

Most organisational examples suggest that the formation of training and development strategy is not something that should be 'owned' by the HR/HRD function. The strategy needs to be owned and worked on by the whole organisation, with the HR/HRD function acting in the roles of specialist/expert and co-ordinator. The function may also play a key role in translating that strategy into action steps. The actions themselves may be carried out by line management, the HR/HRD function or outside consultants.

Involvement from line management in the delivery of the training and development strategy can have a range of advantages. Top management have a key role in introducing and promoting strategic developments to staff, for example, creating an organisation-wide competency identification programme; setting up a system of development centres or introducing a development-based organisational performance management system. Only if management carry out this role can employees see and believe that there is a commitment from the top. At other levels line managers can be trained as trainers, assessors and advisers in delivering the strategy. This is a mechanism not only for getting them involved, but also for tailoring the strategy to meet the real and different needs of different functions and departments.

Consultants may be used at any stage. They may add to the strategy development process, but there is always the worry that their contribution comes down to an offering of their ready-packaged solution, with a bit of tailoring here and there, rather than something which really meets the needs of the organisation. It is useful to have an outside perspective, but there is an art in defining the role of that outside contribution.

In delivery, consultants may make a valuable contribution where a large number of courses have to be run over a short period. The disadvantages are that they can never really understand all the organisational issues, and that they may be seen as someone from outside imposing a new process on the organisation.

WINDOW ON PRACTICE

One large organisation had a well-established training function and on an annual basis they sat down to plan the year ahead. They would plan how many of what types of course would be needed, depending on the demand in the previous year and the availability of appropriate staff. New courses would be introduced where a need had been identified and were piloted. Course evaluation data (collected mainly from participants, but sometimes from their managers) were used to inform course demand and course structure and content.

Individuals were booked on training courses following discussion with their manager regarding their individual needs. There were often problems resulting from long waiting lists and individuals being nominated for courses for which they were not eligible (defined by the nature of their job) – it appeared that individuals sometimes nominated themselves and the manager rubber-stamped this.

Some years later, after efforts on the part of general management and training and development management to employ a more strategic approach to the business, the picture was very different. Performance management had been introduced as the cornerstone of people management, resulting from a multifunctional, high-level working party. A course was devised and delivered in chunks of one and two days and this was delivered to *all* staff, with slightly differing versions for managers and non-managers. The course was an integrating mechanism for all people management activities and most importantly it promoted a cohesive *style and philosophy* of people management that the organisation felt was critical in the achievement of its business objectives. Not only was senior general management involved in the initial stages of the course, but key line managers were involved in delivering the subsequent modules.

WINDOW ON PRACTICE

Holden and Livian (1992) compared some strategic aspects of training across 10 European countries.*

Training as a recruitment strategy

All 10 countries identified training as being used in recruitment strategy. In eight (not including Germany and Sweden) training for new recruits was seen as the most popular method (from a list of 11) of attracting recruits.

Knowledge of investment in training

Although all organisations had increased expenditure on training over the previous year, many were unclear about the actual money spent as a proportion of wages. However this varied by country. The three highest – Sweden (44 per cent of organisations did not know), Denmark (42 per cent of organisations did not know) and the UK (38 per cent of organisations did not know) – compare markedly with the lowest, France, where only 2 per cent of organisations did not know. This no doubt reflects the French taxation system, where a tax is levied if the organisation does *not* spend 1.2 per cent of the paybill on training.

Actual investment in training

In only Sweden and France do more than a quarter of the organisations surveyed spend above 4 per cent of the paybill on training. With the exception of France, the majority of organisations in each of the other countries spent less than 2 per cent of their paybill on training.

Time spent on training

Only some 10 per cent of organisations provided over 10 days' training per year – the exception to this being Spain, where 29 per cent of organisations provided this level of training. In all countries the amount of time for managerial training was greater than for other groups of employees.

*The countries surveyed were Switzerland, Denmark, Germany, Spain, Finland, Italy, Norway, Netherlands, Sweden and the UK.

Source: Summarised from Holden, L. and Livian, Y. (1992) 'Does strategic training policy exist? Some evidence from ten European countries', *Personnel Review*, Vol. 21, No. 1, pp. 12–23.

Approaches to development and national initiatives

The approaches to and methods of development chosen need to be the most effective in achieving the skills and competencies required by the business. They also need to be appropriate to the culture of the organisation, and to promote organisational traditions or encourage innovation.

Another question is the organisation's response to national initiatives such as National Vocational Qualifications, the Investors in People standard, National Training targets, the push for lifelong learning and the national training infrastructure. The work-based nature of NVQs means that organisations adopting and encouraging them are landed with a heavy time commitment, particularly in the assessment process. A further issue is the extent to which the employer decides to tailor the standards specifically to meet their own needs. Similarly, a commitment to Investors in People requires significant time and effort, particularly in relation to the processes involved in development. The initial targets set for the number of employers seeking and achieving the Investors in People recognised status are proving to have been very ambitious. The benefits from gaining recognition of IiP status have been debated. Some studies have found an increase in commitment to HR development, a belief in the value of the process and perceived performance gains (see, for example, Alberga *et al.* 1997); other studies have found significant benefits, although organisations themselves found it difficult to identify these (Down and Smith 1998). Some studies show that organisations struggle with the bureaucracy of the approach, and that the significance of informal development is neglected (see, for example, Ram 2000). Ram also found considerable evidence that the standard is sought after for its 'stamp of approval' rather than because of a genuine commitment to improving training and development. Down and Smith also argue convincingly that it is those organisations that have most to gain from pursuing the standard that are least likely to attempt to do this.

Employers also need to consider the role of the new Learning and Skills Councils (LSCs) and how they can work most effectively with them to enhance development and performance in the organisation.

Summary propositions

24.1 The HR/HRD function does not own HR development strategy – it must be owned by the organisation as a whole.

24.2 HR development strategy needs to focus on the organisation strategy and objectives and involves identifying the skills and competencies required to achieve this, now and in the future. HR development strategy may also be opportunistic and proactive and influence the development of organisational strategy.

24.3 HR development strategy will also be influenced by the external labour market, government initiatives and competitor activity.

24.4 It is important that HR development strategy is reinforced by, and reinforces, other HR strategy.

24.5 The methods of HR development chosen need to be aligned not only with the competencies and skills to be developed, but also with the strategic position of the organisation, its culture, the individuals involved and the context in terms of national training initiatives and infrastructure.

References

Alberga, T., Tyson, S. and Parsons, D. (1997) 'An evaluation of the Investors in People Standard', *Human Resource Management Journal*, Vol. 7, No. 2, pp. 47–60.

Constable, R. and McCormick, R.J. (1987) *The Making of British Managers*. London: BIM.

Department for Education and Employment (1998) *The LEARNING Age: A Renaissance for a New Britain*, Green Paper, Command 3790. London: HMSO.

Down, S. and Smith, D. (1998) 'It pays to be nice to people – Investors in People: the search for measurable benefits', *Personnel Review*, Vol. 27, No. 2.

Garavan, T. (1991) 'Strategic Human Resource Development', *Journal of European Industrial Training*, Vol. 11, No. 9, pp. 17–30.

Handy, C. (1988) *Making Managers*. London: Pitman.

Harrison, R. (1993) *Human Resource Management: Issues and Strategies*. Wokingham: Addison Wesley.

Holden, L. and Livian, Y. (1992) 'Does strategic training policy exist? Some evidence from ten European countries', *Personnel Review*, Vol. 21, No. 1, pp. 12–23.

Journal of Management Education and Development (1994) 'Anticipatory learning: learning for the twenty-first century', Vol. 12, No. 6.

Kaplan, R. and Norton, D. (1992) 'The balanced scorecard – measures that drive performance', *Harvard Business Review*, January–February, pp. 71–9.

Luoma, M. (2000) 'Investigating the Link between strategy and HRD', *Personnel Review*, Vol. 29, No. 6.

Mabey, C. and Iles, P. (1993) 'Development practices: succession planning and new manager development', *Human Resource Management Journal*, Vol. 3, No. 4.

McClelland, S. (1994) 'Gaining competitive advantage through strategic management development', *Journal of Management Development*, Vol. 13, No. 5, pp. 4–13.

McCracken, M. and Wallace, M. (2000) 'Towards a Redefinition of Strategic HRD', *Journal of European Industrial Training*, Vol. 24, No. 5, pp. 281–90.

Mayo, A. (2000) 'The role of development in the growth of intellectual capital', *Personnel Review*, Vol. 29, No. 4.

Miller, P. (1991) 'A strategic look at management development', *Personnel Management*, August.

Pettigrew, A.M., Sparrow, P. and Hendry, C. (1988) 'The forces that trigger training', *Personnel Management*, Vol. 20, No. 12, pp. 28–32.

Rainbird, H. (1994) 'Continuing training', in K. Sisson (ed.), *Personnel Management in Britain*. Oxford: Blackwell.

Ram, M. (2000) 'Investors in People in small firms: Case study evidence from the businesses services sector', *Personnel Review*, Vol. 29, No. 1.

Salaman, G. and Mabey, C. (1995) *Strategic Human Resource Management*. Oxford: Blackwell Business.

Walton, J. (1999) *Strategic Human Resource Development*. Harlow: Financial Times Prentice Hall.

Watkins, J. (1987) 'Management development policy in a fast-changing environment: the case of a public sector service organisation', *Management Education and Development*, Vol. 18, Pt 3, pp. 181–93.

General discussion topics

1 Both the UK as a whole and organisations themselves would benefit if the government adopted an interventionist approach to training.

   ■ Do you agree or disagree? Why?
   ■ How might this intervention be shaped?

2 What opportunities are there for development strategy and reward strategy to be mutually supportive?

   Think of examples (real or potential) where reward strategies undermine development strategies.

Chapter 25 Competencies, competence and NVQs

The words competence, competency and competencies pervade much of the HRM literature, and it is argued that they provide a sound basis for the integration of HRM activities. The terms however are often used confusingly, so we will start with some definitions. The word 'competence' (plural 'competences') relates to the ability to carry out a specific task, and it is this interpretation of competence that forms the foundation for National Vocational Qualifications (NVQs), which could be described as job standards. The concept is therefore output, or performance based. In contrast the word 'competency' and its plural 'competencies' refer to behaviour (see, for example, Whiddett and Hollyforde 1999, p. 5) rather than task achievement, and there is general agreement that this concept is based on the work of Boyatzis (1982). There is a third definition, with which we are not concerned in this chapter, and that is the core competence of the organisation, which relates to the foundation for competitive advantage. In this chapter we will review the context for the concentration on competence and the development of NVQs, and then outline their key characteristics and perceived advantages and disadvantages. We will then turn to the concept of behavioural competencies and review the foundations, advantages and problems with this concept.

Competence and NVQs

The context of the competence movement

There has always been a tension in education and training between what the trainee knows and what the trainee can do after the training is complete. Knowledge has an ancient history of being highly desirable and jealously guarded: look at the trouble the serpent got Eve into in the Garden of Eden. Our literature and our folklore are full of the value of knowledge, including the best-known aphorism in this area, that expressed by Francis Bacon four hundred years ago, that knowledge itself is power. This connection to power and influence is why access to knowledge is often surrounded by elaborate ritual requirements to ensure that possession of the knowledge remains valuable and rare.

In every country of the world education has been developed, with all its mystique and influence, to communicate knowledge and to develop understanding. In developing countries it is usually the first priority of economic growth. For all people the search for better understanding is a human quality that is self-perpetuating once the appetite has first been stimulated.

Many people love studying, but in some places it seems to have become a public nuisance. In a shopping mall on Orchard Road in Singapore a café proprietor concerned about the popularity of the establishment with students has a large notice: 'NO STUDYING IN THE CAFE.'

The search for knowledge also develops a prestige for certain types of knowledge and for the institutions that trade in that knowledge. In Britain and France the areas with the greatest prestige have been those that are closest to the arts and pondering the human condition: English, history, classical civilisation and language, philosophy and theology, followed by those allied to elite professions, like medicine and the law. Science took longer to achieve a similar prestige and it is still physics and chemistry that are valued ahead of engineering. Knowledge rather than practical skills carries status, and the educational institutions with the highest prestige are those universities with the strongest representation in these areas.

This preference for knowledge has carried through into the labour market. We still pay more to people who manipulate words than to those who manipulate materials. Reading the news on television pays much more than making the world's most advanced aircraft or electronic equipment. Writing computer programs for arcade games pays much more than making the equipment on which the games run. It has become very difficult to recruit able students to study physics at university, and it is a bitter frustration for their teachers that many of them will move, on graduation, to merchant banking or accountancy.

Elsewhere it is different. The inevitable comparison is with Germany and Japan, countries where the practical skills of engineering, for instance, carry much greater prestige. This comparison has increasingly led policy makers and those in education to seek ways to shift the emphasis in education away from esoteric knowledge towards practical, vocational skills. This has proved remarkably difficult, as education is a large vested interest in any advanced society and change is resisted, however inevitable it may be. In the last half-century there have been the moves to set up technical schools in the late 1940s, which failed almost completely. We have had technological universities, many of which became universities much like any other. We had degrees in technology that were designated as BSc*, to show that they were not real degrees at all. We had the industrial training boards in the 1960s, rapidly followed by polytechnics in the 1970s, but the training boards were abolished and the polytechnics developed degrees in social sciences more rapidly than in vocational science and engineering.

By the early 1980s government policy achieved an unprecedented degree of centralised control on schooling through the national curriculum and on higher education through controlling student numbers and having differential fee regimes. Central to this control has been a heightened emphasis on practical vocational skills: what the student is able to do that is vocationally useful when the training is complete. The end result should be that the student is competent to do something that is useful. Furthermore, the education and training agenda has been placed under greater employer influence than previously. It is difficult to see that this has produced the desired results.

Activity 25.1
Think of your own schooling. Single out three things you learned at school that have subsequently been useful to you in your working life. Then single out the three topics or subjects which you found most interesting to study. What changes would you make if you could have your time over again?

Characteristics of NVQs

The vehicle for this attempted revolution has been an array of National Vocational Qualifications (NVQs), which have brought together a wide and unstructured range of previous vocational qualifications. Now vocational qualifications either are completed directly by the NVQ competence route itself, or, if they are of a different nature, will be identified as equivalent to a specific NVQ level. NVQs have been developed for all occupational areas, and within each occupation there are five levels of NVQ with level one relating to basic and routine work and level five relating to the most complex tasks. There are standards for the management occupation at levels three, four and five.

The basic idea of training for competence is that it should be criterion related, directed at developing the ability of trainees to perform specific tasks directly related to the job they are in or for which they are preparing, expressed in terms of performance outcomes and specific indicators. It is a reaction against the confetti-scattering approach to training as being a good thing in its own right, concerned with the general education of people dealing with general matters. The design of the standards themselves is somewhat complex. Each standard is first divided into job roles. For example in the updated (1997) level three management standards seven job roles are identified, as shown in Table 25.1. This is a development on the four job roles which were in the original standard. The key roles are then subdivided into units of competence, which are then subdivided into elements of competence with attached performance criteria and range statements.

In the United Kingdom, competence standards have been developed in line with other aspects of change in education, like experiential learning, problem-based learning, the national curriculum and GCSEs, as an attempt to develop the ability of learners to do rather than to know. This introduces greater flexibility into the learning process, so that career aspirants are not restrained by the elitist exclusiveness of either educational institutions or professional associations. The standards are designed so that the vast majority of work can be done 'on the job' with maybe small inputs from educational providers. Where this route is not

Table 25.1 Level three standards

Key roles

22	To manage activities
23	To manage resources
24	To manage people
25	To manage information
26	To manage energy
27	To manage quality
28	To manage projects

possible the standards can be completed as part of a 'course'. Wherever they are done the individual's completed portfolio of work has to be assessed by a qualified and accredited assessor.

The emphasis on practical, demonstrated competence is partly due to a long-standing disappointment about British industrial performance, easily attributable to poor management (Constable and McCormick 1987). There is therefore a political momentum behind the competency movement over and above considerations of education and training. It has been heavily promoted by the Training and Enterprise Directorate of the Department for Education and Employment.

The principles of competencies leading to national vocational qualifications are:

1 **Open access**. There should be no artificial barriers to training, such as that it is available only to people who are members of a professional body, such as the Chartered Institute of Personnel and Development or the Law Society, or those in a particular age group. There are no previous qualifications required in order to embark on the NVQ process.

2 There is a focus on what people can **do**, rather than on the process of learning. Masters students in a university typically cannot graduate in less than 12 months. With competence-based qualifications, you graduate when you can demonstrate competence, however long or short a period it takes you to achieve the standard.

3 **National** vocational qualifications, which are the same wherever the training takes place, so that the control is in the hands of the awarding body rather than the training body, and there is only one strand of qualification for each vocational area: no multiplication of rival qualifications. The overall control is with the National Council for Vocational Qualifications (NCVQ).

4 The feature of performance **standards** as the basis of assessment; not essays or written-up case studies, but practical demonstrations in working situations, or replicas, of an ability to do the job at a specified standard. Although training schemes are littered with euphoria about excellence, the competence basis has only one standard. The only degree of differentiation between trainees is the length of time taken to complete the qualification.

5 **Flexibility and modularisation**. People must be able to transfer their learning more or less at will between 'providers', so that they are not tied to a single institution or by needless regulations about attendance. Candidates can stop and start their work towards the standard as it suits their personal or work needs, and they can begin on any element of the standard and complete the elements in any order. This means that standards can be worked on in line with business demands.

6 **Accreditation of prior experience and learning**. You can accredit prior learning, no matter how you acquired it. If you have been able to acquire a competence by straightforward experience or practice at home, and if you can reach the performance standard, you can receive the credit for it. If prior experience enables you to demonstrate competence, you can receive credit for that as well.

7 The approach to training is the establishment of a **learning contract** between the provider and the trainee, whereby the initiative lies with the

trainee to specify the assistance and facilities that are needed and the provider agrees to provide them. The idea of this is that the learner is active in committing to the learning process.

8 Flexibility in assessment is partly achieved by the **portfolio** principle, as you accumulate evidence of your competence from your regular, day-to-day working and submit it for assessment as appropriate.

9 **Continuous development**. Initial qualification is not enough. Updating and competence extension will be needed and failure to do this will lead to loss of qualification.

10 The standards to be achieved are determined by designated **lead bodies**, which are large committees of practitioners, or professional bodies, so that vocational standards are decided by those in charge of the workplace instead of by those in charge of the classroom.

11 **Assessment**. Written examinations are not regarded as being always the most appropriate means of assessing competence. Assessment of whether or not the learner has attained the appropriate standard must be by a **qualified assessor**, who becomes qualified by demonstrating competence according to two units of the scheme produced by the Training and Development Lead Body. Assessment may be partly by portfolio (see 8 above), but has to be **work based**. Originally it was to be in the workplace, but that proved impracticable to implement in every case.

12 **General National Vocational Qualifications** are school or college based and take the place of BTec and similar qualifications.

The general intention is that NVQs should run alongside traditional academic qualifications at undergraduate level.

The standards have strong support from some quarters as we have already stated, but there have been fewer reports of the benefits of pursuing the standards. Winterton and Winterton (1999) report that organisations adopting the management standards have been able to identify gaps in competence, identify competence development targets, develop a coherent structure for training and development and identify clearer criteria for human resource planning and career progression. In our own studies, again in relation to the management standards, it was found that participants developed self-confidence in their managerial role, became better organised and were motivated to focus on improvement (Hall and Holman 1996). Most critically, we found that following the standards was a rite of passage for those who were new to the managerial world (Holman and Hall 1996).

Problematic aspects of NVQs

NVQs have had a rough ride since the concept was first introduced, coming under some heavy criticism and not being extensively taken up. The most common reservations about NVQs are:

1 **Assessment**. The emphasis has been shifted away from learning towards assessment. The assessment process is itself somewhat laborious. Research by the Institute of Manpower Studies (1994) found that the most common problem about introducing NVQs was finding the time to organise the assessments. The study found that 5 per cent of employers were using NVQs and half of them reported this difficulty. In our own studies (Hall and

Holman 1996) we found that candidates were heavily engaged in a paper chase to gather evidence of their competence, and this seemed to take over from the importance of the learning process and what was being learned.

2 **Bureaucracy.** NVQs have developed an entire vocabulary to bring the concept into action, and this causes difficulties (see, for example, Priddley and Williams 2000). One of the key terms is 'range indicators' and at a meeting of 50 HR practitioners, no one could produce a definition that the rest of the group could accept. Also the assessment process specifies a number of different standards of performance that have to be demonstrated and assessed. Each of these has to be described succinctly and the performance measured.

3 **The generality of the standards.** Those employers who take up NVQs are likely to modify them for their own use. In a three-year research project at UMIST over twenty employer schemes for the management standards were examined, and each one was tailored to the needs of the particular business. This is for two reasons: (a) the national standards are seen as being too general, and (b) employers are concerned to train for their own needs rather than for national needs of skilled human resources. This begins to undermine the concept of a *national* qualification.

4 **The quality of the standards.** It is very difficult to ensure a satisfactory quality of assessment, where so much depends on a large number of individual assessors. The initial emphatic opposition to written examination has lessened, especially as NVQs are contemplated for some of the well-established professions, such as medicine and the law.

5 In relation to the management standards in particular there is a criticism that the standards are **reductionist**. In other words, by trying to spell out the detail of what management entails, the complexity of management gets lost as it is difficult to specify this in the structure and language of the standards.

6 A related criticism is that the **functional** approach (see, for example, Stewart and Hamblin 1992) used to identifying what management is (that is, through specifying management activities) is a narrow and partial approach.

7 The early management standards were also criticised for being an **incomplete** representation of management, and yet in our research we found that those following the pre-1997 standard had not recognised any omissions, for example ethics and politics.

8 **Lack of attention to learning and cognitive processes** has also been identified (for example by Holman and Thorpe 1993), as the emphasis is on doing rather than thinking and understanding.

9 It has also been argued that following the standards rubber stamps the level of competence already achieved, rather than stimulating further development. Currie and Derby (1995) for example, criticise the lack of development in the scheme.

10 **The training agenda.** Within a large vested interest like British higher education, there is obviously some resistance to the idea that educators are not competent to set the training agenda.

> There seems to be a drift towards a training agenda in management education, such that students are technically equipped to take up a task but intellectually incapable of addressing the ideas that have shaped the creation of that task. (Berry 1990)

One quite damning piece of research has been produced by Peter Robinson of the London School of Economics. He demonstrates that the actual take-up of

NVQs is very low and has not been associated with an increase in the training available to individuals.

> Between 1991 and 1995 the only net growth in the number of all vocational qual-ifications awarded was at level 1 and especially level 2. There was no growth at all in the number of awards at level 3, and a slight fall in the number of awards at levels 4 and 5. (Robinson 1996, p. 4)

In 1998/9 there was a 3 per cent drop in the number of all vocational qualifica-tions awarded: 442 thousand were awarded in this period compared with 458 thousand in 1997/8 (DfEE 2000). Awards of traditional vocational qualifications continue to outstrip NVQs by a wide margin, especially at higher levels. There were 501 thousand vocational awards made outside the national framework in 1998/9 which was a 12 per cent increase on those awarded the previous year (DfEE 2000). So currently traditional forms of vocational award are growing while national awards are falling, although GNVQs are increasing.

NVQs are heavily concentrated in clerical and secretarial, personal and protec-tive services, and craft and related occupation. The only other area where they have made an impact is in management and administration (DfEE 2000).

The initial failure of NVQs to take off stimulated a high-level review of the whole process; for example the management standards were redesigned in 1997 to make them more flexible, easy to understand and up to date (Whittaker 1998).

Activity 25.2	Interview at least three people who have followed the NVQ standards. They may be employees of your organisation, but this is not essential, so friends and family can be included. Ask your interviewees:

1 What were the most positive aspects of following the standards, and why?

2 What were the problematic aspects of following the standards, and why?

3 How might these negative aspects be overcome?

Behavioural competencies

The key piece of research on competencies is by Richard Boyatzis, who carried out a large-scale intensive study of 2,000 managers, holding 41 different jobs in 12 organisations. He defines a competency as: 'an underlying characteristic of a person which results in effective and/or superior performance in a job' (Boyatzis 1982, p. 21).

Competency may be a trait, which is a characteristic or quality that a person has, like efficacy, which is the trait of believing you are in control of your future and fate. When you encounter a problem, you then take an initiative to resolve the problem, rather than wait for someone else to do it.

Competency may be a motive, which is a drive or thought related to a par-ticular goal, like achievement, which is a need to improve and compete against a standard of excellence.

Competency may be a skill, which is the ability to demonstrate a sequence of behaviour that is functionally related to attaining a performance goal. Being able to tune and diagnose faults in a car engine is a skill, because it requires the ability to identify a sequence of actions, which will accomplish a specific objective. It

Gwen is a management trainer in a large organisation running a number of in-house management courses. She has just moved into this position from her role as section leader in the research department; the move was seen as a career development activity in order to strengthen her managerial skills.

Gwen is working with her manager to learn from her experiences. Here is an extract from her learning diary based on the learning cycle:

Activity – I've had a go at running three sessions on my own now, doing the input and handling the questions.

Reflection – I find the input much easier than handling questions. When I'm asked a question and answer it I have the feeling that they're not convinced by my reply and I feel awkward that we seem to finish the session hanging in mid-air. I would like to be able to encourage more open discussion.

Theory building – If I give an answer to a question it closes off debate by the fact that I have 'pronounced' what is 'right'. If I want them to discuss I have to avoid giving my views at first.

Planning practice – When I am asked a question rather than answering it I will say to the group: 'What does anyone think about that?' or 'What do you think?' (to the individual who asked) or 'What are the possibilities here?' I will keep encouraging them to respond to each other and reinforce where necessary, or help them change tack by asking another question.

achieve this which identified individuals' learning styles as 'activist', 'reflector', 'theorist' and 'pragmatist', and explain that:

- **Activists** learn best from 'having a go', and trying something out without necessarily preparing. They would be enthusiastic about role-play exercises and keen to take risks in the real environment.
- **Reflectors** are much better at listening and observing. They are effective at reflecting on their own and others' experiences and good at analysing what happened and why.
- **Theorists'** strengths are in building a concept or a theory on the basis of their analysis. They are good at integrating different pieces of information, and building models of the way things operate. They may choose to start their learning by reading around a topic.

Figure 26.1 The learning cycle

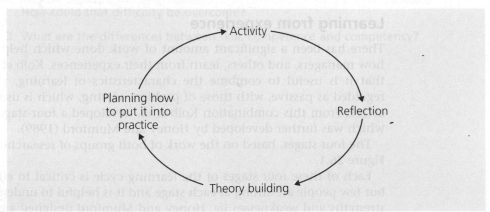

- **Pragmatists** are keen to *use* whatever they learn and will always work out how they can apply it in a real situation. They will plan how to put it into practice. They will value information/ideas they are given only if they can see how to relate them to practical tasks they need to do.

Understanding how individuals learn from experience underpins all learning, but is particularly relevant in encouraging self-development activities. Understanding our strengths and weaknesses enables us to choose learning activities which suit our style, and gives us the opportunity to decide to strengthen a particularly weak learning stage of our learning cycle. While Honey and Mumford adopt this dual approach, Kolb firmly maintains that learners *must* become deeply competent at all stages of the cycle. There has been considerable attention to the issue of matching and mismatching styles with development activities: see, for example, Hayes and Allinson (1996), who also consider the matching and mismatching of trainer learning style with learner learning style.

Activity 26.1	1 If you have not already done so obtain the Honey and Mumford questionnaire and work out your learning style(s).
	2 Select your weakest style and try and identify two different learning activities which fit with this style, but that you would normally avoid.
	3 Seek opportunities for trying out these learning activities. If you practise these activities on a regular basis this should help you strengthen the style you are working on.
	4 Log your experiences and in particular what you have learned about these 'new' learning activities.

Planned and emergent learning

From a different, but compatible, perspective, David Megginson characterises learners by the extent to which they plan the direction of their learning and implement this (planned learning), and the extent to which they are able to learn from opportunistic learning experiences (emergent learning). Megginson (1994) suggests that strengths and weaknesses in these two areas will influence the way individuals react to self-development. These two characteristics are not mutually exclusive, and Megginson combines them to identify four learning types, as shown in Table 26.1.

Warriors are those who are strong at planning what they want to learn and how, but are less strong at learning from experiences they had not anticipated. They have a clear focus on what they want to learn and pursue this persistently.

Table 26.1 Planned and emergent learning

Learner type	Planned learning score	Emergent learning score
Sage	High	High
Warrior	High	Low
Adventurer	Low	High
Sleeper	Low	Low

Source: Adapted from Megginson, D. (1994) 'Planned and emergent learning: A framework and a method', *Executive Development*, Vol. 7, No. 6, pp. 29–32.

On the other hand Adventurers respond to and learn from opportunities that come along unexpectedly, they are curious and flexible. However they tend not to plan and create opportunities for themselves. Sages are strong on both characteristics, and Sleepers display little of either characteristic at present. To be most effective in self-development activities learners need to make maximum use of both planned and emergent learning. For a further explanation of this model also see Megginson and Whitaker (1996).

Activity 26.2	Consider your development over the past year: do you feel that your strengths are in planning your learning or in learning opportunistically?
	Choose your weaker approach, and identify how you could strengthen this.

Learning curves

The idea of the learning curve has been promulgated for some time, and was developed in relation to technical skills development. The general idea was that we tend to learn a new task more rapidly at first, so that the learning curve is steep, and then gradually plateau after we have had significant experience. A slightly different shape of learning is more relevant to personal skills development: the curve is less likely to be smooth, or it may not even be curved. Ideally our learning would be incremental, improving bit by bit all the time; in reality, however, learning is usually characterised by a mix of improvements and setbacks. Although, with persistence, our skills gradually increase, in the short term we may experience dips. These dips are demotivating but they are a necessary part of learning. Developing personal skills usually requires us to try out a new way of doing things. This is risky because, although the skills we are developing may be quite personal to us, we usually have to experiment with new ways of

Figure 26.2 The reality of learning progress

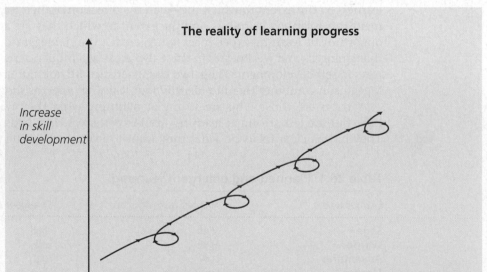

doing things in public. Understanding that sometimes things get worse before they get better helps to carry us through the dips. Figure 26.2 shows the reality of learning progress.

Identifying learning and training needs

While the 'systematic training cycle', as for example described by Harrison (1997, p. 424), which was developed to help organisations move away from ad hoc non-evaluated training, has been less prominent of late, it still has value. We describe an adaptation of such a model to make it more applicable to today's environment. The model is set within an external environment and within an organisation strategy and an HR development strategy. Even if some of these elements are not made explicit, they will exist implicitly. Note that the boundary lines are dotted, not continuous. This indicates that the boundaries are permeable and overlapping. The internal part of the model reflects a systematic approach to learning and to training. Learning needs may be identified by the individual, by the organisation or in partnership, and this applies to each of the following steps

Figure 26.3 A systematic model of learning and training

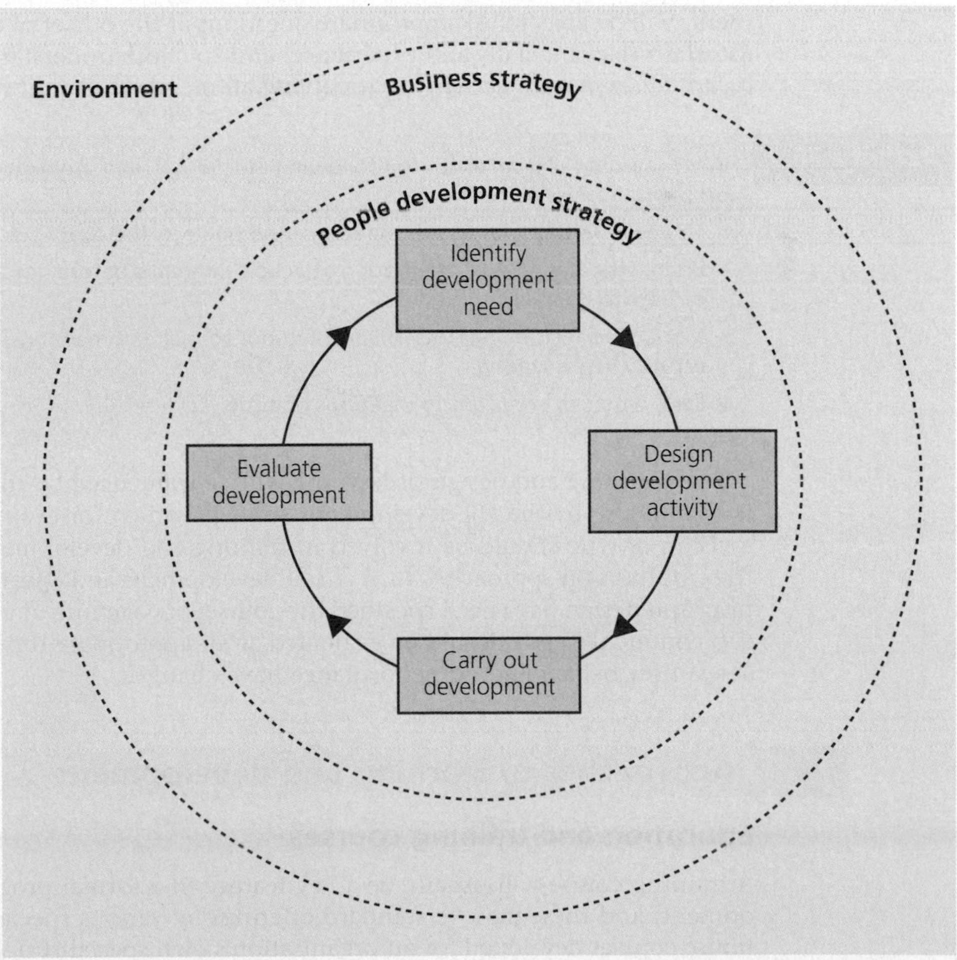

in the circle. This dual involvement is probably the biggest change from traditional models where the steps were owned by the organisation, usually the trainers, and the individual was considered to be the subject of the exercise rather than a participant in it, or the owner of it. The model that we offer does not exclude this approach where appropriate, but is intended to be viewed in a more flexible way. The model is shown in Figure 26.3.

There are a variety of approaches to analysing needs, the two most traditional being a problem-centred approach or matching the individual's competency profile with that for the job they are filling. The problem-centred approach focuses on any performance problems or difficulties, and explores whether these are due to a lack of skills, and if so which. The profile comparison approach takes a much broader view and is perhaps most useful when an individual, or group of individuals, are new to a job. This latter approach is also useful because strategic priorities change and new skills are required of employees, as the nature of their job changes, even though they are still officially in the same role with the same job title. When a gap has been identified, by whatever method, the development required needs to be phrased in terms of a learning objective, before the next stage of the cycle, planning and designing the development, can be undertaken. For example, when a gap or need has been identified around team leadership, appropriate learning objectives may be that learners, by the end of the development, will be able 'to ask appropriate questions at the outset of a team activity to ascertain relevant skills and experience, and to check understanding of the task' or 'to review a team activity by involving all members in that review'.

Activity 26.3	Write learning objectives for the following individuals who are experiencing problems in their performance:

1 Tina, who always dominates meetings, and neglects the contribution of others.

2 Brian, who has never carried out a selection interview before, and is very unsure of how to go about this.

3 Mark, who feels he has lots of contributions to make at meetings, but never actually says anything.

4 Sara, who can never get to meetings on time.

The planning and design of learning will be influenced by the learning objectives and also by the HR development strategy, which for example may contain a vision of who should be involved in training and development activities, and the emphasis on approaches such as self-development and e-learning. Once planning and design have been specified the course, or coaching or e-learning activity can commence, and should be evaluated at an appropriate time in the future to assess how behaviour and performance have changed.

Approaches to learning and development

Education and training courses

A training course will usually be a key feature in a formal programme of development, and these may be standard offerings by various specialist bodies or in-house courses developed for an organisation's own specialist needs. Increasingly, these options are being combined so that there is the possibility of an externally provided course tailored to suit an organisation's particular needs.

First are the pre-experience courses: full-time education leading to academic or vocational qualifications as a preliminary to a career. Second are the post-experience courses undertaken during a career. These may be part- or full-time education usually leading to a diploma or master's degree with a management or business label, and/or qualification for a professional body. An alternative approach to qualification is the NVQ route which we discussed in the previous chapter. Neither pre-experience nor post-experience courses of the type described here will feature strongly the skills element mentioned above, although greater attention is being paid to the skills element of university and further education courses.

The third category can be generally described as consultancy courses. Varying from a half-day to several weeks in length, they are run by consultants or professional bodies for all comers. They have the advantage that they bring together people from varying occupational backgrounds and are not, therefore, as introspective as in-house courses and are popular for topical issues. They are, however, often relatively expensive and superficial, despite their value as sources of industrial folklore, by which we mean the swapping of experiences among course members.

The most valuable courses of this type are those that concentrate on specific areas or knowledge, like developing time management, interviewing or disciplinary skills, or being introduced to a new national initiative. This short-course approach is probably the only way for individuals to come to terms with some new development, such as a change in legislation, because they need not only to find an interpretation of the development, they need also to share views and reactions with fellow employees to ensure that their own feelings are not idiosyncratic or perverse.

A fourth category is in-house courses, which are often similar in nature to the consultancy courses. Such in-house courses are sometimes run with the benefit of some external expertise, but not always. In-house courses can be particularly useful if the training needs to relate to specific organisational procedures and structures, or if it is geared to encouraging employees to work more effectively together in the organisational environment. The drawbacks of in-house courses are that they suffer from a lack of breadth of content, and there is no possibility of learning from people in other organisations.

Lastly, and on the fringe of education and training courses, are outdoor-type (sometimes known as outward-bound) courses. Outdoor courses attempt to develop skills involved in working with and through others, and aim to increase self-awareness and self-confidence through a variety of experiences, including outdoor physical challenges. Courses like these continue to be increasingly used, and their differential value is assumed to hinge on their separation from the political, organisational environment. A natural, challenging and different environment is assumed to encourage individuals to forsake political strategising, act as their raw selves and be more open to new ideas. Burleston and Grint (1996), based on ethnographic research into outdoor programmes, found that while most participants did gain from the experience, the idea of providing a de-politicised environment is a naïve hope rather than a reality. Ibbetson and Newell (1999) did find, however, that non-competitive outdoor programmes were more effective in meeting teambuilding objectives than competitive programmes.

While courses are no longer viewed as the key means of developing staff, they still have an important role to play. In Chapter 28 we therefore explore teaching and instructional skills.

Learning on the job

Coaching

Coaching is an informal approach to individual development based on a close relationship between the individual and one other person, usually their immediate manager, who is experienced in the task. The manager as coach helps trainees to develop by giving them the opportunity to perform an increasing range of tasks, and by helping them to learn from their experiences. They work to improve the trainee's performance by asking searching questions, actively listening, discussion, exhortation, encouragement, understanding, counselling and providing information and honest feedback. The coach is usually in a position to create development opportunities for the trainee when this is appropriate. For example a line manager can delegate attendance at a meeting, or allow a trainee to deputise, where this is appropriate to the individual's development needs. Alternatively they can create the opportunity for a trainee to join a working party or can arrange a brief secondment to another department. Coaches can share 'inside' information with the individual they are coaching to help them understand the political context in which they are working. For example, they are able to explain who will have most influence on a decision that will be made, or future plans for restructuring within a department.

Skilled coaches can adapt their style to suit the individual that they are coaching, from highly directive at one end of the scale to non-directive at the other. MacLennan (1995) suggests that the most appropriate way to determine the style required is to ask the individual which style will help them the most. The needed style may change over time, as the trainee gains more confidence and experience. Useful texts on coaching include MacLennan who provides considerable detail on the nature of achievement, skills required for coaching, coaching issues, barriers to coaching and how to overcome them. Also, Mumford (1994) has written an excellent guide to the ways that managers can help other managers to learn.

Mentoring

Mentoring is seen as offering a wide range of advantages for the development of the protégé, coaching as described above being just one of the possible benefits of the relationship. The mentor would occasionally be the individual's immediate manager, but usually it is a more senior manager in the same or a different function. Kram (1983) identifies two broad functions of mentoring, the first of which is the career function, including those aspects of the relationship that primarily enhance career advancement, such as exposure and visibility and sponsorship. The second is the psychosocial function, which includes those aspects of the relationship that primarily enhance a sense of competence, clarity of identity and effectiveness in the managerial role. Arnold (1997) found that the most common advantages of mentoring were perceived as role-modelling and counselling. There is evidence that mentoring does benefit both parties (see, for example, Johnson *et al.* 1999), and Broadbridge (1999) suggests that mentors can gain through recognition from peers, increased job satisfaction, rejuvenation, admiration and self-satisfaction. The drawbacks to mentoring that were revealed in Broadbridge's research include the risk of over-reliance, the danger of picking up bad habits, the fact that the protégé may be alienated from other sources of expertise and the sense of loss experienced when a mentor leaves. In addition, the difficulty of dealing with conflicting views in such an unequal relationship was identified. Perceived benefits, however, considerably outweighed any drawbacks. Megginson (2000) identifies the issue of dysfunctional mentoring, and the danger of assuming that mentoring is unquestionably good.

Managers are also seen as responsible for developing talent, and while a mentor/protégé relationship might not naturally occur, mentorship may be encouraged or formalised. For example, there are systems where all new graduates are attached to a mentor as soon as they join the organisation. The difficulties of establishing a formal programme include the potential mismatch of individuals, unreal expectations on both sides and the time and effort involved.

Gibb and Megginson (1993) surveyed a number of formal mentoring schemes and explain that such UK schemes offer a slightly different perspective from the US approach. They argue from the literature and from their research that the mentoring relationship is multifaceted, and that in the UK in particular there is greater emphasis than in the USA on learning support, often based around the restructuring of our qualification system. In these situations the protégés were more likely to have specific learning goals. An example might be mentoring in support of achieving NVQ competencies or other competency-based qualifications. In the formal schemes surveyed, just under half the protégés were working on a learning contract. Conway (1998) provides useful advice on planning and implementing a mentoring scheme.

Peer relationships

Although mentor–protégé relationships have been shown to be related to high

---

WINDOW ON PRACTICE

Tony Stott and Jenny Sweeney (1999) report on a structured mentoring scheme with a difference at Shell. While Shell run a very flexible mentoring scheme appropriate for many different types of employee and purposes, they recognise the importance of the design of the scheme and good administration. They suggest that there are five critical elements in a good scheme:

- **A database**: although the scheme is based on natural selection, that is, a mutual decision between a potential mentor and a new recruit, the database appears to be critical, in order to track the flow of mentees and the availability of mentors. Copies of mentor biographies are available for new recruits to read.
- **Mentor support**: Mentors are trained in their role and in recognising the limits of their abilities. There is also a support mechanism for mentors, and mentors meet to share their experiences.
- **Training**: Both mentors and mentees are trained, and this forms a key part of the induction programme for new recruits, with information on reasons for using mentoring, roles and expectations.
- **Resource materials**: these include websites for mentors. Guidance booklets for mentees are also produced.
- **Evaluation**: Shell found that a non-bureaucratic scheme, which gives ownership to the participants, was appreciated.

Source: Summarised from T. Stott and J. Sweeney (1999) 'More than a match', *People Management*, June, pp. 45–8.

levels of career success, not all developing individuals have access to such a relationship, and even formal schemes are often reserved for specific groups such as new graduate entrants. Supportive peer relationships at work are potentially more available to the individual and offer a number of benefits for the development of both parties. The benefits that are available depend on the nature of the peer relationship, and Kram and Isabella (1985) have identified three groups of peer relationships, which are differentiated by their primary development functions. These can be expressed on a continuum from 'information peer', based primarily on information sharing, through 'collegial peer', based on career strategising, giving job-related feedback and friendship, to 'special peer', based on emotional support, personal feedback, friendship and confirmation. Most of us benefit from one or a number of peer relationships at work but often we do not readily appreciate their contribution towards our development. Peer relationships most often develop on an informal basis and provide mutual support. Some organisations, however, formally appoint an existing employee to provide such support to a new member of staff through their first 12–18 months in the organisation. These relationships may, of course, continue beyond the initial period. The name for the appointed employee will vary from organisation to organisation, and sometimes the word 'coach' or 'mentor' is used – which can be confusing! Cromer (1989) discusses the advantages of peer relationships organised on a formal basis and references the skills and qualities sought in peer providers, which include accessibility, empathy, organisational experience and proven task skills.

Activity 26.4	Consider each significant peer relationship that you have at work. Where does each fit on the continuum of relationships described above, and what contributions does it make towards your development? If you are in full-time education consider the contribution that each of your relationships (whether at university, home or work) has to your development.

Action learning

Reg Revans was one of the first professors in the UK to specialise in management. Despairing of how management was being taught, Revans resigned his chair in Manchester and moved to Belgium to start his first action learning project based on his conviction that managers do not need education, but the ability to solve problems (Revans 1974). His method has been basically to organise exchanges, so that a manager experienced in one organisation is planted in another to solve a particular set of problems that is proving baffling. He or she brings a difference of experience and a freshness of approach, and is not dependent on new, temporary, organisational peers for career growth. They work on the problem for a period of months, having many sessions of discussion and debate with a group of other individuals similarly planted in unfamiliar organisations with a knotty problem to solve. The learning stems from the immediate problem that is presented, and from all the others that emerge, one by one, in the steps towards a solution. This presents a need that the student has to satisfy and all the learning is in terms of what they discover they need to know, rather than what someone else feels is necessary. It is an idea of startling simplicity, and has been adapted by both formal educational providers, often in masters courses, and by organisations.

Self-development

Natural learning is learning that takes place on the job and results from an individual's everyday experience of the tasks that they undertake. Natural learning is even more difficult to investigate than coaching, mentoring or peer relationships, and yet the way that we learn from everyday experiences, and our level of awareness of this, is very important for our development To some extent self-development may be seen as a conscious effort to gain the most from natural learning in a job, and to use the learning cycle as a framework. Self-development can be focused in specific skills development, but often extends to attitude development and personal growth: for example Ireland's North Western Health Board is using an approach to action learning to promote a culture of continuous development (O'Hara *et al.* 2001).

Activity 26.4

The video 'Groundhog Day' can be viewed as a journey of self-development. Watch the video and answer the following questions:

■ How did Phil's attitudes change and how was this reflected in his behaviour?

■ What do you think Phil learned?

■ How did he learn it?

■ Why is personal development so difficult?

The emphasis in self-development is that each individual is responsible for, and can plan, their own development, although they may need to seek help when working on some issues. Self-development involves individuals in analysing their strengths, weaknesses and the way that they learn, primarily by means of questionnaires and feedback from others. This analysis may initially begin on a self-development course, or with the help of a facilitator, but would then be continued by the individual back on the job. From this analysis individuals, perhaps with some help at first, plan their development goals and the way that they will achieve them, primarily through development opportunities within the job. When individuals consciously work on self-development they use the learning cycle in a more conscious way than in natural learning. They are also in a better position to seek appropriate opportunities and help, in their learning, from their manager.

Many of the activities included in self-development are based on observation, collecting further feedback about the way they operate, experimenting with different approaches and in particular reviewing what has happened, why and what they have learned. A manager's guide to self-development has been written by Pedler, Burgoyne and Boydell (1991), which provides some structured analyses and activities for managers to work through.

Self-development, however, is not a quick fix for, as Stansfield (1997) suggests, it requires time, patience, tenacity, adjustment and careful planning. Stansfield (1996) also recommends that more attention needs to be paid to the 'scaffolding' which supports the self-development process. To this end she suggests that extensive briefing and explanation of the theoretical underpinning of the self-development are both important. In addition she suggests direct skill development concerning the role, importance and nature of peer feedback, and further support in tracking personal learning needs to ensure a more rigorous learning journey. Woodall (2000) also notes difficulties around the support structure for self-development, and identifies confusion in terminology as unhelpful. Confusion in terminology is also raised by Antonacopoulou (2000) who highlights a much neglected influence on self-development – that the individuals themselves have to be capable of taking on this responsibility.

Self-development groups

Typically, a group of individuals is involved in a series of meetings where they would jointly discuss their personal development, organisational issues and/or individual work problems. Groups may begin operating with a leader who is a process expert, not a content expert, and who therefore acts as a facilitator rather than, but not to the complete exclusion of, a source of information. The group itself is the primary source of information and they may operate without outside help as their process skills develop. The content and timings of the meetings can be very flexible, although they will require a significant level of energy and commitment if they are to operate well.

Self-development groups can be devised in a variety of contexts. They can be part of a formal educational course, for example a Diploma in Management Studies, where a group of managers from different organisations come together to support their development; they constitute the whole of a self-development 'course'; or they can be an informal support group within an organisation. However the group originates, it is important that the members understand what every member hopes to get out of the group, the role of the facilitator (if there is one), the processes and rules that the group will operate by and how they agree to interact.

Learning logs

Learning logs are a mechanism for learning retrospectively as they encourage a disciplined approach to learning from opportunistic events. The log may be focused around one particular activity and is usually designed to encourage the writer to explain what happened, how they have reflected on this, what conclusions they have made and what future learning actions they wish to make. Alternatively logs can be used in the form of a daily or weekly diary.

Activity 26.5

Identify a management skills area that you need to develop. (You may find it particularly helpful to choose an interpersonal area, for example, assertiveness, influencing others, presentation, being more sociable, contributing to meetings, helping others.)

Keep a learning diary over the next few weeks logging anything that is relevant to your development area. Use the framework which Gwen used in a previous example (see Window on Practice box at the beginning of this chapter).

At the end of the period review what you have learned in your development area and also what you have learned about the learning cycle.

Learning contracts

There is increasing use of management learning contracts, sometimes used within more formalised self-development groups; on other management courses; as part of a mentoring or coaching relationship; or in working towards a competency-based qualification. These contracts are a formal commitment by the learner to work towards a specified learning goal, with an identification of how the goal might be achieved. They thus promote a proactive approach to learning. Boak (1991) has produced a very helpful guide to the use of such contracts and suggests that they should include:

- an overall development goal;
- specific objectives in terms of skills and knowledge;
- activities to be undertaken;
- resources required;
- method of assessment of learning.

The value that individuals gain from learning contracts is dependent on their choosing to participate, their identification of the relevant goal and the importance and value they ascribe to achieving it. Only with commitment will a learning contract be effective, because ultimately it is down to the individual learner manager to make it happen.

WINDOW ON PRACTICE

David wanted to improve his influencing skills and has sent the following draft learning contract to his manager for discussion:

Goal

To improve my influencing skills with both peers and more senior managers.

Specific objectives

- To prepare for influencing situations.
- To try to understand better the perspective of the other.
- To identify the interpersonal skills required – probably active listening, reflecting, summarising, stating my needs, collaboration (but maybe more).
- To be able to identify that I have had more influence in decisions made.

Activities

- Watch a recommended video on influencing skills.
- Re-read my notes from the interpersonal skills course I attended.
- Watch how others in my department go about influencing.
- Ask other people (supportive ones) how they go about it.
- Identify possible influencing situations in advance, and plan for what I want and what might happen.
- Reflect back on what happened, and work out how to do better next time.
- Ask for feedback.

Resources

- Video.
- Notes.
- The support of others.

Assessment

- I could ask for feedback from colleagues and my manager.
- My own assessment may be helpful.
- Make a log over time of decisions made and my originally preferred outcome.

Open, distance and e-learning

As technology enables interesting and interactive presentation of distance learn-ing materials, there is evidence of considerable enthusiasm on the part of organ-isations to pursue this approach to development, and take advantage of the opportunities it presents. While e-learning has been characterised as requiring high investment in terms of hardware, software and design time, it has also been characterised as cost-effective in the long run, with the ability to provide speedy and flexible training. Hammond (2001), for example, describes the case of Cisio which is constantly launching new IT based products. The company has moved from 90 per cent classroom-based training for its sales representative to 80 per cent online training so that the large numbers of representatives can experience training immediately the product is launched. Channel Four (Cooper 2001) has a strategy to replace much of its classroom teaching activity with interactive learning, and the London Emergency Services are using virtual reality training to prepare employees for emergency events. For example Prickett (1997) reports how Hendon Police Training College uses virtual reality to prepare officers to deal with siege and hostage situations.

However enthusiasm from the organisation is not sufficient. Sadler-Smith *et al.* (2000), for example, found that managers did not widely use such distance learn-ing methods, and they were perceived as less effective than other methods. The support provided may be well be critical.

<table>
<tr><td>WINDOW
ON
PRACTICE</td><td>Hills and Francis (1999), for example, suggest that computer-based learning is a soli-tary activity, and that social contact and interaction were a necessary ingredient in learning. They assessed the use of their local computer-based training centres in Lloyds TSB, and found that some were used much more than others. The extent of</td></tr>
</table>

use was not related to geographical accessibility, but instead to the support provided by the centre administrator, before, during and after learning sessions, and also the support of local managers.

Evaluation of training and development

One of the most nebulous and unsatisfactory aspects of the training job is eval-uating its effectiveness, yet it is becoming more necessary to demonstrate value for money. Evaluation is straightforward when the output of the training is clear to see, like reducing the number of dispatch errors in a warehouse or increasing someone's typing speed. It is more difficult to evaluate the success of a manage-ment training course or a programme of social skills development, but the fact that it is difficult is not enough to prevent it being done.

A familiar method of evaluation is the post-course questionnaire, which course members complete on the final day by answering vague questions that amount to little more than 'good, very good or outstanding'. The drawbacks with these are, first, that there is a powerful halo effect, as the course will have been, at the very least, a welcome break from routine and there will probably have been some attractive fringe benefits like staying in a comfortable hotel and enjoying rich food. Second, the questionnaire tends to evaluate the course and not the learn-ing, so that the person attending the course is assessing the quality of the tutors and the visual aids, instead of being directed to examine what has been learned.

Hamblin (1974), in a much-quoted work, identified five levels of evaluation:

(1) evaluating the training, as in the post-course questionnaire above; (2) evaluating the learning, in terms of how the trainee now behaves; (3) evaluating changes in job performance; (4) evaluating changes in organisation performance; and (5) evaluating changes in the wider contribution that the organisation now makes. Perhaps the most well-referenced approach to evaluation is Kilpatrick (1959) who suggested four levels of evaluation, somewhat similar to Hamblin: reaction level; learning level (have the learning objectives been met?); behaviour (how has the individual's behaviour changed back in the job?); and results (what is the impact of training on job performance?). Bramley (1996) suggests that performance effectiveness can be measured at individual, team and organisational levels, and that changes in behaviour, knowledge, skills and attitudes need to be considered. He makes the worthwhile point – as do others – that the criteria for evaluation need to be built into development activities from the very beginning, and not tagged on at the end. Bramley is a useful source of practical approaches to evaluation, as is Bee and Bee (1994). Sadler-Smith *et al.* (1999) provides a useful comparison of a wide range of evaluation frameworks.

In 1996 Canning noted that the body of knowledge on evaluation had not grown over the past ten years, and the difficulty of this task is no doubt an influence on lack of progress. Harrison (1997), for example, notes that due to high levels of change and the gap between espoused and actual HR goals, and strategy, it is 'therefore hard, if not impossible, to be certain about the specific outcomes of HR or HRD strategy' (p. 209). There is a need, however, to assess value for money, and this is generally worked out on a pay-back basis, which focuses attention on the short term. Lee (1996) suggests a 'pay-forward' approach to assessing value for money and this concept appears to be more consistent with the nature of training and development strategy and interventions as the outcome may only be observed in the long term.

While organisations may desire a measure of the impact of training on the organisation (Kilpatrick 1996) in practice this appears to be rarely achieved. Sadler-Smith *et al.*, for example, found in their study (1999) that the reasons for evaluating training were more often operational than strategic, and they state that evaluation information was used 'mostly for feedback to individuals, and to inform the training process, and less for return on investment decisions' (p. 369).

Summary propositions

26.1 The emphasis has moved from training to learning, with individuals taking ownership of their own learning needs.

26.2 To be effective learners we need to understand the nature of learning and our own strengths and weaknesses.

26.3 The emphasis on formal development programmes is declining in favour of greater interest in approaches to on-the-job development, such as coaching, mentoring, peer relationships and self-development.

26.4 There has been an upsurge of interest in e-learning. However the extent to which employees take advantage of such opportunities will be affected by the context and the support available.

26.5 Evaluation of development is critical but difficult. It is most effective when built into the design of the development activity rather than tagged on at the end.

References

Antonacopoulou, E. (2000) 'Employee development through self-development in three retail banks', *Personnel Review*, Vol. 29, No. 4.

Arnold, J. (1997) 'Mentoring in early career', *Human Resource Management Journal*, Vol. 7, No. 4, pp. 61–70.

Bee, F. and Bee, R. (1994) *Training Needs Analysis and Evaluation*. London: IPM.

Boak, G. (1991) *Developing Managerial Competencies. The management learning contract approach*. London: Pitman.

Bramley, P. (1996) *Evaluating Training*. London: IPD.

Broadbridge, A. (1999) 'Mentoring in retailing: a tool for success?', *Personnel Review*, Vol. 28, No. 4.

Burleston, L. and Grint, K. (1996) 'The deracination of politics: outdoor management development', *Management Learning*, Vol. 27, No. 2, pp. 187–202.

Canning, R. (1996) 'Enhancing the quality of learning in human resource development', *Journal of European Industrial Training*, Vol. 20, No. 2, pp. 3–10.

Conway, C. (1998) *Strategies for Mentoring*. Chichester: Wiley.

Cooper, C. (2001) 'Connect Four', *People Management*, February.

Cromer, D.R. (1989) 'Peers as providers', *Personnel Administrator*, Vol. 34, Pt 5, pp. 84–6.

Gibb, S. and Megginson, D. (1993) 'Inside corporate mentoring schemes – a new agenda of concerns', *Personnel Review*, Vol. 22, No. 1, pp. 40–54.

Hallier, J. and Butts, S. (1999) 'Employers' discovery of training: self-development, employability and the rhetoric of partnership', *Employee Relations*, Vol. 21, No. 1.

Hamblin, A.C. (1974) *Evaluation and Control of Training*. Maidenhead: McGraw-Hill.

Hammond, D. (2001) 'Reality Bytes', *People Management*, January.

Harrison, R. (1997) *Employee Development*. London: IPD.

Hayes, J. and Allinson, C.W. (1996) 'The implications of learning styles for training and development: a discussion of the matching hypothesis', *British Journal of Management*, Vol. 7, pp. 63–73.

Hills, H. and Francis, P. (1999) 'Interaction Learning', *People Management*, July.

Honey, P. and Mumford, A. (1989) *A Manual of Learning Opportunities*. Maidenhead: Peter Honey.

Ibbetson, A. and Newell, S. (1999) 'A comparison of a competitive and non-competitive outdoor management development programme', *Personnel Review*, Vol. 28, No. 1/2.

Johnson, S., Geory, G. and Griego, O. (1999) 'The Mentoring Model theory: dimensions in mentoring protocols', *Career Development International*, Vol. 04, No. 7.

Kilpatrick, D. (1959) 'Techniques for evaluating training programmes', *Journal of the American Society of Training Directors*, Vol. 13.

Kolb, D.A., Rubin, I.M. and McIntyre, J.M. (1984) *Organization Psychology*, 4th edn. Englewood Cliffs, NJ: Prentice Hall.

Kram, K.E. (1983) 'Phases of the mentor relationship', *Academy of Management Journal*, Vol. 26, No. 4.

Kram, K.E. and Isabella, L.A. (1985) 'Mentoring alternatives: the role of peer relationships in career development', *Academy of Management Journal*, Vol. 28, No. 1.

Lee, R. (1996) 'The pay-forward view of training', *People Management*, pp. 30–2.

MacLennan, N. (1995) *Coaching and Mentoring*. Aldershot: Gower.

Megginson, D. (1994) 'Planned and Emergent Learning: A framework and a method', *Executive Development*, Vol. 7, No. 6, pp. 29–32.

Megginson, D. (2000) 'Current issues in mentoring', *Career Development International*, Vol. 5, No. 4/5.

Megginson, D. and Whitaker, V. (1996) *Cultivating Self-development*. London: IPD.

Mumford, A. (1994) *How Managers Develop Managers*. Aldershot: Gower.

O'Hara, S., Webber, T. and Murphy, W. (2001) 'The joy of sets', *People Management*, 8 Feb, pp. 30–4.

Pedler, M., Burgoyne, J. and Boydell, T. (1991), *A Manager's Guide to Self-development*, 3rd edn. London: McGraw-Hill.

Prickett, R. (1997) 'Screen savers', *People Management*, 26 June, pp. 36–8.

Revans, R.W. (1974) 'Action learning projects', in B. Taylor and G.L. Lippitt (eds), *Management Development and Training Handbook*. Maidenhead: McGraw-Hill.

Sadler-Smith, E., Down, S. and Field, J. (1999) 'Adding value to HRD: evaluation, Investors in People and small firm training', *Human Resource Development International*, Vol. 2, No. 4, pp. 369–90.

Sadler-Smith, E., Down, S. and Lean, J. (2000) ' "Modern" learning methods: rhetoric and reality', *Personnel Review*, Vol. 29, No. 4.

Stansfield, L. (1996) 'Is self-development the key to the future?', *Management Learning*, Vol. 27, No. 4, pp. 429–45.

Stansfield, L. (1997) '"Employee – develop yourself" Experiences of self-directed learners', *Career Development International*, Vol. 2 No. 6.

Stott, T. and Sweeney, J. (1999) 'More than a match', *People Management*, June, pp. 45–8.

Woodall, J. (2000) 'Corporate support for work-based management development', *Human Resource Management Journal*, Vol. 10, No. 1, pp. 18–32.

General discussion topics

1 If learning is an individual process, why is so much training done in groups? What are the implications of moving towards more individualised learning?

2 Discuss the view that the role of the trainer/facilitator is critically important in the effectiveness of a training programme.

Chapter 27   Career development

Mallon (1998) reports on research with 24 ex-managers of one branch of the public sector who now had portfolio careers, and through in-depth biographical interviews set out to understand how they account for their career move. From the data she grouped the participants into three categories: 'refugees', 'missionaries' and 'reluctant missionaries'.

There were only two managers classified as 'refugees' and both were made compulsorily redundant, unexpectedly, from senior positions. Since then they have not reconciled themselves to any alternative form of working other than full-time employment. One found a new job, after a year, in which she hopes to remain until retirement, the other still looks for jobs, but having been unsuccessful so far is developing his portfolio of work. Two others Mallon classified as 'ex-refugees'. Both experienced redundancy, both found other work, but both have since chosen the portfolio route. Their explanation for this centred around growing disillusion with the 'employment' world stimulated by their bitter experiences of redundancy.

Mallon identified five of her respondents as 'missionaries'. All left voluntarily and two of these never felt that they fitted in the 'employed world'. Three made very well-planned decisions to move to a portfolio, reducing hours with their current employer in order to gradually build up work elsewhere, for example. These three felt that there were no further challenges in the organisation for them, they talked about 'new' careers, and about taking control for themselves. They clearly felt pulled by other opportunities.

The final, largest group, 'reluctant missionaries', were somewhere in between. Two were offered the choice between a different job or redundancy, and chose to leave, others felt a growing dissatisfaction with the organisation and being out of step with the organisation, one felt that dismissal was looming. However, although these individuals were pushed into action they did report factors which pulled them towards a portfolio approach, such as integrity, time for childcare and doing the type of work that they wanted to do. Others fled the organisation because they felt their position was untenable, but had, at the time, no idea what they were going to do next, and their decision to go portfolio was a pragmatic response to the situation that they were in.

Source: Adapted from M. Mallon (1998) 'The portfolio career; pushed or pulled to it?', *Personnel Review*, Vol. 27, No. 5.

There is a considerable body of literature indicating that the foregoing examples show a general and substantial move from long-term organisationally based careers to individually managed portfolio or boundaryless careers. In this chapter we consider the support for this proposition, but also consider the evidence against such a dramatic move away from traditional notions of the organisational career. We then consider some definitions of career and the theories which help us understand the concept. The remainder of the chapter explores practical ways in which the individual can manage their career, and the types of support the organisation can provide for career development and management.

How and why are careers changing?

Many writers over the past decade provide a picture of dramatic change in the nature of careers that are possible in today's society. The traditional career within a single organisation, characterised by hierarchical progression, managed on a planned basis by the organisation, is gone, it is argued (see, for example, Arthur and Rousseau 1996a; Adamson et al. 1998). Organisations now have flatter structures and need to be flexible, fluid and cost-effective in the face of an uncertain and unpredictable future. Thus they can no longer offer long-term career progression in return for loyalty, commitment and adequate performance, which was an unwritten deal and part of the traditional psychological contract.

Kanter (1989), for example, suggests that managers can no longer rely on the organisation for their career future and must learn to manage themselves and their work independently as many professionals do. In particular, they must build portfolios of their achievements and skills, develop networks, make a 'name' for themselves and market themselves within the relevant industry sector rather than just within their current organisation. In a different sense Handy (1994) uses the words 'portfolio career' to mean 'exchanging full time employment for independence', which is expressed in the collection of different pieces of work done for different clients. Individuals starting off a portfolio career often continue to do some work for their previous organisation (on a fee-paying basis) and add to this a network of other clients. Arthur (1994) describes the 'boundaryless career' which includes moves between organisations and non-hierarchical moves within organisations where there are no norms of progress or success.

However the evidence to support the reality that careers have fundamentally changed is 'shaky at best' (Mallon 1998). Guest and McKenzie-Davey (1996), for example, found the traditional organisation and the traditional career 'alive and well' (pp. 22–3), with the hierarchy still used for motivation and progression. Also, as we indicated in Chapter 13, where we looked at retention, statistics demonstrate that job tenure and the number of job changes has changed very little over the past thirty years. As yet there is insufficient research into the extent to which new career patterns are developing.

While some argue that the contradictions between the above views are a result of being in transition (see, for example, Burke 1998a), another explanation may be that temporary and contract work are spread more evenly across different sectors (see, for example, Burke 1998b), and have therefore become more visible. Let us not forget that the traditional psychological contract was never available to everyone. Smithson and Lewis (2000) argue that public perceptions of increasing insecurity may have more to do with the characteristics of those whom the insecurity now affects, such as graduates and professional staff, rather than an increase in the phenomenon. Similarly different groups have different sets of expectations and subjective feelings of job insecurity. Younger workers accept insecurity, almost as the norm (see, for example, Smithson and Lewis 2000), but older workers feel the psychological contract has been violated. Older workers may have the same expectations as before but realise that the employer is no longer going to fulfil their part of the bargain (see, for example, Herriot et al. 1997; Thomas and Dunkerley 1999).

A different explanation for these contradictory findings is that organisations project the image of a stable and predictable internal career structure, because it

some possible movement and progress in their work, and perhaps most importantly.
■ Itexploits the full potential of the workforce.

Before looking at how individuals can manage their career development with organisational support, we need to review some of the concepts underlying the notion of career.

Understanding careers

Career development stages

Many authors have attempted to map out the ideal stages of a successful career, matched against an age range for each stage. Schein (1978) offers nine stages of the career life cycle, while other authors, such as Super (1980) and Hall and Nougaim (1968), have suggested five. In this section we review the five stages outlined by Greenhaus and Callanan (1994). Few careers follow such an idealised pattern, and even historically such a pattern did not apply for all employees. However, the stage approach offers a useful framework for understanding career experiences, if we use it flexibly as a tool for understanding careers rather than as a normative model.

Stage 1: occupational choice: preparation for work

Greenhaus and Callanan suggest that the first stage may last until around age 25, or may reappear for those who wish to change career later in life. It involves developing an occupational self-image. The key theme is a matching process between the strengths/weaknesses, values and desired lifestyle of the individual and the requirements and benefits of a range of occupations. One of the difficulties that can arise at this stage is a lack of individual self-awareness. There are countless tests available to help identify individual interests, but these can only complete part of the picture, and need to be complemented by structured exercises, which help people look at themselves from a range of perspectives. Other problems involve individuals limiting their choice due to social, cultural, gender or racial characteristics. Although we use role models to identify potential occupations, and these extend the range of options we consider, this process may also close them down. Another difficulty at this stage is gaining authentic information about careers which are different from the ones pursued by family and friends.

Stage 2: organisational entry

There is some overlap between Stage 1 and Stage 2 which occurs, typically, between the ages of 18 and 25, but is revisited by most of us a number of times. It involves the individual in both finding a job which corresponds with their occupational self-image, and starting to do that job. Problems here centre on the accuracy of information that the organisation provides, so that when the individual begins work expectations and reality may be very different. Recruiters understandably 'sell' their organisations and the job to potential recruits, emphasising the best parts and neglecting the downside. Applicants often fail to test their assumptions by asking for the specific information they really need. In addition, schools, colleges and universities have, until recently, only prepared students for the technical demands of work, ignoring other skills that they will need, such as communication skills, influencing skills and dealing with organisational politics. To aid organisational entry, Wanous (1992) has suggested the idea of realistic recruitment which we refer to in Chapter 13.

Activity 27.1	Think of three different jobs in your organisation (or any organisation with which you are familiar) which have been/may be recruited externally. If a 'realistic recruitment' approach were adopted:

■ What information would you give to the candidates about each job and the organisation so that a balanced picture was presented?

■ What methods would you use to communicate this information?

Stage 3: early career – establishment and achievement

The age band for early career is suggested by Greenhaus and Callanan as between 25 and 40 years.

The establishment stage involves fitting into the organisation and understanding 'how things are done around here'. Thorough induction programmes are important, but more especially it is important to provide the new recruit with a 'real' job and early challenges rather than a roving commission from department to department with no real purpose (as often found on trainee schemes). Feedback and support from the immediate manager are also key.

The achievement part of this stage is demonstrating competence and gaining greater responsibility and authority. It is at this stage that access to opportunities for career development becomes key. Development within the job and opportunities for promotion and broadening moves are all aided if the organisation has a structured approach to career development (not necessarily hierarchical progression) involving career ladders, pathways or matrices. Feedback remains important, as do opportunities and support for further career exploration and planning. Organisations are likely to provide the most support for 'high fliers' who are seen as the senior management of the future and who may be on 'fast track' programmes.

Stage 4: mid-career

Greenhaus and Callanan suggest that the mid-career stage usually falls between the ages of 40 to 55, and may involve further growth and advancement or the maintenance of a steady state. In either case it is generally accompanied by some form of re-evaluation of career and life direction. A few will experience decline at this stage. For those individuals who continue to advance, organisational support as described above remains important. Some people whose career has reached a plateau will experience feelings of failure. Greenhaus and Callanan suggest that organisational support in these cases needs to involve the use of lateral career paths, job expansion, development as mentors of others, further training to keep up to date and the use of a flexible reward system.

Stage 5: late career

The organisation's task in the late career stage is to encourage people to continue performing well. This is particularly important as some sectors are experiencing skills shortages and there are moves by some companies to allow individuals to stay at work after the state retirement age. Despite the stereotypes that abound defining older workers as slower and less able to learn, Mayo (1991) argues that if organisations believe these employees will do well and treat them accordingly they will perform well. Greenhaus and Callanan point out that the availability of flexible work patterns, clear performance standards, continued training and the avoidance of discrimination are helpful at this stage, combined with preparation for retirement.

Activity 27.2

If you had a high degree of choice in terms of your career stages would you prefer to:

1 Remain with one organisation for life, or move around?

2 Stay with one occupation/profession for life or change your occupation/profession once or twice?

3 Prefer hierarchical job moves with more responsibility in the same area, or the opportunity to move into new areas without increasing your responsibility level?

4 Prefer to retire as soon as you can, or work for as long as you can?

Identify the reasons for your choice, and consider its advantages and disadvantages. How likely do you think it is that you will be able to fulfil your choice?

Career anchors

Based on a longitudinal study of 44 male Sloan graduates completed in 1973, 10–12 years after graduation, Schein (1978) identified a set of five 'career anchors' and proposed that these explained the pattern of career decisions that each individual had taken. Schein described career anchors as much broader than motivation, and including the following:

■ self-perceived talents and abilities,
■ self-perceived motives and needs,
■ self-perceived attitudes and values.

Our perception of ourselves in these areas comes from direct experiences of work, from successes, from self-diagnosis and feedback. The conclusions that we draw both drive and constrain future career development. Schein sees career anchors as a holistic representation of the person, which takes into account the interaction between the factors identified above. Career anchors can identify a source of personal stability in the person which has determined past choices and will probably determine future choices.

The problematic aspect of career anchors is the accuracy of the individual's self-perceptions, and the question of what happens in mid-career to those who feel their attitudes and values are changing. Schein acknowledges that career anchors are learned rather than reflecting latent abilities and are the sort of things that people are reluctant to abandon. Not only do we all need to identify and understand what our anchors are in order to make sure we are doing the right thing, we also need to appreciate that there are things that we shall continue to need even if we make a career change.

Schein originally identified five career anchors and later supplemented them with another four. The original five are:

Technical/functional competence

Those who have this as their career anchor are interested in the technical content of their work and their feelings of competence in doing this. They tend not to be interested in management itself, as they prefer to exercise their technical skills. They would, however, be prepared to accept managerial responsibilities in their own functional area.

Managerial competence

For those with this career anchor, the exercising of managerial responsibility is an end in itself, and technical/functional jobs just a way of getting there. These people are most likely to end up in general managerial jobs and possess three key competences: analytical competence to solve problems characterised by incomplete information in areas of uncertainty; interpersonal competence to influence and control; and emotional resilience, with the ability to be stimulated rather than paralysed by crises.

Security and stability

It is characteristic of those with this career anchor to be prepared to do what the organisation wants of them in order to maintain job security and the present and future benefits which go with this. Given the choice, most will therefore remain with one organisation for life, although there are alternative patterns such as remaining in the same geographical area but moving between different employers, and making separate financial provision for the future. Because they have not sought career success in terms of hierarchical promotion those with this career anchor often feel a sense of failure, and find it hard to accept their own criteria for career success. This group are more likely to integrate career with home life.

Creativity

Individuals with creativity as a career anchor feel the need to build something new. They are driven by wanting to extend themselves, get involved in new ventures and projects and could be described as entrepreneurial. Should their new venture turn into a thriving business they may become bored by the need to manage it and are more likely to hand this aspect over to others.

Autonomy and independence

The desire to be free of organisational constraints in the exercise of their technical/functional competence is what drives those with this career anchor. They tend to find organisational life restrictive and intrusive into their personal lives and prefer to set their own pace and work style. They will usually work alone or in a small firm. Consultants, writers and lecturers are typical of the roles that this group occupy.

The four additional anchors which Schein added later are:

Basic identity

Those with this career anchor are driven by the need to achieve and sustain an occupational identity. Typically they are in lower-level jobs where their role is represented visually perhaps with badges or uniforms. In this way their role is defined externally, and some may seek for example to be associated with a prestigious employer.

Service to others

The driving force here is the need to help others, often through the exercise of interpersonal competence or other skills. The need is not to exercise such competence as an end in itself, but for the purpose of helping others; typical examples here would be teachers and doctors.

Power, influence and control

This career anchor can be separate from the managerial anchor or may be a pronounced part of it. Those driven by this career anchor may pursue political careers, teaching, medicine or the church as these areas may give them the opportunity to exercise influence and control over others.

Variety

Those who seek variety may do so for different reasons. This career anchor may be relevant for those who have a wide range of talents, who value flexibility or who get bored very easily.

Other models

Derr (1986) proposed an alternative set of five career types, later updated by BT.Novations, with the emphasis on the development of this aspect of self-identity as an ongoing process.

Driver (1982) proposed a model which describes four shapes of the career lives of individuals. He identified 'transitory' careers where individuals make frequent job changes, and do not display any stability; 'steady state' careers where occupational choice is made early and does not change; 'linear' careers where the field of work is chosen early and upward movement is the imperative; and 'spiral' careers where individuals develop in one area for a time then move on and develop in another area or areas. In some ways these frameworks have stood the test of time better than the career stages theories.

Career balance

Much of the original work done on describing career stages and career anchors was carried out by analysing the experiences of those who were both male and white, so the analyses are clearly inadequate for our contemporary world of work. Schein's development of his original set of career anchors shows understanding is being reshaped, but we still lack satisfactory explanations of career development that can embrace the full variety of ethnic backgrounds, gender and occupational variety.

There is considerable evidence that racial minorities and women limit their career choices, both consciously and unconsciously, for reasons not to do with their basic abilities and career motives. Social class identity may have the same impact. Employers need at least to be aware of such forces and ideally would explore such constraints with their employees to encourage individual potential to be exploited to the full.

The acceptance of such idealised career development stages as described above, particularly in an era of work intensification, leaves little room for family and other interference in career development, and until recently there has been no place in career development and even in the thinking about careers for those who do not conform to the stages outlined. There are hopeful signs of increasing recognition that career and life choices need to be explored in unison. There has also been little recognition of the commercial environment and the impact that this has on career development stages for many individuals. Considerable attention is being paid, currently, to the concept of work-life balance (see IDS 2000) where aspects of work flexibility are considered in relation to other responsibilities and interests that the employee may have. The business case for this is partly concerned with productivity resulting from higher motivation and commitment if personal circumstances are recognised and built around. Second, such an approach is considered to be important in recruitment and retention. Within this concept some attention is being paid to career, although this does not appear to be an explicit focus in many schemes. We briefly consider three major influences below on career choices: parenting; partner's career; lifestyle values.

WINDOW ON PRACTICE

The workplace as a home from home: career balance or a force in the opposite direction? We still work longer hours in the UK than our European counterparts, and some employers are attempting to make the workplace a home from home. This may apply to décor, layout, ambiance or facilities and support. In the context of this move towards 'living at work' Meyerson (2001) describes Thomas Cook's Falkirk callcentre as having a 'palms and sunshield' flavour. Some firms are attempting to create a 'corporate village'. Egg (Meyerson 2001) have designed their office as a city with streets, squares and local neighbourhoods, with areas that cater for passive (chill out rooms and soft seating) and active (table football) retreats. Hilpern (2001) reports workplaces with 'granny creches', desk massage, saunas, and 'nap' areas, and describes BA's Waterside Business Centre as including supermarkets, hairdressers, fitness suites, banks and a flower shop. Some firms reported by Hilpern provide employees with a 'lifestyle manager' who will, amongst other things, make their holidays and restaurant bookings.

Parenting and caring

Parenting is a powerful influence, particularly, but *not only*, on women's careers. This may create the desire to take a few years out from employment; putting a halt on advancement aspirations while children are young; or taking a different career path which combines more effectively with child-raising. Pringle and Gold (1989) note that the interruption of a woman's career pathway is often identified as one of the reasons for the lower status and salary they receive in management positions. Such people are often classified as not interested in their career development. The following quotation from a female chartered accountant, reported by Lewis and Cooper (1989), is telling:

> If you are trying to get back into the profession at the age of 40, there isn't much chance. This is the problem, the child rearing years are the same years when you have to build your career. For a woman who drops out for a period of, say five to ten years, it would be difficult to get back. You would be out of touch anyway.

A more positive reaction would be to view their career development curve as having a different, but equally legitimate shape. Caring for old or sick relatives has been slower to be recognised, but more attention is being paid to this. As with parenting, the evidence suggests that it is women who carry out these roles in the main.

WINDOW ON PRACTICE	IDS (2000) report on six organisations which are actively pursuing work-life balance programmes: Lloyds TSB, the Benefits Agency, Arthur Andersen, Fox's Biscuits, Liverpool City Council and Marks and Spencer. The emphases are different in each company and three of the six make explicit reference to career development:

At Lloyds TSB they recognise the importance of culture when they aim to ensure that flexible forms of work do not act as 'career killers', where employees working flexibly are marginalised. Not only should there be equal access to training for, say, part-time staff, but such flexible contracts should be available for and be used by senior members of the organisation.

At Liverpool City Council career breaks were not normally very common. However the option is now available to all those with over two years' service, and on return staff are appointed on a grade similar to their previous one. However, they are not guaranteed a job. They need to apply as normal, but are given advance notice of posts becoming available so they can apply before they are advertised in the newspapers. The career break can be used for anything as long as it is not other paid employment. For example a career break can be used for studying, voluntary work or other developmental experiences.

Marks and Spencers have introduced career leave as a formal policy. Again to be eligible staff must have at least two years' service, and are normally expected to provide at least six months' warning. Leave can last for up to nine months, and staff have used the opportunity to do such activities as sailing and undertaking charity work. As with Liverpool City Council employment elsewhere is not an option during a career break. Leave counts towards service, so that benefits such as pensions are retained.

Source: Adapted from IDS (2000) *Work-life Balance* IDS Study 698, November.

Partner's career

Career choices are increasingly likely to be taken in combination with the career choice of a partner rather than in isolation, although the burden of adapting one's own career choices to fit in with those of a partner still falls mainly on women. Traditional patterns of job-seeking activity for dual-career couples would be for the man to choose a job first and the woman to follow. Lewis and Cooper (1989) identify a range of alternatives, including direct reversal of the traditional pattern. More egalitarian strategies are that:

- each partner seeks opportunities independently and the best joint option is chosen;
- both partners seek to be employed by the same organisation on a joint basis;
- both partners share the same job;
- each partner selects the best opportunity for them and geographical distance is dealt with by one partner living away from home during the working week.

As alternative strategies become more common, career decisions become more complex and organisations need to work harder at understanding and working with the influences at play. Geographical mobility generally becomes more difficult, and Evans (1986) notes that resistance to being required to be mobile is increasing.

Changing lifestyle values

As we begin the twenty-first century there is increasing evidence that, for some, the value of work is changing. While the 1980s were characterised by the idea that 'lunch is for wimps', there has been a shift, perhaps encouraged by increasing work intensification and pressure, towards valuing a slower and gentler pace, which allows more room for personal interests, environment and family. 'Downshifting' has been described as swapping a life of total commitment to work and possible high rewards, for less demanding, or part-time work or self-employment – or a combination of the three. Guides on how to downshift are increasingly appearing (for example, Ghazi and Jones 1997), which help individuals evaluate the best option for themselves, recognising both the sacrifices and the benefits. To some extent this movement may be rationalising the lack of traditional career opportunities and the need to develop a portfolio career, but the protagonists make a pretty convincing case for downshifting from choice.

Individual career management

If we identify a career as the property of the individual, then clearly the responsibility for managing this rests on the individual, who should identify career goals, adopt strategies to support them and devise plans to achieve the goal.

In reality, however, many people fail to plan. Pringle and Gold (1989), for example, found a lack of career planning in their sample of 50 'achieving' men and women managers. Only around a quarter of people had plans for the future and many identified luck, opportunity or being in the right place at the right time as the reason they had achieved promotions. Harlan and Weiss (1982) found both men and women drifting into positions created through coincidences.

Of course, we do not know how well these people would have done had they planned – they might have done even better. We argue that planning is an essential ingredient of individual career management even if only to provide a framework for decisions about the opportunities that arise through identifying priorities. We also argue that the more an individual attempts to manage their career, the more likely it is that opportunities will arise and the more likely that they are to be able to do something constructive with them.

Mayo suggests that in defining a career goal it is too difficult for a person to try to specify the ultimate goal of their career. Career aiming points are more appropriate if based on a 10–15-year timespan, maybe a shorter period for younger people.

A career goal will be specific to the individual – for example, to become an internal senior organisational consultant by the age of 35. The range of strategies that a person may adopt in pursuit of their goal can be described in terms of more general groups. The list below describes the type of strategies, identified from a review of the literature by Gould and Penley (1984).

- **Creating opportunities**. This involves building the appropriate skills and experiences that are needed for a career in the organisation. Developing those skills that are seen as critical to the individual's supervisor and department are most useful, as is exercising leadership in an area where none exists at present.
- **Extended work involvement**. This necessitates working long hours, both at the workplace and at home, and may also involve a preoccupation with work issues at all times.
- **Self-nomination/self-presentation**. The individual who pursues this strategy will communicate the desire for increased responsibility to their managers. They will also make known their successes, and build an image of themselves as someone who achieves things.

- **Seeking career guidance**. This involves seeking out a more experienced person, either within the organisation or without, and looking for guidance or sponsorship. The use of mentor relationships would come into this category.
- **Networking**. Networking involves developing contacts both inside and outside the organisation to gain information and support.
- **Interpersonal attraction**. This strategy builds the relationship with one's immediate manager on the basis that they will have an impact on career progression. One form of this is 'opinion conformity'; that is, sharing the key opinions of the individual's manager, perhaps with minor deviations. Another is expressed as 'other enhancement', which may involve sharing personal information with one's manager and becoming interested in similar pursuits.

These strategies provide some difficulties for women:

> women in management often find it difficult to break into the male-dominated 'old boy network' and therefore are denied the contacts, opportunities and policy information it provides. (Davidson and Cooper 1992, p. 129)

The career strategies explored above are clearly most appropriate in the early and mid-career stages, and other strategies will best fit other stages.

Activity 27.3

What general types of career strategy would be appropriate for:
- organisational entry?
- late career?

Compare your views with those of people you know who are in each of these career stages.

While the strategies above were derived from careers within an organisational context, similar strategies could be appropriate for employees forced to look more widely in developing their careers. Arthur and Rousseau (1996b) suggest that individuals need to develop career resilience, which he defined as bouncing back from disruptions to one's career, and Waterman *et al.* (1994), in an article on the career-resilient workforce, suggest that individuals need to:

- Make themselves knowledgeable about relevant market trends.
- Understand the skills and knowledge needed in their area and anticipate future needs.
- Be aware of their own strengths and weaknesses.
- Have a plan for increasing their performance and employability.
- Respond quickly to changing business needs.
- Move on from their current employer when a win/win relationship is no longer possible.

Ball (1997) identifies four career management competencies. Three of these are planning, engaging in personal development and balancing work and non-work. The fourth is optimising, which includes intelligence gathering, seeking a mentor, having a positive self-image and gaining the attention of others.

Organisational support for career development

Although career management is primarily the individual's responsibility, organisations can support this. This will be relevant whether careers are offered internally or whether employability is promoted, although the support may be different. Organisations can help individuals with:

- **Career exploration** – providing tools and help for self-diagnosis and supplying organisational information.
- **Career goal setting** – providing a clear view of the career opportunities available in the business, making a wider range of opportunities available to meet different career priorities.
- **Career strategies and action planning** – providing information and support; what works in this organisation; what's realistic.
- **Career feedback** – providing an honest appraisal of current performance and career potential.

Organisations can make this contribution through the following activities.

Career pathways and grids

A career path is a sequence of job roles or positions, related via work content or abilities required, through which an individual can move. Publicised pathways can help people to identify a realistic career goal within the organisation. Traditional pathways were normally presented as a vertical career ladder, emphasising upward promotion within a function, often formally or informally using age limits and formal qualifications for entry to certain points of the ladder. Joining the pathway other than at the normal entry point was very difficult. These pathways tended to limit career opportunities as much as they provided helpful information. The emphasis on upward movement meant that career progress for the majority was halted early on in their careers. The specifications

Figure 27.1 Traditional career pathway

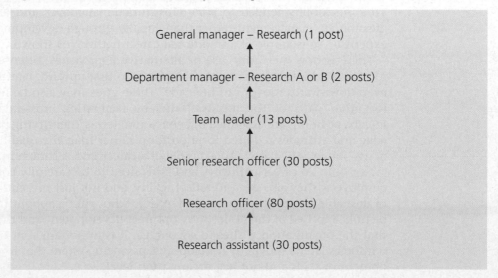

General manager – Research (1 post)

↑

Department manager – Research A or B (2 posts)

↑

Team leader (13 posts)

↑

Senior research officer (30 posts)

↑

Research officer (80 posts)

↑

Research assistant (30 posts)

Figure 27.2 Career grid or matrix

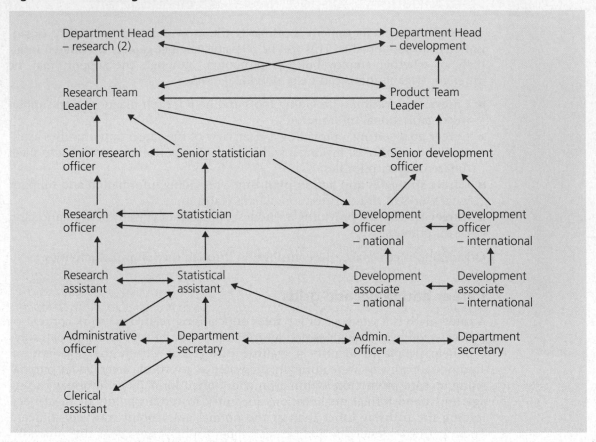

of age and qualification meant that the pathways were restricted to those who had an 'ideal' career development profile but excluded those who had taken career breaks, or who had lots of relevant experience but no formal qualifications. This inflexibility tended to stifle cross-functional moves and emphasised progression via management rather than equally through development of technical expertise. An example of a traditional career pathway is shown in Figure 27.1.

There is now increasing use of alternative approaches, often designed in the form of a grid, with options at each point, so that upward, lateral, diagonal and even downwards moves can be made. These grids may also be linked into grids for other parts of the business, thereby facilitating cross-functional moves. Ideally, positions are described in behavioural terms, identifying the skills, knowledge and attitudes required for a position rather than the qualifications needed or age range anticipated. An example of a career grid is shown in Figure 27.2.

Not only do career pathways and grids need to be carefully communicated to employees, they also need to reflect reality, and not just present an ideal picture of desirable career development. Managers who will be appointing staff need to be fully apprised of the philosophy of career development and the types of move that the organisation wishes to encourage. It is important that the organisation reinforces lateral moves by developing a payment system that rewards the development of skills and not just organisation level.

Fast-track programmes

Fast-track programmes have been considered as a way of developing and retaining high performers. However problems have been found with such accelerated progress. Hall (1999) reports that although individuals on such programmes perform well early on, they tend to experience derailment later in their career. He proposed four reasons for this. First, that moving through the organisation so quickly means that they have never been in one place long enough to develop a network of learning support. Second, that in their rapid progress they will have alienated a lot of people on the way. Third, that they have never been in one position long enough to experience failure and setbacks and learn how to deal with these, and, finally, this means that they have not received sufficient developmental feedback, which is critical to career success. Iles (1997) suggests that to make such careers more sustainable there needs to be greater emphasis on developing empowerment skills and more developmental feedback.

Managerial support

Managerial support is critical, not only in terms of appointing staff, but also in terms of supporting the career development of their current staff. Direct feedback on current performance and potential is vital, especially in identifying strengths and weaknesses, and what improvement would be critical. The immediate manager is in a good position to refer the individual to other managers and introduce them into a network which will support their career moves. In addition the manager is in the ideal position to provide job challenges and experiences within the current job which will equip the incumbent with the skills needed for the desired career move.

> The manager can provide valuable input in terms of honest feedback relative to the individual's capabilities, information about the organisation's needs and future direction, and ideas and suggestions for training and use of company resources.
>
> (Walker 1992, p. 208)

Unfortunately, as Evans (1986) notes, managers often do not see these responsibilites as part of their job and see them as belonging to the HR department. Yarnall (1998) found low levels of support from managers, but also found that employees participating in self-development career initiatives did encourage management support. Managers often feel constrained by their lack of knowledge about other parts of the organisation, and often withdraw from giving accurate feedback about career potential, particularly when they know that what they have to say is not what the individual wishes to hear. Managers are also sometimes tempted, in their own interests, to hold on to good employees rather than encouraging them to develop elsewhere.

Activity 27.4

As a member of the personnel function pursuing an organisational philosophy of flexible career moves and continuous career development, how would you:

■ encourage managers to adopt this philosophy?

■ prepare them for the skills they will need to use?

What other career development support could immediate managers give in addition to the suggestions made above?

Career counselling

Occasionally immediate managers will be involved in career counselling, drawing out the strengths, weaknesses, values and interests of their staff. In many cases, however, those who seek such counselling would prefer to speak in confidence to someone independent of their work situation. In these circumstances a member of the HR department may act as counsellor. In more complex cases, or those involving senior members of staff, professionals external to the organisation may be sought. This is also more likely to be the case if the career counselling is offered as part of an outplacement programme resulting from a redundancy.

Career workshops

Career workshops are usually, but not always, conducted off-site, and offered as a confidential programme to help individuals assess their strengths and weaknesses, values and interests, identify career opportunities, set personal career goals and begin to develop a strategy and action plan. Career goals will not necessarily be restricted to the current employing organisation – and one objective of the workshop is often to broaden career perspectives. Workshops may last 2–3 days, and normally involve individual paper-and-pencil exercises, group discussions, one-to-one discussions and private conferences with tutors. For some people these can be quite traumatic events as they involve whole-life exploration, and often buried issues are confronted which have been avoided in the hurly-burly of day-to-day life. The most difficult part for many individuals is keeping the momentum going after the event by continuing the action planning and self-assessment of progress.

Self-help workbooks

As an alternative to a workshop there is a variety of self-help guides and workbooks which can assist people to work through career issues by presenting a structure and framework. Organisations such as 'Lifeskills' provide a range of workbooks appropriate for different stages of career development.

Another excellent example is the work of Burgoyne and Germain (1982) at Esso Chemicals. The two driving forces here were the need to spend more effective career planning time with employees and the anticipated needs of the organisation in the year 2000.

A guide was produced that staff could work through at their own speed using friends and colleagues to check out their responses and assessments. The guide was designed to help them integrate career planning and self-development, and covered the following areas:

- your skills and job,
- your life and work,
- the world in which you live and work,
- exploring career options,
- what can you learn to help you in the future?
- how do you solve problems?
- what should you be planning to learn?
- how best do you learn?
- how do you keep up to date?

- opportunities and resources for learning,
- planning your self-development.

It was critical that in completing the guide individuals also had a series of meetings with their immediate manager to test out their assessments and assumptions and share information.

Career centres

Career centres can be used as a focal point for the provision of organisational and external career information. The centre may include a library on career choices and exploration, information on organisational career ladders and grids, current opportunities to apply for, self-help workbooks and computer packages.

Assessment and development centres

Assessment centres for internal staff have traditionally taken the form of pass/fail assessment for a selected group of high-potential managers at a specific level. They were focused on organisational rather than individual needs. Recently changes to some of these centres have moved the focus to the individual, with less limitation on who is allowed to attend. These 'development centres' assess the individual's strengths and weaknesses and provide feedback and development plans so that each can make the most of his or her own potential. The outcome is not pass/fail but action plans for personal and career development.

Whatever career activities are in place in the organisation it is important to ensure that:

- There is a clear and agreed careers philosophy communicated to all in the organisation.
- Managers are supported in their career development responsibilities.
- Career opportunities are communicated to staff.
- There is an appropriate balance between open and closed internal recruitment.
- The reasons for the balance are explained.
- Knowledge, skills and attitude development are rewarded as well as achievement of a higher organisational level.
- Attention is given to career development within the current job.

Although all of these activities focus on careers within an organisation, most are still appropriate for employers providing development leading to employability rather than long-term employment. Waterman *et al.* (1994) stress that employers need to move to an adult/adult relationship with their employees from that of parent/child, be prepared to share critical organisational information and let go of the old notion of loyalty, thus accepting that good employees will leave. Hiltrop (1996) provides a good range of suggestions for managing the changing psychological contract.

Activity 27.5	■ What are the advantages and disadvantages of open and closed internal recruitment?
	■ In which circumstances might it be appropriate to give a greater emphasis to closed recruitment?
	■ In which circumstances might it be appropriate to give a greater emphasis to open recruitment?

Perhaps the most outstanding challenge is to come to terms with the fact that careers have changed due to a changing organisation structure and competitive demands; individuals in our current labour market have a greater say in their career and how it relates to their whole life; and that alternative career profiles are equally legitimate. It is a sad reflection that in most research career development activities are not found to have a high profile (see, for example, Atkinson 2000).

Summary propositions

27.1 Careers are owned by individuals and the primary responsibility for managing them falls to the individual; organisations have a role in supporting and encouraging this.

27.2 The context of careers is changing from long-term careers in one organisation with upward movement to careers that are characterised by disruption, movement between employers and the development of portfolios of work. There is a school of though that suggests this move is overstated.

27.3 It is important for individuals and organisations to understand the dynamics of careers and changing psychological contracts in order that they may manage or support them more effectively.

27.4 Career development can be described in stages, for example: occupational choice, organisational entry, early career, mid-career, late career. These stages may follow a traditional pattern but there are equally legitimate alternative forms, and these are becoming increasingly prevalent.

27.5 Career anchors represent the self-perceived talents, values and needs of individuals. They help to explain past career choices and have a bearing on future choices. Individual people usually have a combination of anchors.

27.6 Individuals need to manage their careers and aim to become career resilient, so that they have developed the skills and knowledge to overcome career setbacks.

27.7 Organisations can support and encourage individual career management by providing flexible and realistic career grids, honest feedback, opportunities for individual career exploration and planning.

References

Adamson, S., Doherty, N. and Viney, C. (1998) 'The meanings of career revisited: Implications for theory and practice', *British Journal of Management*, Vol. 9, pp. 251–9.

Arthur, M. and Rousseau, D. (1996a) 'A career lexicon for the 21st century', *Academy of Management Executive*, Vol. 10, No. 4, pp. 28–39.

Arthur, M. and Rousseau, D. (1996b) *The Boundaryless Career: A New Employment Principle for a New Organisational Era*. Oxford: OUP.

Arthur, M. (1994) 'The boundaryless career', *Journal of Organisational Behaviour*, Vol. 15, pp. 295–306.

Atkinson, C. (2000) 'Career management strategies in a major UK plc', paper presented to the British Academy of Management Conference, September, Edinburgh.

Ball, B. (1997) 'Career Management competencies – the individual perspective', *Career Development International*, Vol. 2, No. 2.

Burgoyne, J. and Germain, C. (1982) 'Self-development and career planning: an exercise in mutual benefit', *Personnel Management*, April, pp. 21–3.

Burke, R. (1998a) 'Correlations of job insecurity amongst recent business school graduates', *Employee Relations*, Vol. 20/1, No. 2, pp. 92–100.

Burke, R. (1998b) 'Changing career rules: clinging to the past or accepting the new reality?', *Career Development International*, Vol. 3, No. 1.

Collin, A. and Watts, A. (1996) 'The death and transfiguration of career – and of career guidance?', *British Journal of Guidance and Counselling*, Vol. 24, No. 3, pp. 385–98.

Davidson, M.J. and Cooper, C. (1992) *Shattering the Glass Ceiling*. London: Paul Chapman.

Derr, C.B. (1986) *Managing the New Careerists: The diverse career success orientations of today's workers*. Wokingham: Jossey-Bass.

Doherty, N., Viney, C. and Adamson, S. (1997) 'Rhetoric or reality – shifts in the philosophy and practice of graduate career management?', *Career Development International*, Vol. 2, No. 4.

Driver, M. (1982) 'Career concepts – a new approach', in R. Katz (ed.), *Career Issues in HRM*. Englewood Cliffs, NJ: Prentice-Hall.

Evans, P. (1986) 'New directions in career management', *Personnel Management*, December, pp. 26–9.

Ghazi, P. and Jones, J. (1997) *Getting a Life: a downshifter's guide*. London: Hodder & Stoughton.

Goffee, R. and Nicholson, N. (1994) 'Career development in male and female managers – convergence or collapse?', in M.J. Davidson and R.J. Burke (eds), *Women in Management: Current Research Issues*. London: Paul Chapman.

Gould, S. and Penley, L. (1984) 'Career strategies and salary progression: a study of their relationships in a municipal bureaucracy', *Organisational Behaviour and Human Performance*, Vol. 34, pp. 244–65.

Greenhaus, J.H. and Callanan, G.A. (1994) *Career Management*. London: Dryden Press.

Guest, D. and McKenzie-Davey, K. (1996) 'Don't write off the traditional career', *People Management*, February.

Hall, D.T. (1999) 'Accelerate executive development at your peril', *Career Development International*, Vol. 4, No. 4, pp. 237–9.

Hall, D.T. and Nougaim, K. (1968) 'An examination of Maslow's need hierarchy in an organisational setting', *Organisational Behaviour and Human Performance*, Vol. 13, pp. 12–35.

Handy, C. (1994) *The Empty Raincoat: Making Sense of the Future*. London: Hutchinson.

Harlan, A. and Weiss, C.L. (1982) 'Sex differences in factors affecting managerial career advancement', in P.A. Wallace (ed.), *Women in the Workforce*. London: Auburn House, ch. 4.

Herriot, P. (1998) 'The role of the HRM function in building a new proposition for staff', in P. Sparrow and M. Machington (eds), *Human Resource Management: The New Agenda*. London: Financial Times/Pitman.

Herriot, P. and Pemberton, C. (1996) 'Contracting careers', *Human Relations*, Vol. 49, No. 6, pp. 757–90.

Herriot, P., Manning, W. and Kidd, J. (1997) 'The content of the psychological contract', *British Journal of Management*, Vol. 8, pp. 151–62.

Hilpern, K. (2001) 'Office, sweet office', *The Times magazine,* 28 April, pp. 18–24.

Hiltrop, J.-M. (1996) 'Managing the changing psychological contract', *Employee Relations*, Vol. 18, No. 4, pp. 36–49.

IDS (2000) *Work-life Balance*, IDS Study 698, November. London: IDS.

Iles, P. (1997) 'Sustainable high-potential career development: a resource-based view', *Career Development International*, Vol. 2, No. 7.

Kanter, R.M. (1989) *When Giants Learn to Dance*. New York: Simon and Schuster.

Lewis, S. and Cooper, C.L. (1989) *Career Couples*. London: Unwin Hyman.

Mallon, M. (1998) 'The portfolio career; pushed or pulled to it?', *Personnel Review*, Vol. 27, No. 5.

Malton, M. (1999) 'Going "Portfolio": making sense of changing careers', *Career Development International*, Vol. 4, No. 4.

Mayo, A. (1991) *Managing Careers: strategies for organisations*. London: IPM.

Myerson, J. (2001) 'It's an office, Jim, but not as we know it', *The Times magazine*, 28 April, pp. 48–53.

Pringle, J.K. and Gold, U.O'C. (1989) 'How useful is career planning for today's managers?', *Journal of Management Development*, Vol. 8, No. 3, pp. 21–6.

Schein, E. (1978) *Career Dynamics: Matching individual and organisation needs*. Reading, Mass.: Addison-Wesley.

Smithson, J. and Lewis, S. (2000) 'Is job insecurity changing the psychological contract?', *Personnel Review*, Vol. 29, No. 6.

Sparrow, P. (1996) 'Transitions in the psychological contract: some evidence from the banking sector', *Human Resource Management Journal*, Vol. 6, No. 4.

Super, D.E. (1980) 'A life span, life space approach to career development', *Journal of Vocational Behaviour*, Vol. 16, pp. 282–98.

Thomas, R. and Dunkerley, D. (1999) 'Careering downwards? Middle managers' experiences in the downsized organisation', *British Journal of Management*, Vol. 10, pp. 157–69.

Walker, J.W. (1992) *Human Resource Strategy*. Maidenhead: McGraw-Hill.

Walton, J. (1999) *Strategic Human Resource Development*. Harlow: Financial Times Prentice Hall.

Wanous, J.P. (1992) *Recruitment, Selection, Orientation and Socialisation of Newcomers*. Wokingham: Addison-Wesley.

Waterman, R.H., Waterman, J.A. and Collard, B.A. (1994) 'Toward a career-resilient workforce', *Harvard Business Review*, July–August.

Yarnall, J. (1998) 'Line managers as career developers: rhetoric or reality?', *Personnel Review*, Vol. 27, No. 5.

General discussion topics

1 What is the career management challenge for the early twenty-first century? What appropriate strategies and actions might there be for employers and employees?

2 'No matter how much we encourage individuals to plan their careers, at the end of the day it comes down to opportunity and chance.'

Do you think that this comment is a fair reflection of the way that individuals manage their careers?

Chapter 28

Interactive skill: presentation and teaching

A central function of HRM is to enable people to learn. There are all manner of ways in which this can be done, especially with the development of technical aids, but this chapter concentrates on the face-to-face learning situation: teaching. We use that simple, traditional term despite its connotations of narrowness. Many people visualise teaching as a process in which someone who knows instructs someone who does not. But enabling people to learn goes beyond simple instruction. Learners frequently have to discover for themselves, as this is the only way in which they will understand, and they frequently can only learn by their interaction with other people in a group, as it is the group process alone that can help them develop their social skills.

Teaching a person to do something is different from teaching someone to understand something, and understanding something intellectually is different from understanding and changing how you interact with other people.

> Notwithstanding the amazing developments that have taken place in recent years with alternative modes of delivery, there is still a great demand for classroom-based, tutor delivered training. People do, however, demand and expect training to be lively and stimulating. They will not put up with dull and irrelevant training.
>
> (Truelove 1992, p. 172)

Approaches to learning

Different types of learning require fundamentally different methods and approaches by the teacher. One recent, popular classification is to distinguish between memorising, understanding and doing (MUD). This classification was the result of research by Downs and Perry (1987), who identified blockages to learning, especially by adults, and was widely promoted in the late 1980s by, among others, the Manpower Services Commission. A more detailed classification was shown in the CRAMP taxonomy (ITRU 1976), developed after a study of the work of the Belbins (Belbin and Belbin 1972) and following an earlier analysis by Bloom (1956). This system divides all learning into five basic types.

1 **Comprehension** is where the learning involves knowing how, why and when certain things happen, so that learning has only taken place when the learner understands: not simply when the learner has memorised. Examples would be having enough understanding of how German grammar works to be able to get the words of a sentence in the right order, or knowing enough of the law of employment to decide whether or not someone has been dismissed unfairly.

2 **Reflex learning** is involved when skilled movements or perceptual capacities

have to be acquired, involving practice as well as knowing what to do. Speed is usually important and the task needs constant repetition to develop the appropriate synchronisation and co-ordination. Many of the obvious examples lie outside the interests of most personnel managers, like juggling, gymnastics or icing a cake, but there are many examples in most organisations, such as driving a fork-lift truck, spot welding, fault-finding and typing. One of the most widespread in management circles is the use of a keyboard. It is interesting how the status of the keyboard has altered. On promotion to supervisory, administrative or managerial positions, ex-secretaries have regarded it as essential that they should never use a keyboard again for fear that they would revert to being seen as 'merely a secretary'. Now the use of a keyboard is an essential managerial adjunct to making the most of information technology.

3 **Attitude development** is enabling people to develop the capacity to alter their attitudes and improve their social skills. Much of the customer care training currently being conducted has this as its basis. The theory is that dealing with customers requires people to be confident of their own ability to deal with others, shedding some of their feelings of insecurity and discovering how they are able to elicit a positive response. This can partly be achieved by the process of 'scripting', whereby staff have a set formula to follow. We are all familiar with making a telephone call which brings a response along the lines of, 'Good morning. Bloggs, Blenkinsop, Huggins and Scratchit. Mandy speaking. How may I help you?' The woodenness of that method can be overcome by enabling people to develop positive attitudes about themselves and their relationships with others, so that they can cope effectively with other people in a variety of situations, including the telephone.

4 **Memory training** is a way of enabling trainees to remember how to handle a variety of given situations. Pharmacists learn by rote a series of maximum dosages, for example, and an office messenger will need to remember that all invoices go to Mr Brown and all cheques to Mrs Smith. Police officers remember the registration numbers of cars better than most of us, and we all need to remember telephone numbers and PIN numbers. Memory training is distinguished from comprehension because understanding is not necessary, only recall, and it is worth referring back to the example above of understanding German grammar. Learning grammatical rules by rote does not enable one to use that knowledge, because understanding is also required. Learning your PIN number does not require any understanding at all.

5 **Procedural learning** is similar to memory except that the drill to be followed does not have to be memorised, but located and understood. An example is the procedure to be followed in shutting down a plant at Christmas, or dealing with a safety drill.

Most forms of training involve more than one type of learning, so that the apprentice vehicle mechanic will need to understand how the car works as well as practising the skill of tuning an engine, and the driver needs to practise the skill of co-ordinating hands, feet and eyes in driving as well as knowing the procedure to follow if the car breaks down. Broadly speaking, however, comprehension-type learning is best approached by a method that teaches the whole subject as an entity rather than splitting it up into pieces and taking one at a time. Here the lecture or training manual is typically used. Attitude change is now often handled by group discussion, but reflex learning is best handled by part methods, which break the task down into sections, each of which can be studied and practised separately before putting together a complete performance, just as a tennis player will practise the serve, the smash, the forehand, the backhand and other individual strokes before playing a match in which all are used. Memory and procedural learning may take place either by whole or by part methods, although memorisation is usually best done by parts.

<table>
<tr><td>Activity 28.1</td><td>

1 Think of things that you have learned in the recent past and identify whether the learning was comprehension, reflex, attitude development, memorisation or procedural.

2 How would you classify learning for the following?

■ Swimming	■ Selection interviewing
■ Calorie counting in a diet	■ Learning Russian
■ Parenting	■ Running a business
■ Safe lifting	■ Preparing for retirement

</td></tr>
</table>

Types of learner

Learners differ according to their prior knowledge, the quality and nature of their previous education and their age. CRAMP (comprehension, reflex learning, attitude development, memory training, procedural learning) was based on research among adults and most of the teaching carried out under the aegis of human resource management is with adults, so we need some understanding of how learners differ. An excellent analysis has been produced by Robert Quinn (1988) based on earlier work by Dreyfus *et al.* (1986). It also appears in Quinn's work on management skills (Quinn *et al.* 1990). He believes that mastery of an activity involves a learning process that takes place over an extended period of time and that the capacity to learn evolves at the same time. The inference of this is that our approach to organising facilities for others to learn will be influenced by how far their learning capacity has developed. There are five stages:

1 **The novice** learns facts and rules without criticism or discussion, accepting that there are ways of doing things that others have devised, and that's that.

2 **The advanced beginner** goes a little further by being able to incorporate the lessons of experience, so that understanding begins to expand and embellish the basic facts and rules. As you begin to experience working in an organisation, aspects of cultural norms become apparent that are just as important as the basic rules. You find out the subtleties of the dress code and working relationships and extend competence by trying out very slight departures from the rigidity of the rules.

3 **Competency** represents a further development of confidence and a reduced reliance on absolute rules by recognising a wider variety of cues from the working context. There is a greater degree of learning by trial and error, experimenting with new behaviours. It is not abandoning the rules, but being able to use them more imaginatively and with an interpretation that suits one's own personal strengths and inclinations.

4 **Proficiency** is where the learner transcends analysis and begins to use intuition:

> Calculation and rational analysis seem to disappear. The unconscious, fluid, and effortless performance begins to emerge, and no one plan is held sacred. You learn to unconsciously 'read' the evolving situation. You notice cues and respond to new cues as the importance of the old ones recede. (Quinn *et al.* 1990, p. 315)

5 **Expert** is the term used to describe those rare people who produce a masterly performance simply by doing what comes naturally, because all the learning has fused together to develop a capacity based on having in their heads 'multidimensional maps of the territory' that are unknown to other people; they are thus able to meet effortlessly the contradictions of organisational life.

This is a neat and helpful model, although it could also be an excuse for sloppy thinking and an inability to see that there has been a sea change that undermines the expert's certainties. HR students have ground into them the risks of snap judgements in selection interviewing ('I can tell as soon as they come through the door') and there will always be a temptation for established managers to take short cuts on the basis of their assumed expertise without realising that the rules have been changed and they are now playing the wrong game.

WINDOW ON PRACTICE

David teaches a teacher-training course which has a mixture of students. Most are recent graduates with little working experience but well-developed study skills. A minority are a little older, usually mothers with growing children, who have experience, but whose study skills are rusty. He finds that the mature students tend to dominate discussion at the beginning of the course, as they constantly relate everything to their own experience and circumstances, while the recent graduates feel at a loss and put down. After a few weeks the younger students become more assertive in discussion as they gain confidence from their developing understanding, and the mature students are less dominant because they are beginning to question some of the taken-for-granted certainty of their earlier opinions. Mutual respect gradually develops and both groups learn from each other. David classifies the recent graduates as novices rapidly becoming advanced beginners and the mature students as competents who have to revert to being novices in order to move on to proficiency.

Job instruction

The first step in learning a skill is for the learner to understand the task and what needs to be done to produce a satisfactory performance. This provides the initial framework for, and explanation of, the actions that are to be developed later, although more information will be added to the framework as the training proceeds. The job of the teacher at this point is to decide how much understanding is needed to set up the training routine, especially if part methods are to be used for the later practice. Trainees are usually keen to get started with 'hands-on' experience, so long and detailed preliminaries are best avoided.

The second step is to practise the performance, so the instructor has to decide how to divide the task up into separate units or subroutines to aid learning. Typists begin their training by learning subroutines for each hand before combining them into routines for both hands together, but pianists spend very short periods of practice with one hand only. The reason for this seems to be that typists use their two hands in ways that are relatively independent of each other with the left always typing 'a' and the right always typing 'p', so that co-ordination of the hands is needed only to sequence the actions. In playing the piano there is a more complex integration of the actions performed by the two hands so that separate practice can impair rather than enhance later performance. A further aspect of learning to type is to practise short letter sequences that occur frequently, such as 'and', 'or', 'the', 'ing' and 'ion'. These can then be incorporated into the steadily increasing speed of the typist as the actions become automatic and reliable. The amateur typist will often transpose letters or hit the wrong key, writing 'trasnpose' instead of 'transpose' or 'hte' instead of 'the'. The skilled typist will rarely do this because the effect of the repeated drills during training will have made the subroutines not only automatic but also correct.

The third element is feedback, so that learners can compare their own performance with the required standard and see the progress they are making. The characteristics of good feedback are immediacy and accuracy. If the feedback comes immediately after the action, the trainee has the best chance of associating error with the part of the performance that caused it, whereas delayed feedback will demonstrate what was wrong, but the memory of what happened will have faded. If you are being taught to drive a car, one of the early lessons is changing gear. If you think you understand what the instructor tells you, you need to try it out straightaway, so that you have first the feedback of your own performance in seeing if you execute the manoeuvre effectively and then the feedback from the instructor, who screams in anguish before telling you what you did wrong. If you are learning photography you do not have that element of immediate feedback, so that you have to recall everything that took place in taking the photograph when you eventually receive the prints.

The second characteristic of feedback is that it should be as accurate as possible in the information it provides on the result and the performance. The driving instructor may say, 'That's fine', or may say, 'That was better than last time because you found the gear you were looking for, but you are still snatching. Try again and remember to ease it in.' The second comment provides a general indication of making progress, it provides an assessment of the performance and specific comment that should improve the next attempt.

The job instruction sequence

Preparation

The instructor will have two sets of objectives: organisational and behavioural. Organisational objectives specify the contribution to the business that the learner will make at the end of training. It will be general but necessary. If a company trains its own word processor operators and secretaries, for instance, it might be that the organisational objectives will be to teach people to word process and to transcribe from handwritten copy or dictating machine, but not to take shorthand. These are different from educational objectives, which focus on the trainee or student rather than on organisational needs, so that tutors in secretarial colleges are more likely to arrange training round what will be useful in a number of occupational openings. The instructor will need to work out organisational objectives which may or may not include broader educational features.

Behavioural objectives are specifically what the learner should be able to do when the training, or training phase, is complete. Organisational objectives for trainee word processor operators may be simply to ensure a constant supply of people able to type accurately and at reasonable speed. In behavioural terms that would be made more specific by setting standards for numbers of words to be typed to a predetermined level of accuracy per minute.

Activity 28.2

Think of a training experience involving learning how to *do* something that you are contemplating for yourself or for someone else in your organisation. Note down organisational objectives and behavioural objectives for the training.

Next the instructor will decide what learning methods to use. We have already seen that the main elements of job instruction are understanding, practice and feedback, so the instructor decides how much initial explanation is needed, and how many other explanations will be needed at different stages of the training, together with the form that is appropriate. Words alone may be enough, but audio-visual illustration and demonstration will probably be needed as well. There are rapid developments in computer-based training and interactive video that can provide frequent explanations and feedback on trainee performance.

Two questions about practice are to decide on the subroutines and any necessary simulation, like the working of a flight simulator in pilot training. Most feedback is by the instructor talking to the learner, but it may be necessary to provide greater accuracy or speed to the feedback by methods like television recording or photography. The most common method of job instruction is the *progressive part* method. This had its most comprehensive explanation by Douglas Seymour (1966). The task to be undertaken by the learner is broken down into a series of subroutines. The learner then practises routine 1, routine 2 and then 1 + 2.

The next step is to practise routine 3, 2 + 3 and 1 + 2 + 3, so that competence is built up progressively by practising a subroutine and then attaching it to the full task, which is constantly being practised with an increasing number of the different components included. The components are only practised separately for short periods before being assimilated, so there is no risk of fragmentary performance.

This only works if the job can be subdivided into components. Where this is not possible, *simplification* offers an alternative. In this method the task to be performed is kept as a whole, but reduced to its simplest form. Skilled performance is then reached by gradually increasing the complexity of the exercises. In cookery the learner begins with simple recipes and gradually develops a wider repertoire.

There are some specialised methods of memory training which can be listed here, as well as ways of training for acquiring perceptual skills. Both types of ability appear to be increasing in importance in organisational life.

The most familiar way of memorising is the *mnemonic* or *jingle*, wherein a simple formula provides the clue to a more comprehensive set of data. 'Laser' is much easier to remember than 'light amplification by stimulated emission of radiation'. If the initial letters are not easily memorable, the mnemonic is replaced by the jingle. The denseness of 'ROYGBIV' has led generations of school children to remember that 'Richard Of York Gave Battle In Vain' as a way of recalling the sequence of red, orange, yellow, green, blue, indigo and violet in the spectrum. 'Arthur Spits in Claude's Milk' is a rather less familiar way of remembering that there are five types of arthropod: Arthropods, Spiders, Insects, Crustaceans and Myriapods. One does have to be sure, however, both that the mnemonic or jingle will itself be remembered and that it will subsequently be possible to remember what is to be recalled.

Activity 28.3	What do the following sets of letters mean:

DERV, DFEE, DSS, RADAR, TINA LEA, UNESCO, UNPROFOR?

Apart from the obvious, why should anyone remember the phrase, 'Most Engineers Prefer Blondes'?

For some tasks the use of *rules* reduces the volume of material to be memorised. There are many fault-finding rules, for instance, where the repairer is taught to use a systematic series of rules. The stranded motorist who telephones the vehicle rescue service for assistance will probably be asked a first question, 'Have you run out of petrol?' The answer 'Yes' identifies the fault, while 'No' leads to the second question, 'Is there any spark?' so that the engineer who comes to help already has some areas of fault eliminated.

Deduction is a method that puts information into categories so that if something does not fit into one category the learner then uses deduction to conclude that it must belong in another. At the beginning of this chapter was the example of the office messenger remembering that invoices go to Mr Brown and cheques to Mrs Smith. If there was also a Ms Robinson, who received all sales enquiries, complaints, unsolicited sales promotion material, tax returns, questionnaires, applications for employment, and so on, the messenger would not need to remember what did go to Ms Robinson, but what did not: invoices to Mr Brown, cheques to Mrs Smith and everything else to Ms Robinson. Some interesting examples of using deduction in training are to be found in Belbin and Downs (1966).

For memorisation of information the *cumulative part* method is slightly, but significantly, different from the progressive part method already described in that the learner constantly practises the whole task, with each practice session adding an extra component. This is distinct from the progressive part method in which components are practised separately before being built into the whole. This can be especially useful if the more difficult material is covered first, as it will then get much more rehearsal than that coming later.

A method for the development of perceptual skills is *discrimination*, which requires the learner to distinguish between items that appear similar to the untrained eye or ear. In a rough-and-ready way it is the procedure followed by the birdwatcher or the connoisseur of wine. First the trainee compares two items which are clearly dissimilar and identifies the points of difference. Then other pairs are produced to be compared, with the differences gradually becoming less obvious. Discrimination can be aided by *cueing*, which helps the learner to identify particular features in the early attempts at discrimination by providing arrows or coloured sections. Some people start learning to type with the keys coloured according to whether they should be struck with the left or right hand, or even according to the particular finger which is appropriate. Gradually the cues are phased out as the learner acquires the competence to identify without them.

Magnification is a way of developing the capacity to distinguish small faults in a process or even small components in machinery. Material for examination is magnified at the beginning of training and then reduced back to normal as competence is acquired. Inspectors of tufted carpet start their training by being shown samples of poor tufting that have been produced using much larger material than normal. Later they examine normal material under a magnifying glass and eventually they are able to examine the normal product. A helpful discussion of the magnification method can be found in Holding (1965).

The various training methods to be used are put together in a training programme. This sets out both what the instructor is going to do and the progress the trainee is expected to make. Of critical importance here is pacing; how much material has to be taken in before practice begins, how long the practice period is before the learner is able to proceed to a new part, and how frequently progress is checked by the teacher. Individual trainees will each have their own rate at which they can proceed and will need differing levels of initial explanation and demonstration before practice can start. Training programmes require sufficient flexibility to accommodate the varying capacities that learners bring to their training.

A useful feature of the training programme is providing scope for learners to be involved in determining their own rate of progress and some self-discovery, to avoid spoon-feeding. At the outset trainees are so conscious of their dependency that all measures that build up confidence, independence and autonomy are welcome.

The instruction

When instructor and trainee meet for the first time there is a mutual appraisal. The process is basically 'getting to know you', but the exchanges are important, as the two people have to work together and the learner will be uncertain in an unfamiliar situation, and absolutely dependent upon the instructor. It is essential that learners feel confident in the instructor as someone skilled in the task that is to be learned and enthusiastic about teaching it to others. They will also be looking for reassurance about their own chances of success by seeking information about previous trainees.

The explanation of procedure will follow as soon as the meeting phase has lasted long enough. Here is the first feature of pacing that was mentioned as part of preparation. There has to be enough time for meeting to do its work, but long, drawn-out introductions lead to impatience and wanting to get started.

The procedure is the programme, with the associated details of timing, rate of progress, training methods and the general overview of what is to happen. The most important point to the trainee is obviously the end. When does one 'graduate'? What happens then? Can it be quicker? Do many people fail? What happens to them? The instructor is, of course, more interested in the beginning of the programme rather than the end, but it is only with a clear grasp of the end that the trainee can concentrate on the beginning. Clarifying the goal reinforces the commitment to learning.

With long-running training programmes where an array of skills has to be mastered, the point of graduation may be too distant to provide an effective goal so that the tutor establishes intermediate goals: 'By Friday you will be able to . . .'. This phase benefits from illustration: a timetable, a chart of the average learning curve, samples of work by previous trainees – all make more tangible the prospect of success and more complete the mental picture of the operating framework that the learner is putting together. It is also helpful to ensure that the explanation does not become mechanical, like the tourist guide at a stately home. If the instructor has explained the procedure so often that it has become automatic, it is no longer the vivid stimulus to learning that is so necessary. It is a time for as much interchange as possible, with questions, reiteration, further explanation, clarification and confirmation.

<table>
<tr><td>

WINDOW ON PRACTICE

</td><td>

Repetition does not necessarily make material automatic. Acker Bilk played 'Stranger on a Shore' thousands of times, and many excellent teachers re-use exactly the same material repeatedly. The Scottish playwright James Barrie studied medicine in his youth and took with him to university a set of verbatim anatomy notes

</td></tr>
</table>

that had been compiled by his father thirty years earlier. His father said the lectures were so interesting that it would be better if he did not have to make notes. As Barrie attended the lectures, he was astonished to find that little had changed. At one point the lecturer took hold of a gas bracket and related an anecdote. On looking at his father's notes he saw, 'At this point Professor X took hold of a gas bracket and told this story . . .'.

The task that the trainee has to perform first is demonstrated and explained. The purpose is not to display the teacher's advanced skills, but to provide a basis for the learner's first, tentative (and possibly incorrect) attempts. The demonstration is thus done without any flourishes, and as slowly as possible, because the teacher is not only demonstrating skill but also using skill to convince the trainees that they can do the job. Accompanying the demonstration, an explanation gives reasons for the different actions being used and describing what is being done so that the learners can watch analytically. Their attention is drawn to features they might overlook, the sequence of actions is recounted and key points are mentioned.

The task must be presented to the learner in its simplest possible form, with a straightforward, unfussy, accurate demonstration accompanied by an explanation which emphasises correct sequence, reasons why, features that might be overlooked in the demonstration and the key points that lead to success. Where possible, the tutor should not mention what not to do. Errors can be dealt with later; at this stage the direction should be on what to do.

The presentation is followed, and perhaps interrupted, by questions from the learners on what they did not follow or cannot remember. The success of this stage will depend on the skill of the instructor in going through the opening stages of the encounter. Many trainees are reluctant to question because they feel that the question reveals their ignorance, which will be judged as stupidity. The experienced instructor can stimulate the questioning and confirming by the trainees by putting questions to them. This is effective only when done well, as there is the obvious risk of inhibiting people by confronting them with their lack of understanding. The most unfortunate type of questions are those which cross-examine:

'Now, tell me the three main functions of this apparatus.'
'Can anyone remember which switch we press first?'

Little better are the vague requests for assent:

'Do you understand?'

a series of events. A presentation to an industrial tribunal often follows this pattern.

- **Known to unknown, or simple to complex**. The speaker starts with a brief review of what the audience already knows or can easily understand and then develops to what they do not yet know or cannot yet understand. The logic of this method is to ground the audience in something they can handle so that they can make sense of the unfamiliar. This is the standard method of organising teaching sessions.
- **Problem to solution** is almost the exact opposite of simple to complex. A problem is presented and a solution follows. The understanding of the audience is again grounded, but this time grounded in anxiety that the speaker is about to relieve.
- **Comparison** is a method of organisation which compares one account with another. Selling usually follows this path, as the new is compared with the old.

Whatever the method of organisation for the material, the main body will always contain a number of key thoughts or ideas. This is what the speaker is trying to plant in the minds of the audience: not just facts, which are inert, but the ideas which facts may well illustrate and clarify. The idea that inflation is dangerously high is only illustrated by the fact that it is at a particular figure in a particular month.

The ideas in a presentation can be helpfully linked together by a device that will help audience members to remember them and to grasp their interdependence. One method is to enshrine the ideas in a story. If the story is recalled, the thoughts are recalled with it, as they are integral to the structure. The classic examples of this are the New Testament parables, but every play, novel or film uses the same method. Another method is to use key words to identify the points that are being made, especially if they have an alliterative or mnemonic feature, like 'People Produce Prosperity'. In a lecture it is common to provide a framework for ideas by using a drawing or system model to show the interconnection of points.

Facts, by giving impact, keep together the framework of ideas that the speaker has assembled. They clarify and give dimension to what is being said. The danger is to use too many, so that the audience are overwhelmed by facts and figures which begin to bemuse them. If the presentation is to be accompanied by a hand-out, facts may be usefully contained in that, so that they can be referred to later, without the audience having to remember them.

Humour is the most dangerous of all aids to the speaker. If the audience laughs at a funny story, the speaker will be encouraged and may feel under less tension, but how tempting to try again and end up 'playing for laughs'. Laughter is a most seductive human reaction, but too many laughs are even more dangerous than too many facts. What will the audience remember – the joke, or what the joke was intended to illustrate? Attempted humour is also dangerous for the ineffective comedian. If you tell what you think is a funny story and no one laughs, you have made a fool of yourself (at least in your own eyes) and risk floundering.

Very few people speak effectively without notes. And although there is a tendency to marvel at those who can, relying solely on memory risks missing something out, getting a fact wrong or drying up completely. Notes follow the pattern of organisation you have established, providing discipline and limiting the tendency to ramble. It is both irritating and unhelpful for members of an audience to cope with a speaker who wanders off down a blind alley, yet this is very common. When an amusing anecdote pops up in your brain, it can be almost irresistible to share it.

There are two basic kinds of notes: headlines or a script. Headlines are probably the most common, with main points underlined and facts listed beneath. Sometimes there will also be a marginal note about an anecdote or other type of illustration. The alternative, the script, enables the speaker to try out the exact wording, phrases and pauses to achieve the greatest effect. The script will benefit from some marking or arrangement that will help you to find your place again as your eyes constantly flick from the page to the audience and back again. This can be underlining or using a highlighter.

There are many variations of these basic methods, so that one approach is to use varying line length, while another is to use rows of dots to indicate pause or emphasis.

Some people like to have their notes on small cards, so that they are unobtrusive, but this is difficult if the notes are more than headlines. Standard A4 paper should present no problem, if the notes are not stapled, are well laid out and can be handled discreetly. Never forget to number the pages or cards, as the next time you speak they may slip off your lap moments before you are due to begin.

Summary propositions

28.1 A useful classification of types of learning is CRAMP: comprehension, reflex learning, attitude development, memory training, procedural learning.

28.2 Selecting the right approach to learning is helped by identifying the learner as being at one of these stages: novice, advanced beginner, competent, proficient or expert.

28.3 Alternative methods in job instruction are: progressive part, simplification, mnemonics or jingles, rules, deduction, cumulative part, discrimination and magnification.

References

Belbin, E. and Belbin, R.M. (1972) *Problems in Adult Retraining*. London: Heinemann.

Belbin, E. and Downs, S. (1966) 'Teaching and paired associates', *Journal of Occupational Psychology*, Vol. 40, pp. 67–74.

Bloom, B.S. (1956) *Taxonomy of Educational Objectives: The cognitive domain*. London: Longman.

Downs, S. and Perry, P. (1987) *Helping Adults to Become Better Learners*. Sheffield: Manpower Services Commission.

Dreyfus, H.L., Dreyfus, S.E. and Athanasion, T. (1986) *Mind over Machine: The power of human intuition and expertise in the era of the computer*, New York: Free Press.

Fandt, P.M. (1994) *Management Skills: Practice and Experience*. St Paul, MN: West Publishing.

Holding, D.H. (1965) *Principles of Training: Research in Applied Learning*, Oxford: Pergamon.

ITRU (Industrial Training Research Unit) (1976) *Choose an Effective Style: A self-instructional approach to the teaching of skills*. Cambridge: ITRU Publications.

Quinn, R.E. (1988) *Beyond Rational Management: Mastering the paradoxes and competing demands of high performance*. San Francisco: Jossey-Bass.

Quinn, R.E., Faerman, S.R., Thompson, M.P. and McGrath, M.R. (1990) *Becoming a Master Manager*. New York: John Wiley.

Seymour, W.D. (1966) *Industrial Skills*. London: Pitman.

Truelove, S. (1992) *Handbook of Training and Development*. Oxford: Blackwell.

Winfield, I. (1979) *Learning to Teach Practical Skills*. London: Kogan Page.

Part V
Case study problem

Micropower is a rapidly growing computer software firm, specialising in tailor-made solutions for business. Increasingly training for other businesses in their own and other software packages has occupied the time of the consultants. This it sees as a profitable route for the future and such training is now actively sold to clients. Consultants both sell and carry out the training. As an interim measure, to cope with increasing demand, the firm is now recruiting some specialist trainers, but the selling of the training is considered to be an integral part of the consultant's role.

Micropower has just issued a mission statement which accentuates 'the supply of and support for sophisticated computer solutions', based on a real under-standing of business needs. The firm considers that it needs to be flexible in achieving this and has decided that multiskilling is the way forward.

All consultants need to sell solutions and training at all levels, and be excellent analysts, designers and trainers. Some 200 consultants are now employed; most have a degree in IT and most joined the firm initially because of their wish to specialise in the technical aspects of software development, and they spent some years almost entirely in an office-based position before moving into a customer contact role. A smaller proportion were keen to concentrate on systems analysis, and were involved in customer contact from the start.

In addition there are 300 software designers and programmers who are primar-ily office based and rarely have any customer contact. It is from this group that new consultants are appointed. Programmers are promoted to two levels of designer and those in the top level of designer may then, if their performance level is high enough, be promoted to consultant. There is some discontent amongst designers that promotion means having to move into a customer contact role, and there are a growing number who seek more challenge, higher pay and status, but who wish to avoid customer contact. Another repercussion of the promotion framework is that around a quarter of the current consultants are not happy in their role. They are consultants because they valued promotion more than doing work that they enjoyed. Some have found the intense customer contact very stressful, feel they lack the appropriate skills, are not particularly comfortable with their training role and are unhappy about the increasing need to 'sell'.

Required

1 What immediate steps could Micropower take to help the consultants, particularly those who feel very unhappy, perform well and feel more comfortable in their new roles?

2 In the longer term how can Micropower reconcile its declared aim of multiskilling with a career structure which meets both organisational and employee needs?

3 What other aspects of human resource strategy would support and integrate with the development strategy of multiskilling?

4 Micropower wishes to develop a competency profile for the consultant role. How would you recommend that the firm progress this, and how might the profile be used in the widest possible manner in the organisation?

Part V
Examination questions

Undergraduate introductory

1 Outline the nature and purpose of National Vocational Qualifications. What has been their impact so far?

2 Discuss the advantages and disadvantages of on-the-job training and development compared with off-job training and development. In which circumstances might each be more appropriate?

Undergraduate finals

3 Identify the factors which determine 'skill need' in an organisation. Discuss how managers ensure that workers develop the skills and knowledge necessary for their roles within organisations.

4 What practical steps would you take if you were the human resource manager in an organisation wanting to introduce training for people to enable them to manage their own careers more effectively?

Masters

5 What is a career, how is it changing and how should it be managed?

6 Choose one of the following: (a) career planning workshops; (b) mentoring; (c) succession planning. Define it and briefly describe the forms it can take in an organisation. Discuss the criteria on which its success can be evaluated and consider whether some criteria are (i) more appropriate, and (ii) more easily measured, than others.

Professional

7 Explain to a line manager the value of coaching as a way of developing a subordinate.

8 'Employment development should be handed over to line managers.' Summarise your views on this statement.

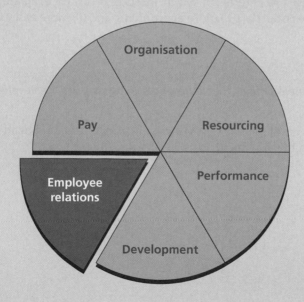

EMPLOYEE RELATIONS

All jobs have the potential to be alienating, making the job holder indifferent or hostile both to the job and to the management, who are seen as responsible for obliging the employee to continue doing the job.

Involvement is largely concerned with preventing or alleviating that type of alienation. Because the issues are often collective, concerning a number of people in a similar situation, many procedures incorporate the recognition of trade unions and ways of making that recognition productive for both parties. Working safely in a healthy environment is included here as there is a legal obligation to involve employee representatives in monitoring management arrangements for safe working. Safe working is ultimately a matter of employees working safely because they understand and follow the practices that are provided for their personal safety.

Whether unions are recognised or not, there are always points of disagreement between managers and the managed and here we have two rather 'heavy' words: grievance and discipline. Few managers like to participate in these processes, but they are very interesting and provide the opportunity of major change and improvement for the manager who handles them well.

Chapter 29   Strategic aspects of employee relations

When we surveyed the activities and priorities of HR specialists in the early 1980s, there was no doubt about the pre-eminence of employee relations as being the activity on which they spent most of their time and as being most central to the human resource function (Mackay and Torrington 1986, pp. 149, 161). Only in recruitment and selection did they feel that they had a slightly greater degree of discretion and scope in decision making (pp. 146–8). Twenty years on the situation has wholly changed. A recent survey of HR managers showed that employee relations issues are now placed well down the agenda in terms of their current and perceived future importance (IRS 2000, pp. 5–11). The emphasis is overwhelmingly on recruitment, staff retention, development and performance management, along with the HR implications associated with the introduction of new technology. The main reason appears to be a widespread perception that employee relations in UK organisations are in a healthy state. The 1998 Workplace Employment Relations (WERS) Survey found that 80 per cent of HR managers believed their own organisations' employment relations climate to be either 'good' or 'very good', while only 2 per cent saw it as being poor – the same proportion who reported industrial action as having taken place during the previous year (Cully *et al.* 1999, pp. 125 and 276–7). Similar findings were reported in the IRS survey (IRS 2000, pp. 10–11), suggesting that the pressures placed on many workforces to become more efficient and flexible are not leading to overt forms of conflict. Employee relations is not therefore seen as being an organisational problem. Interestingly the WERS Survey also found that a majority of employees were positive about the employee relations climate in their own organisations; although theirs was a less enthusiastic endorsement (21 per cent characterised the climate as being 'poor' or 'very poor'). Employee relations activities may not be as significant to HR practitioners as they once were, but they remain important. A good employee relations climate is not created or maintained automatically; ongoing action on the part of managers is required.

Activity 29.1	What do you think are the main reasons for the fall in the perceived importance of employee relations activities? What would need to happen for the position to be reversed?

There are several different perspectives from which to view the management of employee relations. Some see it primarily as being about managing conflict in organisations, resolving the clash of economic interests that will inevitably arise between employer and employee. For others emphasis is placed on corporate governance and the formal constitutional rules (or lack of them) which determine pay and conditions, employment policy and the distribution of power within organisations. A third approach, which we adopt in this chapter, involves viewing the management of employee relations primarily as comprising a set of choices about the extent and nature of employee involvement. The key questions are as follows:

■ How far should employees be involved in decision making?
■ Should their involvement be direct or through representatives such as trade unions?
■ What form should the involvement take?
■ At what organisational level should the involvement take place?
■ Which issues should be the subject of involvement?

The answers vary from workplace to workplace, while in some managers have limited room for manoeuvre if they are to avoid a deterioration in employee relations and/or their position in competitive labour markets. It is possible to run a successful business with minimal employee participation of any kind, but this is often not the best option. A strong case can be put for a substantial degree of worker involvement both directly and through the actions of legitimate representatives.

We begin this chapter with a historical survey of the evolving context for employee relations, looking at ways in which this has affected the actions of employers. We go on to look at the main alternative forms of collective and individual employee involvement. Finally we consider some of the differences that are apparent between employee relations practices in different countries. A more detailed treatment of key legal and operational issues follows in Chapters 30, 31 and 32.

Historical development of employee relations in the UK

Surveys of modern employee relations history usually start with the birth of the trade union movement in the nineteenth century in response to the poor pay levels and working conditions associated with the early industrialisation. The early trade unions were ineffective and seldom lasted, but by 1880 the British trade union movement had established itself and taken on a form that has not been much altered since. Not only were the methods of industrial action set, so too were the subtle class distinctions between the craft and general unions.

The twentieth century

Through the first half of the twentieth century trade unions, employers' associations and the various institutions of collective bargaining developed steadily. The General Strike of 1926 was a trauma from which two main lessons were learned. The union movement learned that a general strike would bring no miracles of social change in a British context and those who had so implacably opposed it, particularly in the employer ranks, learned that 'beating' the strike did not cause the trade unions to wither and die, even though they suffered considerable losses in membership, funds and morale.

Trade union fortunes revived considerably in the years following the Second

World War. Nationalisation of much British industry led to a situation in which the terms and conditions of most UK employees were determined at national level through institutions of collective bargaining. The same was true in industries which remained largely in private hands. Here negotiations to set nationally agreed rates of pay and standard, industry-wide working conditions were negotiated between employers' associations and trade unions.

With little protection being available from the law, employees naturally looked to their unions to represent their interests at work. The ability of a union or group of unions to do so rested on the muscle they could wield in negotiations. The number of members was significant, as was their willingness to become involved in sustained industrial action if and when agreement could not be reached. In around a fifth of workplaces unions became sufficiently powerful to be able to enforce a 'closed shop' in which membership of the appropriate union was a condition of employment. Dismissal from the union meant dismissal from the job. Total trade union membership remained steady in the post-war years at around 10 million. This represented over 40 per cent of the total UK workforce and ensured that collective forms of representation dominated the employee relations scene.

The 1960s

By the 1960s British managers often took a rather defeatist attitude towards the organisation of employment where trade unions were recognised. Bit by bit more was conceded to the unions which, in many organisations, had effected a vice-like grip on production around which nothing could be altered. Restrictive or protective practices were deeply entrenched. This coincided with bad news in the product market. Exports were slipping and the economic growth of other countries was outstripping that of Britain. Productivity bargaining became fashionable as managements sought initiatives with trade unions that had previously seemed impracticable. A very visible symptom of worsening employee relations was the number of days lost as a result of strike action. It averaged 3.5 million a year in the 1960s, reaching nearly seven million in 1969.

A Royal Commission was set up to make proposals for change regarding trade unions and employers' associations. It was chaired by Lord Donovan and the report is always known as the Donovan Report. Here it was argued that the main source of poor employee relations was the nature of the collective bargaining system. National agreements were frequently inadequate as a framework for employment relations as their formality and precision was shadowed by a series of informal, imprecise arrangements that governed what actually happened on the shop-floor. It was these informal understandings that needed attention in order to improve the disorder of the workplace. They should be reviewed and a greater degree of formality introduced so that everyone knew more reliably where they stood. The recommendation was for a more decentralised approach to collective bargaining. The national framework should remain, but more should be determined at plant level by managers and shop stewards.

Activity 29.2 The Donovan analysis drew a distinction between the formal system of industrial relations, which was a series of agreements and procedures agreed and organised at the level of a complete industry, and the informal system, which was the actual behaviour of managers, shop stewards and employees.

To what extent has the usefulness of that distinction altered in the period since 1968, and what has caused the change?

The 1970s

The 1970s saw a deterioration in the industrial relations climate in many organisations. The state of industrial relations also became one of the major political issues of the day, being responsible in large part for the fall of governments in 1974 and 1979. Productivity continued to be lacklustre compared with the rates being achieved in other economies such as Germany and Japan. Competitors were able to produce goods of superior quality in greater numbers and at lower prices, putting UK-based managers and employees under greater pressure to improve their own performance levels. The economic climate also deteriorated as oil prices rose exponentially and fuelled inflation.

In a bid to put downward pressure on inflation rates and to improve productivity, governments started to intervene more actively in employee relations matters than they had previously. The major tool of inflation control that was used was the incomes policy, which sought to control income growth by statute. Norms were set in negotiations carried out at national level between the government, employers' representatives and trade unions. In some years these were adhered to, while in others (notably in 1978) the agreements broke down in the face of industrial action.

Attempts were made to reduce the number of strikes by making collective agreements enforceable in the courts, by setting up ACAS (the Advisory, Conciliation and Arbitration Service) and by introducing new legal remedies for badly treated workers in the form of unfair dismissal and anti-discrimination laws. The first measure, contained in the Industrial Relations Act 1971, was made wholly ineffective by the refusal of most employers and trade unions to accept it. The Act also set out to contain collective bargaining and to control trade unions. The resistance of unions was fierce and the reaction of managements generally apathetic or hostile. Within four years the Act was repealed. The other measures have had positive long-term effects, but did not prevent the general employee relations climate from worsening during the 1970s.

By the late 1970s most industrial disputes concerned pay deals and disagreements over productivity agreements deemed necessary to finance them. Union membership climbed substantially during the decade, reaching a peak of 13.5 million in 1979. This represented over 50 per cent of the total UK workforce. Collective bargaining was now less likely to occur at national level, but it remained the means by which pay and conditions were determined for a clear majority of UK employees.

The last months of 1978 and the first of 1979 have become known 'as the winter of discontent', and are generally acknowledged to be of great historical significance for both employee relations and politics in the UK. A series of bitter strikes occurred involving first private sector workers, and then public sector workers, over pay. Each was eventually settled but only after employers agreed to pay rises that were well in excess of the 5 per cent norm set by government ministers seeking to reduce inflation. In itself this was damaging to the authority of the Callaghan Government, but the situation was made worse by the direct results of some public sector strikes which resulted in rubbish not being collected, grit not being spread on roads and, in one case, corpses not being removed from a hospital's wards. A total of 39 million working days were lost as a result of strike action in 1978 and 1979 (Taylor 1993, p. 380). These events led directly to the election of the Thatcher Government in May 1979, with radical consequences for UK employee relations.

The 1980s

The 1980s saw a sharp reversal in the position of trade unions. They started the decade directly representing over half the employees in the country, having considerable influence on the formation of government policy and dominating the employee relations agenda in most workplaces of any size. By 1990 membership had fallen by a quarter and was to continue declining for a further 10 years, unions were frozen out of government decision making and no longer enjoyed the influence they had wielded in the 1970s. The context of employee relations thus changed considerably during these years.

Several causes of this situation can be identified. First, there was the shift in employment from manufacturing and extraction industries to services. Economic recession led to the closure of thousands of manufacturing plants and the loss of millions of jobs. In their place came jobs in the retail, catering and leisure sectors which had no tradition of union organisation or of any type of collective employee involvement. Many of the new jobs were part-time or temporary, which are also associated with low levels of union membership. Persistently high unemployment made people less inclined to 'rock the boat' for fear of losing their jobs, while relatively low inflation made them less likely to look to unions as a means of protecting their incomes. The position of trade unions was further weakened by government action. A series of new laws came on to the statute books throughout the 1980s which served to reduce both their freedom of manoeuvre and their capacity to sustain industrial action. Closed shops were outlawed, as was secondary action, so that it was no longer possible to spread a dispute to suppliers or customers of the employer concerned. New regulations were introduced to determine the way that trade unions governed themselves and it became necessary to hold a secret postal ballot before embarking on any form of industrial action. Restrictions on picketing were introduced and effective means found of enforcing all the new laws. In addition the Thatcher Government regularly displayed its resolve to fight with and beat any unions which sought to challenge its authority. This resulted in conspicuous defeats for trade unions in strikes such as those undertaken by the miners (1984–5) and newspaper print workers (1986) which further damaged their cause.

The 1980s can thus be characterised as being a revolutionary decade in UK employment relations. By the end trade unions were no longer the dominant force that they had been. Privatisation and recession ensured that national-level collective bargaining was largely restricted to a shrunken public sector, requiring managers to adopt new ways of managing employee relations in their organisations.

Activity 29.3 To what extent do you agree with the proposition that the 1980s assault on trade union influence was either necessary or desirable as a means of halting relative economic decline?

The 1990s

The shift away from manufacturing industry and towards services continued during the 1990s. The manufacturing sector itself became less dominated by large plants and increasingly reliant on new technologies as a means of competing internationally. By 1998 47 per cent of UK workplaces employing over 25 people stated that they employed no union members at all, while unions were recognised in only 45 per cent of cases (Cully *et al.* 1999, pp. 87 and 92). Trade union membership had fallen to 7.8 million. Employee relations thus became characterised by a far greater variety of forms than had been the case throughout much of the century:

> What we find, therefore, is a marked split between the public sector, where traditional industrial relations appears to have survived, albeit with some adaptations, and a private sector which, with the exception of a declining set of large establishments, is predominantly non-union and without worker representation.... Management appears to be firmly in the driving seat, controlling the direction of employment relations. (Guest 2001, p. 99)

In both the union and non-union sectors, the 1990s saw an increased interest in employee relations initiatives which did not rely on the presence of trade unions. Innovations in the field of employee communication were made possible by the development of email and intranet sites, while team briefing and employee attitude surveys became more common. Decision making was decentralised to business units, allowing more employees to have a direct influence in determining practice in their own areas of responsibility. In some cases decentralisation went further, with individual employees or teams of employees being given the autonomy to decide for themselves how their work was to be organised. The proportion of employees working on individually agreed contracts rose as did the numbers working on a subcontracted basis. For many pay became increasingly variable. The annual rise, traditionally negotiated by unions, became less significant than increases resulting from assessments of personal performance or those linked to the organisations' profitability. Steadily, the significance of the collective employment relationship declined while that of the individual employment relationship grew. In a minority of organisations negotiation and consultation with trade unions remained the dominant feature of employee relations practice, in the others unions were either of marginal importance or wholly irrelevant.

The Blair Government came to office in 1997 promising 'fairness not favours' to the trade union movement. It left in place the vast majority of the legislative measures introduced by its Conservative predecessors, accepting that collective bargaining should not be the means used to determine pay and conditions in organisations where trade unions were not strong. However, measures were introduced in 1999 to ensure that collective bargaining did occur where it was clearly demonstrated that this was the will of a majority of employees. This legislation is described in detail in Chapter 30.

Current trends

The first years of the twenty-first century have seen a continuation of established trends in many respects, but also some changes which may turn out to be significant. Most interesting are reports of a reversal in union membership decline and increases in the number of new collective agreements being signed by employers.

After nearly twenty years of year-on-year decline, the total number of trade union members in the UK grew again in 1999 and 2000 by over 100,000 (see Labour Market Trends 2000). However, despite this growth, the level of union density (that is, the proportion of the workforce who are union members) continued to fall slightly because of the large number of new jobs being created. It is too early to tell whether or not this will be a long-term trend, but the trade union movement can certainly take some encouragement. In addition to the successful attraction of more members, Gall and Hammond (2000) report that the number of formal recognition agreements between employers and unions has also begun to increase again. The likely reason is fear on the part of employers that they will be forced to recognise their trade unions under the terms of the Employment Relations Act 1999 if they do not do so voluntarily first.

A number of possible reasons for the new trends can be identified aside from legal changes. First it can be argued that trade unions and their leaders have successfully regained a positive media image. Whereas they used to be commonly portrayed as out of date and a detrimental influence, they now come across as professional and constructive. Second, we can point to relatively low levels of unemployment and to growing skills shortages, and suggest that these are causing employers to take action aimed at improving their records on recruitment and retention. In industries where unions are relatively strong and where collective bargaining is desired by employees, it makes sense for employers to move towards some form of recognition.

A third explanation focuses on the new outlook and policy stances that have been adopted by the trade unions themselves after years of suffering decline. Central here is an acceptance of the principles associated with 'business unionism' which stress ways in which unions can work with employers, rather than against them, for mutual benefit. Instead of being adversaries unions increasingly want to be seen as partners, helping employers to achieve their business goals by 'adding value' to their operations. Following a series of seminars held in 1999 to define 'tomorrow's union', the TUC adopted 'six principles of partnership' which encompass the new approach. Central is a commitment to serve the interests of businesses in which they are recognised. In return they seek from the employers genuine involvement, openness and respect, along with a commitment to promote employment security and the quality of working life as far as is practicable. In short, they are inviting good employers to work with them as a means of achieving greater long-term business success (see IRS 1999a).

Activity 29.4

A central idea behind the business union approach is the notion that employees will be more likely to join a trade union if their employer has first agreed to recognise it. The approach therefore involves 'recruiting' employers as a means of increasing membership.

What success would you consider such an approach enjoys in practice?

Collective employee involvement

Management always needs the collective consent of its employees: it also needs a mandate to manage. This can partly be delivered by trade union recognition, but other approaches are also available. The recent changes in union membership, employment legislation and fluctuating unemployment levels have provided academic analysts with the challenge of describing how employee relations strategies have changed. We still lack a full explanation, but one of the best-known approaches has been the attempt of Purcell and Sisson (1983) to categorise management styles in industrial relations. These are summarised in Table 29.1 and the key distinguishing feature is a collective view of the workforce.

This is a useful set of categories, although some organisations do not fit easily into any one of them. Most large, long-established companies will be in one of the last three; most public sector organisations will be in category 4; and many of the newer businesses will be in some version of category 2.

| Activity 29.5 | Which of the five categories in Table 29.1 most closely fits your establishment? Does the category vary for different groups of employees? |

Taking a strictly managerial view of trade unions and their recognition, the interest is the degree to which recognition will deliver collective consent to a general framework of rules and guidelines within which management and employees operate. Collective consent implies the acceptance of a situation, while agreement has the more positive connotation of commitment following some degree of initiative in bringing the situation into existence. We are not, therefore, necessarily describing active employee participation in managerial decision making. The range is wider, and includes the variety of circumstances in which employees consent collectively to managerial authority, so long as they find it acceptable.

Table 29.1 Categories of management styles in employee relations

Style	Characteristics
Traditional	Fire-fighting approach. Employee relations not important until there is trouble. Low pay. Hostile to trade unions. Authoritarian. Typical in small, owner-managed businesses.
Paternalist	Unions regarded as unnecessary because of employer's enlightenment. High pay. Concentration on encouraging employee identification with business objectives.
Consultative	Union participation encouraged through recognition. Problem-solving, informal approach to employee relations. Emphasis on two-way communications.
Constitutional	Similar to consultative, but emphasis on formal agreements to regulate relationship between two powerful protagonists.
Opportunistic	Large company devolving responsibility for employee relations to subsidiaries, with no common approach but emphasis on unit profitability.

Source: J. Purcell and K. Sisson (1983) 'Strategies and practice in the management of industrial relations', in G.S. Bain (ed.), *Industrial Relations in Britain*, pp. 112–18. Oxford: Blackwell.

employee attitudes or to improved organisational performance. The claim is nonetheless persuasive intuitively, and can explain the growth in direct involvement initiatives over recent years.

How far do you think that your own work performance is/would be affected by the presence of individual employee involvement initiatives at your workplace? What about your level of commitment to the organisation?

The major forms of direct involvement used in the UK are team briefing, the publication of company news sheets (often now web based), quality circles, suggestion schemes and attitude surveys. Team working is less common but has generated considerable interest among researchers because it involves individual workers, together with their colleagues, exercising substantial control over their own areas of work. It can therefore be characterised as the most far-reaching form of individual employee involvement.

Team briefing

Team briefing is an initiative that attempts to do a number of different things simultaneously. It provides authoritative information at regular intervals, so that people know what is going on, the information is geared to achievement of production targets and other features of organisational objectives, it is delivered face to face to provide scope for questions and clarification, and it emphasises the role of supervisors and line managers as the source of information:

> They are often used to cascade information or managerial messages throughout the organisation. The teams are usually based round a common production or service area, rather than an occupation, and usually comprise between four and fifteen people. The leader of the team is usually the manager or supervisor of the section and should be trained in the principles and skills of how to brief. The meetings last for no more than 30 minutes, and time should be left for questions from employees. Meetings should be held at least monthly or on a regular pre-arranged basis.
> (Holden 1997, p. 624)

With goodwill and managerial discipline, team briefing can be a valuable contributor to employee involvement, as it deals in that precious commodity, information. Traditionally, there has perhaps been a managerial view that people doing the work are not interested in anything other than the immediate and short term and that the manager's status partly rests on knowing what others do not know. For this reason all the managers and supervisors in the communications chain have to be committed to making it a success, as well as having the training that Holden refers to above. Team briefing gets easier once it is established as a regular event. The first briefing will probably go very well and the second will be even better. It is important that management enthusiasm and commitment do not flag just as the employees are getting used to the process.

During economic recessions there is a boost to the team briefing process because so many managements have so much bad news to convey. When you are losing money and profitability, there is a great incentive to explain to the workforce exactly how grim the situation is, so that they do not look for big pay rises.

Whatever the economic climate, it continues to be used widely and was found to operate in a majority of organisations featured in the 1998 Workplace Employment Relations Survey.

Quality circles

Originating in Japanese firms, quality circles comprise small groups of employees (10–15 maximum) who meet regularly to generate ideas aimed at improving the quality of products and services and of organisational productivity. They can also be used as problem-solving groups and as a means by which employee opinion is transmitted to senior management. Some quality circles consist of staff who work together within a team or organisational function, others are cross-functional and focus on interdepartmental issues. They can form part of total quality management approaches such as those we assessed in Chapter 17:

> These sorts of practice have several objectives, such as to increase the stock of ideas within an organisation, to encourage co-operative relations at work, and to legitimise change. These practices are predicated on the assumption that employees are recognised as *a* (if not *the*) major source of competitive advantage for organisations, a source whose ideas have been ignored in the past or who have been told that 'they are not paid to think'. (Marchington 2001, p. 235)

Not only, therefore, are quality circles a potential source of useful ideas for improving systems and saving costs. They also give people a welcome opportunity to contribute their thoughts and experience. A general positive impact on employee attitudes should thus result.

News sheets

Another common form of employee involvement occurs through the regular publication of in-house journals or news sheets either in paper or electronic form. On one level they simply provide a means by which information concerning finances, policy and proposed change can be transmitted by managers to employees. This is a limited form of employee involvement which does little more than improve the extent to which employees are informed about what is going on elsewhere in their organisations. This will engender a perception of greater involvement and belonging, but does not directly involve employees in any type of decision making. For that to occur the news sheet must be interactive in some way. It may, for example, be used as a means by which employees are consulted about new initiatives, or may provide a forum through which complaints and ideas are voiced.

Attitude surveys

Regular surveys of employee opinion are very useful from a management point of view, particularly where there are no unions present to convey to management an honest picture of morale and commitment in the organisation. In order to be effective (that is, honest) responses must be anonymous, individuals stating only which department they work in so that interdepartmental comparisons can be made. It also makes sense to ask the same questions in the same format each time a survey is carried out, so that changes in attitude and/or responses to initiatives can be tracked over time.

The major problems with attitude surveys are associated with situations in which they reveal serious problems which are then not properly addressed. This can easily lead to cynicism and even anger on the part of the workforce. The result is a poorer employee relations climate than would have been the case had no survey taken place. The same is true of suggestion schemes. It is counter-productive to involve employees if their contribution is subsequently ignored.

Team working

Team working is a direct descendant of the concept of autonomous working groups, which had their highest profile in the Volvo plant at Kalmar (now closed down), and a rather vague movement of the 1960s, called Quality of Working Life (QWL). At Volvo there were the twin aims of improving the quality of working life and enhancing productivity. The QWL was directed mainly at making life more tolerable, as the title implies, and it is difficult to see what impact it had. More recently team working has become more comprehensive in its approach and its objectives. It is very fully explained in the work of Buchanan (1993; Buchanan and McCalman 1989).

Team working aims to focus work activity among small groups of about a dozen members, who are mutually supportive and who operate with minimal supervision. Management sets performance targets (often after consultation) and allocates tasks, but it is for the team itself to decide exactly how these are to be achieved. The team organises its own activities, appoints its own leaders and works out for itself how to overcome problems. Team working can thus be characterised as a form of worker control, even though it operates within heavily prescribed limits. Managers refrain from giving day-to-day supervision, but are on hand to give advice or to give more direct assistance where necessary. Disciplining staff, for example, is a task carried out by managers and not by team members. Team working is often associated with situations in which several regionally based teams compete with each other to meet or exceed performance targets. Team-based remuneration then accounts for a proportion of the total pay received.

International perspectives

Employee relations, more than other areas of human resource management practice, varies considerably from country to country. Although some analysts believe that there has been a degree of convergence in recent years in response to increased global competition and new technologies, it is clear that substantial differences remain. In important respects different countries have witnessed different responses to the same environmental pressures (see Bamber and Lansbury 1998 for a summary of these debates).

Comparative studies undertaken in the industrialised countries reveal the continued effect of different industrial relations traditions on contemporary practice. They also identify the importance of historical experience and institutional differences in explaining the observed variations. The major dimensions across which national systems vary are as follows:

■ high union membership v. low union membership;
■ single-employer bargaining v. multi-employer bargaining;

■ interventionist government role v. non-interventionist role;
■ adversarial tradition v. consensual (or social partnership) tradition;
■ autocratic management style v. involving management style.

Activity 29.7

Making reference to our historical survey above, consider in which ways the UK employee relations system has evolved along each of these dimensions in recent years.

Clearly, of course, there is a great deal of variation within as well as between national systems in all the above areas. It is also true that things do not remain static over time and that prevailing norms within any country evolve in new directions. However, it remains the case that certain approaches remain associated with particular countries. In Japan, for example, union membership is high and management practices relatively autocratic, but the unions themselves are enterprise based and there is a consensual tradition. In Germany and the Scandinavian countries the social partnership approach is well established, but here it is associated with industry-based unions, national-level bargaining, extensive employee involvement in decision making and heavy government intervention. Hence employers are obliged by law to consult and share decision making with their workforces through works councils. In France, by contrast, union membership is notoriously low, but the unions maintain a role in negotiating terms and conditions because they are empowered to do so in law. The government is further involved through the setting of minimum standards in areas such as training provision, holiday entitlements, wages, hours of work, health insurance and pensions. Government intervention is also extensive in the eastern European countries, but here union membership remains high, while bargaining is often carried out at industry level.

The main practical implications associated with this variation in approach are for multinational organisations. They have an understandable impulse to strengthen their corporate culture by taking a standard approach to employee relations management across their operations, but also have to take account of local conditions. For them, success comes when they find ways of creating a company-wide, international strategy which is adaptable to the requirements of the various countries in which they operate. Employee relations considerations thus play a major role in determining which countries are chosen as the locations for their operations. They can also contribute to decisions about plant closures when retrenchment is deemed necessary.

Summary propositions

29.1 A collective approach to employee relations and employee involvement does not have the emphasis it had in the period before 1980.

29.2 Employee relations practice in the UK was dominated by trade unions and collective bargaining for most of the twentieth century.

29.3 Since 1980 trade union membership has declined along with the significance of collective bargaining. There were some signs of a revival in trade union fortunes in 1999 and 2000.

29.4 As trade unions have become more marginal, managers have sought other forms of employee involvement over which they are able to exert more influence.

29.5 It is possible to identify seven categories of consent to illustrate variations in the level and type of collective employee involvement.

29.6 Individual employee involvement initiatives are direct; they do not operate through workforce representatives. The most common are team briefing, attitude surveys, quality circles, news sheets and team working initiatives.

29.7 Despite some evidence of convergence in recent years, national employee relations systems remain very different from one another in important respects.

References

Bamber, G. and Lansbury, R. (1998) 'An introduction to international and comparative employment relations', in G. Bamber and R. Lansbury (eds), *International and Comparative Employment Relations*, 3rd edn. London: Sage.

Buchanan, D. (1993) 'Principles and practice of work design', in K. Sisson (ed.), *Personnel Management*, 2nd edn. Oxford: Blackwell.

Buchanan, D. and McCalman, J. (1989) *High Performance Work Systems*. London: Routledge.

Cully, M., Woodland, S., O'Reilly, A. and Dix, G. (1999) *Britain at Work: As depicted by the 1998 Workplace Employee Relations Survey*. London: Routledge.

Department for Education and Employment (2000) *Labour Market Trends*. London: The Stationery Office.

Etzioni, A. (1961) *A Comparative Analysis of Complex Organisations*. New York: Free Press.

Fernie, S. and Metcalf, D. (1996) 'Participation, contingent pay, representation and workplace performance: Evidence from Great Britain', *Discussion Paper 232*. London: Centre for Economic Performance, London School of Economics.

Gall, G. and Hammond, D. (2000) 'Spectre of CAC prompts first wave of voluntary recognitions', *People Management*, 7 December, pp. 14–15.

Guest, D. (2001) 'Industrial Relations and Human Resource Management', in J. Storey (ed.), *Human Resource Management: A Critical Text*, 2nd edn. London: Thomson Learning.

Guest, D. and Hoque, K. (1994) 'The good, the bad and the ugly: employment relations in new non-union workplaces', *Human Resource Management Journal*, Vol. 5, No. 1, pp. 1–14.

Holden, L. (1997) 'Employee Involvement', in I. Beardwell and L. Holden (eds), *Human Resource Management*, 2nd edn. London: Pitman.

IRS (1999a) 'Unions in the 21st century', *IRS Employment Trends* 688, September. London: Industrial Relations Services.

IRS (1999b) 'Trends in employee involvement', *IRS Employment Trends* 683, July. London: Industrial Relations Services.

IRS (2000) 'Where next for HR?', *IRS Employment Trends* 704, May. London: Industrial Relations Services.

Mackay, L.E. and Torrington, D.P. (1986) *The Changing Nature of the Personnel Function*. London: IPM.

Marchington, M. (2001) 'Employee Involvement at Work', in J. Storey (ed.), *Human Resource Management: A Critical Text*, 2nd edn. London: Thomson Learning.

Purcell, J. and Sisson, K. (1983) 'Strategies and practice in the management of industrial relations', in G.S. Bain (ed.), *Industrial Relations in Britain*. Oxford: Blackwell.

Taylor, R. (1993) *The Trade Union Question in British Politics*. Oxford: Blackwell.

General discussion topics

1 Why should employees be involved and what should they be involved in?

2 To what extent would you regard the history of employee relations in Britain as a history of failure?

3 Which of the forms of direct employee involvement described in this chapter do you think is most attractive from an employee perspective and why?

Activity 30.1

What do you think should be the main criteria used to establish whether a body should or should not be granted the status of a trade union?

Traditionally the Certification Officer has placed a great deal of importance on independence from management, ensuring that staff associations that are limited to specific companies cannot qualify. Is this fair?

The cases for and against union recognition

When a trade union has recruited a number of members in an organisation, it will seek recognition from the employer in order to represent those members. The step of recognition is seldom easy but is very important as it marks a highly significant movement away from unilateral decision making by the management.

If the employees want that type of representation, they will not readily co-operate with the employer who refuses. In extreme cases this can generate sufficient antagonism to cause industrial action in support of recognition. In such situations the employer may be forced to grant partial recognition or even concede the demand for full negotiating rights over a whole range of issues. Alternatively refusal may lead to a situation in which the employer is forced to recognise the union under the terms of the Employment Relations Act 1999 (see below).

However, there are also positive reasons for considering recognising trade unions, relating to the benefits that can flow as a result: there are employee representatives with whom to discuss, consult and negotiate so that communication and working relationships can be improved:

> There are a number of reasons why employers should choose to work with, rather than against, unions at the workplace. Firstly, management may regard trade union representatives as an essential part of the communication process in larger workplaces. Rather than being forced to establish a system for dealing with all employees, or setting up a non-union representative forum, trade unions are seen as a channel which allows for the effective resolution of issues concerned with pay bargaining or grievance handling. It is also the case that reaching agreement with union representatives, in contrast to imposing decisions, can provide decisions with a legitimacy which otherwise would be lacking. It can also lead to better decisions as well. (Marchington and Wilkinson 1996, p. 237)

There is also a variety of arguments that can be put against choosing to recognise a trade union and resisting doing so. Employers are often apprehensive about the degree of rigidity in employment practice that union aims for security of employment appear to imply, and they therefore consider to what extent collective consent can be achieved by other means, provided that the management work hard at both securing and maintaining that consent.

A survey undertaken by IRS (1995, pp. 3–9) asked company representatives to outline the advantages and disadvantages of trade union recognition. The benefits suggested included the stable structure such a relationship gives to the management of employees, the promotion of smooth industrial relations and its role in providing a mechanism for upward communication from the staff. A further perceived advantage was its cost effectiveness as a communication tool when compared to more individualised approaches. The drawbacks principally related to a perception that unions tend to resist change and take a long time to get things done. The result is a reduction in the ability of managers to respond quickly and flexibly to market pressures and opportunities.

Data from the Workplace Employment Relations Survey shows that managers are split over the issue of trade union recognition. Cully *et al.* (1999, p. 87) report that in 29 per cent of workplaces managers are broadly in favour of union membership and that in 17 per cent they are opposed. The remaining 54 per cent stated either that they were 'neutral' or that it was simply not an issue in their workplaces.

WINDOW ON PRACTICE

An interesting footnote to British industrial relations is the elimination of trade unions at the Government Communications Headquarters (GCHQ) at Cheltenham. GCHQ produces signal intelligence to support the security, defence, foreign and economic policies of the British government. As in most public sector bodies, there has been a strong tradition of union representation among the several thousand staff who are employed there.

In the early 1980s the government became concerned about the possible risk to security of this type of representation in a body where such sensitive data were handled. There was a particular apprehension about the possibility of industrial action impeding urgent defence initiatives. In January 1984 union members were offered £1,000 each to 'buy out' their membership. All but a small number accepted the offer, but the action was regarded as a serious attack on union rights and there were a series of legal moves, including an appeal to the European Court of Human Rights, to have the ban declared invalid. In October 1988, 14 of the employees who had not resigned their union membership were dismissed.

The incoming 1997 government was pledged to restore negotiating rights, and fulfilled the pledge within two weeks of taking office, although maintaining a ban against industrial action. In July those who had been dismissed returned to work.

Forms of trade union recognition

Union recognition comes in various shapes and forms. It may be 'partial', in which case the range of topics subject to negotiation is limited, or it may be 'full', covering pay, conditions and all employer policies relating to the employment relationship. The irreducible minimum is assistance by a union representative for members with grievances, but the extent to which matters beyond that are recognised as being a subject of bargaining depends on the type of management regime that is in place. It also depends on the possible existence of other agreements that could take some matters out of the scope of local recognition. A feature of some collective agreements is an acceptance that certain matters are potentially subject to negotiation with the recognised union (e.g. pay and redundancy), while in other areas the union has the right only to be consulted or informed.

The second fundamental decision to be taken in respect of recognition concerns the number of unions to be recognised and the type of bargaining to be adopted. There are three basic alternatives:

1 **Multi-union bargaining** involves the recognition of several different unions, each of which negotiates separately on behalf of different groups of workers.

Sometimes this leads to a situation in which the separate groups are employed on different sets of terms and conditions. Such an approach has traditionally been common in large public sector organisations such as the NHS, although union mergers in recent years have tended to reduce the overall number that are recognised. As a rule different unions will represent different 'bargaining groups' such as unskilled manual workers, skilled manual grades and white-collar workers.

2 **Single-table bargaining** is a situation in which a number of unions are recognised, but where only one set of negotiations takes place over terms and conditions at a time. The full range of issues is thus determined for all groups of staff around a single table. It is usual for such arrangements to be associated with 'single-status' practices or harmonised terms and conditions, so that all workers enjoy the same basic entitlements as regards matters such as holiday, pensions, hours and sick pay.

3 **Single-union bargaining** is principally associated with situations in which only one union seeks recognition. However, it can also occur where an employer rejects multi-union bargaining and agrees instead only to recognise one union. These are popularly known as 'sweetheart' or 'new style' agreements and have been the subject of some controversy. They are typically found on greenfield sites and in businesses of technological sophistication, their essential novelty being the closeness and extent of the working relationship between management and union. Union officials find that they have less freedom of action on some matters than their members expect, but also find they are involved in the full range of human resource management questions, not simply the familiar terrain of collective bargaining. The agreements are also frequently accompanied by 'no strike' clauses, which supposedly remove the need for industrial action by providing for independent arbitration in situations where management and union fail to reach agreement. Single-status arrangements also often feature in single-union deals.

From a management perspective it is preferable, if possible, to conclude a **partnership agreement** with the union or unions which have been recognised. Such approaches have been actively enouraged by the government and by the TUC in recent years and may well become the dominant form in the future if European Works Councils become a statutory requirement in all larger organisations. Partnership deals represent an attempt to move away from the traditional, adversarial, low-trust form of union–management relationship towards one which is characterised by high trust and a willingness to engage in joint problem solving. Communication and consultation are watchwords, so that employees and their representatives are kept fully aware of the factors affecting management decision making and are themselves involved as far as is possible. Collective bargaining continues but is supplemented with other prominent institutions such as a company council:

> This is a representative body consisting of employer and union representatives, which has a number of functions. These normally include: acting as a negotiating forum; acting as a consultative forum; establishing sub-committees and working parties; facilitating the resolution of grievances and disputes; and promoting the agreed principles of employee relations between the employer and the union(s).
>
> (Farnham 2000, p. 248)

Another feature of many recent collective agreements is the inclusion of specific undertakings relating to flexibility and new technology. **Flexibility agreements** aim to reduce the significance of demarcation between different groups of workers so that greater numbers are willing and able to undertake tasks outside a tightly defined job role. They are typically introduced in response to intense competitive pressures and are concluded as a means of minimising job losses. In return for higher wages and appropriate training, the workforce agrees to become multiskilled and to abandon strict grade definitions which restrict which people can do which kinds of task. **Technology agreements** are concluded in order to facilitate the smooth introduction of new machinery and accompanying working practices. The result is a planned transfer to new systems in which employee representatives are fully involved. Issues that managers might otherwise consider unimportant (such as adjustments in the make-up of production teams) are thus included in discussions, while uncertainty and fears of job losses are kept to a minimum.

The third major way in which collective bargaining arrangements differ is in their level. Three approaches are commonly identified:

- multi-employer bargaining;
- single-employer bargaining;
- workplace bargaining.

All can operate within the same organisation at the same time with different matters being determined at different levels. However, in most organisations which recognise trade unions the most important decisions are taken in one forum.

Multi-employer bargaining used to be very common in the UK and remains so in many European countries. Negotiations over basic pay and conditions of employment take place at industry or national level through the auspices of employers' associations. The result is the presence of industry norms, the same rates of pay and agreements on hours being honoured by all employers in a particular industry. The 1980s and 1990s saw a rapid decline in multi-employer bargaining in the UK, with the collapse of long-established agreements in industries such as engineering and textiles. According to Milward *et al.* (2000, pp. 184–99) only 6 per cent of UK workplaces engaged in manufacturing and 3 per cent of private services operations now determine pay through a multi-employer agreement. The figure for the public sector is a great deal higher (39 per cent), but here too there has been substantial decentralisation in recent years.

Most bargaining therefore takes place within organisations either at employer level, or in multi-site operations at the level of the workplace. The former is best where core terms and conditions are standardised across the organisation. It is also the most efficient approach as it ties up less managerial time than is the case where each workplace carries out its own negotiations.

Activity 30.2

What do you think are the main reasons for the breaking up of so many industry-level collective agreements in the UK over recent decades? Why have they survived in other countries such as Denmark and Italy?

Derecognition

Derecognition of trade unions is often seen in published literature as being redolent of fundamentally undesirable 'macho' approaches to employee relations. While outright derecognition against the stated wishes of the workforce has been relatively rare, the TUC Labour Research Department has formally recorded a number of significant cases in recent years (see IRS 1996a, p. 4; 1996b, p. 4). The comparative rarity of derecognition is also a finding of successive Workplace Employment Relations Surveys (see Millward *et al.* 2000, pp. 103–4). The majority of these have related to specific grades of employees rather than the entire workforce. In other cases partial derecognition has occurred where the scope of matters covered by collective bargaining is narrowed. Such situations often accompany moves by employers to establish personal employment contracts and/or to move towards pay rises based on individual performance or contribution. The result is the retention of collective bargaining machinery, but a tendency for it to be used more and more rarely in important decision making.

It could be argued that partial derecognition of this kind ultimately leads to full derecognition as fewer staff see any particular advantage in joining the union. Over time the union becomes so numerically weak that there is no longer a persuasive case for its continued recognition – even over the limited range of issues for which it retains bargaining rights.

In such circumstances there is a good case for accepting that the union is no longer performing a useful representative function and that employees' interests might thus be better served with the introduction of other forms of collective or individual involvement.

Trade union recognition law

Since 2000 there has been in place a formal legal route which unions can use as a means of forcing employers to recognise them and to bargain with them in good faith about the pay and conditions of the workers they represent. The new law was introduced as part of the Employment Relations Act 1999 and is highly complex. A central role is played by the Central Arbitration Committee (CAC), a statutory body which is independent of government, to which union recognition claims are sent. The CAC is required to consider the claim and to seek voluntary agreement between the parties. Where this cannot be established it can either require management to recognise the union or organise a ballot of the workforce concerned. The law applies in all organisations employing more than 20 people where there is no existing collective bargaining arrangement in place.

The process is started by a union or a group of unions acting together making a formal recognition claim on behalf of a defined bargaining group. Management can then either accept the claim, reject it outright or seek to negotiate a more favourable deal. If necessary the CAC panel dealing with the case will ask officials from the Advisory, Conciliation and Arbitration Service (ACAS) to help the parties reach a voluntary agreement. Only when such avenues fail are formal hearings held and decisions made. The CAC will consider the case if the bargaining group concerned is coherent, includes everyone who should be included and is generally 'compatible with effective management'.

Where it can be shown that over 50 per cent of the workers in the defined bargaining group are members of the union/unions bringing the claim, the CAC will order recognition unless there is evidence to suggest that sufficient members may not want their union to be recognised or where the panel is persuaded that it would not be in the interests of good industrial relations to require recognition without first organising a ballot. Where the union concerned shows that over 10 per cent of the bargaining group are members and produces evidence to suggest that a ballot for recognition stands a good chance of succeeding the CAC will order that a ballot should take place. In most cases the evidence required will be in the form of a petition of workers in the defined bargaining group.

Ballots ordered by CAC panels are funded jointly by employers and unions, and are supervised by independent scrutineers. Ballot papers are sent to employees' home addresses, to which campaigning literature can also be sent. In order to win the ballot, the union side must secure a majority of the votes cast and those of at least 40 per cent of the employees in the bargaining group. Strong support must therefore be shown for recognition among the workers concerned. A majority voting for recognition will not succeed if only a minority decide to vote. Once a ballot has been won and a recognition order served, the employer is obliged to bargain in good faith for at least three years. Only then is it possible to consider derecognition; in which case a further application has to be made to the CAC and another ballot held along similar lines.

In the UK, unlike in most other industrialised countries, collective agreements are not generally legally enforceable. They are binding on the parties 'in honour only', so if one side breaches the agreement no legal action can be taken to ensure that it is honoured. Elsewhere in the world, across Europe and in the United States, this is not the case. As a result collective agreements have the character of a contract and tend to be written in less unambiguous language than in the UK. An important exception to this rule has been made for collective agreements formed as a result of an order by the CAC. Where an employer is forced to recognise a trade union as a result of the legal procedure described above, the resulting agreement can be enforced in a court. Employers are thus prevented from formally recognising a trade union and then subsequently failing to engage with it in meaningful collective bargaining.

WINDOW ON PRACTICE

During the first six months of its operation the CAC received 40 applications from trade unions, of which only four resulted in recognition and in a further two ballots were held. Of the others a majority were withdrawn because a voluntary agreement had been reached with the employer concerned. In addition, over 150 other voluntary recognition agreements were reached during 2000 (double the number in previous years), indicating that employers are seeking to avoid being forced to recognise unions by reaching their own agreements first.

IDS (2000) provides several useful examples of recent recognition agreements. It shows that some employers are organising ballots themselves with the same rules as can be imposed by the CAC as a means of deterring trade unions from making formal applications.

Collective consultation

Among the legal rights that are conferred on unions when they are recognised is a requirement to be consulted over particular issues. However, the duty on employers to consult with their workforces on a collective basis is not only restricted to those which recognise trade unions. The legal requirement to consult thus takes a variety of different forms. In this context the term 'consultation' means formally talking to employee representatives with a view to reaching agreement. There is no obligation on employers to negotiate or to conclude any formal deal, but an attempt must be made in good faith.

Redundancy

Where an employer proposes to make 20 or more people redundant there is an obligation to consult when formal proposals are drawn up. Where a union or unions are recognised, consultation must be with their representatives. In non-union organisations the obligation is to consult with representatives chosen by all relevant sections of the affected workforce. The aim of the consultation is to find ways of avoiding redundancies and/or to mitigate the consequences. Consultation should take place over issues such as the proposed selection procedure, the method used to determine the pool of affected employees and the basis on which redundancy payments are to be calculated.

Transfer of undertakings

The same regulations covering redundancies apply in transfer of undertakings cases (namely, situations in which one organisation is taken over by another, usually as a result of a sale). Consultation is a requirement placed on both the transferor and transferee companies. The duty to consult extends to representatives of employees whose work or conditions will be directly affected by the transfer. There is a more general duty to inform representatives of other workers about the reasons for the transfer and its longer-term implications.

Health and safety

Under the Health and Safety (Consultation with Employees) Regulations 1996 employers have a general duty to consult with worker representatives about all health and safety matters. Here too the obligation is to consult with trade union appointed safety representatives wherever a union is formally recognised. In other organisations employers can either consult with the workforce directly or set up a health and safety committee to which employee representatives are elected. There are specific duties to consult 'in good time' on the introduction of any measure (e.g. new technology or working arrangement) which substantially affects health and safety, and on procedural arrangements for managing health and safety issues.

Pensions

Recognised unions must be consulted where an employer proposes that its occupational pension should 'contract out' of the State Earnings Related Pension

Scheme (see Chapter 37). They also have the right to receive on request information concerning a pension scheme's rules and membership numbers, as well as copies of its accounts and actuarial valuations.

European Works Councils

As of 2001, European Works Councils have to be set up in all 'community scale undertakings', defined as organisations which employ over 1,000 people in the European Union and including at least 150 in two EU states. They are not instruments of industrial democracy and there is no right to co-determination with management over areas of employment policy, as has long been the approach in Germany. The major requirements are as follows:

- Councils must have between three and 30 members.
- These individuals must be elected to the council by the workforce.
- Council meetings are to be held annually at which management are obliged to give reports concerning progress, prospects, the financial situation and plans relating to sales, production, employment, investment and/or the corporate structure.
- Special meetings are to be held in 'exceptional' circumstances when, for example, large-scale redundancies or plant relocations are being contemplated.
- Councils have the right to be informed and consulted about 'any measure liable to have a considerable effect on employees' interests'.
- Only matters that are 'community scale' need be discussed. There is no legal requirement to cover affairs affecting employees in only one EU country.

At the time of writing (early 2001) the governments of the EU states are considering extending the requirement to consult through works councils to all organisations employing more than 50 people.

Activity 30.3

The UK government is known to oppose the extension of works councils beyond community scale undertakings and has sought, with other countries, to block the new directive. Why do you think this is? What arguments could be put for and against requiring all substantial UK employers to operate European Works Councils?

Workplace agreements

Two recent pieces of legislation originating in Europe provide employers with the opportunity to determine their local application via workplace agreements. These are the Working Time Regulations 1998 and the Maternity and Parental Leave etc. Regulations 1999 (as they apply to parental leave). In both cases the basic rights are set out together with a 'default scheme' which contains more detailed rules on their application. However, employers are permitted to develop their own local rules to replace the government's default scheme, provided these are agreed through a formal workplace agreement. Where unions are recognised this can be achieved using established collective bargaining machinery. Otherwise the employer needs either to secure the explicit agreement of a majority of employees or to arrange for representatives to be elected to a consultative forum.

Consultation in practice

Irrespective of legal obligations, consultation is generally regarded as being a hallmark of good management. An employer who fails to consult properly, particularly at times of significant change, is likely to be perceived as being unduly autocratic. The result will be dissatisfaction, low levels of motivation, higher staff turnover and poorer levels of customer service. Moreover, consultation has important advantages as a means by which good ideas are brought forward and weak ones challenged.

In workplaces where unions are recognised it is usual for consultation to take place over a range of issues and for permanent consultative institutions to be established. The joint consultative committee (JCC) is the most common form, being a forum in which managers and union representatives meet on a regular basis. Importantly, JCCs are kept distinct from negotiating forums – despite the fact that the membership is often the same:

> In Britain, voluntary collective bargaining and voluntary joint consultation have traditionally been seen as separate and complementary processes, with collective bargaining focusing on the divergent interests of employers and employees and consultation focusing on their common interests . . . This has meant in many cases that collective bargaining has been concerned with pay determination and conditions of employment and joint consultation with welfare, health and safety, training and efficiency. (Farnham 2000, pp. 81–2)

The partnership approach to recognition outlined above, in seeking to move away from adversarial approaches to employee relations, is associated with a process of strethening or upgrading consulative forums (such as JCCs) at the expense of those used for bargaining.

JCCs are twice as common in union workplaces than in those where unions are not recognised (Millward *et al.* 2000, pp. 108–9), suggesting that they are mostly still used in parallel with collective bargaining machinery. However, research by Marchington (1989) found evidence that they were used in some workplaces as a substitute for collective bargaining or as a means of discouraging the development of a union presence. Managers in such workplaces believe that unions are less likely to gain support and request recognition if the employer keeps its staff informed of issues that affect them and consult with them before taking decisions. Consultative forums in non-union firms also provide a means whereby managers can put their case effectively without the presence of organised opposition.

In many workplaces, union or non-union, JCCs often play a very marginal role from the perspective of most employees. This typically is true where decision making is heavily decentralised to the level of the department or to individual teams of employees. If budgets are devolved too, people may also be uninterested in the outcomes of collective bargaining, because their pay and career prospects are effectively determined by their immediate managers. This poses a problem for management at times of significant change, because there is a need to engage everyone in proper consultation. Without it people will not understand the reasons for the proposed changes or the alternative strategies that are being considered, and will not have the opportunity to contribute their own ideas. From time to time, therefore, managers need to organise one-off consultation exercises as a means of making change management processes as smooth and effective as possible. Common examples would be business reorganisations, major policy changes, the introduction of new product lines, organisational relocations and cultural change programmes.

From a management perspective, the great danger is that people come to believe that management is not genuinely interested in hearing their views or in taking them on board. Rose (2001, p. 391) refers to this approach as a 'pseudo-consultation' in which managers are really doing little more than informing employees about decisions that have already been taken. Cynicism results because there is perceived to be an attempt on the part of managers to use consultative forums merely as a means of legitimising their decisions. They can say that consultation has taken place, when in truth it has not. Pseudo-consultation typically involves assembling employees in large groups with senior managers present. The management message is then put across strongly and a short time is given for others to respond. In such situations employees have no time to give proper consideration to the proposals and are likely to feel too intimidated to articulate criticisms. The result is often worse in terms of employee morale and engagement with the changes than would have been the case had no consultation been attempted.

Even where managers genuinely intend to undertake meaningful consultation, they can very easily create an impression that it is no more than a 'pseudo' exercise. It is therefore important to avoid the approaches outlined in the above paragraph. Employees should be informed of a range of possible ways forward (not just the one favoured by management) and invited to consider them in small groups. The results of their deliberations can then be fed back to senior managers and given proper consideration. In this way the appearance of pseudo-consultation, as well as the reality, can be avoided.

WINDOW ON PRACTICE

An issue of significance for employers recognising trade unions for the first time is the need to reassure non-union members that their voices will still be heard. IDS (2000, p. 7) gives several examples of the way in which employers use consultative machinery to ensure that this is the case.

It is particularly important where a union is recognised despite it representing only a minority of the workforce. While union representatives necessarily dominate the staff side in collective bargaining institutions, this need not be the case with joint consultative committees, company councils or health and safety committees.

IDS describes the way that firms such as Yoplait Dairy Crest and Monarch Aircraft Engineering have reserved specific seats on key consultative committees for the representatives of both union members and employees who do not wish to join the recognised union.

HR roles in recognition and consultation

HR specialists play different roles in the recognition, bargaining and consultation processes, much depending on the status achieved by the HR function within the organisation. Broadly it is possible to identify three types of role: facilitating, advisory and executive.

The **facilitating** role is the most restricted. Here HR staff do little more than manage the administrative aspects of recognition and consultation. They organise the meetings, circulate agendas, take minutes and provide factual information, but do little more than support the line managers who take the leading role. The **advisory** role also involves the HR manager being present in a supporting capacity. Here, however, there is considerably more direct involvement with the substance of employee relations management. Specialist advice is provided on legal matters, procedure and precedent, as well as on the HR implications of different courses of action. Line managers chair meetings and take the lead in negotiations, but are directly assisted and supported by an HR specialist who participates in decision making. The third '**executive**' model is one in which employee relations management is largely devolved to the HR function. Here HR managers lead the negotiations, chair consultative meetings and are chiefly responsible for decision making concerning matters such as recognition and derecognition. The advisory role, in such situations, is played by line managers.

In order to carry out the advisory or executive roles effectively, HR managers need to be able to combine specialist knowledge with detailed knowledge of the organisation and its business strategy. Practical negotiation skills and experience of handling sensitive employee relations matters are also significant. HR managers' role has been enhanced in recent years by the great growth in the volume and complexity of legislation.

In the past HR advice used to be thoughtful and genuinely intended to be helpful, and was sometimes welcome, but its basis was simply general experience and good intentions. The recipient could use or ignore it at will, depending on the commonsense assessment of its value. Legislation has caused the need for advice of the type offered by a professional. This is thoughtful and intended to be helpful, but may not be welcome. It will be based on an informed examination of statute and precedent, and will include a full appreciation of the strategic implications of whatever is being considered. No HR manager can now regard the general company strategy as something of concern only to other members of the management team. Although this is such an obvious point, it needs reiteration as a number of those applying for courses in HRM retain a view that their role is to be much more even-handed, and some commentators castigate personnel managers for adopting a managerial approach. One commentary criticised HR managers for abandoning their social and religious principles, adopting a managerial rather than an independent professional stance, ignoring the pluralistic nature of work organisations and consolidating an exploitative relationship between people at work (Hart 1993). Today's HR manager is inescapably and necessarily a representative of management interests. In union recognition issues in particular, there is no point in having a personnel manager involved who does not adopt that perspective.

The HR manager therefore carries a specific type of authority. As well as receiving advice, the employer needs to see that all employment matters are administered in a way that is consistent with the legislative framework, and part of that requirement is that managerial actions should be consistent with each other. It may also be that people see the need not only for advice, but also for representation by someone who knows the esoteric rules of procedure and behaviour in a highly stylised form of discussion.

Summary propositions

30.1 While trade union recognition is less common than was the case 25 years ago, collective bargaining remains the main means by which pay and conditions are determined in a large minority of workplaces. It is still dominant in the public sector.

30.2 An employer is deemed in law to have recognised a trade union if it negotiates with it about pay, conditions or employment policy. Recognition gives trade unions and their representatives important rights in law.

30.3 There are compelling cases from a management perspective both in favour of and against trade union recognition. Their validity is determined by the circumstances of the organisation.

30.4 Collective bargaining varies in terms of its scope and its level and in the number of unions involved. Recent years have seen moves towards partnership agreements, as well as those designed to achieve flexibility and to facilitate the introduction of new technology.

30.5 Since 2000 there has been in place a legal route for trade unions to use as a means of securing recognition. The result has been an increase in the number of voluntary agreements reached.

30.6 Recognised unions have a right to be consulted about a range of issues. Collective consultation is also a legal obligation in non-union firms.

30.7 Consultation is a hallmark of a good employer. In order to be effective, consultation processes must be meaningful and genuine.

References

Cully, M., Woodland, S., O'Reilly, A. and Dix, G. (1999) *Britain at Work: As depicted by the 1998 Workplace Employee Relations Survey*. London: Routledge.

Farnham, D. (2000) *Employee Relations in Context*, 2nd edn. London: CIPD.

Gall, G. and Hammond, D. (2000) 'Spectre of CAC prompts first waves of voluntary recognition', *People Management*, 7 December.

Hart, T. (1993) 'Human resource management: time to exorcize the militant tendency', *Employee Relations*, Vol. 15, No. 3, pp. 29–36.

IDS (2000) 'Union Recognition', *IDS Study 685*. London: Incomes Data Services.

IRS (1995) 'Employee representation arrangements: the trade unions', *Employment Trends 586*. London: Industrial Relations Services.

IRS (1996a) 'News section', *Employment Trends 612*. London: Industrial Relations Services.

IRS (1996b) 'News section', *Employment Trends 616*. London: Industrial Relations Services.

Marchington, M. and Wilkinson, A. (1996) *Core Personnel & Development*. London: IPD.

Marchington, M. (1989) 'Joint consultation in practice', in K. Sisson (ed.), *Personnel Management in Britain*. Oxford: Blackwell.

Millward, N., Bryson, A. and Forth, J. (2000) *All Change at Work?* London: Routledge.

Rose, E. (2001) *Employment Relations*. London: Financial Times Prentice Hall.

General discussion topics

1 Why has trade union membership remained so high in the public sector when it has declined so markedly in the private sector?

2 How effective do you think the recognition provisions in the Employment Relations Act 1999 will turn out to be?

3 What are the arguments for and against extending the concept of the 'workplace agreement' to fields of employment law beyond working time and parental leave?

Chapter 31   Health, safety and welfare

There is always a conflict between the needs of the employer to push for increased output and efficiency and the needs of the employee to be protected from the hazards of the workplace. In the mid-nineteenth century these tensions centred almost entirely on the long hours and heavy physical demands of the factory system. In the opening years of the twenty-first century the tensions are more varied and more subtle, but concern about them remains as great, being expressed by employers, employees, trade unions, government agencies and campaign groups.

Increasingly, aspects of protection are being provided by statute, much new legislation having a European origin. The most recent addition is the body of measures contained in the Working Time Regulations 1998 which aim to reduce the number of hours we work each week, while also guaranteeing everyone a minimum period of paid holiday each year. In addition some aspects result from the initiatives of managements, employees and their representatives. No matter what the source of the initiative or the nature of the concern, the human resource manager is often the focus of whatever action has to be taken.

In this chapter we first consider definitions of health, safety and welfare, and then discuss the development and importance of this area of work and the role of human resource management. Following this we cover the main legislation relating to health, safety and welfare and then look at the management of health and safety matters – both physical and emotional.

Definitions of health, safety and welfare

The dictionary defines 'welfare' as 'well-being', so health and safety are strictly aspects of employee welfare, which have been separately identified as being significant areas of welfare provision for some time. Others (e.g. Beaumont 1984), have noted that welfare can be very broadly defined. Using Fox (1966) as an example, he notes that welfare has been defined to encompass not only the early concern with workers' physical working conditions (sanitation, canteens, hours of work, rest pauses, etc.), but also the 'human relations school of thought', due to the achievement of job satisfaction being seen as a way to achieve higher productivity. He also notes the importance attached to counselling by early welfare workers and the human relations school.

There are two primary areas of benefit to the individual from the provision of welfare facilities – physical benefits and emotional/psychological benefits. Physical benefits stem primarily from measures to improve health and safety, as well as from the provision of paid holidays, reduced working hours and suchlike.

Emotional welfare stems chiefly from any provisions made to improve mental health, for example, counselling, improved communications, or anything involving the 'human relations' needs of people at work. These benefits are, however, highly interrelated, and most welfare activities would potentially have both physical and emotional benefits. It can also be argued that employers provide for the material and intellectual welfare of their employees, in the material provisions of sick pay and pensions, and in the intellectual benefits that come from the provision of satisfying work and appropriate training and development. However, since these aspects are covered elsewhere in this book, we shall concentrate on physical and emotional welfare in this chapter.

HRM and health, safety and welfare

The development of health, safety and welfare provision is to a large extent interrelated with the development of human resource management itself. As mentioned in Chapter 1, one of the early influences on the development of the profession was the growth of industrial welfare workers at the beginning of the twentieth century. Enlightened employers gradually began to improve working conditions for employees and the industrial welfare worker was often concerned in implementing these changes. Much of this work was carried out voluntarily by employers, although not necessarily from altruistic motives alone. Another influence was that of the 'human relations school', in particular the work of Elton Mayo at the Hawthorne plant of the Western Electric Company. Here there was an employee counselling programme, which operated from 1936 to 1955. It was found that such a programme was beneficial for both the mental health of the employees and their work. Other aspects of welfare provision, particularly in respect of safety, such as limitations on the hours of work of children, were enshrined in the law from as early as the 1840s and these again have become identified with the human resource function.

Our research shows that in 41 per cent of those firms with a safety officer, this person comes within the ambit of the human resource function. In those firms without a health and safety officer the human resource department had a primary responsibility for health and safety. As health and safety legislation has become more pervasive, in particular since the Health and Safety at Work etc. Act 1974, and the surge of regulations stemming from it (many resulting from the need to harmonise health and safety regulation throughout the EU), the human resource department has taken on the role of advising managers on the organisation's legal obligation.

The importance of health, safety and welfare from the employees' point of view is clear because their lives and futures are at risk. Health and safety has thus been given increasing emphasis by the trade unions in recent years and has been covered more extensively in the media. A convincing business case for addressing these issues has been articulated in the human resource management press, while the Health and Safety Executive campaigns vigorously to raise awareness of its validity among employers.

The business case is based on three propositions:

1 Illness and injury which is work related leads to avoidable absence.
2 Serious injury and illness can lead to litigation and substantial compensation being paid out by employing organisations.

3 A poor reputation for safety and welfare makes it harder for an organisation to recruit, retain and motivate its staff.

The number of serious injuries sustained at work by UK employees fluctuates substantially each year. The level has dropped since the 1970s with the fall in manufacturing employment, but the total number remains much higher than it should be. In the year to April 2000, for example, 218 people lost their lives in the UK as a result of accidents sustained at work, 75 of which occurred in the construction industry alone (IRS 2000a, p. 3). In addition, over a million people are reported by the Health and Safety Executive to suffer from some form of work-related illness each year. In 1995/96, for example, 1.3 million workers were taken ill as a result of their work, resulting in the loss of 24.3 million working days (IRS 1999). The total annual cost to employers is estimated to be £2.5 billion, including the costs associated with the early retirement of 27,000 employees forced to give up work on grounds of ill health. If the number of incidents were reduced by only a small percentage, employers would thus save a considerable amount of money and trouble.

The reason that the numbers remain so high is the continual conflict between health, safety and welfare considerations and other business priorities. Leach (1995) reports a line manager who had previously been a safety officer as saying: 'I think in general managers don't see [health and safety issues] as important as . . . other issues that they would deal with disciplinary on. I mean you do take short cuts, I do myself. I mean I am not practising a lot of what I used to preach, there's no doubt about it. Managers know it is a part of their job, but I don't think they personally see [health and safety offences] as an offence as such.'

Activity 31.1

How convincing do you find the business case for the maintenance of a high level of health and safety? What additional arguments, other than those outlined here, could be deployed either for or against its validity in different workplaces?

Health and safety law

In the area of health and safety legislative intervention has existed continuously for well over a century, longer than for any other matter we consider. Prior to 1974 the principal statutes were the Factories Act 1961, the Offices, Shops and Railway Premises Act 1963 and the Fire Precautions Act 1971. These three Acts, along with others relating to specific industries, were all brought up to date by the Health and Safety at Work etc. Act 1974 which remains the major statute governing the law in this area. In addition there is a host of health and safety regulations primarily extending the Health and Safety Act to expand specific areas of the legislation, the most significant of which are the Control of Substances Hazardous to Health (COSHH) Regulations 1988 and the series of 'daughter directives' issued by the EU concerning matters such as noise control, the manual handling of heavy loads, use of visual display units (VDUs) and use of carcinogens and biological agents. In addition there are specific sets of regulations covering matters such as violence at work, fire precautions, ventilation, the provision of sanitary facilities, safety signs and noise at work. In 1998 a major new piece of legislation came into UK law in the form of the Working Time Regulations which also have an EU origin. Many of the regulations are supplemented by Health and Safety Commission codes of practice which are not themselves legally enforceable, but which define the standard against which the authorities judge employer's actions. A readable and up-to-date summary of the main employer obligations is found in *Health and Safety* by Jeremy Stranks (2000).

Health and safety legislation is thus increasing at a high rate and the IPD (1997) notes that 'This is now the most highly regulated area of employment and more proposals are on the table'. The reason that EU directives have increased so rapidly in this area is that the Single European Act 1987 added another article to the Treaty of Rome. This allowed health and safety directives to be accepted by a qualified majority vote as a move towards harmonising EU health and safety legislation.

Health and safety law can be neatly divided into two halves, representing its criminal and civil spheres. The first is based in statute and is policed both by the Health and Safety Executive and by local authority inspectorates. The second relies on the common law and allows individuals who have suffered injury as a result of their work to seek damages against their employers. The former is intended to be preventative, while the latter aims to compensate individuals who become ill as a result of their work.

Criminal law

Health and safety inspectors potentially wield a great deal of power, but their approach is to give advice and to issue warnings except where they judge that there is a high risk of personal injury. They visit premises without giving notice beforehand in order to inspect equipment and make sure that the appropriate monitoring procedures are in place. They have a general right to enter premises, to collect whatever information they require and to remove samples or pieces of equipment for analysis.

Where they are unhappy with what they find, inspectors issue **improvement notices** setting out recommended improvements and requiring these to be put in place by a set date. In the case of more serious lapses, where substantial risk to health is identified, the inspectors issue **prohibition notices** which prevent employers from using particular pieces of equipment until better safety arrangements are established. Breach of one of these statutory notices is a criminal offence, as is giving false information to an inspector. Over a thousand prosecutions are brought each year for non-compliance with a Health and Safety Executive Order, leading to fines of up to £20,000. Prosecutions are also brought after injuries have been sustained where it can be shown that management knew of risks and had not acted to deal with them. Where fatalities result and an employer is found guilty of committing corporate manslaughter, fines of several hundred thousand pounds are levied. Moreover, in some cases custodial sentences have been given to controlling directors held to have been individually liable.

The Health and Safety at Work etc. Act 1974 is the source of most health and safety law in the UK, under which more detailed sets of regulations are periodically issued. Its main purposes are as follows:

■ to secure health, safety and welfare of people at work;
■ to protect the public from risks arising from workplace activities;

- to control the use and storage of dangerous substances;
- to control potentially dangerous environmental emissions.

The Act places all employers under a general duty 'to ensure, as far as is reasonably practicable, the health, safety and welfare at work' of all workers. In addition there are specific requirements to maintain plant and equipment, to provide safe systems of working, to provide a safe and healthy working environment, to consult with trade union safety representatives, to maintain an accident reporting book and to post on a notice board a copy of the main provisions contained in the 1974 Act. Where hazardous substances or equipment are in use, there is a further requirement to train people properly in their use and to have safe arrangements for their 'handling, transport and storage'. Where more than five workers are employed, employers are expected to have a written health and safety policy which must be kept up to date and made available to all staff.

In the case law, judges have interpreted the phrase 'as far as is reasonably practicable' relatively narrowly. Employers are expected to undertake formal risk assessments and to compare the level of risk against the costs involved in making a workplace safer. Wherever there is risk identified improvements must be made unless it would be unreasonable, for example on grounds of excessive cost, to expect an employer to do so.

The management of the organisation carry the prime responsibility for implementing the policy they have laid down; they also have a responsibility under the Act for operating the plant and equipment in the premises safely and meeting all the Act's requirements whether these are specified in the policy statement or not. A duty is also placed on employees while they are at work to take reasonable care for the safety of themselves and others, as well as their health, which appears a more difficult type of responsibility for the individual to exercise. The employee is, therefore, legally bound to comply with the safety rules and instructions that the employer promulgates and can be prosecuted for failing to do so. Employers are also fully empowered to dismiss employees who refuse to obey safety rules on the grounds of misconduct, especially if the possibility of such a dismissal is explicit in the disciplinary procedure.

| WINDOW ON PRACTICE | An employee who refused to wear safety goggles for a particular process was warned of possible dismissal because the safety committee had decreed that goggles or similar protection were necessary. His refusal was based on the fact that he had done the job previously without such protection and did not see that it was now |

necessary. He was dismissed and the tribunal did not allow his claim of unfair dismissal (*Mortimer* v. *V. L. Churchill* (1979)).

Under the 1974 Act recognised trade unions have the right to appoint safety representatives who have specific duties and with whom managers are obliged to consult. Their role is to investigate complaints from staff about health and safety matters, to carry out their own inspections, to liaise with HSE inspectors and to attend meetings of health and safety committees. Managers are not permitted to prevent a representative from carrying out an inspection, but may be present during the process. Safety representatives are legally entitled to reasonable paid time off work to carry out their duties and to undertake necessary training, as well as to have facilities such as a notice board, telephone access, secure filing and photocopying. In 1993 new legislation gave safety representatives protection from victimisation, while case law has determined that managers cannot decide who is appointed to the role or for how long they remain in post.

The First Aid Regulations 1981 place employers under a general duty to provide adequate first aid equipment and facilities. The accompanying code of practice sets out what should be kept in a first aid box and what supplementary equipment is required in different types of workplace. In low-risk environments it is recommended that there should be one person with first aid training for every 50–100 employees, rather more being needed in high-risk workplaces such as construction sites and chemical plants.

The Control of Substances Hazardous to Health (COSHH) Regulations 1988 comprise 19 regulations and four approved codes of practice. The purpose of the legislation is to protect all employees who work with any substances hazardous to their health, by placing a requirement on their employer regarding the way in which and extent to which such substances are handled, used and controlled. The regulations apply to all workplaces, irrespective of size and nature of work – so for example, they would apply equally to a hotel as to a chemical plant, and in firms of a handful of employees as well as major PLCs. The regulations place a responsibility for good environmental hygiene not only on the employer, but on employees too. All substances are included, except for asbestos, lead, materials producing ionising radiations and substances underground, all of which have their own legislation (see Riddell 1989). The regulations require employers to focus on five major aspects of occupation in respect of hazardous substances. These are:

1 Assessing the risk of substances used, and identifying what precautions are needed. This initial assessment of substances already in use, and those that are intended for use is a major undertaking in terms of both the number of substances used and the competency of the assessor. Cherrie and Faulkner (1989) report that one employer in their survey used over 25,000 different substances!

2 Introducing appropriate measures to control or prevent the risk. These may include: removing the substance, by changing the processes used, substituting the substance or controlling the substance where this is practical. Examples include totally or partially enclosing the process, increasing ventilation and instituting safer systems of work and handling procedures.

3 Ensuring that control measures are used – that procedures are observed and that equipment involved is regularly maintained. Where necessary, exposure of employees to the substance should be monitored. This would particularly apply where there could be serious health hazards were the measures to fail or be suboptimal. Records of monitoring should be made and retained.

4 Health surveillance. Where there is a known adverse effect of a particular substance, regular surveillance of the employees involved can identify problems at an early stage. When this is carried out, records should be kept and these should be accessible to employees.

5 Employees need to be informed and trained regarding the risks arising from their work and the precautions that they need to take.

The Management of Health and Safety at Work Regulations 1992 implemented the EU's Framework and Temporary Workers Directives. The Framework Directive is an umbrella directive, in a similar way as the Health and Safety at

Work etc. Act is an umbrella act. Additional rules known as 'daughter directives' covering specific areas have been issued within the framework of this directive. The following are examples of those daughter directives which apply to workplaces generally. Others apply to specific industries such as construction, mining and chemicals.

■ The Workplace (Health, Safety and Welfare) Regulations 1992 set out minimum design requirements, including provision of rest and no-smoking areas.
■ The Provision and Use of Work Equipment Regulations 1992 set minimum standards for the safe use of machines and equipment.
■ The Personal Protective Equipment at Work Regulations 1992 require employers to provide appropriate protective equipment, and workers to use this correctly.
■ The Manual Handling Operations Regulations 1992 require employers to reduce the risk of injury by providing lifting equipment where appropriate and training in lifting.
■ The Health and Safety (Display Screen Equipment) Regulations 1992 require employers to provide free eye tests, glasses where appropriate, regular breaks, appropriate training and organisation of equipment to reduce strain.
■ The Protection of Pregnant Workers Directive 1994 was implemented in 1994 via a range of UK Acts and regulations. The major measures are now incorporated into the Employment Relations Act 1999. The most important element is that requiring employers to offer alternative work to a pregnant employee or to one who has recently given birth where there are identifiable health and safety risks.

The Health and Safety (Consultation with Employees) Regulations 1996 require employers to consult collectively with their employees about health and safety matters irrespective of whether a trade union is recognised. Consultation is defined as discussing issues with employee representatives, listening to their views and taking these into account when decisions are being made which have health and safety implications. Where trade unions are recognised the regulations require that their representatives are consulted. In situations where there are no recognised unions the employer must consult with employees as individuals directly or must make arrangements for employees to elect health and safety representatives. Elected representatives have the same rights to paid time off for training and to information disclosure as trade union appointed safety representatives.

The Working Time Regulations 1998 comprise the most significant recent addition to UK health and safety law. Like the other statutes described above, they are enforced by officers of the Health and Safety Executive, but complaints can also be taken directly to employment tribunals by individuals whose employers deny them the various rights set out in the regulations.

The law on working time originates in the EU's Working Time Directive 1993. This was agreed by the Council of Ministers via qualified majority voting, with the UK government voting against. Moves were subsequently made to challenge the legality of its imposition in the UK on the grounds that it was essentially a social issue (and thus inapplicable in the UK) and not about health and safety at all. Predictably the government's case was turned down by the European Court of Justice, leading to the rather hurried introduction of the new regulations in October 1998.

As of 2001 the basic entitlements are as follows. They apply to all workers whether or not they work under a contract of employment:

- a working week limited to a maximum of 48 hours;
- four weeks' paid annual leave per year (in addition to bank holidays);
- a limitation on night working to eight hours in any one 24-hour period;
- eleven hours' rest in any one 24-hour period;
- an uninterrupted break of 24 hours in any one seven-day period;
- a 20-minute rest break in any shift of six hours or more;
- regular free health assessments to establish fitness for night working.

There are more restrictive, additional regulations relating to those aged between 16 and 18, while other groups such as transport workers, junior doctors and people who determine their own working time are excluded from the 48-hour week. Further complexity derives from the way the regulations permit more than 48 hours to be worked in some weeks and more than eight hours on some nights provided that the average number of hours worked over a 17-week period does not breach these limits. Individuals can agree with their employers in writing that they are excluded from the right to the 48-hour maximum working week, but all must be permitted to opt back into the scheme with reasonable notice if they so wish.

The regulations set out the basic rights, but they also allow for locally agreed variation on detailed matters through the mechanism of **workplace agreements**. Where trade unions are recognised, these can be drawn up and agreed through existing collective bargaining machinery. Where unions are not recognised a workplace agreement can be established in one of two ways:

1 The employer can draw up the text before asking employees to sign their approval. Once over half of the employees' signatures in a workplace are obtained, the agreement becomes valid.
2 The employer can arrange for representatives of employees to be elected to negotiate on behalf of everyone. An existing health and safety committee, provided it is properly elected, can fulfil this function.

It is likely that the EU will seek to tighten these regulations in future years. It is generally agreed that they have had no substantial impact on the UK's 'long hours culture' in their first few years of operation because so many people either opt out or remain unaware of their rights under the regulations. Further restrictions will thus be necessary if the directive's health and safety objectives are to be met.

Activity 31.2	Devise a health and safety policy for your organisation. Include information about:

1 General policy on health and safety.
2 Specific hazards and how they are to be dealt with.
3 Management responsibility for safety.
4 How the policy is to be implemented.

or

Obtain the Health and Safety Policy from any organisation and assess the policy in the light of these four points.

Civil law

While distinct in origin and nature from the criminal sanctions, civil cases relating to health and safety are often brought alongside criminal proceedings in connection with the same incident. When someone is seriously injured or suffers ill health as a direct result of their work the health and safety authorities will bring a criminal prosecution, while the injured party will sue for damages in the civil courts. Most claims are brought under the law of contract (see Chapter 10), the injured party alleging that their employer breached its implied duty of care or its duty to provide safe systems of working. It is also possible in certain circumstances to sue for damages under the law of tort by claiming that an employer is guilty of negligence or of breaching its statutory duty.

Whatever the nature of the claim, the courts have to be satisfied that the employer failed to act reasonably and that the injury or illness was sustained 'during the course of employment'. Central here, as in the criminal law, are the notions of foreseeability and risk assessment. Cases often hinge on what the employer knew at the time the injury was sustained and whether or not reasonable precautions in the form of training or the provision of equipment had been taken. Employers can thus defend themselves effectively by satisfying the court that little else could have been done by any reasonable employer to prevent the accident from occurring. Importantly the principle of vicarious liability applies in this field, as in sexual harassment (see Chapter 21). This means that the employer is legally liable for the negligent actions of employees when they are at work. If one employee causes another to become injured, the claim is therefore brought against the employer and not the fellow employee who was responsible.

There are a number of defences open to employers which can result in no award being made or in reduced damages. These include situations in which an accident was not foreseeable (for example if someone was struck by a piece of masonry during exceptionally heavy winds), where the employee voluntarily assumed a risk despite being warned of possible danger, and where an injury which originated outside the workplace was worsened as a result of working. Most significant of all are situations where the employee is found to have contributed to their own injury in some way. This can happen where illnesses derive from lapses of concentration, professional misjudgement or simply stupid behaviour in the face of dangerous conditions. An example is the extraordinary case of *Jones* v. *Lionite Specialities (Cardiff) Ltd* (1961) where an employee fell into a tank of noxious liquid and died. The court held that he was wholly to blame as he had put himself at risk in order to take big whiffs of the liquid's vapour 'to which he had taken a liking'.

Managing stress and emotional welfare

Workplace stress is the welfare topic which has received the most coverage in recent years. It is also a source of litigation which has led to particularly high amounts of damages being paid to those who have sustained illnesses brought on directly as a result of work-related strain. An out of court settlement worth £175,000 was agreed following the High Court ruling in the landmark case of *Walker* v. *Northumberland County Council* (1995). Here a social work manager who had returned to work following a nervous breakdown was given inadequate support and an increased workload leading to a further breakdown. The court held that this amounted to a breach of the implied duty of care, because the second illness had been clearly foreseeable. More recently, in *Ingram* v. *Worcester County Council* (2000), a settlement of £203,000 was reached after a warden responsible for the regulation of travellers' sites suffered a single breakdown after having been subjected to physical and verbal abuse from site residents. The fact that he had been undermined in his efforts by senior council officials and had suffered 'prolonged and unremitting stress' led to the finding that the duty of care had been breached (see IRS 2000b, p. 4). Guidance published by the Health and Safety Executive (see Willey 2000, pp. 324–5) makes it clear that employers are now expected to treat stress like any other health hazard, and that there is consequently 'a legal duty to take reasonable care to ensure that health is not placed at risk through excessive and sustained levels of stress arising from the way people deal with each other at their work or from the day-to-day demands placed on their workforce'.

Stress at work is not a new idea, although it was originally viewed in terms of executive stress (for example, Levinson 1964), and seen only to apply to those in senior management positions. The literature on the subject of stress at work is large (for example, Cooper and Marshall 1980; Palmer 1989; Nykodym and George 1989; Roney and Cooper 1997; Jex 1998; Macdonald 1999). It is defined by Ganster and Murphy (2000) as a form of 'strain' provoked in response to situational demands labelled 'stressors' which occur 'when jobs are simultaneously high in demands and low in control':

> Stressors generally mean environmental factors that cause the individual to muster a coping response because they pose threat or harm. In the work domain examples of such stressors are high workloads, requirements for working fast and meeting strict deadlines, conflicting demands and interruption . . . Problems are seen to arise when exposure to such demands is chronic and elicits a strong enough pattern of responses to strain the individual's physical and mental resources.
>
> (Ganster and Murphy 2000, p. 36)

According to Willey (2000, p. 324) the incidence of chronic stress is often seen as a 'by-product' of management initiatives adopted in many countries, including the UK, in the past twenty years. These include delayering, downsizing, the intensification of work, increased monitoring of staff, moves towards greater flexibility at work and competitive tendering. Each has placed increased burdens on staff groups who have had to accept lower job security, greater levels of responsibility and longer hours of work. The inability to reconcile such demands with family life is a further cause of strain. The results are twofold:

■ adverse health conditions (such as heart disease, high blood pressure, ulcers, depression and panic attacks);
■ behavioural consequences (such as insomnia, anxiety, poor concentration and increased consumption of alcohol, tobacco and other substances).

Both can lead to increased rates of absence, high staff turnover, low levels of job satisfaction and the sustenance of a low-trust employee relations environment.

Stress and its consequences are often caused by a combination of strains originating in and outside work. A person who is normally able to cope well with the demands of a stressful job may cease to do so when home-based problems come to the fore – the major culprits being bereavement, debt and marital breakdown.

There is thus a good business case for employers to provide formal mechanisms for emotional support, quite aside from the strong ethical case. The following are examples of available approaches.

Someone to talk to/someone to advise

A person to talk to could be the individual's manager, or the human resource manager, but it is often more usefully someone who is distinct from the work itself. Occupational health nurses, welfare officers or specialised counsellors are the sort of people well placed to deal with this area. There are two benefits that come from this, the first being advice and practical assistance. This would be relevant, for example, if the individual had financial problems, and the organisation was prepared to offer some temporary assistance. Alternatively, the individual could be advised of alternative sources of help, or referred, with agreement, to the appropriate agency for treatment. The second benefit to be gained is that of having someone just listen to the individual's problem without judging it – in other words, counselling. De Board (1983) suggests that the types of work-related problems that employees may need to be counselled on are: technical incompetence, underwork, overwork, uncertainty about the future and relationships at work. Counselling aims to provide a supportive atmosphere to help people to find their own solution to a problem.

Reorganisation of work

This is a preventive measure involving reorganisation of those aspects of work that are believed to be affecting the mental health of employees. This may include changes that could be grouped as 'organisational development', such as job rotation and autonomous work-groups. Eva and Oswald (1981) suggest greater control over the speed and intensity of work, an increase in the quality of work and a reduction in unsocial hours. Individually based training and development programmes would also be relevant here. Specifically for the executive, there is growing use of the 'managerial sabbatical'. Some American companies have begun to give a year off after a certain number of years' service in order to prevent 'executive burnout'. In the UK, the John Lewis Partnership has a programme allowing six months away from work.

Positive health programmes

Positive health programmes display a variety of different approaches aimed at relieving and preventing stress and associated problems, and promoting healthy lifestyles. There is increasing activity in terms of healthy eating and no-smoking campaigns and support, together with the provision of resources for physical activity. Corporate wellness programmes have been in place for a longer period in the USA, where the prime motivation was the reduction of medical costs (most employers covering these costs as a benefit for their employees). In the UK the programmes are more often seen as an employee benefit in themselves, with the hope that providing them will also encourage higher productivity and reduce absence levels. However, Mills (1996) argues that although there is a weak positive relationship between healthier lifestyles and the bottom line, there is little evidence that health promotion programmes are actually working. He argues that only a small number of employees are affected by such programmes and that these are likely to be the ones who already have healthier lifestyles. Mills suggests that blue-collar employees, who have the least control over their working lives, also tend to have less healthy lifestyles and are more resistant to health promotion. He suggests that all three factors are interrelated and connected in a complex manner with employee motivation. If Mills is right, this presents a challenge to organisations and suggests at the very least that they should evaluate positive health programmes as well as investigating the impact of the prevailing management style.

Some approaches to corporate wellness include the use of yoga and meditation. Others, like 'autogenic training', are based on these principles, but are presented in a new guise. Autogenic training is developed through exercises in body awareness and physical relaxation which lead to passive concentration. It is argued that the ability to achieve this breaks through the vicious circle of excessive stress, and that as well as the many mental benefits, there are benefits to the body including relief of somatic symptoms of anxiety, and the reduction of cardiovascular risk factors (Carruthers 1982). Another approach is 'chemo feedback', which is geared towards the connection between stress and coronary heart disease, high blood pressure and strokes. Chemo feedback (Positive Health Centre 1985) is designed as an early warning system to pick up signs of unfavourable stress. The signs are picked up from the completion of a computerised questionnaire together with a blood test. This approach, like others such as the Occupational Stress Indicator (see IRS 2000c, pp. 13–16), is being offered as a 'stress-audit' tool for use on a company-wide basis.

Managing physical welfare

There are a number of ways in which managerial responsibility can be discharged to implement the organisation's health and safety policy statement and to ensure compliance with legal requirements.

Making the work safe

Making the work safe is mainly in the realm of the designer and production engineer. It is also a more general management responsibility to ensure that any older equipment and machinery that is used is appropriately modified to make it safe, or removed. The provision of necessary safety wear is also a managerial responsibility – for example, making sure goggles and ear protectors are available.

Enabling employees to work safely

Whereas making the work safe is completely a management responsibility, the individual employee may contribute by his or her own negligence, working unsafely in a safe situation. The task of managers is twofold; first, the employee must know what to do; second, this knowledge must be translated into action: the employee must comply with the safe working procedures that are laid down. To meet the first part of the obligation management need to be scrupulous in communication of drills and instructions and the analysis of working situations to decide what the drills should be. That is a much bigger and more difficult activity than can be implied in a single sentence, but the second part of getting compliance is more difficult and more important. Employee failure to comply with clear drills does not absolve the employer and the management. When an explosion leaves the factory in ruins it is of little value for the factory manager to shake his head and say: 'I told them not to do it.' We examine the way to obtain compliance shortly, in the course of our discussion about training and other methods of persuasion.

In larger organisations the initiative on safe working will be led by the professionals within the management team. They are the safety officer, the medical officer, the nursing staff and the safety representatives. Although there is no legal obligation to appoint a safety officer, more and more organisations are making such appointments. One reason is to provide emphasis and focus for safety matters. The appointment suggests that the management mean business, but the appointment itself is not enough. It has to be fitted into the management structure with lines of reporting and accountability which will enable the safety officer to be effective and which will prevent other members of management becoming uncertain of their own responsibilities – perhaps to the point of thinking that they no longer exist. Ideally, the safety officers operate on two fronts: making the work safe and ensuring safe working, although this may require an ability to talk constructively on engineering issues with engineers as well as being able to handle training and some industrial-relations-type arguments.

The medical officer (if one is appointed) will almost certainly be the only medically qualified person and can therefore introduce to the thinking on health and safety discussions a perspective and a range of knowledge that is both unique and relevant. Second, the medical officer will probably carry more social status than the managers dealing with health and safety matters and he or she will be detached from the management in their eyes and his or her own. Doctors have their own ethical code, which is different from that of the managers. They are authoritative advisers to management on making the work safe and can be authoritative advisers to employees on working safely. They are invaluable members of the safety committee and potentially important features of training programmes. Occupational nurses also deal directly with working safely and often play a part in safety training, as well as symbolising care in the face of hazard.

Safety training and other methods of persuasion

Safety training has three major purposes: (1) employees should be told about and understand the nature of the hazards at the place of work; (2) employees need to be made aware of the safety rules and procedures; and (3) they need to be persuaded to comply with them. The first of these is the most important, because employees sometimes tend to modify the rules to suit their own convenience. Trainers cannot, of course, condone the short cut without implying a general flexibility in the rules, but they need to be aware of how employees will probably respond. In some areas the use of short cuts by skilled employees does not always mean they are working less safely, but there are many areas where compliance with the rules is critical, for example, the wearing of safety goggles.

Safety training needs to be carried out in three settings: at induction, on the job and in refresher courses. A variety of different training techniques can be employed, including lectures, discussions, films, role playing and slides. These methods are sometimes supplemented by poster or other safety awareness campaigns and communications, and disciplinary action for breaches of the safety rules. Management example in sticking to the safety rules no matter what the tempo of production can also set a good example.

Research by Pirani and Reynolds (1976) indicated that the response to a variety of methods of safety persuasion – poster campaigns, film shows, fear techniques, discussion groups, role playing and disciplinary action – was very good in the short term (over two weeks) but after four months the initial improvement had virtually disappeared for all methods except role playing. From this it can be concluded that: first, a management initiative on safety will produce gratifying results in the obeying of rules, but a fresh initiative will be needed at regular and frequent intervals to keep it effective; and second, the technique of role playing appears to produce results that are longer lasting.

WINDOW ON PRACTICE

Health and safety and the use of contractors

As large firms increasingly contract out their operations the Health and Safety Commission is paying greater attention to this area, and Frank Davis, the Chair of the Commission warned: 'No firm – whatever the industrial sector – can afford to be complacent about the activities of contractors' (speaking at the Royal Society for Prevention of Accidents Congress, May 1996).

Lucas Industries (who subcontract a range of activities, some high risk), as part of a major reorganisation, reviewed their health, safety and environment systems in order to improve their performance. They concluded that current systems were reactive, not auditable or integrated with other systems, lacked clear ownership, were too dependent on internal specialists and did not address concerns about high-risk activities.

Their new approach seeks to rectify these problems. They developed a questionnaire for contractors to complete, relating to health and safety issues and they assessed this against what they could reasonably expect from a contractor of that size in that business. This enabled Lucas to take the initiative by assessing the risk and then discussing this assessment with the contractor. Where necessary, contractors were given encouragement and help to improve. Only those contractors who were already operating at the appropriate level, or who would improve to this level, would be on the Lucas Register of Contractors. Contractors were invited to attend a half-day awareness raising workshop based on the questionnaire topics and focused on risk assessment. A newly designed Contractors Registration Form was implemented to be completed jointly by the contractor and Lucas. This covers such issues as the task, materials, substances and equipment used, services needed, work environment and conditions and site hazards. Via this form the contractors and Lucas agree and record controls and precautions and safe systems of work. Where possible these forms are displayed where the work is carried out in order to make the risk assessment visible.

Occupational health departments

Occupational health and welfare is a broad area, which includes both physical and emotional well-being. The medical officer, occupational health nurse and welfare officer all have a contribution to make here. In a broader sense so do the dentist, chiropodist and other professionals when they are employed by the organisation. The provision of these broader welfare facilities is often found in large organisations located away from centres of population, especially in industrial plants, where the necessity of at least an occupational health nurse can be clearly seen.

In terms of physical care the sorts of facility that can be provided are:

1 Emergency treatment, beyond immediate first aid, of injuries sustained at work.
2 Medical, dental and other facilities, which employees can use and which can be more easily fitted into the working day than making appointments with outside professionals.
3 Immediate advice on medical and related matters, especially those connected with work.
4 Monitoring of accidents and illnesses to identify hazards and danger points, and formulating ideas to combat these in conjunction with the safety officer.
5 On-site medicals for those joining the organisation.
6 Regular medicals for employees.
7 Input into health and safety training courses.
8 Regular screening services (e.g. cervical cancer screening).

Summary propositions

31.1 Occupational welfare is the 'well-being' of people at work, encompassing occupational health and safety.

31.2 The history of human resource management is interrelated with the development of welfare. Many HR managers find this association a disadvantage when trying to develop the authority and status of personnel management.

31.3 The legal framework for health and safety includes both the criminal and civil law. The former is policed by health and safety inspectors, the latter provides a vehicle for those who suffer illness or injury as a result of their work to claim damages.

31.4 The Health and Safety at Work etc. Act 1974 is a major piece of UK legislation in this field. The efforts of the EU to ensure harmonisation of health and safety resulted in a major surge of new legislation in the 1990s.

31.5 The period since the 1980s has seen increasing interest in occupational health and welfare, particularly related to stress, alcoholism and counselling.

References

Beaumont, P.B. (1984) 'Personnel management and the welfare role', *Management Decision*, Vol. 22, No. 3.

Carruthers, M. (1982) 'Train the mind to calm itself', *General Practitioner*, 16 July.

Cherrie, I. and Faulkner, C. (1989) 'Will the COSHH regulations improve occupational health?', *Safety Practitioner*, February, pp. 6–7.

Cooper, C.L. and Marshall, I. (1980) *White Collar and Professional Stress*. Chichester: John Wiley.

De Board, R. (1983) *Counselling People at Work: an introduction for managers*. Aldershot: Gower.

Eva, D. and Oswald, R. (1981) *Health and Safety at Work*. London: Pan Books.

Fox, A. (1966) 'From welfare to organization', *New Society*, 9 June.

Ganster, D.C. and Murphy, L. (2000) 'Workplace Interventions to Prevent Stress-Related

Illness: Lessons from Research and Practice', in C. Cooper and E. Locke (eds), *Industrial and Organizational Psychology: Linking Theory with Practice*. Oxford: Blackwell.

Industrial Relations Services (1999) 'Unhappy, unhealthy, not here ...', *Employee Health Bulletin 12*, December.

Industrial Relations Services (2000a) 'Construction deaths mar health and safety figures', *Employee Health Bulletin 17*, December.

Industrial Relations Services (2000b) '£203,000 award for single breakdown', *Employee Health Bulletin 13*, February.

Industrial Relations Services (2000c) 'Stress auditing – the OSI', *Employee Health Bulletin 16*, August.

Institute of Personnel and Development (1997) 'Europe: personnel and development', *IPD Brief*, July.

Jex, S.M. (1998) *Stress and Job Performance: Theory, Research and Implications for Managerial Practice*. Thousand Oaks, Calif.: Sage.

Leach, J. (1995) *Devolution of personnel activities – the reality*, MA Dissertation, Manchester Metropolitan University.

Levinson, H. (1964) *Executive Stress*. New York: Harper & Row.

Macdonald, L. (1999) *Sensitive Issues in Employment*. Dublin: Blackhall.

Mills, M. (1996) 'Body and soul', *People Management*, 2 September, pp. 36–8.

Nykodym, N. and George, K. (1989) 'Stress busting on the job', *Personnel*, July, pp. 56–9.

Palmer, S. (1989) 'Occupational stress', *The Safety and Health Practitioner*, August, pp. 16–18.

Pirani, M. and Reynolds, J. (1976) 'Gearing up for safety', *Personnel Management*, February.

Positive Health Centre (1985) *Chemo Feedback*. London: Positive Health Centre.

Riddell, R. (1989) 'Why COSHH will hit hard on health and safety', *Personnel Management*, September, pp. 46–9.

Roney, A. and Cooper, C. (eds) (1997) *Professionals on Workplace Stress*. Chichester: Wiley.

Stranks, J. (2000) *Health and Safety*, 2nd edn. London: ICSA Publishing.

Willey, B. (2000) *Employment Law in Context*. London: Financial Times/Prentice Hall.

Legal cases

Ingram v. *Worcester County Council* (2000) (in IRS 2000c).

Jones v. *Lionite Specialities (Cardiff) Ltd* (1961) 105SJ 1082.

Mortimer v. *V.L. Churchill* (1979).

Walker v. *Northumberland County Council* [1995] 1 All ER 737; [1995] IRLR 35.

General discussion questions

1 Good health is good business. Discuss.

2 To what extent and by what processes can organisations reduce stress for employees who are members of dual-career families?

3 How can an organisation utilise training and development to foster a culture that is receptive to health and safety?

Chapter 32

Grievance and discipline

Grievance and discipline are awkward words nowadays. They sound rather solemn and forbidding, more suitable for a nineteenth-century workhouse than a twenty-first-century business. They certainly have no place in the thinking of Britain's favourite entrepreneur, Sir Richard Branson:

> If you have the right people in place, treat them well and trust them, they will produce happy customers and the necessary profits to carry on and expand the work.
>
> (quoted in Handy 1999, p. 86)

We use them for their value as technical terms to describe the breakdown of mutual confidence between employer and employee, or between managers and managed. When someone starts work at an organisation there are mutual expectations that form the basis of the forthcoming working relationship. We explained in the opening chapter of this book how the maintenance of those mutual expectations is the central purpose of human resource management. Apart from what is written in the contract of employment, both parties will have expectations of what is to come. Employees are likely to expect, for instance, a congenial working situation with like-minded colleagues, opportunities to use existing skills and to acquire others, work that does not offend their personal value system, acceptable leadership and management from those more senior, and opportunities to grow and mature. Employers will have expectations such as willing participation in the team, conscientious and imaginative use of existing skills and an ability to acquire others, compliance with reasonable instructions without quibbles, acceptance of the authority of those placed in authority and a willingness to be flexible and accept change.

That working relationship is sometimes going to go wrong. If the employee is dissatisfied, then there is potentially a grievance. If the employer is dissatisfied, there is the potential for a disciplinary situation. The two complementary processes are intended to find ways of avoiding the ultimate sanction of the employee quitting or being dismissed, but at the same time preparing the ground for those sanctions if all else fails.

Usually, the authority to be exercised in a business is impersonalised by the use of role in order to make it more effective. If a colleague mentions to you that you have overspent your budget, your reaction might be proud bravado unless you knew that the colleague had a role such as company accountant, internal auditor or financial director. Everyone in a business has a role – most people have several – and each role confers some authority. The canteen assistant who tells you that the steak and kidney pudding is off is more believable than the managing director conveying the same message. Normally in hospitals people wearing white coats and a stethoscope are seen as being more authoritative than people in white coats without a stethoscope.

Dependence on role is not always welcome to those in managerial positions, who are fond of using phrases like, 'I know how to get the best out of people', 'I understand my chaps' and 'I have a loyal staff'. This may partly be due to their perception of their role being to persuade the reluctant and command the respect of the unwilling by the use of personal leadership qualities, and it is indisputable that some managers are more effective with some groups of staff than with others, but there is more to it than personal skill: we are predisposed to obey those who outrank us in any hierarchy.

The Milgram experiments with obedience

Obedience is the reaction expected of people by those in authority positions, who prescribe actions which, but for that authority, might not necessarily have been carried out. Stanley Milgram (1974) conducted a series of experiments to investigate obedience to authority and highlighted the significance of obedience and the power of authority in our everyday lives.

Subjects were led to believe that a study of memory and learning was being carried out which involved giving progressively more severe electric shocks to a learner who gave incorrect answers to factual questions. If the learner gave the correct answer the reward was a further question; if the answer was incorrect there was the punishment of a mild electric shock. Each shock was more severe than the previous one. The 'learner' was not actually receiving shocks, but was a member of the experimental team simulating progressively greater distress, as the shocks were supposedly made stronger. Eighteen different experiments were conducted with over 1,000 subjects, with the circumstances between experiments varying. No matter how the variables were altered the subjects showed an astonishing compliance with authority even when delivering 'shocks' of 450 volts. Up to 65 per cent of subjects continued to obey throughout the experiment in the presence of a clear authority figure and as many as 20 per cent continued to obey when the authority figure was absent.

Milgram was dismayed by his results:

> With numbing regularity good people were seen to knuckle under to the demands of authority and perform actions that were callous and severe. Men who are in everyday life responsible and decent were seduced by the trappings of authority, by the control of their perceptions, and by the uncritical acceptance of the experimenter's definition of the situation into performing harsh acts. (1974, p. 123)

Our interest in Milgram's work is simply to demonstrate that we all have a predilection to obey instructions from authority figures, even if we do not want to. He points out that the act of entering a hierarchical system (such as any employing organisation) makes people see themselves acting as agents for carrying out the wishes of someone else, and this results in these people being in a different state, described as the agentic state. This is the opposite to the state of autonomy when individuals see themselves as acting on their own. Milgram then sets out the factors that lay the groundwork for obedience to authority.

1 **Family**: Parental regulation inculcates a respect for adult authority. Parental injunctions form the basis for moral imperatives as commands to children have a dual function. 'Don't tell lies' is a moral injunction carrying a further

implicit instruction: 'And obey me!' It is the implicit demand for obedience that remains the only consistent element across a range of explicit instructions.

2 **Institutional setting**: Children emerge from the family into an institutional system of authority: the school. Here they learn how to function in an organisation. They are regulated by teachers, but can see that the headteacher, the school governors and central government regulate the teachers themselves. Throughout this period they are in a subordinate position. When, as adults, they go to work it may be found that a certain level of dissent is allowable, but the overall situation is one in which they are to do a job prescribed by someone else.

3 **Rewards**: Compliance with authority is generally rewarded, while disobedience is frequently punished. Most significantly, promotion within the hierarchy not only rewards the individual but also ensures the continuity of the hierarchy.

4 **Perception of authority**: Authority is normatively supported: there is a shared expectation among people that certain institutions do, ordinarily, have a socially controlling figure. Also, the authority of the controlling figure is limited to the situation. The usher in a cinema wields authority, which vanishes on leaving the premises. As authority is expected it does not have to be asserted, merely presented.

5 **Entry into the authority system**: Having perceived an authority figure, an individual must then define that figure as relevant to the subject. The individual not only takes the voluntary step of deciding which authority system to join (at least in most of employment), but also defines which authority is relevant to which event. The firefighter may expect instant obedience when calling for everybody to evacuate the building, but not if asking employees to use a different accounting system.

6 **The overarching ideology**: The legitimacy of the social situation relates to a justifying ideology. Science and education formed the background to the experiments Milgram conducted and therefore provided a justification for actions carried out in their name. Most employment is in realms of activity regarded as legitimate, justified by the values and needs of society. This is vital if individuals are to provide willing obedience, as it enables them to see their behaviour as serving a desirable end.

Managers are positioned in an organisational hierarchy in such a way that others will be predisposed, as Milgram demonstrates, to follow their instructions. Managers put in place a series of frameworks to explain how they will exact obedience: they use *discipline*. Because individual employees feel their relative weakness, they seek complementary frameworks to challenge the otherwise unfettered use of managerial disciplinary power: they may join trade unions, but they will always need channels to present their *grievances*.

In later work Milgram (1992) made an important distinction between obedience and conformity, which had been studied by several experimental psychologists, most notably Asch (1951) and Abrams *et al.* (1990). Conformity and obedience both involve abandoning personal judgement as a result of external pressure. The external pressure to conform is the need to be accepted by one's peers and the resultant behaviour is to wear similar clothes, to adopt similar attitudes and adopt similar behaviour. The external pressure to obey comes from a hierarchy of which one is a member, but which certain others have more status and power than oneself.

> There are at least three important differences ... First, in conformity there is no *explicit* requirement to act in a certain way, whereas in obedience we are *ordered* or *instructed* to do something. Second, those who influence us when we conform are our *peers* (or equals) and people's behaviours become more alike because they are affected by *example*. In obedience, there is ... somebody in *higher authority* influencing behaviour. Third, conformity has to do with the psychological need for acceptance by others. Obedience, by contrast, has to do with the social power and status of an authority figure in a hierarchical situation.
>
> (Gross and McIlveen 1998, p. 508)

In this chapter we are concerned uniquely with discipline and grievance within business organisations, but it is worth pointing out that managers are the focal points for the grievances of people outside the business as well, but those grievances are called complaints. You may complain *about* poor service, shoddy workmanship or rudeness from an employee, but you complain *to* a manager.

HR managers make one of their most significant contributions to business effectiveness by the way they facilitate and administer grievance and disciplinary issues. First, they devise and negotiate the procedural framework of organisational justice on which both discipline and grievance depend. Second, they are much involved in the interviews and problem-solving discussions that eventually produce solutions to the difficulties that have been encountered. Third, they maintain the viability of the whole process which forms an integral part of their work: they monitor to make sure that grievances are not overlooked and so that any general trend can be perceived, and they oversee the disciplinary machinery to ensure that it is not being bypassed or unfairly manipulated.

Grievance and discipline handling is one of the roles in human resource management that few other people want to take over. Ambitious line managers may want to select their own staff without personnel intervention or by using the services of consultants. They may try to brush their personnel colleagues aside and deal directly with trade union officials or organise their own management development, but grievance and discipline is too hot a potato.

The requirements of the law regarding explanation of grievance handling and the legal framework to avoid unfair dismissal combine to make this an area where HR people must be both knowledgeable and effective. That combination provides a valuable platform for influencing other aspects of management. The personnel manager who is not skilled in grievance and discipline is seldom in a strong organisational position.

What do we mean by discipline?

Discipline is regulation of human activity to produce a controlled performance. It ranges from the guard's control of a rabble to the accomplishment of lone individuals producing spectacular performance through self-discipline in the control of their own talents and resources.

First, there is managerial discipline in which everything depends on the leader from start to finish. There is a group of people who are answerable to someone who directs what they should all do. Only through individual direction can that group of people produce a worthwhile performance, like the person leading the community singing in the pantomime or the person conducting an orchestra. Everything depends on the leader.

Second, there is team discipline, where the perfection of the performance derives from the mutual dependence of all, and that mutual dependence derives from a commitment by each member to the total enterprise: the failure of one would be the downfall of all. This is usually found in relatively small working groups, like a dance troupe or an autonomous working group in a factory.

Third, there is self-discipline, like that of the juggler or the skilled artisan, where a solo performer is absolutely dependent on training, expertise and self-control.

Discipline is, therefore, not only negative, producing punishment or prevention. It can also be a valuable quality for the individual who is subject to it, although the form of discipline depends not only on the individual employee but also on the task and the way it is organised. The development of self-discipline is easier in some jobs than others and many of the job redesign initiatives have been directed at providing scope for job holders to exercise self-discipline and find a degree of autonomy from managerial discipline. Figure 32.1 shows how the three forms are connected in a sequence or hierarchy, with employees finding one of three ways to achieve their contribution to organisational effectiveness. However, even the most accomplished solo performer has been dependent on others for training, and advice, and every team has its coach.

Activity 32.1	Note three examples of managerial discipline, team discipline and self-discipline from your own experience.

Figure 32.1 Three forms of discipline

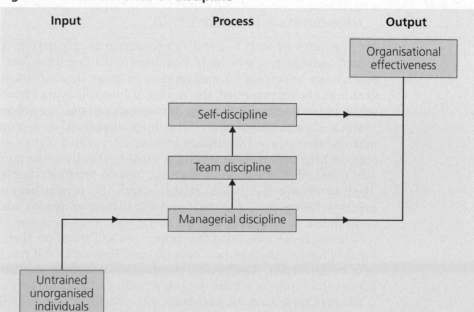

Managers are not dealing with discipline only when they are rebuking late-comers or threatening to dismiss saboteurs. As well as dealing with the unruly and reluctant, they are developing the co-ordinated discipline of the working team, engendering that *esprit de corps* which makes the whole greater than the sum of the parts. They are training the new recruit who must not let down the rest of the team, puzzling over the reasons why A is fitting in well while B is still struggling. Managers are also providing people with the equipment to develop the self-discipline that will give them autonomy, responsibility and the capacity to maximise their powers. The independence and autonomy that self-discipline produces also produces the greatest degree of personal satisfaction – and often the largest pay packet. Furthermore the movement between the three forms represents a declining degree of managerial involvement. If you are a leader of community singing, nothing can happen without your being present and the quality of the singing depends on your performance each time. If you train jugglers, the time and effort you invest pays off a thousand times, while you sit back and watch the show.

What do we mean by grievance?

Contemporary British texts virtually ignore grievance handling, but the Americans maintain sound coverage. Mathis and Jackson (1994) have a particularly helpful review. Some years ago Pigors and Myers (1977, p. 229) provided a helpful approach to the topic by drawing a distinction between the terms dissatisfaction, complaint and grievance as follows:

■ **Dissatisfaction**: Anything that disturbs an employee, whether or not the unrest is expressed in words.
■ **Complaint**: A spoken or written dissatisfaction brought to the attention of the supervisor and/or shop steward.
■ **Grievance**: A complaint that has been formally presented to a management representative or to a union official.

This provides us with a useful categorisation by separating out grievance as a formal, relatively drastic step, compared with commonplace grumbling. It is much more important for management to know about dissatisfaction. Although nothing is being expressed, the feeling of hurt following failure to get a pay rise or the frustration about shortage of materials can quickly influence performance.

Much dissatisfaction never turns into complaint, as something happens to make it unnecessary. Dissatisfaction evaporates with a night's sleep, after a cup of coffee with a colleague, or when the cause of the dissatisfaction is in some other way removed. The few dissatisfactions that do produce complaint are also most likely to resolve themselves at that stage. The person hearing the complaint explains things in a way that the dissatisfied employee had not previously appreciated, or takes action to get at the root of the problem.

Grievances are rare since few employees will question their superior's judgement (whatever their private opinion) and fewer still will risk being stigmatised as a troublemaker. Also, many people do not initiate grievances because they believe that nothing will be done as a result of their attempt.

HR managers have to encourage the proper use of procedures to discover sources of dissatisfaction. Managers in the middle may not reveal the complaints they are hearing, for fear of showing themselves in a poor light. Employees who feel insecure, for any reason, are not likely to risk going into procedure, yet the dissatisfaction lying beneath a repressed grievance can produce all manner of unsatisfactory work behaviours from apathy to arson. Individual dissatisfaction can lead to the loss of a potentially valuable employee; collective dissatisfaction can lead to industrial action.

There are three types of complaint that get progressively harder to handle. The first kind is factual and can be readily tested:

- 'The machine is out of order.'
- 'The stock we're getting now is not up to standard.'
- 'This adhesive won't stick.'

The second type is complaints that are based partly on subjective reactions:

- 'The work is messy.'
- 'It's too hot in here.'
- 'This job is too stressful.'

These statements include terms where the meaning is biologically or socially determined and can therefore not be understood unless the background of the complainant is known; seldom can their accuracy be objectively determined. A temperature of 18 degrees celsius may be too hot for one person but equable for another.

The third, and most difficult, type of complaint is that involving the hopes and fears of employees:

- 'The supervisor plays favourites.'
- 'The pay is not very good.'
- 'Seniority doesn't count as much as it should.'

These show the importance of determining not only what employees feel, but also why they feel as they do; not only verifying the facts ('the manifest content'), but also determining the feelings behind the facts ('the latent content'). An employee who complains of the supervisor being a bully may actually be saying something rather different. In one instance it was revealed that the root of the dissatisfaction was the employee's attitude to any authority figure, not simply the supervisor who was the subject of the complaint.

Each type of dissatisfaction is important to uncover and act upon, if action is possible. Action is usually prompt on complaints of the first type, as they are neutral: blame is placed on an inanimate object so individual culpability is not an issue. Action may be quick on complaints of the second type if the required action is straightforward – such as opening a window if it is too hot – but the problem of accuracy can produce a tendency to smooth over an issue or leave it 'to sort itself out' in time. The third type of complaint is the most difficult, and action is often avoided. Supervisors will often take complaints to be a personal criticism of their own competence, and employees will often translate the complaint into a grievance only by attaching it to a third party like a shop steward, so that the relationship between employee and supervisor is not jeopardised.

Activity 32.2 Think of an example from your own experience of dissatisfaction causing inefficiency that was not remedied because there was no complaint. Why was there no complaint?

The framework of organisational justice

The organisation requires a framework of justice to surround the employment relationship so that managers and supervisors, as well as other employees, know where they stand when dissatisfaction develops. Figure 32.2 shows a framework.

Awareness of culture and appropriateness of style

The culture of an organisation affects the behaviour of people within it, develops norms that are hard to alter and provides a pattern of conformity. If, for instance, everyone is in the habit of arriving ten minutes late, a 'new broom' manager will have a struggle to change the habit. Equally, if everyone is in the habit of arriving punctually, then a new recruit who often arrives late will come under strong social pressure to conform, without need for recourse to management action. Culture also affects the freedom and candour with which people discuss dissatisfactions with their managers without allowing them to fester.

The style of managers in handling grievances and discipline reflects their beliefs. The manager who sees discipline as being punishment, and who regards grievances as examples of subordinates getting above themselves, will behave in a relatively autocratic way, being curt in disciplinary situations and dismissive of

Figure 32.2 The framework of organisational justice

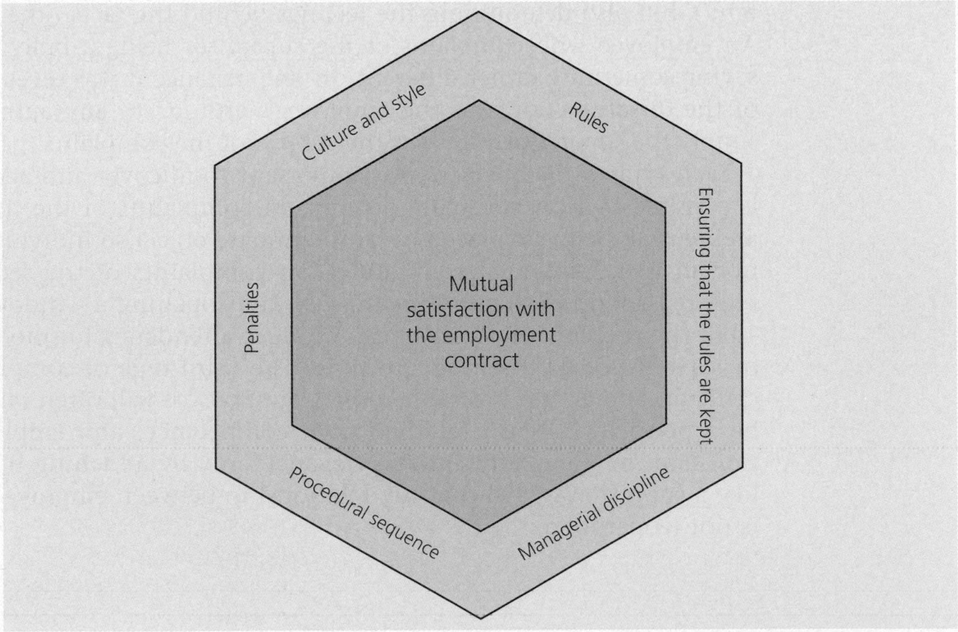

complaints. The manager who sees disciplinary problems as obstacles to achievement that do not necessarily imply incompetence or ill will by the employee will seek out the cause of the problem. That problem may then be revealed as one requiring firm, punitive action by the manager, or it may be revealed as a matter requiring management remedy of a different kind. The manager who listens out for complaints and grievances, gets to the bottom of the problems and finds solutions will run little risk of rumbling discontent from people obsessed by trivial problems.

Rules

Every workplace has rules; the difficulty is to have rules that people will honour. Some rules come from statutes, like the tachograph requirement for HGV drivers, but most are tailored to meet the particular requirements of the organisation in which they apply. For example, rules about personal cleanliness are essential in a food factory but less stringent in a garage.

Rules should be clear and readily understood; the number should be sufficient to cover all obvious and usual disciplinary matters. To ensure general compliance it is helpful if rules are jointly determined, but it is more common for management to formulate the rules and for employee representatives eventually to concur with them. Employees should have ready access to the rules through the employee handbook and notice board, and the personnel manager will always try to ensure that the rules are known as well as published.

In 1973 the Department of Employment suggested that rules fall into six categories, relating to different types of employee behaviour:

1 Negligence is failure to do the job properly and is different from incompetence because of the assumption that the employee can do the job properly, but has not.

2 Unreliability is failure to attend work as required, such as being late or absent.

3 Insubordination is refusal to obey an instruction, or deliberate disrespect to someone in a position of authority. It is not to be confused with the use of bad language. Some of the most entertaining cases in industrial tribunals have involved weighty consideration of whether or not colourful language was intended to be insubordinate.

4 Interfering with the rights of others covers a range of behaviours that are deemed socially unacceptable. Fighting is clearly identifiable, but intimidation may be more difficult to establish.

5 Theft is another clear-cut aspect of behaviour that is unacceptable when it is from another employee. Theft from the organisation should be supported by very explicit rules, as stealing company property is regarded by many offenders as one of the perks of the job. How often have you taken home a box of paper clips or a felt tip pen without any thought that you were stealing from the employer?

6 Safety offences are those aspects of behaviour that can cause a hazard.

The value of rules is to provide guidelines on what people should do, as the majority will comply. The number of people killed on the roads has declined sharply because the great majority of drivers obey the law on wearing seat belts. The date for introducing the legislation was, however, deferred twice to ensure

WINDOW ON PRACTICE	In a recent discussion with a group of senior managers, employees identified the following as legitimately taken at will:

paper clips, pencils, disposable pens, spiral pads, local telephone calls, plain paper, computer disks, adhesive tape, overalls and simple uniform.

Among the more problematic were:

■ Redundant or shop-soiled stock. One DIY store insisted that the store manager should personally supervise the scrapping of items that were slightly damaged, to ensure that other items were not slightly damaged on purpose.

■ Surplus materials. One electricity supplier had some difficulty in eradicating the practice of surplus cable and pipe being regarded as a legitimate perquisite of fitters at the end of installation jobs, as they suspected their engineers were using the surplus for private work. Twelve months later the level of material requisition had declined by 14 per cent.

that it was introduced when there would be general acceptance rather than widespread defiance of the law.

Ensuring that the rules are kept

Although the majority of car drivers wear seat belts, the majority of dog owners never had dog licences, so that legal requirement had to be repealed. It is not sufficient just to have rules; they are only effective if they are observed. How do we make sure that employees stick to the rules?

1 Information is needed so that everyone knows what the rules are and why they should be obeyed. Written particulars may suffice in an employment tribunal hearing, but most people conform to the behaviour of their colleagues, so informal methods of communication are just as important as formal statements.

2 Induction can make the rules coherent and reinforce their understanding. The rule can be explained, perhaps with examples, so that people not only know the rules but also understand why they should be obeyed.

3 Placement or relocation can avoid the risk of rules being broken, by placing a new recruit with a working team that has high standards of compliance. If there are the signs of disciplinary problems in the offing, then a quick relocation can put the problem employee in a new situation where offences are less likely.

4 Training increases awareness of the rules, improving self-confidence and self-discipline. There will be new working procedures or new equipment from time to time, and again training will reduce the risk of safety offences, negligence or unreliability.

5 Review of the rules periodically ensures that they are up to date, and also ensures that their observance is a live issue. If, for instance, there is a monthly staff council meeting, it could be appropriate to have a rules review every 12 months. The simple fact of the rules being discussed keeps up the general level of awareness of what they are.

6 Penalties make the framework of organisational justice firmer if there is an understanding of what penalties can be imposed, by whom and for what. It is

not feasible or desirable to have a fixed scale, but neither is it wise for penalties to depend on individual managerial whim. This area has been partially codified by the legislation on dismissal, but the following are some typical forms of penalty:

(a) **Rebuke:** The simple 'Don't do that' or 'Smoking is not allowed in here' or 'If you're late again, you will be in trouble' is all that is needed in most situations, as someone has forgotten one of the rules, had not realised it was to be taken seriously, or was perhaps testing the resolution of the management. Too frequently, managers are reluctant to risk defiance and tend to wait until they have a good case for more serious action rather than deploy their own, there-and-then authority. They should remember the lessons of Stanley Milgram on obedience.

(b) **Caution:** Slightly more serious and formal is the caution, which is then recorded. This is not triggering the procedure for dismissal, it is just making a note of a rule being broken and an offence being pointed out.

(c) **Warnings:** When the management begin to issue warnings, great care is required, as the development of unfair dismissal legislation has made the system of warnings an integral part of disciplinary practice which has to be followed if the employer is to succeed in defending a possible claim of unfair dismissal at tribunal. For the employer to show procedural fairness there should normally be a formal oral warning, or a written warning, specifying the nature of the offence and the likely outcome of the offence being repeated. It should also be made clear that this is the first, formal stage in the procedure. Further misconduct could then warrant a final written warning containing a statement that further repetition would lead to a penalty such as suspension or dismissal. All written warnings should be dated, signed and kept on record for an agreed period. The means of appeal against the disciplinary action should also be pointed out.

(d) **Disciplinary transfer or demotion:** This is moving the employee to less attractive work, possibly carrying a lower salary. The seriousness of this is that it is public, as the employee's colleagues know the reason. A form of disciplinary transfer is found on assembly lines, where there are some jobs that are more attractive and carry higher status than others. Rule-breakers may be 'pushed down the line' until their contempt is purged and they are able to move back up.

(e) **Suspension:** A tactic that has the benefit of being serious and avoids the disadvantage of being long lasting, like demotion. The employer has a contractual obligation to provide pay, but not to provide work, so it is easy to suspend someone from duty – with pay – either as a punishment or while an alleged offence is being investigated. If the contract of employment permits, it may also be possible to suspend the employee for a short period without pay.

(f) **Fines:** These are little used, because of contractual problems, but the most common is deduction from pay for lateness.

The important general comment about penalties is that they should be appropriate in the circumstances. Where someone is, for instance, persistently late or absent, suspension would be a strange penalty. Also penalties must be within the law. An employee cannot be demoted or transferred at managerial whim, and fines or unpaid suspension can only be imposed if the contract of employment allows such measures.

7 Procedural sequence is essential to the framework of organisational justice. It should be the clear, unvarying logic of procedure, and be well known and trusted. Procedure makes clear, for example, who does and who does not have the power to dismiss. The dissatisfied employee, who is wondering whether or not to turn a complaint into a formal grievance, knows who will hear the grievance and where an appeal could be lodged. This security of procedure, where step B always follows step A, is needed by managers as well as by employees, as it provides them with their authority as well as limiting the scope of their actions.

8 Managerial discipline. Finally, managers must preserve general respect for the justice framework by their self-discipline in how they work within it. With very good intentions some senior managers maintain an 'open door' policy with the message: 'My door is always open ... call in any time you feel I can help you.' This has many advantages and is often necessary, but it has danger for matters of discipline and grievance because it encourages people to bypass middle managers. There is also the danger that employees come to see the settlement of their grievances as being dependent on the personal goodwill of an individual rather than on the business logic or their human and employment rights.

Managers must be consistent in handling discipline and grievance issues. Whatever the rules are, they will be generally supported only as long as they deserve support. If they are enforced inconsistently they will soon lose any moral authority, depending only on the fear of penalties. Equally, the manager who handles grievances quickly and consistently will enjoy the support of a committed group of employees.

The other need for managerial discipline is to test the validity of the discipline assumption. Is it a case for disciplinary action or for some other remedy? There is little purpose in suspending someone for negligence when the real problem is lack of training. Many disciplinary problems disappear under analysis, and it is sensible to carry out the analysis before making a possibly unjustified allegation of indiscipline.

Grievance procedure

Managers, who believe that it introduces unnecessary rigidity into the working relationship, often resent the formality of the grievance procedure: 'I see my people all the time. We work side by side and they can raise with me any issue they want, at any time they want ...'. The problem is that many people will not raise issues with the immediate superior that could be regarded as contentious, in just the same way that managers frequently shirk the rebuke as a form of disciplinary penalty. Formality in procedure provides a framework within which individuals can reasonably air their grievances and avoids the likelihood of managers dodging the issue when it is difficult. It avoids the risk of inconsistent ad hoc decisions, and the employee knows at the outset that the matter will be heard and where it will be heard. The key features of grievance procedure are fairness, facilities for representation, procedural steps and promptness.

1 Fairness is needed, to be just, but also to keep the procedure viable. If employees develop the belief that the procedure is only a sham, then its value will be lost and other means will be sought to deal with grievances. Fairness is

best supported by the obvious even-handedness of the ways in which grievances are handled, but it will be greatly enhanced if the appeal stage is either to a joint body or to independent arbitration – usually by ACAS – as the management is relinquishing the chance to be judge of its own cause.

2 Representation can help the individual employee who lacks the confidence or experience to take on the management single handedly. A representative, such as a union official, has the advantage of having dealt with a range of employee problems and may be able to advise the aggrieved person whether the claim is worth pursuing. There is always the risk that the presence of the representative produces a defensive management attitude affected by a number of other issues on which the manager and union official may be at loggerheads, so the managers involved in hearing the grievance have to cast the representative in the correct role for the occasion.

3 Procedural steps should be limited to three. There is no value in having more just because there are more levels in the management hierarchy. This will only lengthen the time taken to deal with matters and will soon bring the procedure into disrepute. The reason for advocating three steps is that three types of management activity are involved in settling grievances. Having said that, it is quite common for there to be more than three steps where there is a steep hierarchy, within which there may be further, more senior, people to whom the matter could be referred. The reason for more steps has nothing to do with how to process grievances but is purely a function of the organisation structure.

The first step is the preliminary, when the grievance is lodged with the immediate superior of the person with the complaint. In the normal working week most managers will have a variety of queries from members of their departments, some of which could become grievances, depending on the manager's reaction. Mostly the manager will either satisfy the employee or the employee will decide not to pursue the matter. Sometimes, however, a person will want to take the issue further. This is the preliminary step in procedure, but it is a tangible step as the manager has the opportunity to review any decisions made that have caused the dissatisfaction, possibly enabling the dissatisfied employee to withdraw the grievance. In our experience it is rare for matters to be taken any further unless the subject of the grievance is something on which company policy is being tested.

The hearing gives the complainant the opportunity to state the grievance to a more senior manager, who is able to take a broader view of the matter than the immediate superior and who may be able both to see the issue more dispassionately and to perceive solutions that the more limited perspective of the immediate superior obscured. It is important for the management that the hearing should finalise the matter whenever possible, so that recourse to appeal is not automatic. The hearing should not be seen by the employees as no more than an irritating milestone on the way to the real decision makers. This is why procedural steps should be limited to three.

If there is an appeal, this will usually be to a designated more senior manager, and the outcome will be either a confirmation or a modification of the decision at the hearing.

4 Promptness avoids the bitterness and frustration that comes from delay. When an employee 'goes into procedure', it is like pulling the communication cord in a train. The action is not taken lightly and is in anticipation of a swift resolution.

Figure 32.4 Outline disciplinary procedure

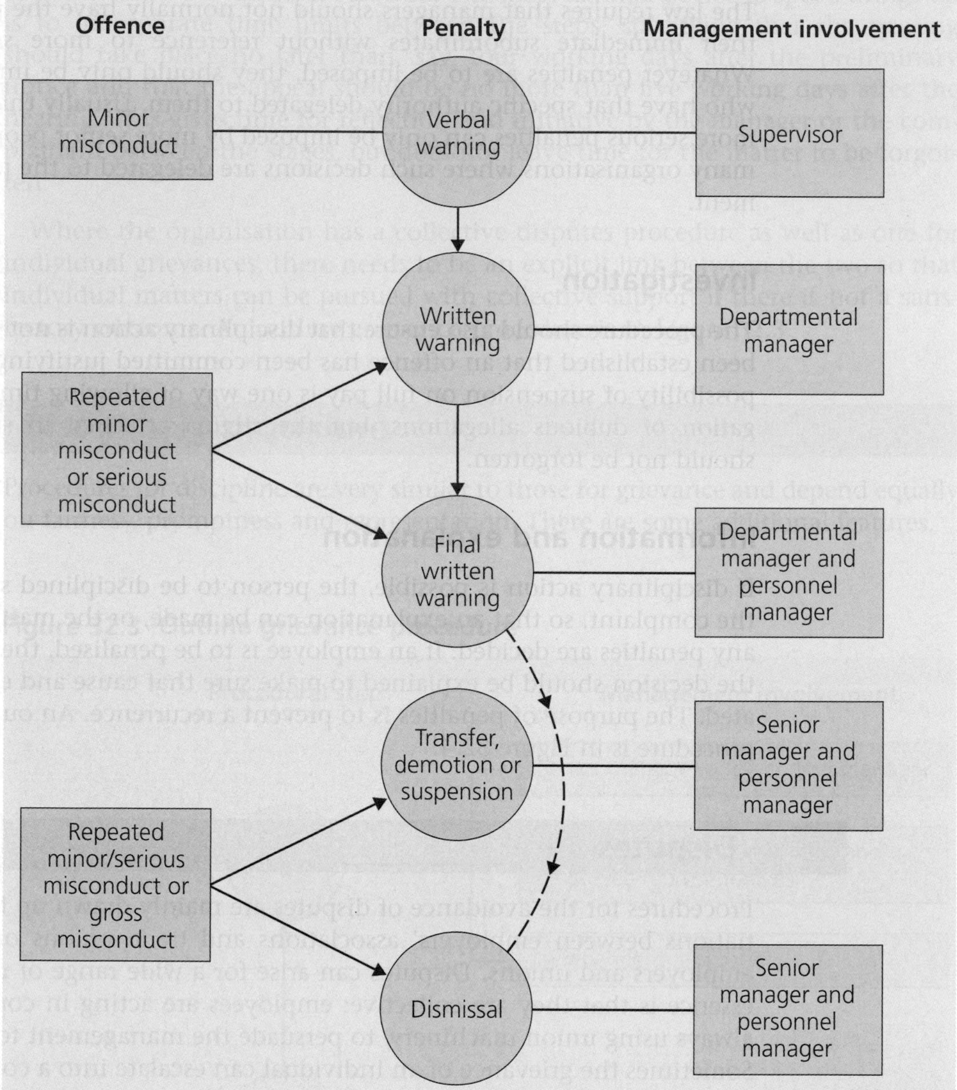

Offence	Penalty	Management involvement
Minor misconduct	Verbal warning	Supervisor
	Written warning	Departmental manager
Repeated minor misconduct or serious misconduct	Final written warning	Departmental manager and personnel manager
	Transfer, demotion or suspension	Senior manager and personnel manager
Repeated minor/serious misconduct or gross misconduct	Dismissal	Senior manager and personnel manager

common in the business, and to the managers who must also perceive the system as equitable if they are to abide by its outcomes.

Procedures have a potential to be fair in that they are certain. The conduct of employee relations becomes less haphazard and irrational: people 'know where they stand'. The existence of a rule cannot be denied and opportunities for one party to manipulate and change a rule are reduced. Procedures also have the advantage that they can be communicated. The process of formalising a procedure that previously existed only in custom and practice clarifies the ambiguities and inconsistencies within it and compels each party to recognise the role and responsibility of the other. By providing pre-established avenues for responses to various contingencies procedures make it possible for the response to be less random and so more fair. The impersonal nature of procedures offers the possibility of removing hostility from the workplace, since an artificial social situation is created in which the ritual displays of aggression towards management are not seen as personal attacks on managers.

The achievement of equity may not match the potential. Procedures cannot, for instance, impart equity to situations that are basically unfair. Thus attempting to cope with an anomalous pay system through a grievance procedure may be alleviating symptoms rather than treating causes. It is also impossible through a grievance procedure to overcome accepted norms of inequity in a company, such as greater punctuality being required of manual employees than of white-collar employees.

A further feature of procedural equity is its degree of similarity to the judicial process. All procedures adopt certain legalistic mechanisms, like the right of individuals to be represented and to hear the case against them, but some aspects of legalism, such as burdens of proof and strict adherence to precedent, may cause the application of standard remedies rather than the consideration of individual circumstances.

There is a nice irony in the fact that equity is best achieved when procedures are not used. Procedure is there in the background and expresses principles for fair and effective management of situations. All the while the **principles** are followed and the framework for organisational justice observed, procedure is not invoked. The advantage of this is that individuals (whether employees or managers) are not named and shamed, so that matters are much easier to deal with. Only when the matter is dealt with badly does the procedural step come closer.

The existence of the procedure becomes the incentive rather than the means for action to be taken: it is not an excuse for inaction. In 1999 and 2000 there were several high profile cases of medical negligence resulting in doctors being struck off the medical register and therefore being no longer able to practise. In each case it appeared that lapses had been allowed to continue for too long before remedial action was taken.

It is accepted that some employment situations require naming and shaming first, with possible remedial action following. In most sports there is on-the-spot penalising of players for breaking the rules.

WINDOW ON PRACTICE	The 'red-hot stove' rule of discipline offers the touching of a red hot stove as an analogy for effective disciplinary action:

1 The burn is immediate. There is no question of cause and effect.
2 You had warning. If the stove was red-hot, you knew what would happen if you touched it.
3 The discipline is consistent. Everyone who touches the stove is burned.
4 The discipline is impersonal. People are burned not because of who they are, but because they touch the stove.

Activity 32.3	Think of an attempt at disciplinary action that went wrong. Which of the features of the red-hot stove rule were missing?

Notions of fairness are not 'givens' of the situation; they are socially constructed and there will never be more than a degree of consensus on what constitutes fairness. Despite this, the procedural approach can exploit standards of certainty and consistency, which are widely accepted as elements of justice. The extent to which a procedure can do this will depend on the suitability of its structure to local circumstances, the commitment of those who operate it and the way that it reconciles legalistic and bargaining elements.

Summary propositions

32.1 The authority of managers to exercise discipline in relation to others in the organisation is underpinned by a general predilection of people to obey commands from those holding higher rank in the hierarchy of which they are members.

32.2 The exercise of that discipline is limited by the procedural structures for grievance and discipline.

32.3 Grievance and discipline handling are two areas of human resource management that few other people want to take over, and provide personnel managers with some of their most significant contributions to business effectiveness.

32.4 Discipline can be understood as being managerial, team or self-discipline, and they are connected hierarchically.

32.5 Dissatisfaction, complaint and grievance is another hierarchy. Unresolved employee dissatisfaction can lead to the loss of potentially valuable employees. In extreme cases it can lead to industrial action.

32.6 Grievance and disciplinary processes both require a framework of organisational justice.

32.7 The procedural framework of disciplinary and grievance processes is one of the keys to their being equitable.

32.8 Effective management of both discipline and grievance is achieved by following the principles of the procedures without invoking them in practice.

References

Abrams, D., Wetherell, M., Cochrane, S., Hogg, M.A. and Turner, J.C. (1990) 'Knowing what to think by knowing who you are: Self categorization and norm formation', *British Journal of Social Psychology,* Vol. 29, pp. 97–119.

Asch, S.E. (1951) 'Effect of group pressure upon the modification and distortion of judgements', in H. Guetzkow (ed.), *Groups, Leadership and Men.* Pittsburgh, Penn.: Carnegie Press.

Department of Employment (1973) *In Working Order.* London: HMSO.

Gross, R. and McIlveen, R. (1998) *Psychology: A New Introduction.* London: Hodder & Stoughton.

Handy, C.B. (1999) *The New Alchemists.* London: Hutchinson.

Mathis, R.L. and Jackson, J.H. (1994) *Human Resource Management,* 7th edn. Minneapolis/St Paul: West.

Milgram, S. (1974) *Obedience to Authority.* London: Tavistock.

Milgram, S. (1992) *The Individual in a Social World*, 2nd edn. New York: Harper & Row.
Pigors, P. and Myers, C. (1977) *Personnel Administration*, 8th edn. Maidenhead: McGraw-Hill.

General discussion topics

1 Do you think Milgram's experiments would have had a different outcome if the subjects had included women as well as men?

2 What examples can individual members of the group cite of self-discipline, team discipline and managerial discipline?

3 'The trouble with grievance procedures is that they encourage people to waste a lot of time with petty grumbles. Life at work is rarely straightforward and people should just accept the rough with the smooth.'

What do you think of that opinion?

Chapter 33   Interactive skill: grievance and disciplinary interviewing

We said earlier that the appraisal interview was the hardest aspect of management for any manager to undertake. The subject of this chapter is the least popular of all management activities: talking to people when things have gone wrong. Reading most books on management you might think that things never go wrong. The writing has such an upbeat tone that it is *entirely* positive, enthusiastic, visionary, forward looking and all the other qualities that are so important. Sometimes, however, things really do go wrong and have to be sorted out. The sorting out involves at some point a meeting between a dissatisfied manager and an employee who is seen as the cause of that dissatisfaction, or between a dissatisfied employee and a manager representing the employing organisation that is seen as the cause of the employee's dissatisfaction. Procedures can do no more than force meetings to take place: it is the meetings themselves that provide answers.

Many contemporary views of discipline are connected with the idea of punishment, as we saw in the last chapter; a disciplinarian is one seen as an enforcer of rules, a hard taskmaster or martinet. To discipline school children is usually to punish them by keeping them in after school or chastising them. Disciplinary procedures in employment are usually drawn up to provide a preliminary to dismissal, so that any eventual dismissal will not be viewed as unfair by a tribunal. This background makes a problem-solving approach to discipline difficult for a manager, as there is always the sanction in the background making it unlikely that the employee will see the manager's behaviour as being authentic. There will always be a feeling – somewhere between outright conviction and lingering uncertainty – that a manager in a disciplinary interview is looking for a justification to punish rather than looking for a more constructive solution. The approach of this chapter is based on the more accurate notion of discipline implied in its derivation from the Latin *discere*, to learn and *discipulus*, learner. In disciplinary interviews the manager is attempting to modify the working behaviour of a subordinate, but the modification does not necessarily involve punishment.

The idea of grievance similarly has problems of definition and ethos. In the last chapter we used the convenient scale of dissatisfaction–complaint–grievance as an explanation, but that is a convenient technical classification. The general sense of the word is closer to the dictionary definitions which use phrases like 'a real or imaginary wrong causing resentment' or 'a feeling of injustice having been unfairly treated'. Notions of resentment and injustice seem too heavy for situations where the basic problem is that the maintenance crew have fallen down on the job or the central heating is not working properly. Where we have unresolved problems about our jobs – even when we are deeply worried by them

– we are often reluctant to construe our feelings as 'having a grievance'. We just want to get more information, or an opportunity for training, a chance to talk to someone a bit more senior. Very few people indeed want to be seen to be grumbling. Customers are generally reluctant to grumble about the service they receive, because it is too much trouble, because no one would listen, or just because they do not want to make a fuss; yet they can simply walk away. Compared with customers, employees are much less inclined to complain, or even to point out problems, for fear of being categorised as a nuisance.

Despite the difficulties, the aim of this chapter is to formulate an approach to the interview that achieves an adjustment in attitude, with the changed attitude being confirmed by subsequent experience. Either the manager believes that the employee's subsequent working behaviour will be satisfactory, or the employee believes that his or her subsequent experience in employment will be satisfactory. The interview only succeeds when there is the confirmation.

In his profound and simple book of 1960, Douglas McGregor advocated an approach to management based on the strategy of *integration and self-control*. He regarded forms and procedures as having little value and emphasised the importance of social interaction as well as the difficulty of achieving any change in people's interactive behaviour:

> Every adult human being has an elaborate history of past experience in this field and additional learning is profoundly influenced by that history. From infancy on, his ability to achieve his goals and satisfy his needs – his 'social survival' – has been a function of his skills in influencing others. Deep emotional currents – unconscious needs such as those related to dependency and counterdependency – are involved. He has a large 'ego investment' and his knowledge and skill in this area, and the defences he has built to protect that investment are strong and psychologically complex.
>   (McGregor 1960, p. 75)

Managers undoubtedly spend a great deal of their time in interviews of one type or another and grievance and disciplinary interviews are among the least popular parts of their managerial day; nearly as difficult as performance appraisal and potentially even less pleasant.

Just as we set grievance and discipline alongside each other in the last chapter, similarly we examine here the grievance/disciplinary encounter in the same framework, as both are trying to tackle dissatisfaction where resolution of the problem is not straightforward. If Jim sets fire to the Plant Director's office and admits to the police that he did it for a lark because he was bored, then any disciplinary interview ought not be too difficult. If Joe is not working as well as he used to, but nobody quite knows why and he refuses to say anything about it to anyone, then there is the less straightforward situation with which the approach of this chapter might help.

| **Activity 33.1** | What grievance or disciplinary incidents can you recall where the situation was not clear-cut and where an interview with a manager produced a resolution to the problem that was effective, although quite different from what had been anticipated by the manager at the beginning of the interview? |

The nature of grievance and disciplinary interviewing

Many grievance or discipline interviews are simple: giving information, explaining work requirements and delivering rebukes, but from time to time every manager will need to use a problem-solving approach, involving sympathy, perception, empathy and the essential further feature that some managers provide only with reluctance: time. The method will be analytical and constructive; not only for the interviews built in to the grievance and discipline procedure, but also for interviews that avoid recourse to the rigid formality of procedure. We see such interviews as one of the means towards *self-discipline* and *autonomy* of employees, reducing the need for supervision. The sequence we advocate has discipline and grievance intertwined for much of the process but diverging in the interview itself.

As we have shown in the previous chapter, a grievance may be expressed only in manifest form, requiring interviewing to understand its latent content in order that appropriate action is taken to remove the underlying dissatisfaction. Discipline problems will have underlying reasons for the unsatisfactory behaviour and these need to be discovered before solutions to the problems can be attempted.

WINDOW ON PRACTICE

There is a risk of some managers looking for problems that do not exist anywhere other than in their own imagination. George was a supervisor in charge of several cleaning gangs and he prided himself on his avuncular concern for their welfare (some of the more cynical cleaners described him as 'bloody nosey').

One day, Mildred stopped at his office to say that she was going to leave at the end of the month, because she had decided to give up work. Mildred had been a cleaner in the company for 15 years and was highly regarded by George. She was 59 and her husband had recently retired. Her two children were both independent, so she and her husband had decided that she would give up work in April, so that they could both get used to retirement during the summer rather than wait until her 60th birthday in November.

George decided that there was 'more to this than met the eye' and spent half an hour asking Mildred a series of questions about her health, her children, her relationship with her husband and how she spent her spare time. Mildred became more and more exasperated, eventually storming out to see her shop steward.

Sometimes people say what they mean, mean what they say and that's that: problem-solving interviewing is definitely not required.

The discipline and grievance sequence

Preparation

The first requirement is to check the procedural position and to ensure that the impending interview is appropriate. In a grievance situation, for instance, is the employee pre-empting the procedure by taking the matter to the wrong person or to the wrong point in the procedure? This is most common when the first-line supervisor is being bypassed, either because the employee or the representative feels that it would be a waste of time, or perhaps because the supervisor is unsure

Figure 33.1 The grievance and disciplinary interviews

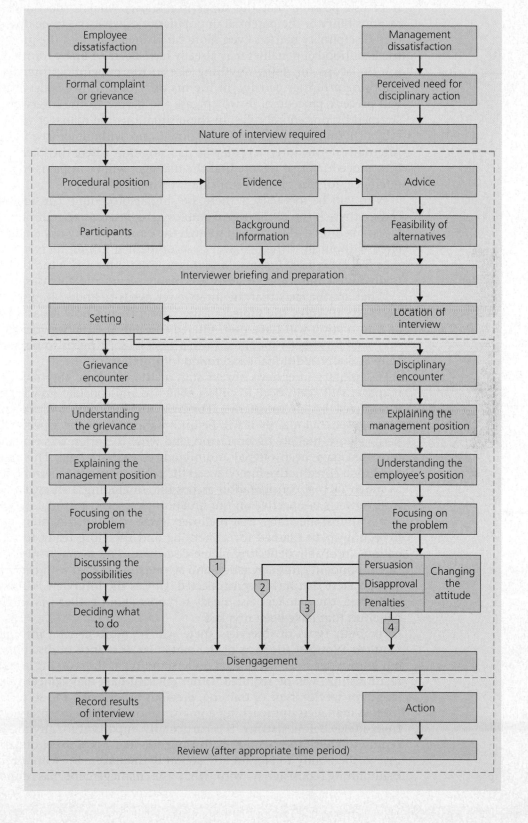

of the appropriate action and is conniving at the procedure being side-stepped. It is also possible that the supervisor knows what to do but is shirking the responsibility or the potential unpopularity of what has to be done.

In disciplinary matters even more care is needed about the procedural step, as the likelihood of penalties may already have been set up by warnings, thus reducing the scope for doing anything else in the impending interview apart from imposing a further penalty. In the majority of cases we believe that interviews will precede procedure, in which case the parties to the interview are less constrained by procedural rules. In these situations the manager will be at pains to establish that the interview is informal and without procedural implications. Alternatively the interview may be in a situation where the likelihood of a move into procedure is so remote that the manager will be at pains to avoid any such reference, for fear of the complainant taking fright.

Who will be there? Here there are similar procedural considerations. In procedure there is the likelihood of employee representation, out of procedure there is less likelihood of that, even though the employee may feel anxious and threatened without it. If the manager is accompanied in the interview, the employee may feel even more insecure, and it is doubtful how much can be achieved informally unless the employee feels reasonably secure and able to speak frankly.

What are the facts that the interviewer needs to know? In grievance it will be necessary to know the subject of the grievance and how it has arisen. This type of information will have been filtered through the management hierarchy and may well have been modified in the process, so it needs to be considered carefully and any additional background information collected.

Disciplinary interviews always start at the behest of the management so the manager will again need to collect evidence and consider how it may have been interpreted by intermediaries. This will include some basic details about the interviewee, but mainly it will be information about the aspects of the working performance that are unsatisfactory and why. Too often this exists only in opinions that have been offered and prejudices that are held. This provides a poor basis for a constructive interview, so the manager needs to ferret out details, with as much factual corroboration as possible, including a shrewd guess about the interviewee's perspective on the situation.

It is almost inevitable that the interviewee will start the interview defensively, expecting to be blamed for something and therefore ready to refute any allegations, probably deflecting blame elsewhere. The manager needs to anticipate the respondent's initial reaction and be prepared to deal with the reaction as well as with facts that have been collected. Unless the interview is at an early, informal stage, the manager also needs to know about earlier warnings, cautions or penalties that have been invoked.

For both types of interview there will be more general information that is required. Not just the facts of the particular grievance or disciplinary situation, but knowledge to give a general understanding of the working arrangements and relationships, will be required. Other relevant data may concern the employee's length of service, type of training, previous experience, and so forth.

Most managers approaching a grievance or disciplinary interview will benefit from advice before starting. It is particularly important for anyone who is in procedure to check the position with someone like a personnel officer before starting, as the ability to sustain any action by management will largely depend on maintaining consistency with what the management has done with other employees previously. The manager may also have certain ideas of what could be done in terms of retraining, transfer or assistance with a domestic problem. The manager needs to verify the feasibility of such actions before broaching them with an aggrieved employee or with an employee whose work is not satisfactory.

Where is the interview to take place? However trivial this question may seem it is included for two reasons. First, because we have seen a number of interviews go sadly awry because the parties arrived at different places; this mistake seems to happen more often with this type of encounter than with others. Second, because there may be an advantage in choosing an unusually informal situation – or an unusually formal location, according to the manager's assessment. A discussion over a pie and a pint in the local pub may be a more appropriate setting for some approaches to grievance and disciplinary problems, although they are seldom appropriate if the matter has reached procedure. Also employees frequently mistrust such settings, feeling that they are being manipulated or that the discussion 'does not count' because it is out of hours or off limits. If, however, one is trying to avoid procedural overtones, this can be a way of doing it.

Unusual formality can be appropriate in the later stages of procedure, especially in disciplinary matters, when proceedings take on a strongly judicial air. An employee is not likely to take seriously a final warning prior to probable dismissal if it is delivered over a pint in a pub. The large, impressive offices of senior managers can provide appropriate settings for the final stages of procedure.

Activity 33.2	What incidents have you experienced or heard about where the location of the interview was clearly unsuitable?

The grievance interview

The first step in the grievance interview is for the manager to be clear about what the grievance is; a simple way of doing this is to state the *subject* of the grievance and get confirmation from the employee that it is correct. The importance of this lies in the probability that the manager will have a different perspective on the affair from the employee, particularly if it has got beyond the preliminary stage. A supervisor may report to a superior that Mr X has a grievance and 'will not take instructions from me', but when the interview begins Mr X may state his grievance as being that he is unwilling to work on Saturday mornings. In other situations it might be the other way round, with the supervisor reporting that Mr X will not work Saturday mornings and Mr X saying in the interview that he finds the style of his supervisor objectionable. Even where there is no such confusion, an opening statement and confirmation of the subject demonstrate that the two parties are talking about the same thing.

Having clarified or confirmed the subject of the grievance, the manager will then invite the employee to state the case, explaining the nature and reasons for the dissatisfaction. This enables the employee to explain why he or she is aggrieved, citing examples, providing further information and saying not just 'what' but also 'why'. Seldom will this be done well. The presentation of a case is not a particularly easy task for the inexperienced, and few aggrieved employees are experienced at making a case of this type. Furthermore there is the inhibition of questioning the wisdom of those in power and some apprehension about the outcome. Because of this the manager will need to ask questions after the declaration of the case in order to fill in the gaps that have been left by the employee and to clarify some points that were obscure in the first telling. As a general rule it seems better to have an episode of questioning after the case has been made, rather than to interrupt on each point that is difficult. Interruptions make a poorly argued case even more difficult to sustain. There may, however, be disguised pleas for assistance that provide good opportunities for questioning to clarify: 'I'm not very good with words, but do you see what I'm getting at?', 'Do you see what I mean?', or 'Am I making myself clear?' Among the communication ploys that the manager will need at this stage could be the method of *reflection* that is described by Beveridge:

> a selective form of listening in which the listener picks out the emotional overtones of a statement and 'reflects' these back to the respondent without making any attempt to evaluate them. This means that the interviewer expresses neither approval nor disapproval, neither sympathy nor condemnation. Because the respondent may be in an emotional state, sympathy is liable to make him feel resentful and angry. Any attempt to get the respondent to look objectively and rationally at his problem at this stage is also likely to fail; he is still too confused and upset to be able to do this and will interpret the very attempt as criticism.
>
> (Beveridge 1968, p. 121)

After all the necessary clarification has been obtained the manager will restate the employee grievance, together with an outline of the case that has been presented, and will ask the employee to agree with the summary or to correct it. By this means the manager is confirming and demonstrating an understanding of what the grievance is about and why it has been brought. This is not agreeing with it or dismissing it; all that has happened is that the grievance is now understood.

This phase of the interview can be summarised in sequential terms:

Manager	Employee
1 States subject of grievance	
	2 Agrees with statement
	3 States case
4 Questions for clarification	
5 Re-states grievance	
	6 Agrees or corrects

The grievance is now understood

The next phase is to set out the management position on the grievance. This is not the action *to be taken* but the action that *has been taken* with the reasons for it, and may include an explanation of company policy, safety rules, previous grievances, supervisory problems, administrative methods and anything else which is needed to make clear why the management position has been what it has been. The manager will then invite the employee to question and comment on the management position to ensure that it is understood and the justifications for it are understood, even if they are not accepted. The objective is to ensure that the parties to the discussion see and understand each other's point of view.

The management position is now understood

Setting out the two opposed positions will have revealed a deal of common ground. The parties will agree on some things, though disagreeing on others. In the third phase of the interview the manager and employee sort through what they have discussed and identify the points of disagreement. At this stage the points on which they agree can be ignored, as the need now is to find the outer limits. It is very similar to the differentiation stage in negotiation.

Points of disagreement are now in focus

As a preliminary to taking action in the matter under discussion, various possibilities can be put up for consideration. It is logical that the employee suggestions are put first. Probably this has already been done either explicitly or implicitly in the development of the case. If, however, specific suggestions are invited at this stage they may be different ones, as the aggrieved employee now understands the management position and is seeing the whole matter clearly following the focusing that has just taken place. Then the manager can put forward alternatives or modifications, and such alternatives may include – or be limited to – the suggestion that the grievance is mischievous and unfounded so that no action should be taken. Nevertheless in most cases there will be some scope for accommodation even if it is quite different from the employee's expectation. Once the alternative suggestions for action are set out, there is time for the advantages and disadvantages of both sets to be discussed.

Alternatives have now been considered

A grievance interview is one that falls short of the mutual dependence that is present in negotiation, so that the decision on action is to be taken by the manager alone; it is not a joint decision even though the manager will presumably be looking for a decision that all parties will find acceptable. In bringing a grievance the employee is challenging a management decision and that decision will now be confirmed or it will be modified, but it remains a management decision.

Before making the decision the manager may deploy a range of behaviours to ensure that the decision is correct. It may be useful to test the employee's reaction by thinking aloud, 'Well, I don't know, but it looks to me as if we shall have to disappoint you on this one . . .'. There may be an adjournment for a while to seek further advice or to give the employee time to reflect further, but the manager has to decide and then explain the decision to the employee. In this way the manager is not simply deciding and announcing, but supporting the decision with explanation and justification in the same way that the employee developed the case for the grievance at the beginning. There may be employee questions, the employee may want time to think, but eventually the management decision will have to be accepted, unless there is some further procedural step available.

Management action is now clear and understood.

The disciplinary interview

Discipline arises from management dissatisfaction rather than employee dissatisfaction with the employment contract, so the opening move is for a statement of why such dissatisfaction exists, dealing with the *facts* of the situation rather than managerial feelings of outrage about the facts. This shows that the interview is being approached by the manager as a way of dealing with a problem of the working situation and not – yet – as a way of dealing with a malicious or indolent employee. If an employee has been persistently late for a week, it would be unwise for a manager to open the disciplinary interview by saying, 'Your lateness this week has been deplorable' as the reason might turn out to be that the employee has a seriously ill child needing constant attendance through the night. Then the manager would be embarrassed and the potential for a constructive settlement of the matter would be jeopardised. An opening factual statement of the problem, 'You have been at least twenty minutes late each day this week . . .' does not prejudge the reasons and is reasonably precise about the scale of the problem. It also circumscribes management dissatisfaction by implying that there is no other cause for dissatisfaction: if there is, it should be mentioned.

WINDOW ON PRACTICE

In the booklet *I'd Like to Have a Word With You*, Tietjen decribes types of difficult interviewee, one of which is 'the professional weeper':

> This is the person who can turn on tears like turning on a tap. Some people are quite unmoved by tears, but lots of bosses find tears and emotion very hard to cope with. They are either very embarrassed or very apologetic that their words could have had such an effect. (1987, p. 26)

Another difficult interviewee is the 'counter-attacker':

> who operates on the maxim that the best defence is attack. Once you have stated your reasons for the interview, he will leap straight into the discussion, relishing the opportunity to 'have it out'. The obvious danger is that you respond to his aggression, that a battle of words will ensue and that nothing else will happen. (p. 28)

Notice that Ms Tietjen leaves the gender open in the first instance and specific in the second!

Now the manager needs to know the explanation and asks the employee to say what the reasons for the problem are, perhaps also asking for comments on the seriousness of the problem itself, which the employee may regard as trivial, while the manager regards it as serious. If there is such dissonance it needs to be drawn out. Getting the employee reaction is usually straightforward, but the manager needs to be prepared for one of two other types of reaction. Either there may be a need to probe because the employee is reluctant to open up, or there may be angry defiance. Disciplinary situations are at least disconcerting for employees and frequently very worrying, surrounded by feelings of hostility and mistrust, so that it is to be expected that some ill feeling will be pent up and waiting for the opportunity to be vented.

First possible move to disengagement

If the employee sees something of the management view of the problem and if the manager understands the reasons for it, the next requirement is to seek a solution. We have to point out that a disciplinary problem is as likely to be solved by management action as it is to be solved by employee action. If the problem is lateness, one solution would be for the employee to catch an earlier bus, but another might be for the management to alter the working shift to which the employee is assigned. If the employee is disobeying orders, one solution would be to start obeying them, but another might be for the employee to be moved to a different job where orders are received from someone else. Some managers regard such thinking as unreasonable, on the grounds that the contract of employment places obligations on individual employees that they should meet despite personal inconvenience. However, the point is not how people *should* behave, but how they do. Can the contract of employment be enforced on an unwilling employee? Not if one is seeking such attitudes as enthusiasm and co-operation, or behaviour such as diligence and carefulness. The disenchanted employee can always meet the bare letter rather than the spirit of the contract.

The most realistic view of the matter is that many disciplinary problems require some action from both parties, some require action by the employee only and a small proportion require management action only. The problem-solving session may quickly produce the possibility for further action and open up the possibility of closing the interview.

This simple, logical approach outlined so far may not be enough, due to the unwillingness of employees to respond to disciplinary expectations. They may not want to be punctual or to do as they are instructed, or whatever the particular problem is. There is now a test of the power behind management authority. Three further steps can be taken, one after the other, although there will be occasions when it is necessary to move directly to the third.

Second possible move to disengagement

Persuasion

A first strategy is to demonstrate to employees that they will not achieve what they want, if their behaviour does not change:

■ 'You won't keep your earnings up if you don't meet targets.'
■ 'It will be difficult to get your appointment confirmed when the probationary period is over if . . .'.

By such means employees may see the advantages of changing their attitude and behaviour. If they are convinced, there is a strong incentive for them to alter, because they believe it to be in their own interests.

Third possible move to disengagement

Disapproval

Another strategy is to suggest that continuing the behaviour will displease those whose goodwill the employee wishes to keep:

■ 'The Management Development Panel are rather disappointed . . .'.

- 'Some of the other people in the department feel that you are not pulling your weight.'

A manager using this method needs to be sure that what is said is both true and relevant. Also the manager may be seen by the employee as shirking the issue, so it may be appropriate to use a version of 'I think this is deplorable and expect you to do better.'

We asked for a restraint from judgement in the early stages of the interview, until the nature of the problem is clear. The time for judgement has now come, with the proper deployment of the rebuke or the caution.

Fourth possible move to disengagement

Penalties

When all else fails or is clearly inappropriate – as with serious offences about which there is no doubt – penalties have to be invoked. In rare circumstances there may be the possibility of a fine, but usually the first penalty will be a formal warning as a preliminary to possible dismissal. In situations that are sufficiently grave summary dismissal is both appropriate and possible within the legal framework.

Disengagement

We have indicated possible moves to disengagement at four different points in the disciplinary interview. Now we come to a stage that is common for both grievance and disciplinary encounters from the point of view of describing the process, although the nature of disengagement will obviously differ. The manager now needs to think of the working situation that will follow. In a grievance situation can the employee now accept the decision that has been made? Are there faces to be saved or reputations to be restored? What administrative action is to be taken? In closing a disciplinary interview, the manager will aim for the flavour of disengagement to be as positive as possible so that all concerned put the disciplinary problem behind them. In those cases where the outcome of the interview is to impose or confirm a dismissal, then the manager will be exclusively concerned with the fairness and accuracy with which it is done, so that the possibility of tribunal hearings is reduced, if not prevented. It can never be appropriate to close an interview of either type leaving the employee humbled and demoralised.

WINDOW ON PRACTICE	The American Eric Harvey has reduced what he calls 'positive discipline' to three simple steps: 1 Warn the employee orally. 2 Warn the employee in writing. 3 If steps 1 and 2 fail to resolve the problem, give the employee a day off, *with pay* (Harvey 1987) A similar, very positive, approach was outlined in a seminal paper by Huberman in 1967.

Summary propositions

33.1 Grievance and disciplinary interviews are central to the process of sorting things out when there is a management/employee problem, but most managers dislike such interviews intensely.

33.2 Grievance and disciplinary interviews are one of the means towards people at work achieving self-discipline and autonomy, reducing the need for supervision and reducing the need for recourse to the formality of procedure.

33.3 The steps in conducting a grievance interview are first to understand the nature of the grievance, then to explain the management position, focus on the problem, discuss possibilities and then to decide what to do.

33.4 The disciplinary interview starts the other way around, first explaining the management position, then understanding the employee's position and focusing on the problem. If that does not produce a satisfactory disposal, the manager may have to move through three more steps: persuasion, showing disapproval or invoking penalties.

References

Beveridge, W.E. (1968) *Problem-Solving Interviews*. London: Allen and Unwin.

Harvey, E.L. (1987) 'Discipline versus punishment', *Management Review*, March, pp. 25–9.

Huberman, J.C. (1967) 'Discipline without punishment', *Harvard Business Review*, May, pp. 62–8.

McGregor, D. (1960) *The Human Side of Enterprise*. Maidenhead: McGraw-Hill.

Tietjen, T. (1987) *I'd Like a Word With You*. London: Video Arts Ltd.

Part VI
Case study problem

Industrial dispute at British Airways

British Airways is an international company by any standards and, by 1990, was the world's most popular and most profitable airline. Because of its extensive network and the salient position of Heathrow as the world's busiest airport, it was relatively straightforward to become the most popular airline, but achieving high profitability was more difficult. There was overstaffing and the need for radical measures:

> The organisation had a bureaucratic style of management, damaging industrial relations and a poor reputation for customer service.... There was a drastic reduction in staff numbers from 60,000 to 38,000. This was achieved by a combination of voluntary severance and natural wastage. (Hopfl 1993, p. 117)

In order to maintain market leadership the airline embarked on a famous programme of staff training to develop commitment to customer service, and the quality of service to the customer improved markedly, so that British Airways was able to maintain its premier position despite ever-increasing competition.

There were, however, mounting problems with the staff as the pressure on margins continued. In 1996 a strike by pilots was narrowly averted, but 1997 brought one stoppage and the threat of another.

On 9 July a 72-hour strike by cabin staff began. It was an official stoppage called by the Transport and General Workers Union following protracted negotiations and a ballot among its members working for the airline. According to British Airways only 142 cabin crew formally joined the strike, but 1,500 (compared with a normal daily average of 120) reported sick – a novel strategy! The number that reported for work as usual was 834.

The management reaction was to announce that all strikers would forfeit travel perks and promotion prospects for three years. Film was also taken of strikers on picket lines. The threats were later withdrawn and the filming was stopped. The situation was complicated by the existence of a rival union, Cabin Crew '89, which had broken away from the TGWU in 1989. This union, known as CC89, supported the management position and all their members worked normally through the stoppage.

Another interesting feature of the dispute was reported by *The Times*:

> During the past few years, BA, like many companies in Britain, has appointed middle and senior managers who fear for their jobs. To get on, they believe, they must show they are tough. I have heard these 'performance managers' brusquely warning vacillating staff that if they follow their union and refuse to work, they will 'face the consequences.' This has irked the cabin crew far more than the dispute over pay and conditions. They no longer feel part of a team and believe they are being bullied. (Elliott 1997, p. 41)

As usual, the dispute moved on to talks to find a resolution, but BA had lost many flights and its reputation was as severely dented as its financial position. The share price dropped from 763p to 583p before recovering to 635p, and there were varying reports about how many millions of pounds the dispute was costing.

Required

1 Do you think it is inevitable that the pressures of international competition drive companies into a situation where unilateral managerial decision making must prevail and there is simply no time for the consultation and compromise that is involved in union negotiation?

2 This case provides an excellent example of the problems that can arise from having two unions representing the same group of employees and competing with each other for membership. How would you try and deal with this situation *now* – not back in 1989?

3 How accurate do you regard Harvey Elliott's views to be as a general comment on current management practice?

References

Elliott, H. (1997) 'BA is Plunging towards Disaster', *The Times*, 10 July.

Hopfl, H. (1993) 'Culture and Commitment: British Airways', in D. Gowler, K. Legge and C. Clegg (eds), *Case Studies in Organizational Behaviour and Human Resource Management*, 2nd edn. London: Paul Chapman Publishing, pp. 117–25.

Part VI
Examination questions

Undergraduate introductory

1 Explain the difference between these four terms:

   (a) Industrial relations

   (b) Employee relations

   (c) Collective bargaining

   (d) Employee involvement

2 What are the aims and objectives of British trade unions?

Undergraduate finals

3 What is meant by the term 'derecognition'? How extensive is derecognition in contemporary Britain, and what employment practices, if any, have employers initiated to take the place of trade unions?

4 'Good health is good business.' Discuss.

Masters

5 How just can the framework of organisational justice ever be when managers have so much more power than employees?

6 Analyse critically the assertion that employers develop employee involvement schemes in order to empower their employees.

Professional

7 Explain the main components of a grievance procedure.

8 Explain the difference between bargaining and grievance handling.

PAY

If we were all paid the same amount for working, life would be very straightforward, but not many of us would be satisfied with the arrangement! This part of the book deals with the ways in which what we are paid differs between us. There must always be a reason to justify the difference.

It may be that one person is paid more than another because of having a higher level of skill, so the skilled artisan is paid more than the labourer, or it may be that the difference is justified by experience, so that the experienced school teacher will be paid more than the newly qualified teacher. Managers have always been interested in making arrangements for the better performer to be paid more than the average performer, and we can see lots of schemes currently that are working towards that objective. Aspects of payment do not only affect our working life; there is an effect also on our pension at the end of our working life and other effects on our attitudes to our work as a result of associated benefits that are provided.

Pay is a feature of management arrangements where fairness is always both important and problematic, so job evaluation is a means of introducing fairness into the calculations.

The elements of payment

Once the mechanisms for determining rates of pay for jobs in an organisation have been settled, the second key strategic decision relates to the make-up of the pay package. Here there is a great deal of potential choice available. What is included and to what extent are matters which should be decided with a view to supporting the organisation's objectives and encouraging the necessary attitudes and actions on the part of employees. The payment of an individual will be made up of one or more elements from those shown in Figure 34.1. Fixed elements are those that make up the regular weekly or monthly payment to the individual, and which do not vary other than in exceptional circumstances. Variable elements can be varied by either the employee or the employer.

Basic rate

The irreducible minimum rate of pay is the basic. In most cases this is the standard rate also, not having any additions made to it. In other cases it is a basis on which earnings are built by the addition of one or more of the other elements in payment. Some groups of employees, such as operatives in the footwear industry,

Figure 34.1 The potential elements of payment

Bonus	Profit allocation		
	Discretionary sum		**Variable elements**
Incentive	Group calculation basis		• Irregular
	Individual calculation basis		• Variable amount
			• Usually discretionary
Overtime payment			
Premia	Occasional		
	Contractual		
Benefits	Fringe benefits		
	Payments in kind	Other	**Fixed elements**
		Accommodation	• Regular
		Car	• Rarely variable
	Benefit schemes	Other	• Usually contractual
		Pension	
		Sick pay	
Plussage	'Fudge' payments		
	Special additions		
Basic rate of payment			**Basic**

have little more than half of their earnings in basic, while primary and secondary schoolteachers have virtually all their pay in this form.

Plussage

Sometimes the basic has an addition to recognise an aspect of working conditions or employee capability. Payments for educational qualifications and for supervisory responsibilities are quite common. There is also an infinite range of what are sometimes called 'fudge' payments, whereby there is an addition to the basic as a start-up allowance, mask money, dirt money, and so forth.

Activity 34.3 If your employer offered you a 'remuneration package', which could be made up from any of the items in Figure 34.1 provided that the total cost was no more than £X, what proportion of each item would you choose and why? Does your answer suggest ideas for further development of salary policies?

Benefits

Extras to the working conditions that have a cash value are categorised as benefits and can be of great variety. Some have already been mentioned; others include luncheon vouchers, subsidised meals, discount purchase schemes and the range of welfare provisions like free chiropody and cheap hairdressing.

Premia

Where employees work at inconvenient times – or shifts or permanently at night – they receive a premium payment as compensation for the inconvenience. This is for inconvenience rather than additional hours of work. Sometimes this is built into the basic rate or is a regular feature of the contract of employment so that the payment is unvarying. In other situations shift working is occasional and short-lived, making the premium a variable element of payment.

Overtime

It is customary for employees working more hours than are normal for the working week to be paid for those hours at an enhanced rate, usually between 10 and 50 per cent more that the normal rate according to how many hours are involved. Seldom can this element be regarded as fixed. No matter how regularly overtime is worked, there is always the opportunity for the employer to withhold the provision of overtime or for the employee to decline the extra hours.

Incentive

Incentive is here described as an element of payment linked to the working performance of an individual or working group, as a result of prior arrangement. This includes most of the payment-by-results schemes that have been produced by work study, as well as commission payments to salespeople, skills-based pay schemes and performance-related pay schemes based on the achievement of agreed objectives. The distinguishing feature is that the employee knows what has to be done to earn the payment, though he or she may feel very dependent on other people, or on external circumstances, to receive it.

ders and steps, whereby different groups or 'families' of jobs in an organisation are identified, each having a separate pay scale. This principle is illustrated in Figure 35.1.

Job families

The first element of the structure is the broad groupings of salaries, each group being administered according to the same set of rules. The questions in making decisions about this are to do with the logical grouping of job holders, according to their common interests, performance criteria, qualifications and, perhaps, bargaining arrangements and trade union membership. Massey (2000, p. 144) suggests the following as a typical seven-way division of jobs into distinct families:

1 Executives
2 Management
3 Professional
4 Technical
5 Administrative
6 Skilled manual
7 Manual

The broad salary ranges are then set against each group, to encompass either the maximum and minimum of the various people who will then be in the group or – in the rare circumstance of starting from scratch – the ideal maximum and minimum levels.

As the grouping has been done on the basis of job similarity, the attaching of maximum and minimum salaries can show up peculiarities, with one or two jobs far below a logical minimum and others above a logical maximum. This requires the limits for the group to be put at the 'proper' level, with the exceptions either being identified as exceptions and the incumbents being paid a protected rate or being moved into a more appropriate group.

Salary groups will not stack neatly one on top of another in a salary hierarchy. There will be considerable overlap, recognising that there is an element of salary growth as a result of experience as well as status and responsibility. No overlap at all (a rare arrangement) emphasises the hierarchy, encouraging employees to put their feet on the salary ladder and climb, but the clarity of internal relativities may increase the dissatisfaction of those on the lower rungs and put pressure on the pay system to accommodate the occasional anomaly, especially if climbing is not well supported. Overlapping grades blur the edges of relativities and can reduce dissatisfaction at the bottom, but introduce dissatisfaction higher up.

Another reason why pay scales for different job families usually overlap is to accommodate scales of different length. A family with a flat hierarchy will tend to have a small number of scales with many steps, while the steep hierarchy will tend to have more scales, but each with fewer steps. One of the main drawbacks of overlapping scales is the problem of migration, where an employee regards the job as technical at one time and makes a case for it to be reclassified as administrative at another time, because there is no further scope for progress in the first classification. Another aspect of migration is the more substantive case of employees seeking transfer to other jobs as a result of changes in the relative pay scales, which reduce rigidity in the internal labour market.

Figure 35.2 Ladders and steps in a salary group

Annual salary (£)	A	B	C	Ladders D
17,100				
				7
16,500				
				6
15,900				
				5
15,300				
			7	4
14,800				
			6	3
14,300				
			5	2
13,800			4	
		7		1
13,400				
		6	3	
13,000				
		5	2	
12,600	7	4	1	
12,300	6	3		
12,000		2		
	5			
		1		
11,700	4			
11,500	3			
11,300	2			
11,100	1			

Ladders and steps

Because employees are assumed to be career-oriented, salary arrangements are based on that assumption, so each salary group has several ladders within it and each ladder has a number of steps (often referred to as 'scales' and 'points'). In the traditional model increments are awarded annually, reflecting individual seniority. Hence the new starter normally enters employment with the organisation at the lowest rung of the ladder in the grade for the job. At the end of each completed year of service they are then awarded an increment until after six or seven years they reach the top of the ladder – the ceiling for the relevant grade. At this point pay progression stops, except for any annual cost of living rise. The only way a higher income can be gained within the organisation is to secure promotion to a more highly graded job. This involves moving up on to a new ladder, at which point annual incremental pay awards commence again. Such

Broadbanding

Attention has recently been given to the introduction of broadbanding as a way of retaining the positive features of traditional pay scales while reducing some of the less desirable effects (see IDS 1996; IPD 1997). One of these is the built-in incentive to focus on getting promoted rather than on performing well in the current job. This can lead to individuals playing damaging political games in a bid to weaken the position of colleagues or even undermine their own supervisors. Inflexibility can also occur when individuals refuse to undertake duties or types of work associated with higher grades. Moreover, in making internal equity the main determinant of pay rates within an organisation, rigid salary structures prevent managers from offering higher salaries to new employees. This tends to hinder effective competition in some labour markets.

Broadbanding essentially involves retaining some form of grading system while greatly reducing the numbers of grades or salary bands. The process typically results in the replacement of a structure consisting of 10 or 12 distinct grades with one consisting of only three or four. Pay variation within grades is then based on individual performance, skill or external market value rather than on the nature and size of the job. The great advantage of such approaches is their ability to reduce hierarchical thinking. Differences in pay levels still exist between colleagues but they are no longer seen as being due solely to the fact that one employee is graded more highly than another. This can reduce feelings of inequity provided the new criteria are reasonably open and objective. As a result, teamwork is encouraged as is a focus on improving individual performance in order to secure higher pay.

In theory, therefore, broadbanded structures increase the extent to which managers have discretion over the setting of internal differentials, introduce more flexibility and permit organisations to reward performance or skills acquisition as well as job size. Their attraction is that they achieve this while retaining a skeleton grading system which gives order to the structure and helps justify differentials. Time will tell how acceptable such approaches are to the courts when it comes to judging equal value claims.

Job evaluation methods

Job evaluation is the most common method used to compare the relative values of different jobs in order to provide the basis for a rational pay structure. Among the many definitions is this one from ACAS:

> Job evaluation is concerned with assessing the relative demands of different jobs within an organization. Its usual purpose is to provide a basis for relating differences in rates of pay to different in-job requirements. It is therefore a tool which can be used to help in the determination of a pay structure.   (ACAS 1984)

It is a well-established technique, having been developed in all its most common forms by the 1920s. In recent years it has received a series of boosts. First, various types of incomes policy between 1965 and 1974 either encouraged the introduction of job evaluation or specifically permitted expenditure above the prevailing norm by companies wishing to introduce it. In the 1980s the use of job evaluation became the hinge of most equal pay cases. More recently organisations have found it useful as part of moves towards single-status contractual arrangements and resolving pay issues following organisational mergers (IDS 2000, p. 2).

Despite its popularity it is often misunderstood, so the following points have to be made:

1 Job evaluation is concerned with the job and not the performance of the individual job holder. Individual merit is not assessed.
2 The technique is systematic rather than scientific. It depends on the judgement of people with experience, requiring them to decide in a planned and systematic way, but it does not produce results that are infallible.
3 Job evaluation does not eliminate collective bargaining. It determines the differential gaps between incomes; it does not determine pay levels or annual pay rises.
4 Only a structure of pay rates is produced. Other elements of earnings, such as premia and incentives, are not determined by the method.

There are many methods of job evaluation in use and they are summarised in Smith (1983, pp. 68–106), Armstrong and Murlis (1998, pp. 81–102), Smith and Nethersall (2000) and IDS (2000). Where a non-analytical or 'whole job' scheme is used a panel of assessors examines each job as a whole, in terms of its difficulty or value to the business, to determine which should be ranked more highly than others. No attempt is made to break each job down into its constituent parts. By contrast, an analytical scheme requires each element or factor of the job to be assessed. Since 1988 it has been the practice of courts only to accept the results of analytical schemes in equal pay cases.

The most widely used analytical schemes are based on points-rating systems, under which each job is examined in terms of factors such as skill, effort and responsibility. Each factor is given a weighting indicating its value relative to the others and for each factor there are varying degrees. A score is then given depending on how demanding the job is in terms of each factor, with the overall points value determining the relative worth of each job – and hence its grade in the organisation's pay structure. Traditionally the analysis was carried out by a panel of managers and workforce representatives examining each job description in turn and comparing it, factor by factor, against grading definitions. In recent years there has been increased interest in computer-assisted job evaluation systems which award scores to each job on the basis of information gathered from job analysis questionnaires.

The best-known set of factors, weightings and degrees is that devised for the National Electrical Manufacturers Association of the United States, but the International Labour Organisation has produced a list of the factors used most frequently. It would be unusual for more than a dozen of these to be used in any one scheme, most taking account of six to ten different factors:

Accountability	Effort	Problem solving
Accuracy	Initiative	Resources control
Analysis and judgement	Judgement	Responsibility for cash/materials, etc.
Complexity	Know-how	Social skills
Contact and diplomacy	Knowledge and skills	Supervision given/received
Creativity	Mental effort	Task completion
Decision making	Mental fatigue	Training and experience
Dexterity	Physical demands	Work conditions
Education	Physical skills	Work pressure
Effect of errors	Planning and co-ordination	

The points values eventually derived for each job can be plotted on a graph or simply listed from the highest to the lowest to indicate the ranking. Then – and only then – are points ratings matched with cash amounts, as decisions are made on which points ranges equate with various pay grades. This process is illustrated in Figure 35.3, each cross representing a job. The most common approach involves using a graph on which one axis represents the *current* salary for each job evaluated and the other the number of job evaluation points awarded. A line of best fit is then drawn and each job assigned to a grade. Salary modelling software is widely available to help with this process.

It is virtually inevitable that some jobs will be found to be paid incorrectly after job evaluation has been completed. If the evaluation says that the pay rate

Figure 35.3 Job evaluation analysis

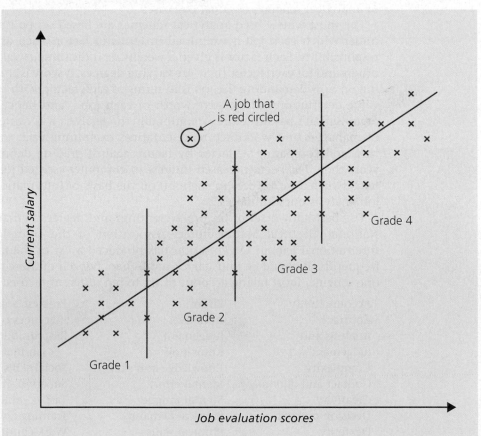

should be higher then the rate duly rises, either immediately or step by step, to the new level. The only problem is finding the money, and introducing job evaluation always costs money. More difficult is the situation where evaluation shows the employee to be overpaid. It is not feasible to reduce the pay of the job holder without breaching the contract of employment. There have been two approaches. The first, which was never widespread and appears almost to have disappeared, is buying out. The overpaid employee is offered a large lump sum in consideration of the fact of henceforth being paid at the new, lower rate. The second and more general device used is that of the personal rate or **red-circling**. An example could be where the rate for the job would be circled in red on the salary administrator's records to show that the employee should continue at the present level while remaining in that post, but a successor would be paid at the lower job-evaluated rate.

The most widely used proprietary scheme is the Hay Guide Chart-Profile Method. IRS (1998a) surveyed the use of job evaluation in 145 organisations and found that 55 employed the Hay method for some or all the jobs covered. It is used particularly widely in the evaluation of management jobs. The method is based on an assessment of four factors; know-how, problem solving, accountability and working conditions. Jobs are assessed by using each of three guide charts, one for each factor. A profile is then developed for the job showing the relationship between the factors, a ranking is eventually produced and the rates of the jobs considered in order to produce a new pay structure. At this stage comes one of the greatest advantages of this system. The proprietors have available a vast amount of comparative pay data on different undertakings using their system, so their clients not only can compare rates of pay within their organisation (differentials and internal relativities); they can also examine their external relativities. This and other proprietary systems developed by firms of consultants are described by Armstrong and Murlis (1998, pp. 602–15) and by IDS (2000).

WINDOW ON PRACTICE

In 1997 the National Joint Council for Local Authority Services agreed in principle to abolish the long-standing division in UK local government between manual workers and white-collar officers. This harmonisation deal included the introduction of a single national pay spine covering all workers. In order to assist local authorities implement the new payment arrangements, the negotiating parties at national level developed a single-status job evaluation scheme which can be used to assess the size of jobs across the various employee groupings. No authority is obliged to evaluate jobs using this particular scheme, but many are doing so. Potentially, 1.5 million workers could ultimately be covered. The main motivation for moving towards a single pay spine was the threat of equal value claims.

The local government scheme contains four principal factors: knowledge and skills, effort demands, responsibilities and environmental demands. Each is broken down into a number of sub-factors which are weighted differently. Under 'effort demands' there are four headings listed: initiative and independence, physical effort, mental effort and emotional effort, the first being weighted as double the significance of the others. The aim is to ensure that different types of 'effort' are rewarded properly, those typically associated with male jobs being given equal standing to those that are characteristic of female-dominated jobs.

Sources: IRS (1998b) 'From status quo to single status: job evaluation in local government', *IRS Employment Trends 663*, September, and S. Hastings (2000) 'Grading Systems and estimating value', in G. White and J. Druker (eds), *Reward Management: A Critical Text*. London: Routledge.

Employee participation in job evaluation

The degree of participation by non-managerial employees in job evaluation varies from one business to another. In some cases the entire operation is conducted from start to finish without any employee participation at all. Some degree of participation is more common and is sensible if acceptance of a new scheme is to be gained. Apart from negotiating on pay levels and bargaining units, the main opportunities for employee contribution are as follows.

Job families

Employees collectively need to consent to the family structure and they can probably add to the deliberations of managers about what that structure should be, as they will be well aware of the sensitive points of comparison.

Job descriptions

Traditionally job descriptions have been crucial to the evaluation and it is common for job holders to prepare their own, using a pro-forma outline, or for supervisors to prepare them for jobs for which they are responsible. Spencer (1990b) reported that 88 per cent of his respondents involved job holders in the preparation of job descriptions and 94 per cent involved supervisors. Superficially, this is an attractive method, as there is direct involvement of the employee, who cannot claim to have been misrepresented. Also, it delegates the task of writing job descriptions, enabling it to be completed more quickly. The drawback is similar to that of character references in selection. Some employees write good descriptions and some write bad ones: some overstate while others understate. Inconsistency in job descriptions makes consistency in evaluation difficult.

An alternative is for job descriptions to be compiled by job analysts after questioning employees and their supervisors, who subsequently initial the job description which the analyst produces, attesting to its accuracy.

Panel evaluation

The awarding of points is usually done by a panel of people who represent between them the interests and expertise of management and employee. This is not only being 'democratic', it is acknowledging the need for the experience and perspective of job holders as well as managers in arriving at shrewd judgements of relative worth. Naturally, panel memberships alter so that employees are not asked to evaluate their own jobs. Although there is an understandable general tendency for employee representatives to push ratings up, and for management representatives to try to push them down, this usually smooths out because both parties are deriving differential rankings and not pay levels. The only potential conflict of interest will be if employee representatives and managers have divergent objectives on the shape of the eventual pay structure, with big or small differential gaps.

Job analysis questionnaires

Proprietary, computer-assisted job evaluation methods involve trained analysts putting a series of detailed questions to job holders from a multiple-choice questionnaire. The results are then fed into a computer which generates a score for each job. There is therefore no need for a panel to reach decisions based on written job descriptions. While there is clearly direct employee involvement in providing answers to the job analysis questionnaire, the absence of a panel including workforce representatives can reduce the level of employee influence on the outcome of the exercise. This is particularly the case with those proprietary schemes which are customised to meet the needs of the purchasing organisation.

Equal value

One of the major reasons for the growth in job evaluation in recent years has been the development of equal pay law. When assessing the validity of equal pay claims, tribunals employ the principles of job evaluation as a starting point, appointing a job analyst to undertake a comparison of the content of different jobs if necessary. Importantly, from the employer perspective, this means that the use by an organisation of an analytical job evaluation scheme can be a very effective defence when an equal pay claim is brought. The employer can simply claim that the jobs in question have both been evaluated and have been found to be of different value for specific reasons. Provided the scheme itself is free of sex bias, this should serve to deter aggrieved employees from bringing cases in the first place.

The Equal Pay Act 1970 established that a woman could bring a case to an employment tribunal claiming entitlement to equal pay with a man working at the same establishment if the claimant and her chosen comparator were engaged in 'like work' or work rated as equivalent under an employer's job evaluation study. A man can equally bring a case comparing his pay to that of a female colleague but this has rarely occurred in practice outside the field of pension entitlements. An amendment to the Act, which came into effect in 1984, broadened the definition of 'equal value' so that it became possible for a case to be brought if the claimant believes that her work is equal to that of her comparator in terms of the demands made upon them. This amendment followed a European Court ruling which judged the existing Equal Pay Act to fall short of the standard established by the EEC Equal Pay Directive. Since then other European Court rulings have further extended the scope of equal value law.

Like work

When presented with a claim for equal pay an employment tribunal will first seek to establish whether the claimant is engaged in 'like work' with the more highly paid man she has named as her comparator. The work does not have to be identical to justify equal pay under this heading, but must be either the same or of a broadly similar nature. In practice this means that the difference in pay can only be justified if there is 'a difference of practical importance' in the work done or if there is 'a genuine material factor' which justifies the higher rate of pay enjoyed by the male comparator.

An example of a difference of practical importance might be the level of responsibility of the man's job when compared to that of the claimant. An employer might, for example, be justified in paying a man more than his female colleague working on a comparable production line if the articles being manufactured by the man were of substantially greater value. Similarly a discriminatory payment could be justified if a man worked under less supervision than a woman engaged in otherwise like work. A common example would be a man working without supervision on night shifts.

Where there is no practical difference of this kind a discriminatory payment can only be justified where there is a 'genuine material factor other than sex' which can explain the difference in pay levels.

Work rated as equivalent

Cases brought under this section of the Act relate to jobs which are different in nature but have been rated as equivalent under the employer's job evaluation study. The existence of such a study can also provide the basis of an employer's defence in equal value claims. A definition of a job evaluation scheme is included in the Act:

> A woman is to be regarded as employed on work rated as equivalent with that of any man if her job and his have been given an equal value, in terms of the demand made on a worker under various headings (for instance, effort, skill, decision), on a study undertaken with a view to evaluating in these terms the jobs done by all or any of the employees in an undertaking. (Equal Pay Act 1970, s. 1.5)

Case law has further narrowed the definition of acceptable job evaluation schemes. In the case of *Bromley* v. *H. & J. Quick* (1988) the Court of Appeal ruled that the identification of benchmark jobs and paired comparisons was 'insufficiently analytical' as this did not involve evaluation under headings as required by the Act. The widely used method of job evaluation whereby only a sample of benchmark jobs are analysed cannot, therefore, be relied upon as a basis for an employer's defence. The jobs of the applicants and their chosen comparators must each have been evaluated analytically. In addition, a tribunal will look at the means by which scores derived from a job evaluation scheme are used to determine the rate of pay and will take account of a job evaluation study which has been completed but not implemented.

To be acceptable to a tribunal the job evaluation scheme in use must also be free of sex bias. Employers should ensure, therefore, that the factor weightings do not indirectly discriminate by over-emphasising job requirements associated with typical male jobs, like physical effort, at the expense of those associated with jobs predominantly undertaken by women, such as manual dexterity or attention to detail.

Work of equal value

A woman who is not engaged in like work, work of a broadly similar nature, or work rated as equivalent is still entitled to bring an equal pay claim if she believes her work to be of equal value. In these cases the claimant names as her chosen comparator a man employed by the same undertaking who may be engaged in work of a wholly different nature. If the tribunal decides that there are grounds to believe that the work is of equal value, it will then appoint an independent expert, nominated by ACAS, to carry out a job evaluation study. The report of the expert will then be used by the tribunal as a basis of the decision on whether or not to make an award of equal pay to the claimant. A woman may bring an equal value claim in this way even if she has male colleagues engaged in like work and paid at the same rate as her.

A number of significant equal value cases have been brought to tribunals over the years. In *Hayward* v. *Cammell Laird* (1984) a cook was awarded pay equal to that of men employed as joiners and laggers, but only after an appeal to the House of Lords three years after making the initial complaint. In 1990 the shop-workers' union USDAW dropped an equal value case against Sainsbury's when the employer agreed to carry out a job evaluation exercise. The union had claimed that predominantly female check-out operators were engaged in work of equal value to that of predominantly male warehousemen. This led to an 11 per cent rise in Sainsbury's retail wage bill and to a series of similar USDAW settlements with other major retailers during 1990 and 1991.

Genuine material factor defences

If it is established, to the satisfaction of an employment tribunal, that the claimant is engaged in like work, work rated as equivalent or work of equal value, the employer must show that the difference in the respective rates of pay is not due to sex discrimination but to a 'genuine material factor not of sex'. There are many defences which potentially fall into this category, some of which are described in Chapter 21. Among the most significant, as far as job evaluation is

WINDOW ON PRACTICE

The Ontario Pay Equity Act

A major purpose of equal pay law is the reduction of inequality between payment for jobs which are principally performed by men and those which are mostly carried out by women. Although improvements have occurred since the 1970s when the legislation was first brought in, women's gross average hourly earnings remain around 80 per cent of men's (Shaw and Clark 2000). Equal pay law is thus failing to achieve one of its principal aims, or is doing so too slowly. This has led many to argue that the current law is inadequate and that more radical approaches are needed.

A model often cited by supporters of change is the approach used in the Canadian province of Ontario, where an inspectorate has a policing role. This means that there is less need for individual women or their representatives to prepare court actions. The following are the key features of the Ontario pay equity regime:

- Employers of more than 100 are required to have written policies which identify 'female' job classes – defined as being over 60 per cent female.
- They then have to carry out job evaluation to establish whether or not there is a discrepancy between male and female classes.
- Where there is, they have to draw up a 'pay equity plan' setting out what they intend to do to narrow the gap – that is, make pay equity adjustments – over a number of years if necessary.
- There are derogations similar in nature to the UK's genuine material factors which employers can deploy to defend unequal pay.

Aileen McColgan (1993, p. 251) makes the following observation about the system:

The potential of Ontario's legislation lies in its effective reversal of the burden of proof. Rather than encouraging employers to ignore issues of equal pay save in the unlikely event of an individual's complaint, the Pay Equity Act obliges them, in co-operation with any bargaining agent, to scrutinise their own pay practices for evidence of discrimination and eliminate it.

concerned, is the practice of red-circling whereby an individual's rate of pay is protected for a period following redeployment or a new job evaluation exercise. In most cases, provided it can be clearly shown that the red circle was awarded for reasons other than the individual's sex, this will be an acceptable material factor defence.

Summary propositions

35.1 Traditional salary structures assign each job to a grade in which there are a number of incremental steps.

35.2 Recent years have seen moves towards single pay spines covering all jobs in an organisation. Separate scales for different 'job families' remain common.

35.3 Another recent development is a move towards broadbanded structures which reduce the number of grades in each salary scale to allow managers greater flexibility in setting pay levels for individual employees.

35.4 Job evaluation involves using a standard system to measure the size or importance of jobs in an organisation. Systems can be analytical or non-analytical. Modern computerised systems are highly analytical in nature.

35.5 Key decisions in designing job evaluation schemes are which factors to include and what weighting to give to each.

35.6 A major reason for the growth in the use of job evaluation in recent years has been the development of equal value law which uses the principles of job evaluation as the basis for deciding cases.

References

ACAS (1984) *Job Evaluation*. London: Advisory, Conciliation and Arbitration Services.

Armstrong, M. and Murlis, H. (1998) *Reward Management*. London: Kogan Page.

Hastings, S. (2000) 'Grading systems and estimating value', in G. White and J. Druker (eds), *Reward Management: A Critical Text*. London: Routledge.

IDS (1996) *Job Evaluation*. IDS Focus. London: Incomes Data Services Ltd.

IDS (2000) *Job Evaluation*. IDS Studies Plus, Autumn. London: Incomes Data Services.

IPD (1997) *The IPD Guide to Broadbanding*. London: Institute of Personnel and Development.

IRS (1998a) 'There is value in job evaluation', *IRS Employment Trends 665*, October.

IRS (1998b) 'From status quo to single status: job evaluation in local government', *IRS Employment Trends 663*, September.

Massey, C. (2000) 'Strategic reward systems – pay systems and structures', in R. Thorpe and G. Homan (eds), *Strategic Reward Systems*. London: Financial Times Prentice Hall.

McColgan, A. (1993) 'Equal Pay: A New Approach', in A. McColgan (ed.), *The Future of Labour Law*. London: Cassell.

Shaw, S. and Clark, M. (2000) 'Women, pay and equal opportunities', in R. Thorpe and G. Homan (eds), *Strategic Reward Systems*. London: Financial Times Prentice Hall.

Smith, I. (1983) *The Management of Remuneration*. London: IPM.

Smith, P. and Nethersall, G. (2000) 'Job Evaluation', in R. Thorpe and G. Homan (eds), *Strategic Reward Systems*. London: Financial Times Prentice Hall.

Spencer, S. (1990a) 'Devolving job evaluation', *Personnel Management*, September.

Spencer, S. (1990b) 'Job evaluation; a modern day genie for management information?', *Employment Gazette*, May.

Legal cases

Bromley v. *H. & J. Quick* [1988] ICR 623.
Hayward v. *Cammell Laird Shipbuilders Ltd* [1984] TLR 52.

General discussion topics

1 'Job evaluation does not produce equitable payment: it merely produces a ramshackle method of justifying the status quo.' Do you agree with this statement?

2 What would be the main arguments for and against introducing legislation that is similar to the Ontario Pay Equity Act in the UK?

3 What do you think would be the major organisational problems associated with a move from a narrow to a broadbanded payment structure?

Another basic choice concerns the extent of the incentive. In practice this is a decision of rather greater importance than the type of incentive scheme to be used, although it is given rather less coverage in the literature. There is the world of difference, in terms of cost and employee perception, between a scheme which rewards people with 3 per cent or 4 per cent of salary and one which pays a sum equivalent to 25 per cent. Studies undertaken in the USA, reported by Bartol and Durham (2000, p. 14) suggest that the minimum level of bonus or pay rise 'necessary to elicit positive perceptual and attitudinal responses' is between 5 per cent and 7 per cent of salary. Lesser payments are thus unlikely to provide meaningful incentives and will only have a peripheral impact. According to Hendry *et al.* (2000, p. 54) this has been a major problem for schemes introduced in the public sector where incentives have tended to be worth a maximum of only 2 per cent or 3 per cent of salary. Armstrong and Murlis (1998) offer the following advice:

> As a rule of thumb, those whose performance is outstanding may deserve and expect rewards of 10% and more in their earlier period in a job. People whose level of performance and rate of development is well above the average may merit increases of between 7 and 9%, while those who are progressing well at the expected rate towards the fully competent level may warrant an increase of between 4% and 6%. Increases of between 0% and 3% may be justified for those who are not making such good progress but who are still developing steadily. Performance-related increases of less than 2–3% are hardly worth giving. Much also depends on current market movement and this affects expectations.   (Armstrong and Murlis 1998, pp. 286–9)

The final choice concerns the level at which the incentive will be paid. Some schemes reward individuals for individual performance, others reward a group of

---

WINDOW ON PRACTICE

Peter and Patrick are sales consultants for a financial services company and both had business targets for a six-month period. Peter met his target comfortably and received the predetermined bonus of £6,000 for reaching on-target earnings. Patrick failed to reach his target because his sales manager boss left the company and poached two of Patrick's prime customers just before they signed agreements with Patrick, whose bonus was therefore £2,000 instead of £6,250.

Joanne was a sales consultant for the same company as Peter and Patrick. Before the sales manager left, he made over to her several promising clients with whom he had done considerable preparatory work and who were not willing to be 'poached' by his new employer. All of these signed agreements and one of them decided to increase the value of the deal tenfold without any reference to Joanne until after that decision was made, and without knowing that she was now the appropriate contact. Her bonus for the period was £23,400.

Henry is a production manager in a light engineering company with performance pay related to a formula combining output with value added. Bonus payments were made monthly in anticipation of what they should be. One of Henry's initiatives was to increase the gearing of the payment by results scheme in the factory. Through peculiarities of company accounting his bonus payments were 'justified' according to the formula, but later it was calculated that the production costs had risen by an amount that cancelled out the value-added benefits. Also 30 per cent of the year's output had to be recalled due to a design fault.

Peter had his bonus made up to £6,250. Joanne had her bonus reduced to £8,000, but took legal advice and had the amount cut restored, whereupon Peter and Patrick both threatened to resign until mollified by *ex-gratia* payments of £2,000 each. Peter resigned three months later. Henry was dismissed.

employees or team for their collective performance. Finally there are schemes which share incentive payments out among all employees in the organisation or within individual business units. These are not mutually exclusive. It is possible, for example, to reward a sales person with three types of incentive, one from each level. The basic pay would thus be enhanced with commission calculated individually, with a performance-based payment made to all in his/her sales team to reflect excellent customer feedback, and finally with a profit-related bonus paid to all employees in the organisation. Team-based incentives have tended to get a better press in recent years than individual incentives, a major problem with the latter being their tendency to undermine team working in situations where it is an important contributor to competitive advantage (see Pfeffer 1998, pp. 218–20).

The extent to which incentives are paid

There is conflicting evidence about how widespread incentive payments are in the UK and about whether or not they are becoming more or less common. Each year the government's New Earnings Survey selects a sample of over 100,000 employees from across the country and asks their employers to fill in a form outlining their earnings in the previous tax year. One of the questions asks about earnings from Inland Revenue-approved profit-sharing schemes, another about other types of incentive payment 'such as piecework, commission, profit sharing (excluding the government scheme), productivity and other incentives/bonuses'. In 2000 the survey results revealed that only 14.9 per cent of employees were receiving incentive payments, a further 3.5 per cent earning bonuses from the government profit-related pay scheme. The proportion of manual workers being paid through incentive schemes (23 per cent) is shown to be considerably higher than is the case for non-manual workers (10 per cent), suggesting that the most common use of incentives involves the use of traditional piecework or payment by results schemes in manufacturing industry. Other approaches, such as individual performance-related pay, appear restricted to relatively small numbers of employees. These results are broadly consistent with those published in previous New Earnings Surveys.

However, other surveys paint a rather different picture. The authors analysing the 1998 Workplace Employment Relations Survey (Millward *et al.* 2000, pp. 212–13) concluded that around 60 per cent of the 2,191 workplaces in their sample operated either a payment by results or a merit pay incentive scheme. They concluded that, on balance, the proportion was similar to that reported in the 1990 survey, indicating no overall change in the extent of incentive schemes. In 1998 an IPD survey of 1,158 organisations found that 40 per cent of the respondents operated a merit pay system and that the median percentage of employees covered by the schemes was between 70 and 80 per cent. This survey also produced evidence of growth, a majority of the schemes in operation having been started within the previous five years. Other smaller surveys described by Brown and Armstrong (2000, pp. 19–23) lead to a similar conclusion – namely that incentive schemes of one kind or another are common and are steadily becoming more widespread.

It is not easy to reconcile the diverse results produced by these surveys. One possibility is that the different results may reflect the different samples used. The between individual effort and individual reward, so that those who are working effectively can have their efforts nullified by others working less effectively or by misfortunes elsewhere.

Commission

The payment of commission on sales is a widespread practice about which surprisingly little is known as these schemes have not come under the same close scrutiny as incentive schemes for manual employees. They suffer from most of the same drawbacks as manual incentives, except that they are linked to business won rather than to output achieved.

Activity 36.3	A problem with sales commission is its tendency to reward the quantity of goods sold without having regard to the quality of service provided by sales staff. In which circumstances might this have negative consequences? How could a commission-based incentive scheme be adapted to incorporate measures of quality as well as quantity?

Disadvantages of PBR schemes

The whole concept of payment by results was set up to cope with a stable and predictable situation, within the boundaries of the workplace. External demands from customers were irritations for others – like sales representatives – to worry about. The factory was the arena, the juxtaposed parties were the management on the one hand and the people doing the work on the other, and the deal was output in exchange for cash. The dramatic changes of the 1980s and 1990s, which have swept away stability, dismantled the organisational boundary and enthroned the customer as arbiter of almost everything have also made PBR almost obsolete.

According to the New Earnings Survey the proportion of manual workers receiving PBR payments has been in steady decline since 1983. This trend can be explained, in part, by changing technologies and changes in working practices. A payment system that puts the greatest emphasis on the number of items produced or on the time taken to produce them is inappropriate in industries where product quality is of greater significance than product quantity. Similarly a manufacturing company operating a just-in-time system will rely too heavily on overall plant performance to benefit from a payment scheme that primarily rewards individual effort.

In addition to the problem of fluctuating earnings, described above, there are a number of further inherent disadvantages which explain the decline of PBR-based remuneration arrangements.

Operational inefficiencies

For incentives to work to the mutual satisfaction of both parties, there has to be a smooth operational flow, with materials, job cards, equipment and storage space all readily available exactly when they are needed, and an insatiable demand for the output. Seldom can these conditions be guaranteed and when they do exist they seldom last without snags. Raw materials run out, job cards are not available, tools are faulty, the stores are full, customer demand is fluctuating or there is trouble with the computer. As soon as this sort of thing happens the incentive-paid worker has an incentive either to fiddle the scheme or negotiate its alteration for protection against operational vagaries.

Quality of work

The stimulus to increase volume of output can adversely affect the quality of output, as there is an incentive to do things as quickly as possible. If the payment scheme is organised so that only output meeting quality standards is paid for, there may still be the tendency to produce expensive scrap. Operatives filling jars with marmalade may break the jars if they work too hurriedly. This means that the jar is lost and the marmalade as well, for fear of glass splinters.

Renewed emphasis on quality and customer satisfaction mean that employers increasingly need to reward individuals with the most highly developed skills or those who are most readily adaptable to the operation of new methods and technologies. PBR, with its emphasis on the quantity of items produced or sold, may be judged inappropriate for organisations competing in markets in which the quality of production is of greater significance than previously.

The quality of working life

There is also a danger that PBR schemes may demotivate the workforce and so impair the quality of working life for individual employees. In our industrial consciousness payment by results is associated with the worst aspects of rationalised work: routine, tight control, hyper-specialisation and mechanistic practices. The worker is characterised as an adjunct to the machine, or as an alternative to a machine. Although this may not necessarily be so, it is usually so, and generally expected. Payment in this way reinforces the mechanical element in the control of working relationships by failing to reward employee initiative, skills acquisition or flexibility. There is also evidence to suggest that achieving high levels of productivity by requiring individuals to undertake the same repetitive tasks again and again during the working day increases stress levels and can make some employees susceptible to repetitive strain injuries.

The selective nature of the incentive

Seldom do incentive arrangements cover all employees. Typically, groups of employees are working on a payment basis which permits their earnings to be geared to their output, while their performance depends on the before or after processes of employees not so rewarded, such as craftsmen making tools and fixtures, labourers bringing materials in and out, fork-truck drivers, storekeepers and so forth. This type of problem is illustrated most vividly by Angela Bowey's study of a garment factory, where employees 'on piecework' were set against those who were not, by the selective nature of the payment arrangement (Lupton and Bowey 1975, pp. 76–8).

The conventional way round the problem is to pay the 'others' a bonus linked to the incentive earned by those receiving it. The reasoning for this is that those who expect to earn more (like the craftsmen) have a favourable differential guar-

Critiques of PRP

Performance-related pay attracted a great amount of criticism from academic researchers in the 1980s and 1990s during a period when its virtues were frequently asserted by HR managers and consultants. The attacks have come from several quarters. Occupational psychologists have tended to question the ability of PRP to motivate positively (e.g. Kohn 1993), while sociologists have seen it as a means of reinforcing management control at the expense of worker autonomy (e.g. Hendry *et al.* 2000). A further source of criticism has come from those who suspect that PRP is used as a means of perpetuating gender inequality in payment matters (e.g. Rubery 1985). However, the most colourful and damning criticisms have come from management thinkers such as W. Edwards Deming who advocate Total Quality Management approaches (see Chapter 17) and for whom PRP represents exactly the wrong kind of initiative to introduce. The whole basis of their philosophy is the substitution of 'leadership' for 'supervision', removing organisational hierarchies and managing people with as little direction and control as possible. They see PRP as having the opposite effect. It reinforces the hierarchy, enhances the power of supervisors and strengthens management control.

For many critics, including those cited above, PRP has fundamental flaws which cannot be overcome. Kohn, for example, argues that incentives can only succeed in securing temporary compliance. Their use cannot change underlying attitudes, while the attempt to do so ultimately damages the long-term health of an organisation by undermining relationships and encouraging employees to focus on short-term aims:

> Managers who insist that the job won't get done right without rewards have failed to offer a convincing argument for behavioural manipulation. Promising a reward to someone who appears unmotivated is a bit like offering salt water to someone who is thirsty. Bribes in the workplace simply can't work.   (Kohn 1993, p. 60)

A second stream of criticism is more moderate, arguing that PRP can have a role to play in organisations, but that its positive effects are limited. Moreover, while not fundamentally flawed, PRP is very difficult to implement effectively in practice. As a result, systems fail as often as they succeed. The arguments are summarised well by Gomez-Mejia and Balkin (1992, pp. 249–55), Cannell and Wood (1992, pp. 66–101), Pfeffer (1998, pp. 203–4) and Purcell (2000). The major points made by these authors are as follows:

1 Employees paid by PRP, especially where the incentive is substantial, tend to develop a narrow focus to their work. They concentrate on those aspects which they believe will initiate payments, while neglecting other parts of their jobs.
2 PRP, because of its individual nature, tends to undermine team working. People focus on their own objectives at the expense of co-operation with colleagues.
3 PRP, because it involves managers rating employees, can lead to a situation in which a majority of staff are demotivated when they receive their rating. This occurs where people perceive their own performance to be rather better than it is considered to be by their supervisors – a common situation. The result is a negative effect on the motivation of the staff who are unexceptional, but loyal and valued. These are often the very people organisations depend on most.

4 Employees are rarely in a position wholly to determine the outcomes of their own performance. Factors outside their control play an important role, leading to a situation in which the achievement or non-achievement of objectives is partially a matter of chance.

5 Even the most experienced managers find it difficult to undertake fair and objective appraisals of their employees' performance. Subjective judgements are often taken into account leading to perceptions of bias. Some managers deliberately manipulate ratings for political reasons, allowing their judgement to be coloured by the effect they perceive the outcome will have on particular employees. Low ratings are thus avoided, as are very high ratings, where it is perceived this will lead to disharmony or deterioration of personal relationships.

6 In organisations subject to swift and profound change, objectives set for the coming year may become obsolete after a few months. Employees then find themselves with an incentive to meet goals which are no longer priorities for the organisation.

7 PRP systems tend to discourage creative thinking, the challenging of established ways of doing things and a questioning attitude among employees.

8 Budgetary constraints often lead managers to reduce ratings, creating a situation in which excellent individual performance is not properly rewarded.

9 It is difficult to ensure that each line manager takes a uniform approach to the rating of their subordinates. Some tend to be more generously disposed in general than others, leading to inconsistency and perceptions of unfairness.

10 When the results of performance appraisal meetings have an impact on pay levels, employees tend to downplay their weaknesses. As a result development needs are not discussed or addressed.

11 PRP systems invariably increase the paybill. This occurs because managers fear demotivating their staff by awarding low or zero rises in the first years of a system's operation. Poorer performers are thus rewarded as well as better performers.

Using PRP effectively

Despite the problems described above it is possible to implement PRP successfully, as is shown by the experience of case study companies quoted by Brown and Armstrong (2000) and IRS (2000). It will only work, however, if it is used in appropriate circumstances and if it is implemented properly. Part of the problem with PRP has been a tendency in the HR press to portray it as universally applicable and as a panacea capable of improving performance dramatically. In fact it is neither, but is one of a range of tools that have a useful if limited role to play in some situations. Gomez-Mejia and Balkin (1992) specify the following favourable conditions:

1 Where individual performance can be objectively and meaningfully measured.
2 Where individuals are in a position to control the outcomes of their work.
3 Where close team working or co-operation with others is not central to successful job performance.
4 Where there is an individualistic organisational culture.

In addition, Brown and Armstrong (2000) rightly point to the importance of careful implementation and lengthy preparation prior to the installation of a scheme. Moreover, they argue that PRP should not be looked at or judged in isolation from other forms of reward, both extrinsic and intrinsic. Success or failure can hinge on what else is being done to maximise motivation, to develop people and to improve their job security.

Ultimately PRP has one great advantage which no amount of criticism can remove: it helps ensure that organisational priorities become individual priorities. Managers can signal the importance of a particular objective by including it in a subordinate's goals for the coming year. If the possibility of additional payment is then tied to its achievement, the chances that the objective concerned will be met increases significantly. Organisational performance is improved as a result. Where the achievement of such specific objectives forms a relatively minor part of someone's job, PRP can form a relatively minor part of their pay packet. Other rewards can then be used to recognise other kinds of achievement.

Many job descriptions for supervisory positions include reference to responsibility for ensuring that the appropriate health and safety at work regulations are adhered to. Few supervisors, however, left to themselves would see this aspect of their work as a priority. In one organisation known to the authors it was decided to try to raise the profile of health and safety issues by including objectives in this field into managers' annual performance targets. It therefore became clear that the level of PRP in the following year would, in part, be determined by the extent to which the health and safety objectives had been met.

The result was the swift establishment of departmental health and safety committees and schemes whereby staff could bring safety hazards to the attention of supervisors.

Skills-based pay

A further kind of incentive payment scheme is one which seeks to reward employees for the skills or competencies which they acquire. It is well established in the United States and, according to an IPD survey undertaken in 1998, is becoming more common among British employers. It is particularly prevalent as a means of rewarding technical staff, but there is no reason why the principle should not be extended to any group of employees for whom the acquisition of additional skills might benefit the organisation.

There are several potential benefits for an employer introducing a skills-based pay scheme. Its most obvious effect is to encourage multiskilling and flexibility enabling the organisation to respond more effectively and speedily to the needs of customers. A multiskilled workforce may also be slimmer and less expensive. In addition it is argued that, in rewarding skills acquisition, a company will attract and retain staff more effectively than its competitors in the labour market. The operation of a skills-based reward system is proof that the sponsoring employer is genuinely committed to employee development.

Most skills-based payment systems reward employees with additional increments to their base pay once they have completed defined skill modules. A number of such schemes are described in detail in a study published by Incomes Data Services (1992). Typical is the scheme operated by Venture Pressings Ltd where staff are employed on four basic grades, each divided into 10 increments. Employees progress up the scale by acquiring specific skills and demonstrating proficiency in them to the satisfaction of internal assessors. New starters are also assessed and begin their employment on the incremental point most appropriate to the level of skills they can demonstrate. In many industries it is now possible to link payment for skills acquisition directly to the attainment of National Vocational Qualifications (NVQs) for which both the setting of standards and the assessment of individual competence are carried out externally.

A skills-based pay system will only be cost effective if it results in productivity increases which are sufficient to cover the considerable costs associated with its introduction and maintenance. A business can invest a great deal of resources both in training its workforce to attain new skills, and in rewarding them once those skills have been acquired, only to find that the cost of the scheme outweighs the benefit gained in terms of increased flexibility and efficiency. Furthermore, in assisting employees to become more highly qualified and in many cases to gain NVQs, an employer may actually find it harder to retain its staff in relatively competitive labour markets.

The other major potential disadvantage is associated with skills obsolescence. Where a business operates in a fast-moving environment and needs to adapt its technology regularly, a skills-based payment system can leave the organisation paying enhanced salaries for skills which are no longer significant or are not required at all. Employers seeking to introduce skills-based systems of payment therefore need to consider the implications very carefully and must ensure that they only reward the acquisition of those skills which will clearly contribute to increased productivity over the long term.

Activity 36.5	A number of commentators praise skills-based pay as a system which avoids some of the pitfalls associated with performance-related pay schemes. Look back at the list of practical problems with PRP schemes above and consider which do and which do not apply to skills-based incentive systems.

Profit sharing

There are a number of different ways in which companies are able to link remuneration to profit levels. In recent years the government has sought to encourage such schemes and has actively promoted their establishment with advantageous tax arrangements. Underlying government support is the belief that linking pay to profits increases the employee's commitment to his or her company by deepening the level of mutual interest. As a result, it is argued that such schemes act as an incentive encouraging employees to work harder and with greater flexibility in pursuit of higher levels of take-home pay. Other potential advantages for employers described by Pendleton (2000, pp. 346–51) are better cost flexibility, changed attitudes on the part of employees and the discouragement of union membership.

Cash-based schemes

The traditional and most common profit-sharing arrangement is simply to pay employees a cash bonus, calculated as a proportion of annual profits, on which the employee incurs both a PAYE and a national insurance liability. Some organisations pay discretionary profit bonuses on this basis, while others allocate a fixed proportion of profits to employees as a matter of policy. **Gainsharing** is a variation on cash-based profit sharing which is widely used in the USA and which can be used in non-profit-making organisations as well as those operating in the commercial sector. Here the bonus relates to costs saved rather than profit generated in a defined period. So if a workforce successfully achieves the same level of output at lower overall cost, the gain is shared between employer and employees.

Between 1987 and 2000 the government operated an approved profit-related pay scheme which became increasingly popular. By 1996 there were over 14,000 schemes in operation, covering 3.7 million employees. The attraction was the ability profit-related pay schemes gave employers to give pay rises to all employees, while recouping the cost through tax concessions. The scheme was phased out and has now been replaced by the All-Employee Share Scheme.

Share-based schemes

There are several methods of profit sharing which involve employees being awarded shares rather than cash. Here too there are government-sponsored schemes in operation which involve favourable tax treatment.

Approved Deferred Share Trusts (ADSTs) were established under the Finance Act 1978. In this arrangement the company allocates a proportion of profit to a trust fund which purchases company shares on behalf of the employees. The shares are then allocated to eligible employees on some agreed formula. The employee shareholder pays tax only when the shares are sold, and there is no additional national insurance contribution by employee or employer. ADST schemes seldom allow shares to be sold in the first two years after purchase and if they are sold in the following year there is no tax obligation. A variant of this arrangement was made possible by the Finance Act 1980 under which Save As You Earn Schemes can be established, enabling employees, if they wish, to purchase company shares through monthly deductions from salary.

From 2001 it has been possible for employers to take advantage of the Inland Revenue approved All-Employee Share Scheme that allows employees to obtain shares in their own companies while avoiding tax and national insurance contributions. Employers can give such shares to employees to a maximum value of £3,000 per year. Some can be given in recognition of individual or team performance, making it possible to award some employees more shares than others. Where employees subsequently hold these shares for three years or more, there is no tax liability when they are sold. In addition, under the scheme, employees can buy shares in their own companies out of pre-tax income and subsequently avoid a proportion of the tax owed if they are sold after three years. Companies are also allowed to give 'free' matching shares for each share purchased by an employee under the scheme. These too are subject to favourable tax treatment if sold after three years. Employers as well as employees gain tax advantages from operating these schemes. Deductions in corporation tax can be made equivalent to the amount of salary used by employees to purchase shares, as well as monies used in establishing and operating the scheme.

Disadvantages of profit-related schemes

The obvious disadvantage of the schemes described above from the employee's point of view is the risk that pay levels may decline if the company fails to meet its expected profit levels. If no profit is made it cannot be shared. Share values can go down as well as up. Companies are not permitted to make guarantees about meeting payments and will have their schemes revoked by the Inland Revenue if they do so. In any event it is likely that profit-based incentives will vary in magnitude from year to year.

For these reasons it is questionable to assert that profit-sharing schemes do in fact act as incentives. Unlike performance-related pay awards they do not relate specifically to the actions of the individual employee. Annual profit levels are clearly influenced by a whole range of factors which are both internal and external to the company. An employee may well develop a community of interest with the company management, shareholders and other employees but it is unlikely to seriously affect the nature of his or her work. It is also the case that both poor and good performers are rewarded equally in profit-related schemes. The incentive effect will therefore be very slight in most cases and will be restricted to a general increase in employee commitment.

Summary propositions

36.1 Incentive schemes should be used where they are appropriate to the needs of the business and where they can clearly contribute to the achievement of organisational objectives.

36.2 Incentive payment schemes either involve the payment of a bonus or form the basis of incremental progression systems. In either case, the reward should represent at least 7 per cent of salary if there is to be a meaningful incentive effect.

36.3 The extent to which different types of incentive arrangement are used in the UK is unclear. There is evidence of growth in recent years, but the majority of employees remain uncovered by such schemes.

36.4 Methods of payment by results include individual time saving, group incentives, measured daywork, plant-wide schemes, productivity schemes and commission.

36.5 Performance-related pay systems are either merit based or goal based. They have been the subject of notable debate in recent years, many researchers finding a mismatch between their theoretical attractions and practical outcomes.

36.6 Skills-based pay involves linking incentives to the achievement of defined competencies or qualifications. It rewards what people bring to the job rather than the results of their efforts.

36.7 Profit sharing has been promoted by governments for many years. The All-Employee Share Scheme is the latest attempt to encourage employees to hold shares in their own companies.

allowances. Where relevant the regulatory environments are considered as well as the HR aspects. Finally we discuss the prospects for increased use of flexible benefits schemes. Another important group of benefits, those which are described as 'family friendly', were discussed in Chapter 13.

Pensions

Occupational pensions are increasingly seen as a form of 'deferred pay' rather than a reward for a lifetime of employment, and as such are attracting more attention from employees and trade unions. As the state pension scheme is changed and changed again, its future form becoming more uncertain, greater attention is being paid to personal and company schemes. The nature of work has changed dramatically since the first company pension schemes emerged. There has been a move from lifetime employment with one employer towards greater job mobility for all groups of employees. Sometimes this movement is deliberate, for example, young executives who join new companies to further their careers; sometimes it is involuntary, as in the case of redundancy. This has prompted an interest in the way that occupational schemes provide for those employees who have had more than one, frequently many, employers. The increasing likelihood of fairly lengthy unemployment between one job and the next, together with increasing attention to the role of women who characteristically have broken records of employment due to family commitments, have highlighted the assumptions on which most occupational pension schemes are based. The plight of those who, having been made redundant at 50 are never to find work again, has made people more aware of the potential role of pensions schemes in financing early retirement.

Our expectations in general have risen, with ideas of early retirement from choice, 'while you're still young enough to enjoy it', and increasing expectations that retirement should not necessarily be a time for 'tightening your belt', but a time to reap the rewards from one's work and to do things that there was never time for before. Retirement is now seen more as a beginning than an end, and consequently the pensions that support this new beginning are seen as more important at an earlier age than before. In addition to this, as information is more generally available, employees expect more information about their pension schemes and about the benefits to which they will eventually become entitled.

> ### Activity 37.1
>
> Robert Noble-Warren (1986) talks about 'lifetime planning' as a series of 'rest and recuperation' periods throughout life as well as the planning of financial provision. Lifetime planning has to start with a statement of your life's objectives. What are your life's objectives and what work, rest and financial plans can you make to achieve these?

State schemes

The state runs two schemes: a basic scheme and SERPS (State Earnings Related Pension Scheme). Every employee is obliged to contribute a standard amount to the basic scheme, which currently provides an old age pension at the age of 65 for men and 60 for women. By 2020 the pensionable age for both men and women will be 65 and in the 10 years prior to this date there will be a gradual phasing in of the new pensionable age for women.

For those employees who earn over a certain amount (known as the lower earnings limit) a percentage of salary earned between this limit and a higher salary level (known as the upper earnings limit) is also payable. Both these payments are deducted from wages as part of the national insurance contribution. The individual who has paid into SERPS as well as the basic scheme will receive a higher pension from the state on retirement in proportion to the additional amount that they have contributed. The employer also makes a contribution to the state pension scheme just as the individual employee does. The state pension scheme is organised on a pay-as-you-go basis. This means that there is no state pension fund as such, and the money that is paid to today's pensioners comes from today's taxes and national insurance contributions. The money that will be paid to today's contributors, when they become pensioners, will come not from the investment of their and their employers' contributions, but from the contributions of the workforce and their employers in the future. This approach to pension provision is causing great concern as the number of pensioners is increasing rapidly. Hopegood (1994) states that there are currently 3.3 people of working age to every pensioner, a figure which will reduce to 2.7 by 2030. Without substantial increases in taxation, the demographic trends mean that it will become increasingly difficult for the state to fund pensions beyond a basic subsistence level, with additional help being targeted at the very poorest pensioners. Most employees currently working are thus well advised to make substantial alternative provision through a company pension scheme or personal pension vehicle. In this respect the UK is better placed than most other European countries whose populations have traditionally enjoyed a higher level of state pension and where the occupational and personal pensions sectors are a good deal less developed.

Occupational schemes

The UK has had, for many years, one of the most extensive and effective systems of occupational pension provision in the world. There are over 150,000 separate schemes in operation with combined assets worth approximately £800 billion. Ten and a half million people are members of occupational pension schemes, while 6.5 million pensioners draw an income from their funds (Government Actuary's Department 1999). Although there has been some reduction recently in the proportion of the workforce covered by occupational pensions, they remain by far the most significant employee benefit in terms of their cost to employers.

In general, occupational schemes provide an additional retirement pension on top of the basic state pension, and sometimes on top of SERPS. Most often, however, the company will avoid employee and employer payments into SERPS by means of 'contracting out'. The Occupational Pensions Board (OPB) issues a contracting-out certificate provided employers pass a test relating to overall scheme quality.

Occupational schemes generally provide better and wider-ranging benefits than the state schemes and they provide some flexibility. They are most often found in large organisations and the public sector, but some smaller organisations also run such schemes. Men and women have equal access to occupational schemes and, since 1990, have had to be treated equally in respect of all scheme rules. In spite of this legislation men and women will continue to fare differently in terms of pensions benefits due to the patterns of women's employment being different from male patterns on which pensions schemes are typically based (see, for example, Ginn and Arber 1996). Women's longer average life expectancy also puts them at a disadvantage to men under certain types of scheme. A higher proportion of managerial and professional workers have occupational pensions than other groups, blue-collar workers being the least likely to be in schemes. It is no longer lawful for an employer to exclude part-time or temporary workers.

Occupational schemes rarely pay their pensioners in the pay-as-you-go manner operated by the state, but create a pension fund, which is managed separately from the business. The advantage of this is that should the organisation go broke, the pension fund cannot be seized to pay debtors because it is not part of the company. The money in the pension fund is invested and held in trust for the employees of the company at the time of their retirement.

Larger organisations administer their own pension funds themselves, and appoint an investment manager or a fund manager. The manager will plan how to invest the money in the fund to get the best return and to ensure that the money that is needed to pay pensions and other benefits will be available when required. An actuary can provide mortality tables and other statistical information in order to assist planning and must be hired regularly to carry out a formal actuarial assessment of the scheme's assets and liabilities. Smaller organisations tend to appoint an insurance company or a bank to administer their pension funds, and so use their expertise. Pension funds can be invested in a variety of different ways, and are often worth more than the market value of their sponsoring companies. As a result they have come to dominate investment on the stock market. Occupational pensions take one of three basic forms.

Defined benefit schemes are the most common, accounting for 80 per cent of all UK schemes in operation (National Association of Pension Funds 1999) and including virtually all public sector schemes. Here contributions are made into a single organisation-wide fund which is invested on behalf of members by a fund manager. Retired employees then draw a pension from the fund calculated according to a defined formula. Most defined benefit schemes take the final salary form, in which the value of the pension is determined by the level of salary being received by each individual at the time of retirement. In the private sector it is common for this to be calculated on a 'sixtieths' basis, whereby the retiree is paid an annual pension equivalent to 1/60th (1.67 per cent) of their final salary multiplied by the number of years' pensionable service they have completed. In the public sector it is usual for the figure to be based on 'eightieths', with a tax-free lump sum being paid in addition at the time of retirement. In either case the size of pension is heavily related to the length of scheme membership, the maximum pension payable equalling two-thirds of final salary. Examples of final salary calculations are given in Figure 37.1.

Another form of defined benefit scheme bases the pension calculation on the average salary earned over a period of five, 10 or 20 years prior to retirement rather than on pay in the final year. Unless most of someone's pensionable service has been spent earning close to the final salary level, such schemes are less generous than the final salary variety in terms of the amount of pension paid. High levels of inflation also reduce the value of pensions calculated on an average salary basis.

Figure 37.1 Final salary schemes – examples of various contribution periods with a 1/60 and a 1/80 scheme

Sixtieths Scheme

Final salary	= £24,000
Contributions for 5 years	= 1/60 × 24,000 × 5
Pension	= £2,000 per year
Final salary	= £24,000
Contributions for 25 years	= 1/60 × 24,000 × 25
Pension	= £10,000 per year
Final salary	= £24,000
Contributions for 40 years	= 1/60 × 24,000 × 40
Pension	= £16,000 per year

Eightieths Scheme

Final salary	= £24,000
Contributions for 25 years	= 1/80 × 24,000 × 25
Pension	= £7,500 per year
Lump sum	= 3/80 × 24,000 × 25 = £22,500

Most defined benefit schemes are contributory. This means that monies are paid into the fund on a regular basis by both the employer and the employee. In the case of employees the contribution is fixed as a percentage of salary (typically 5 per cent) a sum which is subject to tax relief. Employers, by contrast, are obliged only to pay in sufficient funds to ensure that the scheme remains solvent. When the pension fund is in surplus, as many were in the 1980s and 1990s, employers can take 'contribution holidays'. By contrast, when the fund is in deficit, the employer has to contribute whatever is necessary to ensure that assets are sufficient to meet possible liabilities. This means that the amount of employer contribution can vary considerably, year on year, in an unpredictable fashion. Employers, like employees, gain from tax relief on contributions paid.

In some industries, as well as parts of the public sector, it has been traditional for occupational pensions to be non-contributory. In such schemes the employee makes no contribution at all, but nonetheless draws a pension calculated according to the final salary. Civil servants benefit from this kind of arrangement, as do many employees in the banking and finance sectors.

Defined contribution schemes (also known as money purchase schemes) are organised in a totally different way from defined benefit arrangements, and there are no promises about what the final level of pension will be. Employees and employers both contribute a fixed percentage of current salary to these schemes, usually 5 per cent or 7 per cent on a monthly basis. The pension benefits received are then entirely dependent on the money that has been contributed and the way that it has been invested. Where investments perform well, a good level of pension can be gained. Where investments are disappointing, the result is a low level of pension. Further uncertainty derives from the way that money purchase schemes result in the payment of a single lump sum to the employee when he/she retires. This is then used to buy an annuity from an insurance company from which a weekly or monthly income is paid for life. Annuity rates vary considerably from year to year, and there is also considerable variation between the deals offered by different providers. In essence this means that the risk associated with pension investments is carried by the employee in a defined contribution arrangement, rather than by the employer as in a final salary scheme. For this reason it is generally the case that defined contribution schemes are less satisfactory than defined benefit schemes when seen from an employee's perspective. Investments have to perform unusually well while inflation remains low for a money purchase scheme to give an equivalent level of benefit. However, despite these drawbacks, money purchase schemes are more flexible and more easily transferable than defined benefit arrangements. For people changing jobs frequently or working on a self-employed basis for periods of time, particularly during the early years of a career, they can thus be a more attractive option.

During the 1990s there was a strong trend away from defined benefit schemes and towards defined contribution provision. At the time of writing 15 per cent of all UK schemes are of the money purchase variety, compared with only 5 per cent in 1990 (National Association of Pension Funds 1992 and 1999). The majority of newly established schemes take the defined contribution form, while many organisations now offer only a money purchase scheme to new employees. The trend has coincided with a period in which long contribution holidays have come to an end and in which the amount of regulation to which defined benefit schemes are subject has increased substantially. Employers have thus taken the opportunity to reduce their own liabilities and to move to a form of provision which is more predictable financially from their point of view. Many employees are less well served as a result, but the lack of appreciation and understanding of pensions issues referred to above has allowed employers to make the change without becoming any less attractive in the labour market.

Hybrid schemes too are becoming more common, although as yet they represent a small minority of UK pension funds. These, in various different ways, combine elements of the defined benefit and defined contribution forms of provision. The most common form is the 'money purchase underpin' which is basically a final salary arrangement, but one which calculates pensions and transfer values on a money purchase basis where these are higher. Such schemes seek to combine the best aspects of both main types of scheme. They offer a generous, secure and predictable pension, but also incorporate the flexibility associated with defined contribution schemes.

Activity 37.2

Which of these three types of occupational pension scheme would you find most attractive at the current stage in your career? Under what circumstances might you change your preference?

Group personal pensions

Since the 1980s there has been substantial growth in the market for personal pensions. Self-employed people have always needed to be concerned with making their own provisions for retirement, as they are excluded from joining SERPS. More general attention has been focused on this area due to increasing job mobility and the perceived greater portability of personal pensions. A personal pension is arranged, usually through an insurance company, and the individual pays regular amounts into their own 'pension fund' in the same way that they would with a company fund. The employer may also make a contribution to the fund, but at present there are very few employers who have chosen to do so.

An alternative arrangement is a Group Personal Pension plan (GPP) set up by an employer instead of an occupational pension scheme. From a legal and taxation perspective a GPP is no different from any individual personal pension arrangement, but charges are lower because the employer is able to arrange a bulk discount. The scheme is administered by an insurance company, the employer making contributions as well as the employee. Pensions are calculated on the same basis as an occupational money purchase scheme, but tend to be less extensive because employees are responsible for paying some of the administrative charges. From an employee perspective a GPP is inferior to an occupational pension scheme, but is better than a situation in which no employer provision is made at all. Such arrangements are mainly entered into by small firms, but one or two big companies have also set them up in place of conventional occupational pensions.

> ## WINDOW ON PRACTICE
>
> ### Pension scandals
>
> Following the introduction of personal pensions in 1988 many thousands of employees who were members of occupational schemes were persuaded by salespeople working for insurance companies to leave their employers' schemes and take out inferior personal pension products instead. This became known as the 'pensions mis-selling scandal' because so many people lost out as a result. The government has required the companies concerned to compensate the individuals who were mis-sold pensions, but by 2001 there were still thousands of cases outstanding and waiting to be settled. This scandal, combined with the discovery in 1992 of the defrauding of the Mirror Group pension funds by Robert Maxwell, served to harm the reputation of the UK pensions industry. Mr Maxwell had used the funds to prop up ailing businesses owned by his group. Their combined worth was greater than the value of the companies themselves. When the group collapsed, the funds intended to pay past and present pensioners were found to have disappeared. Robert Maxwell committed suicide.
>
> The government responded to public concern by setting up a committee under the chairmanship of Professor Roy Goode to examine the whole field of pension fund regulation. The result was the Pensions Act 1995, which substantially altered UK law on pension funds.

Stakeholder pensions

A new form of government-sponsored pension arrangement, the stakeholder pension, was established in 2001. These are aimed primarily at middle income earners (that is, those earning £9,000 to £18,500 per year) who do not have access to an occupational scheme. The aim is to reduce the number of people in future decades who are reliant on state pensions for their retirement income.

A stakeholder pension scheme can be operated by an employer, a financial services company or a trade union. They operate along money purchase lines and are regulated by established authorities. Charges are kept low because providers are obliged to follow minimum standards set by the government. Employers are not obliged to make contributions to a stakeholder pension, but must provide access to one through their payroll. If employees join a scheme, for example provided by their trade union, the employer is therefore obliged to make deductions via the payroll out of pre-tax income.

Occupational pensions and HRM

While occupational pension schemes are governed by a board of trustees which includes member representatives, in most organisations the pensions manager and pensions department are part of the HR function. It is thus important that HR professionals are familiar with the types of scheme offered and the main operating rules so that they can give accurate and timely advice to staff and to potential recruits. They also need to be familiar with the regulatory environment for occupational pensions, which has changed considerably in recent years. Aside from new legislation outlawing discrimination on grounds of sex or against part-time and temporary staff, several other important regulatory changes have been made and new regulatory bodies established. The Pensions Act 1995 now sets out in detail what information must be disclosed to scheme members on request and what must be sent to them automatically each year. The Act also requires all occupational funds to meet a defined minimum funding level so that they are always able to meet their liabilities in the event of the employing company being wound up. Moreover, strict restrictions are now placed on 'self-investment', making sure that fund assets cannot be invested in property or other business ventures controlled by the sponsoring organisation. However, the most important single piece of recent legislation was the Social Security Act 1985 which put in place a series of measures to protect 'early leavers', ensuring that people who switch employers during their careers do not suffer substantial loss in the value of their pensions.

Early leavers now have one of three options in making their pension arrangements when they begin work for a new employer. One option is to claim back the contributions that the individual has made into the former employer's pension scheme. Deductions are made in accordance with tax laws, and of course, the employer's contribution is lost, but a substantial sum can be reinvested in the new employer's scheme or in a personal pension. Another alternative involves opting for a preserved pension. With a final salary scheme, if there were no inflation, and if the individual progressed very little up the career ladder, a preserved pension from an old employer plus a pension from the recent employer would equate well with the pension they would have received had they been with the new employer for the whole period. However, if these conditions are not met, which in recent times they have not been, individuals who have had more than one employer lose out in the pension stakes. Past employers are required to revalue preserved pensions in line with inflation (to a maximum of 5 per cent), but the value of such a pension remains linked to the level of salary at the date of leaving.

The third option is usually preferable, but is only open to people who have completed two years' membership of a scheme. This involves the transfer of the pension from the old employer's fund into that of the new employer. The process is straightforward in the case of a money purchase scheme, because the worth of each person's pension is readily calculated. It is simply the value of the employee's contributions, plus those of the employer, together with funds accrued as a result of their investment. The process is more complicated in the case of a final salary scheme, the transfer value being calculated according to standard actuarial conventions which take account of the employee's age, their length of pensionable service, the level of salary at the time of leaving and the current interest rate. All things being equal, 'early leavers' still fare worse than 'stayers' in terms of final pensions, but the difference is a great deal less than used to be the case.

Aside from giving advice and taking overall responsibility for pensions issues, HR managers are concerned with determining their organisations' pension policy. Is an occupational pension to be offered? If so, what form should it take? What level of contribution is the employer going to make? It is quite possible to make a judgement in favour of generous occupational provision simply on paternalistic grounds. Many organisations have thus decided that they will offer pensions because it is in the interests of their staff that they should. Occupational schemes provide a convenient and tax-advantageous method of providing an income in old age; it therefore makes sense to include a pension in the total pay and benefits package. The problems with such a commitment, particularly in the case of defined benefit schemes, are the cost and the fact that the long-term financial consequences are unpredictable. This, combined with the fact that many employees do not seem to appreciate the value of an occupational pension, means that many employers are now questioning their commitment to final salary schemes and to pension provision in general.

Research suggests that interest in and understanding of occupational pensions varies considerably from person to person (Goode 1993; Taylor 2000). Older people, professional workers and those working in the financial services sector usually have a clearer perception of their value than other groups of staff. For these groups pensions are important, and their labour market behaviour will be affected as a result. A firm which does not offer a good pension will thus find it harder to recruit and retain them than one which does. By contrast, a firm which largely employs younger people, and/or workers in lower-skilled occupations, may find that it makes more sense to offer additional pay in place of an occupational scheme.

Activity 37.3

It has been argued that by making occupational pensions readily transferable, by increasing the complexity of the regulatory regime and by increasing taxation levied on pension funds, successive governments have provided a major disincentive to employers considering the establishment of a scheme. To what extent do you agree with this point of view?

Sick pay

As with pension schemes, the provision of sick pay is seen as the mark of a good employer. Sick pay is an important issue due to the need for control and administration of absence. Recent figures (Industrial Society 1996) suggest that sickness absence represents 3.9 per cent of working time, although there are large differences between sector and job type. The HR manager and the HR department have a variety of roles to play in relation to sick pay, particularly since the introduction of statutory sick pay in 1983 when state sick pay in addition to occupational sick pay have been managed by the employer.

Statutory sick pay (SSP)

Statutory sick pay is a state benefit that has been in existence for several decades.

It provides a basic income (£60.20 per week in 2001) to employees who are incapable of going to their normal place of work as a result of illness. SSP, however, is not claimed from a benefit office; it is administered by employers and paid through the payroll according to regulations set out in statute.

Since 1994 employers have been required to take full financial responsibility for SSP for the first four weeks of absence, after which they can claim back 100 per cent of sick pay paid from the state through reduced employer national insurance contributions (see IDS 1994). Most employees are entitled to state sickness benefit; however, there are some exceptions: employees who fall sick outside the EU, employees who are sick during an industrial dispute, employees over pensionable age and part-timers whose earnings are below the lower earnings limit (£67 per week in 2001). These groups, as well as self-employed people, are obliged to claim state incapacity benefit instead from the Department of Social Security (DSS). SSP is built around the concepts of qualifying days, waiting days, certification, linked periods, transfer to the DSS and record periods.

Qualifying days are those days on which the employee would normally have worked, except for the fact that he or she was sick. For many Monday-to-Friday employees this is very straightforward. However, it is more complex to administer for those on some form of rotating week or shift system. Sick pay is only payable for qualifying days.

Waiting days have to pass before the employee is entitled to receive sick pay – at present the number of days is three. These three days must be qualifying days, and on the fourth qualifying day the employee is entitled to sickness benefit, should he or she still be away from work due to sickness.

Certification from a doctor is required after seven days of sickness absence. Prior to this the employee provides self-certification. This involves notifying the employer of absence due to sickness by the first day on which benefit is due – that is, immediately following the three waiting days.

Linked periods of illness mean that the three waiting days do not apply. If the employee has had a period of incapacity from work (PIW) within the previous eight weeks, then the two periods are linked and treated as just one period for SSP purposes, and so the three waiting days do not have to pass again.

The employer does not have to administer SSP for every employee indefinitely. Where the employee has been absent due to sickness for a continuous or linked period of 28 weeks the responsibility for payment passes from the employer to the DSS. A continuous period of 28 weeks' sickness is clearly identifiable. It is not so clear when linked periods are involved. An employee who was sick for five days, back at work for four weeks, sick for one day, at work for seven weeks and then sick for two days would have a linked period of incapacity of eight days. Alternatively, an employee who was sick for four days, back at work for ten weeks and then sick for five days would have a period of incapacity this time of five days. The DSS requires employers to keep SSP records for three years so that these can be inspected.

Occupational sick pay

There is no obligation on employers to pay employees for days of absence due to sickness over and above what is required under the state's SSP scheme. However, most employers choose to do so via a benefit known as occupational sick pay (OSP). The most common approach is to continue paying the full salary for a set period of time, but other schemes involve reducing the pay rate for days taken off as a result of illness. In either case a sum in excess of the statutory minimum is paid, the portion accounted for by SSP being reclaimed from the state where possible. Paying the full salary is straightforward for those staff who receive a basic salary with no additions. It is more difficult to define for those whose pay is supplemented by shift allowances or productivity bonuses.

Occupational sick pay arrangements tend to be most generous in unionised environments and in the public sector, although professional and managerial employees are usually well covered in most organisations. The common public sector approach involves paying full pay for the first six months of an illness, once three years' service have been completed, before moving the employee on to half pay for a further six months. Thereafter OSP ceases. At the other end of the scale are employers who pay no OSP at all. They take the view that occupational sick pay will be abused and so pay only what is due under the state scheme. Another approach involves paying a predetermined flat rate in addition to money provided via SSP.

Occupational sick pay schemes also vary according to the period of service required. Some employers provide sick pay for sickness absence from the first day of employment. Others require a qualifying period to be served. For some this is a nominal period of four weeks, but the period may be three or six months, or a year or more. There is a major difference here between OSP and SSP. With SSP pay is available immediately after employment has begun.

In order to ensure that there is minimal abuse of the right to OSP, HR departments need to monitor absence rates carefully and take action where abuse is suspected. The following activities are common.

Home visits involve HR managers or welfare officers visiting employees at home after they have been away sick for a considerable period. Such visits are partly intended to enable the manager to keep in touch with the employee and their progress, but also for the advisory purposes outlined above, and for planning purposes. For example, it might be appropriate to discuss with the employee the possibility of early retirement when sick pay runs out. These visits are some-

Table 37.1 Formulating administrative procedures

- How, to whom and when should employees notify they are sick?
- When is a doctor's certificate required, and to whom should it go?
- Are there any arrangements for return to work interviews?
- How is absence information to be communicated from the line manager to personnel, and from personnel to payroll?
- What should happen if employees are sick while on holiday or on a bank holiday?
- What sickness and absence records are to be kept and who will keep them, and in what form?
- How are poor attenders to be identified, and what investigations should be made and what action taken?
- What methods should be used to keep in touch with long-term sick employees?
- What arrangements are there to transfer older long-term sick employees on to a retirement pension?
- How do the OSP procedures integrate with the SSP procedures?

times organised on a more regular basis, say every month, and may be included as part of the sick pay procedure. In these circumstances they are intended partly as a deterrent to those claiming sick pay under false pretences.

Absence procedures are formulated and communicated by HR managers so that everyone knows where they stand and what are their contractual entitlements. The questions to ask when determining policy are listed in Table 37.1.

Procedures, however, are useless unless they are recognised and adhered to. It is, therefore, essential that employees know what is expected of them when they are sick – that they know whom to inform, when they need to do this and what information they need to give. If there is an employee handbook, the rules of the sick pay scheme and absence procedures should be included, and this information should be emphasised by line managers. Employees need to be aware of sick pay policy, and what is regarded as acceptable and unacceptable behaviour in relation to the scheme. They need to know how the disciplinary procedure will be implemented with regard to abuse of the sick pay scheme, and the type of information that management will use in order to decide when to invoke the procedure. Sick pay should not, however, be presented in a completely negative way, and the reasons why the organisation provides sick pay and the benefits available should be clearly presented to encourage the employee to take a responsible attitude towards the scheme, so that the use of disciplinary procedures is a rare rather than a frequent event.

Absence monitoring can be used in the development of control procedures. For example, lists may be produced of those employees claiming most sick pay entitlement and managers may be asked to interview these employees in order to provide further information and explanation. Monitoring of sickness absence is entirely dependent on the keeping of complete and reliable records. Useful analyses of this information can be produced by comparing different individuals; groups, such as age groups or skill level groups; departments; times of year; or comparing absence over a few years to identify trends. Comparison with the absence levels of other employers may also be illuminating. It is helpful to look at total amount of absence, number of spells of absence and length of each spell of absence.

Activity 37.4	What other steps, aside from home visits and conspicuous monitoring, can be taken by employers to reduce absence levels? Which approach do you think is likely to be most effective?

Company cars

A form of employee benefit which is a great deal more common in the UK than in other countries is the company car, nearly two million employees enjoying this benefit in 2000 (IRS 2000b, p. 2). Managers from overseas often take some persuading that cars are necessary to attract and retain high calibre managers, but the received wisdom is that they are. Their importance to employees is demonstrated by the comparative lack of take-up of cash alternatives where these are offered (Smith 2000a, p. 161). After pensions, they are the second most significant employee benefit in cost terms, and are provided for some employees by over 90 per cent of large and medium-sized companies.

There are a number of sound reasons underlying the provision of company cars. First, for some there is a need as part of their jobs to travel very widely and regularly. Not everyone can be assumed to own a reliable car, so it is sometimes necessary to provide one simply to enable an employee to carry out his/her day-to-day job duties. In the case of sales representatives and senior managers the impression created when travelling on company business can be important. It is therefore often considered necessary to provide them with up-market and up-to-date models to ensure that clients and potential clients are suitably impressed. A case can also be made on cost efficiency grounds for people who clock up a great number of business miles each year. The cost of paying them a reasonable mileage allowance to drive their own cars is often greater than the cost of providing them with a company vehicle; it costs £9,000 a year to reimburse someone who has travelled 30,000 miles at 30p per mile.

However, most possessors of company cars do not fit either of the above categories. Their car entitlements simply come as an expected part of the pay package for middle and senior managers. As such, they signify the achievement of a certain level of status. Indeed, in many companies the cars offered become steadily more imposing as people climb up the corporate hierarchy. Being upgraded car-wise thus signifies in a very manifest way the company's approval. Downgrading, of course, has the opposite effect.

One of the reasons that company cars are so significant in the UK is historical, because prior to April 1994 they were a highly tax-efficient benefit. It was a good deal cheaper to drive a company car than to purchase one's own out of taxed income, so it made sense for people to be 'paid' in part with a car. At the time of writing (2001) company cars are generally considered to be tax neutral, but this situation will change with the introduction of new regulations from April 2002.

The aim of the new regulations is to encourage employers to lease or purchase cars which are more environmentally friendly. At present company cars are taxed according to the number of miles driven on company business. The annual tax paid by the driver is equivalent to a percentage of the car's list price. The more miles are driven on business, the less tax is paid. Someone who drives 20,000 business miles a year pays 15 per cent of the car's list price, whereas someone who clocks up only 2,000 miles pays 35 per cent of the list price in tax. There are then substantial discounts available for people who drive older cars. Most employers offer cash alternatives equal to the tax payable on the car, but only 18 per cent of those eligible choose to take these up (see IRS 2000b, p. 6).

After 2002 the tax paid will depend on carbon emissions or engine size and there will be no reductions for people who drive a great number of miles or use an older vehicle. This means that someone who drives 20,000 miles in a large car under the old system will have to pay more than twice as much tax after April 2002 unless they switch to a smaller car with lower carbon emissions. The new regime is complex, with different rules applying to cars with and without approved carbon emissions figures. A good summary is provided by IRS (2000b).

A major policy choice faced by employers in the provision of cars is whether to buy or lease their fleet. There are advantages and disadvantages associated with both approaches, much depending on the nature of the deal that is struck with a leasing company. Where the company is reputable and where the agreement provides for insurance, maintenance and repair of vehicles, the financial case for leasing is strong.

Activity 37.5 Assume that you have been offered a new job which comes with either the use of a new company car or a cash allowance. The salary is £35,000 per year. The car is worth £15,000, giving you an annual tax bill of £5,250. This is also the amount being offered by way of an annual cash allowance. Which option would you choose and why?

London allowances

Most larger employers pay a standard, organisation-wide allowance or salary weighting to employees working in central London. In some cases such allowances are also paid to employees working in the region around London. The purpose is to attract and retain staff who are obliged to live and commute in the capital where the cost of property, transport and parking is so much higher than it is elsewhere in the country. The typical level of allowance is between £3,000 and £4,000 a year, the highest sums being paid by the finance houses of the City and the lowest by the retailers and public sector employers. According to IDS (1999b), the level of allowances has tended to rise more slowly than wage inflation generally. This has occurred because employers are increasingly moving towards the development of wholly separate London-based salary scales. The flat-rate allowance has thus become a less significant part of the total pay packet, allowing employers to target resources on the groups who are hardest to recruit. In tight labour markets, therefore, there is now a greater differential between pay rates in and out of London than was the case 10 years ago.

Flexible benefits

Flexible benefits or 'cafeteria plans' have proliferated in the United States over recent years where they are specifically recognised in the tax regime. By contrast, take-up of the idea in the UK has been slow (Smith 2000b, p. 379). However, several high profile organisations have moved towards greater flexibility, and the case for others doing so is strong. Such flexibility involves giving individual employees a choice as to how exactly their pay packet is made up. The overall value of the package is set by the employer, but it is for employees to choose for themselves what balance they wish to strike between cash and the different kinds of benefit. Those who have children, for example, can opt for benefits that are of value to them such as childcare vouchers, access to a company crèche or additional holidays. A young person in their first job might well prefer to forgo most benefits in return for higher take-home pay, while an older person may wish to purchase additional years of pensionable service in exchange for cash or perhaps a car.

There are a number of good reasons for considering such an approach. First, it helps ensure that employees are only provided with benefits which they are aware of and appreciate. Resources that would otherwise be wasted providing unwanted benefits are thus saved. The employer gets maximum value per pound spent, while at the same time allowing employees to tailor their own 'perfect' benefits mix. The result should be improved staff retention and a better motivated workforce.

In 1998 a large-scale merger took place between two of the world's largest professional services firms – Price Waterhouse and Coopers & Lybrand. The merged firm, called PricewaterhouseCoopers, employs 150,000 people in 150 different countries. While the two organisations were culturally similar, they had rather different traditions in the provision of benefits. Rather than continue with different people employed on different sets of terms and conditions, partners decided to harmonise everyone as soon as was possible. This process was made a great deal easier and less contentious by the decision to develop a new flexible benefits scheme called 'Choices'. It allows employees to trade cash for additional holiday, a choice of car, childcare vouchers, retail vouchers, insurance of various kinds and a pension. As a result no one was required to alter their existing benefits package as a result of the merger unless they wished to.

Source: O. Franks and D. Thompson (2000) 'Rights and rites of passage', *People Management*, 17 February.

Flexible benefits plans take many different forms, the main distinction being between those that are 'fully flexible' and those that allow a degree of flexibility within prescribed limits. The former allow employees a free hand to make up their own package and to change it at regular intervals. Under such a regime an employee could theoretically swap all benefits for cash, or could double their holiday entitlement in exchange for a pay cut. A degree of restriction is more common, a compulsory core of benefits being compulsory, with flexibility beyond that. Under such a scheme everyone might be required to take four weeks' holiday and invest in a minimal pension, but be allowed freedom to determine whether or not they wished to benefit from private health insurance, gym membership, discounts on company products, etc. Typical plans also permit some choice on the make and model of car.

A third approach is administratively more simple but is more restrictive in terms of employee choice. This involves 'prepackaging' a number of separate benefits menus designed to suit different groups of employees (rather like a preset banquet menu in a Chinese restaurant). Employees must then opt for one package from a choice of five or six, each having the same overall cash value. One is typically tailored to meet the needs of older staff, another for those with young families, a third for new graduates and so on.

A number of disadvantages with flexible benefits systems can be identified which may well explain their slow development in the UK. These are summarised by Smith (2000b) as follows:

> Objections include difficult administration; problems connected with handling individual employee choices; the requirement for complex costing and records; difficulty in getting employees to make effective choices; employees making mistakes (for example leaving themselves with inadequate pension cover); employees' circumstances changing over time leaving his or her package inappropriate and giving the employer the costly headache of re-designing the package; and finally the possible hiring of expensive specialist or consultant skills and financial counselling to support the move to flexibility.

Uncertainty about the future tax position may also be a deterrent, especially where changes have the potential to throw a whole system out of kilter (as happened in 1997 when the Chancellor of the Exchequer substantially extended taxation on pension fund investments). Good advice about how to overcome these obstacles, together with examples of UK-based schemes in operation, is provided in IDS (1998).

Summary propositions

37.1 Between 20 per cent and 50 per cent of the typical employer's paybill is spent on the provision of supplementary benefits. Evidence suggests that most employees do not appreciate the true financial value of such benefits.

37.2 Occupational pensions provide a tax-efficient means of providing funds for retirement over and above what is provided by state and personal pension schemes.

37.3 Occupational pensions take one of three forms: defined benefit, defined contribution and hybrid. Employers can choose as an alternative to set up a group personal pension or to provide a stakeholder pension under the government's scheme.

37.4 Employers are required to facilitate the payment of statutory sick pay to employees who are away from work as a result of an illness. Most pay occupational sick pay in addition either as a result of moral obligation or in order to attract, retain and motivate their workforces.

37.5 Absence control is important, as high absence levels cost money, lower morale and suggest a lack of interest in employees on the part of employers.

37.6 Company cars are commonly provided by UK employers for senior staff. A new tax regime, starting in 2002, aims to discourage demand for larger cars which are not environmentally friendly.

37.7 In theory, flexible benefits plans have a great deal to offer employees. It is likely that their use will grow more widespread in the next few years.

References

Franks, O. and Thompson, D. (2000) 'Rights and rites of passage', *People Management*, 17 February.

Ginn, J. and Arber, S. (1996) 'Patterns of employment, gender and pensions: the effect of work history on older women's non-state pensions', *Work, Employment & Society*, Vol. 10, No. 3, pp. 469–90.

Goode, R. (1993) *Pension Law Reform: The Report of the Pension Law Review Committee*, Volume 2: Research. London: HMSO.

Government Actuary's Department (1999) *Occupational Pension Schemes: Eleventh Survey*. London: HMSO.

Hopegood, J. (1994) 'Money-go-round: solving the age-old SERPS puzzle', *Daily Telegraph*, 19 March.

IDS (1994) *Absence and Sick Pay Policies*, IDS Study 556, June. London: Incomes Data Services.

IDS (1998) *Flexible benefits*, IDS StudyPlus, July. London: Incomes Data Services.

IDS (1999a) *Benefits: costs and values*, IDS Focus 89, March. London: Incomes Data Services.

IDS (1999b) *London allowances*, IDS Study 669, May. London: Incomes Data Services.

Industrial Society (1996) *Maximising Attendance: managing best practice*. London: Industrial Society.

IRS (2000a) 'Managing benefit provision', *IRS Pay and Benefits Bulletin 487*, January. London: Industrial Relations Services.

IRS (2000b) 'Cash or car?', *IRS Pay and Benefits Bulletin 498*, June. London: Industrial Relations Services.

NAPF (1992) *Seventeenth Annual Survey of Occupational Pension Funds*. London: National Association of Pension Funds.

NAPF (1999) *Twenty-Fourth Annual Survey of Occupational Pension Funds*. London: National Association of Pension Funds.

Noble-Warren, R. (1986) 'Lifetime planning', in Institute of Directors, *The Director's Guide to Pensions*. London: The Director Publications Ltd.

Smith, I. (2000a) 'Benefits', in G. White and J. Druker (eds), *Reward Management: A Critical Text*. London: Routledge.

Smith, I. (2000b) 'Flexible plans for pay and benefits', in R. Thorpe and G. Homan (eds), *Strategic Reward Systems*. London: Financial Times/Prentice Hall.

Taylor, S. (2000) 'Occupational pensions and employee retention: debate and evidence', *Employee Relations*, Vol. 22, No. 3, pp. 246–59.

General discussion topics

1 Some organisations are said to have an 'absence culture' while others are said to have an 'attendance culture'. How do these terms differ, and how might an organisation move from an absence to an attendance culture?

2 Why do you think so few people seem to have an appreciation of the value of their occupational pensions and other benefits? What could be done to raise awareness of the costs involved in their provision?

3 Draw up three flexible benefits packages; one aimed at new graduates, one at employees in their thirties, and one for those aged over 50.

Chapter 38   Interactive skill: negotiation

Negotiation is a long-standing art, which has developed into a major mode of decision making in all aspects of social, political and business life, even though there is always a feeling that it is no more than a substitute for direct, decisive action. Henry Kissinger was US Secretary of State when protracted negotiations eventually brought to an end the war in Vietnam. He commented:

> A lasting peace could come about only if neither side sought to achieve everything that it had wanted; indeed, that stability depended on the relative satisfaction, and therefore the relative dissatisfaction, of all the parties concerned.   (Kissinger 1973)

In employment we have developed the institutions of collective bargaining as a means of regulating some parts of the employment relationship between employer and organised employees. The essence of the process is to find not just common ground between two parties but a new relationship with greater constructive potential than the one that preceded it. To some this is the cornerstone of industrial democracy and the effective running of a business, but to others it is seen as impairing efficiency, inhibiting change and producing the lowest, rather than the highest, common factor of co-operation between management and employees. Most of the academic work on negotiation is of relatively long standing, although there is a recent thorough review in Hiltrop and Udall (1995) and a particular angle described in Grint (1997).

Since the summer of 2000 trade unions have had restored to them a statutory right to recognition by an employer that had been removed from them twenty years before. Recognition means the right to require an employer to negotiate on matters like hours, pay and holidays: not to consult, but to negotiate. A useful summary is in Younson (2000).

Is negotiation rightly viewed as an activity that is only second best to unilateral decision making? If the outcome is no more than compromise, the choice seems to be between negotiation and capitulation. Some would argue that capitulation by one side would be a better outcome for both than a compromise that ignores the difficulties and dissatisfies both. There is, however, an alternative to splitting the difference in negotiation and that is where the differences in view and objective of the parties are accommodated to such an extent that the outcome for both is better than could have been achieved by the unilateral executive action of either.

Any negotiation takes place because there are some goals that are common to both parties and some goals that conflict. Between employer and employees the desire to keep the business in operation is a goal they usually have in common, but others of their goals may conflict. Consequently the two parties negotiate a settlement because the attempt by one to force a solution on the other either would fail because of the other's strength or would not be as satisfactory a settlement without the approval of the other party. Many years ago G.C. Homans expressed the situation thus:

> The more the items at stake can be divided into goods valued more by one party than they cost to the other and goods valued more by the other party than they cost to the first, the greater the chances of a successful outcome.
>
> (Homans 1961, p. 62)

Traditionally, negotiation on employment matters has been assumed to deal with the collective aspects of the relationship: the management or the employers being pitched against the unions or the workers. Now, however, we include material on the negotiation of the bargain between the management and an individual person or consultancy selling services. Another recent change has been the growing interest of language specialists in the various processes of negotiation (for instance, Mulholland 1991).

The nature of conflict in the employment relationship

The approach to collective negotiations depends on the view that conflict of interests is inevitable between employer and employee because there is an authority relationship in which the aims of the two parties will at least sometimes conflict. A further assumption is that such conflict does not necessarily damage that relationship.

This has led some commentators to discuss negotiation in terms of equally matched protagonists. The power of the two parties may not actually be equal, but they are both willing to behave as if it were. Negotiation thus has the appearance of power equalisation in the search for a solution to a problem. When both sides set out to reach an agreement that is satisfactory to themselves and acceptable to the other, then their power is equalised by that desire. Where the concern for acceptance by the other is lacking, there comes the use of power play of the forcing type described later in this chapter:

> negotiators seek to increase common interest and expand cooperation in order to broaden the area of agreement to cover the item under dispute. On the other hand, each seeks to maximize his own interest and prevail in conflict, in order to make the agreement more valuable to himself. No matter what angle analysis takes, it cannot eliminate the basic tension between cooperation and conflict that provides the dynamic of negotiation.   (Zartman 1976, p. 41)

The relative power of the parties is likely to fluctuate from one situation to the next; this is recognised by the ritual and face-saving elements of negotiation, where a power imbalance is not fully exploited, both to make agreement possible and in the knowledge that the power imbalance may be reversed on the next issue to be resolved.

The classic work of Ann Douglas (1962) produced a formulation of the negotiating encounter that has been little modified by those coming after her. However, this needs further thought when applied to negotiations between representatives of management and representatives of employees about terms and conditions of employment. Cooper and Bartlett point out the difficulty:

> If equality is available to all . . . conflicting groups can meet. All they need to shed

are their misperceptions and their prejudices. Any differences are psychological rather than economic. The truth of the matter is, of course, that ... there are glaring inequalities of wealth and power. Each society contains its own contradictions which arise from the distribution of money, of status and control. So conflict resolution is not just a matter of clearing away mistrust and misunderstanding, replacing them with communication. It is also concerned with political matters such as the re-allocation of power.   (Cooper and Bartlett 1976, p. 167)

Sources of conflict in the collective employment relationship

Most texts on organisational behaviour include sections on reducing conflict and management talk is full of the need for team working, corporate culture and collaboration, so why do we find one area of working life where conflict is readily accepted, even emphasised?

Although the processes of civilisation tend to constrain it there is a natural human impulse to behave aggressively to some degree at some time. It has a number of outlets, for example, watching football, wrestling or boxing. Another outlet for aggression is in negotiations within the employing organisation, which is a splendid arena for the expression of aggressiveness and bravura without actually incurring the physical risks that would be involved in violent combat. Dr Johnson summed up the attractions of vigorous disagreement when he said, 'I dogmatise and am contradicted, and in this conflict of opinions I find delight'. Probably the main source of industrial relations conflict is divergence of interests between those who are classified as managers and those who are seen as non-managers. One group is seeking principally such things as efficiency, productivity and the obedience of others to their own authority. The members of the other group are interested in these things, but are more interested in features like high pay, freedom of action, independence from supervision, scope for the individual and leisure. To some extent these invariably conflict.

Potential benefits of such conflict

Although it is widely believed that conflict of the type described here is counterproductive, there are some advantages.

Introducing new rules

Employment is governed by a number of rules, formal rules that define unfair dismissal and the rate of pay for various jobs, as well as informal rules like dress codes and modes of address. Management/union conflict is usually a disagreement over the rules and the bargain that is struck produces a new rule: a new rate of pay, a new employment practice or whatever. It may be the only way of achieving that particular change, and it is a very authoritative source of rule making because of the joint participation in its creation.

Modifying the goals

The goals that management set can be modified as a result of conflict with others. Ways in which their goals will be unpopular or difficult to implement may be seen for the first time and modifications made early instead of too late. A greater range and diversity of views is brought to bear on a particular matter so that the capacity for innovation is enhanced, but it can be difficult for the manager to accept:

> I can spend hours working out a proper plan that will be good news for everyone, yet they always pick it to pieces. It is so depressing as everything I propose will be ridiculed. (Operations Manager in a pharmaceuticals company)

Clash of values

More fundamental is the possible clash of values, usually about how people should behave. Frequently the clash is about managerial prerogative. Managers like to believe and proclaim that management is their inalienable right, so that those who question the way their work is done are ignorant or impertinent. Non-managers may regard management as a job that should be done properly by people who are responsive to questioning and criticism.

Competitiveness

One of the most likely sources is the urge to compete for a share of limited resources. Much of the drive behind differential pay claims is that of competing with other groups at a similar level, but there may also be competition for finance, materials, security, survival, power, recognition or status.

Organisational tradition

If the tradition of an organisation is to be conflict prone, then it may retain that mode obdurately, while other organisations in which conflict has not been a prominent feature may continue without it. It is axiomatic that certain industries in the United Kingdom are much more likely to display the manifestations of extreme conflict in industrial relations than others. Indicators like the number of working days lost through strikes show a pattern of distribution which varies little between different industries year by year. The nature of the conflict can range between the extremes of pettiness, secrecy, fear and insecurity on the one hand, to vigorous, open and productive debate on the other, with many organisations exhibiting neither.

Understanding of respective positions

Combatants will come to a better understanding of their position on the issue being debated because of their need to set it forth, develop supporting arguments and then defend those arguments against criticism. This enables them to see more clearly what they want, why they want it and how justifiable it is. In challenging the position of the other party, they will come to a clearer understanding of where they stand, and why.

Potential drawbacks of such conflict

These advantages may not be sufficient to balance the potential drawbacks.

Waste of time and energy

Conflict and the ensuing negotiations take a great deal of time and energy. Conflict can be stressful when over-personalised, and individuals become obsessed with the conflict itself rather than what it is about. Negotiation takes a lot longer than simple management decree.

Emotional stress for participants

People vary in the type of organisational stress to which they are prone. To be involved in negotiation is stressful for some people, while others find it stimulating.

Accommodating conflict often causes some inefficiency through the paraphernalia that can accompany it: striking, working to rule, working without enthusiasm, withdrawing co-operation or the simple delay caused by protracted negotiation.

Risks

Negotiation may be the only way to cope with a conflictual situation, but there is the risk of stirring up a hornets' nest. When conflict is brought to the surface it may be resolved or accommodated, or it may get worse if the situation is handled badly.

The quality and amount of communication is impaired. Those involved are concerned more to confirm their own viewpoint than to convey understanding, and there are perceptual distortions like stereotyping and cognitive dissonance. The attitudes behind the communications may also become inappropriate as there are greater feelings of hostility and attempts to score off others.

Bargaining strategies

Managers and managements adopt various strategies to cope with conflict. We need to recognise these and appreciate some of the likely effects.

Avoidance

To some extent conflict can be 'handled' by ignoring it. For a time this will prevent it surfacing so that it remains latent rather than manifest: the danger being that it is harder to deal with when it eventually does erupt. Opposing views cannot be heard unless there is apparatus for their expression. The management of an organisation can fail to provide such apparatus by, for instance, not having personnel specialists, not recognising trade unions and not recognising employee representatives. If the management organise the establishment as if conflict of opinion did not exist, any such difference will be less apparent and its expression stifled. This strategy is becoming harder to sustain because of the developing legal support for employee representation, but it has obvious short-term advantages.

Smoothing

A familiar strategy is to try and resolve conflict by honeyed words in exhortation or discussion where the emphasis is on the value of teamwork, the assurance that 'we all agree really' and an overt, honest attempt to get past the divergence of opinion, which is regarded as a temporary and unfortunate aberration. This is often an accurate diagnosis and represents an approach that would have broad employee support in a particular employment context, but there is always the risk that smoothing ignores the real problem, like giving a massage to someone who has suffered a heart attack.

Forcing

The opposite to smoothing is to attack expressions of dissent and deal with conflict by stamping it out. This is not easy and has innumerable, unfortunate precedents in both the political and industrial arenas.

Compromise

Where divergence of views is acknowledged and confronted, one possibility is to split the difference. If employees claim a pay increase of £10 and the management say they can afford nothing, a settlement of £5 saves the face of both parties but satisfies neither. However common this strategy may be, and sometimes there is no alternative, it has one major drawback: both parties fail to win.

Confrontation

The fifth strategy is to confront the issue on which the parties differ. This involves accepting that there is a conflict of opinions or interests, exploring the scale and nature of the conflict and then working towards an accommodation of the differences which will provide a greater degree of satisfaction of the objectives of both parties than can be achieved by simple compromise. This sounds ambitious, but we suggest that this is the most productive strategy in many cases and offers the opportunity of both parties winning. It is this strategy that we consider in the remainder of this chapter.

Activity 38.1   Consider an industrial dispute or disagreement which you have recently witnessed or read about.

1 Was the management strategy one of avoidance, smoothing, forcing, compromise or confrontation?

2 Was this an inappropriate strategy?

3 If the answer to the last question was 'yes', why was an inappropriate strategy used?

Bargaining tactics

In preparing for negotiation there are a number of matters that the parties must review before they begin.

Resolution or accommodation

Conflict can be *resolved* so that the original feelings of antagonism or opposition vanish, at least over the issues that have brought the conflict to a head. The schoolboy story of how two boys 'put on the gloves in the gym' after a long feud and thereafter shook hands and became firm friends is a theoretical example of a conflict resolved. This type of outcome has a romantic appeal and will frequently be sought in industrial relations issues because so many people feel acutely uncomfortable when involved in relationships of overt antagonism.

Alternatively, the conflict may be *accommodated*, so that the differences of view persist, but a *modus vivendi*, some form of living with the situation, is discovered. In view of the inevitability of the conflict that is endemic in the employment relationship, accommodation may be a more common prospect than resolution, but an interesting question for a negotiator to ponder when approaching the bargaining table is: which is it – resolution or accommodation?

Tension level

Most negotiators feel they have no chance to determine the timing of encounters. This is partly due to reluctance; managers in particular tend to resort to negotiation only when necessary, and the necessity is usually a crisis. A more proactive approach is to initiate encounters, at least trying to push them towards favourable timings.

A feature of timing is the tension level. Too much, and the negotiators get the jitters, unable to see things straight and indulging in excessive interpersonal vituperation: too little tension, and there is no real will to reach a settlement. Ideal timing is to get a point when both sides have a balanced desire to reach a settlement.

Power balance

Effective negotiation is rarely limited to the sheer exploitation of power advantage. The best settlement is one in which both sides can recognise their own and mutual advantages (Fowler 1990, pp. 11–16). The background to any negotiation includes the relative power of the disputants. Power parity is the most conducive to success:

> Perceptions of power inequality undermine trust, inhibit dialogue, and decrease the likelihood of a constructive outcome from an attempted confrontation. Inequality tends to undermine trust on both ends of the imbalanced relationship, directly affecting both the person with the perceived power inferiority and the one with perceived superiority.
> (Walton 1969, p. 98)

The greater the power differential, the more negative the attitudes.

Synchronising

The approaches and reactions of the two parties need a degree of synchronising to ensure that an approach is made at a time when the other party is ready to deal with it. Management interpretation of managerial prerogative often causes managers to move quickly in search of a solution, virtually pre-empting negotiation. When what they see as a positive overture is not reciprocated, they are likely to feel frustrated, discouraged and cross; making themselves in turn unready for overtures from the other side.

Openness

Conflict is handled more effectively if the participants are open with each other about the facts of the situation and their feelings about it. The Americans place great emphasis on this, as openness is more culturally acceptable in the United States than in the United Kingdom, but we note their concern that negotiators should own up to feelings of resentment and anger, rather than masking their feelings behind role assumptions of self-importance.

WINDOW ON PRACTICE

John Dunlop is known as one of the great theorists of industrial relations and the processes in collective bargaining. David Farnham summarises the ten points of his framework for analysing the negotiating process:

1 It takes agreement within each negotiating group to reach a settlement between them.
2 Initial proposals are typically large, compared with eventual settlements.
3 Both sides need to make concessions in order to move towards an agreement.
4 A deadline is an essential feature of most negotiating.
5 The end-stages of negotiating are particularly delicate, with private discussions often being used to close the gap between the parties.
6 Negotiating is influenced by whether it involves the final, intermediate or first stages of the conflict resolution process.
7 Negotiating and overt conflict may take place simultaneously, with the conflict serving as a tool for getting agreement.
8 Getting agreement does not flourish in public.
9 Negotiated settlements need procedures to administer or interpret the final agreement.
10 Personalities and their interactions can affect negotiating outcomes.

Source: D. Farnham (1993) *Employees Relations*. London: IPM, p. 337.

The negotiation sequence

In the various stages of the negotiating encounter aspects of ritual are especially important. They can make for formality and awkwardness rather than relaxed informality, but these ritual steps are not time-wasting prevarication: they are an inescapable feature of the process.

Preparation

In Figure 38.1 there is a summary of the various stages in the negotiating process itself.

Figure 38.1 The negotiating process

Figure 38.1 The negotiating process

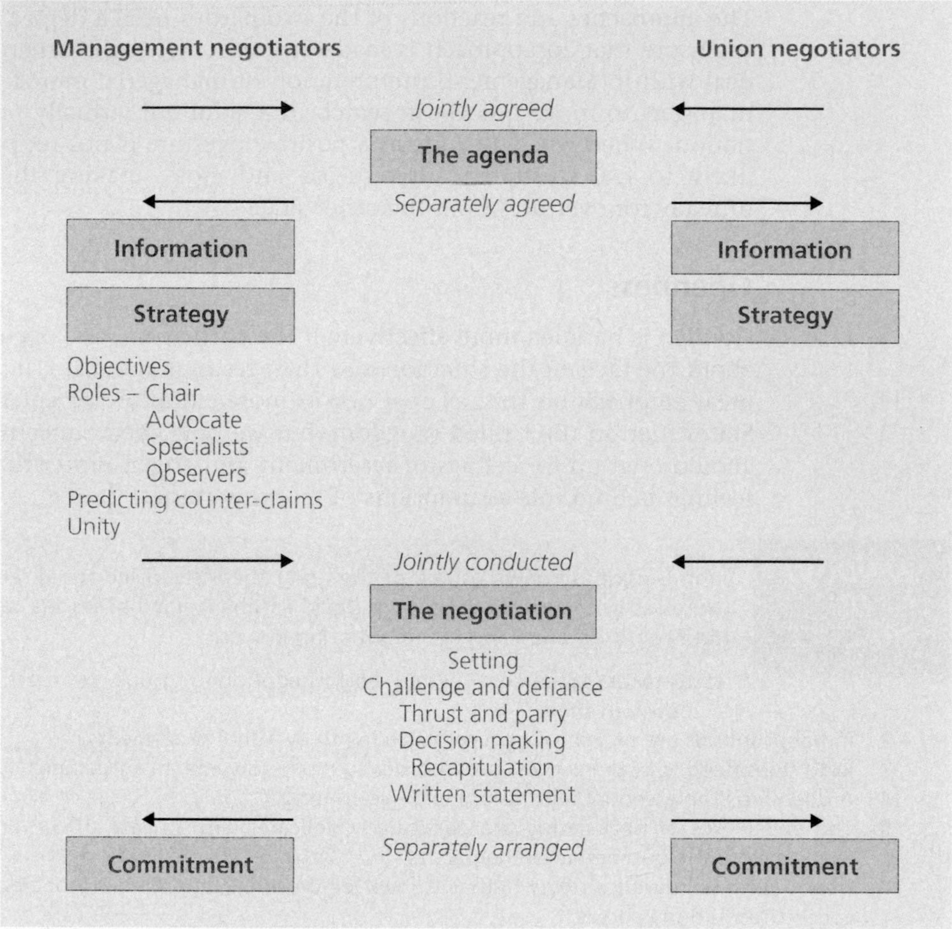

Agenda

The meeting needs an agenda or at least some form of agreement about what is to be discussed. Some people nurture a naïve conviction that there is benefit in concealing the topic from the other party until the encounter begins, believing there is something to be gained from surprise. In fact, this only achieves a deferment of discussion until members of the other party have had a chance to consider their position. The nature of the agenda can have an effect on both the conduct and outcome of the negotiations. It affects the conduct of the encounter by revealing and defining the matters that each side wants to deal with. It is unlikely that other matters will be added to the agenda, particularly if negotiations take place regularly between the parties, so that the negotiators can begin to see, before the meeting, what areas the discussions will cover.

The sequence of items on the agenda will influence the outcome as the possibilities of accommodation between the two positions emerge in the discussion. If, for instance, all the items of the employees' claim come first and all the management's points come later, the possibilities do not turn into probabilities until the discussions are well advanced. An agenda that juxtaposes management and employee 'points' in a logical fashion can enable the shape of a settlement to develop in the minds of the negotiators earlier, even though there would be no commitment until all the pieces of the jigsaw were available. Many negotiations take place without an agenda at all, sometimes because there is a crisis, sometimes because neither party is sufficiently well organised to prepare one. Morley and Stephenson (1977, pp. 74–8) review a number of studies to draw the conclusion that agreement between negotiators is facilitated when there is the opportunity for them to experience 'orientation', considering on what to stand firm and on what to contemplate yielding, or where there is an understanding of the issues involved. An agenda is a prerequisite of orientation.

Information

Both parties need facts to support their argument in negotiation. Some information will be provided to employee representatives for the purposes of collective bargaining and both sets of negotiators have to collect what they need, analyse it so that they understand it, and confirm that the interpretation is shared by each member of their team.

Strategy

The main feature of preparation is for each set of negotiators to decide their strategy. Probably the most helpful work on negotiation strategy has been done by Fowler (1990), with his careful analysis of bargaining conventions and possibilities. In this chapter we limit our considerations to four aspects of strategy.

Objectives

What do the negotiators seek to achieve? They need clear and helpful objectives. When the question has been put to management negotiators entering either real or contrived negotiations in recent years the following have been some of the statements of objectives:

- 'Get the best deal we possibly can.'
- 'Maintain factory discipline at all costs.'
- 'Keep cool.'
- 'See what they want and put up a strong defence.'

All these declarations have a common, negative quality. The initiative is with the other party and the only management strategy is to resist for as long as possible and to concede as little as possible. If this is the best management negotiators can contrive, then their prospects are indeed bleak. They are bound to lose; the only unresolved question is how much. They cannot gain anything because they do not appear to want anything.

More positive objectives are those that envisage improvements which could flow from a changing of the employment rules – changes in efficiency, working practices, manning levels, shiftwork patterns, administrative procedures, flexibility, cost control, and so forth. Unless both parties to the negotiations want something out of the meeting there is little scope for anything but attrition.

Roles

Who will do what in the negotiations? A popular fallacy is that negotiation is

Summary propositions

38.1 The practice of negotiation is based on a need to resolve or accommodate matters on which there is a conflict of interest about the appropriate rate for the job between those who employ and those who are employed.

38.2 In collective issues negotiation can clear the air, introduce new rules, modify an unworkable management position or produce better understanding of respective positions.

38.3 Among the problems of negotiation are the waste of time, the stress and the risks.

38.4 The most common bargaining strategies are avoidance, smoothing, forcing, compromise or confrontation.

38.5 Aspects of preparation are setting the agenda, collecting information, deciding a strategy, agreeing objectives and roles.

38.6 The stages in collective negotiation are challenge and defiance, thrust and parry, decision making, recapitulation, agreeing a written statement and ensuring the commitment of the parties.

38.7 In individual negotiations a negotiator will want to get agreement to an appropriate position of the 'freedom scale'.

References

Cooper, B.M. and Bartlett, A.F. (1976) *Industrial Relations: A study in conflict*. London: Heinemann.

Douglas, A. (1962) *Industrial Peacemaking*. New York: Columbia University Press.

Dunlop, J.T. (1984) *Dispute Resolution*. London: Auburn.

Farnham, D. (1993) *Employee Relations*. London: IPM.

Fisher, R. and Ury, W. (1986) *Getting to Yes: Negotiating agreement without giving in*. New York: Penguin.

Fowler, A. (1990) *Negotiation Skills and Strategies*. London: IPM.

Grint, K. (1997) *Fuzzy Management*. London: Sage.

Hiltrop, J.M. and Udall, B. (1995) *The Essence of Negotiation*. Hemel Hempstead: Prentice Hall International.

Homans, G.C. (1961) *Social Behaviour: Its elementary forms*. London: Routledge & Kegan Paul.

Kissinger, H. (1973) in *New York Times*, 25 January.

Morley, I. and Stephenson, G.M. (1970) 'Strength of case, communication systems and the outcomes of simulated negotiations', *Industrial Relations Journal*, Summer.

Morley, I. and Stephenson, G.M. (1977) *The Social Psychology of Bargaining*. London: George Allen & Unwin.

Mulholland, J. (1991) *The Language of Negotiation*. London: Routledge.

Oncken, W. (1984) *Managing Management Time: who's got the monkey?* Englewood Cliffs, NJ: Prentice Hall.

Walton, R.E. (1969) *Interpersonal Peacemaking: Confrontations and third party consultation*. Reading, Mass.: Addison-Wesley.

Walton, R.E. and McKersie, R.B. (1965) *Towards a Behavioural Theory of Labour Negotiations*. London: McGraw-Hill.

Younson, F. (2000) 'How to handle a union recognition claim', *People Management*, Vol. 6, No. 15.

Zartman, I.W. (1976) *The 50% Solution*. New York: Anchor Press/Doubleday.

Part VII
Case study problem

Salary versus benefits in financial services

We saw in Part VII the way in which there is a balance to be struck between the level of salary and the benefits that are associated with that salary. The case study problem at the close of Part VI was an example, as employees were concerned that a salary increase of more than 20 per cent would not be as satisfactory as the previous situation, where their benefits – including greatly reduced air fares – were much greater. The problem is always in finding the right balance.

You have just been appointed to review the salary and benefits package in a financial services company, where the benefits package includes mortgages and loans at preferential rates, a non-contributory pension scheme and profit sharing. There is some feeling in the company that the value of these benefits has shrunk in recent years as the preferential terms have become less attractive. You have been asked to consider ways in which the benefits arrangements can be made more flexible, so that employees have a degree of choice between the benefits they enjoy, but you are concerned that the increase in costs of administration may be too high to justify such a move.

Research by the consultants Towers Perrin (1996) covered responses from 250 UK companies and showed that half the respondents were now allowing employee choice between different benefits, compared with only one in 10 five years previously. The only significant benefit where individual choice has been reduced is in car benefits.

You carry out a questionnaire survey among staff members which provides you with the following data:

1 Would you be willing to exchange part of your salary for improvements in your benefits package? Yes: 28%. No: 72%.
2 What do you feel about the present combination of salary and benefits: (a) about right as it is? (b) improving benefits more important than improving salaries? (c) improving salaries more important than improving benefits? (a) 42%. (b) 9%. (c) 49%.
3 In reply to a question about the relative value of different types of benefit, the following was the rank order:
   (a) Non-contributory pension.
   (b) Profit sharing.
   (c) Preferential mortgage rates.
   (d) Flexible holiday arrangements.
   (e) Free life insurance.
   (f) Private health care insurance.
   (g) Fees refunded for approved training schemes.
   (h) Sports club membership.
   (i) Extended maternity leave/paternity leave.
   (j) Luncheon vouchers.

Required

1 Why do you think there is such strong preference for improving salary rather than benefits?
2 What are the benefits (and disadvantages) to the employer in increasing the range of choice for individuals between a range of benefits?
3 Do you agree with the rank order of the 10 benefits shown above? What changes would you make to produce your own personal list?

Reference

Towers Perrin (1996) *The Benefits Package of the Future*. London: Towers Perrin.

Part VII
Examination questions

Undergraduate introductory

1 Explain the difference in the objectives of employer and employee when considering the payment arrangements of the employee.

2 What are the differences between wages and salaries?

Undergraduate finals

3 'Job evaluation is redundant: it is only the Equal Pay Act that keeps it going.' Discuss.

4 How effective are payment systems in improving effort levels and performance?

Masters

5 If you are managing a system of payment with the objective that those being paid should regard the system as being fair, would you relate the payment to the demands of the job or to the relative performance of individuals doing the job?

6 'Individual performance pay is only one ingredient of a performance management system and a relatively insignificant one at that.' Do you agree or disagree with this statement? Explain your reasons.

Professional

7 What are the advantages and disadvantages of broadbanded pay structures?

8 What should be the main benefits of an employee benefits policy?

Index